Handbook of Research on Advancements in Organizational Data Collection and Measurements:

Strategies for Addressing Attitudes, Beliefs, and Behaviors

Mihai C. Bocarnea
Regent University, USA

Bruce E. Winston
Regent University, USA

Debra Dean
Regent University, USA

A volume in the Advances in Human Resources
Management and Organizational Development
(AHRMOD) Book Series

Published in the United States of America by
IGI Global
Business Science Reference (an imprint of IGI Global)
701 E. Chocolate Avenue
Hershey PA, USA 17033
Tel: 717-533-8845
Fax: 717-533-8661
E-mail: cust@igi-global.com
Web site: http://www.igi-global.com

Library of Congress Cataloging-in-Publication Data

Names: Bocarnea, Mihai C., 1960- editor. | Winston, Bruce E., editor. |
  Dean, Debra J., editor.
Title: Handbook of research on advancements in organizational data collection
  and measurements: strategies for addressing attitudes, beliefs, and behaviors
  / Mihai Bocarnea, Bruce E. Winston, and Debra Dean, editor..
Description: Hershey, PA : Business Science Reference, [2021] | Includes
  bibliographical references and index. | Summary: "This book will help
  researchers and practitioners understand, assess, and use newly
  developed data collection instruments in organizational management and
  leadership, including human research development"-- Provided by
  publisher.
Identifiers: LCCN 2020056962 (print) | LCCN 2020056963 (ebook) | ISBN
  9781799876656 (hardcover) | ISBN   9781799876670 (ebook)
Subjects: LCSH: Management--Statistical methods. | Social
  sciences--Statistical methods. | Organizational sociology. | Leadership.
Classification: LCC HD30.215 .A299 2021 (print) | LCC HD30.215 (ebook) |
  DDC 658.4/033--dc23
LC record available at https://lccn.loc.gov/2020056962
LC ebook record available at https://lccn.loc.gov/2020056963

This book is published in the IGI Global book series Advances in Human Resources Management and Organizational Development (AHRMOD) (ISSN: 2327-3372; eISSN: 2327-3380)

British Cataloguing in Publication Data
A Cataloguing in Publication record for this book is available from the British Library.

All work contributed to this book is new, previously-unpublished material. The views expressed in this book are those of the authors, but not necessarily of the publisher.

For electronic access to this publication, please contact: eresources@igi-global.com.

Advances in Human Resources Management and Organizational Development (AHRMOD) Book Series

Patricia Ordóñez de Pablos
Universidad de Oviedo, Spain

ISSN:2327-3372
EISSN:2327-3380

MISSION

A solid foundation is essential to the development and success of any organization and can be accomplished through the effective and careful management of an organization's human capital. Research in human resources management and organizational development is necessary in providing business leaders with the tools and methodologies which will assist in the development and maintenance of their organizational structure.

The **Advances in Human Resources Management and Organizational Development (AHRMOD) Book Series** aims to publish the latest research on all aspects of human resources as well as the latest methodologies, tools, and theories regarding organizational development and sustainability. The **AHRMOD Book Series** intends to provide business professionals, managers, researchers, and students with the necessary resources to effectively develop and implement organizational strategies.

COVERAGE

- Personnel Retention
- Corporate Governance
- Process Improvement
- Employee Benefits
- E-Human Resources Management
- Executive Education
- Organizational Learning
- Organizational Development
- Worker Behavior and Engagement
- Succession Planning

IGI Global is currently accepting manuscripts for publication within this series. To submit a proposal for a volume in this series, please contact our Acquisition Editors at Acquisitions@igi-global.com or visit: http://www.igi-global.com/publish/.

Titles in this Series

For a list of additional titles in this series, please visit: www.igi-global.com/book-series

Building Competencies for Organizational Success Emerging Research and Opportunities
Donta S. Harper (University of Washington, USA)
Business Science Reference • © 2021 • 300pp • H/C (ISBN: 9781799865162) • US $195.00

Role of Leadership in Facilitating Healing and Renewal in Times of Organizational Trauma and Change
Lynda Byrd-Poller (Thomas Nelson Community College, USA) Jennifer L. Farmer (Renewed Mindset LLC, USA)
and Valerie Ford (ISP Global Communications LLC, USA)
Business Science Reference • © 2021 • 291pp • H/C (ISBN: 9781799870166) • US $195.00

Impact of Infodemic on Organizational Performance
Muhammad Waseem Bari (Government College University, Faisalabad, Pakistan) and Emilia Alaverdov (Georgian
Technical University, Georgia)
Business Science Reference • © 2021 • 380pp • H/C (ISBN: 9781799871644) • US $195.00

Transgender Discrimination in the Workplace
Qaiser Rafique Yasser (Preston University, Islamabad, Pakistan)
Business Science Reference • © 2021 • 315pp • H/C (ISBN: 9781799873129) • US $195.00

Effective Strategies for Communicating Insights in Business
Ross Jackson (Wittenberg University, USA) and Amanda Reboulet (Jacoulet, USA)
Business Science Reference • © 2021 • 261pp • H/C (ISBN: 9781799839644) • US $195.00

Handbook of Research on Remote Work and Worker Well-Being in the Post-COVID-19 Era
Daniel Wheatley (University of Birmingham, UK) Irene Hardill (Northumbria University, UK) and Sarah Buglass
(Nottingham Trent University, UK)
Business Science Reference • © 2021 • 420pp • H/C (ISBN: 9781799867548) • US $265.00

Cases on Critical Practices for Modern and Future Human Resources Management
Devi Akella (Albany State University, USA) Niveen Eid (Birzeit University, Palestine) and Anton Sabella (Birzeit
University, Palestine)
Business Science Reference • © 2021 • 322pp • H/C (ISBN: 9781799858201) • US $195.00

Asian Women in Corporate America Emerging Research and Opportunities
Sambhavi Lakshminarayanan (Medgar Evers College, City University of New York, USA)
Business Science Reference • © 2021 • 263pp • H/C (ISBN: 9781799843849) • US $185.00

701 East Chocolate Avenue, Hershey, PA 17033, USA
Tel: 717-533-8845 x100 • Fax: 717-533-8661
E-Mail: cust@igi-global.com • www.igi-global.com

List of Contributors

Table of Contents

Detailed Table of Contents

Chapter 1
Mary A. Hansen, Robert Morris University, USA
Gaelebale Nnunu Tsheko, University of Botswana, Botswana

This chapter presents a summary of best practices for the design, development, and analysis of quantitative survey research. The authors provide an overview of sampling procedures, as well as a summary of considerations for researchers as they develop questionnaires. Additionally, they provide descriptions of both qualitative and quantitative analyses that should be used to provide content and construct validity evidence for questionnaires. Finally, they show examples of common descriptive and inferential procedures appropriate for survey research. The goal of the chapter is to summarize factors that survey researchers should consider at all stages of their research project, from design to analysis, in order to improve survey research in practice.

Chapter 2
Debra J. Dean, Regent University, USA

When embarking on this journey, the author had little expectation of finding the topics of validity and reliability to be so complex and convoluted or so interesting. This chapter helps to clear the air and communicate the concepts of validity and reliability more clearly. The challenges seem to include the wording used to introduce and describe the concepts along with the transformation of statistical equations over time and technology. What remains the same is the importance of knowing whether an instrument is valid and reliable. One of the most basic places to start with conducting a robust quantitative research project is to have valid and reliable instruments. This may involve creating your own instrument, using an established instrument, or modifying an existing instrument. This chapter takes a deep dive into the concepts of validity and reliability uncovering some of the cynicism and myths of these topics along the way. The ultimate goal is to communicate clearly so that future research can use the proper technique(s) and describe the output in a more uniform fashion.

Chapter 3
Bruce E. Winston, Regent University, USA

This chapter critiques the use of the Likert response items for scale development. Likert response data when as nominal data and analyzed as nominal data is useful for recording and analyzing participants' attitudes about a topic. However, it is illogical for researchers who use Likert response data as interval data. The typical five or seven-item Likert response provides three response methods for each topic under study: a neutral item that is categorical, a two or three-item negatively worded ordinal scale, and a two or three-item positively worded ordinal scale. While Likert suggested scoring the five-item response with the numbers 1-5 and scoring the seven-item response with numbers 1-7, it places the neutral response in the 3rd or 4th position, which, if treating the data as interval means that 'neutral' scores higher than the Strongly Disagree-Disagree and lower than the Agree-Strongly Agree items, is not a logical outcome.

Chapter 4

Dail Fields, Regent University, USA

This chapter describes in detail the process used to develop and validate a scale that measures servant leadership. The steps covered include construct identification from previous studies, review of previously proposed and developed measures, item selection, survey development, collection of data, scale identification, and evaluation of convergent, discriminant, predictive validity. The chapter provides a hands-on example of the steps required for scale measure development and assessment and includes description of the mechanics involved in completing each step of this process.

Chapter 5

Tanesia R. Beverly, Law School Admission Council, USA

Researchers tend to evaluate psychological instruments in terms of reliability (internal consistency) and construct validity (exploratory factor analysis and confirmatory factor analysis). In many instances, these instruments are used for cross-cultural comparisons such as gender and race—however, many of these studies do not provide evidence of measurement invariance or measurement equivalence. Measurement equivalence is a statistical property of an instrument that indicates that participants interpret and respond to the items similarly or that the same latent construct is being measured across observed groups of people. Partial measurement equivalence is a necessary condition for comparing latent mean differences across cultures. This area of construct validity is often neglected in the literature; therefore, this chapter aims to introduce the concept of measurement invariance. Additionally, it highlights the necessity of testing for measurement invariance when making cross-cultural comparisons on organizational leadership instruments.

Chapter 6

Rodney Reynolds, Independent Researcher, USA

The focus of this chapter is on insights for and evaluation of if the transfer of learning by training and development professionals will sustain the training field. The chapter begins with the need for a model of learning. Then there is a section on a proposed evaluation of the trainer presentation of a model of learning or training development. The chapter then progresses to a proposed measure of the potential for the transfer of learning and the need to assess self-efficacy with gradations of attainments on the training topic. Finally, the chapter turns to trainee engagement and to having a results orientation for a training program.

Chapter 7

The leadership intention measure was developed to help organizations deal with the dynamic and complex realities of the 21st-century competitive global environment, which necessitates a more rapid and effective response to changes to survive. An effective approach for dealing with this reality is to involve employees in the various leadership processes for the organization. However, employees must be prepared to assume the responsibility for a more active leadership role. Before an organization can open their work environment for 'leadership in all', determining whether members have the intention to exhibit leadership is critical. Therefore, this scale is based on the reasoned action behavioral model of Fishbein and Ajzen to determine the intentions of employees for engaging in leadership behavior. The LIM scale was validated in an organization whose stated culture encouraged leadership behavior by all. Results indicate that this measure would be a valuable tool for assessing organization readiness for facilitating and enabling leadership behaviors.

Chapter 8

The authors present three studies that develop the five-scale measurement for holistic ethical leadership questionnaire. Study 1 reports the scale development process using predominately non-Western participants. Study 2 tests the five-scale instrument for convergent and discriminant validity as well as test-retest reliability using a subset of the sample who participated in Study 1. Study 3 used a sample of USA residents for confirmatory factor analysis from which a single factor emerged to measure holistic ethical leadership. The authors concluded that the five-scale instrument should be used when measuring non-Western participants and the single-scale should be used when measuring USA residents. The authors recommended follow-up research using qualitative methods to better understand the reasons why the single-scale measure works well with USA residents.

Chapter 9

The study on which this chapter is based investigated whether there is a connection between hope, self-efficacy, and motivation to lead (MTL) in the development of leaders in South Africa. The data collected for the MTL component were gathered using a revised two-factor model of Chan's MTL instrument, comprising the leading for self-benefit factor (MTL-S) and the group-centered leading factor (MTL-G). The revised two-factor model of Chan's MTL instrument is a meaningful redevelopment of Chan's MTL instrument for the South African context and potentially elsewhere in the world. The MTL-G, which comprises seven items, is of particular interest as a scale for measuring altruism. This research makes a contribution to servant leadership by establishing the connection between MTL-G and altruism, and adds a valuable dimension to the research of Patterson. More recent research has emerged, indicating MTL instrument adaptions and revisions in different contexts.

Chapter 10

Wood and Winston defined leader accountability as the leader's response to (1) his/her willing acceptance of the responsibilities inherent in the leadership position to serve the well-being of the organization; (2) the implicit or explicit expectation that he/she will be publicly linked to his/her actions, words, or reactions; and (3) the expectation that the leader may be called on to explain his or her beliefs, decisions, commitments, or actions to constituents. They developed three scales—the Responsibility, Openness, and Answerability Scales—to form the Leader Accountability Index (LAI). Use of the scales in subsequent research has suggested the possibility of combining the three to form a single factor instrument to measure leader accountability. This chapter updates the literature on leader accountability since the LAI was first published, reviews the data collection and factor analyses involved in creating the new Leader Accountability Scale (LAS), and discusses implications of the new scale's usefulness in leadership research and organizational practice.

Chapter 11

In the ubiquitous mediated world in which we live, we daily encounter organizational leaders through mediated communication. New communication technology and the age of the COVID-19 pandemic have made these mediated encounters even more pronounced, leading to more opportunities for parasocial interaction with organizational leaders by various publics. This chapter provides a theoretical model and quantitative measurement for assessing parasocial interaction in the social scientific tradition of middle range analysis. The leader-follower parasocial interaction scale provided here is a useful tool for assessing the persuasive influence of leaders on those who follow them.

Chapter 12

Spirituality and its relationship to leadership and organizational behavior has been of increasing interest to researchers, but inadequate scales have limited rigorous quantitative studies. Spirituality is complex and involves experiential, emotional, and transformative dimensions that create dynamic cycles of expectancy, behavior, and attitudes that evolve, rendering many existing spiritual practice behavioral measures inadequate. An instrument developed to capture the broader concept of spiritual engagement, the Spiritual Engagement Instrument (SpEI), is presented. Through an overview of SpEI development, and demonstration of SpEI research, a primer to advance spirituality-based organization and leadership research is offered. If spiritual engagement is a transformative cycle, understanding and measuring the phenomena in context will better inform leadership and organization development policy. Toward a theoretical and practical understanding, this chapter guides the researcher in exploring the potential of spirituality in organizations.

Chapter 13
J. Louis Spencer, American Public University System, USA
W. David Winner, Regent University, USA

This chapter presents the development of a scale that measures vision conflict, which refers to the disparity between what a minister anticipates a ministry to be like versus the real-life experience. Vision conflict is correlated with four similar phenomena, including role ambiguity, negative job satisfaction, negative values congruence, and negative ability-job fit. The scale addresses key factors that may affect pastoral terminations and exits from church ministry. It also encourages the understanding of critical elements that hinder pastoral effectiveness and create a stronger resilience to exiting the ministry.

Chapter 14
C. Victor Herbin III, Regent University, USA

Prior studies provided insight on arrogance at the individual level and how arrogant individuals express superiority through (1) overconfidence in capabilities, (2) dismissiveness, (3) and disparagement, and how these behaviors may negatively impact those employees in and around their work teams, yet did not indicate how these behaviors impact organizational culture. Organizational arrogance represents an emerging concept that describes arrogance at the organizational level. Organizational arrogance provides the body of knowledge with a comprehensive and inclusive definition that led to the development and validation of the Organizational Arrogance Scale with a Cronbach Alpha of .922 that accurately measures the presence of organizational arrogance.

Chapter 15
Jamie Brownlee-Turgeon, Point Loma Nazarene University, USA

This chapter describes a new instrument that measures a leader's ability to identify and avert crisis in the pre-crisis stages. There is currently no other instrument that measures leadership ability pre-crisis but rather only leadership attributes during the crisis event. Based on the conceptual model developed by Wooten and James, the measurement focuses on the first two stages of the conceptual model, signal detection and prevention and preparation. This chapter covers multiple aspects of the measurement. First, it provides the framework for the development of the crisis identification and aversion tool. Secondly, it provides an analysis of the inclusive quartiles of the three-factor measurement, which includes the competencies of participatory management, sensemaking, and resourcefulness.

Chapter 16
Sarah E. Walters, Evangel University, USA

This chapter addresses how Winston et al.'s "An Instrument to Measure the Impact of Hope in Strategic Plan Implementation" can be implemented within the workplace. Leaders should have a way to measure the impact of hope on strategic plans. Winston et al.'s instrument include three main theories: hope, expectancy, and value chain theories. This instrument is unlike any other tool to date in its conceptualization of employee hope in the organizational context. This chapter explains the validity, reliability, and practical application steps of Winston et al.'s instrument.

Chapter 17

Taylor et al. evaluated Dupuy's general employee well-being measurement instrument and pointed out two concerns: a combination of positive and negative item wording and two different measurement response methods. Taylor et al. collected new data, ran a principal component analysis, and found three of Dupuy's five reported scales. In this study, the author reworded Taylor et al.'s final 18 items so that all items were worded positively, used a common measurement response, and removed double-barreled wording, which Taylor et al. did not note. The author of this current chapter conducted two studies. The first study's analysis of the new data produced a single eight-item scale with Cronbach alpha of .96 that explained 77% of the variance. The second study used confirmatory factor analysis that showed a four-item scale with GFI = 0.98, AGFI = 0.89, RMSEA = 0.13, and Chi-square = 9.96, df = 9, p < 0.000. The four-item scale had a Cronbach alpha of 0.86.

Chapter 18

Coronavirus has emphasized the importance of nursing contributions and their integral participation in interdisciplinary leadership teams providing patient care in healthcare organizations. Workforce shortages of qualified nurses in healthcare with technology skills are necessary to maintain a high level of patient care and healthcare operations. A validated instrument, Healthcare Information System Self-Efficacy Perception, was created providing a self-assessment tool for measuring an older working nurse's perception of self-efficacy of healthcare information system training within a healthcare environment. The study was the first of its kind to recognize the salient training differences that existed for older workers in a healthcare setting. The instrument was developed using a focus group, pilot study, and validated with registered nurses (RN) in a single healthcare organization. The sample (N=162) was assessed using an online survey tool. After face validity was established for HISSEP, a principal component factor analysis was conducted to determine content validity.

Chapter 19

A review of the current literature showed that clergy effectiveness (CE) instruments were inadequate due to age, insufficient content validity, and/or based on secondary criteria. The premise of this study was that an instrument built upon qualitative data reflective of 21st-century ministry paradigms is needed. Such data did not exist until DeShon identified 64 personal and behavioral characteristics of clergy deemed to enhance effectiveness. The purpose of this study was to operationalize the characteristics identified by DeShon. Staff and lay leaders in churches of various sizes from five different denominations were selected using a snowball technique (N = 397). Scale optimization resulted in a final three-factor instrument consisting of 14 items: professional competence (five items), socially adept (five items), and inclination to lead (four items). Scale reliability was substantiated by Cronbach's alpha scores of .89 (professional competence), .94 (socially adept), and .73 (inclination to lead).

Chapter 20

Corporations have failed to charge human resource officers with the responsibility of facilitating the unique diverse relationships needed for enriching their own workforce. Often, at best, training programs introduce intercultural sensitivity and only suggest the actual need for employee connections with diverse others. The trainers hesitate to discuss how to monitor and facilitate accountability for forming the diverse relationships that make others feel a sense of inclusion and create safe places for voices to be asserted. This chapter calls for a human resources plan for raising the awareness for engaging in the actual networking, accountability, and the building of the human relationships that enrich the vitality of the workplace. This plan sees the corporate diversity mission as a persuasive message and thus looks at how employees may become involved in the mission in different ways related to their values, their relevant impressions, and possible outcomes.

Chapter 21

Machine learning enables organizations to leverage data strategically to improve employee performance, promote continuous improvement, and better fulfill the mission. Opportunities for leveraging machine learning within organizations exist throughout the employee lifecycle but should be pursued with a clear understanding of the strengths and limitations of the methodology. This chapter will review traditional performance management processes, introduce machine learning as a methodology, highlight how machine learning methods could be used in new performance assessment models, and note future research directions to improve the use of machine learning within organizations.

Preface

Advancements in Organizational Data Collection and Measurements: Strategies for Addressing Attitudes, Beliefs, and Behaviors was written by quantitative researchers for quantitative researchers and seeks to inform academics and researchers about quantitative survey-based research tools, new instruments available to social science researchers, and suggests future research topics.

We divided the chapters into three categories: (a) research notes about designing, developing, and analyzing quantitative research; (b) measurement instruments; and (c) suggestions for future research.

RESEARCH NOTES ABOUT DESIGNING, DEVELOPING, AND ANALYZING QUANTITATIVE RESEARCH MEASUREMENT INSTRUMENTS

Chapter 1 by Mary Hansen informs the reader of best practices in designing, developing, and analyzing quantitative survey research. Dr. Hansen posits that while survey research is a common form of research, the tenets of high-quality instrument development, sampling, and data analysis are not consistently implemented in practice. Dr. Hansen discusses best practices for the design, development, and analysis of quantitative survey research. Her chapter provides novice researchers with an overview of options for designing, developing, administering, and analyzing quantitative survey research. At the same time, the chapter introduces more advanced quantitative analyses that can be implemented to improve questionnaires. The overarching goal of this chapter is to describe the principles that are foundational to high-quality survey research.

Chapter 2 by Debra Dean takes a deep dive into the concepts of validity and reliability, uncovering some of the cynicism and myths of these topics along the way. The ultimate goal is to communicate clearly so that future research can use the proper technique(s) and describe the output more uniformly. Dr. Dean's chapter is a good 'next step' from Dr. Hansen's chapter.

Chapter 3 by Bruce Winston critiques the use of the Likert response items for scale development. Dr. Winston presents the origin of Rensis Likert's work and the development of the Likert scale that found a place in marketing research focused on understanding customers' attitudes. Winston points out the flaws of using scales such as the Likert Scale, in which the scale has both negative and positive wording and a scale that does not behave according to conditions of a continuous variable.

Chapter 4 by Dail Fields describes the process used to develop and validate a scale that measures servant leadership from item development, response scale selection, a panel of expert evaluation, collecting data from participants, factor analysis, testing for reliability, and validity to model testing.

Chapter 5 by Tanesia R Beverly explains how to evaluate psychological instruments in terms of reliability (internal consistency) and construct validity (exploratory factor analysis and confirmatory factor analysis). Dr. Beverly's chapter explores the use of structured equation modeling to test measurement and research models.

The overarching theme of this section is an admonition to experienced and developing quantitative researchers to be diligent in the creation and testing of measurements so that their own and others' research can be stronger through appropriate validity and more robust through appropriate reliability.

MEASUREMENT INSTRUMENTS

Chapter 6 by Rodney Reynolds presents a proposed measure of The Potential for the Transfer of Learning and the need to assess Self-Efficacy with gradations of attainments on the training topic. Key to Dr. Reynold's chapter is the desire to understand how trainees move learning from short-term to long-term. Dr. Reynolds focused on Donald Kirkpatrick's Model of learning. Dr. emphasizes the need for learning research to present valid and reliable evidence of the effectiveness of training and development programs.

Chapter 7 by Charles G Sanders presents the Leadership Intention Measure, which was developed to help organizations deal with the dynamic and complex realities of the 21st-century competitive global environment, which necessitates a more rapid and effective response to changes to survive. The Leadership Intention Measure has three valid and reliable scales: (a) organizational complexity, (b) personal responsibility, and (c) influence intention.

Chapter 8 by Tariku Fufa Gemechu and Bruce Winston explains the development and testing of the Five-Factor Holistic Ethical Leadership Questionnaire. Dr. Gemechu developed the holistic leadership scale instrument in an African context. Dr. Winston then tested the instrument in a United States of America context. While Dr. Gemechu found five factors, Dr. Winston found one factor. The two studies conclude that the five-factor measure is appropriate in an African context, and the one-factor solution is appropriate in the United States Culture.

Chapter 9 by Karen Cerff presents the development of the modified Motivation to Lead instrument. The data collected for the MTL component were gathered using a revised two-factor model of Chan's (1999) MTL Instrument, comprising the leading for self-benefit factor (MTL-S) and the group-centered leading factor (MTL-G). The revised two-factor model of Chan's (1999) MTL Instrument is a meaningful redevelopment of Chan's MTL Instrument for the South African context and potentially elsewhere in the world. The MTL-G, which comprises seven items, is of particular interest as a scale for measuring altruism. This research makes a contribution to servant leadership by establishing the connection between MTL-G and altruism

Chapter 10 by James (Andy) Wood and Heidi Ventura explains the development of a single scale to measure leader accountability. Dr. Wood initially developed three separate instruments that measured (a) acceptance of responsibilities (Responsibility Scale), (b) the degree of acceptance by the leader of his/her behaviors being public (Openness Scale), and (c) the level of understanding about the consequences of his/her behaviors (Answerability Scale). Subsequent use of the three scales by other researchers led to a discussion of whether or not there was a single scale that measured accountability. Dr. Wood and Dr. Ventura analyzed data from prior studies and found a single factor (Leader Accountability Scale) that showed validity and reliability to measure leaders' accountability.

Chapter 11 by William Brown and Mihai Bocarnea provides a theoretical model and quantitative measurement for assessing parasocial interaction in the social scientific tradition of middle-range analysis. The leader-follower parasocial interaction scale provided here is a helpful tool for assessing the persuasive influence of leaders on those who follow them.

Chapter 12 by Rick Roof explains the development and use of the Spiritual Engagement Instrument (SpEI). Rick Roof helps the reader understand the potential of spirituality in organizations. Dr. Roof's instrument consists of four scales: (a) five-item Worship scale with $a = .94$ that explained 57.8% of the variance; (b) five-item Meditation scale with $a = .96$ that explained 12.7% of the variance, (c) a five-item Fasting scale with $a = .98$ that explained 9.6% of the variance, and (d) a five-item Rest scale with $a = .99$ that explained 5.2% of the variance. The instrument is useful for researchers seeking to understand leaders' spiritual engagement.

Chapter 13 by J. Louis Spencer and W. David Winner presents the development of the Vision Conflict Scale that measures the disparity between what a minister anticipates a ministry to be like versus the real-life experience. Dr. Spencer and Dr. Winner's scale is based on the consulting/coaching work of Chuck Wickman or Pastors-in-Residence and can help pastors self-examine or consultants/coaches determine if the person-organization fit component of vision conflict may be a risk factor in predicting a pastor's success.

Chapter 14 by C. Victor Herbin III provides the reader with an overview of the development and use of the fine-item Organizational Arrogance Scale with $a = .922$. According to Dr. Herbin, "arrogance represents a collection of thoughts, attitudes, and behaviors that demonstrate an individual's superiority level. The term sense of superiority reflects a consistent theme identified throughout the literature and pertinent to the definition of arrogance.' Dr. Herbin's five-item scale can help leaders and consultants diagnose the presence of organizational arrogance and its possible emergence through dysfunctional behavior at the organizational level.

Chapter 15 by Jamie Brownlee-Turgeon describes a new instrument that measures a leader's ability to identify and avert a crisis in the pre-crisis stages. Dr. Brownlee-Turgeon's literature review led to the conclusion that crisis leaders focus on crisis identification and aversion. Dr. Brownlee-Turgeon's three-dimension instrument consists of: (a) a 17-item participatory management scale with $a = .97$, (b) a seven-item resourcefulness scale with $a = .95$, and (c) an 11-item sensemaking scale with $a = .95$. The instrument can help consultants diagnose a leader's propensity toward guiding the organization through a crisis, or steer the organization away from a crisis.

Chapter 16 by Sarah E Walters addresses how Winston et al.'s (2008) "An Instrument to Measure the Impact of Hope in Strategic Plan Implementation" can be implemented within the workplace. Leaders should have a way to measure the impact of hope on strategic plans. Winston et al.'s instrument includes three main theories: hope, expectancy, and value chain theories. This instrument is unlike any other tool to date in its conceptualization of employee hope in the organizational context. This chapter explains the validity, reliability, and practical application steps of Winston et al.'s instrument.

Chapter 17 by Bruce Winston developed the Modified General Employee Well-being Scale from Dupuy's original general employee well-being measurement instrument. Dupy's instrument' items show content validity but used positive and negative items, some items being double-barreled, and two different response methods were used. Dr. Winston modified the items from Taylor et al.'s (2003) study that used Dubuy's instrument. Dr. Winston converted the items to positive wording, split the double-barreled items into separate items, each with a single focus, and changed the response method to a semantic differential scale. Dr. Winston's principal component and confirmatory analysis of the final four-item scale explained 71.00% of the variance with factor loads ranging from .772 to .872, with $a = .86$, and showed both validity and reliability. The four-item scale can help leaders and consultants measure employee well-being as a part of personnel development and as a pre/post-test in problem-solving interventions.

Chapter 18 by B. J. Weathersby-Holman describes the Healthcare Information System Self Efficacy Perception instrument that was created to provide a self-assessment for measuring an older working nurse's perception of self-efficacy of healthcare information system training within a healthcare environment. The study was the first of its kind to recognize the salient training differences that existed for older workers in a healthcare setting.

Chapter 19 by Samuel P. Dobrotka presents the three-factor Clergy Effectiveness measure consisting of Professional Competence (five items), Socially Adept (five items), and Inclination to Lead (four items). Dr. Dobrotka used the existing literature on ministerial effectiveness and earlier attempts to measure ministerial effectiveness to create and analyze a three-factor instrument consisting of: (a) five-item socially adept scale with $a = .98$. (b) a five-item professional competence scale with $a = .88$. and (c) a four-item inclination to lead scale with $a = .73$.

SUGGESTIONS FOR FUTURE RESEARCH

Chapter 20 by Janet L. Reynolds calls for a human resources plan for raising the awareness for engaging in the actual networking and building of the human resources that enrich the vitality of the workplace. Dr. Reynolds calls for more research using cluster analysis to understand better the collection of values and perceptions within and between groups in organizations and societies, that would lead to a greater understanding of diverse interactions, inclusions, and equity

Chapter 21 by Jason D. Baker reviews traditional performance management processes, introduces machine learning as a methodology, highlights how machine learning methods could be used in new performance assessment models, and presents future research directions to improve machine learning within organizations.

CONCLUSION

Advancements in Organizational Data Collection and Measurements: Strategies for Addressing Attitudes, Beliefs, and Behaviors is a useful collection of research notes, instruments, and suggestions for future research that is meant to inform and guide both experienced and developing researchers explore social science quantitative research efforts. This book is an excellent addition to graduate-level research courses and academic libraries for use as a supporting resource.

REFERENCES

Taylor, T. E., Poston, W. S. C., II, Haddock, C. K., Blackburn, G. I., Heber, D., Heymsfield, S. B., & Foreyt, J. P. (2003). Psychometric characteristics of the general well-being schedule (GWB) with African-American women. *Quality of Life Research, 12*(1), 31-39. doi:http://dx.doi.org.ezproxy.regent.edu:2048/10.1023/A:1022052804109

Chapter 1
A Primer on Survey Research

Mary A. Hansen

https://orcid.org/0000-0003-0051-4039

Robert Morris University, USA

Gaelebale Nnunu Tsheko

University of Botswana, Botswana

ABSTRACT

This chapter presents a summary of best practices for the design, development, and analysis of quantitative survey research. The authors provide an overview of sampling procedures, as well as a summary of considerations for researchers as they develop questionnaires. Additionally, they provide descriptions of both qualitative and quantitative analyses that should be used to provide content and construct validity evidence for questionnaires. Finally, they show examples of common descriptive and inferential procedures appropriate for survey research. The goal of the chapter is to summarize factors that survey researchers should consider at all stages of their research project, from design to analysis, in order to improve survey research in practice.

INTRODUCTION

Survey research is a common form of research, yet the tenets of high quality instrument development, sampling, and data analysis are not consistently implemented in practice (Draugalis et al., 2008; Starr, 2012). Quantitative survey research uses questionnaires as tools for data collection, and serves as one of the primary research designs used to represent views, attitudes, beliefs, or opinions of a population of interest. Across organizations, survey research provides an increased understanding of phenomena, needs, experiences, and best practices; and is commonly used as an evaluation tool to examine current perceptions, attitudes, beliefs, and behaviors, as well as changes in these constructs over time. Survey research studies are one of the most frequently utilized methodologies by educational researchers (Hsu, 2005).

This chapter discusses best practices for the design, development, and analysis of quantitative survey research. The chapter provides novice researchers with an overview of options for design, development, administration, and analysis of quantitative survey research. At the same time, the chapter introduces

DOI: 10.4018/978-1-7998-7665-6.ch001

more advanced quantitative analyses that can be implemented to improve questionnaires. The overarching goal of this chapter is to describe the principles that are foundational to high-quality survey research. More specifically, the purpose is fourfold.

- Provide an overview of the sampling procedures for large scale survey research.
- Present a framework for designing, developing, piloting, and validating questionnaires that reflect the underlying construct(s) being measured.
- Discuss design considerations that will allow for both basic descriptive and inferential analysis.
- Describe and show examples of basic descriptive and inferential analyses that can be conducted for quantitative survey research studies and address cautionary notes about use of these inferential procedures.

The objectives of this chapter are for the reader to be able to:

1. Define and describe errors that commonly occur with survey research and take steps to rectify these errors.
2. Describe and implement sampling strategies used with survey research.
3. Recognize the sample size needed for accurate estimation of parameters.
4. Describe the processes associated with high-quality instrument development.
5. Create high quality items and instruments.
6. Select appropriate analyses for survey data.

BACKGROUND

As methodology, survey research can be driven by both positivist and post-positivist paradigms. These two traditions shaping research are grounded in differing perspectives (Aliyu et al., 2014; Crosson, 2003; McGregor & Murnane, 2010). Positivism generally employs quantitative research designs for investigating phenomena, and stems from the underlying assumptions that research should involve data that are objective and measurable. Positivism differs from post-positivist approaches, which aim to describe and explore in-depth phenomena, often including a qualitative perspective. The decision to implement a specific research design is dictated by a paradigm that drives the topic under investigation, the goals of the research, and the methodological preferences of the researcher. Both positivist and post-positivist paradigms assume that relationships already exist about the phenomenon under investigation, and the purpose of research is to unearth the relationships by measuring them. Thus, survey research can be used with both paradigms. This chapter focuses on large scale, descriptive, quantitative survey research, stemming more from the positivist paradigm.

Survey research is a relatively young field of study, and major advances in the field have been made in the last century (Kalton, 2019). Growth and development in sampling procedures, design elements, electronic administration options, analysis features including technical procedures for handling missing data, examining the internal structure of questionnaires, and visually presenting results, have all increased the popularity and convenience of survey research. While advances in the field have increased the complexity of survey research studies, several foundational aspects underlie instrument development, administration, and analyses used in survey research. This chapter highlights these fundamental aspects, providing a framework for developing and using questionnaires for data collection.

DESIGNING SURVEY RESEARCH STUDIES

Survey research commonly falls under the heading of quantitative, descriptive research and the process for conducting survey research typically involves several steps, each which further encompasses its own set of processes that can vary across studies. Generally the steps are: a) establish project goals; b) determine the survey sample; c) design the questionnaire and develop items; d) pilot and revise items; e) administer the questionnaire; f) clean, analyze and summarize the data; and g) draw conclusions, considering limitations and strengths of the design.

Aligning Instruments with Project Goals

Survey research begins with a determination of the project goals and articulation of the specific research, evaluation, or institution-based questions that will be addressed (Tait & Voepel-Lewis, 2015). Grounding both project goals and these underlying questions in the research literature and/or institution goals ensures the questionnaire dimensions and items will be linked to theory and practice.

To promote alignment across project goals, research questions, and questionnaire items, tabular displays can be utilized. Table 1 provides an example template for presenting evidence of content alignment. Table 1 includes a column for the questionnaire dimension and literature-based support of the topics. Additional columns can be added to address relevant alignment features such as professional standards, institutional missions, or underlying theories being examined by sets of questionnaire items. By displaying the alignment of questionnaire items, such tables provide content validity evidence. Direct alignment of questionnaire items to the underlying project goals and research questions can strengthen instrument quality.

Table 1. Alignment table showing content validity evidence for questionnaire

Program Goal	Research Question	Topic / Dimension	Questionnaire Items	Supporting Literature
1	1	A	1-3,5,7,8 (close ended) 9 (open ended)	Author1 (year)
	2	B	4, 6, 10-14 15 (open ended)	Author2 (year)
		C	16-19 (close ended)	Author3 (year)
2	3	A D	20-27 (close ended) 28-35 (close ended)	Author1 (year); Author4(year)
	3	D	36-39 (close ended) 40 (open ended)	Author1 (year); Author4(year)

Sampling in Survey Research

One main goal of quantitative survey research is to generalize the results from the study sample to the population of interest. Errors associated with survey research are introduced when data from the whole population are not accessed, and when instruments do not perfectly measure the intended construct. Survey research yields accurate results when researchers succeed in limiting four kinds of errors to the greatest possible extent: coverage error, sampling error, measurement error, and non-response error (Assael & Keon, 1982; Famule, 2010; Salant & Dillman, 1994). When these errors are considered at the design stage, each can be minimized.

Errors in Survey Research

Coverage error occurs when the sampling frame or accessible population, which is the source of the population from which a sample is drawn, does not include all elements of the population of interest. Researchers may not have access to the entire population. Therefore, they rely upon a sampling frame to represent the individuals in the population of interest. When the sampling frame is limited or not representative of the population, coverage error can impact the generalizability of the results. Coverage error can be impacted by factors including the availability of internet access, use of land versus cell phones, or completeness of the database used in defining and obtaining the sampling frame (Peytchev et al., 2011; Vicente & Reis, 2012). Coverage error becomes a concern when the sample drawn from the sampling frame does not accurately represent the population of interest, which can result in sample estimates that are biased for the population quantity being estimated. To combat issues stemming from coverage error, researchers should seek as comprehensive a sampling frame as possible. Further, researchers should acknowledge and describe the sampling frame in their studies. Concerns with coverage error may be lessened in organizational research in cases where complete population data are accessible from internal databases.

Sampling error is a common concern in survey research and all research studies that utilize samples. With sampling, there will be a difference between the sample statistic (e.g., the sample proportion or sample mean) and the population parameter (e.g., the population proportion or population mean), due to random differences in data that occur through selection of different samples. Sampling error can be reduced by using large, representative samples. Additionally, sampling error can be quantified using statistical procedures. Researchers should compute the sampling error associated with the study using formulas built into on-line sample size calculators (e.g., https://goodcalculators.com/margin-of-error-calculator) or found in statistics textbooks (e.g., Gravetter & Wallnau, 2017). By estimating sampling error prior to conducting survey research, researchers can determine the sample size needed to conduct their study, and plan ways to attain the desired sample size given likely response rates.

Measurement error must be a consideration in survey research. Measurement error occurs when questions asked do not provide useful information, are not clearly written, do not adequately measure the intended content or underlying construct, or do not include appropriate response choices. For example, if an item on the questionnaire has options that are not mutually exclusive, responses will not provide useful information. Lack of content coverage, poor directions, poorly worded items, and poor item layout are all potential causes of measurement error. Measurement error can be reduced by following sound instrument development procedures, conducting expert reviews to improve validity, and carrying out advanced statistical analyses.

Non-response error occurs when a significant number of those sampled do not respond to some or all of the questionnaire items. Nonresponse is often addressed using response rates, yet wide ranges for expected, acceptable, and reported response rates of 30% to 80% have been found in the literature (Cycyota & Harrison, 2006; Draugalis et al., 2008; Fincham, 2008; Fulton, 2018). Historically, response rates of 80% were desired; but factors such as increased resistance to completion by respondents, increased availability of questionnaires through technological advances, and survey fatigue have resulted in reduced response rates in survey research (Fosnacht et al., 2017; Hendra & Hill, 2019; Kohut et al., 2012; Porter et al., 2004).

Non-response error generates concern if the non-responders differ from responders in a way that would impact results and conclusions, thus creating non-response bias. Often, the effects of non-response error remain unrecognized by researchers, as non-response bias is difficult to detect and non-response analyses are uncommon (Peytchev, 2013; Standish & Umback, 2019; Werner et al., 2007). However, a growing body of research suggests only weak a relationship between response rates and response bias (Groves, 2006; Groves & Peytcheva, 2008; Hendra & Hill, 2019; Massey & Tourangeau, 2013), suggesting that researchers should consider conducting response analyses to examine sample quality rather than focusing only on response rate (Davern, 2013; Halbesleben & Whitman, 2013).

To minimize these various errors in survey research designs, researchers must be aware of potential errors; attempt to reduce the errors when possible; and acknowledge them when drawing conclusions. To that end, researchers should purposefully target high quality samples and construct high quality, technically sound questionnaires. Questionnaire development requires that considerations of item quality, questionnaire layout and other factors as described in this chapter and throughout the book are made. In addition, choosing an adequately sized, representative sample can reduce errors in survey research. While it is not possible to completely avoid any of these errors, researchers can reduce their impact through high quality design.

Probability Sampling Procedures

Sampling procedures should be determined early in the design stage of survey research. In general, potential respondents are identified based on the topic under investigation. A sample in survey research should be representative of the population from which it is drawn (i.e., sampling frame or accessible population) as well as the population to which results will be generalized (i.e., target population). Probability samples, commonly called random samples, provide the best way of obtaining representative samples (Colton & Covert, 2007; Mills & Gay, 2019). The power of survey research is that information from a relatively small sample can be used to describe the characteristics, attitudes, or perceptions of an entire population. However, this benefit is not generally attained unless the sample is both representative of the population and large enough to minimize sampling error.

Common random sampling methods include: 1) simple random sampling, where subjects are selected randomly from the sampling frame; 2) cluster sampling, where existing clusters are randomly sampled; 3) systematic random sampling, where every nth subject is randomly selected; and 4) stratified random sampling, where subjects are randomly selected within certain demographics, or strata, to obtain a sample that reflects the population based on the specified strata (Mills & Gay, 2019; Privitera & Ahlgrim-Delzell, 2019). Stratified random sampling incorporates either a) proportional sampling that results in samples from each strata being selected proportionally to how they exist in the population; or b) quota sampling, where subjects in each strata are collected until a pre-set quota, or percent, from each strata is obtained.

Results from non-random samples cannot be indisputably generalized to populations of interest. This being said, although non-random sampling techniques are less desirable, they can provide useful information and are widely used in practice (Colton & Covert, 2007; Druckman, 2005). Some levels of generalizability are often possible with non-random samples. However, given a choice between a random and a non-random procedure, random sampling is recommended.

An exception to this guideline would be survey research that is conducted at a single site, organization, or institution where the entire population might be accessible. In organizational research, using a census sample would likely yield a larger sample size and make results more generalizable. Within an organization, census surveys may be preferred over surveys that implement random sampling.

Sample Size

Choosing an appropriate sample size should not be overlooked in survey research, as having an appropriate sample size is crucial for running inferential statistical procedures. Thus, an adequate sample size, accounting for the likely response rate, must be planned from the start of the study. The determination of the final needed sample size depends on population size, sampling error tolerance, and variability in populations with respect to the characteristics of interest (Salant & Dillman, 1994).

As an example, when planning the sample size, the researcher selects the degree of confidence (90%, 95%, or 99%) and will have to estimate the variation in the characteristic of interest. Fortunately, online sample size calculators are available for computing the sample size for survey research studies (e.g., https://www.calculator.net/sample-size-calculator.html). Table 2 shows the needed sample size to estimate the population proportion with two levels of confidence (i.e., 95%, 99%) and three specified margins of error (i.e., 5%, 2.5%, 1%), given different population sizes, when no prior estimate of the proportion is needed. The values in Table 2 were generated using the formula $n = (Z_{\alpha/2})^2 * (.25) / E^2$ where $Z_{\alpha/2}$ is the critical value from the standard normal (Z) table based on the desired level of confidence (e.g., 95%, 99%) and E is the desired margin of error (e.g., 5%, 2.5%, 1%). While the computation is not meant to be the central focus here, readers should plan for final sample sizes, after nonresponses, in the hundreds for adequate estimation of population parameters for quantitative survey research designs where the goal is to generalize to large populations.

Table 2. Sample size needed for 95% and 99% confidence intervals for specified margins of errors (5%, 2.5%, 1%) for different population sizes

Population Size	Margin of Error, 95% Confidence			Margin of Error, 99% Confidence		
	5%	2.5%	1%	5%	2.5%	1%
100	80	94	99	87	96	99
500	217	377	475	285	421	485
1,000	278	606	906	399	727	943
10,000	370	1,332	4,899	622	2,098	6,239
100,000	383	1,513	8,762	659	2,585	14,227
500,000	384	1,532	9,423	663	2,640	16,055
1,000,000	384	1,534	9,512	663	2,647	16,317

Instrument Development

Regardless of whether cross-sectional or longitudinal survey research is conducted, questionnaire development must receive adequate time and care. When beginning questionnaire development, the goals of the survey research study should be articulated. As a first step, the relevant dimensions of the questionnaire must be specified.

Questionnaire Dimensions

Concept development is foundational to questionnaire development. That is, determining the concepts, constructs, or dimensions to be assessed by the questionnaire is a necessary first step in questionnaire development. This process involves determining what can and should be measured by the instrument, and entails extensive review of related literature. Additional means beyond literature can also be used to establish questionnaire dimensions, such as organizational missions, theories, or experience.

Literature-Based Dimensions

Content validity for questionnaires can be increased by grounding questionnaire dimensions and items in existing literature (e.g., see Kim et al., 2015). Particularly for topics that are under debate, controversial, undergo changes over time, or show inconclusive results across published studies, using existing literature as the basis for item development can result in questionnaire items that more completely address the dimensions under study. Aligning the dimensions under study as well as individual items to ideas and findings from existing literature as shown in Table 1 can increase the relevance and content validity of the instrument.

Experience-Based Dimensions

Questionnaire dimensions may also be based on personal or organizational experience. Experience plays a role in instrument development, but must be used with caution, as it remains important that the experiences asked about apply across individuals, settings, organizations, time, and other factors. When experienced-based topics are explored, researchers should attempt to ground the dimensions and items to existing literature or theories.

Expert-Informed Dimensions: Delphi Method

Experts can also play a role in instrument development. To this end, the Delphi Method can provide insight into concept and item development for questionnaires (Hasson et al., 2000; Hsu & Sandford, 2007). The Delphi Method is a structured, formatted means of communication that involves multiple rounds of data collection from experts in order to achieve a consensus of opinion. In the first round, opinions from a panel of experts are solicited. Data from the first round can be used to generate a draft questionnaire. In the second and subsequent rounds of expert review, items are rated, and ratings and their justification or rationale are shared across the group. Panelists receive the group information before making their new judgments about the relevance of topics.

Hsu and Sanford (2007) recommend the Delphi Method during questionnaire development because it allows for 1) anonymity of respondents; 2) a structured process for providing and receiving feedback, and 3) statistical analysis of data in order to put limits on the feedback process. Researchers must take care when implementing the Delphi Method for questionnaire development to include only experts or highly qualified panelists, and to ensure that the panel members do not feel pressure to conform to the group as a result of the iterative process itself, rather than because of a true change in opinion. While not without limitations, the Delphi Method can be used effectively during questionnaire development to provide both construct validity evidence related to overall questionnaire dimensions and content related validity evidence at the item level.

User Informed Dimensions Focus Groups / In-depth Interviews / Cognitive Interviews

Focus groups and cognitive interviews can also be used to inform questionnaire development (Beatty & Willis, 2007; Desimone & LeFloch, 2004; Drennan, 2003; Gehlbach & Brinkworth, 2011; Orovio-goicoechea et al., 2010; Renberg et al., 2008; Sherman et al., 2014; Thompson et al., 2011; Willis, 2005). Generally, informants for focus groups and interviews should be similar to those in the target population. Informing instrument development with information from likely respondents can help ensure that relevant topics are addressed and proper language and terminology are used in the questionnaire. Further, using cognitive interviews or think-alouds during or prior to the pilot stage can provide insight about respondent understanding and interpretation of questionnaire items. Information gathered from cognitive interviews can help researchers refine their scale.

The Delphi technique, focus groups, in-depth interviews, and cognitive interviews can be used independently or in combination to inform questionnaire development. For instance, Lindsay and colleagues (2012) used focus groups, in-depth interviews, and cognitive interviews to develop a child-feeding questionnaire appropriate for low-income, Latina mothers. Collecting data for the purpose of instrument development from the intended response group can inform the overall dimensions of the questionnaire, and limit problems respondents might have with interpretation, language, and word choice. Using one or more of these techniques during questionnaire development provides both construct and content related validity evidence.

Internal Structure

Using literature, the Delphi Method, focus groups, and/or interviews, questionnaire developers can refine the underlying constructs or dimensions to assess. The number of dimensions measured by a questionnaire will depend on several factors including the scope of the research questions, the precision by which each dimension can be measured, and the theoretical framework from the literature. After determining the desired number and defining dimensions, item development can begin. Instrument developers should generate between three and twelve items to represent each dimension; using only one item per dimension is not recommended (Marsh et al., 1998). Recommended practice suggests that additional items be written to measure each dimension, in case items need to be deleted after pilot testing (see Fraser et al. (2021) for an example). Nunnally (1978) recommends a starting item pool that is between one and a half and two times as large as desired for the final instrument. Planning and developing additional items in the design stage will help to ensure the final instrument will yield reliable and valid overall and subscores.

Item Quality

Writing clear and measurable items is central to high-quality survey research (Colton & Covert, 2007; Haladyna & Rodriguez, 2013). The items constructed must be derived from the research questions. It is therefore important to first identify the type of information being sought and decide on the format (closed- or open-ended) that best addresses that content. This is followed by a focus on wording of actual questions making sure language is kept simple and focused. Avoiding leading and double-barreled questions, making sure options are mutually exclusive, and ensuring that the provided response options cover all possible responses, are considerations during item development. Additionally, using parallel phrasing across items by framing all items from the same perspective (e.g., using *I* or *you* consistently when referring to the respondent), maintaining consistent verb tense, and using common vocabulary can increase item quality.

Table 3 provides example questionnaire items that do not satisfy these item writing guidelines. Piloting the questionnaire and having respondents think-aloud during the pilot administration can reduce and eliminate poorly constructed items. Considering feedback from a pilot group of respondents during individual think-alouds as they complete the questionnaire can be especially helpful in clarifying item wording.

Table 3. Problem questionnaire items

Item	Response Choices	Problem
Do you recommend online instruction?	a. Yes b. No	Leading towards socially acceptable response
I liked the content and the modality of the courses in the doctoral program.	a. Yes b. No	Double-barreled
Circle the letter of the response that shows the number of totally online classes you had as part of your doctoral program.	a. 0-3 b. 3-6 c. 6-9 d. 10 or more	Overlapping Categories
Which of the following types of instructional materials were part of your weekly instruction?	a. Video lecture b. Journal writing c. Tests	Too few response options to satisfy all respondents

Item Types

Questionnaire items are created to address the aims of the survey research study, which may include describing opinions, attitudes, perceptions, or feelings about one or more underlying constructs. There are two main categories of questions: closed- and open-response items. Closed-response items have fixed responses from which a respondent can choose while open-response items are less structured and allow respondent to construct their responses.

A common type of closed-response item utilizes a Likert scale. The decision of whether to include an even or odd number of response option closed-ended items that utilize Likert scales is a debated topic. That is, whether to include a middle score point or *neutral* category has been a topic of discussion and debate for questionnaire designers and data analysts. By forcing respondents to choose a preference, questionnaire developers can address the concern that respondents will choose a response option that takes less effort (Mason, 1996). For analysis purposes, researchers can often gain more information from the data by omitting a *neutral* response; but this is a philosophical determination that the researcher must make.

Open-ended questions are useful when the researcher is exploring a topic in-depth. Open-ended comments supplement information received with closed-ended items with reasons, rationale, or examples. Open-ended questions are valuable if used strategically (Druckman, 2005), such as in exploratory studies or at the end of sections of questionnaires to obtain respondents' overall views about specific questionnaire dimensions.

Unit of Analysis

During instrument development, researchers must determine the smallest unit of analysis at which they intend to summarize results. While categories of demographic variables can be collapsed or aggregated during data analysis, the categories cannot be separated into smaller units once data are collected. The smallest unit of analysis must therefore be decided upon during instrument development so that it can be built into the questionnaire.

For instance, if subjects' ages are of interest, the smallest unit of analysis the researchers could collect would be birthdate, as this variable would allow for an exact measure, even to the number of days, of the subject's age. During analysis and reporting, researchers could describe summary statistics of individual ages such as means, standard deviations, and ranges; researchers could also summarize respondents by collapsing the ages into age groups and reporting the counts and percentages of respondents in each age group. Alternatively, researchers may collect only age group information, rather than exact birth date. In this case, the smallest unit of analysis that could be reported is age group, where counts and percentages of respondents in each age group could be summarized in the results. However, neither the average age of participants nor the exact range of ages of respondents could be found by just knowing respondents' age groups.

When deciding on the unit of analysis, researchers must simultaneously consider the sensitivity of the item and the value of the summarized information. For sensitive data such as age or salary, researchers may choose to collect data categorically rather than exact values, in order to increase the likelihood of response; knowing that precision in the reporting of statistical summaries will be lost.

Questionnaire Formatting

Questionnaire layout is an important quality issue (Colton & Covert, 2007; Fowler, 2014; Haladyna & Rodriguez, 2013; Rea & Parker, 2014). The cover of the questionnaire, title, introductory statement, and directions for responding in each section all require consideration. Again, these attributes can be improved through piloting.

Item order must be a consideration to ensure the questionnaire structure is presentable to respondents, as some studies have found different results based on item order (Bowman & Schuldt, 2014; Chen, 2010; Kaplan et al., 2013). Dillman (1978) suggested that items in a questionnaire be ordered in a way that will build the confidence of respondents. The first question on a questionnaire is important and can determine whether the respondent will continue. Starting with demographic information like age, sex, or income may not build such confidence, and as such those items should be placed towards the end or strategically within a questionnaire (Colton & Covert, 2007; Dillman, 1978). Ordering items by their social importance, response scale, content, and question type is desirable. Items of social importance are those that address issues that would undoubtedly be deemed important and foundational to the research. Item order must be planned and adjusted as needed during instrument development to improve formatting.

Closed-ended items should be presented before the open-ended items related to the same topic. For a survey that addresses several dimensions, sets of closed-ended items related to a single topic can be presented followed by open-ended item(s) that relate to the same content. The pattern of closed-response followed by open-ended can be repeated throughout the questionnaire in order to maintain a parallel nature, and obtain both quantitative and qualitative information about each dimension.

In addition, in order to ensure that respondents are completing the questionnaire seriously and honestly, reverse-coded items, or items phrased in the negative, can be incorporated. Including negatively worded items periodically provides evidence about whether respondents are answering truthfully and reading all items. Any reverse-coded items must be recoded before data analysis. Subsequent analyses using person-fit statistics or formal examinations of low quality data can also be conducted (DeSimone & Harms, 2018; Felt et al., 2017).

Piloting the Questionnaire

Once developed, questionnaires should be piloted on a small sample with similar characteristics as the target population. The pilot sample should not be included in the main data collection. Ideally, the pilot sample should be large enough to allow for reliability indices to be established. Even when this pilot sample size is not attainable, a small pilot will be worthwhile. Through a pilot, information about question wording and content, instructions, questionnaire length and layout, and logistical administration issues such as cost and time for administration is gathered.

Addtionally, conducting a think-aloud or cognitive interview with a small number of individuals during the pilot can provide specific information that can aid in item refinement. Pilot data are then analyzed and results used to alter and refine the questionnaire before actual administration. Common responses to open-ended items can also be transformed into closed-ended items as the result of a pilot. Piloting and revising problem items based on feedback provides additional validity evidence.

Administering a Questionnaire

Administration considerations for questionnaires encompass several decisions about sampling procedures, modality, cost, logistics, and time frames.

Cover Letter

A questionnaire should be accompanied by a cover letter. Online questionnaires often include the required introductory information in the initial screen. This letter or introductory information should include the purpose of study, why the respondent is important to the study, benefits and risks associated with participation, confidentiality and/or anonymity clauses, notification of voluntary participation, affiliation, timeframe for responding, and contact information of the researcher. A well-crafted cover letter should increase response rate. Figure 1 presents an example cover letter for an online questionnaire that obtains consent.

Cost and Other Logistics

Questionnaires can be administered via mail, face-to-face, telephone or online. Each modality has advantages and disadvantages researchers must carefully weigh. The decision should be based mainly on increasing response rate and reducing response bias. Literature related to the response rates associated with paper-and-pencil versus electronic modalities has been mixed, with several studies suggesting lower response rates for online surveys (Manfreda et al., 2008) and others showing comparable response rates when both formats were preceded by an advance mail notification (Kaplowitz et al., 2004).

Figure 1. Example consent letter for a survey research study

Perceptions about Online Instruction for Doctoral Program

Dear Doctoral Student,

You are invited to participate in a survey research study that will collect information about your perceptions, satisfaction, and needs related to online instruction in your doctoral program. You are being asked to participate in this study because you are currently enrolled in an online doctoral program at XXX institution.

This questionnaire contains demographic items as well as items that relate to your experiences with online instruction before and during our program. A variety of item formats are included. The results will show which instructional and assessments methods are currently being used most often in courses, how effective students believe these methods to be, and a breakdown of preference for these methods based on demographic and course-related features.

You will not be asked to identify yourself on the survey, so all responses will be anonymous and will remain confidential. Electronic copies of the questionnaires will be kept in a password protected site on a password protected computer for five years. There are no anticipated risk factors or benefits for your participation in this study.

The investigator in this study is NAME and the research is being conducted to fulfill PROJECT at INSTITUTION. If you have any questions, you may contact me at email@researcher.email or the INSTITUTION IRB at XXX-XXX-XXXX or IRB@irb.email . This study has been approved by RESEARCHER INSTITUION IRB.

Entering the questionnaire by clicking on the CONTINUE button below indicates that you have chosen to participate in this study and have read and understood this consent form. You may withdraw consent and terminate your participation in completing this questionnaire at any time. If you choose to participate, please complete and return the survey by Month, date, year.

Thank you for your time.

CONTINUE

Online survey packages contain many features that allow for ease of administration for the researcher and respondent. Web-based questionnaires also have issues of concern such as security and being recognized as junk mail or spam (Sills & Song, 2002). For mailed questionnaires, a personalized letter showing potential respondents how important they are to the study and subsequent follow-up reminders for non-respondents are necessary, which can increase cost. QR codes can be included within paper mailings to allow for electronic entry by the respondent. For face-to-face and telephone administration, issues of timing for visits or calls and procedures for handling matters when potential respondents are not available are important. For face-to-face surveys, there are additional travel and labor expenses.

The cost and other logistical matters play roles in determining the modality of administration. Multiple administration types can also be utilized. Finally, incentives can help increase response rates, and can be considered when resources are available. Incentives for all respondents or for a small number of randomly selected respondents can be included, and when applicable, information about incentives should be included in the cover letter or introductory material.

Time Frame for Data Collection

The timeline for data collection requires consideration. Launching a questionnaire during a particularly busy time for an organization may impact both responses and response rates. Waiting too long to administer a survey to a particular population (e.g., graduates) may limit the applicability of the instrument topics. While a perfect administration time may not exist, the researcher should consider factors that may limit applicability or response rates, and work around those factors to select the best time for administration.

Additionally, the researcher must determine how long the questionnaire should remain open for responses. Generally, timelines ranging from three to eight weeks will allow ample time for data collection, including reminders and possible resampling to increase response rates. Timelines and reminders for electronically administered instruments can be automatically set in online survey software packages and instruments can be closed to additional entry; timelines for paper and pencil administration will have to be determined and set, and decisions about questionnaires received in the mail after the end date will have to be made.

Analysis of Questionnaire Data

Data Cleaning

Data must be cleaned before analysis. Cleaning data involves checking for data entry errors, missing values, incomplete responses, and outliers in the data (Fowler, 2014; Williams, 2003). In practice, an initial step of data cleaning can utilize frequency distributions of the items to verify that all closed-ended item responses are valid. In addition, data cleaning involves checking for duplicate and invalid cases. Further, researchers should recode all negatively worded items so that higher numeric codes on all items reflect more positive responses; and lower numeric codes on all items reflect less positive responses.

Restrictions such as item response validation can be built into online survey packages to reduce the types and amount of data cleaning that are required for electronically administered instruments. For instance, defined item formats for dollar amounts, zip codes, email addresses, and numbers can force correct formatting during administration. As an example, the number ten could have a forced format to require entry of "10" and not permit entry of text data in the form "ten." Because analysis requires a number format, cleaning would be necessary to change "ten" to 10 if the entry format is not required during administration.

During data cleaning for paper-and-pencil instruments, incorrect data must be fixed or deleted. To ease this task, researchers should assign an identification code to each paper instrument that is also entered into an electronic file. If the results yield responses that were not possible response options (e.g., a mark between two response categories; or multiple response categories selected for a single item), the researcher traces the data back to the hard copy of the questionnaire and corrects or excludes data accordingly. Failing to record the identification field on both the hard copy and the electronic file can hinder data cleaning to the point that data entry will have to be redone.

Researchers must also determine how to deal with partial response data. The rule for including or excluding partial responses should be implemented consistently, independent of the actual questionnaire responses. That is, researchers cannot include partially completed positive responses, while excluding partially completed negative responses.

Additionally, statistically centered techniques for handling missing data include deletion, mean substitution, regression substitution, and multiple imputation. Researchers should examine each of these methods and determine which, if any, will be used, prior to data analysis (Montiel-Overall, 2006; Tsikriktis, 2005).

Reliability Analysis and Inter-item Correlations

After data cleaning, researchers should summarize reliability and validity evidence showing the quality of the questionnaire. A widely used measure of reliability is Cronbach's coefficient alpha (Cronbach & Shavelson, 2004; Liu et al., 2010; Taber, 2018; Yang & Green, 2011). Coefficient alpha is commonly used as a measure of internal consistency associated with the construct or dimension underlying the questionnaire and can be computed for the overall instrument and individual subscales.

Researchers have suggested that Cronbach's coefficient alpha has some flaws, in that it can be inflated by outliers, misunderstood, or used inappropriately when underlying assumptions are not met (Cronbach & Shavelson, 2004; Liu et al., 2010; Taber, 2018; Yang & Green, 2011). Additional analyses that require more quantitative expertise using structural equation modeling (SEM) can provide evidence about the assumptions underlying coefficient alpha and additional reliability evidence (Yang & Green, 2011).

Researchers can utilize inter-item and item-to-total correlations to target items for elimination or modification. Items measuring the same underlying construct should positively correlate with the total questionnaire score or the total subscale score (Rattray & Jones, 2007). While specific guidelines for elimination of items based only on inter-item correlation values are not strictly enforced, item-to-total correlations that are less than .30 often do not add a great deal to the explanatory power (Ferketich, 1991; Kline 1993; Rattray & Jones, 2007). An exception to this guideline would be items that exhibited strong content validity, supported by the literature and expert review.

Classical Item Analysis and Item Response Theory

Along the lines of more advanced statistical and psychometric analyses of survey data, classical test theory (CTT) and item response theory (IRT) principles can be implemented to provide statistical evidence about the quality of questionnaires (Becker et al., 2007; DeVellis, 2006; Edelen & Reeve, 2007; Sharkness & Deangelo, 2011). IRT includes a set of modeling techniques that offer benefits over CTT and can aid researchers in evaluating instrument quality (Edelen & Reeve, 2007; Hambleton, et al., 1991; Lavrakas, 2012). IRT can be used to examine item and scale quality, optimally shorten instruments by providing precision in item measurement throughout the measurement range, and examine item performance across subgroups (Becker et al., 2007; Edelen & Reeve, 2007). The novice researcher may need to seek additional quantitative support to implement IRT procedures as well as the more advanced statistical procedures associated with factor analysis that are discussed next.

Validity Evidence

Questionnaire quality is established by reporting evidence of validity and reliability. The most common validity evidence for questionnaires is content validity. Content validity reflects evidence of the degree to which the responses from the questionnaire can appropriately be said to measure the construct they represent. Content validity is not established statistically but rather established through expert judgment. Use of the Delphi Method, cognitive interviews, and focus groups can provide evidence of content validity. Item alignment maps (see Table 1) can visually show content alignment of items. General review and critique of the questionnaire by experts in the field can also provide content related validity evidence. When more advanced content- and construct-related evidence is desired, researchers can utilize more advanced statistical methods.

Factor Analysis

Factor analytic techniques provide researcher with one way to examine the underlying internal structure of the questionnaire using statistical modeling. Such analyses require fairly advanced quantitative analysis skills. Rather than relying only on expert judgment, these more advanced statistical analyses can provide strong evidence of the internal structure. With both expert judgment and quantitative validation of the structure, use of questionnaire results for decision making is better justified. Factor analytic studies are characterized as being exploratory or confirmatory. The overview of factor analysis that follows does not provide in-depth descriptions of the analysis; thus, additional reading and statistical proficiency are recommended before conducting these analyses.

Exploratory Factor Analyses (EFA)

The goal of exploratory factor analysis (EFA) is to find an underlying structure that could account for the intercorrelations of an observed set of variables. In terms of questionnaire data, the item responses would be used to determine which items tend to correlate with each other, thus forming a factor structure, and an attempt would be made to describe the resulting factors. A factor structure is not verified in this exploratory analysis, but sought out (Cromrey & Lee, 1992; Loehlin, 1998; Streiner, 2006).

Confirmatory Factor Analysis (CFA)

In confirmatory factor analysis (CFA), a factor structure for the data is hypothesized, and the goal is to verify the intended internal structure (Cromrey & Lee, 1992; Loehlin, 1998; Thompson, 1997). CFA falls under the broader umbrella of analyses called structural equation modeling (SEM). In CFA, the number of constructs or factors that underlie the questionnaire, as well as the relationships between and among the constructs, must be determined in advance of analysis, and the relationships are tested during analysis. CFA is useful for verifying the intended structure of widely utilized instruments whose structure has not been verified since its initialization (Herbert et al., 1995); examining whether an instrument may yield a different structure for subgroups of the population such as men and women (Miller & Krieshok, 1989); or comparing different versions of instruments (Streiner, 2006).

Guidelines for the sample size needed to conduct CFA range from approximately five times to twenty times as large as the number of items in a model (Hair et al., 1995; Mundfrom et al., 2005; Nunnally, 1975). This sample size recommendation should be used in conjunction with the information provided in Table 2 when the underlying structure of the questionnaire will be examined. Additionally, at least two (Bollen, 1989) but more likely three (Marsh et al., 1998) or four or more items per factor are needed to run CFA adequately. The number of items, factors, and items per factor all play a role in determining the needed sample size (Mundfrom et al., 2005). In all cases, large sample sizes are required to run factor analyses.

CFA is recommended over EFA for a variety of reasons. EFA is often seen as being data-driven. CFA instead forces the researcher to be precise when defining constructs, before analysis of the data begins (Thompson, 1997). Additionally, CFA allows a number of models to be hypothesized which can aid in understanding an instrument's construct validity (Daniel & Siders, 1994). After testing various models that support different structures, one can have a stronger argument that the structure of the data exists as expected. The most parsimonious model, which is more likely to be replicated, can be selected as the best fitting (Thompson, 1997). Models that do not fit can be modified based on the output of the CFA, and a new model could be tested. However, since the goal of CFA is to verify the structure of a questionnaire, model changes should not be so great that they indicate model fit for a model which is not representative of the intended structure (Cromrey & Lee, 1992). Thus, with this cautionary note in mind, CFA can be used to verify the structure of questionnaires.

Graphical Representations

In descriptive research, graphical representations of response patterns can be useful. Bar charts, pie charts, histograms, line graphs and scatterplots are common graphical displays that can be generated for questionnaire data, and the graphical displays can be presented for the full data set overall and to compare subgroups. Infographics and data visualization software provide additional means of graphically showing results.

Descriptive Statistics

Clean data can be analyzed and results used to describe the characteristics of the sample and their response patterns. For nominal scale variables including basic demographics like gender or ethnicity, frequency counts and percentages can be presented. As the measurements collected from survey research get more specific, additional analyses can be run. For example, for ordinal level variables including those measured on Likert scales, both frequencies, percentages, and measures of center and spread can be used to summarize data. For analysis of interval and ratio scale variables, the expectation is that means and standard deviations will be provided.

Tables 4 presents an example summary table for all respondents for items measured on a five-point scale. Table 4 shows item level descriptive statistics including frequencies, percentages, medians, means (*M*), and standard deviations (*SD*). In addition to providing numeric summaries of item level data in tabular form, researchers should provide written summaries of meaningful findings including take-away messages for the reader. These summaries should not duplicate tabular summaries, but should instead complement them.

Table 4. Summary of responses about overall satisfaction with course work (n = 131)

Item	Strongly Dissatisfied (1)		Slightly Dissatisfied (2)		Neither Satisfied nor Dissatisfied (3)		Slightly Satisfied (4)		Strongly satisfied (5)		Overall		
	n	%	*n*	%	*n*	%	*n*	%	*n*	%	*Mdn*	*M*	*SD*
Item 1	20	15.3%	10	7.6%	42	32.1%	30	22.9%	29	22.1%	2	2.3	1.3
Item 2	35	26.7%	8	6.1%	23	17.6%	41	31.3%	24	18.3%	2	2.1	1.5
Item 3	31	23.7%	13	9.9%	28	21.4%	22	16.8%	37	28.2%	2	2.2	1.5
Item 4	53	40.5%	12	9.2%	13	9.9%	15	11.5%	38	29.0%	2	1.8	1.7
Item 5	16	12.2%	29	22.1%	34	26.0%	29	22.1%	23	17.6%	2	2.1	1.3

Inferential Statistics

In addition to running basic descriptive analyses, when samples sizes are adequate and evidence supporting the quality and structure of the questionnaire has been established, researchers can answer inferential questions about the populations from which the samples were drawn. Two common types of inferential procedures used with survey data are tests on means and proportions.

Tests of Means: T tests and ANOVA

Tests of means are prevalent in survey research. For instance, a common research question looks at differences in mean responses across subgroups of respondents. However, researchers should be cautious when running such analyses, and need to take steps to ensure that the assumptions underlying the use of *t* tests and analysis of variance (ANOVA) procedures are met. The assumptions underlying independent samples *t* tests and ANOVA are:

- the underlying data are normally distributed
- the groups for which comparisons are being made are independent
- the variances between the groups are the same

For survey research, especially when responses to single Likert item are compared for two more ore subgroups of responses, the underlying distribution is not normally distributed. This is because Likert items are based on a discrete scale that usually has between three and seven categories. In addition, the assignment of meaning of numbers to Likert items is arbitrary. Therefore, *t* tests and ANOVA are inappropriate for individual item level Likert response data because ordinal scales do not satisfy the underlying assumption of normality. Thus, graphical displays of data coupled with chi-square analyses at the individual item level which are discussed below are recommended (Mircioiu & Atkinson, 2017). At the item level, nonparametric tests such as the Mann-Whitney-Wilcoxon U test can also be used to compare responses (de Winter & Dodou, 2012) instead of parametric *t* tests.

Rather than use tests of means for individual questionnaire items, a new variable that represents the total or average response to the full set of items representing the dimension can be created and used for analysis. This computation for a total subscale score should be justified by the reliability and validity evidence gathered from previous steps articulated in this chapter. Aggregating responses across items within a dimension of the questionnaire creates a new variable which can represent either a total or average subscale score. This aggregated score will have a distribution much closer to a normal distribution than single three to seven point Likert items, making the use of *t* tests and ANOVA more appropriate.

Table 5 shows a subset of individual questionnaire items that relate to one dimension or subscale of the questionnaire, as well as a variable called TOTAL_SUB1 that represents each individual's total score across the seven items constituting the first subscale on the questionnaire. Comparisons for each gender (coded Male = 1, Female = 2) can then be carried out using an independent samples *t*-test, with TOTAL_SUB1 as the dependent variable.

Table 5. Computation of subscale scores across 5-point Likert items that measure one dimension

ID	Gender	Item 1	Item 2	Item 3	Item 4	Item 5	Item 6	Item 7	TOTAL_SUB1
001	2	5	5	5	4	5	5	5	34
002	2	4	5	5	5	5	5	5	34
003	1	2	1	2	2	2	2	1	12
004	2	4	4	3	4	4	3	4	26
005	1	3	3	3	3	3	3	3	21
006	2	4	4	4	3	4	4	4	27
...		...	...	...	...	...	...	...	...
525	1	3	2	2	2	3	2	2	16

Tests of Proportions: Chi Square Tests

Chi-square tests examine relationships between variables measured on nominal and ordinal levels. The chi-square test of association involves the cross-tabulation of the frequencies with which the variables co-occur in a sample. Like t-tests and ANOVA, chi-square tests also have assumptions that must be met for appropriate use of the statistical test:

- Each observation is independent of all the others (i.e., one observation per subject)
- All expected cell counts must be greater than 5.

With respect to the second assumption, statistical texts suggest that chi-square tests can be run appropriately as long as no more than 20% of the expected counts are less than five, as long as all individual expected counts are one or greater. In ideal situations, the needed sample size to satisfy these assumptions will be obtained. For cases when this is not possible, the process of collapsing categories may help. To collapse categories, two or more rows or column categories are combined. For example, a strongly agree and agree category could be combined into one category, and the new count of the collapsed category would be the sum of the respondents who agreed to any degree with the item content. Care must be taken during data analyses to ensure that the assumptions of any inferential statistical procedures are met.

Drawing Conclusions from Survey Research

Descriptive research including large scale survey research does not permit causal inferences. Further, the extent to which results generalize to the target population will be dependent on the quality of the study design. When high quality samples are coupled with strong reliability, content and construct validity evidence, generalizability arguments are stronger.

FUTURE RESEARCH DIRECTIONS

This chapter presents a primer for questionnaire development for quantitative survey research. While the chapter introduces important design, development, administration, and analysis procedures, additional readings and exploration into these aspects are recommended. The authors presented an overview of the topics that should be considered, and encourage instrument developers and data analysts to explore these aspects in greater depth.

CONCLUSION

While there has been an increase in the use of questionnaires and survey research across fields, there is not strong evidence that adequate time, review processes, and analyses have been allocated to questionnaire development. Failure to develop a high-quality instruments or access representative samples may lead to incorrect conclusions. This chapter addresses the principles of high-quality survey research design, development, and analysis. By addressing sound design, development and analysis practices, the authors aim to inform future researchers of factors and steps they should consider throughout the survey research process.

REFERENCES

Aliyu, A., Bello, M., Kasim, R., & Martin, D. (2014). Positivist and non-positivist paradigm in social science research: Conflicting paradigms or perfect partners. *Journal of Management and Sustainability*, *4*(3), 79–95. doi:10.5539/jms.v4n3p79

Assael, H., & Keon, J.Sampling Errors in Survey Research. (1982). Nonsampling vs. sampling errors in survey research. *Journal of Marketing*, *46*(2), 114–123. doi:10.1177/002224298204600212

Beatty, P., & Willis, G. (2007). Research synthesis: The practice of cognitive interviewing. *Public Opinion Quarterly*, *71*(2), 287–311. doi:10.1093/poq/nfm006

Becker, J., Schwartz, C., Saris-Baglama, R., Kosinski, M., & Bjorner, J. (2007). Using item response theory (IRT) for developing and evaluating the pain impact questionnaire (PIQ-6™). *Pain Medicine*, *8*(s3), 129–144. doi:10.1111/j.1526-4637.2007.00377.x

Bethlehem, J., & Schouten, B. (2016). Nonresponse error: detection and correction. In *The SAGE handbook of survey methodology* (pp. 558–578). Sage Publications Ltd. doi:10.4135/9781473957893.n35

Bollen, K. A. (1989). *Structural equations with latent variables*. John Wiley. doi:10.1002/9781118619179

Bowman, N. A., & Schuldt, J. P. (2014). Effects of item order and response options in college student surveys. *New Directions for Institutional Research*, *2014*(161), 99–109. doi:10.1002/ir.20070

Brick, J. M., & Tourangeau, R. (2017). Responsive survey designs for reducing nonresponse bias. *Journal of Official Statistics*, *33*(3), 735–752. doi:10.1515/jos-2017-0034

Chen, P. H. (2010). *Item order effects on attitude measures* (Dissertation thesis). University of Denver.

Colton, D., & Covert, R. W. (2007). *Designing and constructing instruments for social research and evaluation*. Jossey-Bass.

Comrey, A. L., & Lee, H. B. (1992). *A first course in factor analysis*. Erlbaum.

Cronbach, L. J., & Shavelson, R. J. (2004). My current thoughts on coefficient alpha and successor procedures. *Educational and Psychological Measurement*, *64*(3), 391–418. doi:10.1177/0013164404266386

Crossan, F. (2003). Research philosophy: Towards an understanding. *Nurse Researcher*, *11*(1), 46–55. doi:10.7748/nr2003.10.11.1.46.c5914 PMID:14533474

Cycyota, C., & Harrison, D. (2018). What (not) to expect when surveying executives: A meta-analysis of top manager response rates and techniques over time. *Organizational Research Methods*, *9*(2), 133–160. doi:10.1177/1094428105280770

Czajka, J. L., & Beyler, A. (2016). *Declining response rates in federal surveys: Trends and implications (background paper)*. Mathematica Policy Research. https://mathematica.org/publications/declining-response-rates-in-federal-surveys-trends-and-implications-background-paper

Daniel, L. G., & Siders, J. A. (1994). Validation of teacher assessment instruments: A confirmatory factor analytic approach. *Journal of Personnel Evaluation in Education*, *8*(1), 29–40. doi:10.1007/BF00972707

Davern, M. (2013). Nonresponse rates are a problematic indicator of nonresponse bias in survey research. *Health Services Research*, *48*(3), 905–912. doi:10.1111/1475-6773.12070 PMID:23656501

de Winter, J., & Dodou, D. (2012). Five-point Likert items: T test versus Mann-Whitney-Wilcox on. *Practical Assessment, Research & Evaluation*, *15*(11), 1–16. doi:10.7275/bj1p-ts64

Desimone, J., & Harms, P. (2018). Dirty data: The effects of screening respondents who provide low-quality data in survey research. *Journal of Business and Psychology*, *33*(5), 559–557. doi:10.100710869-017-9514-9

Desimone, L. M., & Kerstin Carlson, L. F. (2004). Are we asking the right questions? Using cognitive interviews to improve surveys in education research. *Educational Evaluation and Policy Analysis*, *26*(1), 1–22. doi:10.3102/01623737026001001

DeVellis, R. F. (2006). Classical test theory. *Medical Care*, *44*(11, Suppl 3), S50–S59. doi:10.1097/01.mlr.0000245426.10853.30 PMID:17060836

Dillman, D. A. (1978). *Mail and telephone surveys: The total design method*. John Wiley & Sons, Inc.

Draugalis, J., Coons, S., & Plaza, C. (2008). Best practice for survey research reports: A synopsis for authors and reviewers. *American Journal of Pharmaceutical Education*, 72(1), 1–6. doi:10.5688/aj720111 PMID:18322573

Drennan, J. (2003). Cognitive interviewing: Verbal data in the design and pretesting of questionnaires. *Journal of Advanced Nursing*, 42(1), 57–63. doi:10.1046/j.1365-2648.2003.02579.x PMID:12641812

Druckman, D. (2005). *Doing research: Methods of inquiry for conflict analysis*. Sage Publication., doi:10.4135/9781412983969

Edelen, M., & Reeve, B. (2007). Applying Item Response Theory (IRT) modeling to questionnaire development, evaluation, and refinement. *Quality of Life Research: An International Journal of Quality of Life Aspects of Treatment, Care and Rehabilitation*, 16(5), 5–18. doi:10.100711136-007-9198-0 PMID:17375372

Famule, F. D. (2010). Assessing and reducing survey error in mail surveys. *Pacific Journal of Science and Technology*, 11(2), 422–428.

Felt, J., Castaneda, R., Tiemensma, J., & Depaoli, S. (2017). Using person fit statistics to detect outliers in survey research. *Frontiers in Psychology*, 8, 863. doi:10.3389/fpsyg.2017.00863 PMID:28603512

Ferketic, S. (1991). Focus on psychometrics: Aspects of item analysis. *Research in Nursing & Health*, 14(2), 165–168. doi:10.1002/nur.4770140211 PMID:2047538

Fincham, J. E. (2008). Response rates and responsiveness for surveys, standards, and the journal. *American Journal of Pharmaceutical Education*, 72(2), 1–3. doi:10.5688/aj720243 PMID:18483608

Fosnacht, K., Sarraf, S., Howe, E., & Peck, L. K. (2017). How important are high response rates for college Surveys? *Review of Higher Education*, 40(2), 245–265. doi:10.1353/rhe.2017.0003

Fowler, F. J. (2014). *Survey Research Methods* (5th ed.). Sage.

Fraser, B. J., McLure, F. I., & Koul, R. B. (2021). Assessing classroom emotional climate in STEM classrooms: Developing and validating a questionnaire. *Learning Environments Research*, 24(1), 1–21. doi:10.100710984-020-09316-z

Fulton, B. (2018). Organizations and survey research: Implementing response enhancing strategies and conducting nonresponse analyses. *Sociological Methods & Research*, 47(2), 240–276. doi:10.1177/0049124115626169

Gehlbach, H., & Brinkworth, M. (2011). Measure twice, cut down error: A process for enhancing the validity of survey scales. *Review of General Psychology*, 15(4), 380–387. doi:10.1037/a0025704

Gravetter, F. J., & Wallnau, L. B. (2017). *Statistics for the Behavioral Sciences* (10th ed.). Thomson/Wadsworth.

Groves, R. M. (2006). Nonresponse rates and nonresponse bias in household surveys. *Public Opinion Quarterly*, 70(5), 646–675. doi:10.1093/poq/nfl033

Groves, R. M., & Peytcheva, E. (2008). The impact of nonresponse rates on nonresponse bias: A meta-analysis. *Public Opinion Quarterly*, 72(2), 167–189. doi:10.1093/poq/nfn011

Hair, J., Anderson, R., Tatham, R., & Black, W. (1995). *Multivariate data analysis*. Prentice-Hall.

Haladyna, T. M., & Rodriguez, M. C. (2013). *Developing and validating test items*. Taylor & Francis. doi:10.4324/9780203850381

Halbesleben, J. R. B., & Whitman, M. V. (2013). Evaluating survey quality in health services research: A decision framework for assessing nonresponse bias. *Health Services Research*, 48(3), 913–930. doi:10.1111/1475-6773.12002 PMID:23046097

Hambleton, R. K., Swaminathan, H., & Rogers, H. J. (1991). Fundamentals of Item Response Theory. *Sage (Atlanta, Ga.).*

Hasson, F., Keeney, S., & McKenna, H. (2000). Research guidelines for the Delphi survey technique. *Journal of Advanced Nursing*, 32(4), 1008–1015. doi:10.1046/j.1365-2648.2000.t01-1-01567.x PMID:11095242

Hendra, R., & Hill, A. (2019). Rethinking response rates: New evidence of little relationship between survey response rates and nonresponse bias. *Evaluation Review*, 43(5), 307–330. doi:10.1177/0193841X18807719 PMID:30580577

Herbert, J. T., Ward, T. J., & Hemlick, L. M. (1995). Confirmatory factor analysis of the supervisory style inventory and the revised supervision questionnaire. *Rehabilitation Counseling Bulletin*, 38(4), 334–349.

Hsu, C., & Sandford, B. A. (2007). The Delphi technique: Making sense of consensus. *Practical Assessment, Research & Evaluation*, 12(10), 1–8. http://pareonline.net/pdf/v12n10.pdf

Hsu, T. (2005). Research methods and data analysis procedures used by educational researchers. *International Journal of Research & Method in Education*, 28(2), 109–133. doi:10.1080/01406720500256194

Kalton, G. (2019). Developments in survey research over the past 60 Years: A personal perspective. *International Statistical Review*, 87(S1), S10–S30. doi:10.1111/insr.12287

Kaplan, S. A., Luchman, J. N., & Mock, L. (2013). General and specific question sequence effects in satisfaction surveys: Integrating directional and correlational effects. *Journal of Happiness Studies*, 14(5), 1443–1458. doi:10.100710902-012-9388-5

Kaplowitz, M., Hadlock, T., & Levine, R. (2004). A comparison of web and mail survey response rates. *Public Opinion Quarterly*, 68(1), 94–101. doi:10.1093/poq/nfh006

Keusch, F., Bähr, S., Haas, G., Kreuter, F., & Trappmann, M. (2020). Coverage error in data collection combining mobile surveys with passive measurement using apps: Data from a German national survey. *Sociological Methods & Research*, ●●●, 1–38. doi:10.1177/0049124120914924

Kim, J., Egan, T., & Tolson, H. (2015). Examining the dimensions of the learning organization questionnaire: A review and critique of research utilizing the DLOQ. *Human Resource Development Review*, 14(1), 91–112. doi:10.1177/1534484314555402

Kline, P. (1993). *The handbook of psychological testing*. Routledge.

Kohut, A., Keeter, S., Doherty, C., Dimock, M., & Christian, L. (2012). *Assessing the representativeness of public opinion surveys*. Pew Research Center. https://www.pewresearch.org/politics/2012/05/15/assessing-the-representativeness-of-public-opinion-surveys/

Lavrakas, P. J. (2012). *Encyclopedia of survey research methods.* SAGE Publications.

Lie, H. C., Rueegg, C. S., Fosså, S. D., Loge, J. H., Ruud, E., & Kiserud, C. E. (2019). Limited evidence of non-response bias despite modest response rate in a nationwide survey of long-term cancer survivors—Results from the NOR-CAYACS study. *Journal of Cancer Survivorship: Research and Practice, 13*(3), 353–363. doi:10.100711764-019-00757-x PMID:30993649

Lindsay, A. C., Sussner, K. M., Greaney, M., Wang, M. L., Davis, R., & Peterson, K. E. (2012). Using qualitative methods to design a culturally appropriate child feeding questionnaire for low-income, Latina mothers. *Maternal and Child Health Journal, 16*(4), 860–866. doi:10.100710995-011-0804-y PMID:21512780

Liu, Y., Wu, A. D., & Zumbo, B. D. (2010). The impact of outliers on Cronbach's coefficient alpha estimate of reliability: Ordinal/Rating scale item responses. *Educational and Psychological Measurement, 70*(1), 5–21. doi:10.1177/0013164409344548

Livingston, E. H., & Wislar, J. S. (2012). Minimum response rates for survey research. *Archives of Surgery, 147*(2), 110. doi:10.1001/archsurg.2011.2169 PMID:22351903

Loehlin, J. C. (1998). *Latent variable models: An introduction to factor, path and structural analysis.* Erlbaum.

Manfreda, K., Berzelak, J., Vehovar, V., Bosnjak, M., & Haas, I. (2018). Web surveys versus other survey modes: A meta-analysis comparing response rates. *International Journal of Market Research, 50*(1), 79–104. doi:10.1177/147078530805000107

Marsh, H. W., Hau, K.-T., Balla, J. R., & Grayson, D. (1998). Is more ever too much? The number of indicators per factor in confirmatory factor analysis. *Multivariate Behavioral Research, 33*(2), 181–220. doi:10.120715327906mbr3302_1 PMID:26771883

Mason, G. (1996). Recent advances in questionnaire design for program evaluation. *The Canadian Journal of Program Evaluation, 11*(1), 73–84.

McGregor, S. L. T., & Murnane, J. A. (2010). Paradigm, methodology and method: Intellectual integrity in consumer scholarship. *International Journal of Consumer Studies, 34*(4), 419–427. doi:10.1111/j.1470-6431.2010.00883.x

Miller, D. M., & Krieshok, T. S. (1989). Sex differences in the second-order factor structure of the 16 PF: A confirmatory maximum likelihood analysis. *Measurement & Evaluation in Counseling & Development, 2*(2), 73–80. doi:10.1080/07481756.1989.12022914

Mills, G. E., & Gay, L. R. (2019). *Educational Research: Competencies for analysis and applications* (12th ed.). Pearson Education, Inc.

Mircioiu, C., & Atkinson, J. (2017). A comparison of parametric and non-parametric methods applied to a Likert scale. *Pharmacy (Basel, Switzerland), 5*(2), 26–38. doi:10.3390/pharmacy5020026 PMID:28970438

Montiel-Overall, P. (2006). Implications of missing data in survey research. *Canadian Journal of Information and Library Science, 30*(3/4), 241–269.

Mundfrom, D., Shaw, D., & Ke, T. L. (2005). Minimum sample size recommendations for conducting factor analyses. *International Journal of Testing*, 5(2), 159–168. doi:10.120715327574ijt0502_4

Nunnally, J. (1978). *Psychometric Theory*. McGraw-Hill.

Oroviogoicoechea, C., Roger, W., Beortegui, E., & Remirez, S. (2010). Nurses' perception of the use of computerised information systems in practice: Questionnaire development. *Journal of Clinical Nursing*, 19(1–2), 240–248. doi:10.1111/j.1365-2702.2009.03003.x PMID:20500261

Peytchev, A. (2013). Consequences of survey nonresponse. *The Annals of the American Academy of Political and Social Science*, 645(1), 88–111. doi:10.1177/0002716212461748

Peytchev, A., Carley-Baxter, L. R., & Black, M. C. (2011). Multiple sources of nonobservation error in telephone surveys: Coverage and nonresponse. *Sociological Methods & Research*, 40(1), 138–168. doi:10.1177/0049124110392547

Porter, S. R., Whitcomb, M. E., & Weitzer, W. H. (2004). Multiple surveys of students and survey fatigue. *New Directions for Institutional Research*, 2004(121), 63–73. doi:10.1002/ir.101

Privitera, G. J., & Ahlgrim-Delzell, L. (2019). *Research methods for education* (1st ed.). Sage.

Rattray, J., & Jones, M. C. (2007). Essential elements of questionnaire design and development. *Journal of Clinical Nursing*, 16(2), 234–243. doi:10.1111/j.1365-2702.2006.01573.x PMID:17239058

Rea, L., & Parker, A. (2014). *Designing and conducting survey research: A comprehensive guide* (4th ed.). John Wiley & Sons, Inc., Jossey-Bass.

Renberg, T., Kettis-Lindblad, A., & Tully, M. (2018). Testing the validity of a translated pharmaceutical therapy-related quality of life instrument, using qualitative 'think aloud' methodology. *Journal of Clinical Pharmacy and Therapeutics*, 33(3), 279–287. doi:10.1111/j.1365-2710.2008.00921.x PMID:18452415

Salant, P., & Dillman, D. A. (1994). *How to construct your own survey*. John Wiley & Sons, Inc.

Sharkness, J., & Deangelo, L. (2011). Measuring student involvement: A comparison of Classical Test Theory and Item Response Theory in the construction of scales from student surveys. *Research in Higher Education*, 52(5), 480–507. doi:10.100711162-010-9202-3

Sherman, K., Eaves, E., Ritenbugh, C., Hsu, C., Cherkin, D., & Turner, J. (2014). Cognitive interviews guide design of a new CAM patient expectations questionnaire. *BMC Complementary and Alternative Medicine*, 14(1), 39–55. doi:10.1186/1472-6882-14-39 PMID:24460709

Sills, S. J., & Song, C. (2002). Innovations in survey research. An application of web survey. *Social Science Computer Review*, 20(1), 22–30. doi:10.1177/089443930202000103

Standish, T., & Umbach, P. D. (2019). Should we be concerned about nonresponse bias in college student surveys? Evidence of bias from a validation study. *Research in Higher Education*, 60(3), 338–357. doi:10.100711162-018-9530-2

Starr, S. (2012). Survey research: We can do better. *Journal of the Medical Library Association: JMLA*, 100(1), 1–2. doi:10.3163/1536-5050.100.1.001 PMID:22272152

Streiner, D. L. (2006). Building a better model: An introduction to structural equation modelling. *Canadian Journal of Psychiatry*, *51*(5), 317–324. doi:10.1177/070674370605100507 PMID:16986821

Taber, K. S. (2018). The use of Cronbach's alpha when developing and reporting research instruments in science education. *Research in Science Education*, *48*(6), 1273–1296. doi:10.100711165-016-9602-2

Tait, A. R., & Voepel-Lewis, T. (2015). Survey research: It's just a few questions, right? *Paediatric Anaesthesia*, *25*(7), 656–662. doi:10.1111/pan.12680 PMID:25929546

Thompson, B. (1997). The importance of structure coefficients in structural equation modeling confirmatory factor analysis. *Educational and Psychological Measurement*, *57*(1), 5–19. doi:10.1177/0013164497057001001

Thompson, J. J., Kelly, K. L., Ritenbaugh, C., Hopkins, A. L., Sims, C. M., & Coons, S. J. (2011). Developing a patient-centered outcome measure for complementary and alternative medicine therapies II: Refining content validity through cognitive interviews. *BMC Complementary and Alternative Medicine*, *11*(1), 136–153. doi:10.1186/1472-6882-11-136 PMID:22206409

Tsikriktsis, N. (2005). A review of techniques for treating missing data in OM survey research. *Journal of Operations Management*, *24*(1), 53–62. doi:10.1016/j.jom.2005.03.001

Vicente, P., & Reis, E. (2012). Coverage error in internet surveys: Can fixed phones fix it? *International Journal of Market Research*, *54*(3), 323–345. doi:10.2501/ijmr-54-3-323-345

Werner, S., Praxedes, M., & Kim, H.-G. (2007). The reporting of nonresponse analyses in survey research. *Organizational Research Methods*, *10*(2), 287–295. doi:10.1177/1094428106292892

Williams, A. (2003). How to write and analyse a questionnaire. *Journal of Orthodontics*, *30*(3), 245–252. doi:10.1093/ortho/30.3.245 PMID:14530423

Willis, G. (2005). *Cognitive interviewing: A tool for improving questionnaire design.* Sage Publications. doi:10.4135/9781412983655

Yang, Y., & Green, S. B. (2011). Coefficient alpha: A reliability coefficient for the 21st century? *Journal of Psychoeducational Assessment*, *29*(4), 377–392. doi:10.1177/0734282911406668

KEY TERMS AND DEFINITIONS

Construct Validity: Validity evidence that addresses the extent to which the instrument measures the underlying construct, generally examined through a variety statistical and judgmental sources of information.

Content Validity: Validity evidence that addresses the extent to which the instrument measures the intended content area, generally examined through professional judgement.

Descriptive Statistics: Statistical analysis used to describe results using summary statistics and graphical displays.

Factor Analysis: Advanced statistical analysis used to explore or confirm the internal structure of a questionnaire.

Inferential Statistics: Statistical analysis used to generalize results using statistical tests of significance.

Questionnaire: An instrument used to collect data in survey research.

Random Sample: Sample selected using probability sampling techniques.

Reliability: Consistency of results often examined using Cronbach's coefficient alpha.

Survey Research: A type of descriptive research design that utilizes data from questionnaires.

Chapter 2
Clearly Communicating Conceptions of Validity and Reliability

Debra J. Dean
Regent University, USA

ABSTRACT

When embarking on this journey, the author had little expectation of finding the topics of validity and reliability to be so complex and convoluted or so interesting. This chapter helps to clear the air and communicate the concepts of validity and reliability more clearly. The challenges seem to include the wording used to introduce and describe the concepts along with the transformation of statistical equations over time and technology. What remains the same is the importance of knowing whether an instrument is valid and reliable. One of the most basic places to start with conducting a robust quantitative research project is to have valid and reliable instruments. This may involve creating your own instrument, using an established instrument, or modifying an existing instrument. This chapter takes a deep dive into the concepts of validity and reliability uncovering some of the cynicism and myths of these topics along the way. The ultimate goal is to communicate clearly so that future research can use the proper technique(s) and describe the output in a more uniform fashion.

INTRODUCTION

The general purpose of this chapter is to begin the conversation of why and how the topics of reliability and validity became so confusing and to clarify some of the muddy waters by examining the history of these concepts in addition to the current status. In the end, a recommendation is made to all scholars to do better with their rhetoric and selection of tests moving forward. It is important to note that this is not the end-all, be-all chapter on reliability and validity. To accomplish the major feat of an ultimate source for reliability and validity, it will be necessary to collaborate with subject matter experts for each test and develop a complete book or manual to communicate how to do the tests properly and how to communicate the findings in a consistent manner. However, this is the start of that conversation.

DOI: 10.4018/978-1-7998-7665-6.ch002

USING AN ESTABLISHED INSTRUMENT

The author teaches Quantitative Research Methods and coaches students through the dissertation process. She is often asked how to find an established instrument. There are several ways to go about finding an instrument to meet the needs of your research. First, go to the academic library and search for keywords of the item(s) of interest along with keywords of "quantitative" and "development." This is because many empirical articles that introduce a new questionnaire to the world have these keywords in the title. Another way to find an instrument is to include keywords of "index," "inventory," "instrument," "questionnaire," "scale," or "survey." When reviewing empirical articles for the literature review, it is also helpful to note the instruments being used to measure the construct(s) of interest, as other scholars may have already used survey(s) that would fit your research needs. And, it is generally helpful to look at published dissertations that have used similar instruments as many of the survey questions will be published in the appendix. Before using an established instrument, reach out to the developer(s) for permission, an updated version of the questionnaire, and the interpretation documents to know how to score the results.

CREATING AN INSTRUMENT

There are several other textbooks available if planning to develop an instrument. This chapter is far too short to include all the information needed for developing a scale. Therefore, consult DeVellis (2017), Kline (2005), and/or Streiner and Norman (2008). DeVellis (2017) wrote that Step 1 of the scale development process is to "determine clearly what it is you want to measure" (p. 105). Step 2 is to "generate an item pool" (p. 109). Step 3 is to "determine the format for measurement" (p. 118). Step 4 is to "have [the] initial item pool reviewed by experts" (p. 134). Step 5 is to "consider inclusion of validation items" (p. 136). Step 6 is to "administer items to a development sample" (p. 137). Step 7 is to "evaluate the items" (p. 139). And, step 8 is to "optimize scale length" (p. 146).

MODIFYING AN INSTRUMENT

Scholars might find a need to modify an instrument for a variety of reasons. Some want to use an existing survey with a different language group and will need to translate the questions. Others will want to modify an instrument used for a particular demographic to use with a different group of participants; for example, a survey designed for teachers may be appropriate to use with healthcare workers if the wording is slightly changed. Creswell (2009) cautioned that when modifying an established instrument, the original validity and reliability may not sustain the changes made; therefore, there is a need to re-establish the validity and reliability of the newly modified instrument. Pergert, Bartholdson, Wenemark, Lutzen, and Sandeberg (2018) wrote that translating an instrument to a different language or adapting the content poses a dilemma. It is important to keep the new version as close to the original version as possible to "achieve a good functional level and trustworthiness" (p. 2).

THEORETICAL FOUNDATION

The Classical Test Theory (CTT) examines the objectivity, reliability, and validity for the construction, evaluation, and comparison of instruments. Lord (1955) conceptualized the true score, also known as the Universe Score, as the absolute truth. The observed score is derived from the instrument when the participant completes the survey. Ideally, the true score and the observed score would be exact; however, that is not realistic as no instrument can measure reality with 100% accuracy. Instead, the presence of an error is the person's true score minus the observed score. The ultimate goal with determining reliability is to establish the true score and error components to understand how valid and reliable the scores are from the chosen instrument(s).

VALIDITY

Yes, validity comes before reliability in this chapter for a reason. Scholars must first ensure the instrument is valid before being concerned with the reliability of the instrument. Uraschi, Horondic, and Zait (2015) wrote that "validity implies reliability, but the reciprocal is not true; a valid measurement is reliable, but a reliable measurement isn't necessarily valid" (p. 680). Evans (2013) explained that validity represents reality. In other words, how well does the instrument represent "one's perception of the real world" (p. 292)? Creswell (2009) wrote that validity "refers to whether one can draw meaningful and useful inferences from scores on particular instruments" (p. 235). According to Creswell, the "three traditional forms of validity" include content validity, predictive or concurrent validity, and construct validity (p. 149). Hair, Black, Babin, Anderson, and Tatham (2014) wrote that "the three most widely accepted forms of validity are convergent, discriminant, and nomological" (p. 137). Messick explained that the traditional concept of validity is divided "into three separate and substitutable types – namely, content, criterion, and construct validities" and highlighted the following six aspects of construct validity as a unified concept: "content, substantive, structural, generalizability, external, and consequential" (1995, p. 741).

Hair, Black, Babin, Anderson, and Tatham (2014) defined validity as the "extent to which a measure or set of measures correctly represents the concept of study – the degree to which it is free from any systematic or nonrandom error" (p. 3). The authors continued by saying, "validity is concerned with how well the concept is defined by the measure(s), whereas reliability relates to the consistency of the measure(s)" (p. 3). In other words, validity is "the degree to which a measure accurately represents what it is supposed to" (p. 8). Field (2015) wrote that validity is "evidence that a study allows correct inferences about the question it was aimed to answer or that a test measures what it is set out to measure conceptually" (p. 886). The two broadest categories of validity are external and internal. Overall, this section of the chapter is to broaden the horizon of the concept of validity to share information and reinforce the need for additional research beyond this chapter to completely understand internal and external validity.

External Validity

External validity is largely absent from empirical research literature. Perhaps the reason is the vagueness behind what it is and how to do it. However, the author of this chapter argues that external validity is the bridge between theory and practice. External validity is the "basis for generalizability to other populations, settings, and times" (Ferguson, 2004, p. 16). Campbell and Stanley (1963) question external validity regarding if the study is generalizable to other "populations, settings, treatment variables, and measurement variables." External validity, according to Uraschi, Horondic, and Zait (2015), "checks if results can be generalized or extrapolated for a whole population, for all similar situations or contexts, outside those in which the research took place" (p. 680). To improve external validity, Campbell and Stanley (1963), as well as Ferguson (2004), focus on the research design itself. In addition to using the Solomon four-group design to rule out threats of internal and external validity, Ferguson (2004) notes that random sampling can increase the generalizability of findings. Additionally, Ferguson (2004) encourages researchers to address issues of internal validity to enhance external validity. She also acknowledges how historical events taking place during the study can threaten external validity (Ferguson, 2004). In other words, what worked in 2020 and 2021 during COVID may not work post-pandemic. Hair, Black, Babin, Anderson, and Tatham (2014) documented the hit ratio, the jackknife method, and the profiling of group differences as ways to test external validity. Shadish, Cook, and Campbell (2002) provided five guiding principles for researchers to following regarding generalizations: (a) surface similarity, (b) ruling out irrelevancies, (c) making discriminations, (d) interpolation and extrapolation, and (e) causal explanation.

Internal Validity

Internal validity refers to the instrument itself. Internal validity is also known as content validity. This section of the chapter will expand on internal validity. Uraschi, Horondic, and Zait (2015) eloquently wrote that content (also called face, intrinsic or curricular) validity is:

present when the content of the research is related to the studied variables, has a logic; criterion validity (sometimes called concurrent validity) – how meaningful are the chosen research criteria comparing to other possible criteria; construct validity (or factorial validity) – which checks what underlying construct is actually being measured, and has three important parts – convergent validity (the degree to which two instruments designed to measure the same construct are related, convergence being found when the two analyzed instruments are highly correlated); discriminant validity – the degree to which two measures designed to measure similar, but conceptually different constructs are related, a low to moderate correlation being the proof of discriminant validity; nomological validity – the degree to which predictions from a formal theoretical network containing the analyzed concept are confirmed, which means that constructs theoretically related are also empirically related, as well. (p. 680)

Criterion Validity

Field (2015) explained that criterion validity is "evidence that scores from an instrument correspond with (concurrent validity) or predict (predictive validity) external measures conceptually related to the measured construct" (p. 873). Pallant (2005) wrote that criterion validity is concerned with "the relationship between scale scores and some specified, measurable criterion" (p. 6). DeVellis (2003) referred to criterion validity as more practical than scientific and referred to the correlation coefficient as the "traditional index of criterion-related validity" (p. 92). The correlation coefficient evaluates the relationship between two variables, and one of the more popular methods is Pearson's correlation, also known as Pearson's R or Pearson product-moment correlation coefficient. The most significant facet of criterion validity, according to DeVellis (2003), "is not the time relationship between the measure in question and the criterion whose value one is attempting to infer but, rather, the strength of the empirical relationship between the two events" (p. 92). Criterion validity can include three other types of validity: concurrent validity, predictive validity, and retrospective validity. For example, evaluating the criterion validity of an instrument measuring *joy* would involve currently being joyful, predicting joy in the future, or having been joyful in the past.

Construct Validity

Peter (1981) spoke of the "convolution in the measurement literature," saying some view constructs as "no more than labels for different measures" and clarifying that "a construct is a term specifically designed for a special scientific purpose, generally to organize knowledge and direct research in an attempt to describe or explain some aspect of nature" (pp. 133-134). Creswell (2009) wrote that construct validity refers to the items on the survey and if they measure hypothetical constructs or concepts. Hair, Black, Babin, Anderson, and Tatham (2014) defined construct validity as "the extent to which a set of measured items actually reflects the theoretical latent construct those items are designed to measure" (p. 776). Pallant (2005) explained that construct validity does not involve testing a scale against a single criterion; instead, testing the scale relationships with other constructs, including those related (convergent validity) and unrelated (discriminant validity). A form of construct validity is known as nomological validity. In the example of measuring for *joy*, construct validity would indicate how well or to what extent the instrument actually measures joy. According to Atkinson, Rosenfeld, Sit, Mendoza, Fruscione, Lavene, Shaw, Yuelin, Hay, Cleeland, Scher, Breitbart, and Basch (2011), exploratory factor analysis is commonly used with construct validity when the relationship between variables is not known or is ambiguous; whereas confirmatory factor analysis can also be used with construct validity to "reduce the overall number of observed variables into latent factors based on commonalities within the data" (p. 559).

Concurrent Validity

Creswell (2009) wrote that predictive or concurrent validity refers to the scores predicting the criteria being measured. Cozby and Bates (2020) explained that concurrent validity is the "relationship between the measure and a criterion behavior at the same time (concurrently)" and recommend testing two different groups of people, at the same time, where the researcher would expect different results from each group (p. 103). In the example of measuring for *joy*, the instrument could be administered to two different groups at one time. An ideal example might be those attending the Super Bowl. Group A might be the fans that won the game, and Group B would be the fans that lost the game. It is expected that Group A would score higher on the joy measurement than Group B.

Content Validity

Creswell (2009) wrote that content validity looks at the items on the instrument and asks if the questions measure what they intend to measure. Cozby and Bates (2020) further explained that content validity compares the content of the instrument to the construct to ensure they align.

Field (2015) explained that content validity is the "evidence that the content of a test corresponds to the content of the construct it was designed to cover" (p. 872). For the example of measuring *joy*, one could examine the extent that joy is represented with the instrument using exploratory factor analysis or another multivariate statistical approach.

Convergent Validity

Hair, Black, Babin, Anderson, and Tatham (2014) stated that convergent validity evaluates "the degree to which two measures of the same concept are correlated" (p. 137). In short, convergent validity is whether or not the "scale correlates with other like scales" (p. 139). Cozby and Bates (2020) further explained that convergent validity occurs when "measures of similar constructs converge" (p. 103). For example, a measure of *joy* should converge at some point with a separate instrument measuring happiness. Although joy and happiness are not one-in-the-same, they are similar constructs.

Discriminant Validity

Hair, Black, Babin, Anderson, and Tatham (2014) wrote that discriminant validity "is the degree to which two conceptually similar concepts are distinct" (p. 137). In short, discriminant validity is whether or not the "scale is sufficiently different from other related scales" (p. 139). Cozby and Bates (2020) wrote, "the measure should discriminate between the construct being measured and other unrelated constructs" (p. 103). Using the example of measuring for *joy*, the discriminant validity should appear when comparing the joy instrument results to the results of an instrument measuring for sadness.

Face Validity

Hair, Black, Babin, Anderson, and Tatham (2014) declared that "face validity is the most important validity test" and explained that "face validity must be established prior to any theoretical testing when using confirmatory factor analysis" (p. 778). Cozby and Bates (2020) state that face validity is not a sophisticated technique. Instead, it is a judgment call at face value to decide if the instrument is measuring what it is supposed to measure. In the example of measuring for *joy*, face validity would evaluate the questions for apparent soundness of the relation between the questions and the construct of joy.

Nomological Validity

Hair, Black, Babin, Anderson, and Tatham (2014) explained that nomological validity refers to the "degree that the summated scale makes accurate predictions of other concepts in a theoretically based model" (p. 138). In short, nomological validity is whether or not the "Scale predicts as theoretically suggested" (p. 139). Hagger, Gucciardi, and Chatzisarantis (2017) explained that nomological validity is the "degree to which predictions in a formal theoretical network are confirmed" and argue that "few researchers formally test the nomological validity of theories or outline conditions that lead to model rejection" (p. 1). The nomological network will include antecedents, mediators, and outcome variables or consequents. While testing the network, the theory can be abandoned or modified. Hagger, Gucciardi, and Chatzisarantis (2017) recommend using "confirmatory analyses based on regression and covariance structures, such as path analysis and structural equation modeling" to test for nomological validity (p. 4). In the example of measuring *joy*, the nomological network may hypothetically include an antecedent of receiving flowers, a mediator of gathering in large groups, and a consequent of smiling. However, the network may not prove accurate if the receipt of flowers, gathering in a large group, and smiling has to do with attending a funeral. While the initial construct validity may show significance, the nomological validity could falsify the theory or lead to modification of further defining the boundaries of joy.

Postdictive Validity

Postdictive validity is also referred to as retrospective validity and is the least common type of criterion validity (Lilienfeld, 2016). The concept of postdictive validity is that the instrument can accurately assess occurrences from the past. Lilienfeld (2016) wrote that postdictive validity "examines the extent to which a test is associated with variables measured long before the test was administered" (p. 165). For example, postdictive validity assumes a person can take a test today to measure their level of *joy* from an event that occurred in the past.

Predictive Validity

Cozby and Bates (2020) explained that predictive validity answers the question of if the instrument can measure future behavior or outcomes. In other words, will the test took today predict an outcome in the future. Predictive validity is a type of criterion validity. Popular assessments designed to predict the future include the ACT, SAT, or GRE exams aimed at identifying students that are more likely to succeed. Field (2015) wrote that predictive validity looks for evidence that the instrument can predict an external measure related to the construct of interest. Using the example of *joy*, the researcher would examine the instrument to see if it can predict joy in the future.

RELIABILITY

As with the section for validity, this chapter is not the end-all, be-all. Instead. It is an eye-opener to the complexity of the concepts of validity and reliability and the confusion that has penetrated academic journals for decades. This chapter is designed to start the conversation to simplify verbiage and streamline the processes to ensure studies have valid and reliable scores from the chosen instruments. The toolbox of reliability instruments is complex and not easy to understand. These tools have evolved over the years and, thankfully, no longer require pencil and paper to compute exhausting mathematical equations. However, complexity still exists in understanding which tool to use to measure the reliability of an instrument. Cho and Kim (2015) explained the evolution is, in part, due to the fact that "in the 1940s, calculation with computers was unimaginable, and the ease of the calculation was a virtue in a world in which all calculations were performed by hand" (p. 210). Regardless of the evolution of the reliability tools, Cho and Kim (2015) referred to numerous studies seeking to find the best approach only to "give an impression that even among experts, there is no consensus on which methodology is superior to others" (p. 218). They urge scholars to take matters into their own hands noting, it "is not merely a matter of personal choice but a matter of academia consciously responding to the issue" (p. 225).

The most common reliability test is by far Cronbach's alpha. Taber (2018) states that "many researchers who use alpha may have a nuanced appreciation of its affordances and limitations" (p. 1295). He explained that "alpha is routinely being quoted, but often without its use being explained or the value quoted being fully interpreted" (p. 1293). This section of the chapter will help researchers "avoid the impression that alpha is sometimes calculated simply because that is what is routinely done" and challenge scholars to become more familiar with the reliability protocols, including an explanation of the supposed threshold limit of .70. As an example of the challenge of writing the results properly, reliability is a characteristic of the data collected by an instrument and not the instrument itself. Therefore, instead of stating the instrument is reliable, it is best to say the data collected by the instrument is reliable or that reliable data has been collected using the instrument in the past.

This section of the chapter will focus entirely on reliability. DeVellis (2017) explains that "a reliable instrument is one that performs in consistent, predictable ways" (p. 39). Hair, Black, Babin, Anderson, and Tatham (2014) defined reliability as the "extent to which a variable or set of variables are consistent in what it is intended to measure. If multiple measurements are taken, the reliable measures will all be consistent in their values" (p. 3). The authors clarified that reliability "differs from validity in that it relates not to what should be measured, but instead to how it is measured" (p. 3).

Reliability, according to Creswell (2009), "refers to whether scores of items on an instrument are internally consistent (i.e., are the item responses consistent across constructs), and whether there was consistency in test administration and scoring (test-retest correlations)" (p. 233). In other words, reliability is "the degree to which the observed variables measure the *true* value and is *error-free*" (p. 8). Pallant (2005) explained that "the reliability of a scale indicates how free it is from random error" (p. 6). Field (2015) wrote that reliability is "the ability of a measure to produce consistent results when the same entities are measured under different conditions" (p. 882). In summary, reliability is about data and not measures. When reporting a reliability score, it is correct to state "the reliability of the subscale scores was .78;" however, it is not correct to say, "the reliability of the subscale was .78" (Gignac, 2015). There are four types of reliability that will be reviewed in the remainder of this chapter: internal consistency (are the individual items of the test reliable), interrater reliability (is the test reliable if different people conduct the same test), parallel forms reliability (are different versions of the test equal), and test-retest reliability (is the test the same if administered more than once).

Internal Consistency Reliability (Equivalence)

Internal consistency refers to the extent that responses to items designed to measure a single construct are consistent with each other. It is important to note that the goal is consistency, not redundancy. In an instrument, the best items should be used, not the most or least number of items. Factor analysis can help a scale developer choose the right items for each construct within their scale. Cho and Kim (2015) offered three definitions of internal consistency in an effort to defend the phrase "item interrelatedness" instead of internal consistency starting with homogeneity (p. 216). The three definitions include "(a) homogeneity, (b) interrelatedness of a set of items, and (c) general factor saturation" (Cho and Kim, 2015, p. 215). Homogeneity refers to the unidimensionality or the "existence of one latent trait underlying a set of items" (Hattie, 1985). The interrelatedness of a "set of items is an arithmetic mean of interitem correlation coefficients" (Cronbach, 1951). And, general factor saturation is the proportion of test variance that is due to a general factor (Revelle & Zinbarg, 2009).

There are many different tests available to measure internal consistency. The most common test is Cronbach's alpha, which measures the interrelatedness of the items in the scale. This section of the chapter will review Cronbach's alpha in addition to several other tests to provide a broad understanding of internal consistency and how to measure it. Creswell (2009) wrote that internal consistency refers to the items on the survey and whether or not the item's responses are consistent across constructs. Hair, Black, Babin, Anderson, and Tatham (2014) stated that a common way to measure reliability is internal consistency; this refers to the "consistency among the variables in a summated scale" (p. 137). Hair, Black, Babin, Anderson, and Tatham (2014) further explained that "the rationale for internal consistency is that the individual items or indicators of the scale should all be measuring the same construct and thus be highly intercorrelated" (p. 137). There are several assumptions of internal consistency. First, it assumes unidimensionality, whereas all items measure a single dimension. According to Hattie (1985), "one of the most critical and basic assumptions of measurement theory is that a set of items forming an instrument all measure just one thing in common" (p. 139). It does not prove unidimensionality; it only assumes it. It does not measure dimensionality. For an interpretable result, the items in the scale must be similar in reflecting the same construct. Next, it assumes items are correlated with each other. Third, it assumes a composite score is either the sum or average of two or more items on the instrument. Fourth, it does not measure homogeneity. The following subsections of Internal Consistency Reliability will explore the historical transformation of the formulas from the early 1900s to the current day, starting with the Spearman-Brown formula, moving into the Kuder-Richardson era, which includes many scholars attempting to find a better way to measure reliability, followed by Cronbach's Alpha, and stepping into the modern-day Omega Coefficient. Keep in mind, there are many other methods that may be of interest, including bootstrapping, factor analysis, and structural equation modeling; however, to keep this rather complex topic as simple as possible, this section is streamlined with four of the more popular approaches.

Spearman-Brown Split-Half Reliability

To understand more about the reliability of an instrument, the historical emergence of formulas will need to take place. Cronbach and Shavelson (2004) credits "Charles Spearman, just after the start of the 20th century," who realized the need to "evaluate the accuracy of any measuring instrument" that was used (p. 395). Revelle and Zinbarg (2009) wrote that Spearman appeared on the scene in 1904 in pursuit of addressing the issue of reliability. In response, the Spearman split-half reliability procedure was invented. This process involved dividing an instrument in half. Briefly, the survey is split into two random sets of items. If a scale is reliable, the participant will score similarly on both halves (Field, 2015). For example, the total item score of hypothetical questions 1, 3, and 5 would equal the same as those on items 2, 4, and 6. Cronbach (1951) wrote that the Spearman-Brown formula had been "a standard method of test analysis for 40 years" prior to his developing the Cronbach's alpha (p. 298). Cho and Kim (2015) explained that the Spearman-Brown formula was first published in 1910. Spearman and Brown each published an independent article in the same journal that year. Their formula "states that the reliability of the full-length test scores can be estimated by correcting the correlation between the two half-test scores (Cho & Kim, 2015, p. 209). For decades, it was the only method to test reliability; however, it was complex, especially without a calculator, and was thought to be unreliable.

Kuder-Richardson Coefficient of Equivalence

Cronbach and Shavelson (2004) explained that "in the 1930s, investigators became increasingly uncomfortable with the Spearman-Brown method. The Kuder and Richardson formula was published in 1937 as a source for dichotomously scored items (Cho & Kim, 2015, p. 209). Dichotomous variables assume only two responses such as male/female, dead/alive, or yes/no. One major criticism of the Kuder-Richardson model is that they did not give their formula a specific name. It was referred to as the Kuder-Richardson Formula 20 or KR-20. Between 1937 and 1951, several other scholars attempted to solve the reliability formula crisis. Fisher, Flanagan, Gulliksen, Guttman, Mosier, Hoyt, Jackson and Ferguson, and Rulon published their own formulas. Some were considered to be identical to the KR-20. By the time Cronbach's alpha came around, the KR-20 and other similar or exact formulas fell to the wayside. It is believed their efforts diminished in importance due to the complexity of the calculations, the naming convention, and ease of communication. Let's face it, the reliability of an instrument is difficult enough to read about in a journal article or textbook and understand in modern times when computers or calculators do the heavy lifting. Prior to the 1950s, this concept of developing internal consistency formulas must have seemed like a foreign language.

Cronbach's Alpha / Coefficient Alpha

As explained in the introduction of this reliability section, Cronbach's alpha is the most common test for internal consistency. It was introduced in 1951 and stood out as one test that "gave a result identical with the average coefficient that would be obtained if every possible split of a test were made and a coefficient calculated for every split" (Cronbach & Shavelson, 2004, p. 396). The alpha formula was also "identical to KR 20 when it was applied to items scored one and zero" (Cronbach & Shavelson, 2004, p. 396). Thus, it is easy to see why Cronbach's alpha replaced Spearman-Brown and Kuder-Richardson. The naming convention, however, was never intended to be "Cronbach's alpha," and Cronbach stated that "it is an embarrassment to me that the formula became conventionally known as Cronbach's α" (Cronbach & Shavelson, 2004, p. 397). Instead, the name could be just "α" or "coefficient alpha." This is part of the confusion with some articles, books, and dissertations that call this reliability method various names. For the purpose of this chapter, the remaining text will only use α.

Some argue that α is the most common reliability method because it is easy and because SPSS has a program readily available. However, many scholars believe the sun is setting on the α, and it is time for the omega to shine on the horizon. Nevertheless, α is still, by far, the most common reliability test for internal consistency, and this section of the chapter will attempt to define more about when and where it should be used.

Cho and Kim (2015) note the conditions that must be met to use α. Those conditions, according to Cho and Kim (2015, p. 219), include the following:

- The test measures a single factor (unidimensionality).
- The test items are essentially tau-equivalent in statistical similarity. Tau-equivalent means the contribution to the underlying construct is equal.
- The error scores of the items are uncorrelated (independence between errors).

If these assumptions are violated, Cho and Kim (2015) recommend using the structural equation model estimators of reliability instead of α. Another option to use in lieu of α is bootstrapping. Field (2015) claims that bootstrapping "is a very simple and elegant" method to use with "irksome data" (pp. 198-199).

The range of α is .00 to 1.0. According to Hair, Black, Babin, Anderson, and Tatham (2014), the "generally agreed upon lower limit for α is .70" (p. 137). Hair, Black, Babin, Anderson, and Tatham (2014) explained that a score as low as .60 could be applied in exploratory research. Gignac (2015) notes that Nunnally is often cited as the one who set the threshold at .70. However, Gignac believes that is misunderstood, and the minimally acceptable level is .70 for exploratory research, .80 for basic research, and .90 for applied scenarios. This argument for the Standards of Reliability is reinforced by Lance, Butts, and Michels (2006), who refer to this threshold as an urban legend. The scholars explained that .70 is modest reliability arguing that "Nunnally clearly recommended a reliability standard of .80" (Lance, Butts, & Michels, 2006, p. 206). Cho and Kim (2015) argue that the accepted minimum range of

.70 is due to "an immunity standard, which 'legally' excuses [researchers] from having to think further about reliability when α values above .7 or .8 are obtained" (p. 217).

To get back to the source, Nunnally stated that an α score below .70 is "miserably low" and specified that when "important decisions must be made about humans on the basis of test scores, even a reliability of .90 is not high enough" (1975, p. 10). His 1978 text confirmed that "what a satisfactory level or reliability is depends on how a measure is being used" and wrote that for modest reliability, ".70 or higher will suffice" yet for the purpose of applied settings, a score of ".80 is not nearly high enough;" however, "a reliability of .90 is the minimum that should be tolerated, and a reliability of .95 should be considered the desirable standard" (Nunnally, 1978, pp. 245-246). In other words, it is time to raise the standards for reliability.

It is common knowledge that α assesses the consistency of the entire scale and is the "most widely used measure" (Hair et al. 2014, p. 137). This test is appropriate for dichotomous and continuously scored variables. As noted above, dichotomous assumes two options for responses such as male/female, dead/alive, or yes/no. Continuous variables are common with instruments that use Likert-type scales; whereas, the data is numerical and can be measured with an infinite number of smaller segments between two bookend values.

In 1951, Cronbach offered a solution to antiquated methods that measured internal consistency. The α is sensitive to the number of items in the scale. Typically, the more items in the scale, the higher the α, which can skew the number if the items are not unidimensional. As the first rule of thumb with α, the researcher should examine the items in the scale to ensure they are all measuring only one construct. Taber (2018) explained that "calculating α across multiple scales tends to inflate the value obtained" (p. 1286). Below are questions proposed in a checklist by Taber to improve rigor when assessing reliability using α (2018, p. 1294).

- As α does not offer any guide to the validity of a scale or instrument, do authors offer complementary evidence that the scale or instrument measures what it is claimed to measure?
- Are high values of α a reflection of redundancy in a scale or instrument where a large number of items are used when fewer might suffice?
- As α does not offer evidence of dimensionality, do authors who claim that instruments include components that elicit distinct factors provide evidence of dimensionality (i.e., that subscales are supported by factor analysis)?
- Where subscales are pooled and overall values of α reported, does a high overall value of α likely largely reflect the shared variance within the subsidiary subscales rather than across items between subscales?
- Could a high overall α value that is quoted for the administration of an instrument intended to test knowledge and understanding across a science topic or concept area indicate that the main construct being elicited might be a more generic feature of the student response to items (e.g., intelligence) rather than indicating that learning across the particular topic or concept area should be considered as a single dimension?
- Alternatively, could a high overall α value that is quoted for the administration of an instrument intended to test knowledge and understanding across a science topic or concept area indicate that the instrument may not sufficiently test the full range of learning objectives across the topic?

Omega Coefficient

The Omega Coefficient was developed by McDonald (1999). Some scholars argue that α has been superseded by omega (Gignac, 2015). According to Trizano-Hermosilla and Alvarado (2016), the "omega coefficient is always a better choice than α" and recommend using omega when test scores are normally distributed (p. 769). However, α "has proved very resistant to the passage of time, even if its limitations are well documented" (p. 769). The omega coefficient does not "require the assumption of uncorrelated item errors" (Cho & Kim, 2015, p. 214). DeVellis (2017) wrote that the α and omega "both essentially define reliability as the proportion of true score variance, relative to total observed variance" (p. 59). The difference between the two starts with the formula, whereas α examines the correlation between the items that make up the scale, and omega uses the common factor approach to ensure that all items in the scale reflect only one common factor. The issue of the omega truly surpassing the α is the complexity of the calculation and the lack of computer technology to make it easy. The most convenient software platform, at this time, for using omega coefficients is the psych package in R. The symbol for omega is ω.

Inter-Rater Reliability

Many tests can be used to determine inter-rater reliability, also known as an inter-rater agreement, inter-rater concordance, and inter-observer reliability. Cozby and Bates (2020) explained that "when multiple raters agree in their observations of the same thing, reliability is present. Cohen's Kappa is the most common test; however, concordance correlation coefficient, Fleiss' Kappa, interrater correlation, intraclass correlation, Krippendorff's Alpha, and Scott's pi are also options. Cohen's Kappa is on a scale of 0.0 to 1.0. The general rule of thumb, according to Landis and Koch (1977), is 0.41 to 0.60 is considered moderate, 0.61 to 0.80 is considered substantial, and 0.81 to 1.0 is considered almost perfect.

Parallel/Alternative Forms

The parallel or alternative forms type of reliability is concerned with the consistency of data when using different versions of an instrument. The Pearson r correlation coefficient is appropriate for this type of reliability too. The goal for this alternate form of reliability is to first have two separate versions of a scale known as parallel forms. Each form will measure the same latent variables, the α would be the same for both instruments, and so would the means and variances. If these parallel forms exist, the second step is to have the same people complete both of the forms as they should yield similar results, thus deeming it reliable.

Test-Retest Correlations (stability)

Hair, Black, Babin, Anderson, and Tatham (2014) stated that one way to test for reliability is test-retest. This is where "consistency is measured between the responses for an individual at two points in time" (p. 137). The authors explained that "the objective is to ensure that responses are not too varied across time periods so that a measurement taken at any point in time is reliable" (p. 137). Field (2015) explained that an easy way to think of test-retest is that a person taking a test on day one should have similar answers when they retake the test on day two. Creswell (2009) wrote that the test-retest correlations examine if the test results are stable over a period of time when the survey is administered at one point in time and then again with the same group of participants at a second time. Cronbach (1951) explained that a "retest after an interval, using the identical test, indicates how stable scores are and therefore can be called a coefficient of stability" (p. 298). And Pallant (2005) explained that the "test-retest reliability of a scale is assessed by administering it to the same people on two different occasions" (p. 6),

Correlation Coefficient

One way to calculate test-retest reliability is to compute the correlation between the two tests. A Pearson r correlation coefficient is appropriate. Cozby and Bates (2020) explained that the most common correlation coefficient is the Pearson product-moment correlation coefficient, also known as a Pearson r correlation coefficient. To assess the reliability of an instrument, "at least two scores on the measure from many individuals" are needed (p. 99). The Pearson correlation coefficient, also called the reliability coefficient, compares the relationship between the scores on a scale of 0.00 to +/- 1.00. The higher the score (regardless of the +/- sign), the better the relationship. A score of zero indicates no relationship. When scores fall between .00 and .29, there is a degree of correlation. Scores falling between .30 and .49 indicate a medium correlation. And scores between .50 and 1 indicate a strong correlation.

CONCLUSION

This chapter offers a glimpse into the concepts of validity and reliability. It is not the final answer but the start of a conversation to dig deeper into the concepts of validity and reliability. This topic started out of curiosity as the author was personally confused over the various terminology used in articles, books, and dissertations. The author of this chapter actually thought she was the only one confused, but what was found is that many people are confused with the topics of validity and reliability, and a better job is needed going forward. It is clear that this one chapter does not do justice to the complexity of the concepts of validity and reliability; however, it is a start. The main takeaways from this chapter are (a) there are many different techniques to use for validity and reliability, and they are not a one-size-fits-all approach, (b) in addition to reliability, internal and external validity are separate and necessary methods that should have attention with each and every single research project, (c) communication has been messy in the past, and scholars can do a better job communicating clearly and concisely, (d) the alpha threshold of .70 should no longer be quoted as the threshold.

This chapter covers much on both the validity and reliability fronts. However, the untidiest communication of them all revolve around Cronbach's alpha, which was never intended to be called Cronbach's alpha, but coefficient alpha or just plain α (Cronbach & Shavelson, 2004). Reliability assesses the data within the instrument, not the instrument itself. Instead of stating the instrument is reliable, scholars should say the data collected by the instrument is reliable or that reliable data has been collected using the instrument. The symbol for Cronbach's alpha is α. The α threshold cannot be stated as .70 or above as acceptable levels because it "depends how a measure is being used" (Nunnally, 1978). In fact, Nunnally appears to have been misquoted for decades. When scholars get back to the original text, Nunnally clearly said that a score below .70 is "miserably low" and specified that when "important decisions must be made about humans on the basis of test scores, even a reliability of .90 is not high enough" (1975, p. 10). His 1978 text confirmed that "what a satisfactory level or reliability is depends on how a measure is being used" and wrote that for modest reliability, ".70 or higher will suffice" yet for the purpose of applied settings, a score of ".80 is not nearly high enough;" however, "a reliability of .90 is the minimum that should be tolerated, and a reliability of .95 should be considered the desirable standard" (Nunnally, 1978, pp. 245-246). In other words, scholars, including the author of this chapter, need to raise the standards for reliability.

This example of how one reliability test has gone so astray demonstrates how scholars must take more time to understand the concepts of validity and reliability to ensure they are doing the tests properly and communicating the results clearly and concisely. While there are lots of articles that document the lack of knowledge or understanding around these two concepts, the goal is to move forward with a better understanding of what is needed for the future to establish and/or re-establish rigorous testing practices so that the field of research, especially at the Ph.D. level, is always considered as the highest standard resulting in trustworthy findings and recommendations.

REFERENCES

Atkinson, T. M., Rosenfeld, B. D., Sit, L., Mendoza, T. R., Fruscione, M., Lavene, D., Shaw, M., Li, Y., Hay, J., Cleeland, C. S., Scher, H. I., Breitbart, W. S., & Basch, E. (2011). Using confirmatory factor analysis to evaluate construct validity of the Brief Pain Inventory (BPI). *Journal of Pain and Symptom Management, 41*(3), 558–565. doi:10.1016/j.jpainsymman.2010.05.008 PMID:21131166

Campbell, D., & Stanley, J. (1963). *Experimental and quasi-experimental designs for research.* Houghton Mifflin Company.

Cho, E., & Kim, S. (2015). Cronbach's coefficient alpha: Well-known but poorly understood. *Organizational Research Methods, 18*(2), 207–230. doi:10.1177/1094428114555994

Cozby, P., & Bates, S. (2020). *Methods in behavioral research.* McGraw-Hill Education.

Creswell, J. (2009). *Research design: Qualitative, quantitative, and mixed methods approaches.* Sage.

Cronbach, L. (1951). Coefficient alpha and the internal structure of tests. *Pschometrika, 16*(3), 297–334. doi:10.1007/BF02310555

Cronbach, L. J., & Shavelson, R. J. (2004). My current thoughts on coefficient alpha and successor procedures. *Educational and Psychological Measurement, 64*(3), 391–418. doi:10.1177/0013164404266386

DeVellis, R. F. (2017). *Scale development: Theory and applications.* SAGE.

Evans, J. R. (2013). *Statistics, data analysis, and decision modeling.* Pearson Education.

Ferguson, L. (2004). External validity, generalizability, and knowledge utilization. *Journal of Nursing Scholarship, 36*(1), 16-22. http://dx.doi.org.ezproxy.regent.edu/10.1111/j.1547-5069.2004.04006.x

Field, A. (2015). *Discovering Statistics Using IBM SPSS Statistics.* SAGE Publications.

Gignac, G. (2015). *What is Cronbach's Alpha.* Retrieved February 18, 2021, from https://youtu.be/PCztXEfNJLM

Hagger, M. S., Gucciardi, D. F., & Chatzisarantis, N. L. D. (2017). On nomological validity and auxiliary assumptions: The importance of simultaneously testing effects in social cognitive theories applied to health behavior and some guidelines. *Frontiers in Psychology*, 8, 1933–1933. doi:10.3389/fpsyg.2017.01933 PMID:29163307

Hair, J., Black, W., Babin, B., & Anderson, R. (2014). *Multivariate data analysis*. Pearson Education.

Hattie, J. (1985). *Methodology review: Assessing unidimensionality of tests and items*. doi:10.1177/014662168500900204

Kline, T. (2005). *Psychological testing: A practical approach to design and evaluation*. Sage Publications.

Lance, C. E., Butts, M. M., & Michels, L. C. (2006). The sources of four commonly reported cutoff criteria: What did they really say? *Organizational Research Methods*, 9(2), 202–220. doi:10.1177/1094428105284919

Landis, J., & Koch, G. (1977). The measurement of observer agreement for categorical data. *Biometrics*, 33(1), 159–174. doi:10.2307/2529310 PMID:843571

Lilienfeld, S. (2016). *Forensic interviewing for child sexual abuse: Why psychometrics matters*. Springer International Publishing. doi:10.1007/978-3-319-21097-1_9

Lord, F. M. (1955). Estimating Test Reliability. *Educational and Psychological Measurement*, 15(4), 325–336. doi:10.1177/001316445501500401

McDonald, R. (1999). *Test theory: A unified treatment*. Lawrence Erlbaum Associates.

Messick, S. (1995). Validity of psychological assessment: Validation of inferences from persons' responses and performances as scientific inquiry into score meaning. *The American Psychologist*, 50(9), 741–749. doi:10.1037/0003-066X.50.9.741

Nunnally, J. (1975). Psychometric theory. 25 years ago and now. *Educational Researcher*, 4(10), 7–21. doi:10.2307/1175619

Nunnally, J. (1978). An Overview of Psychological Measurement. In B. B. Wolman (Ed.), *Clinical Diagnosis of Mental Disorders*. Springer., doi:10.1007/978-1-4684-2490-4_4

Pallant, J. F. (2005). *SPSS survival manual: A step-by-step guide to data analysis using SPSS for Windows (Versions 12-14)*. Allen & Unwin.

Pergert, P., Bartholdson, C., Wenemark, M., Lützén, K., & Af Sandeberg, M. (2018). Translating and culturally adapting the shortened version of the hospital ethical climate survey (HECS-S) - retaining or modifying validated instruments. *BMC Medical Ethics*, 19(1), 35–35. doi:10.118612910-018-0274-5 PMID:29747639

Peter, J. P. (1981). Construct validity: A review of basic issues and marketing practices. *JMR, Journal of Marketing Research*, 18(2), 133–145. doi:10.1177/002224378101800201

Revelle, W., & Zinbarg, R. E. (2009). Coefficients alpha, beta, omega, and the glb: Comments on sijtsma. *Psychometrika*, 74(1), 145-154. http://dx.doi.org.ezproxy.regent.edu/10.1007/s11336-008-9102-z

Shadish, W. R., Cook, T. D., & Campbell, D. T. (2002). *Experimental and quasi-experimental designs for generalized causal inference*. Houghton Mifflin.

Streiner, D. L., & Norman, G. R. (2008). *Health measurement scales: A practical guide to their development and use*. Oxford University Press. doi:10.1093/acprof:oso/9780199231881.001.0001

Taber, K. (2018). The use of Cronbach's alpha when developing and reporting research instruments in science education. *Research in Science Education*, *48*(6), 1273–1296. doi:10.100711165-016-9602-2

Trizano-Hermosilla, I., & Alvarado, J. M. (2016). Best alternatives to Cronbach's alpha reliability in realistic conditions: Congeneric and asymmetrical measurements. *Frontiers in Psychology*, *7*, 769–769. doi:10.3389/fpsyg.2016.00769 PMID:27303333

Uraschi, G., Horodnic, I., & Zait, A. (2015). How reliable are measurement scales? External factors with indirect influence on reliability estimators. *Procedia Economics and Finance*, *20*, 679-686. doi:S2212567115001239

Chapter 3
A Critique of Likert–Response Items in Social Science Research:
A Research Note

Bruce E. Winston
Regent University, USA

ABSTRACT

This chapter critiques the use of the Likert response items for scale development. Likert response data when as nominal data and analyzed as nominal data is useful for recording and analyzing participants' attitudes about a topic. However, it is illogical for researchers who use Likert response data as interval data. The typical five or seven-item Likert response provides three response methods for each topic under study: a neutral item that is categorical, a two or three-item negatively worded ordinal scale, and a two or three-item positively worded ordinal scale. While Likert suggested scoring the five-item response with the numbers 1-5 and scoring the seven-item response with numbers 1-7, it places the neutral response in the 3rd or 4th position, which, if treating the data as interval means that 'neutral' scores higher than the Strongly Disagree-Disagree and lower than the Agree-Strongly Agree items, is not a logical outcome.

INTRODUCTION

The purpose of this chapter is to present the origin, use of, and problems with the Likert-response method. Specific problems include the neutral item in a five/seven-item Likert-response, the use of both positive and negative wording in a Likert-response item, the problems with participants' psychological reaction to negative wording in a Likert-response, and the problems with treating Likert-response items as parametric data. Throughout the chapter, 'Likert-response' is used rather than 'Likert scale' to avoid confusion when a measurement scale is referenced in the text.

DOI: 10.4018/978-1-7998-7665-6.ch003

BACKGROUND

In 1932, Rensis Likert developed the Likert-response as a means of measuring people's attitudes (Chyung et al., 2017). According to Chyung et al. (2017), the Likert-response rapidly grew in popularity and its use expanded into measuring employee performance, communication studies, political opinion research, marketing surveys, and psychometric studies. The Likert-response presented by Likert (1932) was a five-item response with each item scored as 1, 2, 3, 4, or 5. Likert made it clear that ambiguity of the extremes of the attitude is similar to the extremes in a semantic differential scale:

So far as the measurement of the attitude is concerned, it is quite immaterial what the extremes of the attitude continuum are called; the important fact is that persons do differ quantitatively in their attitudes, some being more toward one extreme, some more toward the other. Thus, as Thurstone has pointed out in the use of his scales, it makes no difference whether the zero extreme is assigned to "appreciation of" the church or- "depreciation of" the church, the attitude can be measured in either case, and the person's reaction to the church expressed. (Likert 1932, p. 91)

Likert (1931) posited that Likert-responses could be correlated and that split-half reliability could be measured. DeVellis (2017) discussed both dichotomous and continuous variables and presented reliability measures for each type of scale.

Likert-type responses with an odd number of choices (3, 5, 7, 9, etc.) offer three types of responses within the Likert-response: (a) a dichotomous choice between having an opinion and not having an opinion. (b) ordinal positive, and (c) ordinal negative. The two sub-response types (positive and negative) present a combination of positive and negatively worded responses. Taylor et al. (2003) pointed out the problems with using a mixture of positively and negatively worded items in a scale, and the present-chapter author posits that a similar concern applies to the response items as well. The present-chapter author, in a study of servant leadership and perceived organizational support's relationship with employee well being used Meyers et al. (2019) eight-item measurement scale in which four items were positively worded and four items were negatively worded. Meyers et al.'s scoring instructions called for reverse scoring the four negatively-worded items and then averaging the score of eight items (four positively-worded and four reversed-scored items.) A post-study analysis for this present chapter showed that a principal component analysis of the eight items produced two factors, each with four items. The positively worded items loaded on factor one and the four negatively worded items loaded on factor 2. The current chapter author recalls similar results from prior studies where negative words were reverse-scored. This outcome may relate to participants' psychological reaction to negative wording that may also apply to how participants react to negative responses such as (a) extremely disagree, (b) disagree, and (somewhat disagree). The use of three types of responses also creates problems with treating the data as parametric rather than categorical data. Mayerl and Giehl (2018) caution researchers that negatively worded items may produce a factor of their own, which is what this current chapter author experienced.

MAIN FOCUS OF THE CHAPTER

Positive and Negative Wording of Response Items

Three response types in a 7-point Likert-Response: (a) ordinal decreasing disagreement, (b) categorical Yes/No Neutral, and (c) ordinal increasing agreement.

The Likert-response analysis assigns scores of 1-7 for a 7-point Likert Response. The assignment of a score of 1 for 'strongly agree' and 4 for the neutral position implies that the neutral position is greater than Strongly Disagree, Disagree, or Somewhat Disagree. The decision to make the neutral position higher in order than strongly disagree, disagree, or somewhat disagree and to make the neutral position less than somewhat agree, agree, or strongly agree is illogical since disagree is not a choice along an 'ordered' scale. Also, if a Likert-response is meant to show order from strongly disagree to strongly agree, it fails to show logic since the typical seven-item Likert-response consists of two ordinal scales: (a) a negatively worded Strongly Disagree – Disagree – Somewhat Disagree and (b) a positively worded Somewhat Agree – Agree – Strongly Agree.

Finsted (2010) cautioned about participants not treating positive and negative scoring options in a similar manner with positive scoring items. In other words, participants were less willing to select strongly disagree as often as they were willing to accept strongly agree. Thus, it is likely that negatively worded statements may form a different cluster of scores that may alter the results of principal component analysis. Noting van Sonderen et al.'s (2013) concern about using reversed scored items and considering Wen-Chung Wang et al.'s (2015) admonition about not using mixed response ratings. The use of Likert-response items should be drawn into question.

Problems with Participants' Psychological Reaction to Negative Wording in a Likert-Response and Suggested Alternative Approaches

Mayerl and Giehl, C. (2018) posited that "mixing item directions may come along with some serious methodological problems, leading to low correlations between positively and negatively worded items and multidimensional instead of unidimensional constructs"(p. 193), and Böckenholt (2017) pointed out that:

For example, some respondents may avoid using extreme response categories even if they feel strongly about a topic, whereas other respondents may prefer to select extreme response categories. Although these reactions are driven by the question format and not by the question content, it is important to account for them because they complicate the interpretation and affect the commensurability of ratings across respondents (p. 69).

Böckenholt went on to test participants as to their likelihood to select extreme negative compared to their likelihood to select extreme positively worded items. Böckenholt's results led him to suggest a response-tree approach, discussed in the next section.

Mayerl and Giehl (2018) said that a measure of a latent should include response items that produce consistent responses between negatively and positively worded options (p 194). As noted above, Mayerl and Giehl commented that negatively worded items might produce a factor of their own, thus showing that the participants' responses are possibly not consistent.

Alternative to Using Likert-Response items

Böckenholt (2017) suggested a modification of the Likert-response items so that the survey item was addressed in two steps. The participant would first have to select 'Disagree' or 'agree' with the survey statement (no neutral item was allowed) and then a separate selection as to how much the participant agrees or disagrees using a three-item slider of 'Somewhat – Strongly.' This removes the neutral item but still has the problem of the use of both positive and negative wording. The result is a choice of one of the two response options. A concern about Bökenholt's option is that the analysis process would have to consider which scale the participant selected.

Ding and Ng (2008) proposed a blend of the Likert-response and the semantic differential method by labeling each of the selected categories between the two opposite anchors. Table 1 below is a representation of a figure from Ding and Ng (pg.1222)

Table 1. Ding and Ng's suggested changes to a Likert-response format

	Extremely	Slightly	Quite	Neither	Slightly	Quite	Extremely	
High Professional Competence	1	2	3	4	5	6	7	Weak Professional Competence

Ding and Ng's suggestion is the same as the Likert-response item but with the opposing anchor terms. The problems with the neutral item (choice 4) and the combination of positive and negative items in each statement/response.

An alternative to using Likert-response items is to use semantic differential responses. Devellis (2017) described semantic differential scales as continuous scales with two related but opposite terms such as shown below:

(No Agreement) – 1 2 3 4 5 6 7 – (Complete Agreement)

The choices 1 – 7 represent seven equally distant grades between 'no agreement' and 'complete agreement' with 'no' and 'complete' being the opposite terms. The semantic differential approach removes the option of 'disagreement' but includes 'no agreement,' which could be interpreted as a neutral score found on the Likert-response method. Thus, a selection of '1' could mean no agreement or neutral.

According to Stoklasa et al. (2019):

The semantic differential [sic] is a tool for the extraction of attitudes of respondents towards given objects or of the connotative meaning of concepts. Semantic differential [sic]-type scales are also frequently used in social science research (p. 435),

Stoklasa et al.'s claim that semantic differential responses are used for measuring attitudes; the semantic differential response could be a useful substitute for the Likert-response method. Stoklasa et al. cautioned that the opposing anchor terms in the semantical differential method might be culturally constrained. This caution implies that semantic differential response surveys should be field-tested to determine if participants in the sample frame interpret the terms the same way as the scale development author(s) intended. Stoklasa et al. considered semantic differential scale data to be interval data. Thus, the data would be suitable for mathematical analysis.

Treating Likert-Response Data as Parametric

Soland (2017) cautioned researchers about treating ordinal data as interval or ratio data. Wu and Leung (2017), when describing a Likert-response, said: "It is usually treated as an interval scale, but strictly speaking it is an ordinal scale, where arithmetic operations cannot be conducted (p. 527). Wu and Leung pointed out that there is nothing inherent about the Likert-response items being anything but a list of options in order. Wu and Leung went on to explain that an interval scale must have an equal distance between items; hence the name 'interval.' Since only interval and ratio data can be described as continuous, Likert-response measures cannot be treated as continuous variables. Wu and Leung went on to say:

Computing means and standard deviations for Likert scale data are considered to be inappropriate. Instead, nonparametric statistics should be used. Kuzon, Urbanchek, and McCabe (1996) maintained that one of the seven deadly sins of statistical analysis is using parametric analysis for ordinal scales (p. 528).

Wu and Leung's (2017) concerns were preceded by Briggs (2013), who discussed measurements used to evaluate students' academic progress. Briggs, who based his concerns on Ballou's (2009) emphasis on the importance of using interval data for measurement, expressed the same concerns that were later echoed by Wu and Leung.

An Example of Treating Likert-Response Data as Parametric

This example consists of data from 94 fictitious participants who scored a Likert-response topic, as shown in Table 2. Table 3 shows a mean of 4.0 and a standard deviation of 1.8. The standard deviation shows the dispersion of the data around the mean of 'Neutral.'

Table 2. Example frequency scores

Title	Score	Frequency	Percent
Strongly Disagree	1	10	10.6
Disagree	2	12	12.8
Somewhat Disagree	3	15	16.0
Neutral	4	20	21.3
Somewhat Agree	5	15	16.0
Agree	6	12	12.8
Strongly Agree	7	10	10.6

Notes: N=94

Table 3. Example descriptive statistics

	N	Mean	Std. Deviation
Question 1	94	4.00	1.814
Valid N (listwise)	94		

The histogram shown in Figure 2 indicates that the data is parametric, with the Mean, Mode, and Median being 'neutral.'

Figure 1. Histogram of example Likert-response data

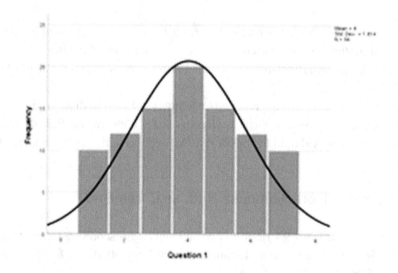

In this example, while the data appears as parametric when examining the histogram, the data is anything but parametric. The frequency data in table 2 shows that the same percentage of participants strongly disagree as strongly agree; likewise, the same percentage of participants disagree as agree; and the same percentage of participants somewhat disagree as agree. All of this is a useful insight into people's attitudes until you see that the same percentage of participants don't have an opinion as to the combined percentage of strongly disagree and strongly agree.

Actions based on the sample of neutral would mislead the future researchers and practitioners who would make decisions based on the average, but a report of frequencies and bar-charts would provide valuable insight into the sample members' attitudes about the statement under study.

TREATING LIKERT-RESPONSE SCORES AS CATEGORICAL DATA

The concerns described above are only valid when performing mathematical analysis as if the data are ordinal or interval. Going back to Likert's original work on the scales, while Likert claimed that the data functioned as ordinal data, which led to analysis problems, those problems do not occur when Likert-response items were treated as categorical data. Going back to the example offered in Figure 1 in the section 'Treating Likert-response Data as Parametric' and examining the bar-graph histogram as categorical data shows valuable information about the participants' attitudes toward the survey item. Then, follow-up research might use qualitative methods to more fully understand why the participants felt the way they do.

FUTURE RESEARCH DIRECTIONS

Future research could include modifying measurements that used Likert-responses to semantic differential responses and conduct paired t-tests to see if participants score the two types of items differently. In addition, qualitative interviews and focus groups could explore how participants interpret the Likert-response items to explore if participants are reluctant and why they are reluctant to select 'strongly disagree' responses compared to 'strongly agree' items.

CONCLUSION

Likert-response data may not be interval data as Likert (1932) implied. Further, Likert-response items have the problems of positive and negative wording raised by van Sonderen et al. (2013). Scale development researchers should consider using response methods that are interval, and all items in a measure should be either positively or negatively worded. While there is a place for Likert-response methods, it is not the best response method for scale development where interval-based mathematics is necessary.

REFERENCES

Ballou, D. (2009). Test scaling and value-added measurement. *Education Finance and Policy*, *4*(4), 351–383. doi:10.1162/edfp.2009.4.4.351

Böckenholt, U. (2017). Measuring response styles in Likert items. *Psychological Methods*, *22*(1), 69–83. doi:10.1037/met0000106 PMID:27893218

Briggs, D. C. (2013). Measuring growth with vertical scales. *Journal of Educational Measurement*, *50*(2), 204–226. doi:10.1111/jedm.12011

Chyung, S. Y., Roberts, K., Swanson, I., & Hankinson, A. (2017). Evidence-Based survey design: The use of a midpoint on the Likert scale. *Performance Improvement*, *56*(10), 15–23. doi:10.1002/pfi.21727

DeVellis, R. F. (2017). *Scale development: Theory and application* (4th ed.). SAGE.

Ding, Z., & Ng, F. (2008). A new way of developing semantic differential scales with personal construct theory. *Construction Management and Economics*, *26*(11), 1213–1226. doi:10.1080/01446190802527522

Finsted, K. (2010). Response Interpolation and Scale Sensitivity: Evidence Against 5-Point Scales. *Journal of Usability Studies*, *5*(3), 104–110.

Likert, R. (1933). The Method of Constructing an Attitude Scale. In the Appendix to A Technique for the Measurement of Attitudes. *Archives of Psychology,* (140), 44-53. Downloaded February 5, 2021, from http://www.sfu.ca/~palys/Likert-1933-TheMethodOfConstructingAnAttitudeScale.pdf

Mayerl, J., & Giehl, C. (2018). A closer look at attitude scales with positive and negative items and response latency perspectives on measurement quality. *Survey Research Methods*, *12*(3). Advance online publication. doi:10.18148rm/2018.v12i3.7207

Meyers, M. C., Adams, B. G., Sekaja, L., Buzea, C., Cazan, A.-M., Gotea, M., Stefenel, D., & van Woerkom, M. (2019). Perceived Organizational Support for the Use of Employees' Strengths and Employee Well-Being: A Cross-Country Comparison. *Journal of Happiness Studies*, *20*(6), 1825–1841. doi:10.100710902-018-0026-8

Soland, J. (2017). Is Teacher Value-Added a Matter of Scale? The Practical Consequences of Treating an Ordinal Scale as Interval for Estimation of Teacher Effects. *Applied Measurement in Education*, *30*(1), 52–70. doi:10.1080/08957347.2016.1247844

Stoklasa, J., Stoklasa, J., Talášek, T., Talášek, T., Stoklasová, J., & Stoklasová, J. (2019). Semantic differential for the twenty-first century: Scale relevance and uncertainty entering the semantic space. *Quality & Quantity*, *53*(1), 435–448. doi:10.100711135-018-0762-1

Taylor, T. E., Poston, W. S. C., II, Haddock, C. K., Blackburn, G. I., Heber, D., Heymsfield, S. B., & Foreyt, J. P. (2003). Psychometric characteristics of the general well-being schedule (GWB) with African-American women. *Quality of Life Research,* *12*(1), 31-39. doi:http://dx.doi.org.ezproxy.regent.edu:2048/10.1023/A:1022052804109

van Sonderen, E., Sanderman, R., & Coyne, J. C. (2013). Ineffectiveness of reverse wording of questionnaire items: Let's learn from cows in the rain. *PLoS One,* *8*(7). Retrieved from https://search-proquest-com.ezproxy.regent.edu/docview/1440999743/fulltextPDF/A7D6467A73644490PQ/1?accountid=13479

Wen-Chung Wang, W., Chen, H., & Jin, K. (2015). Item Response Theory Models for Wording Effects in Mixed-Format Scales. *Educational and Psychological Measurement*, *75*(1), 157–178. doi:10.1177/0013164414528209 PMID:29795817

Wu, H., & Leung, S. (2017). Can Likert scales be treated as interval scales? A simulation study. *Journal of Social Service Research*, *43*(4), 527–532. doi:10.1080/01488376.2017.1329775

Chapter 4

An Illustration of the Actual Steps in Development and Validation of a Multi-Item Scale for Quantitative Research:
From Theory to Practice

Dail Fields

Regent University, USA

ABSTRACT

This chapter describes in detail the process used to develop and validate a scale that measures servant leadership. The steps covered include construct identification from previous studies, review of previously proposed and developed measures, item selection, survey development, collection of data, scale identification, and evaluation of convergent, discriminant, predictive validity. The chapter provides a hands-on example of the steps required for scale measure development and assessment and includes description of the mechanics involved in completing each step of this process.

INTRODUCTION

Over the years, research resources have prescribed the steps involved for development and validation of multi-item scale measures for use in quantitative research (Arnold, Arad, Rhoades & Drasgow, 2000; Fields, 2002). Multi-item scale measures operationalize a construct, which in quantitative research means the scale provides a measure or single numerical of the construct and/or its constituent parts for each study subject. Multi-item summated scale measures include examples such as the Job Diagnostic Survey (Hackman & Oldham, 1980), The Burnout Measure (Pines & Aronson, 1988), and the Minnesota Satisfaction Questionnaire (Weiss, Dawis, England & Lofquist, 1967). These measures all use multiple items (statements or questions) to describe a respondent's perception of an attitude, condition or behavior to improve the internal consistency reliability of the scale and increase the chances that the

DOI: 10.4018/978-1-7998-7665-6.ch004

scale measure covers the meaning of the construct as interpreted by a variety of individuals (Cortina, 1993; Spector, 1992). These measures are very critical to successful quantitative research designs as they enable analysis of possible relationships between each construct and other constructs of interest and theoretical relevance (DeVellis, 2003; Fields, 2002).

There are seven steps specified in the measurement literature that provide critical reassurances to possible users that a scale measure of a construct in the social and behavioral sciences has been rigorously developed, evaluated, and is indeed ready to use (DeVellis, 2003; Kraimer, Seibert, & Liden, 1999; Spector, 1992; Walumbwa, Avolio, Gardner, Wernsing, & Peterson, 2008). To one extent or other, these steps are presented to students in the process of quantitative research training. But how does one go about performing each of these steps correctly? That is the focus of this chapter. Specifically, this chapter reviews and illustrates the 'nuts and bolts' involved in performing each of the steps required in the course of developing a measure of the construct describing a particular set of leadership behaviors.

BACKGROUND

Meyer and Allen (1997) presented requirements for the psychometric evaluation of measures used in quantitative research in the social and behavioral sciences. The process generally consists of two stages. The first is identification of a pool of possible descriptors of the construct of interest and analysis of the applicability of the descriptors based on the views of a sample of subjects familiar with the construct. The second stage consists of evaluating statistically the internal consistency of the new measure as well as its construct validity. The construct validity of a measure, which provides evidence that the derived scale in fact measures what it purports to measure, can be assessed by examining its correlations with other constructs and comparing these correlations with what is expected theoretically (Kerlinger & Lee, 2000). Specifically. construct validity assesses the extent to which a focal measure is significantly related to another validated of a very similar construct (convergent validity), is not related to other distinct different constructs (discriminant validity), and the measure is positively related to an outcome with which the construct is known to be associated (predictive validity). For example, a newly derived measure of job satisfaction should be significantly positively associated with other previously validated measure of job satisfaction, should be negatively associated with a measure of resentment towards and employer, and should be predictive of employee organizational commitment (Scarpello & Vandenberg, 1992).

In addition, confirmatory factor analysis is appropriate for investigating construct validity of multi-item scales because it allows for direct examination of the degree to which specific items jointly are associated with hypothesized factors (i.e. convergent validity) and display minimal cross-loadings on other factors (i.e. discriminant validity). For example, in a four-dimensional measure, if the dimensions do not have discriminant validity, the fit of a single-factor model will be no worse than will the fit of a four-factor model (Kraimer, Seibert, & Liden, 1999).

Starting with a theoretically based description of the construct, the steps generally advocated for development and validation of a quantitative measure of a construct include the following (Arnold, Arad, Rhoades, & Drasgow, 2000; Devillis, 2003; Strauss & Smith, 2009):

1. Use theory and previous empirical research to develop a 'pool' of possible statements or questions that could possibly describe the nature of the construct.

2. If necessary, ask a group of third-party specialists to rate the applicability of the items in order to reduce the number to be further evaluated.

3. Present the reduced set of items to a large sample of respondents who would be knowledgeable about the construct and ask for their individual ratings of the items useful in determining connection to the construct. Assuming that resources are not available for collection of other measures using alternative methods for multitrait-multimethod validation (Shen, 2017), include items in the survey from other validated measures to be used for construct validation (convergent, discriminant, and predictive).

4. Analyze the responses to the items to identify those that group together for the new measure of interest. This is typically done with exploratory factor analysis.
   If single or multiple dimensions group together that on their 'face' measure the construct of interest, assess the internal consistency reliability (Cronbach's alpha) of each dimension. Items that form a scale must measure the same construct and thus should have acceptable internal reliability, typically assessed with coefficient alpha (Cortina, 1993).

5. If the internal consistency is adequate, assess the extent the new measure(s) are positive related with other measures of very similar (or the same) constructs (convergent validity).

6. Assess the extent to which the new measure(s) are different from measures of constructs that differ from the construct interest (discriminant validity). This is generally done using confirmatory factor analysis performed with LISREL of another structural equation modeling (SEM) software.

7. Finally, assess the extent to which the new measure is related to a construct that should be predicted by the construct of interest (predictive validity).

The example discussed in detail in this chapter was used in a research study which was aimed at identification and development of a single relatively parsimonious measure of a set of leadership behaviors known as 'servant leadership.'' Although alternative measures of servant leadership had previously been proposed and published, many seemed overly complex and perhaps embodying other elements than the behaviors of servant leadership. This study was undertaken from the premise that there a 'core' set of essential behaviors of servant leadership and if scale development research might produce a parsimonious measure of servant leadership helpful in leadership assessment and development. The results of the entire study have been published as a research paper in the leadership field (Winston & Fields, 2015). This chapter focuses on the details involved in the 'hands on' performance of the seven steps for measure development and validation described above. The details involved in performing these steps are presented as an example for use by researchers faced with the challenges of scale measure identification and development in order to carry out a quantitative research study.

By way of background, it is useful to know that at the time of this study, there were several previously developed measures used to characterize servant leadership behaviors. These are summarized in Table 1. Previous theoretical and empirical studies aiming to measure servant leadership presented divergent perspectives. On one hand, the concept of servant leadership as explained in both modern and ancient texts requires few words (Keith, 2008). Specifically, servant leadership describes the extent to which a leader exhibits key behaviors that convey service to subordinates so that when goals are accomplished, followers claim the achievement as their own (Keith, 2008; Andersen, 2008; Liden et al., 2009). In essence, the concept of servant leadership suggests that a leader should fulfill an organization's expectations by developing the capabilities of persons he/she is charged with guiding. Greenleaf (1977) summarized the test for servant leadership as whether all involved in an achievement have grown as individuals. He also added, perhaps redundantly, that the undertaking needed to be moral in nature, adding to, rather than subtracting from, society. The focus on serving followers was emphasized by Bass (2000) as a distinction from transformational leadership.

Given the relative simplicity of the essential nature of servant leadership, these previous efforts had been criticized as vague and undefinable, leaving those interested in the concept to figure out its content and nature (Van Dierondonck, 2011). For example, Page and Wong (2000), Sendjaya and Sarros (2006), Dennis and Bocarnea (2005), Barbuto and Wheeler (2006), Hale and Fields (2007), Van Dierendock and Nuitjen (2011), and Liden, et al. (2008) all utilized multi-dimensional operationalizations. The 50 different dimensions included in these views of the same phenomenon are summarized in Table 1.

Table 1. Comparison of domains/categories/factors of multi-dimensional servant leadership instruments

Page and Wong (2003)	Sendjaya and Sarros (2002)	van Dierendonck and Nuitjen (2011)	Dennis and Bocarnea (2005)	Barbuto and Wheeler (2006)	Hale and Fields (2007)	Liden, Wayne, Zhao, and Henderson (2008)
Integrity	Voluntary subordination	Empowerment	Leader's agapao	Wisdom	Humility	Emotional healing
Humility	Authentic self	Standing back	Humility	Persuasion mapping	Service	Creating value for the community
Servant-hood	Covenantal relationship	Accountability	Altruism	Organizational stewardship	Vision	Conceptual skills
Caring for others	Responsible morality	Humility	Vision for followers	Altruistic calling		Empowering
Empowering others	Transcendent spirituality	Authenticity	Trusting	Emotional healing		Helping subordinates grow and succeed
Developing others	Transforming influence	Courage	Empowering others			Putting subordinates first
Visioning		Forgiveness	Service			Behaving ethically
Goal-setting		Stewardship				
Leading						
Modeling						
Team-building						
Shared decision making						

MAIN FOCUS OF THE CHAPTER

As noted above the purpose of this chapter is to describe the details involved in implementing the seven steps for development and validation of a multi-item scale measure of servant leadership (Winston & Fields 2015).

Step 1: Use Theory and Previous Empirical Research to Develop a 'Pool' of Possible Statements or Questions that Could Possibly Describe the Nature of the Construct

First, the 225 items were assembled that were contained in the servant leadership measures previously proposed by Page and Wong (2003), Sendjaya and Saros (2002), Dennis and Bocarnea (2005), Barbuto and Wheeler (2006), Hale and Fields (2008) and Liden et al. (2008). These previously used measures of servant leadership had been subjected to varying degrees of validation. The measure developed and assessed by Liden and colleagues (2008) had been subjected to the most rigorous construct validation evaluation. This list of 225 items was then reduced by removing those statements that were identical or provided duplicate measurement of a specific behavior. This process yielded 116 items that are presented below:

1. Sees serving as a mission of responsibility to others.
2. Is genuinely interested in employees as people.
3. Trusts employees to keep a secret.
4. Models service to inspire others.
5. Shows unselfish regard for employees' well-being.
6. Desires to develop employee potential.
7. Creates a culture that fosters high standards of ethics.
8. Is willing to endure hardships, e.g., political, "turf wars," etc. to defend employees.
9. Is open to receiving input from employees
10. Lets workers make decisions with increasing responsibility.
11. Does not overestimate her or his merits.
12. Seeks employee views regarding the organization's vision.
13. Understands that serving others is most important.
14. Voluntarily gives of him/her self, expecting nothing in return.
15. Shows his or her care by encouraging employees.
16. Gives of his/her self with no ulterior motives.
17. Shows compassion in his or her actions toward employees.
18. Is not interested in self-glorification.
19. Makes others feel important.
20. Is humble enough to consult others in the organization.
21. Is willing to make personal sacrifice(s) for employees.
22. Gives an employee authority to do his/her job.
23. Turns over some control so employees may accept more responsibility.
24. Is willing to make sacrifices to help others.
25. Shows concern for employees.
26. Empowers employees with opportunities so they develop skills.
27. Understands that service is the core of leadership.
28. Communicates trust to employees.
29. Seeks to instill trust rather than fear or insecurity.
30. Encourages employees to participate in determining and developing a shared vision.
31. Entrusts employees to make decisions.

32. Works with employees to write a clear and concise vision for our company.
33. Aspires not to be served but to serve others.
34. Asks employees what the future direction of our organization should be.
35. Does not center attention on his or her own accomplishments.
36. Models service in his or her behaviors, attitudes, or values.
37. Has a demeanor of humility.
38. Lets employees know they are above corruption.
39. Seeks employee views concerning the shared vision of our organization.
40. Can tell if something is going wrong.
41. Makes employee career development a priority.
42. Seems to care more about employee success than his/her own.
43. Holds high ethical standards.
44. Is someone I would seek help from if I had a personal problem.
45. Emphasizes the importance of giving back to the community.
46. Is able to effectively think through complex problems.
47. Encourages employees to handle important work decisions on their own.
48. Is interested in making sure that employees achieve employee career goals.
49. Is always honest.
50. Cares about employee personal well-being.
51. Is always interested in helping people in our community.
52. Has a thorough understanding of our organization and its goals.
53. Gives employees the freedom to handle difficult situations in the way that they feel is best.
54. Provides employees with work experiences that enable them to develop new skills.
55. Sacrifices his/her own interests to meet employee needs.
56. Would not compromise ethical principles in order to achieve success.
57. Takes time to talk to employees on a personal level.
58. Is involved in community activities.
59. Can solve work problems with new or creative ideas
60. Lets employees make important decisions at work without prior consultation.
61. Wants to know about employee career goals.
62. Does whatever she/he can to make employee jobs easier.
63. Values honesty more than profits.
64. Can recognize when employees are down without asking them.
65. Encourages employees to volunteer in the community.
66. Puts employee best interests ahead of his/her own.
67. Does everything he/she can do to serve employees
68. Sacrifices his/her own interests to meet employee needs.
69. Goes above and beyond the call of duty to meet employee needs.
70. Is one I would turn to if I had a personal trauma.
71. Is good at helping employees with employee emotional issues.
72. Is talented at helping employees to heal emotionally.
73. Is willing to help mend employee hard feelings.
74. Seems alert to what's happening.
75. Is good at anticipating the consequences of decisions.

76. Has great awareness of what is going on.
77. Seems in touch with what's happening.
78. Seems to know what is going to happen.
79. Offers compelling reasons to get employees to do things.
80. Encourages employees to dream "big dreams" about the organization.
81. Is very persuasive.
82. Is good at convincing employees to do things.
83. Gifted when it comes to persuading employees.
84. Believes that the organization needs to play a moral role in society.
85. Believes that our organization needs to function as a community.
86. Sees the organization for its potential to contribute to society.
87. Encourages employees to have a community spirit in the workplace.
88. Is preparing the organization to make a positive difference in the future.
89. Is not defensive when confronted.
90. Is driven by a sense of higher calling.
91. Takes a resolute stand on moral principles.
92. Uses power in service to others, not for his/her own ambition.
93. When criticized, tends to focus on the message rather than the messenger.
94. Accepts me as I am, irrespective of my failures.
95. Helps me to find clarity of purpose and direction.
96. Emphasizes doing what is right rather than looking good.
97. Leads by personal example.
98. Practices what he/she preaches.
99. Is more conscious of his/her responsibilities than rights.
100. Promotes values that transcend self-interest and material success.
101. Employs morally justified means to achieve legitimate ends.
102. Inspires me to lead others by serving.
103. Serves people without regard to their nationality, gender, or race.
104. Is willing to say "I was wrong" to other people.
105. Helps employees generate a sense of meaning out of everyday life at work.
106. Has confidence in employees, even when the risk seems great.
107. Encourages employees to engage in moral reasoning.
108. Demonstrates care for employees through sincere, practical deeds
109. Is willing to take control of situations when it is necessary.
110. Treats employees as equal partners in the organization.
111. Enhances employee capacity for moral actions.
112. Listens to employees with intent to understand.
113. Draws out the best from employees.
114. Gives employees the right to question his/her actions and decisions.
115. Minimizes barriers that inhibit employee success.
116. Assists employees without seeking acknowledgement or compensation.

Step 2: Ask a Group of Third-Party Specialists to Rate the Applicability of the Items in Order to Reduce the Number of Items

A panel of 23 researchers attending a conference focused on the study of servant leadership was engaged to evaluate the 116 items drawn from previously developed operationalizations of servant leadership. Each participant was asked to independently rate each item using a 4-point scale where 1 = not useful in describing servant leaders and 4 = contributes greatly to describing servant leaders. The following instructions were provided to each of the expert raters:

Evaluating Questionnaire Items

The following list contains detailed characteristics that various researchers have suggested are good descriptors of servant leaders. Please rate the contribution of each characteristic in uniquely describing and distinguishing servant leaders from other types of leaders. To do this, on the line next to each characteristic write the number from the scale below that best describes how important that characteristic is for describing a person as a servant leader.

Possible Responses

4 This characteristic contributes greatly to describing a servant leader
3 This characteristic contributes somewhat to describing a servant leader
2 This characteristic contributes slightly to describing a servant leader
1 This characteristic is not useful in describing a servant leader

The expert raters were then provided with the list of 116 possible items describing servant leadership. The responses were tabulated in an EXCEL spreadsheet and the ratings averaged for each item. We reduced the items to those descriptors that each had an average rating of 3.5 or above (on a 4-point response scale), were rated '4' by 75% or more of the panel members, and which had within rater agreement (r_{wg}) of at least .70. This resulted in retention of 22 leader behaviors for further analysis. These items selected by the expert panel are shown below:

1. Sees serving as a mission of responsibility to others
2. Is genuinely interested in employees as people
3. Models service to inspire others
4. Understands that serving others is most important
5. Is willing to make sacrifices to help others
6. Understands that service is the core of leadership
7. Seeks to instill trust rather than fear or insecurity
8. Aspires not to be served but to serve others
9. Models service in his or her behaviors, attitudes, or values
10. Holds high ethical standards
11. Is always honest
12. Would not compromise ethical principles in order to achieve success.
13. Values honesty more than profits.
14. Shows concern for employees.

15. Is driven by a sense of higher calling.
16. Takes a resolute stand on moral principles.
17. Emphasizes doing what is right rather than looking good
18. Leads by personal example
19. Practices what he/she preaches
20. Promotes values that transcend self-interest and material success
21. Inspires me to lead others by serving
22. Serves people without regard to their nationality, gender, or race.

Step 3. Present the Items to a Large Sample of Respondents who would be Knowledgeable about the Construct and Ask for Their Individual Ratings of the Items Useful in Determining Connection to the Construct. Include Items from Other Validated Measures that will be Used Later for Construct Validity Tests (Convergent, Discriminant, and Predictive).

A questionnaire was developed that included these 22 items as well as items measuring transformational leadership behaviors, transactional leader behaviors, servant leadership as measured by the instrument developed by Liden and colleagues (2008), and a measure of leadership effectiveness developed and used by Ehrhart and Klein (2001). The questionnaire was placed in internet-based survey software and the link provided to adult working students and faculty at a private mid-Atlantic university as well as to university alumni and colleagues in a variety of organizations. Each respondent was asked to describe a leader he/she had worked for in the past 5 years and included specification of the job role for both the respondent and the leader.

The survey presented to the sample of employees contained the following scales collected in order to conduct tests of construct validity (Liden, et al, 2008; Schaufeli, & Van Dierendonck, 1993.Shen, 2017). It should be noted that the items for the other validated measures were includes at this time because it was extremely unlikely that the same respondents would be available for collection of these other validation measures using alternative methods. That is, multitrait-multimethod validation is generally considered the 'gold standard' for construct validation (Campbell & Fiske, 1959; Shen, 2017). This method of construct validation requires that data collected for other measures of servant leadership (to test convergent validity), measures of other alternative leadership styles (to test discriminant validity) and measures of leadership effectiveness (to test predictive validity) be collected from the same respondents using a different method of collection (Shen, 2017). This project suffered under the constraint that the our large sample of respondents were contacted via an on-line survey which allowed respondents to be anonymous. Knowing in advance that the extremely small likelihood of reaching the same sample for multi-method data collection, the decision was made to collect multi-trait validation data at one time. This approach does open the possibility that the correlations among some items could be inflated by common method variance (Conway & Lance, 2011; Spector, 2006)). The net effects of CMV are of course subject to debate in the literature (Spector, 2006), but nonetheless, this strategic consideration is one that must be kept in mind when planning the execution of the 7 steps of scale development.

The additional measures included in the instrument for validation purposes were:

Transformational Leadership

Sixteen items drawn from the Multifactor Leadership Questionnaire (Avolio, Bass, & Jung, 1999) were used to measure inspirational motivation (4 items, $\alpha = .65$), individualized consideration (4 items, $\alpha = .77$), idealized influence (4 items, $\alpha = .84$), and intellectual stimulation (4 items, $\alpha = .84$).

Transactional Leadership

Eleven items drawn from a study by Avolio and colleagues (1999) to measure 'active' transactional leadership, forming a single dimension scale ($\alpha = .95$). This measure approximates the contingent reward and management by objectives approaches to transactional leadership.

Multi-Dimensional Operationalization of Servant Leadership

Twenty-seven items were used to measure the seven dimensions of servant leadership previously investigated and tested by Liden and associates (2008). As mentioned above, of the alternative measures published at the time of this study, this alternative measure of servant leadership had received the most rigorous evaluation and construct validation. Thus, we used this measure to examine convergent validity for our ultimate product. One item originally used in this study was redundant with the twenty-two rated highly by the expert panel and therefore was not used in the seven dimensions. The measure developed and assessed by Liden and colleagues contains seven scales for: (a) conceptual skills (4 items, $\alpha = .88$), (b) empowering employees (4 items, $\alpha = .85$), (c) helping subordinates grow (3 items used in the scale, $\alpha = .95$; a fourth item reduced scale reliability), (d) putting subordinates first (4 items, $\alpha = .87$), (e) behaving ethically (3 items, $\alpha = .89$), (f) emotional healing (4 items, $\alpha = .87$) and (g) creating community value (4 items, $\alpha = .73$).

Leadership Effectiveness

A six-item scale developed by Ehrhart and Klein (2001) measured leadership effectiveness ($\alpha = .90$). The measure asked each respondent to think of the referent leader and state the extent to which the respondent believed he/she worked at a high level of performance under this leader, enjoyed working for this leader, got along well with the leader, found the leader's style compatible with his/her own, and admired the leader, and felt the leader was similar to his/her ideal leader. Responses were on a scale of 1 (to little or no extent) to 5 (to a great extent).

The large sample yielded responses from 456 working adults. Due to missing values on some key variables, the usable sample contained 443 responses. The average age of the respondents was 45 years. Forty-seven percent were male and seventy-seven percent were white. Seven percent live outside of the United States. Seventy-six percent have 15 or more years of work experience. On average, respondents have worked for the leader they described for three to five years, while 27.5% have worked for the leader over five years and 92% have been with the leader for more than one year. Fifty percent of respondents currently work for the leader they described in our survey. Twenty-one percent of the respondents worked in commercial firms; 13% in government entities including the military, 36% worked in education, 15% in religious organizations, 11% in community non-profit organizations, and 4% in the healthcare field.

Step 4: Analyze the Responses to the Items in Order to Identify Those that Group Together for the New Measure of Interest. This is Typically Done with Exploratory Factor Analysis. If Single or Multiple Dimensions Group Together that on Their 'Face' Measure the Construct of Interest, Assess the Internal Consistency Reliability (Cronbach's Alpha) of Each Dimension.

After providing the 22 items to our large diverse sample of current employees, the extent to which these items might be further reduced was examined by conducting exploratory factor analysis of the items. Since the study sought to find the minimum number of factors required to account for the variance in the variables, principal components extraction was used. (Bandalos & Boehm-Kaufman Hair, 2009: Anderson, Tatham & Black, 1998; Kerlinger & Lee, 1992). Prior to conducting the factor analysis, the appropriateness of the data for exploratory factor analysis was examined by reviewing the Kaiser-Meyer-Olkin (KMO) measure of sampling adequacy. The KMO value was .97, far exceeding the minimum KMO guidelines value of .70 (Watkins, 2018) The responses to the items describing possible servant leadership behaviors was also examined for univariate outliers. In this case, outliers were defined as cases where the pattern of responses would suggest a case was not reasonably representative of the sample of respondents. Statistical examination of standardized variables revealed some cases with uniformly low levels of scores on the servant leader behaviors, however, these low scores were plausible since servant leadership behaviors may be exhibited in organizations to varying degrees, including very low levels. The Mahalanobis D^2 for each case was also examined to investigate the occurrence and possible significance of multivariate outliers. We did find 4 cases with Mahalanobis test values (D2/d.f.) values larger than the 3.5 cutoff suggested by Hair and colleagues (2010). Again, we examined these cases for evidence that they should be removed from the analysis. In all cases, the responses about the frequency of experience of servant leadership behaviors were plausible. The results of the factor analysis were also examined with these cases both included and removed with no discernable differences found in the factor extraction or loadings after rotation.

The initial factor analysis of the 22 prospective items for a measure of servant leadership items produced two factors with eigenvalues greater than 1.0, the first accounting for 74.4% of the total variance in the items and the second accounting for 4.8%. In the interest of developing the most parsimonious measure of essential servant leadership behaviors, varimax rotation (which assumes orthogonal factors) was first used in order to identify possible items which cross-loaded on both extracted factors. Upon close examination, we decided to eliminate from further analysis items that cross-loaded on both extracted factors (showed rotated factor loadings exceeding .50 on both factors). We also examined the inter-items correlations and eliminated pairs of items whose inter-item correlation exceeded .87. This level of correlation indicates shared variance exceeding 75% and therefore likely redundancy in what the items measure (Hair, et al., 2010).

These efforts reduced the item pool to 13 statements describing possible servant leadership behaviors. these remaining items were then re-analyzed yielding one factor containing 10 items accounting for 75% of the total variance across the items. Since items that form a scale must measure the same construct and thus should have acceptable internal consistency reliability, assessed with coefficient alpha (Cortina, 1993). The 10 items in this factor all contributed positively to a scale reliability of alpha = .96. The 10 items representing the new measure of . (abbreviated ESLB) are:. .

1.   Practices what he/she preaches

2. Serves people without regard to their nationality, gender, or race
3. Sees serving as a mission of responsibility to others
4. Genuinely interested in employees as people
5. Understands that serving others is most important
6. Willing to make sacrifices to help others
7. Seeks to instill trust rather than fear or insecurity
8. Is always honest
9. Is driven by a sense of higher calling
10. Promotes values that transcend self-interest and material success

Response scale for the extent to which this statement described the behavior of a focal leader:

1 = definitely no; 2 = no; 3 = neutral; 4 = yes; 5 = definitely yes

Step 5: If the Internal Consistency is Adequate, Assess the Extent the New Measure(s) are Positive Related with Other Measures of Very Similar (or the Same) Constructs (Convergent Validity).

The convergent validity of the new 10-item measure of essential servant leader behaviors was examined by calculating and assessing the relationships of the new measure (ESLB) with the seven dimensions of a servant leadership measure previously developed and validated by Liden and colleagues (2008). The dimensions of this measure cover seven categories of leader behaviors which include conceptual skills, empowering employees, helping subordinates grow, putting subordinates first, behaving ethically, emotional healing and creating community value (Liden et al., 2008). The Essential Servant Leadership Behaviors measure value for each of the 443 subjects in the study sample was calculated by averaging the values for the 10 items. Similarly, the values of each of the seven dimensions of the Liden and colleagues measures of servant leadership were calculated as the mean of the items comprising each dimension. The zero order correlations among these study variables are shown in table 2.

Table 2. Means, standard deviations, and correlations (N = 443) of the ESLB and 7 dimensions of an alternative servant leadership measure (Liden et al., 2008)

Variable	Mn	s.d	1	2	3	4	5	6	7	8
1. Essential Servant Leader Behaviors	3.74	1.12	.----							
2. Conceptual skills	3.80	1.11	.85	----						
3. Empowerment	3.59	1.09	.84	.91	----					
4. Subordinates grow	3.11	1.25	.85	.80	.82	----				
5. Subordinates first	2.72	1.10	.91	.75	.79	.83	----			
6. Behave ethically	3.93	1.18	.89	.85	.79	.82	.86	----		
7. Emotional healing	3.94	1.01	.87	.81	.79	.81	.83	.90	----	
8. Value to community	3.89	.86	.81	.73	.72	.72	.77	.74	.81	----

All correlations shown are significant at p < .01

In this table, the ESLB measure is positively significantly correlated with all 7 dimensions of the alternative measures of servant leadership (Liden et al., 2008) The positive correlations of the essential servant leader behaviors with the 7 dimensions of the existing measure of servant leadership averaged .83 (p < .001). These positive significant correlations support convergent validity of the essential servant leader behaviors with a previously validated existing multi-dimensional measure of servant leadership (Fields, 2002; Kerlinger & Lee, 2000).

Step 6: Assess the Extent to which the New Measure(s) are Different from Measures of Constructs that Differ from the Construct Interest (Discriminant Validity).

The discriminant validity of the ESLB measure was assessed by conducting a confirmatory factor analysis of a model that included the essential servant leadership behaviors, behaviors describing four dimensions of transformational leadership (individualized consideration; intellectual stimulation, idealized influence, inspirational motivation), and behaviors describing a single dimension of transactional leadership (Avolio, Bass, & Jung, 1999). The model of 6 distinct factors (ESLB, 4 dimensions of transformational leadership, and one dimension of transactional leadership) indicated adequate fit to the data (comparative fit index (CFI) =.97; normed fit index (NFI) = .97; Root mean error of approximation (RMSEA) = .10). Moreover, this six-factor model fit the data better than any of 10 alternative models estimated which contained a smaller number of factors. Specifically, these alternative models tested the discriminant validity of the ESLB measure by considering combinations of the ESLB with transactional leadership as well as a combination of the ESLB with each of the dimensions of transformational leadership. The smallest change in fit between the model of 6 distinct sets of behaviors with any of these alternative models was $\Delta\chi^2 = 78.5$, d.f = 5, p < 01). These results are shown in table 3.

Table 3. Fit of alternative confirmatory factor models

Model	χ^2 (df)	$\Delta\chi^2$ (df)	RMSEA	NFI	CFI
6 factor model (Servant, Transactional, and 4 dimensions of Transformational Leadership)	3067.17(545)**	—	0.10	0.97	0.97
5 factor model (Combining Servant and Transactional Leadership with 4 dimensions of Transformational Leadership)	3145.28(550)**	78.11 (5)**	0.10	0.97	0.97
3 factor model (Servant, Transactional, and Transformational Leadership)	3188.76(557)**	121.59 (12)	0.10	0.97	0.97
2 factor model (Combining Servant and Transactional leadership and a single factor for Transformational Leadership)	3261.55(559)**	194.38(14)**	0.10	0.97	0.97
1-factor model	3284.11(560)**	216.94(15)**	0.12	0.96	0.97

RMSEA = Root Mean Squared Error of Approximation

NFI = Normed Fit Index

CFI = Comparative Fit Index

Confirmatory factor analysis was also used to examine the distinctiveness of the essential servant leader behaviors from the seven dimensions servant leadership operationalization developed by Liden and colleagues (2008). An eight-factor model fit the data reasonably well (CFI = .96; NFI = .95; RMSEA

= .06) and significantly better than any of a series of seven-factor models, each combining the ESLB with each of the seven dimensions of this alternative previously validated measure of servant leadership behaviors. The difference in fit between the eight-factor model and the best fitting confirmatory model with essential servant leadership behaviors combined with each of the dimensions of the Liden et al. (2008) model was $\Delta\chi^2 (7) = 1666.02$ (p < .001). These results support distinction of the ELSB from other alternative forms of leadership (transformational and transactional) as well as an alternative multi-dimensional measure of servant leadership behaviors.

Step 7: Assess the Extent to which the New Measure is Related to a Construct that should be Linked with the Construct of Interest (Predictive Validity).

Both theory and previous research suggest that essential servant leadership behaviors should predict the extent to which employees view the leaders described in our survey as an effective leader. As previously noted, the survey included a previously developed and tested six item measure of leader effectiveness (Ehrhart & Klein, 2001). The predictive validity of the ESLB was examined by assessing the extent to which this measure incrementally contributed to explanation of the variance in leader effectiveness over and above the variance explained by other alternative sets of leadership behaviors (transformational and transactional leadership) and the variance explained by an alternative measure of servant leadership (seven dimensions by Liden et al, 2008). The extent to which the ESLB measure make a unique contribution in explaining ratings of leader effectiveness was examined by the parameters estimated for several alternative regression models. These models are presented in Table 4

The models in columns a, b, and c of Table 4 show that the ESLB makes a significant incremental contribution in explaining the variance in leadership effectiveness after entry of the transformational leadership dimensions ($\Delta R^2 = .15$, p < .01), transactional leadership ($\Delta R^2 = .02$, p < .01), and both transformational and transactional leadership ($\Delta R^2 = .01$, p < .01). The regression model in column d of Table 4 shows that the essential behaviors also make an incremental contribution ($\Delta R^2 = .02$, p < .01) in explaining leadership effectiveness ratings over and above the seven dimensions of an existing validated servant leadership operationalization (Liden et al, 2008). While the incremental contributions of the essential servant leadership behaviors over and above transactional leadership and the existing measure of servant leadership are small from a practical viewpoint, they nonetheless provide evidence of incremental predictive validity. However, to further test the extent to which the incremental contribution of the ESLB was a statistical artifact attributable to the relatively large sample size (443 cases) used in the regression models shown in Table 4, half of the cases were randomly selected and the regression models re-estimated. In the regression models with 220 cases, the incremental contribution of the ESLB was approximately the same as in the models using the entire sample (443 cases) and remained statistically significant (p < .01).

CONCLUSION

This chapter set out to provide a 'hands on' description of the way that a project to develop and validate a new measure of a construct was designed and executed. The chapter has provided a detailed description of the activities conducted and the rationale underlying each. This hopefully will be useful to other students and active researchers considering measure development and validation. Unfortunately, space did

Table 4. Regression models predicting leader effectiveness examining the incremental contribution of the ESLB

Predictor Variables	Model A	Model B	Model C	Model D
Transformational Leadership				
Inspirational Motivation	.08**		-.06**	
Intellectual Stimulation	.08*		.04	
Individualized Consideration	.11**		.01	
Idealized Influence	.04		.01	
ΔR^2	.67**			
Transactional Leadership		.57**	.43**	
ΔR^2		.82**	.16**	
Liden et al. Servant Leadership				
Conceptual Skills				.23**
Empowering				.10*
Subordinates Grow				.02
Subordinates First				.07
Behave Ethically				.17**
Emotional Healing				-.06
Value of Community				.05
ΔR^2				.84**
Essential Servant Leadership Behaviors	.71**	.36**	.35**	.41**
ΔR^2	.15**	.02**	.01**	.02**

Notes: * - $p = .05$; ** - $p = .01$

not allow for inclusion of the actual syntax used in the SPSS and LISREL programs used in conducting the seven steps. However, the constantly changing nature of these software tools would make today's syntax somewhat obsolete in a short time.

There are two additional areas of concern that go beyond the seven steps in measure development and validation that future efforts should consider and be prepared to address. Thus, the efforts made in this previous study (Winston & Fields, 2015) are included here for reference. These areas of concern are:

1. The extent to which the data used in many of the statistical analysis may in some what be peculiar in nature.
2. The extent to which the statistical relationships among variables in the study may be inflated by common method variance.

With regard to the first concern, previous studies have expressed concern that the perceptions of servant leadership by employees may be context specific, tending to occur more frequently in spiritually oriented organizations (Andersen, 2008; Hale & Fields, 2007). To investigate this concern, the levels of servant leader behaviors and the levels of leader effectiveness reported by respondents across six major industry categories (commercial, government, education, religious, non-profit, and healthcare) we investigated. There were no significant differences in the reported levels of servant leadership across these industries.

The sample used in this study was dominated by relatively experienced workers and less experienced employees might view leadership behaviors other than those associated with servant leadership as more important to their success. Although this concern is difficult to address directly, some patterns in the descriptions of focal leaders was examined. In the study sample, respondents who had worked for a focal leader for less than one year rated the frequency of ESLB behaviors significantly higher than those who had worked for a leader more than five years. Over longer time periods of association, it is possible that employees observe leaders dealing with varying situations where each leader has differing degrees of success. An employee's greater familiarity with a leader's failures may take some of the 'bloom off the rose', leading to lower ratings of servant leader behaviors by longer tenured followers. In the sample, ratings of essential servant leader behaviors were also significantly lower for those who were currently working for the focal leader (F = 17.01, p < .01). It is possible that retrospective reports about experiences with former leaders are upwardly biased by a halo effect or downwardly biased by day-to-day experiences (Hunter, Bedell-Avers & Mumford, 2007; Johns, 2006).

The second area of concern arises because the data used in this study were collected using a single questionnaire by persons responding voluntarily at a single point in time. In this instances, statistical relationships among the key variables may be affected by common method variance (CMV). Although the magnitude of possible CMV effects have been debated (Spector, 2006), using post hoc techniques suggested by Richardson, Simmering, and Sturman (2009), Lindell and Whitney (2001), and Conway and Lance (2010), the evidence for CMV effects was investigated. Richardson and colleagues (2009) proposed that the 'marker variable' method for assessing effects of CMV within data such as our sample had the best performance. Thus, the marker variables approach was applied to the study sample to identify and adjust for the effects of CMV (Lindell & Whitney, 2001; Richardson, et al., 2009). Although we did not identify and include a specific an 'ideal' marker variable a priori, we followed the procedure suggested by Lindell and Whitney (2001) and we isolated some variables that should be unrelated to leader effectiveness and examined the correlations of these variables with the outcome of leader effectiveness. This approach attempts to provide an indirect indication of the extent that CMV may be inflating relationships such as correlations among variables of the study. Of the variables examined, respondent age had the smallest correlation with leaders' effectiveness (r = .041, n.s.). Thus, this variable was used as a marker and the adjusted correlations estimated among the key constructs (Richardson et al, 2009). After adjustment, the relationships of the predictor variables (essential servant leader behaviors, transformational leadership dimensions, transactional leadership, and Liden and colleagues (2008) servant leadership dimensions) with leadership effectiveness all remained statistically significant at p < .01. While CMV may play some role in the statistical relationships among study variables, the true scores of the variables remain significantly related and not significant altered by CMV (Lindell & Whitney, 2001; Spector, 2006).

Finally, the data collected for this study did not take into account the context within which leader-follower relationships are established and implemented. As Meindl (1993) pointed out, there may be a significant social influence component to the acceptance of a leader and development of subsequent productive relationships. In the case of a relatively non-traditional approach such as servant leadership, the process of social contagion deserves further explication and investigation. These are all examples of healthy skeptical considerations that need to be taken into account when venturing into development and validation of new means of measurement. In other words, it is as important in doing such as study to be recognize what we do not know, as much as what we do know.

REFERENCES

Andersen, J. A. (2009). When a servant-leader comes knocking. *Leadership and Organization Development Journal, 30*(1), 4–15. doi:10.1108/01437730910927070

Arnold, J. A., Arad, S., Rhoades, J. A., & Drasgow, F. (2000). The empowering leadership questionnaire: The construction and validation of a new scale for measuring leader behaviors. *Journal of Organizational Behavior, 21*(3), 249–269. doi:10.1002/(SICI)1099-1379(200005)21:3<249::AID-JOB10>3.0.CO;2-#

Avolio, B. J., Bass, B. M., & Jung, D. I. (1999). Re-examining the components of transformational and transactional leadership using the Multifactor Leadership Questionnaire. *Journal of Occupational and Organizational Psychology, 72*(4), 441–462. doi:10.1348/096317999166789

Barbuto, J. E. Jr, & Wheeler, D. W. (2006). Scale development and construct clarification of servant leadership. *Group & Organization Management, 31*(3), 300–326. doi:10.1177/1059601106287091

Campbell, D. T., & Fiske, D. W. (1959). Convergent and discriminant validation by the multitrait-multimethod matrix. *Psychological Bulletin, 56*(2), 81–105. doi:10.1037/h0046016 PMID:13634291

Conway, J. M., & Lance, C. E. (2010). What reviewers should expect from suthors regarding common method bias in organizational research. *Journal of Business and Psychology, 25*(3), 325–334. doi:10.100710869-010-9181-6

Cook, J. D., Hepworth, S. J., Wall, T. D., & Warr, P. B. (1981). *The experience of work: A compendium of 249 measures and their use.* Academic Press.

Cortina, J. M. (1993). What is coefficient alpha? An examinationof theory and applications. *The Journal of Applied Psychology, 78*(1), 98–104. doi:10.1037/0021-9010.78.1.98

Dennis, R. S., & Bocarnea, M. (2005). Development of the servant leadership assessment instrument. *Leadership and Organization Development Journal, 26*(8), 600–615. doi:10.1108/01437730510633692

DeVellis, R. F. (2003). *Scale development: Theory and applications.* Sage Publications, Inc.

Ehrhart, M. G., & Klein, K. J. (2001). Predicting Followers' Preferences for Charismatic Leadership: The Influence of Follower Values and Personality. *The Leadership Quarterly, 12*(2), 155–179. doi:10.1016/S1048-9843(01)00074-1

Fields, D. L. (2002). *Taking the Measure of Work.* Sage Publications.

Greenleaf, R. K. (1977). *Servant leadership: A journey into the nature of legitimate power and greatness.* Paulist Press.

Greenleaf, R. K. (1998). *The power of servant-leadership.* Berrett-Koehler.

Hair, J., Black, W., Babin, B. J., & Anderson, R. E. (2010). *Multivariate Data Analysis.* Prentice Hall.

Hale, J. R., & Fields, D. L. (2007). Exploring servant leadership across cultures: A study of followers in Ghana and the USA. *Leadership, 3*(4), 397–417. doi:10.1177/1742715007082964

Hunter, S. T., Bedell-Avers, K., & Mumford, M. D. (2007). The typical leadership study: Assumptions, implications, and potential remedies. *The Leadership Quarterly, 18*(5), 435–446. doi:10.1016/j.leaqua.2007.07.001

Kerlinger, F. N., & Lee, H. B. (2000). *Foundations of Behavioral Research* (4th ed.). Cengage Learning.

Liden, R. C., Wayne, S. J., Zhao, H., & Henderson, D. (2008). Servant leadership: Development of a multidimensional measure and multi-level assessment. *The Leadership Quarterly, 19*(2), 161–177. doi:10.1016/j.leaqua.2008.01.006

Lindell, M. K., & Whitney, D. J. (2001). Accounting for common method variance in cross-sectional research designs. *The Journal of Applied Psychology, 86*(1), 114–121. doi:10.1037/0021-9010.86.1.114 PMID:11302223

Meindl, J. (1993). Reinventing leadership: A radical, social psychological approach. In J. K. Murnighan (Ed.), *Social Psychology in Organizations*. Prentice-Hall.

Page, D., & Wong, P. (2000). A conceptual framework for measuring servant-leadership. In S. Adjibolosoo (Ed.), *The human factor in shaping the course of history and development*. University Press of America.

Richardson, H. A., Simmering, M. J., & Sturman, M. C. (2009). A tale of three perspectives: Examining post hoc statistical techniques for detection and correction of common method variance. *Organizational Research Methods, 12*(4), 762–800. doi:10.1177/1094428109332834

Scarpello, V., & Vandenberg, R. J. (1992). Generalizing the importance of occupational and career views to job satisfaction attitudes. *Journal of Organizational Behavior, 13*(2), 125–140. doi:10.1002/job.4030130203

Schaufeli, W. B., & Van Dierendonck, D. (1993). The construct validity of two burnout measures. *Journal of Organizational Behavior, 14*(7), 631–647. doi:10.1002/job.4030140703

Sendjaya, S., & Sarros, J. C. (2002). Servant leadership: It's origin, development, and application in organizations. *Journal of Leadership & Organizational Studies, 9*(2), 57–64. doi:10.1177/107179190200900205

Shen, F. (2017). Multitrait-Multimethod matrix. In The International Encyclopedia of Communication Research Methods. John Wiley & Sons. doi:10.1002/9781118901731.iecrm0161

Spector, P. (2006). Method variance in organizational research: Truth or urban legend? *Organizational Research Methods, 9*(2), 221–232. doi:10.1177/1094428105284955

Spector, P. E. (1992). Summated Rating Scale Construction. In Quantitative Applications in the Social Sciences. Sage Publications. doi:10.4135/9781412986038

Strauss, M. E., & Smith, G. T. (2009, April 27). Construct validity: Advances in theory and methodology. *Annual Review of Clinical Psychology, 5*(1), 1–25. doi:10.1146/annurev.clinpsy.032408.153639 PMID:19086835 van Dierendonck, D. (2011). Servant leadership: A review and synthesis. *Journal of Management, 37*(4), 1228–1261. doi:10.1177/0149206310380462

van Dierendonck, D., & Nuijten, I. (2011). The Servant Leadership Survey: Development and Validation of a Multidimensional Measure. *Journal of Business and Psychology, 26*(3), 249–267. doi:10.100710869-010-9194-1 PMID:21949466

Walumbwa, F. O., Avolio, B. J., Gardner, W. L., Wernsing, T. S., & Peterson, S. J. (2008). Authentic leadership: Development and validation of a theory-based measure. *Journal of Management, 34*(1), 89–126. doi:10.1177/0149206307308913

Watkins, M. W. (2018). Exploratory factor analysis: A guide to best practice. *The Journal of Black Psychology, 44*(3), 219–246. doi:10.1177/0095798418771807

Winston, B. E., & Fields, D. (2015). Seeking and measuring the essential Behaviors of Servant Leadership. *Leadership and Organization Development Journal, 36*(4), 413–434. doi:10.1108/LODJ-10-2013-0135

Chapter 5
Statistical Techniques for Making Cross-Cultural Comparisons on Organizational Instruments

Tanesia R. Beverly
Law School Admission Council, USA

ABSTRACT

Researchers tend to evaluate psychological instruments in terms of reliability (internal consistency) and construct validity (exploratory factor analysis and confirmatory factor analysis). In many instances, these instruments are used for cross-cultural comparisons such as gender and race—however, many of these studies do not provide evidence of measurement invariance or measurement equivalence. Measurement equivalence is a statistical property of an instrument that indicates that participants interpret and respond to the items similarly or that the same latent construct is being measured across observed groups of people. Partial measurement equivalence is a necessary condition for comparing latent mean differences across cultures. This area of construct validity is often neglected in the literature; therefore, this chapter aims to introduce the concept of measurement invariance. Additionally, it highlights the necessity of testing for measurement invariance when making cross-cultural comparisons on organizational leadership instruments.

INTRODUCTION

Researchers often use self-reported survey instruments (e.g., surveys and questionnaires) to measure different latent constructs (e.g., attitudes, grit, self-efficacy). These researchers utilize factor analytic procedures to determine the factor structure of survey or Likert scale data. Researchers spend a great deal of energy ensuring that their newly developed survey instrument has strong psychometric properties such as internal consistency and validity. However, these instruments are typically used to compare mean differences across observed demographic groups (e.g., gender, race, and nationality), but many research-

DOI: 10.4018/978-1-7998-7665-6.ch005

ers fail to ensure that their instrument meets the basic level of scrutiny to make such comparisons. To make valid group comparisons, researchers must ensure that the instrument has the same structure across groups or that the survey questions function similarly for all respondents regardless of their demographic characteristics. Some researchers apply traditional methods, such as ANOVA, when making cross-cultural comparisons based on a composite or summed score from the instrument. Statistical analyses like ANOVA and t-tests assume measurement invariance or measurement equivalence (Borsboom, 2006) or that the instrument is measuring the same latent constructs across multiple populations (Marsh & Hocevar, 1985). For instance, measurement equivalence ensures that differences in latent scores across observed demographic groups result from true latent differences rather than an artifact of the instrument. Measurement equivalence testing provides construct validity evidence and allows researchers to draw inferences about group similarities and differences on these measured constructs. Neglecting to test for measurement invariance can affect the validity of the inferences being made, including inflation of Type I and II error rates.

This chapter introduces the concept of measurement invariance (i.e., equivalence). It also highlights the necessity of testing for measurement invariance when comparing groups (i.e., gender, race, nationality) on new and existing survey instruments. In this chapter, cross-cultural comparisons refer to observable characteristics such as race, gender, ethnicity. The same procedures apply regardless of the groups being compared.

BACKGROUND

The next section details the statistical underpinnings of the measurement equivalence procedure. It starts by introducing the foundations of the model and then details the procedure for testing for measurement equivalence.

Measurement Model

The multiple-group confirmatory factor analysis (MGCFA) was introduced to test measurement equivalence across observable groups (Jöreskog, 1971). Jöreskog's (1971) hierarchical tests for measurement equivalence excluded the mean structure or tests for equality of intercepts and latent means. Sorböm (1974) extended this technique to incorporate means and covariance structures (MACS) or compare intercepts and latent means across groups. In the MACS, equality constraints for factor loadings and intercepts across groups are imposed to detect latent mean differences (Sorböm, 1974).

MGCFA allows researchers to test a priori hypotheses about model parameters across groups. The confirmatory factor analysis model (CFA) provides a framework for evaluating equality constraints across groups. The CFA is defined as:

$$X_g = \tau_g + \Lambda_g \xi_g + \delta_g \tag{1}$$

where X_g is the vector of observed scores, τg is the vector of intercepts or observed means on items, Λg is a matrix of factor loadings or the regression of the observed variables on the latent factors ξ, and δ is the vector of measurement errors for each group g. The mean and variance-covariance matrices of the observed are defined as:

$$E\left(X_g\right) = \tau_g + \Lambda_g \cdot_g \qquad (2)$$

$$\Sigma_g = \Lambda_g \Phi_g \Lambda_g' + \Theta_g \qquad (3)$$

where $E(X_g)$ is a vector of observed means, Σ_g is a matrix of observed variances and covariances, κg is a vector of factor means, Φg_i s a matrix of factor variances and covariances, and Θg is a diagonal matrix of unique variances.

Model Identification and Scaling

Latent variables must be assigned a scale of measurement, and some constraints must be introduced to scale these variables (Bollen, 1989). Two commonly used scaling techniques are factor variance (FV) and referent indicator (RI). The factor variance method constrains the factor variance to one, and the factor means to zero while freely estimating all other parameters. In contrast, the referent indicator method constrains a single factor loading or indicator to 1 and the corresponding item intercept to zero or the latent mean to zero and freely estimates all other parameters. The factor variance method assumes that means and variances are invariant across groups.

   In contrast, the referent indicator method assumes that the indicator chosen to scale the latent construct is invariant across groups (Wang, Whittaker, & Beretvas, 2012). Since the scaling constraints are not assessed in the measurement invariance tests, these assumptions can lead to erroneous conclusions (Kline, 2011). Researchers should be careful when choosing a referent indicator as it can impact conclusions. Several researchers have investigated this phenomenon and argue that invariance violations of the factor scaling technique causes rescaling of the factor loadings. This rescaling can lead to invalid conclusions about measurement invariance (Wang, Whittaker, & Beretvas, 2012). See Cheung and Rensvold (2001) for ways to identify an invariant referent indicator. One caveat of using the different scaling methods in structural equation modeling (SEM) is that they will produce different parameter estimates; however, the model fit statistics will remain unchanged due to statistically equivalent models (Little, 2013). Scaling methods produce different parameter estimates due to the assumptions of each method.

Levels of Measurement Equivalence

This section discusses four levels of measurement equivalence. These tests are hierarchical, and more restrictive levels of equivalence can be imposed once less restrictive invariance has been established. They usually start with the least restrictive, the configural model, which has no equality constraints and becomes increasingly more restrictive until reaching the most restrictive level of invariance, in this case, scalar. A description of the types of invariances is outlined in Table 1 and discussed below.

Table 1. Measurement invariance definitions and constraints

Definition: Measurement invariance tests the assumption that an underlying construct is measured similarly across multiple populations (Marsh & Hocevar, 1985) and allows one to draw inferences about group similarities and differences on these measured constructs.			
Level of Invariance	**Constraints**	**Meaning**	**Interpretation**
Configural	No constraints.	Same patterns of fixed and free parameters.	The construct is related to the same set of indicators.
Metric	$H_0: \Lambda_A = \Lambda_B = \ldots = \Lambda_G$	The magnitude of the relationship between the indicator and the latent construct is the same.	The construct has the same meaning across groups. Item responses (intercepts when $\kappa = 0$) can be meaningfully compared.
Scalar	$H_1: \Lambda_A = \Lambda_B = \ldots = \Lambda_G,$ $\tau_A = \tau_B = \ldots = \tau_G$	Populations respond similarly to observed responses—no systematic measurement biases.	Respondents with the same latent factor score will obtain the same score on the observed variables despite their group demographic.
Latent Means (κ)	$H_2: \Lambda_A = \Lambda_B = \ldots = \Lambda_G$ $\tau_A = \tau_B = \ldots = \tau_G,$ $\kappa A = \kappa B = \ldots = \kappa G$	Latent means are the same across groups.	There are/are not true mean differences in factor scores.

Configural Equivalence

The first step in assessing measurement equivalence is to fit a configural invariance model. The configural model serves as a baseline model in the invariance tests (Horn & McArdle, 1992). This model is equivalent to fitting separate measurement models for each group; the only difference is that these models are estimated simultaneously. This model is not expected to be identical across groups. The configural model determines whether the constructs are conceptualized in the same manner across groups or, in other words, that the factor structure is the same. This model estimates all parameters freely across groups other than those necessary for model identification and scaling. The configural model is more qualitative, requiring that the same number of latent factors and the same pattern of zero and non-zero loadings are specified across groups. This means that the same items should load on the same factors; hence, the same factors should represent each group. For only those latent trait variables that support configural invariance, metric invariance is tested. There is no point in testing measurement equivalence if there is not a similar factor structure.

Metric Equivalence

The next step is to test for weak or metric invariance. In this model, the strength of the relationship between the observed scores and the factors is tested across groups. Metric invariance places equality constraints on the units of measurement or factor loadings across groups and tests the null hypothesis,

$$H_0 : \Lambda_1 = \Lambda_2 \ldots = \Lambda_G.$$

If metric invariance is tenable, a one-unit change in one group or time is equivalent to a one-unit change in the other group. That item response (intercepts) can be meaningfully compared across groups

(Dimitrov, 2010). However, some researchers argue that metric invariance is enough to test for latent mean differences (Byrne, Shavelson, Muthén, 1989).

Scalar Equivalence

Lastly, the scalar invariance model equates the item intercepts (observed score) across the groups for measurement equivalence. The item intercepts represent the point of origin (Bollen, 1989) and test the null hypothesis,

$$H_0 : \tau_1 = \tau_2 \ldots = \tau_G .$$

Evidence of scalar invariance suggests that no group responds systematically higher or lower than the other group. Scalar invariance implies that individuals with the same latent factor score will obtain the same score on the observed variables despite their demographic variable (Milfont & Fischer, 2010). Additionally, it allows one to make meaningful comparisons across latent parameters (Little, 1997). This level of invariance allows researchers to see mean differences across groups as the relative difference between the reference and focal groups. The reference group will have a mean of zero, and the focal group will have a negative or positive mean, indicating that the mean of the focal group is lower or higher.

Mean Equivalence

Once scalar invariance is established, the invariance of factor means is testable by constraining the latent means to equality across groups,

$$H_0 : \kappa_1 = \kappa_2 \ldots = \kappa_G .$$

If this hypothesis is tenable, it suggests that the means across groups are similar.

Evaluating Equivalence Constraints

Evaluating measurement equivalence constraints requires estimating a series of hierarchically nested models (those with parameter constraints) and comparing them with a less restrictive model (those with freely estimated parameters). Measurement equivalence is tenable if the cross-group equality constraints have little influence on model fit (Little, 1997). Researchers rely on model fit statistics such as chi-square statistics, root mean squared error of approximation (RMSEA), comparative fit index (CFI), and the Tucker Lewis Index (TLI) to assess the tenability of invariance constraints. The CFI and TLI are ratios of the misfit in the tested model to the misfit in the null model. Values greater than 0.95 are considered adequate (Little, 2013). Values less than or equal to 0.08 for the RMSEA are considered adequate as well.

The model with the equality constraints is compared to the unconstrained model using fit indices. Typically, the Chi-Square test of differences (with degrees of freedom equal to the difference in the degrees of freedom between the models) and the decrement in model fit (ΔCFI) between the two models are used to assess the tenability of the more restrictive model. The chi-square test of differences is the most used method. If the chi-square difference value is significant, the null hypothesis is rejected, and the equality constraints do not hold. If the chi-square test of differences is nonsignificant, the equality constraints are tenable, and the researcher can place more restrictive constraints on the model. Cheung and Rensvold (2002) recommend that equality constraints hold if the ΔCFI less than or equal to the absolute value of 0.01. Cheung and Rensvold (2009) assert that the ΔCFI is a robust statistic for testing measurement equivalence for MGCFA models. It is robust because the CFI statistic is independent of model parameters and sample size.

Assessing Full Measurement Equivalence

Full measurement equivalence is difficult to attain in practice; only 40% of applied studies achieved full metric invariance (Chen, 2008). Vandenberg and Lance's (2000) extensive literature review revealed the most researchers often ignore scalar equivalence and only test for configural and metric equivalence before testing for latent mean differences. This phenomenon is likely due to early researchers arguing that metric invariance is enough to test for latent mean differences (Byrne, Shavelson, Muthén, 1989; Muthén & Christoffersson, 1981). However, more recently, researchers have expressed the importance of testing for scalar invariance before assessing mean differences (Bollen, 1989). Even proponents of full measurement equivalence have argued that scalar invariance is restrictive and unrealistic (Horn & McArdle, 1983; Horn, 1991). Researchers also believe strict equivalence (equality of error variances) is unnecessarily restrictive (Bollen, 1989; Horn & McArdle, 1992) even though some researchers suggest it is required for valid interpretations of latent mean differences (Meredith, 1993). Because strict invariance is deemed unrealistic in practice, it will not be discussed in this chapter.

Failure to achieve full metric equivalence indicates that researchers should not move onto scalar invariance and that latent mean differences should not be assessed. However, Muthén and Christoffersson (1981) introduced partial measurement equivalence to deal with this issue. Partial measurement equivalence violates the assumption of full equivalence in that it allows the researchers to relax the equality constraints on a subset of indicators. The basic consensus for those supporting partial measurement equivalence is that some level of equivalence needs to be met to allow latent mean comparisons. When the constrained model is the worse fitting model, researchers can relax the assumption of full invariance. If the restrictive model is not better, researchers should look at the modification indices and substantive theory to determine which equality constraints can be relaxed or that parameter estimates are noninvariant. There is limited information on the magnitude of partial measurement equivalence on latent mean differences. However, Byrne, Shavelson, and Muthén (1989) and Steenkamp and Baumgartner (1998) argued that only two indicators, including the referent indicator, need to exhibit at a bare minimum invariance for meaningful latent mean comparisons.

An Example

The example presented in this chapter uses data from a study investigating the measurement properties of a newly created survey instrument called the Perceptions of Test-Taking Ability (PTTAS). Beverly and McCoach (2015) describe the recruitment procedures of the sample. The groups are compared based on a self-identified demographic characteristic, race. The measured variables are five items (X_1 to X_5) from the Time Management scale on the PTTAS. This scale measures respondents' confidence to complete standardized tests within the specified time limits. This scale was chosen because previous analyses suggest a single factor solution with adequate internal consistency and a lack of measurement invariance for race. The response scale is a 1- to 5-point Likert scale, with one being *strongly disagree* and five *strongly agree*. In this analysis, two items were reversed-scored because they had a negative relationship with the total score. They were also reverse-scored so that higher scores were associated with greater time management capabilities. Participants included 1006 White and Black college and graduate students in the Northeastern United States. Most of the sample was White (n = 621, 60.9%) and female (n = 704, 69.1%). All confirmatory factor analyses were conducted using the R *lavaan* package (Rosseel, 2012) and maximum likelihood (ML) estimation.

Table 2 provides the means, standard deviations, and correlations for the Black and White participants. The means show that the White participants rated themselves higher on all-time management items than the black participants. For the most part, inter-item correlations were higher for white participants than Black, and apart from x_4 and x_5, the variability in item scores was also higher for White participants than Black participants.

Table 2. Descriptive statistics for the time management scale for black and white samples.

	x_1	x_2	x_3	x_4	x_5
	Correlations for Black Participants (n = 391)				
x_1	1.00				
x_2	0.46	1.00			
x_3	0.53	0.38	1.00		
x_4	0.47	0.52	0.44	1.00	
x_5	0.49	0.45	0.47	0.60	1.00
Mean	2.68	2.47	2.32	2.68	3.26
SD	1.19	1.04	1.07	1.14	1.05
	Correlations for White Participants (n = 615)				
x_1	1.00				
x_2	0.57	1.00			
x_3	0.48	0.46	1.00		
x_4	0.56	0.56	0.50	1.00	
x_5	0.53	0.55	0.46	0.57	1.00
Mean	3.09	3.02	2.52	3.04	3.49
SD	1.20	1.18	1.08	1.08	0.90

A series of multigroup confirmatory factor models were fit to the data. The *configural model* (*Model 1*) was used as the baseline model and was specified as a single factor with five items for each group. The purpose of this model is to determine whether the models have the same dimensions and patterns of free and constrained parameter estimates (Bollen, 1989). The configural model does not impose any constraints on the factor loadings or intercepts. The factor loading for x_3 and latent mean and the latent mean were fixed to 1 and 0 respectively across each group to scale the latent variable or for identification purposes. A graphical depiction of the model is shown in Figure 1, which shows that the only constraints on the model are for identification purposes only; the factor loadings, intercepts, and residual variances were freely estimated across groups. Table 3 provides the fit results for the configural model and subsequent models. The configural model has a mediocre fit; the RMSEA is below the 0.08 threshold but above the optimal 0.05 threshold. The χ^2 statistic is statistically significant ($p = 0.004$), likely due to the large sample size (Little, 2014). However, the CFI, TLI, and SRMR indices are below the threshold values at 0.991, 0.982, and 0.016, respectively. This model will be retained as the baseline model for illustrative purposes since most fit indices indicate a good fit.

Figure 1. Parameter estimates from the configural model where a) and b) are the estimates for white and black participants, respectively

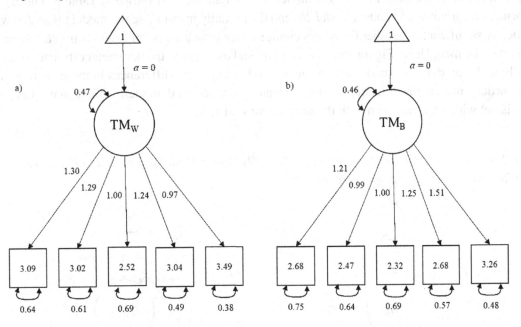

Table 3. Model

	χ^2	df	$\Delta\chi^2$	Δdf	RMSEA (90% CI)	CFI	ΔCFI	Decision
Model 1	26.159	10	--	--	0.057 (0.03 - 0.08)	0.991	--	Accept
Model 2	45.092	14	18.933	4	0.066 (0.05 - 0.09)	0.983	-0.008	Reject
Model 2b	32.340	13	6.181	3	0.054 (0.03 - 0.08)	0.989	-0.002	Accept
Model 3	37.082	16	4.742	3	0.051 (0.03 - 0.07)	0.988	-0.001	Accept
Model 4	65.373	17	28.291	1	0.075 (0.06 - 0.10)	0.973	-0.015	Reject

Since the configural model held, the next form of measurement equivalence is a weak or metric equivalence (*Model 2*). This model imposes equality constraints on the factor loadings ($\Lambda_w = \Lambda_B$) and indicates that the strength of the relationship of each item is the same in each group. The model fit for this model deviated from the model fit for *Model 1*. The $\Delta\chi^2$ is statistically significant at $p < 0.01$, and the ΔCFI is close to the cut-off of the absolute value of 0.01. The metric equivalence does not hold, and the next step is to locate which item violates the equivalence assumption. Upon assessing the modification indices, x_2 has a modification index ($\chi^2 = 12.92$, df = 1) that is statistically significant, indicating significant differences across race. Black and white participants are not interpreting x_2 similarly. Therefore, a partially invariant weak model (*Model 2b)* was created by relaxing the constraint on x_2.

Model fit improved for the partially invariant weak model with the χ^2 decreasing and the other fit indices increasing. The $\Delta\chi^2$ between the configural model (*Model 1)* and the partially invariant weak model (*Model 2)* was not statistically significant, and this model was retained. A partially invariant *strong* or *scalar* model was executed without an equality constraint on x_2. This invariance level focuses on the observed means of the items and helps determine whether one group tends to answer higher or lower than the other (Bollen, 1989). This model fits the data well, as shown in Table 3. The $\Delta\chi^2$ from the partially invariant weak model (*Model 2b)* and the partially invariant scalar model (*Model 3)* was not statistically significant. The other fit indices changed very little because of this constraint. The partially invariant scalar model held. Figure 3 presents a graphical model with the parameter estimates of the final partially scalar model. This model allows the researcher to see the differences in means across groups. Black participants had lower latent meantime management scores than their white counterparts, which is consistent with what was seen with the descriptive statistics.

Figure 2. Parameter Estimates from the Final Partially Scalar Model where a) and b) are the estimates for White and Black participants, respectively

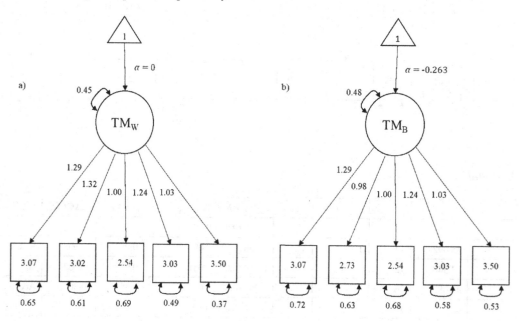

The final step is to test whether there are latent mean differences across races (*Model 4)*. The partial strong invariant model was used to assess latent mean differences, and equality constraints were placed on latent means across race. Equality constraints on the latent means led to a statistically significant $\Delta\chi2$ (28.291, df = 1, p < 0.01) and a decrement in other model fit indices. This statistically significant result indicates statistically significant mean differences between Black and White participants on the time management scale.

CONCLUSION

The purpose of this chapter was to describe the next steps after examining an instruments' internal structure and reliability when researchers are interested in cross-cultural comparisons such as race and gender. While traditional methods can test observed mean differences, measurement invariance aims to test for latent mean differences. One can always use traditional statistical analysis such as ANOVA; however, one needs to be careful with their conclusions because they can be erroneous. After all, it assumes measurement equivalence. Therefore, partial weak equivalence must hold to make valid comparisons across observed groups at a bare minimum. The lack of weak and strong measurement invariance can lead to spurious differences in latent means (Chen, 2008). However, when strong measurement invariance is supported, different cultures similarly interpret the items.

REFERENCES

Beverly, T., & McCoach, D. B. (2015). *Perceptions of standardized test-taking ability survey (PTTAS): Development, validation, and replication* [Paper presentation]. American Educational Research Association.

Bollen, K. A. (1989). *Structural equations with latent variables*. Wiley. doi:10.1002/9781118619179

Borsboom, D. (2006). When does measurement invariance matter? *Medical Care, 44*(11, Suppl 3), S176–S181. doi:10.1097/01.mlr.0000245143.08679.cc PMID:17060825

Byrne, B. M., Shavelson, R. J., & Muthén, B. (1989). Testing for the equivalence of factor covariance and mean structures: The Issue of partial measurement invariance. *Psychological Bulletin, 105*(3), 456–466. doi:10.1037/0033-2909.105.3.456

Chen, F. F. (2008). What happens if we compare chopsticks with forks? The impact of making inappropriate comparisons in cross-cultural research. *Journal of Personality and Social Psychology, 95*(5), 1005–1018. doi:10.1037/a0013193 PMID:18954190

Cheung, G. W., & Rensvold, R. B. (1998). Cross-cultural comparisons using noninvariant measurement items. *Applied Behavioral Science Review, 6*(1), 93–110. doi:10.1016/S1068-8595(99)80006-3

Dimitrov, D. M. (2010). Testing for factorial invariance in the context of construct validation. *Measurement & Evaluation in Counseling & Development, 43*(2), 121–149. doi:10.1177/0748175610373459

Horn, J. L., & Mcardle, J. J. (1992). A practical and theoretical guide to measurement invariance in aging research. *Experimental Aging Research, 18*(3), 117–144. doi:10.1080/03610739208253916 PMID:1459160

Jöreskog, K. G. (1971). Simultaneous factor analysis in several populations. *Psychometrika, 36*(4), 409–426. doi:10.1007/BF02291366

Kline, R. B. (2011). *Principles and practice of structural equation modelling*. Guilford.

Little, T. (1997). Mean and covariance structures (MACS) analyses of cross cultural data: Practical and theoretical issues. *Multivariate Behavioral Research, 32*(1), 53–76. doi:10.120715327906mbr3201_3 PMID:26751106

Little, T. (2013). *Longitudinal structural equation modeling*. Guilford.

Marsh, H. W., & Hocevar, D. (1985). Application of confirmatory factor analysis to the study of self-concept: First-and higher-order factor models and their invariance across groups. *Psychological Bulletin, 97*(3), 562–582. doi:10.1037/0033-2909.97.3.562

Meredith, W. (1993). Measurement invariance, factor analysis and factorial invariance. *Psychometrika, 58*(4), 525–543. doi:10.1007/BF02294825

Milfont, T. L., & Fischer, R. (2010). Testing measurement invariance across groups: Applications in cross-cultural research. *International Journal of Psychological Research, 3*(1), 111–130. doi:10.21500/20112084.857

Muthén, B. O., & Christoffersson, A. (1981). Simultaneous factor analysis of dichotomous variables in several groups. *Psychometrika, 46*(4), 407–419. doi:10.1007/BF02293798

Rosseel, Y. (2012). lavaan: An R Package for Structural Equation Modeling. *Journal of Statistical Software, 48*(2), 1–36. doi:10.18637/jss.v048.i02

Sorböm, D. (1974). A general method for studying differences in factor means and factor structure between groups. *British Journal of Mathematical & Statistical Psychology, 27*(2), 229–239. doi:10.1111/j.2044-8317.1974.tb00543.x

Steenkamp, J. E. M., & Baumgartner, H. (1998). Assessing measurement invariance in cross-national consumer research. *The Journal of Consumer Research, 25*(1), 78–90. doi:10.1086/209528

Vandenberg, R. J., & Lance, C. E. (2000). A review and synthesis of the measurement invariance literature: Suggestions, practices, and recommendations for organizational research. *Organizational Research Methods, 3*(1), 4–70. doi:10.1177/109442810031002

Wang, D., Whittaker, T. A., & Beretvas, S. N. (2012). The impact of violating factor scaling method assumptions on latent mean difference testing in structured means models. *Journal of Modern Applied Statistical Methods; JMASM, 20*(1), 108–130. doi:10.22237/jmasm/1335844920

Chapter 6
The Transfer of Learning:
Designs and Assessment

Rodney Reynolds

Independent Researcher, USA

ABSTRACT

The focus of this chapter is on insights for and evaluation of if the transfer of learning by training and development professionals will sustain the training field. The chapter begins with the need for a model of learning. Then there is a section on a proposed evaluation of the trainer presentation of a model of learning or training development. The chapter then progresses to a proposed measure of the potential for the transfer of learning and the need to assess self-efficacy with gradations of attainments on the training topic. Finally, the chapter turns to trainee engagement and to having a results orientation for a training program.

INTRODUCTION AND BACKGROUND

The major premise for this chapter is that training materials and training assessment should have a base in a model of long-term learning and training development. Any use of a model of learning should draw a consistent focus on how trainees are most likely to transfer their learning from their training(s) to their self-development while becoming an added-value to their profession and, thus, their employers. Evidence is essential (Reynolds & Reynolds, 2002; Reynolds, 2020) especially of post-training achievements (Kirkpatrick, 1994) Thus, any assessment of the potential for the transfer of learning must involve an evaluation of the introduction and projection of the future learning and development. The timing, method, and wording of any measure or the transfer of learning must also be based on the model of learning and training development that forms the base for the training sessions.

DOI: 10.4018/978-1-7998-7665-6.ch006

Model of Learning or Training Development

Most education and learning professionals are familiar with Bloom's Taxonomy (Bloom, Engelhart, Furst, Hill, & Krathwohl, 1956; Anderson & Krathwohl, 2001). Many learning professionals prefer one of the variations and extensions of Vygotsky's (1978) Constructivist Learning Theory. Previously, I argued (Reynolds, 2017) that Training and Development professionals should be well acquainted with Donald Kirkpatrick's Model (Kirkpatrick, 1994; 1998; Kirkpatrick & Kirkpatrick, 2007; 2010). Praslova (2010) adapted Kirkpatrick's thinking to curriculum development. Thus, Prasolva drew a tie between learning theory and advancements for educators as well as training and development professionals.

A Vision for Long-Term Learning

Use of an approach to learning, training, and development is essential for being able to cast a perspective for trainees on where they are starting from, what they can accomplish in the specific training sessions, and their subsequent steps for development. There is an underlying concern here about trainers who lack sufficient background in learning theories that enables their capacity to cast a vision of the long-term path(s) to trainee development. Trainers need to plan, forecast, and embed self-improvement processes that connect to later blended learning processes. In short, without a vision for their long-term learning and development 'curve', trainees cannot be expected to persist in the long-tern transfer of leaning. Therefore, any assessment of the transfer of learning must involve some index of the trainees' sense that they have gained a vision for their long-term development.

There are multiple potential examples of the levels and depths of learning that can illustrate how the specific training session might influence the assessment of the potential transfer of learning and development. Training for novices with survey research should probably not carry an expectation that trainees will be able to 'transfer' their early learning to address complex issues related to potential avoidance of, detection of, or corrections for measurement and sampling errors. Intermediate statistics training should surely not be expected the trainees to offer solutions for the analyses of mixed-nested experimental designs. Similarly, asking advanced and skilled public advocates to explain basic concepts of social influence and persuasion (e.g., the general concept of source credibility) would never be considered evidence of their level of the transfer of their training and development to their current practices.

Proposed Post-Training Measure of Trainer Presentation of a Model of Learning or Training Development

1. The [Training Team] provided a graph/chart of at least four stages of expected development on [Persuasive Speaking Skills].
    Strongly Disagree 1 2 3 4 5 Strongly Agree
2. *2. The content of the training sessions seemed <u>far below</u> my prior stage of development on [Persuasive Speaking Skills].
    Strongly Disagree 1 2 3 4 5 Strongly Agree
3. The [Training Team] explained that the current session[s] are at a specific stage of expected development on [Persuasive Speaking Skills].
    Strongly Disagree 1 2 3 4 5 Strongly Agree

4. At the end of the training session[s], I understood what to work on for the next stage of my development on [Persuasive Speaking Skills].
    Strongly Disagree 1 2 3 4 5 Strongly Agree
5. *5. It was odd that the [Training Team] seemed to occasionally throw in advanced complex material/skill exercises about [Persuasive Speaking Skills].
    Strongly Disagree 1 2 3 4 5 Strongly Agree
    *Reflected item

Definition of Terms

The Transfer of Learning: The transfer of learning happens when learners develop the abilities to mature their applications and synthesizes of information, strategies, and skills to contexts beyond their previous training environments. In short, the transfer of learning requires self-adaptation and adoption of prior learning as the trainee[s] move on to the next stage of learning and development. This approach to the transfer of learning is far beyond simplistic early models about basic uses and applications of training 'on-the-job.' The transfer of learning requires a constant vision (and revision) of the learning curve for the expected training and development.

Post Training Assessments are perhaps the most devalued aspect of training processes. For many, training evaluations are just an after-thought. "Assessment" can be an odd term. Some use "assessment" as a synonym (if not a neologism) for the process of the documentation of the learning of specific knowledge or skills. "Assessment" sometimes carries connotations about verdicts on competency. "Assessment" is also a common reference to compelled financial obligations (especially following tax audits). In the most innocent sense, learning assessment is a broader more holistic term than 'evaluation' because assessment involves multiple evaluation processes based on a vision of learning benchmarks (or standards) with a focus on improvement. At root, training assessment is an appraisal of the trainees' achievements for a specific stage of training and development. Such a training assessment should include appraisal of the trainees' preparation, self-motivation, and perceived self-efficacy to move on to the next level of stage of training and development. It is important to keep in mind that assessment of the transfer of learning must extend beyond the specific training session 'content'. Berg and Chyung (2008) point out that much of the actual learning takes place outside of formal training sessions and, therefore, outside of the traditional model of training evaluation

Perceived Self-Efficacy: Bandura (2006) defines perceived self-efficacy as "a judgment of capability to execute given types of performances" (309). Self-efficacy is not self-confidence (self-esteem), intent to perform, or an expectation of results.

Training Assessment and Reverse Mapping

Training and development professionals can partially track the program value with a general measure of the transfer of learning. Such a measure must include . . . application, synthesis, innovation, and transfer efficacy.

A Proposed Post-Training General Measure of The Potential for the Transfer of Learning

After this training on [Persuasive Speaking Skills],

1. I have ideas on how I can directly apply these [Persuasive Speaking Skills] in my work.
    Strongly Disagree 1 2 3 4 5 Strongly Agree
2. I doubt I could ever adapt these [Persuasive Speaking Skills] to my job.
    Strongly Disagree 1 2 3 4 5 Strongly Agree
3. I will enjoy talking with my colleagues about how I can activate the use of these skills.
    Strongly Disagree 1 2 3 4 5 Strongly Agree
4. *4. There is little from this training program on [Persuasive Speaking] that I can use in my job.
    Strongly Disagree 1 2 3 4 5 Strongly Agree
5. There are unique ways I can synthesize these [Persuasive Speaking Skills] with my current work practices.
    Strongly Disagree 1 2 3 4 5 Strongly Agree
6. I am capable to integrate the {Persuasive Speaking Skills] into the challenges I will face in my career.
    Strongly Disagree 1 2 3 4 5 Strongly Agree
7. *7. The training program seems to suggest [Persuasive Speaking] ideas that are clearly at odds with our normal work routines.
    Strongly Disagree 1 2 3 4 5 Strongly Agree
8. I am looking forward to moving up to the next level of [Persuasive Speaking Skills] at work.
    Strongly Disagree 1 2 3 4 5 Strongly Agree
9. I have a clear vision of the strategies and tactics of [Persuasive Speaking Skills] that I can develop for me in my future.
    Strongly Disagree 1 2 3 4 5 Strongly Agree
10. I now can help my colleagues at work with building their unique [Persuasive Speaking Skills].
    Strongly Disagree 1 2 3 4 5 Strongly Agree
    *Reflected item

Self-Efficacy Measure

Bandura (2006) argues that self-efficacy measures should be specific to the potential impediments to performance. Unfortunately, "there is no all-purpose measure of perceived self-efficacy" (p.307). Thus, the measure below is specific to persuasive speaking as an example of the type of measure of self-efficacy trainer should develop for their specific training topic. Trainers will need to follow Bandura's principals for developing their own measure of self-efficacy specific to their indented training program. The questions in the measure need to address: a specific domain of behaviors addressed by the training; the actual qualities of functioning with the skills and practices; the gradations of progressive accomplishments, difficulties, challenges, and impediments when developing the skills and practices See also (Nye, Chernyshenko, Stark, Drasgow, Phillips, Phillips, & Campbell, 2020).

Proposed Self-Efficacy to Develop Persuasive Speaking Skills

Below are number of situations that can make it hard to perform as a persuasive speaker.

Please rate how certain you are that you can adapt and perform well as a persuasive speaker.

Rate your degree of confidence by recording a number from 0 to 100 using the scale given below:

0 10 20 30 40 50 60 70 80 90 100

Cannot do at all Moderately can do Highly certain can do

Confidence

Table 1. (0-100)

1.	When being 'evaluated' on my speaking	____
2.	When I am feeling under pressure to get 'Yes' answers	____
3.	When I have not rehearsed my arguments many times	____
4.	When I must speak immediately after a highly successful competitor speaks	____
5.	When I am speaking to people who have a critical spirit	____
6.	When I have an unexpected 'visit' to my presentation from a very powerful person	____
6.	When I have not prepared for the people that I need to persuade	____
7.	When I know one of the people in the room will try to make fun of my message	____
8.	When I did not know that I would be asked to give a presentation	____
9.	When there is an error in one of my visual aids	____
10.	When I know the audience is strongly predisposed to resist my message	____
11.	When just before I stand to speak, someone tells the joke I planned to use in my introduction	____

A key here is that the transfer of learning should result in subsequent increases in self efficacy over time.

With a clear vision for subsequent stages of learning and development, the training team can reverse map how their materials and experiential elements are appropriate for the needs of the trainees. Reynolds (2017) argued that reverse mapping or backwards design (Wiggins & McTighe, 2005) is progressively essential to training and development professionals. If we begin with our performance skills and favorite content, materials, and activities "rather than deriving those means from what is implied in the desired results" (p. 15), we place the emphasis on the teacher/trainer and on the content instead of on the actual learning or any sense of development. The focus of training ought not to be on enjoyable yet ephemeral experiences with little lasting effects. The participants in the "learning" may smile with appreciation or a sense of completion, but will later report that they gained little to nothing from the experience.

Seeking Self-Improvement

While various constituencies of clients and trainees demand evidence of quality, the core of success-ful training is the trainee engaged with seeking self-improvement. Kirkpatrick and Kirkpatrick (2007) argue that trainers must refine the justification for training by answering the "in order to?" question. The seeking of quality is essential to any set of learning events. Speaking to an apathetic audience is the black hole of rhetorical moments (Lashbrook, Snavely, & Sullivan, 1977). Without a focus on quality, even high-level professionals find assessment processes threating to the point of emotionally inflamed resistance (Payne & Hysong, 2016). The trainee perception of the utility of the training is essential to the transfer of training to actual applications and future developments on the job and in the career (Yelon, Ford, & Bhatia, 2014). Learners who center on increasing quality are far more likely to adopt and share a vision for enduring and high-level goals. Motivated learners, in turn, are far more likely to provide valid reports on assessments of their learning (Finn, 2015). Without a vision for the multiple and long-range goals for a training program, trainees will not accept, adopt, adapt, and apply their training experiences. Long-term visions for the effects of a training program are essential for supervisors to guide and elicit higher levels of performance. In sum, without beginning with a clear envisioning of the potential levels of a training program, we can never adequately document that our training efforts matter.

Results Orientation

Evidence of the actual transfer of learning (Alliger et al., 1997) would ideally come from subsequent training sessions designed around trainees implementing and adapting what they have learned (e.g., capstone experiences such as a college seniors doing a thesis/project). Evidence of the potential for the transfer of learning would also come from asking supervisors to review the potential utility and transferability of the training exercises and assignments. In the higher education environment, we ideally want at least three levels which should be evident in the curriculum design for the learning outcomes for the university and for the major (e.g., introduced, reinforced, and proficiency).

The *Results* criterion is coming on fast in training and development. Trainee and supervisor reports and evaluations of subsequent progress and accomplishments should become a common practice. Alumni trainee accomplishments might include tracking their promotions and career advancements. An interesting development in higher education asks for evidence that the education on their campus serves the public good (see Kezar, Chambers, & Burkhardt, 2005; WASC Senior College and University Commission, 2015 -- particularly criterion for review 1.1). Training and Development professionals might also track how their training alumni have adapted their learning to outside public service and advancement. Application of the Kirkpatrick Model (see Kirkpatrick & Kirkpatrick, 2007; and especially Kirkpatrick & Kirkpatrick, 2010) definitively calls for training and development professionals to find and report actual corporate returns on training investments. Kirkpatrick (1994) was specific that training and development professionals need to connect the results of their training to actual corporate profits.

Such a vision of finding evidence of *Results*, implies the need to include training alumni, (future) supervisors, and public agencies in the development of new training content and exercises. Kirkpatrick and Kirkpatrick (2007) promote further 'moving the needle' of training attainments with post-training mentoring and motivating. Since post-training progress depends on the trainee development (Papaloizos & Nicholls, 1970), trainers must vary post training strategies. For example, trainers should taylor training and post training strategies across the corporations and agencies they serve (van Rooij & Merkebu, 2015; Taylor, Haywood, Shulruf, 2019). In short, training evaluation requires knowledge about the expected results for training programs and what would count as acceptable and useful evidence of effectiveness.

Reynolds (2017) advocated that training and development professionals should include *expert external reviews* of their training programs. Done well, an 'External Review Reports' will help improve training program content and materials. External reviewers should be independent from the trainer. Usually, the trainers would prepare a detailed self-evaluation 'Training Program Report' on the design, conduct, and effectiveness of the program. The report should address the concerns of multiple audiences (e.g., trainees; supervisors; future clients; external publics, those holding the trainers accountable). Members of the audience for the report should be asked to guide the external review process (initial review of the training program report; selection of reviewers; final approval of the external reviewer report).

Knowing the audiences for both the training program report and the external reviewer report is the key to finding appropriate external reviewers. Criteria for nominating external reviewers should be in the program report (e.g., expertise, qualifications; supervisory experience, commitments to quality standards; familiarity with similar training situations; capability to offer suggestions for practical improvements). The program training report typically contains details on the training/curriculum plan (especially the developmental sequences of knowledge, application, and analysis), the standards set for the content learning and performance by program participants, and the archived evidence from the evaluations of the various parts of the program, the participants, and the extended constituents of the program.

There should be multiple forms and levels of evaluations. Key components of external reviewing process would be: (1) the program improvement plans; (2) the external reviewer recommendations for improvements, (3) how the trainers/educators will adopt those recommendations, (4) the process for the approvals/support for the new initiatives, and finally (5) the overall evaluation of the planning and conduction of the self-study and review process. Training and development associations are moving toward external reviewer models that lead to accreditation for trainers or their programs. It is valuable to note that external reviewers often provide insights about the comparative strengths and accomplishments of programs (often in ways that pleasingly surprise the team and the trainees).

SUMMARY AND CONCLUSION

Reverse mapping for training program planning is essential to the training and development business. The days of merely thrilling and enjoyable training sessions are evaporating. There is a need for unequivocal evidence of effectiveness of training and development programs. Thinking about the long-term reception and utility of feedback over the full course of trainee career development should occur near the beginning of the development of a training programs (Ramani & Krackov, 2012). Training and development practices must consistently match training s to work experiences in order to facilitate the transfer of learning (Locht, Dam, & Chiaburu, 2013). Finally, the perceived value for training (Kirkpatrick & Kirkpatrick, 2007; Stawarski, 2012) and the potential for return training and development contracts, depends on being able to answer questions about how a training program 'pays-off' for the organization (Phillips, 1996; Phillips & Stone, 2002; Phillips and Phillips, 2008; Phillips, 2010; 2012).

REFERENCES

Alliger, G. M., & Janak, E. A. (1989). Kirkpatrick's levels of training criteria: Thirty years later. *Personnel Psychology, 41*, 331-342. doi:10.1111/j.1744-6570.1989.tb00661.x

Anderson, L. W., & Krathwohl, D. R. (2001). *A taxonomy for learning, teaching, and assessing: A revision of Bloom's taxonomy of educational objectives*. Longman.

Bandura, A. (2006). Guide for constructing self-efficacy scales. In F. Pajares & T. Urdan (Eds.), Adolescence and education: Vol. 5. Self efficacy and adolescence (pp. 307-337). Greenwich, CT: Information Age.

Bloom, B. S., Engelhart, M. D., Furst, E. J., Hill, W. H., & Krathwohl, D. R. (1956). *Taxonomy of educational objectives: The classification of educational goals. Handbook I: Cognitive domain*. David McKay Company.

Finn, B. (2015). *Measuring motivation in low-stakes assessments*. ETS Research Report Series No. RR-15-19. Available from https://onlinelibrary.wiley.com/ doi:10.1002/ets2.12067

Kezar, A. J., Chambers, A. C., & Burkhardt, J. C. (2005). *Higher education for the public good: Emerging voices from a national movement.* Jossey-Bass.

Kirkpatrick, D. L. (1994). *Evaluating training programs.* Berrett-Koehler Publishers.

Kirkpatrick, D. L. (1998). *Evaluating training programs: The four levels* (2nd ed.). Berrett-Koehler Publishers.

Kirkpatrick, D. L., & Kirkpatrick, J. D. (2007). *Implementing the four levels.* Berrett-Koehler Publishers.

Kirkpatrick, J. D., & Kirkpatrick, W. K. (2010). *Training on trial: How workplace learning must reinvent itself to remain relevant.* AMACOM.

Lashbrook, W. B., Snavely, W. B., & Sullivan, D. L. (1977) The effects of source credibility and message information quantity on attitude change of apathetics. *Communication Monographs, 44,* 252-261. doi:10.1080/03637757709390136

Locht, M. V. D., Dam, K. V., & Chiaburu, D. S. (2013, July). Getting the most of management training: The role of identical elements for training transfer. *Personnel Review, 42*(4), 422–439. doi:10.1108/PR-05-2011-0072

Nye, C. D., Chernyshenko, O. S., Stark, S., Drasgow, F., Phillips, H. L., Phillips, J. B., & Campbell, J. S. (2020). More than g: Evidence for the Incremental Validity of Performance-Based Assessments for Predicting Training Performance. *Applied Psychology: An International Review, 69*(2), 302–324. doi:10.1111/apps.12171

Papaloizos, A., & Nicholls, J. (1970). An approach to measuring the effectiveness of participative methods in teaching managerial skills. *Training and Development Journal, 24*(6), 10.

Payne, V. L., & Hysong, S. J. (2016). Model depicting aspects of audit and feedback that impact physicians' acceptance of clinical performance feedback. *BMC Health Services Research, 161*(12). doi:10.118612913-016-1486-3

Phillips, J., & Stone, R. (2002). *How to measure training results: A practical guide to tracking the six key indicators.* McGraw-Hill.

Phillips, J. J. (1996). How much is the training worth? *Training & Development, 50*(4), 20–24. https://www.questia.com/magazine/1G1-18434799/how-much-is-the-training-worth

Phillips, J. J., & Phillips, P. P. (2008). *Beyond learning objectives: Develop measurable objectives that link to the bottom line.* ASTD Press.

Phillips, P. P. (Ed.). (2010). *ASTD handbook of measuring and evaluating training.* ASTD Press. Available from https://www.td.org/Publications/Books/ASTD-Handbook-of-Measuring-and-Evaluating-Training

Phillips, P. P. (2012). *Bottomline on ROI* (2nd ed.). HRDQ Press.

Praslova, L. (2010). Adaptation of Kirkpatrick's four level model of training criteria to assessment of learning outcomes and program evaluation in higher education. *Educational Assessment, Evaluation and Accountability, 22*(3), 215-225. doi:10.100711092-010-9098-7

Ramani, S., & Krackov, S. K. (2012). Twelve tips for giving feedback effectively in the clinical environment. *Medical Teacher, 34*(10), 787-791. doi:10.3109/0142159X.2012.684916

Reynolds, R. A. (2017). Begin with the end in mind: Conducting post training evaluations. In S. K. Camara (Ed.), *Communication training and development: Exploring the cutting edge*. Kendall/Hunt Publishing Co.

Reynolds, R. A. (2020). The centrality of evidence in the communication discipline. *Western Journal of Communication, 84*(5), 521-527. doi:10.1080/10570314.2020.1771411

Reynolds, R. A., & Reynolds, J. L. (2002). Evidence. In J. P. Dillard & M. Pfau (Eds.), *The persuasion handbook: Developments in theory and practice* (pp. 427–444). Sage. doi:10.4135/9781412976046.n22

Stawarski, C. A. (2012). *What's the difference between return on expectations and return on investment?* https://www.td.org/Publications/Blogs/L-and-D-Blog/2012/10/Whats-the-Difference-Between-Return-on-Expectations-and-Return-on-Investment

Taylor, S., Haywood, M., & Shulruf, B. (2019). Comparison of effect between simulated patient clinical skill training and student role play on objective structured clinical examination performance outcomes for medical students in Australia. *Journal of Education Evaluation Health Professionals, 16*(3), 30665274. doi:10.3352/jeehp.2019.16.3 PMID:30665274

van Rooij, S., & Merkebu, J. (2015). Measuring the business impact of employee learning: A view from the professional services sector. *Human Resource Development Quarterly, 26*(3), 275-297. doi:10.1002/hrdq.21211

Vygotsky, L. S. (1978). *Interaction between learning and development. Mind in society: the development of higher psychological processes*. Harvard University Press.

WASC Senior College and University Commission. (2015). *2013 Handbook of Accreditation (revised)*. https://www.wscuc.org/resources/handbook-accreditation-2013

Wiggins, G., & McTighe, J. (2005). Understanding by design (2nd ed.). Alexandria, VA: Association for Supervision and Curriculum Development (ASCD).

Yelon, S., Ford, J. K., & Bhatia, S. (2014). How trainees transfer what they have learned: Toward a taxonomy of use. *Performance Improvement Quarterly, 27*, 27-52. doi:10.1002/pfi.21605

Chapter 7
Measurement of the Intention to Exhibit Leadership Behavior

Charles G. Sanders
Spring Arbor University, USA

ABSTRACT

The leadership intention measure was developed to help organizations deal with the dynamic and complex realities of the 21st-century competitive global environment, which necessitates a more rapid and effective response to changes to survive. An effective approach for dealing with this reality is to involve employees in the various leadership processes for the organization. However, employees must be prepared to assume the responsibility for a more active leadership role. Before an organization can open their work environment for 'leadership in all', determining whether members have the intention to exhibit leadership is critical. Therefore, this scale is based on the reasoned action behavioral model of Fishbein and Ajzen to determine the intentions of employees for engaging in leadership behavior. The LIM scale was validated in an organization whose stated culture encouraged leadership behavior by all. Results indicate that this measure would be a valuable tool for assessing organization readiness for facilitating and enabling leadership behaviors.

INTRODUCTION

This chapter describes a scale to measure the intention of an individual in an organization to exhibit leadership behavior. The Leadership Intention Measure was developed to help organizations deal with the dynamic, complex, and multicultural realities of the 21st-century competitive global environment, which necessitates a more rapid response to changes to survive (Rost, 1991). An effective approach for dealing with this reality is to involve employees in the various leadership processes for the organization (Pearce & Conger, 2003; Raelin, 2003). However, employees must be prepared to assume the responsibility for a more active leadership role (Raelin). The leadership role described based on everyday influence processes by anyone in the organization derived from knowledge, the recognition of the need for a specific change, and the intention to influence others to accept the change idea and take implementation action. Before an organization can open their work environment for 'leadership in all', determining whether members

DOI: 10.4018/978-1-7998-7665-6.ch007

have the intention to exhibit leadership is critical. Therefore, this scale is based on the reasoned action behavioral model of Fishbein and Ajzen (2010) to determine the intentions of employees for engaging in leadership behavior so that organizations can determine how best to facilitate and enable their more active involvement in organization success.

BACKGROUND

Leadership has been studied and debated for many years with numerous attempts to define what it means and how leadership theory should be developed and used in organizations. An extensive examination of leadership literature (Bass, 1990; Burns, 1978, 1998, 2003; Day, Harrison, & Halpin, 2009; Goethals & Sorenson, 2006; Greenleaf, 1977; Harter, 2006; Heifetz, 1994; Hickman, 1998; Hogan, Curphy, & Hogan, 1994; Hollander, 1992; House & Aditya, 1997; Jacobs, 1970; Locke, 1991; McCrimmon, 2006; Murrell, 1997; Northouse, 2004; Pearce & Conger, 2003; Raelin, 2003; Rost, 1991; Selznik, 1957; Stogdill, 1948, 1974; Uhl-Bein, 2006; Yukl, 2006) leads to two conclusions: (a) the predominant leadership perspective is based on authority positions with associated assumptions about the appropriate leadership traits, characteristics, and behaviors and (b) everyday individual leadership behaviors in organizations have not been adequately addressed in the literature, and little is understood about the factors that encourage and facilitate the leadership behaviors that support organizational effectiveness (Heifetz), particularly in complex and dynamic work environments.

Leadership Perspective Appropriate to Complex and Dynamic Situations

This chapter views leadership from a non-positional perspective, as an influence process by anyone in the organization, not as something reserved for individuals in authority positions. In this perspective, any individual can offer an idea, question a weak or bad idea, stand up for a virtue, or even help a new employee figure out how to deal with a problem. These are all leadership acts. Leadership occurs when an individual recognizes the need for change and influences others to accept the change idea and take action to effect the change (McCrimmon, 2006). In this context, leadership is clearly not about authority or based on one individual. It is based on the situation and the specific change idea.

This perspective also changes how power is viewed and used in organizations. Power is often defined in the organizational literature as the influence of one person over another or group; where one has power and the other does not. In the positional perspective of leadership, power is mostly held and exercised by individuals in authority positions. In the non-positional perspective, power is based more on knowledge, expertise, or an excellent idea; where it is considered as a factor of competitive or cooperative interdependencies of people in the organization (Stacey, 2007). To Stacey, power is created within the relationships between individuals, rather than within the individuals themselves.

As we learned from Burns (1978), leadership is about influence. Influence is a form of persuasion. O'Keefe (1990) defined persuasion as a human communication designed to influence others by modifying their beliefs, values, or attitudes. Perloff (1993) added the context in which the person being persuaded has a degree of free choice. Greenleaf (1977) differentiated persuasion from coercion, as a response that is voluntary (based on free choice) as opposed to the overt compulsion or covert manipulation of coercion. Thus, persuasion carries with it the idea that the person being persuaded accepts the change voluntarily. Therefore, manipulation or coercion can cause followers to change, but only temporarily. Because the followers were not persuaded, the change is only likely to last as long as the power to force the change is maintained. As soon as pressure is removed, the tendency is for behavior to return to that desired by the individual, as his or her beliefs and attitudes about the behavior have not been influenced. This reinforces the argument that coercion or manipulation cannot be viewed as an aspect of leadership. Therefore, actions that reflect or are based on an ethical or moral position, where individuals choose to follow through influence, are good indicators of leadership.

When regarding leadership simply as an influencing process, other factors, such as traits and characteristics of the person doing the leadership, or leadership methods, only impact the effectiveness of the leadership behavior, not whether the behavior is leadership. If the other person is influenced for a change that is evaluated as moral and ethical, there is leadership (Cuilla, 1998; Murrell, 1997; Rost, 1991; Uhl-Bein, 2006).

As leadership is an act, not a role, it is also very temporary, lasting only the time it takes to convince another to act (McCrimmon, 2006). Note that to be considered a leadership act, the person being engaged must be convinced and choose to act according to the influence from the person exhibiting the leadership behavior. Once the other decides to act accordingly, the need for leadership is ended. McCrimmon also emphasized that leadership is not based on any traits, but only on having a change idea, and the courage to share it. The intention to communicate a change idea (leadership) can range from a minor change to something very significant, requiring major change or transformation.

According to McCrimmon (2006), courage is a trait, but also a type of motivation. Someone needs to really want to share an idea to overcome the innate desire to fit in with the group and take the risk to propose an idea that challenges the status quo. The most important point to understand is that leaders (influencers) do not make decisions, they promote ideas. Managers decide and implement change ideas. McCrimmon argued that executives usually make decisions based on ideas presented or proposed to them. This perspective makes them followers, rather than leaders. The ones proposing the ideas are the actual leaders in this context.

MAIN FOCUS OF THE CHAPTER

Why Leadership in All is Critically Important

The 21st-century competitive global environment is dynamic, complex, and multicultural and necessitates a more rapid response to changes to survive (Rost, 1991). This rapid rate of change and high uncertainty are well beyond the capabilities of the individual manager to effectively deal with them and know what appropriate actions are required at any given time (Cashman, 2008; Childs & McGrath, 2001; Davis & Blass, 2006; Kaiser & Kaplan, 2007; Lombardo & Eichinger, 2000; McCrimmon, 2006). This is even more critical for organizations that operate in competitive environments and need to take advantage of opportunities and/or enable innovations. One approach for dealing with these situations is to involve all employees in the organizational leadership processes (Pearce & Conger, 2003; Raelin, 2003). However, the leadership role described is not the common view based on authority; rather, the required leadership is based on everyday influence processes by anyone in the organization derived from knowledge and the recognition for the need for a specific change.

Raelin (2003) argues that employees need to be prepared to assume the organizational performance responsibility and play a more active leadership role in their organization. Development of employees is usually addressed through a human development intervention process (Gilley, Eggland, & Gilley, 2002). Interventions can be in the form of education, training, coaching, mentoring, or self-development. In any case, the first human development intervention step is the assessment of the current state of the employees (Gilley et al.). The most important predictive precursor to a given behavior is to know the individual's intention towards that behavior (Bandura, 1986; Fishbein & Ajzen, 1975, 2010). If employees are not observed demonstrating leadership in the organization, at least knowing if they had the intention to do so would provide insight into why their intention is not manifested in the desired action. If employees do not have the intention to demonstrate leadership, then the issue is with factors that contribute to intention formation (Fishbein & Ajzen, 2010). If they do have the intent to demonstrate this form of leadership, then the issue is sustainment of the volition to influence others to accept their change idea (Bandura, 1986). Therefore, this study examines the precursors and conditions that foster leadership behavior and propose a scale to determine the leadership intentions of employees, so that managers can determine the best method to develop their ability to contribute to the success of the organization through leadership behavior.

Predicting Leadership Behavior

Fishbein and Ajzen (1975) introduced a model to explain and/or predict behaviors based on beliefs, attitudes, and intentions. According to their model, beliefs about a behavior help shape attitudes towards the behavior, which are defined as an evaluative response to an object, person, or situation. Attitudes in turn lead to development of behavioral intentions for engaging in specific behaviors. Intention is defined as the immediate determination to perform certain activities or to bring about a certain future state condition or solution (Bandura, 1986; Fishbein & Ajzen). The model of Fishbein and Ajzen has been successfully used to explain or predict behavior. Their causation model has been widely accepted as the relationship of factors building up to desired behaviors. The Fishbein and Ajzen model was updated in 2010 (Fishbein & Ajzen, 2010) and is useful for understanding the factors that contribute to influencing (leadership) behaviors by individuals in organizations. More detailed discussion of this model is provided in Sanders (2012).

In the context of the model of reasoned action approach (Fishbein & Ajzen, 2010), leadership behavior is preceded by the intention to demonstrate leadership through influencing another to engage in a specific action or change their behavior in some specific way. There are attitudes and beliefs that precede and contribute to the development of the intention to demonstrate leadership. However, leadership does not occur in a vacuum. People do not develop the intention to lead unless they perceive a need for some change in others' behavior. This means there is always change associated with leadership behavior. But there are also beliefs and attitudes that are associated with the specific change proposal that is the basis for the specific leadership behavior. Leadership exists and is associated with change. There is a difference between someone recognizing the need for change, perhaps even taking action to effect the change, and deciding to influence others to make the change. When someone influences another to change their behavior, it is leadership. Other factors, such as background factors, social norms, and perceived control, influence the development of the intention for leadership, but are not the leadership cause. It all starts with the change idea and the courage to share it.

For organizations where leadership is desired and expected by those not in positions of authority as well as those in positions of authority, the challenge with changing from the traditional positional model of leadership, to the non-positional model of leadership is having some degree of certainty that the employees will actually demonstrate leadership when the situation requires. Unfortunately, past studies of leadership have either attempted to predict leadership potential by assessing if individuals possess certain traits or characteristics required of effective 'leaders' (in reality, managers), or actually demonstrate the ability to be effective managers. Neither of these approaches adequately answers the question of predicting leadership behavior from the non-positional perspective.

Predicting readiness for leadership through observed behavior is problematic because it is always after the fact, based on past behavior. Unless an individual is placed in a situation where the opportunity is presented for them to demonstrate leadership, there is no effective method for determining if they will likely demonstrate the required leadership when the situation requires. A significant benefit of the reasoned action approach (Fishbien & Ajzen, 2010) is the excellent framework through which observed or expected leadership behaviors can be explained. If certain behaviors are expected, but not observed, this model illustrates what factors may be impacting the likelihood of individuals behaving as expected.

To develop a better understanding of the factors which contribute to leadership behaviors by all individuals in organizations, this chapter focuses on leadership as an influencing process based on the non-positional perspective. The Leadership Intention Measure (LIM) was developed to assess an individual's intention to engage in leadership behavior, even if this behavior is not an explicit responsibility of the individual, or they lack the resources or time to solve problems or initiate necessary changes in the organization. Development of the LIM followed the proven scale development steps explained by DeVellis (1991, 2012). It is expected that this scale will provide insight into why individuals who are expected to demonstrate leadership in organization are not manifesting that behavior. This measure will help determine if the issue is with intention formation or volition of the intention.

Leadership Intention Measurement

Fishbein and Ajzen (2010) explained that behavioral intentions are indications of a person's readiness to perform a behavior. They showed that if an organization wants to know whether or not an individual will likely perform a given behavior, the simplest and most efficient method is to ask the individual if he or she intends to perform that behavior. Therefore, the best single predictor of behavior is a measure of intention. Fishbein and Ajzen also found that self-reports are better devices for measuring intention than objective measures of behaviors. Intention can be expressed as: I will engage in the behavior, I intend to engage in the behavior, or I plan to engage in the behavior. The essential element is the individuals estimate of the likelihood of exhibiting the given behavior. However, they acknowledge that intention does not automatically lead to the behavior. There are external factors that can diminish actual control and inhibit the individual with intention from following through to exhibit the intended behavior. An individual may have the intention to influence others to take a desired action for a specific change proposal. However, this individual will be less likely to attempt to influence others if the environment is not conducive to that kind of initiative or behavior. For example, if managers feel threatened by employees demonstrating leadership, they will discourage that kind of behavior, either intentionally or unintentionally. This will have the consequence of maintaining the tendency on the part of the employees to wait for direction, rather than taking the initiative to solve problems and make changes that need to be done when they need to be done.

Given the diversity and confusion over the definitions and understandings of leadership, any leadership intention measure needs to focus on the action that constitutes leadership: influence. Therefore, scale development followed the steps of DeVellis (1991, 2012) to create items that indicate an individual's intention to influence another person(s) to change their belief, attitude, and intention with respect to a specific change proposal for the good of the organization. Measuring intention at a very general level for a specific behavior focused on a specific target, situation, or time will result in a weak relationship. For example, asking if someone intends to engage in leadership generally (without context), would show a weak relationship to leadership intention. Whereas, asking about their intention to influence others in a specific situation would show a stronger relationship.

Good test construction practice dictates the use of as few item types as possible (Tinkelman, 1971). Items for the scale were constructed from a theoretical base to establish construct validity. The model for construction of the items for the leadership intentions scale follows using the Delphi results as a guideline. After review by a panel and a pretest, the items were revised and assembled. During the test, the scale was administered to a sample sufficient for testing reliability and validity.

These responses were then subjected to item analysis and factor analyzed using a combination of principal components and confirmatory procedures and oblique rotation. The items were then reviewed and revised. Mean, standard deviation, and reliability for the scale were estimated based on the item data.

Scale Details and Validation

In compliance with DeVellis (2012), items were developed to address all the aspects of the measurement goal and relevant theories were considered when developing the scale. Also, multiple items provide necessary redundancy to constitute a more reliable test than single items. This places more burden on the researcher to think creatively about how items could be worded differently to get at the same construct. Because each initial item is potentially measuring a slightly different aspect of the concept being tested and also accounts for the various participant interpretations of the question, it is important to develop more items than required for the final scale to ensure, through statistical analysis, the superior items are kept and less ideal items discarded. The complete scale is shown in Appendix 1, and items are explained below in the context of their associated factors.

Organizational Complexity Items. This scale was predicated on the assumption that non-positional leadership, as an influencing process, is required for organizations in dynamic and complex situations. Therefore, the scale measures each respondent perspective of their organization with respect to this assumption, the degree to which respondents see their organization as operating in a complex and dynamic environment. The following items are included for assessing organizational complexity:

1   My organization rarely seems to settle into a routine, as something is always or often changing.
2   I feel like my active involvement in idea generation and/or decision making is required in order to help my manager keep up with the pace of change and make good decisions.
3   My involvement in the generation and communication of change ideas in my organization is required to be successful now and in the future.
4   I feel I am encouraged or expected to be involved in contributing to my organization's performance improvement.
5   My organization frequently encounters situations for which my manager needs help in dealing.

6   Our work processes are frequently subject to change. We seldom do exactly the same thing for each task.

7   Most work gets done through informal communications, rather than formal channels, as the formal channels are too slow or cumbersome to keep up with necessary changes.

8   Even with careful planning, there always seems to be some unforeseen event or problem that requires a significant change in a project plan.

9   The knowledge and/or skills required to effectively get our work done is well beyond any single individual in our organization; and requires the cooperative effort of many.

Personal Responsibility Items. As Raelin (2003) explained, leadership begins with an individual feeling responsible for the performance and/or success of the group or organization. An active approach to problem solving reflects the tendency to take responsibility for the development of a solution to a problem (Frese, 1997; Ponton, 1999). Taking responsibility for a solution is reflected in the behavior of acting to solve a problem or lead others to initiate change without being told to take appropriate action. Without the opportunity to observe such behavior, a measure could assess the individual intention to act if the situation presented itself. The following items are included for assessing personal responsibility:

10   If I see change that needs to be made in the workplace, I feel responsible for ensuring that action is taken to initiate the change.

11   If I see action that needs to be taken, and it is not my assigned task, I do not feel responsible for ensuring that action is taken (reverse coded).

12   I feel responsible for the performance of my group.

13   I feel responsible for the performance of my organization.

14   I feel at least partially responsible for the performance of my organization.

15   If I see behavior that I feel is inconsistent with an established goal of the organization, I feel responsible to influence others to change their behavior towards that goal.

Influence Intention Items. Behavioral intention is an indication of a person's readiness to perform a given behavior (Fishbein & Ajzen, 2010). Different indicators can be used to assess intention. Therefore, items were worded to ask the person to estimate the likelihood or probability of performing the given behavior, in this case, leadership. However, because this measure is focused on leadership as an influencing process for a specific change idea, items also asked the person to estimate the likelihood of influencing others to act according to a given change idea. The following items are included to assess influence intention:

16   If I see the need for a specific change in my organization, I will attempt to influence others to accept my change idea.

17   If I recognize the need for a specific change in my organization, I will influence others to accept my change idea.

18   If I see the need for a specific change in my organization, I intend to influence others to accept my change idea.

19   I will try to influence others to agree with my change ideas.

20   I intend to influence others to accept my change ideas.

21   I intend to exhibit leadership in my organization whenever necessary.

22   I will try to exhibit leadership in my organization whenever necessary.

23   I believe it is my responsibility to demonstrate leadership in my organization whenever the situation requires.

24   I intend to demonstrate leadership in my organization if the situation requires.

25   I feel that my organization expects me to exhibit leadership whenever necessary.

26   I feel that my organization expects me to influence others to do what I think is right in a given situation.

27   I feel that my organization expects me to just do my job and leave leadership to the managers (reverse coded).

28   There is no expectation in my organization for employees to propose change ideas to others (reverse coded).

29   If I see something that needs to change or an action that needs to be taken, I tend to wait for someone else to take the lead before I join the action.

30   If I see something that needs to change or an action that needs to be taken, I will postpone attempting to influence others to accept the change idea as long as I can.

Reliability Assessment

Internal Consistency of the LIM. In the initial use of the scale (Sanders, 2012), the scale was administered to a random sample of individuals in a technology industry company: employees, supervisors, managers, and executives. This was done to test the scale against both the positional and non-positional leadership perspective.

Nunnally (1978) suggested that 300 responses would normally be an adequate number for testing a scale. However, a smaller number of repondents may be sufficient for instruments with a lower number of items, which is anticipated for this scale of only 25 items. Tinsley and Tinsley (1987) suggested a ratio of 5 to 10 subjects per item up to 300 subjects. For the LIM, with 21 items, the sufficient number of respondents should be between 105 and 210. One hundred sixty seven out of the approximately 300 employees of one group in the company completed the survey.

An organization was selected that was assessed by the researcher to fit the context of the 21st-century organization described in this paper. This was known through over 10 years of personal experience working in the company. However, demographic data was also collected to include respondent assessments about whether they perceive their organization to be operating in a complex and dynamic environment. This contributes to the validation of the researcher's organizational context assumption.

The internal consistency of the LIM was computed via Cronbach's alpha measure of internal consistency with all 30 items. The Chronbach's alpha for all 30 items was computed to be 0.94. Hair et al. (2010) indicated that the generally accepted minimum value for Chronbach's alpha is 0.7, which means the LIM demonstrated very good reliability and is deemed internally consistent.

External Reliability of the LIM. The external reliability of the LIM, normally verified through the test–retest method with a paired t-test (DeVellis, 2012), could not be conducted due to the constraints of the organization for the test. Kline (1994) cautioned that the test and retest administering of the scale should be done with little time between the test and retest to limit the chances of other factors influencing the results. The organization for this test changes at a high rate and could not provide the same individuals to retest the measure.

Reliability

The reliability of the LIM was deemed to be very good based on internal consistency as measured by Cronbach's alpha. The 30-item LIM, $\alpha = 0.94$. Kerlinger and Lee (2000) indicated that there is no set minimum for reliability coefficient but that .7 is considered by many researchers as the minimum acceptable level. George and Mallory (2003) identified a score greater than 0.8 as "good."

Scale Limitation

The following scale limitation was identified:

Inability to test the external reliability of the scale. Normally test–retest reliability would be verified by administering the scale again to the same participants after a short time. This was not completed, which leaves open the question of the scale external reliability.

Implications for Future Research

The LIM is a valid instrument that can measure an individual's intention to exhibit leadership behavior, defined as influencing others to accept a change idea (McCrimmon, 2006) in a manner not previously possible. While the factor analysis indicated that some item modification would improve the measure, the findings of this study are still promising. However, modifications of the current measure may be required for validity as this instrument is used in other organizations. Future research will be required to validate the modified measure, as well as identify the factors that contribute or inhibit development of leadership intention.

A long-term goal of the LIM is to establish predictive validity and aid in identifying the factors that contribute to or inhibit the development of the intention to exhibit leadership behavior. This measure will also assist in isolating whether those external factors are contributing to development of intention or the volition to sustain the leadership intention to behavior. This will enable the use of the LIM as an intervention tool for organizations desiring to better deal with complex and dynamic situations.

The greatest potential for the LIM is to assist organizations in determining if the lack of observed leadership behavior on the part of the individuals is due to factors effecting the development of leadership intention or the factors that affect volition to actually demonstrate leadership behavior once intention has been developed. For example, if individuals have the intention to demonstrate leadership behavior, but do not demonstrate that behavior, there are factors affecting their volition to follow through to influence others. Knowing which case is present will facilitate identification of the appropriate interventions to achieve leadership in all.

FUTURE RESEARCH DIRECTIONS

Discuss future and emerging trends. Provide insight about the future of the book's theme from the perspective of the chapter focus. Viability of a paradigm, model, implementation issues of proposed programs, etc., may be included in this section. If appropriate, suggest future research opportunities within the domain of the topic.

CONCLUSION

Many organizations struggle to deal with the complexity and pace of change in the workplace. In these environments, more active change-seeking and decision-making involvement of employees is required. However, this desired leadership behavior is sometimes not observed. The LIM shows great promise as a research and diagnostic tool for organizations that require leadership behavior from more than just those in positions of authority. As the LIM is refined and validated, new levels and degrees of specificity will be available to researchers and practitioners in the field of organizational leadership and development. It is expected that this measure will facilitate a better understanding of the factors that contribute to, as well as inhibit, the development of leadership intention by individuals in an organization, particularly those not in positions of authority. This measure is also expected to facilitate a better understanding of what makes organizations more effective in dealing with complex and dynamic work environments.

This research received no specific grant from any funding agency in the public, commercial, or not-for-profit sectors.

REFERENCES

Bandura, A. (1986). *Social foundations of thought & action: A social cognitive theory*. Prentice-Hall.

Bass, B. M. (1990). *Bass and Stogdill's handbook of leadership: Theory, research, and managerial applications* (3rd ed.). Free Press.

Burns, J. M. (1978). *Leadership*. Harper & Row.

Burns, J. M. (1998). Foreword. In J. B. Ciulla (Ed.), *Ethics: The heart of leadership* (pp. x–xii). Praeger.

Burns, J. M. (2003). *Transforming leadership*. Atlantic Monthly Press.

Cashman, D. (2008). *The effects of vertical leadership, team demographics, and group potency upon shared leadership emergence within technical organizations* [Unpublished doctoral dissertation]. Available from ProQuest Dissertations and Theses database. (UMI No. 3320543)

Childs, J., & McGrath, R. (2001). Organizations unfettered: Organizational forming an information-intensive company. *Academy of Management Journal, 44*(6), 1134–1148.

Cuilla, J. B. (1998). *Ethics: The heart of leadership*. Praeger.

Davis, A., & Blass, E. (2006). The future workplace: Views from the floor. *Futures, 39*(1), 38–52. doi:10.1016/j.futures.2006.03.003

Day, D. V., Harrison, M. M., & Halpin, S. M. (2009). *An integrative approach to leader development*. Routledge.

DeVellis, R. F. (1991). *Scale development: Theory and practice*. Sage.

DeVellis, R. F. (2012). *Scale development: Theory and practice* (3rd ed.). Sage.

Fishbein, M., & Ajzen, I. (1975). *Belief, attitude, intention and behavior: An introduction to theory and research*. Adisson-Wesley.

Fishbein, M., & Ajzen, I. (2010). *Predicting and changing behavior: The reasoned action approach*. Psychology Press.

Frese, M. (1997). Dynamic self-reliance: An important concept for work in the twenty-first century. In C. L. Cooper & S. E. Jackson (Eds.), *Creating tomorrow's organizations: A handbook for future research in organizational behavior* (pp. 399–416). John Wiley & Sons.

George, D., & Mallery, P. (2003). *SPSS for Windows step by step: A simple guide and reference: 11.0 update* (4th ed.). Allyn and Bacon.

Gilley, J. W., Eggland, S. A., & Gilley, A. M. (2002). *Principles of human resource development* (2nd ed.). Basic Books.

Goethals, G., & Sorenson, G. (2006). *The quest for a general theory of leadership*. Edward Elgar. doi:10.4337/9781847202932

Greenleaf, R. K. (1977). *Servant leadership*. Paulist Press.

Hair, J., Black, W., Babin, B., & Anderson, R. (2010). *Multivariate data analysis* (7th ed.). Prentice Hall.

Harter, N. (2006). *Clearings in the forest: On the study of leadership*. Purdue University Press.

Heifetz, R. A. (1994). *Leadership without easy answers*. Harvard University Press.

Hickman, G. R. (Ed.). (1998). *Leading organizations: Perspectives for a new era*. Sage.

Hogan, R., Curphy, G. J., & Hogan, J. (1994). What we know about leadership. *The American Psychologist, 49*(6), 493–504. doi:10.1037/0003-066X.49.6.493 PMID:8042818

Hollander, E. P. (1992). The essential interdependence of leadership and followership. *Current Directions in Psychological Science, 1*(2), 71–75. doi:10.1111/1467-8721.ep11509752

House, R. J., & Aditya, R. N. (1997). The social scientific study of leadership: Quo vadis? *Journal of Management, 23*(3), 409–473. doi:10.1177/014920639702300306

Jacobs, T. O. (1970). *Leadership and exchange in formal organizations*. Human Resources Research Organization. doi:10.21236/AD0725584

Kaiser, R. B., & Kaplan, R. E. (2007). *Leadership versatility index: Facilitator's guide*. Kaplan DeVries.

Kerlinger, F. N., & Lee, H. B. (2000). *Foundations of behavioral research* (4th ed.). Nelson Thomson Learning.

Kline, P. (1994). *An easy guide to factor analysis*. Routledge.

Locke, E. A. (1991). *The essence of leadership*. Lexington Books.

Lombardo, M. M., & Eichinger, R. W. (2000). *The leadership machine*. Lominger Limited.

McCrimmon, M. (2006). *Burn! 7 leadership myths to ashes*. Self Renewal Group.

Murrell, K. L. (1997). Emergent theories of leadership for the next century: Towards relational concepts. *Organization Development Journal, 15*(3), 35–42.

Northouse, P. G. (2004). *Leadership: Theory and practice* (4th ed.). Sage.

Nunnallly, J. C. (1978). *Psychometric theory* (2nd ed.). McGraw-Hill.

O'Keefe, D. J. (1990). *Persuasion*. Sage.

Pearce, C., & Conger, J. (2003). *Shared leadership: Reframing the how's and why's of leadership*. Sage.

Perloff, R. M. (1993). *The dynamics of persuasion*. Lawrence Erlbaum. doi:10.4324/9781410606884

Ponton, M. K. (1999). *The measurement of an adult's intention to exhibit personal initiative in autonomous learning* [Unpublished doctoral dissertation]. The George Washington University, Washington, DC.

Raelin, J. A. (2003). *Creating leaderful organizations*. Berrett-Koehler.

Rost, J. C. (1991). *Leadership for the twenty-first century*. Praeger.

Sanders, C. G. (2012). *Measurement of the intention to exhibit leadership behavior: Development of a scale* [Unpublished doctoral dissertation]. Regent University, Virginia Beach, VA, USA.

Selznick, P. (1957). *Leadership in administration: A sociological interpretation*. Row, Peterson.

Stogdill, R. M. (1948). Personal factors associated with leadership: A survey of the literature. *The Journal of Psychology, 25*(1), 35–71. doi:10.1080/00223980.1948.9917362 PMID:18901913

Stogdill, R. M. (1974). *Handbook of leadership: A survey of the literature*. Free Press.

Tinkelman, S. N. (1971). Planning the objective test. In R. L. Thorndike (Ed.), *Educational measurement* (2nd ed., pp. 46–80). American Council on Education.

Uhl-Bein, M. (2006). Relational leadership theory: Exploring the social processes of leadership and organizing. *The Leadership Quarterly, 17*(6), 654–676. doi:10.1016/j.leaqua.2006.10.007

Yukl, G. (2006). *Leadership in organizations* (6th ed.). Pearson-Prentice Hall.

ADDITIONAL READING

Hackman, M., & Johnson, C. (2013). *Leadership: A communication perspective* (6th ed.). Waveland Press.

Kellerman, B. (2012). *The End of Leadership*. HarperCollins.

MacGregor, M. (2015). *Building Everyday Leadership in All Teems: Promoting Attitudes and Actions for Respect and Success*. Free Spirit Publishing.

Muls, A., Dougherty, L., Doyle, N., Shaw, C., Soanes, L., & Stevens, A. (2015). Influencing organisational culture: A leadership challenge. *British Journal of Nursing (Mark Allen Publishing), 24*(12), 633–638. doi:10.12968/bjon.2015.24.12.633 PMID:26110855

Pfeffer, J. (2015). *Leadership BS: Fixing Workplaces and Careers One Truth at a Time*. HarperCollins.

Stiel, S., Gatzka, M., Elprana, G., & Felfe, J. (2015). Personality and Leadership Intention: The mediating role of motivation to lead in careers. *Zeitschrift für Arbeits- und Organisationspsychologie A&O, 59*, 188-205.

Wang, D., Waldman, D. A., & Zhang, Z. (2014). A meta-analysis of shared leadership and team effectiveness. *The Journal of Applied Psychology, 99*(2), 181–198. doi:10.1037/a0034531 PMID:24188392

KEY TERMS AND DEFINITIONS

Influence: The capacity to have an effect on the character, development, or behavior of someone or something, or the effect itself.

Leadership: Influence process by anyone in the organization derived from knowledge, the recognition of the need for a specific change, and the intention to influence others to accept the change idea and take appropriate action.

Persuasion: One person voluntarily changing their mind about something based on arguments or evidence presented by another person.

APPENDIX

Revised Leadership Intention Scale

Instructions:

Consider your organization and how ideas are generated and/or decisions are made in dealing with changes in the work environment. For each statement, select the response that best reflects your agreement with the statement. Possible responses are as follows: 1 (definitely not true), 2 (generally not true), 3 (somewhat not true), 4 (somewhat true), 5 (generally true), and 6 (definitely true).

ITEMS:

1 My organization rarely seems to settle into a routine, as something is always changing.

2 I feel like my active involvement in idea generation and/or decision making is required in order to help my manager keep up with the pace of change and make good decisions.

3 My involvement in the generation and communication of change ideas in my organization is required to be successful now and in the future.

4 I feel I am encouraged or expected to be involved in contributing to my organization performance improvement.

5 If I see change that needs to be made in the workplace, I feel responsible for ensuring that action is taken to initiate the change.

6 If I see action that needs to be taken, and it is not my assigned task, I do not feel responsible for ensuring that action is taken. (reverse coded)

7 I feel responsible for the performance of my group.

8 I feel responsible for the performance of my organization.

9 I feel at least partially responsible for the performance of my organization.

10 If I see behavior that I feel is inconsistent with an established goal of the organization, I feel responsible to influence others to change their behavior towards that goal.

11 If I see the need for a specific change in my organization, I will attempt to influence others to accept my change idea.

12 If I recognize the need for a specific change in my organization, I will influence others to accept my change idea.

13 If I see the need for a specific change in my organization, I intend to influence others to accept my change idea.

14 I will try to influence others to agree with my change ideas.

15 I intend to influence others to accept my change ideas.

16 I intend to exhibit leadership in my organization whenever necessary.

17 I will try to exhibit leadership in my organization whenever necessary.

18 I believe it is my responsibility to demonstrate leadership in my organization whenever the situation requires.

19 I intend to demonstrate leadership in my organization if the situation requires.

20 I feel that my organization expects me to exhibit leadership whenever necessary.

21 I feel that my organization expects me to influence others to do what I think is right in a given situation.

22 I feel that my organization expects me to just do my job and leave leadership to the managers (reverse coded).

23 There is no expectation in my organization for employees to propose change ideas to others (reverse coded).

24 If I see something that needs to change or an action that needs to be taken, I tend to wait for someone else to take the lead before I join the action.

25 If I see something that needs to change or an action that needs to be taken, I will postpone attempting to influence others to accept the change idea as long as I can.

26 My organization frequently encounters situations for which my manager needs help in dealing.

27 Our work processes are frequently subject to change. We seldom do exactly the same thing for each task.

28 Most work gets done through informal communications, rather than formal channels, as the formal channels are too slow or cumbersome to keep up with necessary changes.

29 Even with careful planning, there always seems to be some unforeseen event or problem that requires a significant change in a project plan.

30 The knowledge and/or skills required to effectively get our work done is well beyond any single individual in the organization and requires the cooperative effort of many.

Chapter 8
Development of the Five–Factor Holistic Ethical Leadership Questionnaire

Tariku Fufa Gemechu
Regent University, USA

Bruce E. Winston
Regent University, USA

ABSTRACT

The authors present three studies that develop the five-scale measurement for holistic ethical leadership questionnaire. Study 1 reports the scale development process using predominately non-Western participants. Study 2 tests the five-scale instrument for convergent and discriminant validity as well as test-retest reliability using a subset of the sample who participated in Study 1. Study 3 used a sample of USA residents for confirmatory factor analysis from which a single factor emerged to measure holistic ethical leadership. The authors concluded that the five-scale instrument should be used when measuring non-Western participants and the single-scale should be used when measuring USA residents. The authors recommended follow-up research using qualitative methods to better understand the reasons why the single-scale measure works well with USA residents.

INTRODUCTION

Scale development consists of three broad steps: (a) development of content-related items through the use of literature review, factor analysis, and scale reliability tests; (b) concurrent and discriminate validity testing through the use of correlation; and (c) validity across populations that can be done with confirmatory factor analysis using one or more populations different from the population used in the development of the instrument. The purpose of this chapter is present the development and testing of the Holistic Ethical Leadership Questionnaire. The authors conducted three studies that follow the flow of scale development presented above. The first study shows the initial development, validity testing,

DOI: 10.4018/978-1-7998-7665-6.ch008

and reliability testing. The second study shows a test-retest reliability study using the same population as used in the first study. The third study presents a confirmatory factor analysis of the instrument but with a different population used in the first and second studies.

The lead author of this chapter developed the Holistic Ethical Leadership Questionnaire (HELQ) to help researchers and leadership development consultants measure all aspects of ethical leadership. The lead author encountered unethical leadership in his interactions with leaders in several Africa countries in which there was a disconnect between leaders espoused and practiced values, with regard to integrity and ethics. In the first study, Gemechu (2019) created a pool of 224 items, of which 81 items were approved by a panel of experts and administered pool of items to 628 participants. Principle component analysis, followed by scale optimization, resulted in five factors: (a) a five-item holistic service scale, a five-item ethical influence scale, a five-item integrated competence scale, a three-item financial stewardship scale, and a five-item healthy life scale. Gemechu et al. (2020) conducted the second study that correlated the five HELQ scales with the 10-item Essential Servant Leadership Behavior (ESLB) scale (Winston & Fields) and the eight-item extraversion scale of the Big-Five Personality test (John & Srivastava, 1999) as well as a test-retest of the five scales of the HELQ. The third study conducted by the present chapter authors conducted a confirmatory analysis of the HELQ's five factors and multiple regression of the five scales of HELQ with the five-item person-supervisor fit scale (P-S) of the Person-Environment fit instrument (Chuang et al., 2016).

This chapter reviews the three studies' processes and results and then offers a discussion of the contribution of the HELQ to researchers and leadership development consultants

STUDY 1: THE DEVELOPMENT OF THE HOLISTIC ETHICAL LEADERSHIP QUESTIONNAIRE

Gemechu (2019) developed the Holistic Ethical Leadership Questionnaire in response to observed and reported corruption across Africa, a concern previously stated by Mantzaris (2016) and since then by Ifedapo et al. (2020). Gemechu sought to add to the body of knowledge for ethical leadership by building upon the work of Trevino and Ball (1992), Trevino and Weaver (2003), and Ciulla (2014), in which ethical principles focused on respect for people, showing justice, manifesting honesty, serving others, and Northouse' (2016) concept of building community. Gemechu chose to extend the understanding of ethical leadership by broadening the view to be holistic, in which Gemechu incorporated the work of Priesmeyer et al. (2012), who examined the 'wholeness' of systems, along with the work of Auyang (1999) and Mankey (2007) whose research focused on understanding holistic leadership/influence as impacting the whole of individuals, groups, organizations, and society. Dhiman (2017) summarized the holistic focus in his definition of holistic leadership as follows:

Holistic leadership is a voyage of inner discovery that begins with the self-knowledge that serves as a prelude to leading from within. This journey begins with knowing oneself and culminates in living one's deepest values at the personal, team, and organizational level. We believe that effective leaders holistically engage the body, mind, heart, soul, and spirit of those whom they lead. (p. 6)

According to the work of Ciulla (2009), Eisenbeiß and Brodbeck (2014) and Treviño et al. (2000) describe the process of developing ethical leadership as first developing the moral person and then leadership development shapes the moral leader. Ethical leaders focus on the organization's ethical values that result in moral codes of conduct (Mo & Shi, 2017). In general terms, ethical leadership explains "what leaders do and who leaders are. It has to do with the nature of leaders' behavior, and with their virtuousness" (Northouse, 2016, p. 330).

Gemechu (2019) presented a literature review of 52 sources on holistic as well as ethical leadership from which Gemechu developed 224 statements the scale development pool. The next section provides an overview of the literature Gemechu used. A full review of Gemechu's review can be found in his 2019 study.

Literature Supporting the Development of the Holistic Ethical Leadership Item Pool

The concept of holistic leadership emerged from the concept of wholism that states that components of a system continually interact with one another, thus, according to Priesmeyer et al. (2012): "The wholeness view draws attention to the interdependencies among the parts. Problems are viewed as problems of the whole rather than associated with any single part. Solutions, likewise, emerge from a better understanding of the whole" (p.555). Northouse (2016) and Yukl (2013, contented that since leadership is an influence process the leader needs to touch the whole aspect of individuals, groups and organizational systems. Dhiman (2017) defined holistic leadership as:

holistic leadership is a voyage of inner discovery which begins with the self-knowledge that serves as a prelude to leading from within. This journey begins with knowing oneself and culminates in living one's deepest values at the personal, team, and organizational level. We believe that effective leaders holistically engage the body, mind, heart, soul, and spirit of those whom they lead. (p.6)

Holistic leadership's focus is on the systematic development of self, followers, and the environment for individual, group and organizational transformation (Best, 2011; Wheeler, 2013). Scouller (2014) posited that holistic leaders lead from the mind, heart, and soul flowing from within to without by exercising personal leadership over self, others, and groups (Scouller, 2014; Wapner & Demick, 2003). According to Lee and Miller (2013, Mankey (2007), and Rogers et al. (2006), holistic leadership takes an integrated approach to leadership and addresses the personal wellness of both self and others concerning the body, mind, and spirit. Adadevoh (2006) stressed the importance of authenticity and consistency between the private and public self of the leader. Finally, holistic leadership seeks the well-being of people through healthy organizational processes and outcomes (Chiavenato, 2001; Goodwin et al., 2015).

Development of the Item Pool

Gemechu's (2019) literature review on ethical leadership and holistic leadership resulted in an item pool of 224 statements from 52 published sources. Gemechu submitted the 224 statements to a panel of three experts who had published studies in the discipline of ethical and holistic leadership. Gemechu followed the advice of the three experts and reduced the item pool to 117 items, and then submitted the reduced item pool back to the panel for another review. After following the three experts' recommendations, Gemechu ended up with a pool of 81 items.

Gemechu (2019) chose to use a semantic differential response method with the ranking based on a continuum from 1 (never) to 7 (always) to collect participants' perceptions of their leaders' Holistic Ethical Leadership. DeVellis (2017) stated that scales, scored on a continuum, are highly compatible for measuring values, attitudes, behaviors, and attributes that people espouse and demonstrate. The response scale for the HELQ items is:

never— 1 2 3 4 5 6 7 —always

Data Collection

According to DeVellis (2017), the sample size for scale development should be five participants per item in the item pool, which for this study was 405 participants. Gemechu (2019) sent the survey of the 81 items to participants in 13 regions of the world who work in various organizations under the umbrella of Campus Crusade for Christ International. Gemechu employed a snow-ball design and asked participants to send the request to participate to other people. The data collection process resulted in 628 responses.

Participant Sample

Table 1 shows the participant demographics of gender, age, geographic region, leadership role, education, and organization.

Table 1. Demographic profile of participants

Demographics	n = 628	%
Gender		
Female	252	40.1
Male	376	59.9
Age		
18-30	112	17.8
30-40	162	25.8
40-50	170	27.1
50-60	113	18.0
60-90	71	11.3
Area		
Central and Eastern Europe	72	11.5
East Asia Opportunities	13	2.1
East Asia Orient	16	2.5
Francophone Africa	31	4.9
Latin America and the Caribbean	35	5.6
NAME (North Africa & Middle East)	24	3.8
PACT (Persia, Armenia, Central Asia & Turkey)	10	1.6

continues on following page

Table 1. Continued

Demographics	n = 628	%
South Asia	21	3.3
Southeast Asia	20	3.2
Southern and Eastern Africa	154	24.5
US, Canada & Oceania	163	26.0
West Africa	48	7.6
Western Europe	21	3.3
Leadership Role		
Global	62	9.9
Regional	127	20.2
National	211	33.6
Local	228	36.3
Education		
First Degree	331	52.7
Master Degree	221	35.2
Doctoral Degree	23	3.7
Diploma	53	8.4
Organization		
Great Commission Movement	50	8.0
Great Commission Ministry	24	3.8
Life Ministry	45	7.2
Cru	167	26.6
Power to Change	45	7.2
Campus Pour Christ	39	6.2
Campus Crusade for Christ	201	32.0
Agape	22	3.5
LifeAgape	22	3.5
Tandem	13	2.1

Item Correlation

Gemechu (2019) conducted a Pearson-r correlation of the 81 items and found a high correlation (r > .50). According to Brown (2009), when the scale development items are correlated, it is best to use an oblique rotation when conducting a principal component analysis. Gemechu used a direct oblimin rotation.

Factor Analysis

The first principal component analysis showed the KMO measure of sample adequacy of .987 and Bartlett's test of Sphericity's X^2 of 51,581 with degrees of freedom of 3,240 and *p-value* = .000. Both KMO and Bartlett's test results imply that the data will benefit from factor analysis.

The first principal component analysis using the direct oblimin rotation and suppressing factor loadings below .40 resulted in seven factors explaining 68.52% of the variation. Four items cross-loaded on at least two factors. Hair et al. (2010) stated, "If a variable persists in having cross-loadings, it becomes a candidate for deletion" (p. 136). The 7th factor had only two items, which Gemechu (2019) removed because Hair et al. stated that "good practice dictates a minimum of three items per factor" (Hair et al., 2010, p. 676).

After removing the items that did not load on a factor and the four items that cross-loaded, Gemechu (2019) conducted a second principal component analysis using the direct oblimin rotation and suppressing factor loadings below .40 that resulted in the KMO measure of sample adequacy of .982 and Bartlett's test of Sphericity's X^2 of 26,584 with degrees of freedom of 946 and *p-value* = .000 that implied that the data would benefit from factor analysis. The second principal component analysis showed five factors with eigenvalues above 1.0 -- factor 1 had six items, factor 2 had 14 items, factor 3 had 14 items, factor 4 had three items, and factor 5 had six items, as seen in Table 2.

Table 2. Rotated pattern matrix for five-factor model

Item	Component				
	1	2	3	4	5
57. My boss serves others.	.52				
52. My boss perceives other's feelings and needs.	.50				
19. My boss practices servant leadership.	.49				
55. My boss shows concerns and acts with care.	.48				
23. My boss is encouraged by agapao love (a moral love) to meet emotional needs.	.46				
6. My boss cares about health and wellbeing of organizational members.	.42				
8. My boss is perceived as a moral person who embodies traits of integrity, honesty, and trustworthiness.		.88			
18. My boss displays strong moral character.		.88			
9. My boss is a strong moral person as well as a moral leader.		.86			
14. My boss is a person of integrity.		.85			
45. My boss applies ethical thinking.		.73			
20. My boss does what is right no matter the cost.		.72			
38. My boss is ethically intelligent.		.71			
15. My boss considers the ethics of the outcome.		.63			
11. My boss demonstrates behaviors of honesty, trustworthiness, fairness, and care in personal actions.		.63			
76. My boss facilitates for the followers to earn income legally.		.60			

continues on following page

Table 2. Continued

Item	Component				
	1	2	3	4	5
13. My boss promotes behaviors of honesty, trustworthiness, fairness, and care when making decisions	.	.57			
12. My boss promotes behaviors of honesty, trustworthiness, fairness, and care in two-way communication.		.52			
71. My boss upholds human dignity.		.51			
68. My boss believes that individuals have unconditional human worth.		.44			
36. My boss articulates the organizational vision clearly.			.78		
44. My boss practices creative thinking.			.74		
37. My boss inspires hope.			.65		
5. My boss equips for personal, interpersonal, organizational and societal successes.			.60		
47. My boss is self-aware.			.59		
57. My boss develops others.			.58		
69. My boss develops oneself.			.58		
24. My boss thinks how to lead well at both individual and group level.			.57		
61. My boss understands and manages team leadership.			.56		
34. My boss helps the followers to make meaning out of work.			.55		
33. My boss inspires a deep sense of calling vocationally.			.54		
42. My boss engages in critical thinking.			.52		
7. My boss practices self-mastery.			.48		
35. My boss facilitates membership where the followers feel understood and appreciated.			.42		
77. My boss communicates the importance of having job as it provides wages and salaries.				.76	
80.My boss encourages saving of money.				.71	
21.My boss is motivated by agapao love (a moral love) to meet physical needs.				.47	
25.My boss values sleep because it contributes to physical wellbeing.					.86
26. My boss understands the benefits of rest to physical health.					.82
27. My boss facilitates opportunities to rest.					.71
66. My boss believes he or she has inherent value and significance by virtue of being a human being.					.51
48. My boss regulates personal emotions.					.50
50. My boss regulates emotions.					.50

Note: Extraction Method: PCA.
Note: N=628

The Cronbach's alphas shown in table 3 indicate that all factors are reliable using DeVellis' (2017) acceptable range of .7 to .9. DeVellis suggested that scale developers should consider shortening scales, above .90, (p.145). Gemechu (2019) used the five factors of the final instrument and defined Holistic Ethical Leadership as: "an ethical influence process that brings about physical, spiritual, mental, emotional, social, psychological, and financial sense of wholeness to oneself and others" (Gemechu, 2019, p.9

Table 3. Cronbach's alpha scores for five-factor model

Factor	Cronbach's Alpha	n
Holistic Service	.94	6
Ethical Influence	.96	14
Integrated Competence	.96	14
Financial Stewardship	.74	3
Healthy Life	.89	6

Scale Optimization

Following DeVellis' (2017) guidelines, Gemechu (2019) reduced factors 1, 2, 3, and 5 to five-items by retaining the five highest loading items and left factor 4 as 3-items. Gemechu conducted another principal component analysis using the oblimin direct rotation and suppressing factor loadings below .40 that resulted in the KMO measure of sample adequacy of .971 and Bartlett's test of Sphericity's X^2 of 11,287 with degrees of freedom of 253 and *p-value* = .000 that implied the data would benefit from factor analysis. The third Principal Component analysis found that the 23 items resulted in five factors explaining 70% of the variation. Table 4 shows the factors, items, and table 5 shows the Cronbach's Alphas 5.

Gemechu (2019) conducted a descriptive analysis and a Pearson-r correlation of the five factors. The skewness and kurtosis results, shown in table 6, revealed that the data is parametric. Kim (2013) wrote that skewness describes the asymmetry of "the distribution of a variable," and kurtosis describes the "peakedness of a distribution of a variable" (p.52). Kim indicated that "an absolute skew value larger than 2 or an absolute kurtosis (proper) larger than 7 may be used as reference values for determining substantial non-normality" (p.53). The five factors have a skew measure of less than 2 and Kurtosis measure of less than 7, thus the data is parametric.

The Pearson-r analysis showed a strong correlation between the factors, and all correlations are statistically significant at the .01 level.

Gemechu et al. (2020) used the five-factor 23-item HELQ instrument to test the instrument for concurrent and discriminant validity as well as test-retest reliability.

Study 2: Testing Concurrent and Discriminant Validity as well as Test-Retest Reliability

Gemechu et al. (2020) continued working on the Holistic Ethical Leadership Questionnaire (HELQ) to determine if the instruments' scales had concurrent and discriminant validity as well as test-retest reliability. Gemechu et al. contacted the people in the sample frame from study one and asked for volunteers to complete the resultant 23-item, five-factor instrument along with Winston and Fields' (2015) Essential Servant Leadership Behavior (ESLB) scale and John and Srivastava's (1999) Extraversion Scale. Gemechu et al. asked the participants if they would also retake the HELQ two weeks after the first take so that Gemechu et al. could analyze the test-retest reliability of the five HELQ scales. 131 participants completed data for the concurrent and discriminant validity analysis, and 81participants provided data for the test-retest reliability analyses.

Table 4. Five-factor holistic ethical leadership questionnaire

Factor	Item
Holistic Service	1. My boss serves others.
	2. My boss perceives other's feelings and needs.
	3. My boss shows concerns and acts with care.
	4. My boss is encouraged by agapao love (a moral love) to meet emotional needs.
	5. My boss cares about health and wellbeing of organizational members.
Ethical Influence	6. My boss is perceived as a moral person who embodies traits of integrity, honesty, and trustworthiness.
	7. My boss displays strong moral character.
	8. My boss applies ethical thinking.
	9. My boss does what is right no matter the cost.
	10. My boss promotes behaviors of honesty, trustworthiness, fairness, and care when making decisions.
Integrated Competence	11. My boss articulates the organizational vision clearly.
	12. My boss practices creative thinking.
	13. My boss inspires hope.
	14. My boss equips for personal, interpersonal, organizational and societal successes.
	15. My boss is self-aware.
Financial Stewardship	16. My boss communicates the importance of having job as it provides wages and salaries.
	17. My boss encourages saving of money.
	18. My boss is motivated by agapao love (a moral love) to meet physical needs.
Healthy Life	19. My boss values sleep because it contributes to physical wellbeing.
	20. My boss understands the benefits of rest to physical health.
	21. My boss facilitates opportunities to rest.
	22. My boss regulates personal emotions.
	23. My boss believes he or she has inherent value and significance by virtue of being a human being.

Table 5. Cronbach's alpha for each of the five factors after optimization

Factor	Cronbach's Alpha	n
Holistic Service	.93	5
Ethical Influence	.92	5
Integrated Competence	.88	5
Financial Stewardship	.74	3
Healthy Life	.87	5

Table 6. Descriptive analysis with skewness and kurtosis test for the final five-factor instrument

	Min	Max	Mean	SD	Skewness	SE	Kurtosis	SE
Holistic Service	1.00	7.00	5.5	1.23	-1.07	.10	.79	.20
Ethical Influence	1.40	7.00	5.8	1.13	-1.36	.10	1.56	.20
Integrated Competence	1.20	7.00	5.6	1.12	-.98	.10	.46	.20
Financial Stewardship	1.00	7.00	5.2	1.19	-.69	.10	.23	.20
Healthy Life	2.67	11.67	9.1	1.87	-.96	.10	.42	.20

Note: Min = Minimum
Note: Max = Maximum
Note: SD = Standard Deviation
Note: SE = Standard Error
Note: N=628

Table 7. Correlation test the items of the final five-factor instrument

	Holistic Service	Ethical Influence	Integrated Competence	Financial Stewardship	Healthy Life
Holistic Service	--				
Ethical Influence	.77**	--			
Integrated Competence	.81**	.76**	--		
Financial Stewardship	.69**	.61**	.63**	--	
Healthy Life	.78**	.73**	.74**	.62**	--

Note: N=628

Concurrent and Discriminant Validity

Concurrent validity is a measure of whether a scale measures what it is supposed to measure. The analysis for concurrent validity requires correlating the scale(s) under study with a concept that should be somewhat similar to the scale(s) under study (Krabbe, 2017). For the second study of the HELQ instrument, Gemechu et al. (2020) used Winston and Fields (2015) ten-item ESLB scale that measures employees' perception of their supervisor's essential servant leadership behaviors. Winston and Fields reported Cronbach's Alpha of 0.96 for the ESLB, and Gemechu et al. reported Cronbach's Alpha of 0.93 for the ESLB

Discriminant validity tests determine if the scale(s), under study, do not measure what the scales are not meant to measure (Russell et al., 1980). Russell et al. (1980) recommended testing to determine that no significant correlation exists between the scale under study with unrelated measures. Gemechu et al. (2020) used John and Srivastava's (1999) extraversion scale since there is no known similarity between extraversion and holistic ethical leadership.

According to Cozby and Bates (2014), "test-retest reliability is assessed by measuring the same individuals at two points in time" (p.102) using both a paired t-test and a correlation. The paired t-test measures if there is a significant difference between each participant's first and second test and the correlation test determines if there is a significant similarity between all participants' first and second test scores (Cozby & Bates, 2014).

Table 8 shows the correlation of the five scales from the HELQ along with the ESLB and Extraversion scale. The high correlation of the five HELQ scales with ESLB indicates that the HELQ scales have concurrent validity. The lack of a significant correlation of three of the five HELQ with the extraversion indicates discriminant validity.

Table 8. Correlation of the HELQ scales with the ESLB scale and the extraversion scale.

	HS	EI	IC	FS	HL	ESLB	E
HS	--						
Ei	.76**	--					
IC	.76**	.72**	--				
FS	.61**	.62**	.66**	--			
HL	.80**	.68**	.76**	.61**	--		
ESLB	.85**	.81**	.80**	.60**	.79**	--	
E	.04	.11	.24**	.20*	.03	.13	--

Notes: N = 133
Note: ** = Correlation is significant at the 0.01 level (2-tailed)
Note: * = Correlation is significant at the 0.05 level (2-tailed).
B=Note: N=133
HS = Holistic Service
EI = Ethical Influence
IC = Integrated Competence
FS = Financial Stewardship
ESLB = Essential Servant Leadership Behaviors
E = Extraversion

Table 9 shows that the paired t-test analysis of the 81 participants who submitted a retest of the five HELQ scales. The lack of significant differences between the test and retest data implies there is test-retest reliability.

Table 9. Paired T-test of the Five HELQ scales

	Mean	Std. Deviation	Std. Error Mean	95% Confidence Interval of the Difference		t	df	Sig. (2-tailed)
				Lower	Upper			
Holistic_Service test-retest	0.02	0.53	0.06	-0.10	0.14	0.37	80	0.709
Ethical_Influence test-retest	0.07	0.56	0.06	-0.05	0.20	1.19	80	0.236
Integrated_Competence test-retest	0.03	0.57	0.06	-0.10	0.16	0.47	80	0.641
Financial_Stewardship test-retest	-0.15	0.84	0.09	-0.34	0.03	-1.63	80	0.107
Healthy_Life test-retest	-0.09	0.61	0.07	-0.23	0.04	-1.35	80	0.182

Table 10 shows that there is significant correlation between the test and re-test scores, thus indicating test-retest reliability

Table 10. Correlation of the test with the re-test of the five scales

		Correlation	Sig.
Pair 1	Holistic_Service test-retest	0.92	0.000
Pair 2	Ethical_Influence test-retest	0.91	0.000
Pair 3	Integrated_Competence test-retest	0.88	0.000
Pair 4	Financial_Stewardship test-retest	0.75	0.000
Pair 5	Healthy_Life test-retest	0.89	0.000

Note: N=81

The findings from study 2 indicated that the five HELQ scales have concurrent and discriminant validity as well as test-retest reliability.

Study 3: Confirmatory Factor Analysis

Confirmatory factor analysis usually uses structured equation modeling. Confirmatory factor analysis determines the fit between exogenous (independent) variables with endogenous (dependent) variables after the exploratory factor analysis process (Byrne, 2016) and, according to Harrington (2009), is useful for social science research where psychometric measurements are used. The quality of the model-fit can be determined using the Goodness of Fit Index (GFI), a measure of variance and covariance, and the Absolute Goodness of Fit Index (AGFI). The AGFI differs from GFI in that AGFI considers the degrees of freedom. The GFI and AGFI test the model against not having a model at all. A good model has GFI and AGFI of 0.95 or higher but is considered acceptable at 0.90-094. Also, Root Mean Square Error of Approximation (RMSEA) measures the model's fit with the population covariance. A good fit occurs when RMSEA is at or below .06. (Byrne, 2016).

Hair et al. (2010) and Tabachnick and Fidell (2019) (2019) suggested a sample size of 200 when using a maximum likelihood estimation process. Byrne (2016) posited that the minimum sample size for structured equation modeling "should be greater than 10 times the number of estimated parameters; otherwise, the results from the ADF method generally cannot be trusted" (Byrne, 2016 p. 194). The current chapter authors contracted with Qualtrics to collect data from 260 people over 18 years of age who had worked for at least one year. The sample size exceeds both Hair et al.'s and Tabachnick and Fidell's, recommendation of a sample size.

The Person-Supervisor Fit Scale

Kristof-Brown et al. (2005) built on Pervin's (1968) work. They explained that person-environment fit examined the notion that people do better when there is a good fit between themselves and the environment in which they find themselves. Collins (2001) presented his 'bus' metaphor that is based on person-organization fit and person-job fit and posited that great leaders seek out and hire those that are 'right' for the bus (person-organization fit) and then the great leaders put those 'right' people into the right seats (person-job fit). Extending Collins' metaphor further, great leaders would put the 'right' people into the right group and align people with the right supervisor. The second author for this present chapter has used the concept of person-environment fit to advise consulting clients how to see dysfunctional behavior as unconscious expressions of the wrong person-environment fit. Chuang et al.'s (2016) person-environment fit measure is helpful for researching organizational leadership issues as well as helping diagnose organizational behavior problems.

Caldwell et al. (2004) discussed the importance of person-environment fit and specifically how changes in the environment, due to mergers, economic upheaval, etc., can change the fit between the organization and the employees. Gemechu (2019) discussed how the ethics, or lack of ethics, in leaders/ supervisors can impact the attitude and commitment of the employee to the organization. Theoretically, it seems that a similar 'fit' might impact the employee's fit with the supervisor. Thus in this third study of the HELQ, the chapter authors chose to see if there was a correlation between the five scales of the HELQ and Chuang et al.'s person-supervisor fit scale.

Chuang et al. (2016) developed a four-dimension instrument to measure person-environment fit. One of the dimensions is person-supervisor fit, measured with a five-item scale. The other three dimensions are (a) person-job fit, (b) person-organization fit, and (c) person-group fit. The person-supervisor fit had a Cronbach's Alpha of .92. All items used a 7-point response method -- 1 meaning "no match" and 7 meaning "complete match."

Two of the five items in the person-supervisor fit scale are:

- How would you describe the match between your work style and your supervisor's work style?
- How would you describe the match between your supervisor's leadership style and the leadership style you desire?

Sample Demographics and Variable Descriptives

Table 11 shows the descriptive demographics of the sample. A notable difference in the sample is that 74% of Gemechu's (2019) sample was from non-North American countries, all of the study 3 sample was from North America.

The skewness and kurtosis scores for all six variables are below 2.0, which indicates that the data can be treated as normal data (Kim, 2013).

Scale Reliability

Scale reliability indicates the items' internal consistency within a scale (DeVellis, 2017, p. 39). According to DeVellis (2017) Cronbach's Alpha is a suitable means of measuring scale reliability (DeVellis, 2017) and scores above .65 are considered to be reliable (Vasle et al., 2017). Each of the five HELQ scales and the person-supervisor fit scale are above .65

Table 11. Descriptive demographics of the sample

Demographics	n = 260	100%
Gender		
Female	138	52.9
Male	120	46.0
Prefer not to say	3	1.1
Age		
18-30	142	54.4
31-40	54	20.7
41-50	29	11.1
51-60	21	8.0
61and older	12	41.6
Prefer not to say	3	1.1
Tenure with Supervisor		
Less than 1 year	54	20.7
2-5 years	122	46.7
6-10 years	48	18.4
11-15 years	15	5.7
16 or more years	9	3.4
Prefer not to say	13	5.0

Table 12. Descriptive analysis with skewness and kurtosis test for the final five-factor instrument

	Min	Max	Mean	SD	Skeness	SE	Kurosis	SE
Holstic Service	1	7	4.8	1.45	-.36	-.51	-.19	.30
Ethical Influence	1	7	4.9	1.51	-.42	-.51	-.41	.30
Integrated Competence	1	7	4.9	1.46	-.42	-.51	-.23	.30
Financial Stewardship	1	7	4.8	1.48	-.39	-.51	-.18	.30
Healthy Life	1	7	4.9	1.40	-.45	-51	-.01	.30
Person-Supervisor Fit	1	7	4.9	1.43	-.43	-.51	-.05	.30

Note: Min = Minimum
Note: Max = Maximum
Note: SD = Standard Deviation
Note: SE = Standard Error
Note: N=260

Convergent Validity

Convergent validity explains if a measure measures what it is supposed to measure (Krabbe, 2017). Convergent validity can be determined if the measure correlates with another measure similar to the measure under study. The current chapter authors used the five-item person-supervisor fit scale (P-S) of the Person-Environment fit instrument (Chuang, et al., 2016).

Table 13. Cronbach's alphas for the variables

Factor	Cronbach's Alpha	n
Holistic Service	.91	5
Ethical Influence	.93	5
Integrated Competence	.91	5
Financial Stewardship	.84	3
Healthy Life	.91	5
Person-Supervisor fit	.91	5

Note: N = 260

Table 14 shows the correlation results of the five factors of Gemechu's HELQ and Chuang et al.'s Person-supervisor fit scale. All of the correlations shown in table 14 are strong, according to Taylor (1990), who posited that Pearson-r correlations above +/-.70 are strong correlations. The high correlations led the present chapter authors to wonder if there might be a single factor for holistic ethical leadership that might be appropriate for samples taken from North American participants. The results of a single factor are in the confirmatory factor section.

Table 14. Correlation of the HELQ scales with the ESLB scale and the extraversion scale.

	HS	EI	IC	FS	HL	PSF
HS	--					
Ei	.88**	--				
IC	.84**	.89**	--			
FS	.78**	.82**	.87**	--		
HL	.81**	.83**	.84**	.83**	--	
PSF	.81**	.85**	.85**	.82**	.89**	--

Notes: N = 260

Note: ** = Correlation is significant at the 0.01 level (2-tailed).

B=Note: N=133

HS = Holistic Service

EI = Ethical Influence

IC = Integrated Competence

FS = Financial Stewardship

PSF = Person-Supervisor Fit

Study 3: Exploratory Factor Analysis

The current chapter authors conducted an exploratory principal component analysis on the data and found a single factor of all 23 items with an eigenvalue of 15.10, explaining 65.64% of the variance. Of interest, all five items of the Ethical Influence dimension were within the eight highest-loading items. The difference in sample frame for study 1 and study 3 might be a contributing cause for the change in the principal component outcomes. While more research is called for, within a North American sample frame, HELQ could be measured with the single Ethical Influence scale. The five scales could be used to measure the holistic ethical leadership concept.

Confirmatory Factor Analysis

Byrne (2016) said that structured equation modeling, used for confirmatory factor analysis, follows exploratory factor analysis, and, according to Jackson et al. (2009) "plays an essential role in measurement model validation in path or structural analyses" (p. 6). Confirmatory factor analysis is the process of determining the fit between exogenous (independent) variables with endogenous (dependent) variables after there is an understanding of the variables, usually determined in the exploratory factor analysis process (Byrne, 2016) and, according to Harrington (2009) is useful for social science research where psychometric measurements are used. The quality of the model-fit is usually determined using the Goodness of Fit Index (GFI), a measure of variance and covariance, and the Absolute Goodness of Fit Index (AGFI). The AGFI differs from GFI in that AGFI considers the degrees of freedom. The GFI and AGFI test the model against not having a model at all. A good model has GFI and AGFI of 0.95 or higher but is considered acceptable at 0.90-094. Also, Root Mean Square Error of Approximation (RMSEA) measures the model's fit with the population covariance. A good fit requires RMSEA at or below .06. (Byrne, 2016). A good model also requires CFI above 0.9. The current chapter authors used IBM's AMOS Version 27 for confirmatory factor analysis.

The current chapter authors decided to conduct a confirmatory factor analysis for the five-factor model and the one-factor (ethical influence) model. Table 15 shows the GFI, AGFI, RMSEA, and CFI for both models.

Table 15. Confirmatory factor analysis for the five-factor and one factor model

	GFI	AGFI	RMSEA	CFI
Five-Factor Model	1.00	.02	.29	1.00
One-Factor Model	.96	.88	.13	0.98

The one-factor model is a better fit than the five-factor model but it would be stronger with RMSEA below .06.

Contribution of the HELQ to Future Research Studies

The results from study 3 imply that there may be two options for the HELQ: (a) a five-factor model for non-North American sample frames and the five-item ethical influence scale when measuring North American participants. Replication studies in various contexts could certainly help refine our understanding of the HELQ, as would hierarchical multiple regression models of both the five-factor and one-factor instruments with dependent variables such as employees' self-report of continuance commitment, employees' self-report of affective commitment, and employees' perception of supervisor's benevolent leadership.

The five-factor model may provide a useful base for leader/supervisor development programs, where action research designs can measure a baseline for leaders/supervisors, follow-up with training sessions, and then conduct post-intervention measurement of leaders/supervisors' scores on the HELQ.

Qualitative bounded-case studies and focus groups could help understand how leaders'/supervisors' holistic ethical behaviors are observed and interpreted by the employees. This may lead to additional studies seeking to understand how employees' perceptions of leaders'/supervisors' ethical attitudes/ behaviors impact the employees' sense of person-supervisor fit and affective commitment.

CONCLUSION

The current chapter authors followed up on Study 1 and Study 2 of the HELQ development steps with an additional convergent validity and confirmatory factor analysis study. The five-factor instrument that emerged from the first study ended up as a single-factor instrument with five items of the Ethical Influence scale among the eight highest-loading items of the single factor. Both the five-factor and one-factor instruments were analyzed using items. It may be that the differences between the Study 1 sample frame and the study 3 sample frame may contribute to the different resultant measurements. Perhaps cultural differences between the non-North American sample and the North American sample may be a confounding variable.

The one-factor instrument showed a better model fit than the five-factor instrument for the North American sample that may lead to additional research that seeks to better understand the role of holistic ethical leadership's impact on employees' sense of person-supervisor fit and employees' self-report of affective commitment and continuance commitment.

REFERENCES

Adadevoh, D. (2006). *Leading transformation in Africa*. International Leadership Foundation.

Auyang, S. Y. (1999). *Foundations of complex-system theories: in economics, evolutionary biology, and statistical physics*. Cambridge University.

Best, K. C. (2011). Holistic Leadership: A Model for Leader-Member Engagement and Development. *Journal of JVBL, 4*(1).

Brown, J. D. (2009). Choosing the right type of rotation in PCA and EFA. Shiken. *JALT Testing & Evaluation SIG Newsletter, 13*(3), 20–25.

Byrne, B. M. (2016). Structural Equation Modeling With AMOS (3rd ed.). Taylor and Francis. doi:10.4324/9781315757421

Caldwell, S. D., Herold, D. M., & Fedor, D. B. (2004). Toward an understanding of the relationships among organizational change, individual differences, and changes in person-environment fit: A cross-level study. *The Journal of Applied Psychology, 89*(5), 868–882. doi:10.1037/0021-9010.89.5.868 PMID:15506866

Chiavenato, I. (2001). Advances and Challenges in Human Resource Management in The New Millennium. *Public Personnel Management, 30*(1), 17–26. doi:10.1177/009102600103000102

Chuang, A., Shen, C., & Judge, T. A. (2016). Development of a Multidimensional Instrument of Person–Environment Fit: The Perceived Person–Environment Fit Scale (PPEFS). *Applied Psychology, 65*(1), 66–98. doi:10.1111/apps.12036

Ciulla, J. B. (2009). Leadership ethics: Mapping the Territory. *Business Ethics Quarterly, 5*(1), 5–28. doi:10.2307/3857269

Ciulla, J. B. (2014). *Ethics, the heart of leadership* (2nd ed.). Praeger.

Collins, J. C. (2001). *Good to great: Why some companies make the leap—and others don't* (1st ed.). HarperBusiness.

Cozby, P. C., & Bates, S. C. (2014). *Methods in behavioral research* (12th ed.). McGraw-Hill.

DeVellis, R. F. (2017). *Scale development: Theory and application* (4th ed.). SAGE.

Dhiman, S. (2017). *Holistic leadership: A new paradigm for today's leaders*. Palgrave Macmillan US. doi:10.1057/978-1-137-55571-7

Eisenbeiß, S., & Brodbeck, F. (2014). Ethical and unethical leadership: A cross-cultural and cross-sectoral analysis. *Journal of Business Ethics, 122*(2), 343–359. doi:10.100710551-013-1740-0

Gemechu, T. F. (2019). *Creating an instrument to measure holistic ethical leadership* (Order No. 13805441). Available from Dissertations & Theses @ Regent University. (2193421074). Retrieved from http://eres.regent.edu/login?url=https://www-proquest-com.ezproxy.regent.edu/dissertations-theses/creating-instrument-measure-holistic-ethical/docview/2193421074/se-2?accountid=13479

Gemechu, T. F., West, G., Winner, W. D., & Winston, B. E. (2020). Creating an Instrument to Measure Holistic Ethical Leadership. *International Leadership Journal, 12*(4). http://internationalleadership-journal.com/

Goodwin, B., Cameron, G., & Hein, H. (2015). *Balanced leadership for powerful learning*. Association for Supervision & Curriculum Development.

Hair, J. F., Black, W. C., Babin, B. J., & Anderson, R. E. (2010). *Multivariate data analysis*. Pearson Prentice Hall.

Harrington, D. (2009). *Confirmatory factor analysis*. Oxford University Press.

Ifedapo, A., Luiz, J., Judy, M., & Kenneth, A. (2020). Business ethics in africa: The role of institutional context, social relevance, and development challenges. *Journal of Business Ethics, 161*(4), 717-729. http://dx.doi.org.ezproxy.regent.edu/10.1007/s10551-019-04338-x

Jackson, D. L., Gillaspy, J. A., & Purc-Stephenson, R. (2009). Reporting practices in confirmatory factor analysis: An overview and some recommendations. *Psychological Methods, 14*(1), 6–23. doi:10.1037/a0014694 PMID:19271845

John, O. P., & Srivastava, J. (1999). The big- five trait taxonomy, History, measurement, and theoretical perspectives. In Handbook of personality: Theory and research (2nd ed.). New York: Guilford Press.

Kim, H.-Y. (2013). Statistical notes for clinical researchers: assessing normal distribution (2) using skewness and kurtosis. *PMC Website*. https://www.ncbi.nlm.nih.gov/pmc/articles/PMC3591587/

Krabbe, P. F. M. (2017). *The Measurement of Health and Health Status*. Elsevier. doi:10.1016/B978-0-12-801504-9.00006-4

Kristof-Brown, A. L., Zimmerman, R. D., & Johnson, E. C. (2005). Consequences of individuals' fit at work: A meta-analysis of person–job, person–organization, person–group, and person–supervisor fit. *Personnel Psychology*, *58*(2), 281–342. doi:10.1111/j.1744-6570.2005.00672.x

Lee, J. J., & Miller, S. E. (2013). A Self-Care Framework for Social Workers: Building A Strong Foundation for Practice. *The Journal of Contemporary Social Services*, *94*(2), 96–103. doi:10.1606/1044-3894.4289

Mankey, R. C. (2007). *Understanding holistic leadership: A collaborative inquiry* (Order No. 3269093). Available from ProQuest Central; ProQuest Dissertations & Theses Global. (304859685). Retrieved from http://eres.regent.edu:2048/login?url=https://search-proquest-com.ezproxy.regent.edu/docview/304859685?accountid=13479

Mantzaris, E. (2016). Development and trust in ethical leadership and the fight against corruption: The case of South Africa. *European Conference on Management, Leadership & Governance*. Kidmore End: Academic Conferences International Limited.

Mo, S., & Shi, J. (2017). Linking ethical leadership to employee burnout, workplace deviance and performance: Testing the mediating roles of trust in Measuring Holistic Ethical Leadership 138 leader and surface acting. *Journal of Business Ethics*, *144*(2), 293–303. doi:10.100710551-015-2821-z

Northouse, P. G. (2016). *Leadership theory and practice* (7th ed.). Sage.

Pervin, L. A. (1968). Performance and satisfaction as a function of individual–environment fit. *Psychological Bulletin*, *69*(1), 56–68. doi:10.1037/h0025271

Priesmeyer, R. H., Seigfried, R. J., & Murray, M. A. (2012). The supply chain as a wholistic system: A case study. *Management & Marketing*, *7*(4), 551–564.

Rogers, G., Mentkowski, M., & Hart, J. R. (2006). Adult holistic development and multidimensional performance. In C. H. Hoare (Ed.), *Handbook of adult development and learning* (pp. 498–534). Oxford University.

Russell, D., Peplau, L. A., & Cutrona, C. E. (1980). The revised UCLA loneliness scale: Concurrent and discriminant validity evidence. *Journal of Personality and Social Psychology*, *39*(3), 472–480. doi:10.1037/0022-3514.39.3.472 PMID:7431205

Scouller, J. (2014). The three levels of leadership. Oxford, UK: Management Books 2000.

Tabachnick, B. G., & Fidell, L. S. (2019). *Using Multivariate Statistics* (7th ed.). Pearson Publishing.

Taylor, R. (1990). Interpretation of the Correlation coefficient: A basic review. *Journal of Diagnostic Medical Sonography: JDMS*, *1*(January/February), 1–39. doi:10.1177/875647939000600106

Treviño, L. K., & Ball, G. A. (1992). The social implications of punishing unethical behavior: Observers' cognitive and affective reactions. *Journal of Management*, *18*(4), 751–768. doi:10.1177/014920639201800409

Treviño, L. K., Hartman, L. P., & Brown, M. (2000). Moral person and moral manager: How executives develop a reputation for ethical leadership. *California Management Review*, *42*(4), 128–142. doi:10.2307/41166057

Treviño, L. K., & Weaver, G. R. (2003). *Managing ethics in business organizations: Social scientific perspectives*. Stanford University Press.

Vasle, J. J., Beaman, J., & Sonarski, C. C. (2017). Rethinking Internal Consistency in Cronbach's Alpha. *Leisure Sciences*, *39*(2), 163–173. doi:10.1080/01490400.2015.1127189

Wapner, S., & Demick, J. (2003). Adult development: The holistic, developmental, and systems-oriented perspective. In J. Demick & C. Andreoletti (Eds.), *Handbook of adult development* (pp. 63–83). Kluwer Academic/Plenum.

Wheeler, J. V. (2013). A Holistic, Organic Process of Personal Growth and Leadership. *OD Practitioner*, *45*(4), 38–42.

Yukl, G. (2013). *Leadership in organizations* (8th ed.). Pearson.

Chapter 9
The Revised Two–Factor Motivation to Lead Instrument

Karen Cerff

Transformational Leadership Institute, South Africa

ABSTRACT

The study on which this chapter is based investigated whether there is a connection between hope, self-efficacy, and motivation to lead (MTL) in the development of leaders in South Africa. The data collected for the MTL component were gathered using a revised two-factor model of Chan's MTL instrument, comprising the leading for self-benefit factor (MTL-S) and the group-centered leading factor (MTL-G). The revised two-factor model of Chan's MTL instrument is a meaningful redevelopment of Chan's MTL instrument for the South African context and potentially elsewhere in the world. The MTL-G, which comprises seven items, is of particular interest as a scale for measuring altruism. This research makes a contribution to servant leadership by establishing the connection between MTL-G and altruism, and adds a valuable dimension to the research of Patterson. More recent research has emerged, indicating MTL instrument adaptions and revisions in different contexts.

INTRODUCTION

A study undertaken by Cerff in 2006 investigated whether there is a connection between hope, self-efficacy and motivation to lead (MTL) in the development of leaders in South Africa. The Hope Instrument (Winston et al., 2005), the New General Self-Efficacy (NGSE) Instrument (Chen et al., 2001), and the Motivation to Lead Instrument (Chan, 1999) were utilized for the data collection.

Chan's (1999) study in Singapore and the United States utilizing the MTL Instrument indicated high reliability for the three subscales of MTL. Following the differences in reliability between Chan's study and the South African context, a revised two-factor model of Chan's (1999) MTL Instrument, comprising the leading for self-benefit factor (MTL-S) and the group-centered leading factor (MTL-G), was developed and utilized in the study.

DOI: 10.4018/978-1-7998-7665-6.ch009

This chapter discusses the contribution that Cerff's 2006 study makes to servant leadership through establishing the connection between MTL-G and altruism, and adds a valuable dimension to the research of Patterson (2003). Details are provided of the process leading to the revised two-factor model of Chan's (1999) MTL Instrument, and the development thereof. Background information, including the role of cultural demographics utilized in the study as potential causes leading to discrepancies found prior to the revision, are also explored.

Commonalities relating to the study of Bobbio and Manganelli Rattazzi (2006), who utilized the MTL Instrument in the Italian context, are considered. The chapter also discusses two studies in which the MTL Instrument was utilized in a military context, namely the study of Amit et al. (2007) in relation to the Israeli army, and that of Kasemaa (2016) in relation to the Estonian army. Most recently, Badura et al.'s (2020) research focused on a meta-analysis and distal-proximal model of motivation and leadership in relation to the MTL Instrument.

BACKGROUND

The research on which this chapter is based investigated the role of hope and self-efficacy as two variables on the MTL in the development of leaders in the South African college context. The 2006 study focused on college students due to their potential and capacity to form a significant core of the future leader pool in South Africa.

The development of future leaders in South Africa is closely linked to the concept of the African Renaissance, which "was born following the progressive regaining of power by the ethnic people in the nations of Africa" (Cerff, 2004, p. 6). A former South African president, Thabo Mbeki, articulated it as "a means to Africa's empowerment" (as cited in Boloka, 1999, p. 4). It is notable that the concept "encompasses a recognition of the need for increased leadership and MTL as well as the development of future leaders to whom the baton may be handed in the pursuit of a better future for the nation and continent" (Cerff, 2006, p. 1).

Chan (1999) developed an empirical model that introduced MTL as a new general differences construct. MTL provides a framework for "understanding the relationship between individual differences and various leader behaviors" (p. iii). Chan and Drasgow (2001) defined MTL as "an individual-differences construct that affects a leader's or leader-to-be's decisions to assume leadership training, roles and responsibilities that affect his or her intensity of effort at leading and persistence as a leader" (p. 486).

According to Chan (1999), the factors that affect each of these behavioral criteria could include individual differences and situational variables. Chan focused on clarifying individual differences that affect MTL. These individual differences in MTL may be "relatively stable over time, barring any major interventions or life events" and may "interact with the person's vocational or life-domain interests and abilities to predict leadership behaviors" (p. 4). It follows that these individual differences in MTL will "interact with characteristics of the situation" and affect "individual decisions to lead in specific situations" (p. 5). Chan argued that individual differences can change through training and experience in leadership and pointed out that "individual differences are an immediate outcome of one's leadership self-efficacy and accumulated leadership experience which are in turn affected by cultural values and beliefs, personality, cognitive and social responsibilities" (p. 5).

According to Chan et al. (2001), MTL can be "conceptualized and measured in terms of three correlated-dimensions: Affective/Identity, Social-Normative, and Non-calculative MTL" (p. 228). Chan et al.

(2001) concluded that individuals' interests in leading are general rather than specific to any domain of activity. Chan and Drasgow (2001) noted that "leadership skills and leadership style are learned and that MTL can be changed" (p. 486) and acknowledged that the concept of self-efficacy is "borrowed from Bandura's (1986, 1997) general social cognitive theory to account for individual differences in MTL" (p. 486). Since MTL can change, is subject to individual differences, and is affected by self-efficacy, Cerff's (2006) study included hope as a likely variable that can exercise influence on an individual's MTL.

Ericksen (2005) undertook an exploratory study of the relationships between individual differences, leadership self-efficacy, leadership experience, collective efficacy, and MTL. Ericksen's (2005) study demonstrated a similarity to Chan's (1999) previous research; thereby suggesting that "the MTL construct is valid and reliable in settings similar to this sample and those studied previously" (Ericksen, p. 91). Ericksen noted that this finding "represents a significant contribution to literature since it broadens the applicability of the MTL construct" (p. 91) and subsequently examined the effects of situational influence on a leader's MTL, noting that the research of Chan and associates (Chan, 1999; Chan et al., 2001) had left "external validity and situational effects" (p. 5) untested. Ericksen made a variety of recommendations for research in the MTL field, one of which concerned the influence of training on MTL, that relates to the development of leaders in the South African context.

The study on which this chapter draws examined the antecedents of hope and self-efficacy on MTL, and explored the situational effects that these relationships have on the development of leaders. The high reliability indicated for the three subscales of MTL of Chan's (1999) study in Singapore and the United States was in contrast to the differences in reliability encountered in the South African context. This prompted the development of a revised two-factor model of Chan's (1999) MTL Instrument, comprising the MTL-S and the MTL-G (Cerff, 2006).

The findings from the 2006 study indicated the potential ability of the revised two-factor MTL Instrument to identify certain character traits present in individuals, including the tendency for Christians to demonstrate higher levels of MTL-G, hence the seven items for the MTL-G could be utilized as a scale for altruism. The presence of altruism as a more common Christian behavioral trait finds support in the biblical roots of altruism, as the construct indicates the motivation for a behavior change away from self-centered tendencies towards embracing and advancing the principles described in the Bible. It would be expected that practicing Christians as well as other individuals who demonstrate a selfless motivation would demonstrate altruistic behavior or the ethics of reciprocity.

Sykes (1980) defines the concept of altruism, which is derived from the Latin *alter*, meaning other, as a "regard for others as a principle of action; unselfishness" (p. 29). The concept is central to many religious traditions. Limited scholarly literature exploring altruism is available. Monroe (1994) points out that self-interest and altruism are at two ends of a continuum, and notes that "this juxtaposition of altruism with self-interest is important precisely because so much social and political theory is constructed on the norm of self-interest" (p. 863).

Patterson (2003), who lists altruism as one of the seven constructs of servant leadership in her theoretical model, points out that "scholarly interest in altruism dates back to the early 1800's" (p. 16) and defines altruism as "helping others just for the sake of helping" (p. 17). Monroe (1994) points out four critical factors relating to altruism: (1) it must involve action; (2) "the goal of the act must be furthering the welfare of the other" (p. 862); (3) "intentions count more than consequences" (p. 862), hence a well-intentioned action that has negative consequences remains altruistic; (4) "the act must carry some form of diminution to my welfare" (p. 863), since an act which does not cost the individual extending altruism anything would fall into the category of "collective welfare" (p. 863).

DeYoung (2000) adds to the traditional view of altruism by including the concept that a motive of altruism "involves getting pleasure from helping behavior" (p. 516), indicating the personal fulfillment derived from serving others. Patterson (2003) notes that "altruism seeks the fulfillment of others with behavior directed toward the benefit of others, and identifies this behavior as consistent with servant leadership" (p. 17). According to Berry and Cartwright (2000), servant leaders seek radical equality in the treatment of all people, thereby demonstrating an altruistic approach.

Bobbio and Manganelli Rattazzi (2006) undertook a study in the Italian context comprising 624 university and post-graduate students who completed MTL questionnaires. These researchers investigated the factorial structure of the MTL Instrument and found disappointing reliability following the analyses, which led to the development of a reduced 15-item form to produce satisfactory reliability. Mull (2018) notes that Bobbio and Manganelli Rattazzi's (2006) revision of the MTL Instrument included that the "affective–identity MTL could be reduced to a 5-item sub-scale" (p. 63).

Amit et al.'s (2007) study, in which the three factors, affective MTL, social-normative MTL and calculative MTL were tested, utilized a sample from the Israel Defense Forces. The researchers expanded Chan's model after finding two additional motivational factors present, being ideological and patriotic. The study also found that MTL factors differed between leaders and non-leaders in the sample.

Kasemaa (2016), having studied the research of Amit et al. (2007), considered an adaptation of the MTL Instrument in the Estonian military context. Kasemaa's study sought to make a contribution to the validation of the Chan and Drasgow's (2001) MTL scale and include the additional motivational factors, ideological and patriotic, in the first application of the adapted MTL scale in the Estonian context.

Ozgen Novelli et al. (2017) undertook a study focusing on the reliability of the MTL Instrument through performing meta-analytic reliability generalization on the MTL questionnaire to provide an aggregate estimate of the reliability of the MTL scores across studies and to identify study and sample characteristics that affect reliabilities. The authors focused on identifying study and sample characteristics that affect the reliability of the MTL Instrument in different applications through an in-depth examination of 95 independent samples from 82 studies.

DEVELOPMENT AND REVISION OF THE MOTIVATION TO LEAD INSTRUMENT

The chapter focuses mainly on aspects relating to the context and redevelopment of Chan's (1999) MTL Instrument to produce the revised two-factor model applicable in a South African context. The value of the 2006 study and the potential for further research are discussed. In addition, findings in more recent studies utilizing the MTL Instrument in other contexts and cultural demographics are highlighted.

In the development of his MTL scale, Chan (1999) commenced with 46 MTL items that were included in the survey "constructed by the researcher through focus group interviews with American and Singaporean students in the University of Illinois during the Spring-semester of 1998" (p. 26).

Following Chan's initial survey, he conducted three small-scale surveys with students from the same university that led to the identification of three factors underlying MTL, namely Affective-Identity MTL (AIMTL), Social-Normative MTL (SNMTL), and Non-Calculative MTL (NCMTL). In his 1999 study, Chan found strong, significant and direct relationships between AIMTL, extraversion, vertical-individualism, leadership self-efficacy and experience. He also found strong, significant and direct relationships between SNMTL, agreeableness, conscientiousness, horizontal-collectivism, vertical-collectivism, horizontal-individualism, vertical-individualism, leadership self-efficacy and experience, as well as strong, significant and direct relationships between NCMTL and agreeableness, emotional stability, horizontal-collectivism, vertical-collectivism, horizontal-individualism and vertical-individualism.

At this stage Chan dropped 19 items and rewrote others to produce an MTL scale that comprised 27 items. Chan's 1999 study consisted of three samples, namely Singapore military recruits, Singapore junior college students, and undergraduate students from the University of Illinois, thus comprising a variety of ethnicities representing different cultures on two continents.

Chan (1999) recorded the Cronbach alpha scores for the three subscales of the MTL scale, as being .84 for the AIMTL, .83 for the SNMTL, and .74 for the NCMTL. Chan's Cronbach alpha scores indicate high reliability of the instrument.

Distinctive Steps Taken in Data Collection Process

In Cerff's (2006) study, the researcher utilized three instruments, and planned a unique sample of respondents. From a demographic perspective, the quota sample size for the study was 200 college and graduate students enrolled in colleges and universities in Cape Town, South Africa. The participants comprised a cross-section of the three main ethnic groups in the nation: Black, White, and Colored people. The study included practicing Christians, non-Christians, English speakers, and Afrikaans speakers. The size of the study was determined by representation of 25 participants per category for each of the three data groups covering ethnicity, language and religiosity, thereby producing a 3 x 3 x 2 study, but not all cells were filled (e.g., Black-Afrikaans). The study consequently required a total of 200 participants.

The data collection process was planned based on the need for all participants to be conversant with English and/or Afrikaans regardless of ethnicity. South Africa has 11 official languages, nine of which are ethnic languages. It is of interest that for some of the participants, English or Afrikaans would have been, at best, their third language. The educational institutions targeted for the data collection have English and/or Afrikaans as the medium of instruction.

Since the sample required was a quota sample, prearranged steps were taken to locate and select the sample. Participants were specifically invited to participate in the study. In order to invite participants covering the White, Black, and Colored groups of both language groups who are practicing Christians, student members of a church that functions on a number of the college campuses in Cape Town and the vicinity were approached through their minister to participate in the research. These participants comprise a 3 x 2 x 1 factorial of 4 categories with a total of 100 participants.

In order to invite participants covering the White, Black, and Colored groups of both language groups who are non-Christians, students were invited to participate in the study by approaching faculty members at a local college to assist in inviting the selected group by approaching students who were standing in a queue to register at a local college for the new academic year and by inviting students relaxing on campus during their lunch break. These participants comprise a 3 x 2 x 1 factorial of 4 categories with a total of 100 participants. More participants made themselves available than were required by the sample size. Some of these extra questionnaires were used where incomplete or incorrectly completed surveys were received from participants. The extra surveys were discarded. Due to sensitivity of certain individuals to answering questions relating to ethnicity and religious affiliation, the availability of additional completed surveys was very useful.

Participants were provided with survey packs consisting of a copy of an English survey and a copy of a professionally translated Afrikaans survey. Participants could choose to answer either the English or the Afrikaans survey. The language in the English survey represents South African English spelling.

A back translation was made to ensure uniformity and understanding between the English and Afrikaans translations. Consequently, the survey pack for each respondent to complete comprised 15 pages.

For each of the various groups of participants who completed the surveys, paper copies and pens were provided and the procedure explained before the participants commenced reading the instructions. Participants were seated in lecture theaters when possible, and an administrator was available to answer any questions that arose.

The researcher personally planned, arranged, supervised and attended each of the data collection sessions. To ensure clarity of language and vocabulary for all participants, given the multi-ethnic composition of the respondents and the potential to misinterpret certain language innuendos and nuances, the researcher's presence was beneficial to the successful outcome of the data collection process. Many of the details described in the preparation, supervision and data collection process relate directly to the researcher's intent to alleviate the potential presence and impact of the role of context, cultural demographics and cultural sensitivity that would exercise a negative influence on the quality of the data. Additionally, a hands-on approach is more respected in some ethnic cultures, and therefore culturally sensitive in the context of the data collection process and commitment requested of participants by the researcher.

Participants were approached to complete the survey packs without remuneration and students willingly gave their time to complete these packs. The professional atmosphere created through the researcher's presence and attention to detail contributed to the conscientious attitude of participants and consequently the integrity of the data collection process. The participants believed that they were making a valuable contribution to research through their commitment and honest participation and many thanked the researcher for the opportunity to participate in the process.

The researcher collected the surveys after completion for data capturing. A direct consequence of the methodical data collection approach that was utilized, including the significant investment of time required in a non-electronic approach, was that very few survey packs were incomplete or incorrectly completed, thereby reinforcing the value of a meticulous preparation and data collection process within the unique context to ensure accuracy.

The data were then entered into SPSS Graduate Pack, version 12 for Windows. The analyses that were performed were the ANOVA tests and Bonferroni post hoc tests for hypotheses 1a, 2a and 3a; *t* tests for hypotheses 1b, 2b and 3b; and multiple regression analysis for hypothesis 4. Hypotheses 3a and 3b were directly linked to MTL, while hypothesis 4 integrated the three variables of hope, self-efficacy and MTL.

The Revision of the Motivation to Lead Instrument

In Cerff's (2006) study carried out in a South African context, some differences between the reliability in the Singapore and USA contexts and that of the South African context were found in relation to the MTL Instrument. In the initial analyses, the Cronbach alpha scores that were reported were disappointing. The Cronbach alpha score for the AIMTL subscale was .09, for the NCMTL subscale .26, and for the SNMTL subscale .59. Following this poor to mediocre reliability, further analyses were conducted. The SNMTL subscale indicated weakness, but by removing MTL item 23, the reliability improved and a Cronbach alpha score of .68 was reported. This finding prompted further analysis.

MTL factor analysis was then conducted using factor loadings of .5 and two factors emerged that explained 54% of the variance. Consequently, a revised two-factor model of Chan's (1999) MTL Instrument comprising the leading for self-benefit factor (MTL-S) and the group-centered leading factor (MTL-G), was developed and utilized in the study. The first new factor, leading for self-benefit, is abbreviated as

MTL-S, indicating the focus on self. The second new factor, group-centered leading factor, is abbreviated as MTL-G indicating the focus on the group.

The MTL-S factor is characterized by a self-centered motivation in leading and comprises six items, namely 14, 19, 27, 29, 33 and 45 with a Cronbach alpha score of .75. Cerff (2006) lists the six items that represent MTL-S as follows: "(14) I would want to know 'what's in it for me' if I am going to lead a group; (19) I am only interested in leading a group if there are clear advantages for me; (27) I will lead the group only when I want to lead and never when the group asks me to lead; (29) Leading others is really more of a dirty job rather than an honorable one; (33) I will never agree to lead if I cannot see any benefits from accepting that role; (45) Leading others is a waste of one's personal time and effort" (pp. 56-58).

The MTL-G factor is characterized by leading focused on the group's interests and comprises seven items, namely 6, 11, 25, 30, 32, 39 and 44 with a Cronbach alpha score of .77. Cerff (2006) lists the seven items that represent MTL-G as follows: "(6) Most of the time, I prefer being a leader rather than a follower when working in a group; (11) I have a tendency to take charge in most groups or teams in which I work; (25) I am the type of person who likes to be in charge of others; (30) I usually want to be the leader in the groups in which I work; (32) I agree to lead whenever I am asked or nominated by the other members; (39) I like the experience of leading others; (44) When chosen as group leader, I will usually accept the job" (pp. 56-58).

The new Cronbach alpha scores indicate high reliability and thereby greatly increase confidence in the empirically derived revised model that was adapted for the South African context. Since the factor analysis of the items did not match Chan's findings and the new factor analysis seems to explain the variance with two factors, the hypotheses associated with the motivation to lead concept were tested with the two new factors, MTL-S and MTL-G.

Consequences of the Need to Revise the Motivation to Lead Instrument

A number of direct and indirect consequences arose from the need to revise the MTL Instrument. On discovery of the poor to mediocre reliability described, significant further analyses were undertaken. A direct consequence was a delay in the timeline for the completion of the study. At the outset of the study, the author developed seven hypotheses of which two were directly linked to MTL, and a third hypothesis comprised an integration of the three variables, hope, self-efficacy and MTL, based on Chan's (1999) model of MTL. The dilemma of encountering one of three reputable instruments delivering disappointing Cronbach alpha scores in the context in which it was applied at a late stage in a project of this nature was a challenge comprising a variety of dimensions.

The successful completion of the entire study was potentially at risk since the application of the three instruments was intricately linked and motivated through the historical, cultural and leadership contexts within which the study was established. Since the discovery of the disappointing reliability of the MTL Instrument in the context took place at an advanced stage of the study, this necessitated insightful and well-founded solutions to ensure the success of the study for the researcher and the institution involved, and to avoid incurring further significant costs in the completion of the study. The dilemma provided an opportunity for an innovative revision of the MTL Instrument that could add further value to the body of knowledge, and provide researchers with additional insights into the role of possible cultural and contextual demographics that may be applicable in other nations and environments, thereby highlighting awareness and opening avenues for further research and development in this and related fields.

Findings Associated with MTL-S and MTL-G

Cerff's (2006) study utilized the two new factors, MTL-G and MTL-S in a two-part hypothesis as follows (pp. 46-48):

H4a: There is a causal relationship in which hope, self-efficacy, Christian and ethnicity predict MTL-S.

In order to determine whether this hypothesis is accepted or rejected, interval data were collected using Winston et al.'s (2005) Hope Instrument, Chen et al.'s (2001) NGSE, and the revised MTL model comprising the six items for MTL-S. A multiple regression analysis was carried out for MTL-S. The predictors were Black, White-Afrikaans, White-English, Colored, hope total score, self-efficacy, and Christian. A stepwise regression analysis was subsequently conducted for MTL-S. The analysis confirmed the three predictors of MTL-S. The results show that hope, self-efficacy, and Christian are predictors of MTL-S. The regression model including these three predictors is significant, $F (1.198) = 33.46, p < .001; R^2 = .21$. These results indicate that 45% of the variance in the dependent variable can be explained with the new model.

The most important predictor of MTL-S is hope ($\beta = -.29; t = -4.15, p < .001$). The other two significant predictors are Christian ($\beta = -.20; t = -3.09, p < .01$) and self-efficacy $\beta = -.15; t = -2.30, p < .05$). The negative regression coefficients indicate an inverse relationship between independent variables and the dependent variable; the more hope and self-efficacy, the less MTL-S. Table 1 provides the standardized regression coefficients for MTL-S predictors.

Table 1. Standardized regression coefficients for MTL-S predictors

Predictor	β	T	Sig.
Hope	-.29	-4.15	$p < .001$
Christian	-.20	-3.09	$p < .01$
SE	-.15	-2.30	$p < .05$

The religious affiliation independent variable was dummy coded with 1 for Christians and 0 for non-Christians. Therefore, the negative regression coefficient indicates that Christians have lower MTL-S scores than non-Christians. The results of the analyses for hypothesis 4a show that the variables of hope, self-efficacy, and Christian are predictors of MTL-S; on the basis of these results, hypothesis 4a is accepted.

$H_4{}^b$: There is a causal relationship in which hope, self-efficacy, Christian, and ethnicity predict MTL-G.

In order to determine whether this hypothesis is accepted or rejected, interval data were collected using Winston et al.'s (2005) Hope instrument, Chen et al.'s (2001) NGSE, and the revised model comprising the seven items for MTL-G to establish whether there is a causal relationship in which hope, self-efficacy, and the dummy variable Christian as well as the dummy variables Black, White-Afrikaans, White-English, and Colored predict MTL-G. A multiple regression analysis was carried out for MTL-G.

The predictors were Black, White-Afrikaans, White-English, Colored, hope total score, self-efficacy, and Christian.

A stepwise regression analysis was run for MTL-G, and the results show that self-efficacy is the only significant predictor of MTL-G. The regression model including this predictor is significant $[F(1.198) = 29.43, p < .001; R^2 = .13]$. The standardized regression coefficient for self-efficacy is $\beta = .36; t = 5.43, p < .001$. The positive regression coefficient indicates a positive relationship between the independent and the dependent variables; indicating that the more self-efficacy, the more MTL-G. Table 2 provides the standardized regression coefficients for MTL-G predictors.

Table 2. Standardized regression coefficients for MTL-G

Predictor	β	T	Sig.
SE	.36	5.43	$p < .001$

The results of the analyses for hypothesis 4b show that self-efficacy is a predictor of MTL-G. On the basis of these results, hypothesis 4b is accepted.

H_4^b: There is a causal relationship in which hope, self-efficacy, Christian, and ethnicity predict MTL-G.

The outcome of the further work required for the revision of the MTL Instrument for the completion of Cerff's (2006) study was successful and rendered results that added value to the body of knowledge, prompting further research.

The Significance Associated with MTL-S and MTL-G

Cerff (2006) reported that the results of the analyses associated with the potential predictors of the MTL-S factor indicated that the variables of hope, self-efficacy and Christian are predictors. The most important predictor of the MTL-S factor is hope, thereafter Christian and self-efficacy. Since each of these variables had a negative beta reported, this indicates an inverse relationship between independents and the dependent, therefore the more hope and self-efficacy, the less motivation to lead for self-benefit is present.

Cerff and Bocarnea (2007) noted that the findings of the analyses "also indicate the potential ability of the revised 13 item, two-factor Motivation to Lead Instrument to identify certain character traits present in individuals. Since the findings of Cerff's (2006) research indicate a tendency for Christians to demonstrate higher levels of MTL-G, the 7 items for the MTL-G could be utilized as a scale for altruism" (p. 14).

Winston (2017) alluded to the presence of unique cultural complexities when he observed that the "motivations to lead in South African college students show a bifurcated value-base – what is in it for me and what is in it for others" and notes the need for current leaders in Africa to intentionally develop leaders of future generations who emulate "credibility, integrity and accountability" (p. 186).

A limited number of other studies utilizing Chan's (1999) MTL Instrument have also encountered the need for adaptations of the MTL Instrument within certain contexts.

Commonalities Encountered and Adaptations to the MTL Instrument

Amit et al.'s (2007) study that centered on the Israel Defense Forces and utilized Chan's (1999) three original MTL factors included a revision that added two factors to the existing model.

The study comprised 402 male soldier participants and included a focus on the following two questions: "What are the sources of motivation to lead and are there additional sources beyond those mentioned in the literature? Is there a significant difference between leaders and non-leaders in motivation to lead?" (Amit et al., 2007, p. 138). The researchers examined the responses within the framework of Chan's (1999) research which led to the expansion and empirical testing with the sample. The first additional factor that was added was Ideological Motivation to Lead (IMTL). The researchers noted that "although Chan mentions values as an important component of motivation to lead, in his discussion he narrows this aspect to individualism–collectivism only, ignoring a wide range of possible and relevant values that are usually put under the title of ideology." (p. 141). The researchers further noted that an "ideology, composed of an organized system of values and ideas, may be a powerful motivational factor for its adherents" (p. 141). The second additional factor that was added was Patriotic Motivation to Lead (PMTL). The researchers pointed out that PMTL

… may be particularly relevant to organizations such as armies acting in the service of the state. This factor differs from ideological motivation to lead in that IMTL may derive from social, political, or religious beliefs and ideas, whereas patriotic motivation to lead stems from beliefs directly related to love of the homeland (pp. 141-142).

Amit et al.'s (2007) findings indicated that

… the basic structure of Chan's three-factor model remains stable in the Israeli sample. The addition of the two motivational factors (ideological and patriotic) expanded and stabilized the model. The ideological and patriotic factors, although they appear to be related in content, were found to be in low correlation with each other. The difference between these two factors, which we had located in our pilot study, stems from the conception underlying the motive. The leader who is motivated by ideological values sees his role through the prism of his ideals, and these determine his choice of actions. In contrast, the leader motivated by patriotic values will do anything to serve the good of the nation and the homeland, even at the cost of rejecting a certain ideology in favor of a practical approach or another ideology (p. 155).

Another dimension of interest to the researchers was that of differences between leaders' versus non-leaders' MTL. The findings showed that "all the participants in the assignment rated the group that was higher in all the measures as higher in leadership and the group that was lower in all the measures as lower in leadership" (p. 142).

Kasemaa (2016) investigated the adaptation of the Motivation to Lead Instrument to the Estonian military, modelling his study on that of Amit et al. (2007) that focused on the Israel Defense Forces. Kasemaa principally sought to validate the Chan and Drasgow (2001) MTL scale. His was also the first study beyond the Israel Defense Force to utilize the additional motivational factors, namely ideological and patriotic, that Amit et al. had identified.

Kasemaa's (2016) study involved a sample of 517 military and non-military individuals from the Estonian Defense Forces, the Estonian Police and students from Tallinn University who participated in the study. The researcher reported that "the results confirmed that both three- and five-component MTL scales are applicable in the Estonian context; the pool of 35 items was reduced into 25 items with good internal reliability" (p. 64). In addition, the results "showed correlations between leadership self-efficacy and MTL components, and differences between leaders' and non-leaders' MTL" (p. 64). Kasemaa concluded that the MTL scale "can be a reliable and useful instrument to measure leadership motivation in the Estonian military context" (p.64). The results showed that both Chan and Drasgow's (2001) MTL version and the expanded MTL version that Amit et al. (2007) developed "have sufficient reliability and validity to be used as research tools in the leadership domain" (Kasemaa, p. 83).

Mull (2018) points out that Bobbio and Manganelli Rattazzi (2006) and Ozgen Novelli et al. (2017) "conducted further validity analyses on the instrument" (p. 62). Ozgen Novelli et al. (2017) "conducted a meta-analysis of 82 studies and found that affective–identity MTL had the highest sample-size weighted mean reliability coefficient ($M = 0.85$, $SD = 0.05$, $K = 76$) among the three subscales of MTL" (p. 62).

Mull's (2018) study utilized an adapted portion of Chan and Drasgow's (2001) model, and was integrated with constructs from Felfe and Schyns's (2014) model with a focus on the intention to apply for a leadership position (IALP). Mull (2018) noted that the IALP model

[… provided] a framework with which to examine the relationships between the independent variables of personality (extraversion, conscientiousness, openness to experience, agreeableness, emotional stability), and values (vertical individualism, horizontal individualism, vertical collectivism, horizontal collectivism), as they relate to the intervening variables of past leadership experience, perceptions of leadership (leadership self-efficacy, personal initiative, and Romance of Leadership), and affective–identity motivation to lead with the dependent variable of intention to apply for a leadership position (p. 51).

Mull's study is an example of a revision of the MTL Instrument in which the Affective-identity MTL portion was utilized in conjunction with IALP. A significant contribution of Mull's (2018) study was in utilizing the adapted portion of Chan and Drasgow's (2001) model in establishing that "affective–identity motivation to lead was found to have a direct effect on intention to apply for a leadership position" (p.126).

The study by Badura et al. (2020) used a meta-analysis and distal-proximal model of motivation and leadership in relation to the MTL instrument. According to Badura et al. (2020), "the 3 types of MTL (affective identity, social-normative, and non-calculative) had a unique pattern of antecedents and were only modestly correlated, indicating that MTL may be best operationalized as three separate motivational constructs instead of as one overarching construct" (p. 331). This study pointed to the distinctiveness of the "three MTL types, establishing MTL's relationship with leadership outcomes, and identifying MTL's role within the broader leadership domain" (p. 331).

FUTURE RESEARCH AND EMERGING TRENDS

Amit et al. (2007) recommended that qualitative methods be used to investigate the sources of motivation to lead directly, since such research "may expand the range of motivational factors beyond what has been discussed in the few studies hitherto conducted. Furthermore, qualitative methods can expose more complex and hidden motives to lead, beyond the factors described in cognitive models" (p. 158).

Kasemaa's (2016) study reduced the number of items in the MTL Instrument and consequently the "findings also introduced the possibility to use fewer items than the original instrument, which would be easier to administer" (p. 83).

Kasemaa raised a significant consideration in his discussion, relating to context and the relevance of the two additional factors, ideological and patriotic:

In order to compare the results with the Israeli military (PaMTL and IdMTL subscales), we need to bear in mind Israel's unique historical and political context. Therefore, these two additional components, still weakly correlated with others, cannot be applied to other countries without careful examination. Thus, we argue that these results indicate that organisational and contextual variables influence the motivation to lead. It could explain why Bobbio and Manganelli Rattazzi (2006) found the model acceptable in the Italian context. They also reported a moderate correlation between MTL and the social desirability scale; thus, we think that these findings should be taken into consideration, with special attention to the samples where a leadership role is more desirable (such as military) (p. 83).

The deeply emotive dimensions involved in this statement offer opportunities for various further studies in the military and other national service institutions in particular.

Badura et al. (2020) study concluded that the "three MTL types are meaningful components of the leadership emergence/effectiveness processes" (p. 347) and their findings indicate further potential research opportunities in the three types of MTL in various organizational contexts.

The MTL studies listed and described indicate certain commonalities and challenges that have led to adaptions and redevelopments, and provide opportunities for researchers to further investigate and develop Chan's (1999) model as well as other models that were inspired through his original research. A variety of trends that are emerging from the application of the MTL Instrument inspire further investigation. These potential studies include those that emanate from mixed ethnic groups, samples from different continents and those from different organizational cultures. The listed studies provide a rich source of insight into the challenges encountered and future research opportunities that exist.

CONCLUSION

In conclusion, the observation by Cerff and Bocarnea (2007) seems opportune:

[T]he revised two-factor model of Chan's (1999) MTL Instrument, comprising the leading for self-benefit factor (MTL-S) and the group-centered leading factor (MTL-G) is a meaningful redevelopment of Chan's MTL instrument for the South African context and potentially in other nations as well. The group-centered leading factor, comprising seven items, is of particular interest as a scale for measuring altruism. This research makes a contribution to servant leadership by establishing the connection between MTL-G and altruism, and adds a valuable dimension to the research of Patterson (2003) (pp.13-14).

REFERENCES

Amit, K., Lisak, A., Popper, M., & Gal, R. (2007). Motivation to lead: Research on the motives for undertaking leadership roles in the Israel Defense Forces (IDF). *Military Psychology, 19*(3), 137–160. doi:10.1080/08995600701386317

Badura, K. L., Grijalva, E., Galvin, B. M., Owen, B. P., & Joseph, D. L. (2020). Motivation to lead: A meta-analysis and distal-proximal model of motivation and leadership. *The Journal of Applied Psychology, 105*(4), 331–354. doi:10.1037/apl0000439 PMID:31393147

Bandura, A. (1986). *Social foundations of thought & action: Social cognitive theory*. Prentice Hall.

Bandura, A. (1997). *Self-efficacy: The exercise of control*. Freeman and Company.

Berry, A. J., & Cartwright, S. (2000). Leadership: A critical construction. *Leadership and Organization Development Journal, 21*(7), 342–349. doi:10.1108/01437730010377881

Bobbio, A., & Manganelli Rattazzi, A. M. (2006). A contribution to the Validation of the Motivation to Lead Scale (MTL): A research in the Italian context. *Leadership, 2*(1), 117–129. doi:10.1177/1742715006057240

Boloka, G. M. (1999). African Renaissance: A quest for (un)attainable past. *Critical Arts, 13*(2), 92–103. doi:10.1080/02560049985310151

Cerff, K. (2004). Exploring Ubuntu and the African Renaissance: A conceptual study of servant leadership from an African perspective. In *Proceedings of the Servant Leadership Research Roundtable*. Retrieved October 5, 2004, from https://www.regent.edu/acad/sls/publications/journals_and_proceedings/proceeding/servant_leadership_roundtable/pdf/Cerff-2004SL.pdf

Cerff, K. (2006). *The role of hope, self-efficacy and Motivation to Lead in the development of leaders in the South African college student context* [Unpublished doctoral dissertation]. Regent University, Virginia Beach, VA.

Cerff, K., & Bocarnea, M. C. (2007). Group-centered leading factor as a scale for measuring altruism. In *Proceedings of the Servant Leadership Roundtable*. Retrieved December 7, 2007 from https://www.regent.edu/acad/global/publications/sl_proceedings/2007/cerff-bocarnea.pdf

Chan, K. (1999). *Toward a theory of individual differences and leadership: Understanding the motivation to lead* [Unpublished doctoral dissertation]. University of Illinois, Urbana, IL.

Chan, K., & Drasgow, F. (2001). Toward a theory of individual differences and leadership: Understanding the motivation to lead. *The Journal of Applied Psychology, 86*(3), 481–498. doi:10.1037/0021-9010.86.3.481 PMID:11419808

Chan, K., Rounds, J., & Drasgow, F. (2001). The relation between vocational interests and the motivation to lead. *Journal of Vocational Behavior, 57*(2), 226–245. doi:10.1006/jvbe.1999.1728

Chen, G., Gully, S., & Eden, D. (2001). Validation of a new general self-efficacy scale. *Organizational Research Methods, 4*(1), 62–83. doi:10.1177/109442810141004

DeYoung, R. (2000). Expanding and evaluating motives for environmentally responsible behavior. *The Journal of Social Issues*, *56*(3), 509–526. doi:10.1111/0022-4537.00181

Ericksen, R. W. (2005). *Exploring the antecedents of motivation to lead and the affects of collective efficacy* [Unpublished doctoral dissertation]. Regent University, Virginia Beach, VA.

Felfe, J., & Schyns, B. (2014). Romance of leadership and motivation to lead. *Journal of Managerial Psychology*, *29*(7), 850–865. doi:10.1108/JMP-03-2012-0076

Kasemaa, A. (2016). The adaptation of the motivation to lead instrument to the Estonian military context. *Journal of Management and Business Administration. Central Europe*, *24*(1), 64–88.

Monroe, K. R. (1994). A fat lady in a corset: Altruism and social theory. *American Journal of Political Science*, *38*(4), 861–893. doi:10.2307/2111725

Mull, M. (2018). *Testing an adapted and integrated model of Motivation to Lead and intention to apply* [Unpublished doctoral dissertation]. University of Texas, Tyler, TX.

Ozgen Novelli, S., Laginess, A., & Viswesvaran, C. (2017). The Motivation to Lead Questionnaire: A meta-analytic examination of score reliability. *Academy of Management Proceedings*, *2017*(1).

Patterson, K. (2003). *Servant Leadership: A theoretical model* [Unpublished doctoral dissertation]. Regent University, VA.

Sykes, J. B. (Ed.). (1980). *The concise Oxford dictionary of current English*. Clarendon.

Winston, B. E. (2017). The stage is set for African Renaissance. In K. Patterson & B. E. Winston (Eds.), *Leading an African Renaissance: Opportunities and challenges* (p. 186). Palgrave Macmillan. doi:10.1007/978-3-319-40539-1_11

Winston, B. E., Bekker, C., Cerff, K., Eames, D., Helland, M. R., & Garnes, D. (2005). *Hope as a possible factor in the implementation of strategic plans*. Unpublished manuscript.

ADDITIONAL READING

Clemons, A. B. (2008). *Values as determinants of Motivation to Lead* [Unpublished doctoral dissertation]. Regent University, Virginia Beach, VA.

Snyder, C. R., Lopez, S. J., Shorey, H. S., Rand, K. L., & Feldman, D. B. (2003). Hope theory, measurements, and applications to school psychology. *School Psychology Quarterly*, *18*(3), 122–139. doi:10.1521cpq.18.2.122.21854

KEY TERMS AND DEFINITIONS

Hope Theory: Hope theory emanated from the research of C.R. Snyder, that commenced in the field of positive psychology in the 1980s. Hope is regarded as the perceived ability of an individual to navigate a route to achieve a desired outcome. The greater the individual's belief in their own ability to achieve their desired outcome, the greater their level of hope will be. Hope theory on which this construct is based, comprises both affective and cognitive dimensions.

NGSE Instrument: The New General Self-Efficacy Instrument is a five-point scale that examines predicted self-efficacy in different contexts and tasks. For the purpose of reporting results in the study, the abbreviation, SE, has been used.

Self-Efficacy: Self-efficacy is an individual's perception of their ability. A. Bandura developed self-efficacy theory in the 1980s. It is based on the principle of an individual's belief in their capacity to achieve specific performance outcomes, and reflects confidence in the individual's own behavior and motivation.

Chapter 10
Development of a Single-Factor Scale to Measure Leader Accountability

James A. (Andy) Wood
Regent University, USA

Heidi R. Ventura
Trevecca Nazarene University, USA

ABSTRACT

Wood and Winston defined leader accountability as the leader's response to (1) his/her willing acceptance of the responsibilities inherent in the leadership position to serve the well-being of the organization; (2) the implicit or explicit expectation that he/she will be publicly linked to his/her actions, words, or reactions; and (3) the expectation that the leader may be called on to explain his or her beliefs, decisions, commitments, or actions to constituents. They developed three scales—the Responsibility, Openness, and Answerability Scales—to form the Leader Accountability Index (LAI). Use of the scales in subsequent research has suggested the possibility of combining the three to form a single factor instrument to measure leader accountability. This chapter updates the literature on leader accountability since the LAI was first published, reviews the data collection and factor analyses involved in creating the new Leader Accountability Scale (LAS), and discusses implications of the new scale's usefulness in leadership research and organizational practice.

INTRODUCTION

Accountability continues to be a proposed social structure that can influence individual behavior to either comply with established behavioral norms and expectations or restore trust and credibility once lost (Wood & Winston, 2005). This is particularly true in the field of leadership. Calls for and examinations of leader accountability continue to go forth in virtually every leadership domain, including business (cf. Steinbauer et al., 2014; Molinaro, 2018), clergy (cf. Senander, 2017; Silliman, 2021), public

DOI: 10.4018/978-1-7998-7665-6.ch010

utilities (cf. Walsh, 2019), the non-profit sector (cf. Saddiq et al., 2013), healthcare (cf. Andersson & Wikstrom, 2014), education administration (cf. Knapp & Feldman, 2012; Lee et al., 2012), building trades (cf. Chapman, 2019), non-government organizations (cf. Ghela & Bhanderi, 2016), accounting (cf. Ahrens & Ferry, 2015), and government (Byrne, 2014; Lewis & Steinhoff, 2019). Despite repeated public scandals in various fields throughout the early part of the century and the perceived importance of leader accountability, Molinaro's (2017) Global Leadership Accountability Survey indicates that only 37% of respondents were satisfied with the level of accountability demonstrated by their leaders.

Wood and Winston (2005) contributed to this field in two ways. First, following a rigorous literature review in which leader accountability was described in a wide variety of ways, they defined the construct upon which leader accountability could be further researched and measured. Wood and Winston define leader accountability as the leader's response to (a) his/her willing acceptance of the responsibilities inherent in the leadership position to serve the well-being of the organization; (b) the implicit or explicit expectation that he/she will be publicly linked to his/her actions, words, or reactions; and (c) the expectation that the leader may be called on to explain his or her beliefs, decisions, commitments, or actions to constituents (Wood & Winston, 2005). Out of this research, Wood and Winston (2007) developed three scales to measure leader accountability – the Responsibility Scale, the Openness Scale, and the Answerability Scale – which, combined, form the Leader Accountability Index (LAI). These scales gave organizations and researchers the ability to move the conversation about leadership and accountability past buzzwords and reactive postures to a more proactive one. Having such a tool also provides organizational leaders and consultants a resource to help select or promote accountable individuals to positions of leadership and a framework by which to train and develop leaders in this critical area.

Use of the three LAI scales in subsequent research has suggested the possibility of combining the three to form a single factor instrument to measure leader accountability. This chapter updates the literature on leader accountability since the LAI was first published, particularly in the ways the three scales have been used in research, reviews the data collection and factor analyses involved in creating the new Leader Accountability Scale (LAS), and discusses the implications of the new scale's usefulness in leadership research and organizational practice. Having such a tool creates the possibility of increased use and usefulness as organizational leaders and researchers continue to address a significant leadership issue.

LITERATURE REVIEW: USE OF THE LAI IN SUBSEQUENT RESEARCH

This study is a response to a call from Frederick et al. (2017), who examined the three factors of leader accountability – acceptance of responsibility, openness, and answerability – as potential antecedents to employees' perception of their leaders' authentic leadership.

Responding to the call from Gardner et al. (2011) for stronger theory building, specifically in empirical studies regarding potential causal relationship with authentic leadership, Frederick et al. investigated the possible predictive role of accountability (responsibility, openness, and answerability) to authentic leadership, noting that the constructs share many common terms and concepts. A convenience sample of employees from six faith-based higher education institutions was asked to complete a questionnaire consisting of the Authentic Leadership Questionnaire (ALQ; Avolio et al., 2008) and the Leader Accountability Index (Wood and Winston, 2007). After eliminating data from employees who had less than a year of tenure due to anomalies in the data, Frederick et al. performed a multiple regression analysis on the 265 remaining surveys to predict variance on perception of authentic leadership associated with the accountability elements. Their analysis revealed that openness accounted for 80% of the variance in explaining authentic leadership. The other two factors – acceptance of responsibility and answerability – contributed 1% of the variance each. Their data also noted that authentic leadership has a high level of correlation with each of the three accountability measures – responsibility (r=.89), openness (r=.89), and answerability (r=.89). The results indicated that responsibility, openness, and answerability do indeed predict the perceived level of authentic leadership in the context of Christian higher education, with 82% of the variance in authentic leadership being predicted by leader accountability.

Frederick et al. (2017) also found that respondents with less than one year with the leader did not rate the authentic leadership or accountability of their leader consistently with followers with longer tenure. Moreover, as the leader's tenure increases, up to 10 years, respondents tend to rate authentic leadership, responsibility, openness, and answerability lower. At the 10-12-year mark, ratings increase. Respondents rated senior and executive leaders significantly higher in authentic leadership; this calls for more research. Perhaps most revealing for this study's purposes, the almost nonexistent effects of two of the three scales, combined with a near-identical correlation with authentic leadership, calls further investigation into the relationship among the three variables. They conclude with a call for further analysis of the data to reflect leader accountability with one scale rather than seeing leader accountability as a latent variable with three distinct observable variables.

Other researchers have used the LAI scales since their publication. A search for citations on Google Scholar revealed 72 instances in which the LAI has been cited in the literature. Many of those, as is typical, are in passing, but several addressed the operative definition of leader accountability (Wood & Winston, 2005) and the LAI scales (Wood & Winston, 2007), and some used them in their own research. The results demonstrated a degree of usefulness in the three-scale design, along with some curious editorial license in some cases. This section will review the experiences and observations that different researchers have described with the three scales of the LAI and the outcomes of their research. It will conclude with a consideration of whether the call from Frederick et al. (2017) for consideration of a single scale is called for and why.

Chen (2011) listed accountability, as defined by Wood and Winston (2005), as one of the four core components of corporate social responsibility. The other components were transparency, competitiveness, and responsibility. Olkers (2013), in developing an instrument to measure psychological ownership, also included accountability as defined by Wood and Winston in her original model. Factor analysis of the pilot test, however, did not retain accountability in the final instrument.

Thompson (2013) conducted a quantitative comparative study of organizational culture and leader accountability within public and private organizations. Citing both the definition of leader accountability (Wood & Winston, 2005) and the descriptions of the three factors that make up the LAI (Wood & Winston, 2007), she strangely asserted that the search for a data collection survey for leadership accountability was unsuccessful, and one had to be developed.

This was not the case for Saddiq et al. (2013), who recognized the LAI as a ready instrument for research. In a proposal at the International Conference on Management, Leadership, & Governance, Saddiq et al. called attention to the lack of research on the relationship between leader accountability and authentic leadership, particularly in the British non-profit sector. They hypothesized that the four components of authentic leadership – self-awareness, internalized moral perspective, balanced processing, and relational transparency – acting as independent variables, have a positively significant relationship with each of the components of leader accountability – acceptance of responsibility, openness, and answerability – acting as dependent variables. They further proposed adopting the ALQ – Self and Rater (Gardner et al., 2011) and the LAI (Wood & Winston, 2007) to include both a Self and Rater scale in conducting their research. The analysis would conclude Multiple Linear Regression and Multivariate Analysis of Variance (MANOVA). It is unclear, however, whether this research was ever actually completed.

Meanwhile, in the United States, Ndlovu (2013) conducted a quantitative, non-experimental, correlational study of 43 nursing leaders to examine the relationship between perceived effectiveness of the balanced scorecard (BSC) and nursing leaders' demonstration of accountability. She incorrectly asserted that Wood and Winston (2005) do not see a distinction between accountability and responsibility while others do. (Wood and Winston maintain that *acceptance* of responsibility and external responsibility are two different constructs.) Ndlovu nevertheless adopted the three scales of the LAI (Wood & Winston, 2007) as one of the data-collection instruments, along with the BSC Organizational Scale (Blackmon, 2008). Rather than the 10-point scoring per item in the original design, Ndlovu used a 7-point Likert scale, with the lowest value of 0 for "strongly disagree" and a 6 for "strongly agree." This scoring is in alignment with the scoring in the BSC Organizational Effectiveness Scale. The research indicated there is no correlation between demographic variables of nurse leaders and accountability. However, the research demonstrated a significant positive relationship between the acceptance of responsibility and all BSC effectiveness variables except employee learning and growth, which also demonstrated a positive association that approached significance. The openness scale showed positive correlations between the mission achieve, customer perspective, and financial perspective variables in the BSC effectiveness scale, with no significant relationship between openness and the internal processes variable and between openness and employee learning and growth variable. A similar pattern was shown with correlation between answerability and the mission achievement, customer perspective, and financial perspective variables and no significant correlation between answerability and internal process and employee learning variables.

Bodenmiller (2015) investigated potential relationships between employee and volunteer perceptions of leadership style and leader accountability in three Louisiana-based non-profit organizations. Using a cross-sectional survey that combined the three LAI measures as the dependent variables and the nine factors of the Full Range Leadership Measure (Bass & Avolio, 1993) as the independent variables, he performed a multivariate linear regression analysis to measure the strength of the relationships between the variables based on 65 responses to his survey. He found no statistically significant relationship between the responsibility scale results and any of the nine types of leadership. He did discover a significant positive relationship between the openness scale results and idealized behaviors and individual consideration, suggesting further consideration of the influence of transformational leadership on perceptions of leader accountability. At the same time, Bodenmiller found a statistically significant negative relationship between the results of the openness scale and the management-by-exception (active) approach to leadership. Moreover, Bodenmiller found a statistically significant positive relationship between answerability and the individual consideration approach to leadership; this was the only positive relationship between answerability and any of the nine independent variables.

Bodenmiller (2015) summarized that two of the five transformational leadership qualities – idealized behaviors and individual consideration – were associated with at least one of the three accountability measures. Individual consideration was found to have a significant positive relationship with both the openness and answerability scales. While it is difficult to argue from silence, the lack of any positive relationship with the acceptance of responsibility scale and any of the nine factors of leadership calls for further study. Nevertheless, Bodenmiler's findings support previous research that demonstrated transformational leadership's effectiveness in improving organizational accountability (cf. Geer, Maher, & Cole, 2008). The negative relationship between management-by-exception (active) – a transactional leadership factor – and the accountability domain of openness points out the difference between a leader who quickly implements corrective action in follower behaviors when errors are detected and one who allows for self-monitoring and correction. Bodenmiller concludes that "transformational leadership might be the only style that stimulates accountability, and only through application of idealized behaviors and individual consideration to demonstrate openness, and through individual consideration to demonstrate answerability" (p. 167).

Wang (2016) created a new leader accountability scale because she maintained that the current understanding of studies (including the LAI) built on Tetlock's (1992) social contingency model of accountability to be incomplete. Noting Wood and Winston's (2005) definition of leader accountability as "willingness to accept responsibility" as distinct from being held responsible by an external set of expectations, she maintains that the literature still mostly focuses on external expectations. Wang adds:

Wood and Winston (2007) developed their scale of leader accountability with three dimensions: (1) responsibility (e.g., sense of obligations and avoid making excuses), (2) openness (e.g., open to communication), and (3) answerability (e.g., answer questions from others). They mixed acceptance of responsibility with obligations and external expectations and did not distinguish how acceptance of responsibility is different from external expectations... In a nutshell, researchers still largely ignore the extent to which people accept and take ownership of responsibility (i.e., "the buck stops here"), as well as associated rewards or disciplinary actions in their discussion of external expectations. As such, my definition of accountability emphasizes a leader's ownership of good or poor performance and acceptance of associated rewards or disciplinary actions (pp. 10-11).

Teh et al. (2017) identified and interpreted leader accountability as a dimension of servant leadership, applying it to educational leadership and management. While much of the research on accountability in that context has to do with outcome accountability or task performance, they add that accountability "accentuates the congruence of 'words' and 'deeds' of the leader in order to build trust in interpersonal relationship" (v. 51). Citing Wood and Winston's (2005) definition of leader accountability and description as evidenced in the LAI (Wood & Winston, 2007), they conclude that "servant leader is tantamount to accountable leader" (v. 51).

Research published in 2018 focused on leader accountability in school counseling and nursing. Sink (2018) built his call for accountability leadership in school counseling on the definition of leader accountability (Wood & Winston, 2005). He notes that leaders who value accountability have a high level of personal ownership in forming, maintaining, and answering for organizational commitments. They also assume ownership beyond past activities, situations, and outcomes, also embracing ownership of future outcomes. Effective leaders help create a shared organizational vision; they create an environment that motivates all colleagues to contribute to the tasks at hand.

Meanwhile, Drach-Zahavy et al. (2018) created an alternative scale to the LAI to measure accountability in nursing, citing problems with the LAI. They defined accountability using similar language to the LAI as comprising acceptance of responsibility, *transparency*, and answerability. In evaluating the LAI for purposes of their research, they made a distinction between transparency and openness – that openness is not part of the definition of transparency. They also note the lack of a survey (including the LAI) that produces a factor analysis delineating three separate sub-constructs.

Eliya and Bibu (2019) adopted Wood and Winston's (2007) definition and three dimensions of accountability in their exploration of the relationship between accountability and a climate of service in

Israeli Public organizations. Determining that the number of items in the LAI was too great, they reduced the number of items in each scale from 10 to 5. . Following Wood and Winston's factor analysis, they used the five items in each scale with the highest factor load. They also changed the scoring, using a Likert scale ranging from 1 to 5, with the lowest polar answer being "completely disagree" and the highest (5) meaning "completely agree." Eliya and Bibu found a positive correlation between employees' accountability for their actions and a service climate of the public organization, thus increasing citizen confidence in the respective public institutions and creating public system fairness.

Summary of the Literature and Recommendations

The three scales to measure leader accountability that comprise the LAI have demonstrated some usefulness in leadership research. Leader accountability has demonstrated a significant correlation with most of the variables in the Balanced Scorecard Organizational Effectiveness Scale, though not with all of them (Ndlovu, 2013). Moreover, two of the five factors of transformational leadership as measured by the Full Range Leadership Measure (Bass & Avolio (1993) – idealized behavior and individual consideration - demonstrated a significantly positive correlation to the openness scale, while the answerability scale had a significantly positive correlation to individualized consideration (Bodenmiller, 2015). The management-by-exception (active) factor associated with transactional leadership revealed a negative correlation with the openness scale (Bodenmiller). Authentic leadership has a high degree of correlation with leader accountability (Frederick et al., 2017). Finally, employees' who demonstrate accountability for their actions are perceived to model a service climate in public organizations (Eliya and Bibu, 2019).

Despite some promising examples of useful research results, however, several issues have arisen that may call for consideration of a more effective instrument. The most glaring of these is Frederick et al.'s (2017) note of a near-nonexistent effect of two of the three scales, combined with a statistically identical correlation of all three of the scales to authentic leadership. The call for further analysis begs the question whether one scale measuring leader accountability can be a more useful tool for measuring and researching leader accountability against the larger context of leadership and organizational research.

Another issue demonstrated in the literature is a lack of precision regarding the meaning of constructs, including accountability, leader accountability, openness, transparency, responsibility, and acceptance of responsibility. At times researchers appear to nitpick distinctions between terms that could be interchangeable, such as openness and transparency (cf. Drach-Zahavy et al., 2018). At other times researchers seem to use terms interchangeably and perhaps use the LAI in ways it was not intended, nor validated for use. Wood and Winston (2005) clearly stated that accountability and responsibility are two separate constructs. Leaders can be *held* responsible by external or internal authorities for the outcomes of their decisions or actions, but that does not make them accountable. Leader accountability is a choice or mindset in which the leader *willingly accepts* the responsibilities inherent in the leadership role. Unfortunately, Wang (2016) either completely missed that fact, or the responsibility scale needs more precise language. Perhaps the desire to simplify terminology by naming the first scale the "Responsibility Scale" may have created more confusion than clarity. In addition, the LAI was intended to demonstrate whether someone in a leadership role (formal or informal), who may well exhibit accountability to his or her supervisors or the organization as a whole, is also willing to hold him/herself as accountable to employees, volunteers, or other manifestations of followership. The LAI was designed to measure *leader* accountability *as a leader*, not organizational accountability as a follower. The fact that those who use either the definition of leader accountability (Wood & Winston, 2005) or the scales of the LAI (Wood & Winston, 2007) in ways that do not align with the precision or lack thereof originally intended suggests a need to review the instrument(s) for clarity and accuracy.

Length of the scale(s) is another issue. The LAI is comprised of three scales of 10 items each. The selection of 10 items was somewhat arbitrary (Wood & Winston, 2007), and in one case (Eliya and Bibu, 2019) the three scales were re-created, using the factor analysis from Wood and Winston's original research, to exhibit five items each instead of 10. Acknowledging the potential for test fatigue, particularly in more complex research projects, if a construct measured with 30 items can be measured with the same precision using 10 (or even less), reducing the length and number of the scale(s) is worth considering. DeVellis (2016), in his call to optimize scale length, notes the tension between placing a burden on respondents when the scale is too long and losing reliability when the scale is too short. Some consideration on optimal length is worthy of a review.

Another reconsideration may be the means by which items are measured and data recorded. On at least two separate occasions, the 10-point range scale was replaced by either a five-point (Eliya and Bibu, 2019) or a seven-point (Ndlovu, 2013) Likert scale. While Likert scales are often preferred for ease of use and near-universal popularity in gauging respondents' attitudes or behaviors, they lack precision in gauging the difference between the points. That said, the ubiquity and popularity of Likert scales for use in questionnaires, combined with the audacity of a researcher changing the data collection design of the instruments, calls for a fair reconsideration, which will follow.

In conclusion, the research results and factors noted above called for a new examination of the Leader Accountability Index, first to determine whether a single scale could be created out of the three subscales, then to determine which items and how many give researchers the best opportunity for a valid single-factor scale. The sections that follow will loosely revisit Devellis's (2016) process for scale development. The author will (a) review the definition of the construct, (b) review the item pool comprised of the 30 items currently in the LAI, (c) reconsider the format for measuring the items, (d) analyze a development sample, (e) conduct a factor analysis to determine, if possible, what would comprise a resultant new Leader Accountability Scale (LAS), and (f) optimize for length.

REVIEWING THE DEFINITION OF THE CONSTRUCT

The strength of any psychometric measurement is its *validity* – that is, whether it actually measures what it claims to measure (DeVellis, 2016). This starts with a clear, robust definition of the construct – something DeVellis (2003) calls "deceptively obvious" (p. 60). Drawing from accountability theory and servant and transformational leadership theory, Wood and Winston (2005) proposed a definition of leader accountability that limits the construct to the *behavior* and *communication* of leaders *as leaders*. This distinguishes leader accountability from other related constructs such as trust, responsibility, obligation, or other accountability forms. Leader accountability is the leader's willing acceptance of the responsibilities inherent in the leadership position to serve the well-being of the organization, the leader's implicit or explicit expectation that he/she will be publicly linked to his/her actions, words, or reactions, and the leader's expectation that he/she may be called on to explain his or her beliefs, decisions, commitments, or actions to constituents. The definition emphasizes that such willingness and expectations inherent in leader accountability manifest in the leader's observable behavior and communication, not in their intentions. As such, leader accountability is observable by constituents and the leader alike; thus, the scale should be usable by both constituents and self-raters.

While calls for accountability in praxis and new definitions of the construct in research continue to emerge, as noted above, nothing has changed the fundamental core construct that this research intends to measure. Leaders demonstrate accountability when they accept responsibility for their leadership role in the ways they act and communicate with employees or other constituents. When they take ownership for being publicly linked to their actions, words, or reactions (demonstrate openness or transparency) and they willingly explain their choices, actions, or commitments to constituents, they are, by definition, accountable leaders. The following section will examine the pool of items from which a new single scale may be designed.

REVIEWING THE ITEM POOL – THE THREE CURRENT SCALES

In their original research, Wood and Winston (2007) generated item pools of 21 items for the responsibility scale, 26 items for the openness scale, and 19 items for the answerability scale. These items were the results of a rigorous review of the literature, mostly from accountability theory as it relates to leadership. After having the items reviewed by a panel of experts, the authors reduced the pools to 18 items for the responsibility scale, 25 items for the openness scale, and 16 items for the answerability scale. A factor analysis of the 148 respondents for each of the scales revealed a remarkably high coefficient alpha score, suggesting a very high degree of reliability for each scale. Following another analysis of the items for face validity, item uniqueness, and scale optimization, the authors settled on 10 items for each scale. The resultant items for the Responsibility, Openness, and Answerability Scales combined are as follows:

The leader:

R1. Demonstrates a sense of obligation to constituents when making decisions.
R2. Accepts responsibility for his/her actions within the organization.
R3. Clearly defines for constituents where his/her responsibilities end and theirs begin.
R4. Provides constituents with safe ways to address grievances against him/her.
R5. Avoids making excuses for mistakes.
R6. Avoids blaming others for mistakes.
R7. Is willing to face the truth, even when it does not fit his/her personal preferences.
R8. Accepts responsibility for the future direction and accomplishments of the group.
R9. Accepts ownership for the results of his/her decisions and actions.
R10. Looks to himself/herself first when the group's results are disappointing.
O1. Behaves consistently from one person to the next.
O2. Demonstrates consistency in public and private behavior.
O3. Identifies personal actions – popular or not – as his/her own.
O4. Openly listens when people offer perspectives that are different from his/her own.
O5. Avoids isolating from constituents in performing his or her duties.
O6. Openly explains his/her decisions.
O7. Openly declares his/her values.
O8. Is a role model.
O9. Interacts openly and candidly with constituents.
O10. Keeps records that are accessible to constituents.
A1. Apologizes to constituents for his/her mistakes.

A2. Explains the reasons for his/her decisions.

A3. Answers questions from constituents.

A4. Provides explanations for the performance shortfalls without making excuses.

A5. Informs constituents of the process by which he/she arrives at decisions.

A6. Explains to constituents why suggested action was not taken.

A7. Provides regular progress reports about personal commitments he/she has made to constituents.

A8. Welcomes constructive feedback of his/her actions.

A9. Openly admits his/her mistakes to constituents.

A10. Takes quick action to deal with the consequences of a mistake.

REVIEWING THE FORMAT FOR MEASUREMENT

One of the more surprising observations of researchers who have used the LAI to this point has been the decision of some to arbitrarily change the scoring format to a Likert Scale (cf. Ndlovu, 2013; Eliya and Bibu, 2019). In both cases, the scale's redesign was simply reported, with no justification or consideration of the advantages or disadvantages of such a change. This is not intended to be a full review of the advantages and disadvantages of Likert scales for measuring attitudes and observations. Nevertheless, the ubiquitous use of that type of measurement and the apparent bias of some calls for a brief reexamination of how items should be scored to measure leader accountability observations.

Chimi and Russell (2009) addressed three specific limitations of Likert items:

1. They provide coarsely granular, qualitative responses when a finer degree of granularity is not only possible within each Likert item category but is likely.
2. The qualitative data generated by the scales limits quantitative analysis; summary statistics can only be inferred, and then only if there is some numeric basis for each response category. The assumption that each response category is interval in nature is flawed.
3. Neutral responses provide ambiguous, insufficient information. As most Likert scales offer a middle response, they do not account for *why* the middle response is chosen.

Chimi and Russell (2009) propose a quasi-continuous quantitative variable of 0-100, using computer technology, to record a subject's relative response in light of two poles. Zorzi et al. (2002) had previously suggested that numerical response choices, arrayed in sequence, correspond to fundamental neural processes. For this reason, while an accountability scale may not need to be dependent on too fine a granularity, evidence still indicates that a quantitative instrument should be scored by quantitative means. Therefore, in piloting the revised scale we held firm on choosing between two polar responses on a zero-10 range, focusing on observable leader behavior – zero meaning the leader *never* demonstrates that type of behavior and 10 indicating the leader *always* demonstrates it.

DEVELOPMENT SAMPLE TEST AND RESULTS

The sample for this analysis was collected by Frederick (2015) on October 20-29, 2014. It involved 324 complete responses to a survey that included the LAI and the Authentic Leadership Questionnaire, along with demographic questions. This provided an appropriate number of responses to validate the instrument as DeVellis (2016) called for a minimum of five respondents per item in the pool; a minimum number for this analysis would be 150. Respondents were among the employees of six faith-based, private, not-for-profit organizations that require employees to be committed to the Christian faith. Participant ages ranged from 18 to over 65, with the largest group in the 46-55 age group. The sample was two-thirds (67%) female, while the leaders being rated were nearly two-thirds (61%) male. Respondents were comparatively highly educated, with 93% having at least a bachelor's degree. The position most commonly rated was a middle manager, which in a university setting included chairpersons and deans. The most frequent tenure reported by the respondents was 1 to 3 years. Table 1 reflects Frederick's collected demographic data.

Table 1. Demographic characteristics of participants

Variable	Percentage	Frequency
Age		
18 to 25	7.4%	24
26-35	20.1%	65
36-45	18.8%	61
46-55	26.2%	85
56-65	20.7%	67
More than 65	6.8%	22
Gender of the Respondent		
Male	32.7%	106
Female	67.3%	218
Gender of the Leader		
Male	61.4%	199
Female	38.6%	125
Education		
High school diploma or equivalency	0.9%	3
Some college	2.8%	9
Associates degree	2.8%	9
Bachelor degree	28.1%	91
Master degree	33.0%	107

continues in next column

Table 1. Continued

Variable	Percentage	Frequency
Doctoral degree	28.7%	93
Postgraduate degree	3.7%	12
Position of the Leader		
Front-line manager/ supervisor	24.1%	78
Middle manager (including dean, chairperson)	39.2%	127
Senior manager (including vice president, provost)	20.4%	66
Executive (including president)	11.4%	37
Other (please specify)	4.9%	16
Respondent's Length of Tenure With the Leader		
Less than 1 year	18.2%	59
1 to 3 years	38.0%	123
4 to 6 years	20.7%	67
7 to 9 years	13.0%	42
10 to 12 years	3.7%	12
13 to 15 years	3.1%	10
More than 15 years	3.4%	11

A Principal Component factor analysis on all 30 items in the present version of the LAI showed three factors in all, with more than 95% loading to one factor. Factors 2 and 3 were subsequently eliminated. The researcher then narrowed the number of items to those with Cronbach Alpha scores at or above .90. This resulted in 11 items. The researcher then assigned an optimized length of the scale at 10 items, by removing the lowest-loading item. Given a 0-10 possible score per item, this provides a potential Leader

Accountability score of 0-100. The subsequent 10-item scale reflected a Cronbach Alpha of .98, reflecting an extremely high level of reliability.

Four of the items came from the Responsibility Scale. They are as follows:

R5. The leader avoids making excuses for mistakes.
R7. The leader is willing to face the truth, even when it does not fit his/her personal preferences.
R9. The leader accepts ownership for the results of his/her decisions and actions.
R10. The leader looks to himself/herself first when the group's results are disappointing.

Two of the items came from the Openness Scale. They are as follows:

O8. The leader Is a role model.
O9. The leader interacts openly and candidly with constituents.

Four of the items came from the Answerability Scale. They are as follows:

A1. The leader apologizes to constituents for his/her mistakes.
A4. The leader provides explanations for performance shortfalls without making excuses.
A8. The leader welcomes constructive feedback of his/her actions.
A9. The leader openly admits his/her mistakes to constituents.

Table 2 shows the component matrix for the 10 items, sorted by factor load.

Table 2. Component matrix for single-factor accountability scale

Item	Component 1
The leader: - Openly admits his/her mistakes to constituents.	.955
The leader: - Provides explanations for the performance shortfalls without making excuses.	.942
The leader: - Apologizes to constituents for his/her mistakes.	.934
The leader: - Welcomes constructive feedback of his/her actions.	.931
The leader: - Is willing to face the truth, even when it does not fit his/her personal preferences.	..928
The leader: - Accepts ownership for the results of his/her decisions and actions.	..924
The leader: - Is a role model.	.916
The leader: - Interacts openly and candidly with constituents.	.912
The leader: - Avoids making excuses for mistakes.	.911
The leader: - Looks to himself/herself first when the group's results are disappointing.	..908

Following the factor analysis, the authors conducted a reliability analysis on each item, using Chronbach's coefficient alpha. They simultaneously tested each item with an "alpha if deleted" score to determine if the scale's reliability would increase if one or more items were deleted. The coefficient alpha score for the accountability scale was remarkably high, suggesting, with a coefficient alpha score of .98, that the scale has a very high degree of reliability. Table 3 reflects the results of the reliability analysis.

Table 3. 10-item reliability analysis using coefficient alpha and "alpha if deleted

Item	Scale Mean if Item Deleted	Scale Variance if Item Deleted	Corrected Item-Total Correlation	Cronbach's Alpha if Item Deleted
The leader: - Avoids making excuses for mistakes.	67.0	582.55	.89	.98
The leader: - Is willing to face the truth, even when it does not fit his/her personal preferences.	66.9	583.86	.91	.98
The leader: - Accepts ownership for the results of his/her decisions and actions.	66.4	592.36	.91	.98
The leader: - Looks to himself/herself first when the group's results are disappointing.	67.3	581.56	.89	.98
The leader: - Is a role model.	66.7	583.67	.89	.98
The leader: - Interacts openly and candidly with constituents.	66.7	591.81	.89	.98
The leader: - Apologizes to constituents for his/her mistakes.	67.0	574.57	.92	.98
The leader: - Provides explanations for the performance shortfalls without making excuses.	67.0	581.97	.93	.978
The leader: - Welcomes constructive feedback of his/her actions.	67.4	564.07	.91	.98
The leader: - Openly admits his/her mistakes to constituents.	67.3	561.97	.94	.98

OPTIMIZING THE SCALE LENGTH

With ten items all with a factor load greater than .90, the question arises what the optimal scale length should be. DeVellis (2003) notes the tension between ease of response for respondents and the need for reliability. The ideal scale length helps avoid test fatigue, but not at the expense of accurately measuring what the scale proposes to measure. DeVellis advises that shortening a scale length for the sake of brevity should be confined to situations in which the researcher has "reliability to spare" (p. 97).

In the case of the scale in question, the researcher is hard-pressed to identify an advantage in reliability that the scale would gain using ten items that would not already be present using five. For this purpose, the author will retain top five items sorted by factor load in the LAS. They are as follows:

In his or her interactions with employees, constituents, or followers, the leader:

1. Openly admits his/her mistakes.
2. Provides explanations for the performance shortfalls without making excuses.
3. Apologizes for his/her mistakes.
4. Welcomes constructive feedback of his/her actions.
5. Is willing to face the truth, even when it does not fit his/her personal preferences.

SUMMARY OF RESULTS

This study was designed to test whether items comprising three scales to measure leader accountability (Wood & Winston, 2007) could be merged into a single-factor scale. Also considered was a review of the construct's definition and a reconsideration of how the items are scored. After a thoughtful review, the scoring method remained unchanged as a range of scores per item from zero to 10, with 10 meaning "always" and 0 meaning "never." A component matrix from the data and the elimination of Cronbach alpha scores below .90 yielded eleven items. These were optimized to provide a tentative Leader Accountability Scale with 10 items, with a Cronbach alpha score of .98. Because of the unusually high consistency of alpha scores, the scale was optimized further to contain five items, with a potential "accountability score" ranging from 0 to 50.

While the sample size was more than adequate, the results are limited to employees of six Christian universities, all of whom are required to identify as being committed to the Christian faith as a term of employment. All respondents were English-speaking people at least 18 years of age, most all Caucasian, and far more educated than the general population. Further studies using the new instrument among a broader range of respondents may differ in reliability. It is also vitally important to note that the Leader Accountability Scale is limited strictly to observable behavior among leaders (even allowing for the possibility of a self-rated scale of leader behavior). Moreover, the scale focuses on leaders' behavior *as leaders* – toward those who answer to their authority or follow their influence. Other potential forms of accountability a leader may demonstrate should be examined using other instruments.

DISCUSSION

Accountability remains a term with varied definitions, depending on the nature and role of the person called to account and the focus of the accountability (e.g., toward the organization, toward peers, toward self, toward the public, or, in the case of leaders, toward followers). Accountability also remains the go-to panacea in the wake of leadership scandals, clergy sexual misconduct, political and public service issues, ethical violations in for-profit and non-profit organizations, or any other type of violation of leader trust. As is its predecessor, the Leader Accountability Scale is built on the conviction that accountability is *always* important for leaders to display to constituents, whether the organization is in crisis or not. Use of the scale provides the opportunity for potential leaders to demonstrate a readiness to be promoted or an opportunity to be coached to develop certain key behaviors that may be missing. As demonstrated by leaders or leaders in the making, proactive accountability is much more valuable to an organization, even if it is in the process of development, than reactive accountability following a breach of trust. The scale can be a useful tool in leadership development, particularly in training prospective leaders and managers to be accountable leaders. And research to this point has demonstrated early indications that leader accountability correlates with authentic leadership, some aspects of transformational leadership, and fostering perceptions of a climate of service in public institutions.

This scale has potential for use in a variety of ways, including leader coaching and development, 360 feedback, and organizational decision making. Leaders who score high in leader accountability at one level of the organization's hierarchy have a greater chance of demonstrating that quality in a higher level of responsibility; thus the LAS offers organizations an excellent resource for evaluating potential candidates for hiring or promotion.

For further research, the new single-factor scale should be re-tested for correlation to authentic leadership and transformational leadership. Also, an exploration of the relationship between leader accountability and servant leadership is warranted, particularly since accountability is presented as a servant leadership characteristic (cf. Teh et al., 2017). In addition, the new scale makes it possible to examine the relationship between leader accountability and trust, especially if that trust has been lost due to a breach by the leader. Accountability has been routinely prescribed, but does it actually make a difference in restoring lost credibility and trust? The literature here remains virtually silent. In addition, in light of the specific focus of the LAS on leader behavior toward constituents, other potential scales could be developed to gauge the leader's demonstration of accountability in other respects. Finally, the impact of leader accountability on employee perceptions such as satisfaction, team performance, corporate profitability, and general leader effectiveness is even riper for study with a simplified tool.

CONCLUSION

The results of this study are a reminder that leaders can and should be accountable to their followers, and that such accountability can be measured. Leader accountability is not just a punitive or fix-it approach to leadership; it should be part of the very fabric of a leader's character. Such an approach gives hope to a generation long-ago jaded by story after story of disappointment and embarrassment brought on by a leader who remains insistent that the rules do not apply to him or her.

REFERENCES

Ahrens, T., & Ferry, L. (2015). Newcastle City Council and the grassroots: Accountability and budgeting under austerity. *Accounting, Auditing & Accountability Journal, 28*(6), 909–933. doi:10.1108/AAAJ-03-2014-1658

Andersson, J., & Wikström, E. (2014). Constructing accountability in inter-organisational collaboration. *Journal of Health Organization and Management, 28*(5), 619–634. doi:10.1108/JHOM-10-2013-0220 PMID:25735421

Bass, B. M., & Avolio, B. J. (1993). Transformational leadership and organizational culture. *Public Administration Quarterly, 17*(1), 112–121.

Blackmon, V. Y. (2008). *Strategic planning and organizational performance: An investigation using the balanced scorecard in non-profit organizations* (Publication No. 3311386) [Doctoral Dissertation, Capella University]. ProQuest Dissertations and Theses Global.

Bodenmiller, J. J. (2015). *A Quantitative relational analysis of leadership style and leader accountability in non-profit organizations* (Publication No. 3714860) [Doctoral Dissertation, University of Phoenix]. Proquest Dissertations and Theses Global.

Byrne, T. P. (2014). Ethical dilemmas in a California city: Lessons in leadership transparency and accountability. *California Journal of Politics and Policy, 6*(4), 577–598. doi:10.5070/P26K5N

Chapman, K. (2019). Accountability-based leadership. *Plumbing & Mechanical, 4*(37), 22–26.

Chen, C. H. (2011). The major components of corporate social responsibility. *Journal of Global Responsibility, 2*(1), 85–99. doi:10.1108/20412561111128546

Chimi, C. J., & Russell, D. L. (2009, November). *The Likert scale: A proposal for improvement using quasi-continuous variables.* Paper presented at the ISECON 2009, Washington, DC.

DeVellis, R. F. (2003). *Scale development: Theory and applications* (2nd ed.). Sage.

DeVellis, R. F. (2016). Scale development: Theory and applications (4th ed.). Thousand Oaks, CA: Sage.

Drach-Zahavy, A., Leonenko, M., & Sruloviet, E. (2018). Towards a measure of accountability in nursing: A three-stage validation study. *Journal of Advanced Nursing, 74*(10), 2450–2464. doi:10.1111/jan.13735 PMID:29869349

Eliya, Y., & Bibu, N. (2019). The relation between accountability and the climate of service in Israeli Public organisations. *Review of International Comparative Management, 1*(20), 31–51. doi:10.24818/RMCI.2019.1.30

Frederick, H., West, G., Winston, B. E., & Wood, J. A. (2016). The Effects of Accountability Variables on Authentic Leadership. *Journal of Research on Christian Education, 25*(3). Advance online publication. doi:10.1080/10656219.2016.1237907

Frederick, H. R. (2015). *The Effect of the Accountability Variables of Responsibility, Openness, and Answerability on Authentic Leadership* (Publication No. 3671894) [Doctoral Dissertation, Regent University], ProQuest Dissertations Publishing.

Gardner, W. L., Cogliser, C. C., Davis, K. M., & Dickens, M. P. (2011). Authentic leadership: A review of the literature and research agenda. *The Leadership Quarterly, 22*(6), 1120–1145. doi:10.1016/j.leaqua.2011.09.007

Geer, B. W., Maher, J. K., & Cole, M. T. (2008). Managing non-profit organizations: The importance of transformational leadership and commitment to operating standards for non-profit accountability. *Public Performance & Management Review, 32*(1), 51–75. doi:10.2753/PMR1530-9576320103

Ghela, K. G., & Bhanderi, R. (2016). Leadership practices in NGOs: Issues of accountability. *Sankalpa: Journal of Management & Research, 6*(1), 1–8.

Knapp, M. S., & Feldman, S. B. (2012). Managing the intersection of internal and external accountability. *Journal of Educational Administration, 50*(5), 666–694. doi:10.1108/09578231211249862

Lee, M., Walker, A., & Chui, Y. L. (2012). Contrasting effects of instructional leadership practices on student learning in a high accountability context. *Journal of Educational Administration, 50*(5), 586–611. doi:10.1108/09578231211249835

Lewis, A. E., & Steinhoff, J. C. (2019). The next frontier in government accountability: Impact reporting. *Journal of Government Financial Management, 68*(1), 22–27.

Molinaro, V. (2017). *The leadership accountability gap: A global study exploring the real state of leadership in organizations today.* Lee Hecht Harrison.

Molinaro, V. (2018). *The leadership contract: The fine print to becoming an accountable leader* (3rd ed.). John Wiley & Sons.

Ndlovu, C. (2013). *Examining relationships between balanced scorecard effectiveness and nursing leaders' accountability* (Publication No. 3599543) [Doctoral Dissertation, Capella University]. ProQuest Dissertations and Theses Global.

Olckers, C. (2013). Psychological ownership: Development of an instrument. *SA Journal of Industrial Psychology, 39*(2), 1–13. doi:10.4102ajip.v39i2.1105

Senander, A. (2017). Beyond scandal: Creating a culture of accountability in the Catholic church. *Journal of Business Ethics, 146*(4), 859–867. doi:10.100710551-016-3217-4

Siddiq, K., Meyer, E., & Ashleigh, M. (2013, February). What is the impact of authentic leadership on leader accountability in a non-profit context? In *International Conference on Management, Leadership & Governance*. Academic Conferences International Limited.

Silliman, D. (2021, January 5). *Inside RZIM, staff push leaders to take responsibility for scandal.* Retrieved February 16, 2021, from https://www.christianitytoday.com/news/2021/january/rzim-ravi-zacharias-turmoil-spa-allegations-investigation.html

Sink, C. A. (2018). School Counselors as Accountability Leaders: Another Call for Action. *Professional School Counseling, 13*(2), 68–74. Advance online publication. doi:10.5330/PSC.n.2010-13.68

Steinbauer, R., Renn, R. W., Taylor, R. R., & Njoroge, P. K. (2014). Ethical leadership and followers moral judgment: The role of followers perceived accountability and self-leadership. *Journal of Business Ethics, 120*(3), 381–292. doi:10.100710551-013-1662-x

Teh, K. P., Kareem, O. A., & Tai, M. K. (2017). *Identifying and interpreting the servant leadership dimensions for educational leadership and management.* UKM Journal of Management.

Tetlock, P. E. (1992). The impact of accountability on judgment and choice: toward a social contingency model. In M. P. Zanna (Ed.), Advances in Experimental Social Psychology (vol. 25). Harcourt Brace Jovanovich. doi:10.1016/S0065-2601(08)60287-7

Thompson, L. M. (2013). *A quantitative comparative study of organizational culture and leadership accountability within public and private organizations* (Publication No. 3572907) [Doctoral Dissertation, University of Phoenix]. ProQuest Dissertations Publishing.

Walsh, S. L. (2019, October 29). Accountability would help in PG&E fiasco. *Wall Street Journal Online.* Retrieved February 16, 2021, from https://search-proquest-com.ezproxy.regent.edu/abicomplete/publication/publications_105983?accountid=13479

Wang, D. (2016). *The Buck Stops Where? Examining Leader and Collective Accountability in Teams* (Publication No. 10106401) [Doctoral Dissertation, Arizona State University]. ProQuest Dissertations Publishing.

Wood, J. A. Jr, & Winston, B. E. (2005). Toward a new understanding of leader accountability: Defining a critical construct. *Journal of Leadership & Organizational Studies, 3*(11), 84–94. doi:10.1177/107179190501100307

Wood, J. A., & Winston, B. E. (2007). Development of three scales to measure leader accountability. *Leadership and Organization Development Journal, 28*(2), 167–185. doi:10.1108/01437730710726859

Zorzi, M., Priftis, K., & Umilita, C. (2002). Brain damage: Neglect disrupts the mental number line. *Nature, 417*(09), 138–139. doi:10.1038/417138a PMID:12000950

Chapter 11
Leader–Follower Parasocial Interaction Scale

William J. Brown
Regent University, USA

Mihai C. Bocarnea
(iD) https://orcid.org/0000-0002-1889-1177
Regent University, USA

ABSTRACT

In the ubiquitous mediated world in which we live, we daily encounter organizational leaders through mediated communication. New communication technology and the age of the COVID-19 pandemic have made these mediated encounters even more pronounced, leading to more opportunities for parasocial interaction with organizational leaders by various publics. This chapter provides a theoretical model and quantitative measurement for assessing parasocial interaction in the social scientific tradition of middle range analysis. The leader-follower parasocial interaction scale provided here is a useful tool for assessing the persuasive influence of leaders on those who follow them.

INTRODUCTION

The rapid diffusion of new communication technology within organizations and the expanded need for mediated organizational communication brought about by the COVID-19 pandemic has expanded the development of mediated relationships in organizations seeking to effectively serve their customers (Oyeniran, Jayesimi, Ogundele, & Oyeniran, 2020). Leaders of both large corporate entities and of medium-sized businesses have had to develop and maintain interpersonal relationships with their employees, customers, and service providers through computer-mediated communication and internet-based media platforms. Interpersonal communication today with national, organizational, and community leaders is primarily mediated through some form of communication technology. The purpose of this chapter is to provide a theoretical framework for understanding these mediated interactions and a research tool for measuring them.

DOI: 10.4018/978-1-7998-7665-6.ch011

BACKGROUND

Organizational leaders in the 21st century have increasingly shifted their concern and organizational resources to building and maintaining good relationship with their employees, customers, and various publics (Schweitzer& Lyons, 2008; Tjosvold & Wong, 2000). Research on organization-public relationships (OPRs) situated within an interpersonal relationship context has been proliferating (Swart, 2012). One negative Twitter message chain, or errant Facebook post, or unflattering Instagram picture, can send an organization's reputation and stock value into a tailspin. Ledingham and Brunig (1998) describe an organization-public relationship (OPR) as "the state which exists between an organization and its key publics, in which the actions of either can impact the economic, social, cultural, or political well-being of the other." Other organizational scholars have expanded their discussion of OPRs to include the exchange of resources between organizations in order to achieve mutual benefit, leading to the development of a theory of relationship management (Broom, Casey & Ritchey, 1997; El-Kasim & Idid, 2017).

Relationship management theorists are concerned with how organizations strategically interact with their publics (Huang, 2009). The study of communication outputs from organizations is insufficient for understanding interpersonal communication with organizational leaders and building relationships with them, which also should include the measurement of behavioral outcomes (Broom & Dozier, 1990). Relational goals are now a primary concern of organizations seeking to build symmetry with stakeholders (Ledingham & Brunig, 2000) and create loyalty by meeting the needs of their publics (Ledingham, 2003) in a highly mediated environment.

Walther's (1996) hyperpersonal model of computer-mediated communication (CMC) provides a useful theoretical framework to study how CMC may facilitate relational intimacy. Extensions and revisions to the model during the past 20 years have extended its application into the study of online organizational relationships, providing both conceptual and empirical contributions that reveal the important role these relationships have in leader-follower online communication (Walther, 2011). Walther and his colleagues argue that four concurrent routines explain how CMC's support of relationships produces a high degree of desirability and intimacy (Walter, Van Der Heide, Ramirez, Burgoon, & Peña, 2015).

Inadequate understanding of the powerful mediated relationships that organizations are establishing with their publics is a serious threat to the health and success of any organization. Relational management necessitates a proper perspective of how organizational leaders develop relationships with customers, employees, and other stakeholders through mediated forms of communication. Such relationships begin with inducing the involvement of various publics with organizational leaders. We will consider how involvement takes placed in mediated communication contexts and how mediated interaction takes place between organizational leaders and their followers.

INVOLVEMENT WITH LEADERS

Involvement is a fundamental conceptual and measured variable in communication study (Wirth, 2006) that is multidimensional and complex (Salmon, 1986). The concept of *involvement* has a rich history in social science research and is closely related to the theoretical variables of *engagement*, *absorption*, and *presence*. Definitions of involvement in communication study commonly focus on both cognitive and emotional responses to a message, person, or media persona. Broadly defined, involvement is "the degree of psychological response of a person to a mediated message or persona" and "is a dynamic process that incorporates both consuming media and coproducing media through mediated interactions" (Brown, 2015, p. 260).

During the past two decades, there has been an increased interest in psychological and emotional forms of mediated involvement (Nabi & Wirth, 2008). One of the important emotional experiences of engagement with mediated communication is media enjoyment (Tamborini, Bowman, Eden, Grizzard, & Organ, 2010)). Tan (2008) posits emotion at the center of media enjoyment and argues that some of the most important mediated encounters are pleasurable experiences that feature narrative forms of communication. It is no mystery, for example, that the most influential organizational leaders are the best storytellers that engage the imagination of their followers to create their brand (Peterson, 2019).

Study of involvement of followers with leaders in communication research encompasses both individual and collective mediated experiences. These experiences are facilitated by many kinds of mediated contexts; for example, text messaging on mobile phone devices, web blogs, and posting text, pictures, and videos on corporate websites and on social media websites (Stever & Lawson, 2013). Researching the degree of involvement of followers with leaders requires an assessment of these mediated interactions and study of the mediated relationships that such interactions produce.

The ubiquitous presence of new communication technology in organizations has blurred the clear demarcation of knowing an organizational leader through direct face-to-face interaction and knowing that person through indirect mediated encounters. The online communication networks we now can access through mobile phones, tablets, and other mobile technologies provide more opportunities for leaders and followers to create and exchange messages continually (see Vorderer, Hefner, Reinecke, & Klimmt, 2018). Followers of leaders can now read their words, listen to them speak, and see photographs and watch video productions that they post at any time of the day or night, provided they have internet access. Face-to-face interaction is no longer a necessary condition to create strong leader-follower relationships. Savvy media professionals, for example, strategically use online websites (Markel, McCann, & Wasserman, 2015), blogs (Hanukov, 2015; Kanai, 2015), and social media platforms (Click, Lee, & Holladay, 2013; Wright, 2015; Jin & Phua, 2014; Marwick, 2011) to craft their images and communicate to their followers, creating strong attachment bonds (Chia & Poo, 2009).

Involvement Processes

Several important processes of involvement with media personae have emerged during the past many decades of communication research. One of these involvement processes, *parasocial interaction*, has a well-defined theoretical framework developed through extensive research in multiple communication contexts and social science disciplines, including communication science, social psychology, psychology, political science, and sociology. Parasocial interaction is one of several distinct yet closely related forms of involvement along with identification and worship (Brown, 2015). These involvement processes provide a useful theoretical model for studying the influence of leaders on followers. In the following section, we will consider the process of parasocial interaction and its antecedents and consequences.

Parasocial Interaction with Media Personae

Parasocial interaction describes the perceived relational engagement that media consumers have with media personae, both real people and fictional characters, resulting in the development of *parasocial relationships* with them. Parasocial interaction was first observed by Robert Merton during his study of the 1943 radio War Bond Drive led by the nationally renowned singer Kate Smith, who raised an astounding amount of money in a short time. Merton (1946), observing that radio listeners related to Smith as if she was a close personal friend, described the strong emotional and psychological bond that Smith developed with her radio audience as a *pseudo-relationship*.

A decade after Merton's radio study, two psychologists observed the same phenomenon in a television study. They identified the pseudo-relationship that formed between television viewers and television personalities as a *parasocial relationship* that resulted from *parasocial interaction*, which they described as imaginary interaction in the minds of television viewers with people they regularly watched on television, both real and fictional characters (Horton & Wohl, 1956). Horton and Wohl's (1956) seminal research revealed that perceived interpersonal intimacy can be achieved with mediated personalities like television characters, also called *personae*. A *persona* is a social construction of an individual whose identity is manifested as "public performances and projections of individuality" that "we inhabit individually and collectively" (Marshall, Moore & Barbour, 2019, p. 2). Head (2003) describes media personae as hypothetical archetypes who represent real people. *Media personae* are therefore the social constructions that form the identities of real people or fictional characters that we are regularly exposed to through mediated communication.

Other media scholars have documented that very strong relational bonds can form between television viewers and television personalities or *personae* over time (Brown & Cody, 1991; Cohen, 2003; Giles, 2002; Gumpert & Cathcart, 1986; Levy, 1979; Rubin & McHugh, 1987; Rubin, Perse, & Powell, 1985; Shefner-Rogers, Rogers, & Singhal, 1998; Sood & Rogers, 2000). Levy (1979) observed that the *pseudo-relationships* formed from parasocial interaction are based on a false sense of intimacy created during television viewing. Visual forms of mediated communication like television, film, video, and pictures provide a rich media landscape for parasocial interaction and the development of parasocial relationships (Gumpert & Cathcart, 1986).

Leader-Follower Parasocial Interaction

Organizational communication scholars are increasingly turning their attention to exploring parasocial interaction between organizational leaders and their various publics (Labrecque, 2014; Yuksel, & Labrecque, 2016). Understanding the mediated nature of all human relationships provides insight into understanding parasocial interaction and the development of prosocial relationships within organizational contexts. Organizational leaders, especially founders and CEOs, personify the organizations they represent and become the chief spokespersons who communicate to various publics both the organization's vision and their responses to various issues and needs (Park & Berger, 2004). Sustaining strong relationships with various publics is now an important leadership skill since the reputation of an organization is influenced by the tenure of its CEO (Conte, 2018). A successful CEO not only enhances publics' identification with the organization and creates a favorable corporate reputation, but also forges positive relations with various stakeholders that contribute to the company's bottom line (Ranft, Zinko, Ferris, & Buckley, 2006).

Publics now expect corporate leaders to communication authentically through social media and to be transparent about their policies and actions and open to dialogue (Coker, Howie, Syrdal, Vanmeter, & Woodroof, 2017). The image of an organizational leader is extremely important and must be managed carefully through social media (Brandfog, 2013), a primary venue where parasocial interaction takes place and where parasocial relationships are formed.

CEOs' communication via social media networks like Facebook, Twitter and Linkedin (Tsai & Men, 2017; Yue, Thelen, Robinson & Men, 2019) and through web blogs (Vidgen, Sims & Powell, 2013) provide opportunities for leaders to create a persona that is attractive and liked by their organizations' stakeholders. These mediated relationship-building strategies between CEOs and their publics, especially through social media platforms, have been understudied to date. Tsai and Men (2017) note that the potential for social media use by organizational leaders to strengthen organization–public relationships (OPRs) "lies in its power of enabling and encouraging interpersonal communication and interaction" (p. 1850). They also argue that leadership communication through social networking sites can enhance the reputation of organizations and facilitate relationship building with their stakeholders (Men & Tsai, 2015; Verčič & Verčič, 2007).

Antecedents to Leader-Follower Parasocial Interaction

Parasocial interaction studies have explored both the predictors of parasocial interaction (PSI) and their consequences. Consistent exposure over time to a media persona is a primary predictor of PSI, allowing media consumers to "come to believe that they know and understand the media persona" (Derrick, Gabriel & Tippin, 2008, p. 261). Similar to the way in which face-to-face interactions produce friendships, PSI meets the attachment needs of followers by creating parasocial relationships over time and fills their interpersonal relationship desires (Bond, 2016). Therefore, organizational leaders must continually be present and highly visible in the media.

A second group of important predictors of PSI is the perceived similarity and homophily of the media consumer and media persona. Media consumers are more attracted to personae they perceive to be similar to themselves (Sokolova & Kefi, 2020). Similarity-attraction theory is a well-established phenomenon in interpersonal relationships also established in leader-follower relationships (Parent-Rocheleau, Bentein, & Simard, 2020). Various types of homophily of media consumers with media personae are predictors of audience involvement with them (Eyal & Rubin, 2003; Schiappa, Gregg, & Hewes, 2005; Turner, 1993).

A third important factor affecting involvement with media personae is perceived realism. Schiappa, Gregg and Hewes (2005) found that the perceived realism of personae is an important predictor of parasocial interaction. In leader-follower communication, leaders who are not perceived to be genuine will not do well in inducing parasocial interaction with their followers.

Interpersonal needs present a fourth set of predictors of leader-follower parasocial interaction. These include the need for companionship, relieving boredom, overcoming loneliness, seeking understanding, searching for inspiration, and gaining life focus and direction (Liwski, 2010, p. 11; Stever, 2009, p. 6).

A fifth set of predictors of leader-follower parasocial interaction is the communication style of the leader. Tsai and Men (2017) found that more assertive and responsive CEOs established stronger PSI and PSRs with social media users than CEOs who are less assertive and less responsive in their online communication. They conclude that organizational leaders whose social communication is more responsive, empathetic, accountable, and decisive will nourish the development of close PSRs.

Finally, demographic characteristics represent a sixth set of predictors of leader-follower parasocial relationships (Liwski, 2010, p. 11). In his study of parasocial breakups, Cohen (2003) found that women and adolescents tend to develop stronger PSRs than do men and older people. In their study of PSI with Princess Diana, Brown, Basil and Bocarnea (2003) found that women experienced stronger PSI with Princess Diana then did men. Organizational leaders must be cognizant of how their gender, age, ethnicity, and other demographic characteristics may affect their ability to strengthen parasocial relationships with their publics.

Consequences of Leader-Follower Parasocial Interaction

One of the most important consequences of PSI is *identification*, a second powerful type of involvement of media consumers with media personae. The study of identification has a long history in a variety of academic disciplines, dating back to the work of Freud (1922, 1940/1989), Lasswell (1931, 1935/1965), and Kelman (1958) in the social sciences and to the work of Burke (1969) in the humanities. Kelman (1958, 1961) developed a theory of social influence based on his studies of compliance, identification, and internalization during the 1950s. His robust theory of identification provides a useful theoretical framework for understanding how identification with media personae like organizational leaders can lead to belief and behavior change.

Kelman (1958, 1961) conceptualized identification as the process of adopting the beliefs and behavior of another person who is the object of one's identification. For example, if an Apple product user had formed a strong parasocial relationship with Apple Founder Steve Jobs before his death, and as a result, decided to explore Buddhism as Steve Jobs had done, we could conclude "identification" had occurred. Kelman (1961) explained that identification took place when a person who has formed a "self-defining" relationship with another person or group of people adopts the attitudes, beliefs and behavior of that other person or group (p. 63).

Thus, there must be a transfer of beliefs and behavior from one person to another person in order for identification to take place. Identification is not simply saying "I want to be like Facebook CEO Mark Zuckerberg." Rather, it means role modeling Mark Zuckerberg so that you adopt some aspect of Zuckerberg's beliefs or behavior into your own life; for example, like taking up the sport of fencing because Zuckerberg likes fencing. Kelman discovered that the internalization of beliefs that served to maintain a desired connection to the object of identification also led to adopting the behavior of other individuals or groups (Brown, 2015). Kelman (1961) explained: "by saying what the other says, doing what he does, believing what he believes, the individual maintains this relationship and the satisfying self-definition that it provides him" (p. 63). It is important to note that the individual or group who is the object of identification is seldom aware that another individual is adopting their beliefs and behavior.

Considering how followers are often profoundly influenced by the leaders they follow, Kelman's identification theory is pertinent to the study of the consequences of parasocial interaction with organizational leaders. Corporate founders, CEOs, and other organizational leaders should be aware that identification is a powerful form of social change that often results from strong leader-follower parasocial interaction.

A second consequence of strong leader-follower parasocial interaction is worship. Worship is the most powerful form of involvement with media personae and is the most recently conceptualized form of involvement studied by social scientists (Brown, 2015). Research by John Maltby, Lynn McCutcheon and their colleagues indicates that media consumers can idolize media personae with such intensity that it emulates worship (Giles & Maltby, 2004; Maltby, Giles, Barber, & McCutcheon, 2005; Maltby, Houran, Lange, Ashe, & McCutcheon, 2002; Maltby, Houran, & McCutcheon, 2003; Maltby et al., 2004; McCutcheon, Ashe, Houran, & Maltby, 2003; McCutcheon, Lange, & Houran, 2002).

The worship of a media persona takes place when media consumers devote their time and attention to a persona that is normally given to God, a god, or some other form of deity (Maltby et al., 2002). Intense worship is a phenomenon described by Maltby et al. (2003) as "an abnormal type of PSR, driven by absorption and addictive elements and which potentially has significant clinical sequelae" (p. 25) that often manifests through relationships with celebrities. McCutcheon, Ashe, Houran & Maltby (2003, p. 309) describe strong celebrity worship in a similar manner, using the words "obsessed" and "delusional" to describe how individuals become deeply involved with celebrities.

However, not all worship of mediated personae like celebrities is characterized as a psychological pathology. Maltby, Giles, Barber and McCutcheon (2005) describe the first two levels of worship as quite common, as when media consumers closely follow the lives of famous people and exhibit intense personal feelings toward them. It is not until one progresses to the third and most intense level of celebrity worship that it is referred to mildly pathological (Maltby et al., 2005, p. 1166). There are many examples of famous CEOs and organizational founders who have been worshipped by their followers. For example, the late soccer legend Diego Maradona, who led Argentina to a historic World Cup victory over England and who coached Argentina's national soccer team, has been worshipped as a hero by many followers (Brown & de Matviuk, 2010). In Sonnenfeld's (1991) study of corporate heroes who retire, he explains:

What business heroes have in common with the heroes of myth and religion is that they not only symbolize dreams and aspirations to their firms, and even to general society, but also are accomplishers of pragmatic goals. Society, it seems, admire inspirational leaders who can translate hazy visions into concrete realities. (p. 6)

In summary, three closely related involvement processes are pertinent to the study of relationships between leaders and followers. These processes begin with leader-follower parasocial interaction that eventually lead to the formation of parasocial relationships between leaders and followers. When these relationships become strong, they often lead to identification with the leader and sometimes even worship of the leader, the most intense form of involvement. Both identification and worship are characterized by changes in beliefs and behaviors of the leader follower. A theoretical model of the antecedents and consequences of PSI is provided later in this chapter in Figure 1.

Leader-Follower Parasocial Experiences

Parasocial interaction theory predicts that when media consumers become involved with media personae, they have certain perceived experiences with them. First, media consumers who regularly engage media personae through mediated forms of communication experience a sense of social presence. In leader-follower parasocial interaction, followers are expected to also experience social presence and feel that their leaders are socially present in their lives (Kim & Song, 2016). This sense of social presence created by leaders provides a type of companionship.

A second anticipated experience of leader-follower parasocial relationships is a sense of attachment to organizational leaders who engage with followers through media. *Parasocial attachment* (PSA) is one dimension of a parasocial relationship that has been studied by psychologists for the past fifty years (Bowlby, 1969). PSA occurs within parasocial relationships when the media persona begins to fulfill the attachment needs of the media consumer such as a sense of intimacy, comfort, security, and safety (Stever, 2017, p. 98; Rosaen & Dibble, 2016).

Horton and Wohl (1956) characterized PSA as "finding safe haven and felt security through a relationship that is with a person not known in a real life face-to-face way" (p. 96). The theoretical construct of PSA predicts that followers of media personae like organizational leaders will seek relationships with them when they believe the personae can provide security and safety (Stever, 2017, p. 97). Followers of organizational leaders who lack meaningful interpersonal relationships in their lives will be more likely to satisfy their attachment needs through PSI with them.

In addition to social presence and parasocial attachment experiences, a third anticipated experience of leader-follower parasocial interaction is the formation of a meaningful friendship that followers develop with leaders. Fans of Steve Irwin, for example, the former star of *Animal Planet's* hit program *Crocodile Hunter,* felt as if Irwin was a member of their family (Brown, 2010). Likewise, fans of NASCAR driver Dale Earnhardt regarded him as a close a friend or family member (Brown, Barker, & Presnell, 2008). Their tragic deaths brought forth strong feelings of genuine friendship by those who followed these two innovative leaders who touched the lives of millions of people who followed them.

Organizational leaders should expect that many of their followers will regard them as friends. This dynamic is an important consideration since with perceived friendship comes an expectation of loyalty. Leaders who disregard the needs of those who follow them will not merely produce feelings of disappointment among their followers; but also will produce feelings of betrayal.

ASSESSING LEADER-FOLLOWER PARASOCIAL INTERACTION

Before developing a measure of leader-follower parasocial interaction, it is important to have a clear definition of this variable. The involvement of media consumers with media personae provides a valuable conceptual domain for the assessment of leader-follower parasocial interaction. One of the challenges of current scholarship is that although there is widespread support for identifying distinct processes of audience involvement, the academic literature reveals conceptual inconsistencies, inadequate theoretical integration, and a lack of shared definitions (Dibble, Hartmann, & Rosaen, 2016; Klimmt, Hartmann, & Schramm, 2006; Murphy, Frank, Moran, & Patnoe-Woodley, 2011).

A review of the measures for PSI shows that knowing a persona is a core attribute of this form of involvement. Audiences would not be expected to identify with a persona who was unknown. Relating to a persona as a friend or as an enemy implies that one knows that persona's attitudes, values, beliefs, or behavior.

Middle-Range Theory and a Theoretical Model

Middle-range theories are developed based on working hypotheses that emerge from many studies seeking to systematically develop a unified theory that will explain the observed uniformities of social behavior, social organization, and social change (Merton, 1986, p. 39). The basic task of conducting a middle-range analysis of a theory is to develop empirical measurements that adequately test conceptual variables of the theory. Middle-range theory testing focuses research on exploring the empirical relationships among a limited number of variables. Middle-range theory analysis in organizational research is a powerful tool for examining multiple theories (Bourgeois, 1979) and provides a framework for studying the involvement processes at work in leader-follower relationships.

In the present discussion of measuring leader-follower parasocial interaction, a conceptual variable, an empirical measurement for leader-follower parasocial interaction must be developed from a theoretical model that includes the antecedent variables or predictors of parasocial interaction and the outcome variables or consequences of parasocial interaction. Definitional clarity is an important requirement for developing theoretically coherent, empirically sound, meaningful, and useful middle-range field studies (Lenz, 1996). Therefore, the following definition is used to construct an empirical measurement for leader-follower parasocial interaction:

Leader-follower parasocial interaction is defined as the process by which a follower develops an imaginary relationship with a leader persona both during and after media consumption, which begins with spending time with the leader persona through media or participation in mediated events, and is characterized by perceived relational development of the follower with the leader-persona.

Drawing from the theoretical model of involvement with media personae presented by Brown (2015) and in the tradition of middle-range theory testing, a theoretical model that will be used for developing a leader-follower parasocial interaction scale is presented in Figure 1.

Figure 1. Theoretical model of involvement processes with media personae

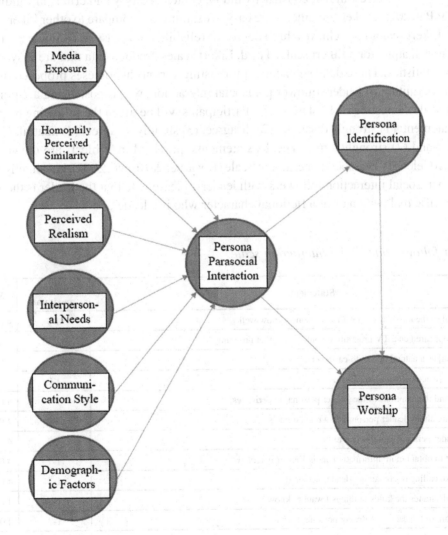

Note that the variable of leader-follower parasocial interaction as defined above is presented with both its antecedent variables and its predicted outcome variables.

DEVELOPING A MEASUREMENT SCALE

One of the most widely used measurement devices in social science research is the Likert-scale (Joshi, Kale, Chandel & Pal, 2015). The Likert scale has a long history of producing reliable data suitable for inferential statistics. The typical Likert scale consists of a set of statements, also called survey items, that require study participants to record their level of agreement (from strongly disagree to strongly agree) with the given statements (items) on a metric scale (Croasmun, & Ostrom, 2011). When used correctly, the combination of Likert scale statements reveal the specific dimension of an attitude or belief towards whatever subject is being studied.

Likert-scale measures are popular for three primary reasons. First, Likert-scales can achieve a high degree validity, including face validity, construct validity, content validity and criterion validity (Joshi, Kale, Chandel & Pal, 2015). Likert statements are easy to examine and compare to other Likert measurements. Second, Likert scales can achieve a high degree of reliability. It is easy to compute the reliability coefficient Cronbach alpha for a Likert scale. Third, Likert scales produce data that are easy to analyze using inferential statistics. These data are excellent for testing various hypotheses proposed in a study.

Based on the definition of leader-follower parasocial interaction, we propose using a 7-point agree-disagree Likert scale consisting of 12 statements. Participants will be given the following response options to each statement: (1) strongly disagree, (2) disagree, (3) slightly disagree, (4) neutral, (5) slightly agree, (6) agree, and (7) strongly agree. The 12 statements, provided in Table 1, are drawn from the Bocarnea-Brown Celebrity Parasocial Interaction Scale (Bocarnea & Brown, 2007), but slightly modified to measure the parasocial interaction followers with leaders. Please note that the leader is the mediated persona of a specific real person or of a fictional character who is a leader.

Table 1. Leader-follower parasocial interaction scale

Statement	minimum maximum	Midpoint
[leader persona] makes me feel as if I am with a someone I know well.	1-7	4.0
If [leader persona] appeared on a TV program, I would watch that program.	1-7	4.0
I see [leader persona] as a natural down -to-earth person.	1-7	4.0
I would like to meet [leader persona] in person.	1-7	4.0
I feel that I understand the emotions of the [leader persona] experiences.	1-7	4.0
I find myself thinking about [leader persona] on a regular basis.	1-7	4.0
Learning about [leader persona] is important to me.	1-7	4.0
I search the Internet to obtain more information about [leader persona].	1-7	4.0
Sometimes I feel like calling or contacting [leader persona]	1-7	4.0
[leader persona] understands the kinds of things I want to know.	1-7	4.0
I am very much aware of the details of [leader persona]'s life.	1-7	4.0
I look forward to seeing [leader persona] posts on social media.	1-7	4.0

Instruction: When administering the leader-follower parasocial interaction scale (LFPIS), the following instruction should be given to study participants along with the 1-7 Likert scale provided below: Please think of a leader that you relate to, either a real person or fictional character (persona), read each statement below, and indicate the degree to which you disagree or agree with each statement using the 1-7 measurement scale shown below:

strongly disagree	disagree	slightly disagree	neutral	slightly agree	agree	strongly agree
1	2	3	4	5	6	7

If using an online survey company like Survey Monkey, Qualtrics, Zoho or similar service to build your survey, the 1-7 Likert scale can be easily converted into a matrix question in which the column headings represent the seven disagree-agree response choices and the rows represent the scale statements. In order to make matrix questions more readable, we recommend no more than six row items per questions. Therefore, we would recommend using two matrix questions to build the online parasocial interaction scale.

Scoring: There are no reverse-coded questions in the leader-follower parasocial interaction scale. Many social science scholars have documented the reliability issues associated with reserve coded items and recommend caution about the inclusion of such items in a measurement scale (Weijters & Baumgartner, 2012). Calculating a total score on the LFPIS is simply achieved by adding up all the numeric responses. The scale has a range of 72, with a minimum possible score of 12 and a maximum possible score of 84. The midpoint on the scale is 48. Although many scholars report measurement scale statistics on a 1-7 basis by dividing the total score by the number of scale items, this is unnecessary and not recommended. Instead, report the actual scale statistics for a sample of respondents, including the minimum score, maximum scale, mean, standard deviation, and variance.

Reliability and Validity: A Cronbach alpha reliability coefficient should also be reported for the sample data. Previous versions of this scale have yielded high Cronbach alpha coefficients, with most studies achieving a 0.75 or higher (Bocarnea & Brown, 2007). Rigorous analysis should be conducted to establish the validity of the scale (Kimberlin, & Winterstein, 2008), focusing on discovering any unique attributes of leader-follower parasocial relationships in organizational settings.

CONCLUSION

Study of the emotional and psychological bonds developed between leaders and followers through mediated interaction can be measured effectively on a parasocial interaction scale. The theoretical model that provided the framework for this scale can be used to assess both the predictors and consequences of leader-follower parasocial interaction.

The global diffusion of new communication technology and social media networks is increasing the opportunities for followers to experience PSI with leaders. When PSI leads to the formation of strong parasocial relationships, identification and worship can result, accompanied by substantive belief and behavior change. As more people become involved with leader-personae, organizational communication scholars and other social scientists should continue to study the nature and effects of leader-follower parasocial interaction and the relationships they produce.

REFERENCES

Bocarnea, M. C., & Brown, W. J. (2007). Celebrity-Persona Parasocial Interaction Scale. In R. A. Reynolds, R. Woods, & J. D. Baker (Eds.), *Handbook of research on electronic surveys and measurements* (pp. 309–312). Idea Group Reference. doi:10.4018/978-1-59140-792-8.ch039

Bourgeois Iii, L. J. (1979). Toward a method of middle-range theorizing. *Academy of Management Review*, 4(3), 443–447. doi:10.5465/amr.1979.4289127

Bowlby, J. (1969). Attachment and loss, Vol. 1, attachment. Holgarth.

BRANDfog. (2013). *CEO, Social media and leadership survey*. Retrieved Feb. 7, 2021, from https://brandfog.com/resource/2013-ceo-social-media-and-leadership-survey/

Broom, G. M., Casey, S., & Ritchey, J. (1997). Toward a concept and theory of organization-public relationships. *Journal of Public Relations Research*, 9(2), 83–98. doi:10.12071532754xjprr0902_01

Broom, G. M., & Dozier, D. M. (1990). *Using research in public relations: Applications to program management*. Prentice-Hall.

Brown, W. J. (2010). Steve Irwin's influence on wildlife conservation. *Journal of Communication*, 60(1), 73–93. doi:10.1111/j.1460-2466.2009.01458.x

Brown, W. J. (2015). Examining four processes of audience involvement with media personae: Transportation, parasocial interaction, identification and worship. *Communication Theory*, 25(3), 259–283. doi:10.1111/comt.12053

Brown, W. J., Barker, G., & Presnell, K. K. (2008). *The social impact of mediated celebrities: Cognitive and emotional responses to the death of Dale Earnhardt*. Paper presented to the National Communication Association, San Diego, CA.

Brown, W. J., Basil, M. D., & Bocarnea, M. C. (2003). Social influence of an international celebrity: Responses to the death of Princess Diana. *Journal of Communication*, 53(4), 587–605. doi:10.1111/j.1460-2466.2003.tb02912.x

Brown, W. J., & Cody, M. J. (1991). Effects of an Indian television soap opera in promoting women's status. *Human Communication Research*, 18(1), 114–142. doi:10.1111/j.1468-2958.1991.tb00531.x PMID:12319295

Brown, W. J., & de Matviuk, M. A. C. (2010). Sports celebrities and public health: Diego Maradona's influence on drug use prevention. *Journal of Health Communication*, 15(4), 358–373. doi:10.1080/10810730903460575 PMID:20574875

Burke, K. (1969). *A rhetoric of motives*. University of California Press.

Chia, S. C., & Poo, Y. L. (2009). Media, celebrities, and fans: An examination of adolescents' media usage and involvement with entertainment celebrities. *Journalism & Mass Communication Quarterly*, 86(1), 23–44. doi:10.1177/107769900908600103

Click, M. A., Lee, H., & Holladay, H. W. (2013). Making monsters: Lady Gaga, fan identification, and social media. *Popular Music and Society*, 36(3), 360–379. doi:10.1080/03007766.2013.798546

Cohen, J. (2003). Parasocial breakups: Measuring individual differences in responses to the dissolution of parasocial relationships. *Mass Communication & Society, 6*(2), 191–202. doi:10.1207/S15327825MCS0602_5

Coker, K., Howie, K., Syrdal, H., Vanmeter, R., & Woodroof, P. (2017, May). The truth about transparency and authenticity on social media: how brands communicate and how customers respond: an abstract. In *Academy of Marketing Science Annual Conference* (pp. 659-660). Springer.

Conte, F. (2018). Understanding the influence of CEO tenure and CEO reputation on corporate reputation: An exploratory study in Italy. *International Journal of Business and Management, 13*(3), 54–66. doi:10.5539/ijbm.v13n3p54

Croasmun, J. T., & Ostrom, L. (2011). Using Likert-type scales in the social sciences. *Journal of Adult Education, 40*(1), 19–22.

Derrick, J. L., Gabriel, S., & Tippin, B. (2008). Parasocial relationships and self-discrepancies: Faux relationships have benefits for low self-esteem individuals. *Personal Relationships, 15*(2), 261–280. doi:10.1111/j.1475-6811.2008.00197.x

Dibble, J. L., Hartmann, T., & Rosaen, S. F. (2016). Parasocial interaction and parasocial relationship: Conceptual clarification and a critical assessment of measures. *Human Communication Research, 42*(1), 21–44. doi:10.1111/hcre.12063

El-Kasim, M., & Idid, S. A. (2017). PR practitioners' use of social media: validation of an online relationship management model applying structural equation modeling. *Jurnal Komunikasi: Malaysian Journal of Communication, 33*(1). doi:10.17576/JKMJC-2017-3301-15

Eyal, K., & Rubin, A. M. (2003). Viewer aggression and homophily, identification, and parasocial relationships with television characters. *Journal of Broadcasting & Electronic Media, 47*(1), 77–98. doi:10.120715506878jobem4701_5

Freud, S. (1922). *Group psychology and the analysis of ego*. Norton. doi:10.1037/11327-000

Freud, S. (1989). *An outline of psychoanalysis* (J. Strachey, Trans.). Norton. (Original work published 1940)

Giles, D. C. (2002). Parasocial interaction: A review of the literature and a model for future research. *Media Psychology, 4*(3), 279–305. doi:10.1207/S1532785XMEP0403_04

Giles, D. C., & Maltby, J. (2004). The role of media figures in adolescent development: Relations between autonomy, attachment, and interest in celebrities. *Personality and Individual Differences, 36*(4), 813–822. doi:10.1016/S0191-8869(03)00154-5

Gumpert, G., & Cathcart, R. (1986). The interpersonal and media connection. In G. Gumpert & R. Cathcart (Eds.), *Inter/Media: Interpersonal communication in a media world* (3rd ed., pp. 17–25). Oxford University Press.

Head, A. J. (2003). Personas: Setting the stage for building usable information sites. *Online (Bergheim), 27*(4), 1–7.

Horton, D., & Wohl, R. R. (1956). Mass communication and parasocial interaction: Observations on intimacy at a distance. *Psychiatry, 19*, 215–229. doi:10.1080/00332747.1956.11023049 PMID:13359569

Jin, S. A. A., & Phua, J. (2014). Following celebrities' tweets about brands: The impact of twitter-based electronic word-of-mouth on consumers' source credibility perception, buying intention, and social identification with celebrities. *Journal of Advertising, 43*(2), 181–195. doi:10.1080/00913367.2013.827606

Joshi, A., Kale, S., Chandel, S., & Pal, D. K. (2015). Likert scale: Explored and explained. *Current Journal of Applied Science and Technology*, 396-403. doi:10.9734/BJAST/2015/14975

Kelman, H. (1958). Compliance, identification, and internalization: Three processes of attitude change. *The Journal of Conflict Resolution, 2*(1), 51–60. doi:10.1177/002200275800200106

Kelman, H. (1961). Process of opinion change. *Public Opinion Quarterly, 25*(1), 57–78. doi:10.1086/266996

Kim, J., & Song, H. (2016). Celebrity's self-disclosure on Twitter and parasocial relationships: A mediating role of social presence. *Computers in Human Behavior, 62*, 570–577. doi:10.1016/j.chb.2016.03.083

Kimberlin, C. L., & Winterstein, A. G. (2008). Validity and reliability of measurement instruments used in research. *American Journal of Health-System Pharmacy, 65*(23), 2276–2284. doi:10.2146/ajhp070364 PMID:19020196

Klimmt, C., Hartmann, T., & Schramm, H. (2006). Parasocial interactions and relationships. In J. Bryant & P. Vorderer (Eds.), *Psychology of entertainment* (pp. 291–314). Routledge.

Labrecque, L. I. (2014). Fostering consumer–brand relationships in social media environments: The role of parasocial interaction. *Journal of Interactive Marketing, 28*(2), 134–148. doi:10.1016/j.intmar.2013.12.003

Lasswell, H. D. (1931). The measurement of public opinion. *The American Political Science Review, 25*(2), 311–326. doi:10.2307/1947659

Lasswell, H. D. (1965). *World politics and personal insecurity.* Free Press. (Original work published 1935)

Lenz, E. (1996). Middle range theory: Role in research and practice. In: *Proceedings of the Sixth Rosemary Ellis Scholar's Retreat, Nursing Science Implications for the 21st century*. Cleveland, OH: Frances Payne Bolton School of Nursing, Case Western Reserve University.

Levy, M. (1979). Watching television news as parasocial interaction. *Journal of Broadcasting, 23*(1), 69–80. doi:10.1080/08838157909363919

Liwski, N. T. (2010). *College Students' Television Friends: Parasocial Relationships as Attachment Bonds* (Doctoral dissertation). Purdue University.

Maltby, J., Day, L., McCutcheon, L. E., Gillett, R., Houran, J., & Ashe, D. D. (2004). Personality and coping: A context for examining celebrity worship and mental health. *British Journal of Psychology, 95*(4), 411–428. doi:10.1348/0007126042369794 PMID:15527530

Maltby, J., Giles, D. C., Barber, L., & McCutcheon, L. E. (2005). Intense-personal celebrity worship and body image: Evidence of a link among female adolescents. *British Journal of Health Psychology, 10*(1), 17–32. doi:10.1348/135910704X15257 PMID:15826331

Maltby, J., Houran, J., Lange, R., Ashe, D., & McCutcheon, L. E. (2002). Thou shalt worship no other gods - unless they are celebrities: The relationship between celebrity worship and religious orientation. *Personality and Individual Differences, 32*(7), 1157–1172. doi:10.1016/S0191-8869(01)00059-9

Maltby, J., Houran, J., & McCutcheon, L. E. (2003). A clinical interpretation of attitudes and behaviors associated with celebrity worship. *The Journal of Nervous and Mental Disease, 191*(1), 25–29. doi:10.1097/00005053-200301000-00005 PMID:12544596

Markel, D., McCann, M., & Wasserman, H. M. (2015). Catalyzing fans. *Harvard Journal on Sports & Entertainment Law, 6*(1), 1–40.

Marshall, P. D., Moore, C., & Barbour, K. (2019). *Persona studies: An introduction.* Wiley-Blackwell.

Marwick, A. E., & boyd. (2011). I tweet honestly, I tweet passionately: Twitter users, context' collapse, and the imagined audience. *New Media & Society, 13*(1), 114–133. doi:10.1177/1461444810365313

McCutcheon, L. E., Ashe, D. D., Houran, J., & Maltby, J. (2003). A cognitive profile of individuals who intend to worship celebrities. *The Journal of Psychology, 137*(4), 309–322. doi:10.1080/00223980309600616 PMID:12943182

McCutcheon, L. E., Lange, R., & Houran, J. (2002). Conceptualization and measurement of celebrity worship. *British Journal of Psychology, 93*(1), 67–87. doi:10.1348/000712602162454 PMID:11839102

Men, L. R., & Tsai, W. S. (2015). Infusing social media with humanity: Corporate character, public engagement, and relational outcomes. *Public Relations Review, 41*(3), 395–403. doi:10.1016/j.pubrev.2015.02.005

Merton, R. K. (1946). *Mass persuasion: The social psychology of a war bond drive.* Harper & Brothers Publishers.

Merton, R. K. (1968). On sociological theories of the middle range. In R. K. Merton (Ed.), *Social Theory and Social Structure* (pp. 39–72). Free Press.

Oyeniran, S. T., Jayesimi, O. S., Ogundele, R. A., & Oyeniran, O. A. Computer mediated communication for effective and efficient organization service delivery amid Covid-19 pandemic. *International Journal of Engineering and Artificial Intelligence, 1*(3), 44-49.

Parent-Rocheleau, X., Bentein, K., & Simard, G. (2020). Positive together? The effects of leader-follower (dis) similarity in psychological capital. *Journal of Business Research, 110*, 435–444. doi:10.1016/j.jbusres.2020.02.016

Peterson, J. J. (2019). *StoryBrand narrative marketing: An examination of the influence of narrative marketing on organizations* (Unpublished doctoral dissertation). Virginia Beach, VA: Regent University.

Ranft, A. L., Zinko, R., Ferris, G. R., & Buckley, M. R. (2006). Marketing the image of management: The costs and benefits of CEO reputation. *Organizational Dynamics, 35*(3), 279–290. doi:10.1016/j.orgdyn.2006.05.003

Rubin, A. M., Perse, E. M., & Powell, R. A. (1985). Loneliness, parasocial interaction, and local television viewing. *Human Communication Research, 12*(2), 155–180. doi:10.1111/j.1468-2958.1985.tb00071.x

Rubin, R. B., & McHugh, M. P. (1987). Development of parasocial interaction relationships. *Journal of Broadcasting & Electronic Media, 31*(3), 279–292. doi:10.1080/08838158709386664

Salmon, C. T. (1986). Perspectives on involvement in consumer and communication research. In B. Dervin & M. J. Voigt (Eds.), *Progress in communication sciences* (Vol. 7, pp. 234–268). Ablex.

Schiappa, E., Gregg, P. B., & Hewes, D. E. (2005). The parasocial contact hypothesis. *Communication Monographs, 72*(1), 92–115. doi:10.1080/0363775052000342544

Schweitzer, L., & Lyons, S. (2008). The market within: A marketing approach to creating and developing high-value employment relationships. *Business Horizons, 51*(6), 555–565. doi:10.1016/j.bushor.2008.03.004

Shefner-Rogers, C. L., Rogers, E. M., & Singhal, A. (1998). Parasocial interaction with the television soap operas 'Simplemente Maria' and 'Oshin.'. *Keio Communication Review, 20,* 3–18. Retrieved January 30, 2021, from http://utminers.utep.edu/asinghal/ Articles%20and%20Chapters/ shefnerrogers_rogers_singhal.pdf

Sokolova, K., & Kefi, H. (2020). Instagram and YouTube bloggers promote it, why should I buy? How credibility and parasocial interaction influence purchase intentions. *Journal of Retailing and Consumer Services, 53,* 1-16. doi: .2019.01.011 doi:10.1016/j.jretconser

Sonnenfeld, J. (1991). *The hero's farewell: What happens when CEOs retire.* Oxford University Press. doi:10.1093/acprof:oso/9780195065831.001.0001

Sood, S., & Rogers, E. M. (2000). Dimensions of parasocial interaction by letter-writers to a popular entertainment-education soap opera in India. *Journal of Broadcasting & Electronic Media, 44*(3), 386–414. doi:10.120715506878jobem4403_4

Stever, G. S. (2009). Parasocial and social interaction with celebrities: Classification of media fans. *Journal of Media Psychology, 14*(3), 1–39. https://gstever. sunyempirefaculty.net/ parasocial-and-social-interaction-with-celebrities/

Stever, G. S. (2017). Evolutionary theory and reactions to mass media: Understanding parasocial attachment. *Psychology of Popular Media Culture, 6*(2), 95–102. doi:10.1037/ppm0000116

Stever, G. S., & Lawson, K. (2013). Twitter as a way for celebrities to communicate with fans: Implications for the study of parasocial interaction. *North American Journal of Psychology, 15,* 339–354.

Swart, C. (2012). Building organisation–public relationships: Towards an understanding of the challenges facing public relations. *Communicatio, 38*(3), 329–348. doi:10.1080/02500167.2012.687751

Tamborini, R., Bowman, N. D., Eden, A., Grizzard, M., & Organ, A. (2010). Defining media enjoyment as the satisfaction of intrinsic needs. *Journal of Communication, 60*(4), 758–777. doi:10.1111/j.1460-2466.2010.01513.x

Tjosvold, D., & Wong, A. S. H. (2000). The leader relationship: Building teamwork with and among employees. *Leadership and Organization Development Journal, 21*(7), 350–354. doi:10.1108/01437730010377890

Tsai, W. H. S., & Men, L. R. (2017). Social CEOs: The effects of CEOs' communication styles and parasocial interaction on social networking sites. *New Media & Society*, *19*(11), 1848–1867. doi:10.1177/1461444816643922

Turner, J. R. (1993). Interpersonal and psychological predictors of parasocial interaction with different television performers. *Communication Quarterly*, *41*(4), 443–453. doi:10.1080/01463379309369904

Verčič, A. T., & Verčič, D. (2007). Reputation as matching identities and images: Extending Davies and Chun's (2002) research on gaps between the internal and external perceptions of the corporate brand. *Journal of Marketing Communications*, *13*(4), 277–290. doi:10.1080/13527260701300151

Vidgen, R., Sims, J. M., & Powell, P. (2013). Do CEO bloggers build community? *Journal of Communication Management (London)*, *17*(4), 364–385. doi:10.1108/JCOM-08-2012-0068

Vorderer, P., Hefner, D., Reinecke, L., & Klimmt, C. (Eds.). (2018). *Permanently Online, Permanently Connected. Living and Communicating in a POPC World*. Routledge.

Walther, J. B. (1996). Computer-mediated communication: Impersonal, interpersonal, and hyperpersonal interaction. *Communication Research*, *23*(1), 3–43. doi:10.1177/009365096023001001

Walther, J. B. (2011). Theories of computer-mediated communication and interpersonal relations. The handbook of interpersonal communication, 4, 443-479.

Walther, J. B., Van Der Heide, B., Ramirez, A., Burgoon, J. K., & Peña, J. (2015). Interpersonal and hyperpersonal dimensions of computer-mediated communication. In S. Shyam Sundar (Ed.), *The handbook of the psychology of communication technology* (pp. 1–22). John Wiley & Sons Inc. doi:10.1002/9781118426456.ch1

Wang, B., Liu, Y., & Parker, S. K. (2020). How does the use of information communication technology affect individuals? A work design perspective. *The Academy of Management Annals*, *14*(2), 695–725. doi:10.5465/annals.2018.0127

Weijters, B., & Baumgartner, H. (2012). Misresponse to reversed and negated items in surveys: A review. *JMR, Journal of Marketing Research*, *49*(5), 737–747. doi:10.1509/jmr.11.0368

Wirth, W. (2006). Involvement. In J. Bryant & P. Vorderer (Eds.), *Psychology of entertainment* (pp. 199–214). Routledge.

Yue, C. A., Thelen, P., Robinson, K., & Men, L. R. (2019). How do CEOs communicate on Twitter? A comparative study between Fortune 200 companies and top startup companies. *Corporate Communications*, *24*(3), 532–552. doi:10.1108/CCIJ-03-2019-0031

Yuksel, M., & Labrecque, L. I. (2016). "Digital buddies": Parasocial interactions in social media. *Journal of Research in Interactive Marketing*, *10*(4), 305–320. doi:10.1108/JRIM-03-2016-0023

Chapter 12
The Influence of Spirituality:
Measuring Spirituality in Leadership With the SpEI

Rick Roof
Liberty University, USA

ABSTRACT

Spirituality and its relationship to leadership and organizational behavior has been of increasing interest to researchers, but inadequate scales have limited rigorous quantitative studies. Spirituality is complex and involves experiential, emotional, and transformative dimensions that create dynamic cycles of expectancy, behavior, and attitudes that evolve, rendering many existing spiritual practice behavioral measures inadequate. An instrument developed to capture the broader concept of spiritual engagement, the Spiritual Engagement Instrument (SpEI), is presented. Through an overview of SpEI development, and demonstration of SpEI research, a primer to advance spirituality-based organization and leadership research is offered. If spiritual engagement is a transformative cycle, understanding and measuring the phenomena in context will better inform leadership and organization development policy. Toward a theoretical and practical understanding, this chapter guides the researcher in exploring the potential of spirituality in organizations.

INTRODUCTION

The influence of spirituality has been of increasing interest to leadership and organizational behavior scholars and practitioners, but research has been hindered by inadequate scales (Nicolae et al., 2013) that often capture only limited spiritual disciplines or other behaviors. When considering the complex nature of spirituality as experiential, emotional, and transformative, manifested as a cycle of expectancy, behavioral practices, attitudes, and deepening spirituality, simple behavioral measures are inadequate (Roof et al., 2017). For researchers interested in capturing a complex, multi-dimensional construct of human spirituality as an antecedent to leadership effectiveness, authenticity, identity, organizational outcomes, or other constructs of interest in leadership or organizational science, the Spiritual Engage-

DOI: 10.4018/978-1-7998-7665-6.ch012

ment Instrument (SpEI) is offered. The SpEI was developed to assess the motivating beliefs, attitudes, intentions, expectations, and actions that comprise an active cycle of spirituality that results in greater connectedness with God, deeper spirituality, and individual affective and cognitive change through core character development (Gould, 2005; Roof et al., 2017).

This chapter will briefly present the theory, development, and initial validation of the SpEI as foundational to an illustration of how the measure can be applied to explore the spirituality-leadership relationship. An examination of spiritual engagement in an organizational setting through the use of the SpEI will then be demonstrated using a previous study that explored spiritual engagement and authentic leadership relationships (Roof, 2016). Through the lenses of the theoretical and practical intersection, scholars seeking to advance the understanding of human spirituality will find options for measuring the complexity of dynamic spiritual constructs in new, active, dynamic ways. The ability to measure the spiritual engagement concept with a validated, multi-dimensional instrument can offer the researcher fresh perspectives with which to explore complex spirituality influences to advance leadership and organizational behavior theories globally.

BACKGROUND

Researchers have been increasingly interested in understanding the higher order needs of individuals and how related motivators may influence organizations and their leaders. Reflecting a growing awareness of intrinsic drives, attention has turned to the less materialistic motivations (Crossman, 2010), leadership spirituality dimensions (Conger, 1994; Fry, 2003; Posner, 2009; Reave, 2005) and spiritual wholeness and workplace meaning within the framework of positive psychology (Garcia-Zamor, 2003; Karakas, 2010).

Scholars are increasingly aware that effective leadership is "grounded in the spiritual dimension of the individual leader" (Strack & Fottler, 2002, p. 4) which allows leaders to develop humility, wisdom, a moral compass, servanthood, self-awareness, and the relational transparency to advance their leadership effectiveness (McNeal, 2000). Considering that leadership is a projection of the leader's identity, Ashmos and Duchon (2000) suggested that spirituality provides an inner nourishment that clarifies identity, and Hoppe (2005) connected that developing inner self with the spiritual connectedness necessary for true authenticity. In addition, the resulting integration of core beliefs from deepening spirituality helps the leader align espoused theory with behaviors connecting heart and mind to deliver effective, authentic leadership (Fry, 2003).

Work life benefits through the integration of spirituality as purpose, ethics, performance, and moral outcomes are elevated and aligned (Garcia-Zamor, 2003). As Byrne et al. (2014) noted, spiritual engagement can bolster leaders' resources and enable desirable behaviors that reflect normative leadership practices contained in theories such as ethical, authentic, transformational, and servant leadership (Roof, 2016). Psychological resources are replenished (Byrne et al., 2014), core beliefs shaped and strengthened (Issler, 2009), and identity-driven authentic behaviors demonstrated (Fields, 2007; Walumbwa et al., 2008) through spiritual engagement. Reave (2005) concluded that effective leadership and spirituality are connected throughout research as leader performance, resiliency, authenticity, emotional intelligence, integrity, and identity are related through the connection of "...inner values and outer behavior" (p. 668).

When considering the relationship or influence of spirituality with leadership or other organizational constructs, spirituality is anything but simple. Spirituality is not static, a simple behavior, or a condition, but should be considered as a complex construct involving emotional, experiential, and transformative elements (Roof et al., 2017). It is that complex, metaphysical, dynamic nature of spiritual phenomena that challenges researcher and demands approaches and instruments that reflect the complexity.

The Need to Measure

Giacalone and Jurkiewicz (2003) argued that advancing research in workplace spirituality demanded that rhetoric be replaced by clear and precise construct definitions and related validated instruments. Inadequate scales that are not rigorously developed and validated, or measures that capture only behaviors or some limited facet of spiritual engagement restrict the insights and power of spirituality research (Nicolae et al., 2013). Quality research demands the use of valid, reliable measures that properly capture well defined constructs of interest (Girden, 2011).

Monod et al. (2011) offered a survey of instruments used in clinical research that captured general spirituality, spiritual coping, spiritual needs, or other elements of spirituality. Some of the instruments that have been widely used to capture some of the elements of spiritual engagement include the Daily Spiritual Experience Scale (DSES) which is focused on spiritual feelings, awareness, or experiences as viewed by both theists and non-theists (Underwood & Teresi, 2002) and the Multidimensional Measure of Religiousness/Spirituality (MMRS) or the shortened version, the Brief Multidimensional Measure of Religiousness/Spirituality (BMMRS) which capture beliefs, religiousness, commitment, practices, and spirituality (Fetzer Institute on Aging, n.d.). There are also measures of specific practices such as prayer as captured by the Multidimensional Prayer Inventory (MPI) (Laird et al., 2004). Such existing instruments should be reviewed to determine if they capture the spirituality constructs of interest to the researcher, but if the study is to capture the richness and breadth of spiritual engagement as a transformative force, a valid, reliable instrument suited to such complexity may be more appropriate and one such instrument is the Spiritual Engagement Instrument (SpEI) (Roof et al., 2017).

The Spiritual Engagement Instrument Development

Leadership and organizational research that considers the influence of spirituality offers relatively unexplored opportunities to examine antecedents to leadership effectiveness, authenticity, humility, leader identity, organizational behavior, work engagement, servanthood, organizational change, and a plethora of other dynamic organizational concepts (Roof et al., 2017), but effective research will require the ability to measure spirituality in all of its richness. Without valid, reliable, complex measures, research will be constrained to investigating limited religious practices, ethical practices, or spiritual feelings leaving deeper understanding of this human experience untouched. In addition, as Reave (2005) noted, without clear definitions, spirituality research will blend with constructs such as ethics, morality, values, and vague metaphysical concepts rendering little of value toward understanding spirituality and the related organizational phenomena. Much of past research that found positive relationships between spirituality and organizational constructs suffered from validity and definitional issues.

Previous calls for instrumentation led to the development of the Spiritual Engagement Instrument (SpEI) (Roof et al., 2017). The SpEI is intended to offer not just a psychometrically sound instrument, but one that measures the behaviors and transformative nature of the spiritual engagement as an evolutionary cycle. Spiritual engagement affects both cognitive and affective transformation through the cycle of beliefs and attitudes shaping behavior, and behaviors then reshaping beliefs and attitudes as the individual draws closer to God (Foster & Griffin, 2000; Whitney, 2014). The SpEI considers practices that connect heart and head, that deepen and awaken intimacy with God as it measures motivating beliefs, attitudes, intentions, and expectations rather than just the rituals or disciplines that reflect traditional spiritual behaviors (Roof et al., 2017). It captures active spirituality, not just either the actions or meta-physical phenomena of faith-based engagement with the transcendent. The SpEI explores the dynamic, transformational nature of spiritual engagement which is driven by underlying attitudes and beliefs, the heart, emotions, cognition, and behaviors (Eck, 2002; Foster & Griffin, 2000; King, 2008) that impact identity (Roof, 2016). Spiritual engagement is not religious by nature, but neither does it reject religion. The SpEI was designed as faith-neutral with participants encouraged (in survey instructions) to respond within the framework of their own worldview and faith traditions. Whitney (2014) observed that spiritual disciplines have been practiced for thousands of years, and when applied collectively and with proper focus, can grow one's spiritual condition (Foster & Griffin, 2000). As Schwanda (2010) suggested, it is the active, intentional, emotional, and intellectual connection of heart and head, brought on by active piety that makes spiritual engagement more than just a feeling. Spiritual engagement, properly practiced, is to the spirit what a gymnasium is to the body (Whitney, 2014).

The Spiritual Engagement Instrument was developed to offer researchers an instrument that transcends limited spiritual practices as measured by many existing instruments, yet still captures action as one part of a greater transformative cycle, (Roof et al., 2017). The scale development efforts are described briefly and only generally in the following sections, but the interested reader should assess the instrument thoroughly to ensure applicability to their research. If needed, researchers can find additional details on the SpEI theoretical constructs and development efforts in Roof, Bocarnea, and Winston's (2017), *The spiritual engagement instrument.*

The six common practices or behaviors that are active elements of spiritual engagement, were identified in the literature as: meditation (Gould, 2005), prayer (Chandler, 2008; Neal, 2000), sacred text study (Gould, 2005; Neal, 2000), fasting (Chandler, 2008; Gould, 2005), worship (Chandler, 2008; Fetzer Institute on Aging, n.d.), and rest or sabbath (Chandler, 2008; Schwanda, 2010). Each of these practices have been connected with personal wellness, spiritual growth, identity development, and leadership or organizational advancement (Ai et al., 2002; Bussing et al., 2005; Chandler, 2008; Foster & Griffin, 2000; Gould, 2005; Underwood, 2011).

Scale development proceeded rigorously while integrating methods described by Devellis (2012) and Hair et al. (2010) beginning with creating 106 potential items developed from theory, and then refining the list to 30 scale items based on a review by three experts in spirituality scholarship. An initial scale development survey used a 6-point Likert scale intended to represent equal response intervals yielding 197 usable surveys exceeding the required sample size. Also included in the initial survey were items from the Daily Spiritual Experience Scale (DSES) (Underwood & Teresi, 2002) and Brief Multidimensional measurement of religiousness/spirituality (BMMRS) (Fetzer Institute on Aging, n.d.) to be used during analysis for convergent validity testing. In addition, five items from the Socially Desirable Response Set (SDRS-5) (Hays et al., 1989) were integrated into the survey to allow for testing social desirability bias. The sample population was 82.2% Caucasian and 76.1% Christian, requiring future users to especially examine the instrument for generalizability for populations that likely will vary from the development and initial validation testing samples (Roof et al., 2017). That is, while the SpEI was developed on sound theoretical foundations and is therefore expected to be effective across a wide range of populations, future users should closely examine the instrument theoretically as well as through thorough reliability and validity testing (Roof et al., 2017).

Robust initial analyses were performed on the initial survey data including the Kaiser-Meyer-Olkin Measure of Sampling Adequacy and Bartlett's Test of Sphericity (Roof et al., 2017). From the published work of Roof et al. (2017, pp. 224-225), the 30 initial survey items were assessed through Principal Component Analysis (PCA) with Oblimin rotation and as is common for such complex concepts, the development resulted in a four-factor solution explaining 85.24% of the variance with the resulting components:

1. Worship – including prayer elements explaining 57.8% of the variance (Cronbach's Alpha of .94)
2. Meditation – explaining 12.7% of the variance (Cronbach's Alpha of .96)
3. Fasting – explaining 9.59% of the variance (Cronbach's Alpha of .98)
4. Rest – explaining 5.16% of the variance (Cronbach's Alpha of .99)

The four scales were tested for convergent validity by examining their correlation with the BMMRS and DSES and all demonstrated significant correlation confirming convergent validity (Roof et al., 2017). Social desirability bias was evaluating using the data from the SDRS-5 and appeared within the normal range. Finally, for the initial scale development sample, demographic variables including age, race, gender, and tenure were used to examine for differences across the four factors using t-tests and ANOVAs with no significant differences noted.

To further validate the SpEI, a supplemental study was performed collecting 134 samples from leaders in the United States (Roof et al., 2017). Using confirmatory factor analysis (CFA) to evaluate model fit including chi-square value, the Comparative Fit Index (CFI), Root Mean Square Error of Approximation (RMSEA) and Tucker-Lewis Index (TLI), the four factor model satisfied criteria suggested by Hair et al. (2010). Convergent validity, discriminant validity (comparing to a single factor CFA model), and Cronbach Alpha values for the four scales all confirmed the SpEI psychometric properties. As with the original development effort, the BMMRS (Fetzer Institute on Aging, n.d.) and DSES ((Underwood, 2011) were included in the sample and used to confirm convergent validity.

The development of the SpEI resulted in a sound, validated instrument to capture spiritual engagement constructs, the transformative cycle of beliefs, expectations, behaviors, and attitudes that offer researchers the ability to assess important human spirituality concepts across faith traditions as they seek to understand the complex relationships with leadership and organizational constructs. As with all instruments, proper application is necessary to render sound theoretical research results.

The Spiritual Engagement Instrument Application

For the researcher interested in the intersection of spirituality with leadership or organization constructs, the spiritual engagement instrument may be useful. The SpEI was designed to be of particular interest to the spirituality researcher interested in capturing more than spiritual behavior as the SpEI assesses the rich, complex, transformational phenomena that may more often intersect with organizational and leadership concepts (Roof et al., 2017). Assessing Spiritual Engagement using the SpEI could be useful in the organizational setting where the concept may relate to leadership practices, organizational development efforts, culture, ethical constructs, servant leader behaviors, or other phenomena that reflect relationships connected to deeper spirituality or spiritual identity.

Of course, when considering use of a particular scale, no matter how rigorously the instrument has been developed and validated, the decision to use the instrument should reflect the focus of the research, the research question(s) to be explored, and the theoretical support for the constructs to be measured. That applies especially to relatively new theories like spiritual engagement and fresh instruments such as the Spiritual Engagement Instrument (SpEI). Assuming an interest in spiritual engagement as a research construct, what relationships might be of interest and supported in the literature?

Reave (2005) discovered in analyzing a wide range of literature, that many of the effective leadership dimensions were connected to spirituality concepts. Prior research connected resiliency, emotional intelligence, integrity, character, trust, self-management, performance, and identity with spiritual practices. Identity, the strength of which is fundamental to effective leadership, clarity of purpose, and personal success, is related to spirituality in that they are "shared ontological concepts" (Sheep & Foreman, 2012, as cited in Roof, 2016, p. 31). Literature also supports investigating the relationship of spiritual engagement to wide-ranging personal and organizational constructs such as burnout (Chandler, 2008), wisdom development (Sanders, 2007), character (Eck, 2002), employee and work engagement (Roof, 2014b), organizational culture (Sass, 2000), authenticity, and authentic leadership (Posner, 2009; Reave, 2005). Piedmont (1999) even argued that spirituality was significant enough to consider it as a sixth personality factor (in addition to the 5-factor model). Spiritual engagement may also serve as a moderating or mediating influence in various personal and organizational relationships.

As a demonstration of how the SpEI may be applied in research, an actual study conducted to examine the relationship between authentic leadership and spiritual engagement will be explored. The research, *The relationship between spiritual engagement and authentic leadership: Exploring the core of leadership* (Roof, 2016), responded to calls to examine authentic leadership antecedents (Gardner et al., 2011) including Reave's (2005) encouragement for researchers to seek greater understanding of the spirituality-leadership relationship. Many scholars (Conger, 1994; Fry, 2003; Giacalone & Jurkiewicz, 2003; Issler, 2009; Posner, 2009; Reave, 2005) theorized that spiritual dimensions are the true basis for leadership despite the lack of sound, empirical research using valid instrumentation. Spirituality has been connected with authentic leadership elements such as identity integrity, self-awareness, moral clarity, and core values (Reave, 2005; Walumbwa et al., 2008). Gould (2005) wrote that effective leadership development required the reshaping of the inner self, core motives, and implicit concepts and not simply behavior modification. Spiritual efforts, such as those measured by the SpEI target the authentic, inner self allowing that leadership growth through discovery, shaping, and deepening core identity (Conger, 1994). Fulfilling a primary consideration of research using the SpEI, the research example was based on sound, scholarly literature support for the potential relationships of interest.

As a reminder, even if a particular instrument meets the theoretical and practical needs of a research project, that scale should also be validated thoroughly to ensure it retains validity in the particular application and population. That validity testing should include the common measures such as Cronbach Alpha, but also apply advanced methods such as confirmatory factor analysis (CFA), convergent validity, and discriminant validity. Of course, face validity will require considering the theoretical foundation of instruments such as the SpEI to assess whether accurately capturing the scale's associated constructs will satisfy the research design. That is, statistical tools, even if rigorously applied, are only a part of the validity assessment for any particular study.

The Relationship Between Spiritual Engagement and Authentic Leadership – An Example in Application

Our example research (Roof, 2016) demonstrated how the SpEI could be used to offer insight into the relationship of the transformative nature of spirituality and an organizational leadership construct. We will often refer to the example as the 'study' for simplicity. In the example research, the use of authentic leadership offered some interesting insights since authentic leadership is not only viewed as a 'root construct' of positive leadership (Avolio & Gardner, 2005), but is comprised of four dimensions allowing for a more complex analysis of not only the second order concept, but first order individual elements of the normative leadership theory (Roof, 2016).

The Design

The design of research must ponder a wide range of considerations, but it begins with the research question to be answered. In the example, the interest was in the intersection of spiritual engagement and contemporary normative leadership. That is, is a leader who commits to spiritual engagement perceived by followers to demonstrate greater positive leadership characteristics? Since prior work with spiritual engagement informed the spiritual construct of interest, the question of what specific leadership theory might illustrate positive leadership characteristics to followers was explored in the literature. Authentic leadership emerged as the theory of interest based on its theoretical constructs and significant recent use, its breadth of positive characteristics for organizations, and its complex relationships with ethical, servant, transformational, and charismatic leadership and related concepts including trust, personality, implicit leadership theories, leader-member exchange, emotional intelligence, and follower motivation (Walumbwa et al., 2008). The authentic leadership constructs from Walumbwa et al.'s work included self-awareness, balanced processing, relational transparency, and internalized moral perspective which were of particular interest since they presented complex dimensions from which to explore the spiritual engagement-leadership intersection. The connection of authentic leadership to spiritual engagement through the leader's spiritual center was supported by Stonecipher (2012) who suggested that incorporating spiritual development would be effective for authentic leadership development since authentic leadership emerges from the spiritual center of the leader. For the research study, robust literature review led to the selection of the specific theories to explore (spiritual engagement and authentic leadership), as use of spiritual engagement and authentic leadership would specifically and properly engage the research question. Similarly, future researchers considering use of the SpEI should fully investigate spiritual engagement and the instrument to ensure they best address their research question(s). For many theories, there may be multiple instruments to consider, each of which captures different theoretical constructs. Therefore, exploring the theoretical underpinnings and development of the specific instrument to be used is just as important as identifying the theories and relationship of interest. For quantitative work, proper hypothesis testing requires theoretical aligned measurements.

The interest into the relationship of spiritual engagement and authentic leadership (Roof, 2016) was reflected in the study's research questions and hypotheses and provided the framework for the methods to be employed. A cross-sectional survey was chosen for the nonexperimental, quantitative research due to its economy and practicality (Creswell, 2009). The SpEI was selected to capture the spiritual engagement constructs and the Authentic Leadership Questionnaire (ALQ) was chosen to capture authentic leadership since it was widely validated, psychometrically sound, and measured second order authentic leadership as well as the four first order dimensions of interest (Roof, 2014a). While both instruments (SpEI and ALQ) were validated during development, and in the case of the ALQ, in prior research, all instruments should also be tested for reliability and validity in each study and for each population. Such reliability and validity confirmatory work was performed within the study.

For exploring the spiritual engagement-authentic leadership intersection, the study design involved capturing spiritual engagement as self-reported by the leader (since observation of the practices, attitudes, and expectations by others would prove unreliable) and the associated follower-reported authentic leadership (Roof, 2016). The survey method and size were established considering the type of hypotheses testing and analysis needed for the research. When designing the data collection survey, in addition to the primary instruments (20 items for the SpEI for leaders, 16 items in the ALQ for followers), the necessary additional items for validation and analysis were incorporated. Potential confounders (from the literature) including age, gender, race, marital status, religious affiliation, and type organization (profit, non-profit) were included. To support testing for concurrent validity of the SpEI since it was an early stage measure, the BMMRS (Fetzer Institute on Aging, n.d.) and DSES (Underwood & Teresi, 2002) were also integrated. The SDRS-5 (Hays et al., 1989) was also incorporated into the leaders' survey to evaluate social desirability bias. Including a number of items in addition to the core instruments is often advisable and requires, as with selection of the core instrumentation, researchers to carefully evaluate inclusion of items such as potential confounders or items to validate scales, the likelihood of social desirability responses, and any other sampling needs. In adding additional items to data collection, the researcher should consider the cost-reward, weighing the value of the information against possible impact on sample response, respondent fatigue, or other unintended biases.

For the analysis (Roof, 2016), an adequate sample size was planned considering the type testing to be performed. Since multiple regression was the primary method for testing the hypotheses, 15-20 samples were needed per variable requiring at least 60-80 surveys (leaders). Increased response rates were promoted through soliciting organizational support for the survey, personalized invitations, follow-up queries to the initial invitations, and reasonable financial incentives (gift cards). The result was 65 leader and 266 associated follower responses that were usable. Designing the collection, population, survey length, solicitation method, and incentives can be critical to successful research. In particular, when using a measure such as the SpEI, sensitivity to individual respondents view of personal questions should be addressed through the survey instructions (see Appendix A – Spiritual Engagement Instrument, (Roof, 2014a)), email solicitations explaining of the purpose of the research, assurance of survey confidentiality, and stressing the volunteer nature of survey response. Such efforts can assist in the harvesting of candid, meaningful survey responses. For the example study, identifying follower participants was a bit unusual in that they had to be identified (and connected during analyses) with their leaders so the relationships of interest could be evaluated.

The Analysis

Each step of the analysis is critical for sound research and it all begins with evaluating the initial response data. In the example (Roof, 2016), both leader and follower responses were reviewed for completeness, and any identified missing data evaluated for patterns of bias with appropriate action taken. Since the missing responses revealed no discernable pattern of bias, incomplete responses were eliminated including, for incomplete leader responses, the associated followers. Further preparation in this unique research design involved aggregating the average follower authentic leadership ratings for each leader. The resulting working file had all individual identifiers removed to support confidentiality.

Following collection, initial examination and analysis of the data was performed in preparation for the actual hypotheses testing (Roof, 2016). Briefly, these preparatory steps included:

- Social desirability responses were examined for each leader to determine extreme response patterns (Hays et al., 1989).
- Descriptive statistics were generated to evaluate representation of sample and generalizability.
- Outliers from the spiritual engagement data from the SpEI and authentic leadership responses from the ALQ were identified using descriptive statistics and 5% trimmed mean analysis followed by evaluation of whether outliers were population characteristics or aberrations to be removed (Hair et al., 2010; Pallant, 2010).
- Authentic leadership data was evaluated for normality assumptions using normality graphs, skewness and kurtosis values, Kolmogorov-Smirmov test of normality and later, plots of normality residuals (Hair et al., 2010; Pallant, 2010; Tabachnik & Fidell, 2001).
- Cronbach Alpha values for all scales (SpEI, ALQ) were computed to confirm values were .7 or greater supporting reliability.
- Correlations were computed between all variables to be used for initial insight into relationships and multicollinearity evaluation.

With the initial data evaluated, hypothesis testing was then conducted. In the example, the hypotheses included:

- Those hypotheses considered social desirability in the SpEI responses (H_1) using one-way ANOVA, and potential confounders (H_2) using correlation, t-tests, and ANOVA depending on the nature of the data.
- The research hypotheses (H_3 through H_7) were tested using simple correlation for each SpEI construct and authentic leadership followed by multiple regression to test the relationships of all four spiritual engagement constructs and authentic leadership.

In the example study (Roof, 2016), none of the research hypotheses were supported so the hypothesized relationship between each of the four spiritual engagement constructs and second-order authentic leadership (the combined authentic leadership values) did not indicate that spiritual engagement was a significant predictor of authentic leadership collectively. While research may not result in support for the theoretically expected outcomes as was the case with the example, with sound and robust data collection involving populations of interest, often there are opportunities through post hoc analyses to reveal other meaningful insights. In the case of the example research, post hoc analyses were pursued to better understand the spiritual engagement-leadership and leader identity formation phenomena within the sampled population. Of note, the SpEI provided insight into the leaders' spiritual engagement, yet the theorized underlying relationships to second order authentic leadership was unsupported, so the value of the spiritual engagement insight allowed further investigation and learning.

Post Hoc Analysis – What Else Might Be Learned?

To explore what else might be discovered from the data collected, it can be interesting and sometimes fruitful to review the data, theories, and findings to determine if some ad hoc tests might reveal fresh insights. For the example research (Roof, 2016), two general areas were identified as warranting additional analysis. With data collected and identified from different profit-structure types of organizations, evaluating their leaders' leadership and spiritual engagement characteristics could potentially yield findings of interest. Also, while the research hypotheses were focused on how spiritual engagement might relate to second-order authentic leadership (which proved not to yield significant relationships), a deeper or perhaps broader understand of spiritual engagement and leadership might emerge from further analysis involving the four first order constructs of authentic leadership. Both of those avenues were pursued (Roof, 2016).

The survey participants in the study were relatively homogeneous in their race and religion (Roof, 2016), so further investigation based on those characteristics was not expected to be meaningful. However, one question that emerged from the demographic characteristics of the sample population was whether there were differences in the characteristics of leaders in for-profit (FP) and not-for-profit (NFP) organizations in terms of their perceived authentic leadership practices and in their spiritual engagement measures. An independent sample t-test revealed no significant difference in second order authentic leadership between the not-for-profit and for-profit leaders in the sample. In fact, perceived mean authentic leadership values were remarkable close (FP=3.30, NFP=3.32) indicating that leaders in the two classes of organization were perceived virtually the same by their followers in terms of authentic leadership. For those who believe non-profit leadership may be motivated differently than for-profit leaders, that would be a surprising finding worthy of additional future examination, perhaps using qualitative methods.

A second area of interest for comparing FP and NFP leaders was in their self-reported measures of spiritual engagement. Evaluation of differences in each of the four spiritual engagement constructs yielded significant differences between FP and NFP leaders in the areas of worship and fasting with NFP leaders reporting greater spiritual engagement in those constructs. While meditation did not exhibit significant differences between NFP and FP leaders, the rest component did indicate fairly meaningful differences with NFP reporting greater spiritual engagement, but they did not quite meet the threshold for significance at 95% confidence. These findings in reported spiritual engagement combined with the lack of difference in authentic leadership observed between the FP and NFP leadership populations raises significant questions related to how spiritual engagement influences leadership, especially within these different organizational communities.

In seeking to understand more fully the possible intersection of spiritual engagement and authentic leadership (AL), ad hoc testing of first order AL was undertaken (Roof, 2016). Authentic leadership as measured by the authentic leadership questionnaire exhibits four dimensions; relational transparency (RT), internal moral perspective (MP), balanced processing (BP), and self-awareness (SA) although adequate discriminant validity of the first order constructs has not been supported consistently in the literature (Roof, 2014a). The original survey data was used to create composite variables for the first order authentic leadership dimensions and Cronbach Alpha values computed (Roof, 2016). Good reliability was indicated for RT, MP, and SA (all >.70), but BP inter-item correlation was only 0.59 indicating that any analysis of the BP dimension be approached cautiously (Pallant, 2010). Correlation was performed between all spiritual engagement dimensions and all authentic leadership first order dimensions and the analysis found significant correlation only between worship and both relational transparency (RT) and balanced processing (BP). As Roof (2016) noted in the original post hoc work, "The implications of correlation with only some authentic leadership dimensions may provide the study's greatest contribution to theory by indicating complexities in the authentic leadership–spiritual engagement relationship or in measurement of the constructs of interest" (p. 67).

One explanation for the first order relationships of RT and BP with worship and not MP and SA may relate to the underlying force driving those authentic leadership dimensions. Yukl (2010) suggested that moral behavior such as that which followers might perceive as internal moral perspective (MP) or even self-awareness (SA) could be more affected by social alignment than moral identity or deepened identity insights, relationships that would minimize the connection of spiritual engagement with observed 'moral' behaviors or self-awareness as was found in the study (Roof, 2016). In earlier supportive qualitative work, Vasconcelos (2010) suggested that spirituality resulted in more effective decision making as might be observed as balanced processing (BP) and greater relationships such as would be seen as the authentic leadership construct of relational transparency (RT).

In the end, these uneven post hoc findings related to the first order authentic leadership dimensions might suggest that authentic leadership as defined by Walumbwa et al. (2008) may incorporate first order dimensions that involve a mix of both identity and socially influenced leader behaviors. Within the normative leadership theories, such characteristics could suggest that other, more identity-driven, humility based, power sharing theories (or authentic leadership definitions) where leaders act contrary to expected societal norms may better relate to spiritual engagement leader identity shifting than that measured by the ALQ. Research into relationships between spiritual engagement and theories such as transformational leadership or servant leadership may yield additional insight into the spiritual engagement-leadership intersection.

As can be seen through the experience of the example, rigorous design, data preparation, confounder testing, and hypothesis testing using the proper analytical techniques is necessary for sound research using the SpEI or other instruments (Roof, 2016). In some cases, as in the example, analysis may involve a wide variety of statistical, graphical, and interpretive methods such as correlation, differences testing (ANOVA, t-test), multiple regression, and other specialized tests for normality or other characteristics (Creswell, 2009; Hair et al., 2010; Pallant, 2010; Tabachnik & Fidell, 2001). Of particular note from the example is that research can reveal unexpected insights if robust, valid, data is viewed with an inquisitive perspective. That is, pursuit beyond the initial framework of the research can be fruitful and yield fresh ideas for refining theory or launching new research endeavors, especially with early stage theories such as spiritual engagement or even authentic leadership.

CONCLUSION

Research interest in the influence of spirituality and how it may connect with positive leadership and organizational constructs has led to increased activity by scholars, but rigorous examination, especially quantitative study has been hindered by inadequate scales (Nicolae et al., 2013). Many existing scales capture behaviors, but do not consider the complex, transformational, experiential nature of human spirituality (Roof et al., 2017). This chapter examined transformational spirituality theoretically and presented the SpEI as a valid instrument with which to explore the spirituality-organizational construct relationships. The scale offers the promise of advancing understanding of how spirituality engages organizational culture, leader identity, authenticity, trust, and the range of normative leadership theories.

By presenting spirituality theory, reviewing the development and validation of the SpEI, and illustrating its use in research into authentic leadership, the reader can garner an understanding of the theory and application of spiritual measures, especially the SpEI, and how it may be used to explore and advance important organizational and individual concepts. The particular example presented as an illustration also demonstrated how research can often yield unexpected insights and, in the process, identify areas for future research. That is, despite research not supporting expected relationships, insights into the true underlying theoretical dimensions may advance understanding in greater, more insightful ways. Discoveries may present deeper understanding of core theoretical dimensions as the example did in examining Walumbwa et al.'s (2008) authentic leadership constructs.

The subject of this chapter, the SpEI, is unique in its focus on spirituality as a transformative force with expectations, attitudes, practices, and outcomes forming a cycle of spiritual growth (Roof et al., 2017). The resulting connectedness with God offers the promise of affective and cognitive transformation. This transformation is a dynamic concept, so the SpEI offers the researcher and interested organizations a device to be used as a pre/post-test of a spiritual development program or in semi-experimental or longitudinal research related to leadership characteristics, organizational culture, employee development efforts, ethics, or any of the normative leadership theories. Understanding the effects of spiritual development may reveal innovative approaches to develop more effective, trusted leaders who lead from an ever-evolving identity, and also assist organizations in evaluating programs directed at cultural shaping or spiritual wellness.

This chapter on measuring the complexity of spirituality through both theoretical and practical perspectives, provides the reader with a framework in which to consider study of these important, emerging principles. The SpEI instrument as a validated, multi-dimensional instrument provides the researcher with a fresh tool with which to contribute to the knowledge of human spirituality in contemporary organizations. Until recently, understanding spirituality in organizational settings has been hindered by the lack of robust, validated scales, so the SpEI with its focus on the transformative nature of spiritual practices contributes a new tool that if applied in rigorous, well-designed, validated research can advance our understanding.

ACKNOWLEDGMENT

This research received no specific grant from any funding agency in the public, commercial, or not-for-profit sectors.

REFERENCES

Ai, A. L., Peterson, C., Bolling, S. F., & Koenig, H. (2002). Private prayer and optimism in middle-aged and older patients awaiting cardiac surgery. *The Gerontologist, 42*(1), 70–81. doi:10.1093/geront/42.1.70 PMID:11815701

Ashmos, D. P., & Duchon, D. (2000). Spirituality at work. *Journal of Management Inquiry, 9*(2), 134–145. doi:10.1177/105649260092008

Avolio, B. J., & Gardner, W. L. (2005). Authentic leadership development: Getting to the root of positive forms of leadership. *The Leadership Quarterly, 16*(3), 315–338. doi:10.1016/j.leaqua.2005.03.001

Bussing, A., Matthiessen, P. F., & Ostermann, T. (2005). Engagement of patients in religious and spiritual practices: Confirmatory results with the SpREUK-P 1.1 questionnaire as a tool of quality of life research. *Health and Quality of Life Outcomes, 3*(53). PMID:16144546

Byrne, A., Dionisi, A. M., Barling, J., Akers, A., Robertson, J., Lys, R., Wylie, J., & Dupré, K. (2014). The depleted leader: The influence of leaders' diminished psychological resources on leadership behaviors. *The Leadership Quarterly, 25*(2), 344–357. doi:10.1016/j.leaqua.2013.09.003

Chandler, D. J. (2008). Pastoral burnout and the impact of personal spiritual renewal, rest-taking, and support system practices. *Pastoral Psychology, 58*(3), 273–287. doi:10.100711089-008-0184-4

Conger, J. A. (1994). *Spirit at work: Discovering the spirituality in leadership*. Jossey-Bass.

Creswell, J. W. (2009). *Research design: Qualitative, quantitative, and mixed methods approaches* (3rd ed.). SAGE Publications, Inc.

Crossman, J. (2010). Conceptualising spiritual leadership in secular organizational contexts and its relation to transformational, servant and environmental leadership. *Leadership and Organization Development Journal, 31*(7), 596–608. doi:10.1108/01437731011079646

Devellis, R. F. (2012). *Scale development: Theory and applications* (3rd ed.). Sage Publications.

Eck, B. E. (2002). An exploration of the therapeutic use of spiritual disciplines in clinical practice. *Journal of Psychology and Christianity, 21*(3), 266–280.

Fetzer Institute on Aging. (n.d.). *Multidimensional measurement of religiousness/spirituality for use in health research*. Retrieved July 25, 2014, from http://www.fetzer.org/resources/multidimensional-measurement-religiousnessspirituality-use-health-research

Fields, D. L. (2007). Determinants of follower perceptions of a leader's authenticity and integrity. *European Management Journal, 25*(3), 195–206. doi:10.1016/j.emj.2007.04.005

Foster, R. J., & Griffin, E. (Eds.). (2000). *Spiritual classics: Selected readings on the twelve spiritual disciplines*. HarperOne.

Fry, L. W. (2003). Toward a theory of spiritual leadership. *The Leadership Quarterly, 14*(6), 693–727. doi:10.1016/j.leaqua.2003.09.001

Garcia-Zamor, J.-C. (2003). Workplace spirituality and organizational performance. *Public Administration Review, 63*(3), 355–363. doi:10.1111/1540-6210.00295

Gardner, W. L., Cogliser, C. C., Davis, K. M., & Dickens, M. P. (2011). Authentic leadership: A review of the literature and research agenda. *The Leadership Quarterly, 22*(6), 1120–1145. doi:10.1016/j.leaqua.2011.09.007

Giacalone, R. A., & Jurkiewicz, C. L. (2003). *Handbook of workplace spirituality and organizational performance*. M.E. Sharpe., doi:10.4324/9781315703817

Girden, E. R. (2011). *Evaluating research articles from start to finish* (3rd ed.). Sage Publications, Inc.

Gould, J. (2005). Becoming good: The role of spiritual practice. *Philosophical Practice: Journal of the American Philosophical Practitioners Association, 1*(3), 135–147. doi:10.1080/17428170600595846

Hair, J. F., Black, W. C., Babin, B. J., & Anderson, R. E. (2010). *Multivariate data analysis* (7th ed.). Prentice Hall.

Hays, R. D., Hayashi, T., & Stewart, A. L. (1989). A five-item measure of socially desirable response set. *Educational and Psychological Measurement, 49*(3), 629–636. doi:10.1177/001316448904900315

Hoppe, S. L. (2005). Spirituality and leadership. *New Directions for Teaching and Learning, 104*(104), 83–92. doi:10.1002/tl.217

Issler, K. D. (2009). Inner core belief formation, spiritual practices, and the willing-doing gap. *Journal of Spiritual Formation and Soul Care, 2*(2), 179–198. doi:10.1177/193979090900200203

Karakas, F. (2010). Spirituality and performance in organizations: A literature review. *Journal of Business Ethics, 94*(1), 89–106. doi:10.100710551-009-0251-5

King, J. E. Jr. (2008). (Dis)missing the obvious: Will mainstream management research ever take religion seriously? *Journal of Management Inquiry, 17*(3), 214–224. doi:10.1177/1056492608314205

Laird, S. P., Snyder, C. R., Rapoff, M. A., & Green, S. (2004). Research: "Measuring private prayer: Development, validation, and clinical application of the multidimensional prayer inventory. *The International Journal for the Psychology of Religion, 14*(4), 251–272. doi:10.120715327582ijpr1404_2

McNeal, R. (2000). *A work of heart: Understanding how god shapes spiritual leaders*. Jossey-Bass.

Monod, S., Brennan, M., Rochat, E., Martin, E., Rochat, S., & Büla, C. J. (2011). Instruments measuring spirituality in clinical research: A systematic review. *Journal of General Internal Medicine, 26*(11), 1345–1357. doi:10.100711606-011-1769-7 PMID:21725695

Neal, J. (2000). Work as service to the divine. *The American Behavioral Scientist, 43*(8), 1316–1333. doi:10.1177/00027640021955883

Nicolae, M., Ion, I., & Nicolae, E. (2013). The research agenda of spiritual leadership. Where do we stand? *Journal of International Comparative Management, 14*(4), 551–566.

Pallant, J. (2010). *SPSS survival guide: A step-by-step guide to data analysis using the SPSS program* (4th ed.). McGraw-Hill.

Piedmont, R. L. (1999). Does spirituality represent the sixth factor of personality? spiritual transcendence and the five-factor model. *Journal of Personality, 67*(6), 985–1013. doi:10.1111/1467-6494.00080

Posner, B. Z. (2009). From inside out. *Journal of Leadership Education, 8*(1), 1–10. doi:10.12806/V8/I1/TF1

Reave, L. (2005). Spiritual values and practices related to leadership effectiveness. *The Leadership Quarterly, 16*(5), 655–687. doi:10.1016/j.leaqua.2005.07.003

Roof, R. (2014a). Authentic leadership questionnaire (alq) psychometrics. *Asian Journal of Business Ethics*, *3*(1), 57–64. doi:10.100713520-013-0031-2

Roof, R. A. (2014b). The association of individual spirituality on employee engagement: The spirit at work. *Journal of Business Ethics*, *130*(3), 585–599. doi:10.100710551-014-2246-0

Roof, R. A. (2016). *The relationship between spiritual engagement and authentic leadership: Exploring the core of leadership* (1791976131) [Doctoral dissertation, Regent University]. Proquest Dissertations & Theses Global.

Roof, R. A., Bocarnea, M. C., & Winston, B. E. (2017). The spiritual engagement instrument. *Asian Journal of Business Ethics*, *6*(2), 215–232. doi:10.100713520-017-0073-y

Sanders, J. O. (2007). *Spiritual leadership: Principles of excellence for every believer* (1st ed.). Moody.

Sass, J. S. (2000). Characterizing organizational spirituality: An organizational communication culture approach. *Communication Studies*, *51*(3), 195–217. doi:10.1080/10510970009388520

Schwanda, T. (2010). "Hearts sweetly refreshed": Puritan spiritual practices then and now. *Journal of Spiritual Formation and Soul Care*, *3*(1), 21–41. doi:10.1177/193979091000300103

Sheep, M. L., & Foreman, P. O. (2012). An integrative framework for exploring organizational identity and spirituality. *Journal of Applied Business and Economics*, *13*(4), 11–29.

Stonecipher, P. (2012). The development of the leader and the spirit. *Journal of Leadership Education*, *11*(2), 88–101. doi:10.12806/V11/I2/RF5

Strack, G., & Fottler, M. D. (2002). Spirituality and effective leadership in healthcare: Is there a connection? *Frontiers of Health Services Management*, *18*(4), 3–18. doi:10.1097/01974520-200204000-00002 PMID:12087690

Tabachnik, B. G., & Fidell, L. S. (2001). *Using multivariate statistics* (4th ed.). Allyn & Bacon.

Underwood, L. G. (2011). The daily spiritual experience scale: Overview and results. *Religions*, *2*(1), 29–50. doi:10.3390/rel2010029

Underwood, L. G., & Teresi, J. A. (2002). The daily spiritual experience scale: Development, theoretical description, reliability, exploratory factor analysis, and preliminary construct validity using health-related data. *Annals of Behavioral Medicine*, *24*(1), 22–33. doi:10.1207/S15324796ABM2401_04 PMID:12008791

Vasconcelos, A. F. (2010). The effects of prayer on organizational life: A phenomenological study. *Journal of Management & Organization*, *16*(3), 369–381. doi:10.5172/jmo.16.3.369

Walumbwa, F. O., Avolio, B. J., Gardner, W. L., Wernsing, T. S., & Peterson, S. J. (2008). Authentic leadership: Development and validation of a theory-based measure†. *Journal of Management*, *34*(1), 89–126. doi:10.1177/0149206307308913

Whitney, D. S. (2014). *Spiritual disciplines for the Christian life*. NavPress.

Yukl, G. A. (2010). *Leadership in organizations* (7th ed.). Prentice-Hall.

KEY TERMS AND DEFINITIONS

Authentic Leadership: A contemporary normative leadership theory that is considered by some researchers to be at the root of normative leadership and reflects principles such as self-awareness, consistency in word and action, fairness, and ethical practices. Like most leadership theories, precise constructs vary among researchers.

Convergent Validity: An element of construct validity that refers to whether theoretically similar constructs are in fact statistically related. That is, do the related constructs 'converge'?

Differences Testing: Class of analysis using statistical tools that assess whether there are statistically significant differences between two or more groups of data. Different tests such as ANOVA, t-tests, or MANOVA are used depending on the nature of the data and groups.

Discriminant Validity: Like convergent validity, an element of construct validity. Discriminant validity refers to whether theoretically dissimilar constructs are in fact statistically different. That is, can the related constructs be shown to 'diverge'?

Social Desirability Response Bias: A bias in social science surveys that results as respondents answer in ways viewed as socially favorable.

Spiritual Disciplines or Exercises: Spiritual practices such as prayer, reading scripture, or worship that are intended to develop the inner being, the spiritual identity.

Spiritual Engagement: The transformational cycle of expectations (faith), attitudes, behaviors, and deeper spirituality that is theorized to elevate spiritual identity and empower leaders to practice positive leadership more consistently.

Validity: In research validity refers to how well the construct of interest is in fact measured by the method used. That is, does the study measure what it is intended to capture.

APPENDIX

Spiritual Engagement Instrument (SpEI) (Roof et al., 2017)

This survey is intended to capture within your own faith tradition, worldview, or philosophy, those spiritual practice and association beliefs and attitudes that draw you closer to God or the divine. While you may feel strongly theologically or have specific ideas of how the spiritual practices or disciplines should be conducted, the survey was designed to measure across a wide range of such perspectives, so please do your best not to be distracted by the nature of any specific question.

Rate the following statements using the categories of Strongly Agree, Moderately Agree, Mildly Agree, Mildly Disagree, Moderately Disagree, and Strongly Disagree as indicated on the survey form.

Worship

Prayer helps me feel closer to God.

I make requests of God in my prayers.

Worship is refreshing to me spiritually.

Worship is a regular practice for me.

Worship is a priority in my spiritual life.

Meditation

Meditation helps me experience peace.

My attitude is often helped by meditation.

Meditation is an important part of my spiritual life.

Meditation helps me be more genuine or authentic.

I get along better with others when I meditate.

Fasting

When I fast I experience more clarity.

My spirit is cleansed by my fasting.

What is truly important becomes clear when I fast.

My values or morals are strengthened by fasting.

I feel closer to my God when I fast.

Rest

My time off for religious/spiritual rest is important to me.

I am more patient and focused when I have my time off for religious/spiritual rest each week.

My spirit is refreshed by my dedicated weekly rest.

My weekly time for religious/spiritual rest leaves me in a better place.

Life's priorities are clearer as a result of my dedicated time off weekly for my faith practices.

Chapter 13
Vision Conflict Scale:
Instrument Profile

J. Louis Spencer
American Public University System, USA

W. David Winner
Regent University, USA

ABSTRACT

This chapter presents the development of a scale that measures vision conflict, which refers to the disparity between what a minister anticipates a ministry to be like versus the real-life experience. Vision conflict is correlated with four similar phenomena, including role ambiguity, negative job satisfaction, negative values congruence, and negative ability-job fit. The scale addresses key factors that may affect pastoral terminations and exits from church ministry. It also encourages the understanding of critical elements that hinder pastoral effectiveness and create a stronger resilience to exiting the ministry.

A PASTORAL MINISTRY CRISIS

Evangelical clergy from a cross-section of denominational traditions are increasingly withdrawing from the ministry due to significant difficulties related to various spiritual, physical, emotional, and social issues manifested in maladies such as burnout, depression, discouragement, immorality, poverty, inadequacy, conflict, and stress (Elkington, 2013; Farley, 2016; Joynt, 2017; Krejcir, 2016; Wickman, 2011). The struggles facing pastoral ministry are not new, but according to a landmark study by London and Wiseman (2003), pastors in the 21st century are facing diverse challenges and adversities associated with contemporary ministry, coupled with fluctuating perceptions that create conflict among clergy:

Unprecedented shifts in moral, social, and economic conditions are battering congregations. These changing circumstances and declining values directly affect pastors and their way of life . . . At the same time, pastors' concepts of ministry are in flux. Now, clergy expect personal fulfillment and meaning, where former generations seemed satisfied with sacrifice and even expected to suffer. Clearly, this new

DOI: 10.4018/978-1-7998-7665-6.ch013

breed of pastors views their world, their work, and themselves differently than their preaching parents and grandparents did. (p. 34)

Pastors progressively appear ill-prepared to fulfill congregational expectations while also answering to their family, denomination, community, and self, since resources and ministry partners are diminishing (Lee, 2017; London & Wiseman, 2003; Tanner, 2016). Hoge and Wenger's (2005) study of 963 pastors from five different evangelical denominations found that there is typically a combination of issues that contribute to pastoral exits. Their study concluded that secularization of the church coincides with a changed view of the pastorate as "a religious vocation based on lifelong calling, self-sacrifice, and personal holiness to a new professional ideal stressing learning, certification, and identity" (Hoge & Wenger, 2005, p. 4). Three important findings come from the Hoge and Wenger (2005) study. First, conflict with parishioners, church staff, and denominational leadership is the primary cause of pastoral exits. Second, women tend to leave the ministry more often than men, with family-oriented issues being the main factor. However, the women in the study reported stronger feelings of disillusionment related to denominational systems and resistance to women as clergy. The third important finding was that more minister exits are associated with institutional or interpersonal complications, not because of a loss of faith or financial shortfall.

Reed (2016) examined the antecedents associated with longevity of ministry and its association with numerous elements such as spiritual practices, lifestyle habits, vocational crises, the role of calling, personal relationships, and congregational characteristics. The qualitative study concludes that healthy relationships with God, family, friends, and congregational members, are key indicators as to whether a minister is likely to remain in the pastorate.

Joynt (2017) found calling as a significant antecedent affecting pastoral exits because of the variation of ways in which calling is viewed. According to Joynt (2017):

Some respond to the call yet leave for various reasons; some consider the call to be seasonal (e.g., a set time frame) or bi-vocational in nature (e.g. both pastoral and business or both pastoral and missions); and some were never called in the first place but merely followed the only route they considered to be a means to serve God. (p. 5)

Another work by Joynt (2018) examines the multi-level role of conflict in creating a negative environment for ministry—conflict stemming from miscommunication with the congregation and/or denomination, including "role ambiguity, role conflict and leadership conflict" (p. 6)—that can result in clergy exiting the ministry. A treatise by Greenfield (2001) focuses on pastor abuse and notes the occurrence of discord between congregations and ministers. According to Greenfield, typical pastor abuse is characterized by "a set of problems in the church that serves as background for the conflict that develops between the minister and one or more laypersons who begin identifying the minister as the cause of the problems" (p. 24). The senior ministers tend to receive the majority of abusive treatment associated with feelings of rejection, questioning their calling, and occasionally, clinical depression. Greenfield's (2001) qualitative work underscores the emotional and social nature of negative confrontations with pastors, and it supports the conclusion that the issues facing ministers are unique from leaders in other sectors. For members of the clergy, the congregation is also the de facto employer and may contribute to a greater sense of devastating attack.

The role of the clergy also plays a significant role in pastoral exits. When the exiting is a result of a congregational decision to terminate the pastor, there tends to be more association with lower-than-expected performance expectations (Croucher, 2002; Elkington, 2013; Rosendahl, 2019). Sheffield (2008) found that the decision to terminate a pastor typically involves at least one of several major issues: (a) control issues in the church, (b) inadequate people skills, (c) domineering leadership style, (d) the church's resistance to change, and (e) ongoing conflict in the church. When the exiting is the personal decision of the minister, psychological dynamics within the pastor's life typically play a certain level of influence. Psychological dynamics affect how the clergy deals with the social expectations of their role as reflected in the degree to which they can differentiate themselves from ministry work (Beebe, 2007). According to Beebe's (2007) study of 343 ministers, lower levels of differentiation between the perception of self and ministry role contributed to a greater likelihood that the clergy will consider exiting the ministry, whereas a higher level of differentiation between the perception of self and ministry role results in a lesser likelihood of exiting the ministry. Beebe's (2007) research concluded that ministers who function at a higher level of differentiation tend to lead with increased collaborative efforts when dealing with conflict, which results in a lower perceived likelihood of exiting the ministry.

The antecedents that contribute to the exiting of clergy from the ministry have limited similarity to those that affect leaders in other sectors. All leaders have some shared experiences in terms of working with other people and organizational boards; clergy tend to experience a peculiar blend of issues and circumstances associated with the church and its ongoing ministry. A study of 108 evangelical pastors by Barfoot et al. (2005) found that the top sources of tension that most likely contribute to pastoral exits were: music/worship style differences, conflicting visions for the church, personality conflicts with members of the board, and conflict with non-board members of the church. Palser (2005) found that the unique blend of circumstances experienced by clergy results in attrition among the clergy that exceeds those of other service professionals.

Some ministry experiences run counter to the original expectations held by the clergy, which can cause a sense of conflict and hopelessness may emerge. Kisslinger (2007) studied 114 ministers and concluded that role ambiguity and mismatched role expectations of the clergy were significant factors in ministry continuance. According to Kisslinger, matters of church doctrine and church personality also add to whether a minister becomes overwhelmed by a sense that ministry expectations and actual ministry experiences do not match. Rediger (2003) encountered the recurring statements from pastors that obedience to God's call to seminary and then to the pastorate ultimately resulted in role confusion, burnout, depression, lack of appreciation, challenges to authority, anger, and frustration. One pastor's remarks typified the expression of colleagues by stating that he and his peers "felt called to be pastors, but we graduated depressed and confused because that's the mood of our day" (Rediger, 2003, p. 16). Kisslinger's research and Rediger's practitioner work among pastors reinforce the idea that there are numerous overlapping variables that affect ministerial service and that those variables positively and negatively contribute to anticipation about the ministry. This supports the idea that the expected and the actual experiences of the ministry may affect the tenure of a minister. This difference between the expected and the actual experiences of the ministry is described as vision conflict.

THE GENESIS OF THE VISION CONFLICT SCALE (VCS)

The initial steps toward identifying vision conflict as a new leadership construct originated in conjunction with Chuck Wickman (2004), his 20 years of practitioner work observing clergy, and studying the forced and unforced exiting of pastors from vocational ministry. According to Wickman (as cited in "Ministry Retrains," 1997), most of the clergy who leave the ministry do so because of conflicts involving their church. The rise of conflict is connected with a sense of irregularity between expectations of the ministry's service versus what actually occurs in the ministry.

Forced and unforced exits from the ministry represent an interplay between various causal elements in a person's life (C. Wickman, personal communication, July 23, 2008). According to Wickman, a clergy member's personality, personal history, the physical location of the church, the culture associated with the church and the community, and acceptance of the minister by those receiving the ministry are typical antecedents that contribute to the vision conflict in a minister's life. Of the numerous clergy interviewed by Wickman, repeated phenomena linked with forced and unforced exits from a ministry included loss of energy, growing cynicism, increasing apathy and feeling like they do not care, feeling more and more like a robot going through the motions of ministry, a rising sense of feeling bothered about ministry, increased desire to procrastinate, the perception that trust is slowly turning into suspicion, tendency to withdraw from stressful situations, more distance between self and people in the church, more impatience with congregants, loss of a sense of humor, increased callousness toward people, a feeling of increasing stress, feelings of helplessness to stop being overwhelmed, difficulty in saying no, and the desire to be liked.

Wickman's (2014) work on clergy resulted in a breadth of data related to the clergy's ability to persist in the ministry in a variety of contexts and denominational groups. Based on a grounded theory approach and established qualitative tradition Creswell (1998, 2014), a quantitative instrument—the Pastors at Risk Inventory (PaRI)—was gradually developed by Wickman using the interrelationship of an array of categories that emerged from the data (Netemeyer et al., 2003). Spencer et al. (2009, 2012) conducted research using Wickman's (2004) 42-item instrument and received 285 responses from a cross-section of evangelical clergy. An analysis of the data (using factor analysis with varimax rotation and Kaiser normalization) concluded that the ten items ($\alpha = .90$) collectively measure vision conflict. Table 1 summarizes the results of the initial research that provided a reference point for creating the Vision Conflict Scale (VCS). Although the research by Spencer et al. (2009, 2012) was used to examine the relationships that exist between the original vision conflict items by Wickman, a further qualitative investigation was necessary to produce a survey for data collection and analysis leading to the validation of the VCS.

The initial research conducted by Spencer et al. (2009, 2012) based on Wickman's (2004) instrument examined vision conflict as a discriminant dimension that negatively affects clergy, and it explored whether it is distinguishable from other similar variables affecting individuals within organizations in other work sectors (Barfoot et al., 2005; Palser, 2005). As a result, four theoretical areas were identified that substantially contribute to an understanding of the vision conflict turf, namely, role stress, motivation, person-organization fit, and environmental determinism. A closer look at each of these theories reveals nine associated variables that demonstrate how vision conflict is distinguishable as a unique dimension associated with clergy. For instance, role stress theory—particularly role conflict (Addae et al., 2008), role ambiguity (Kahn et al., 1964), and role overload (Peterson et al., 1995)—may be suggested by the following items: "I am confused about my major role in the church," "I feel my work is futile," "I feel I would like to leave the church I now serve," and "I seriously consider leaving the ministry entirely."

Table 1. Summary list of original vision conflict items (taken from Wickman's survey)

Item statement	Load
I am confused about my major role in the church.	.57
I have lost the sense of meaning in my work.	.78
I feel my work is futile.	.64
I wonder about my calling as a pastor.	.78
Ministry doesn't bring me satisfaction.	.81
I find little joy in my work.	.79
I feel I would like to leave the church I now serve.	.67
I seriously consider leaving the ministry entirely.	.76
I feel my hope for success has not developed.	.67
I feel my personal relationship with Christ is a real problem.	.44

Note. Factor analysis was conducted using varimax rotation with Kaiser normalization.

Next, motivational theory—particularly job satisfaction (Bacharach et al., 1991) and career commitment (Somers & Birnbaum, 1998)—may be suggested by the following items: "I have lost the sense of meaning in my work," "I wonder about my calling as a pastor," "Ministry doesn't bring me satisfaction," "I find little joy in my work," and "I feel my hope for success has not developed."

A third theoretical area, P–O fit—particularly values congruence (Chatman, 1989, 1991) and abilities–job fit (Abdel-Halim, 1981)—may be suggested by the following items: "I am confused about my major role in the church," "I have lost a sense of meaning in my work," "I feel my work is futile," "I wonder about my calling as a pastor," "I feel my hope for success has not developed," and "I feel my personal relationship with Christ is a real problem." Finally, environmental determinism—including political skill (Ferris et al., 2005) and various environmental determinant items (Northouse, 2007)—may be suggested by the following items: "I feel my work is futile," "I feel I would like to leave the church I now serve," "I seriously consider leaving the ministry entirely," and "I feel my hope for success has not developed." The overall purpose of the suggested associations is to establish the potential relationship between each of these theories and the proposition that vision conflict, although similar in some way to each of these theories, is a discriminant dimension experienced by clergy in the ministry.

THEORETICAL FOUNDATIONS AND ANTECEDENTS

Identifying the antecedents associated with vision conflict is critical to developing a useful instrument. Vision conflict is a distinctive phenomenon that affects the likelihood of pastoral persistence in the ministry. However, vision conflict is a term not previously associated with research involving clergy. In fact, until the development of the VCS, compassion fatigue and burnout were the typical antecedents featured in research associated with pastoral exiting. Spencer et al. (2009, 2012) used Wickman's (2004) PaRI, which found that compassion fatigue was distinct from vision conflict. The presence of compassion fatigue as affecting the ministry survival of at-risk pastors is supported by the literature and suggests its relationship to burnout, but its breadth does not include much of the vision conflict territory. Spencer et al. (2009, 2012) showed that variables related to pastoral termination might originate from other causes not necessarily related to either compassion fatigue or burnout. A closer look at the independent variables associated with the outcome of the Spencer et al. (2009) research shows an array of potential antecedents that are associated with four primary areas warranting theoretical discussion.

First, role stress and its three associated elements—role conflict, role ambiguity, and role overload—impact how events and responsibilities in ministry may impact pastors. Role conflict is perhaps the most frequently mentioned role stressor in the literature (Ivancevich et al., 2005). Mohr and Puck (2007) identify three kinds of role conflict: inter-role conflict (e.g., when the expectations of a person's different roles are incompatible with one another), intra-role conflict (e.g., when different expectations within a single role are incompatible with one another), and person-role conflict (e.g., when expectations of one of the individual's roles are incompatible with the person's own needs, aspirations, and ethics, such as may occur when a person is asked to perform work that conflicts with their sense of values). The role conflict arena tends to be the most difficult when pastors do not characterize the social qualities associated with their work (Francis & Rodger, 1994) and when too many different role expectations are present (Kay, 2000).

Role ambiguity, which is similar to role conflict, is the level of structure and definition associated with a particular work in the pastorate (Chang, 2000; Peterson et al., 1995). Bauer (2000) found that greater role ambiguity correlates with an increase in withdrawal behaviors and that less role ambiguity results in greater job performance. Bray and Brawley (2002) found that role ambiguity has a moderating effect on the role efficacy–role performance relationship. In relation to persistence in one's role, Caykoylu, Egri, and Havlovic (2007) found that less role ambiguity results in greater organizational commitment. The third role stressor, role overload, refers to what takes place when perceived stakeholder expectations exceed what an individual's time and resources can effectively address so that work performance declines. Noteworthy is the relationship between role overload and burnout, as shown in the literature (Hang-yue, Foley & Loi, 2005).

Motivation Theory

Motivation theory is a second theoretical area with some overlap in elements with vision conflict, and it is associated with vision conflict because of evidence that both involve the idea of expectancy (Bartram & Casimir, 2007; Spencer et al., 2009, 2012). Just like with vision conflict, motivation theory includes examining the relationship between what motivates a person to work and what they expect to receive as a reward, whether as a written or unwritten psychological contract or as a career contract (Hall & Moss, 1998). Of the variety of motivational variables that may relate to vision conflict, job satisfaction, and career commitment most closely express similar elements. An example of the relationship between job satisfaction and vision conflict is shown by Locke and Latham (1990), who state that "satisfied people will be more likely than dissatisfied people to both remain with the organization and to accept any new challenges that it might offer" (p. 244). Additionally, Locke and Latham (2002) posit that an association exists between exceeding work goals, increased job satisfaction, and growing positive discrepancy, and also between failure to fulfill goals, increased dissatisfaction, and increasing negative discrepancy.

Job Satisfaction Theory

Job satisfaction theory also relates to the perception that clergy are responsible for a certain level of satisfaction in the lives of their congregants. Croucher (2002) found that forced termination of the clergy was a primary result of performance dissatisfaction on the part of the congregation. On the other hand, Mueller and McDuff (2004) and Zondag (2004) show that positive change and satisfaction experienced by the congregation produces clergy job satisfaction, and this leads to a greater likelihood of perseverance in the ministry. Career commitment—the second of two elements of motivation theory that connect to some extent with vision conflict—is positively correlated to job involvement and organizational commitment (Blau, 1989; Reilly & Orsak, 1991).

Career commitment is a significant element to consider in the context of ministry since individual differences, contexts, and situational characteristics vary greatly from church to church and from ministry to ministry (Hoge & Wenger, 2005; London & Wiseman, 2003). Shehan, Wiggins, and Cody-Rydzewski (2007) note the sacred calling typically attached to the idea of ministry and defines all aspects of clergy life as contributors to high career commitment, but that "the pressure to succeed in circumstances that are extraordinarily demanding but produce few external rewards can create emotional dissonance" (p. 641). The extent of the relationship between career commitment and vision conflict (just like between job satisfaction and vision conflict) may be affected by the changing conditions throughout the ministry.

Person-Organization Fit

Person-organization fit (P-O fit) is a third theoretical area related to vision conflict because of an individual's perception of fit with their respective work situation. According to Kristof (1996), the interaction between an individual's needs, desires, or preferences and what the organization demands from the individual affects the determination of compatibility. Chan (1996) explains how higher or lower perception of fit extends to the congruence of problem-solving style between individuals and organizations. The significance of P-O fit and its association with turnover among the clergy (Wildhagen, Mueller & Wang, 2005) is compounded by the demands faced by ministers amid a society of constantly changing values and social change inside and outside of the church (Snyder, 1979; The Barna Group, 2008). The two most pronounced elements of P-O fit among the likely antecedents of vision conflict appear to be values congruence (alignment) and ability-job fit.

Values congruence is the most pronounced form of P-O fit related to vision conflict since the fundamental connection of values to culture affects attitudes and behavior (Chatman, 1989). According to Chatman (1991), "although people's values in an organization better enable them to make sense of organizational situations, values transcend any particular situation" (p. 460). The level of values congruence provides insight into the different experiences among clergy in terms of leadership style, decision-making, goals, and behaviors within a particular ministry organization context (Schmidt, 1993). Wheeler's (2001) study shows that increased incongruity between seminary graduates and their prospective ministry organizations correlates with a lower standard of orthodoxy and spiritual maturity within seminaries. Moreover, values congruence also differentiates between those values that contribute to a minister's attachment with a particular church in contrast to an attachment to the profession of being a member of the clergy (McDuff & Mueller 2000). The pursuit of understanding how values congruence affects the attachment between the minister and the congregation or occupation also helps to explain their perception of person-organization fit and whether there is a relationship with vision conflict.

The second element is ability-job fit, which refers to the degree to which there is a perceived match between a person's job and their ability or competence. Although a direct link between ability-job fit and vision conflict does not appear in the literature per se, the unique blend of circumstances, personalities, tasks, and skills representative of a typical ministry scenario demonstrates how a decrease of ability-job fit may relate to an increase of vision conflict. Abdel-Halim (1981) and Xie and Johns (1995) show how the relationship of ability-job fit and other variables associated with the vision conflict dimension (e.g., job satisfaction and role stressors) is clear. Abdel-Halim (1981) concluded that high perceived ability-job fit results in greater job satisfaction and greater resilience to role stressors. Xie and Johns (1995) showed that "individuals who perceived a misfit between job demands and their abilities consistently experienced higher stress than those who perceived better demands–ability fit" (p. 1300). These studies, along with additional research by Xie (1996), show that ability–job fit addresses a variety of pertinent issues, such as whether an individual's training, competence, and range of skills match the work demand of the organization and provide the individual an opportunity to do the things they feel they do best. This contributes to the explanation of why the anticipation of job performance in the ministry does not necessarily match the actual experience of ministry. For clergy, where high job demand and high control tend to be typical, a certain degree of ability–job fit may emerge with a significant relationship to the experience of vision conflict.

Environmental Determinism

The last of four theoretical streams associated with vision conflict is environmental determinism, which suggests two areas of focus concerning vision conflict: individual environmental determinants and political skill. Environmental determinism may be described as the extent that human activities within an organization are influenced by environmental or contextual conditions of a given organization. Northouse (2007) likens environmental determinism in terms of the effectiveness of a leader within their organizational context, stating that "environmental influences represent factors that lie outside the leader's competencies, characteristics, and experiences" (p. 52). According to Yukl (2006), the ability to effectively address organizational challenges within a changing environment requires a plan that "builds on core competencies, is relevant to long-term objectives, and is feasible in terms of current capabilities" (p. 381). Clergy are typically seen as key responders to organizational needs that represent long-term objectives amid changing organizational circumstances, and therefore may experience a certain degree of vision conflict as their ability to lead may be affected depending on the environmental determinants involved.

Although the literature does not indicate any particular set of determinants related to the likelihood of clergy termination, the literature does show how certain environmental and contextual factors appear similar to the antecedents of vision conflict. According to personal communication with researchers in this field (e.g., Anne S. Tsui, James R. Detert, Peter G. Northouse, and Carole Lalonde), several environmental determinants describe the work of clergy within a changing milieu of ministries, such as demographic parity, community culture, ministry location, geographic consideration, financial capability, facility issues, denominational support, and local church government. Each of these describes a potential environmental determinant that lies outside of what a minister may directly be able to control. Political skill, a secondary but distinctive environmental determinant, significantly relates to the work of clergy because they are required to navigate relationships between individuals and coalitions that have varying amounts of influence within the ministry's organizational context. Perrewé et al. (2004) define political skill as "the ability to effectively understand others at work and to use such knowledge to influence others to act in ways that enhance one's personal and/or organizational objectives" (p. 142). Ferris et al. (2005) concluded that social astuteness and networking ability are the strongest predictors of political skill. Effectively managing potential challenges from individuals and coalitions in the ministry's organizations may contribute to a feeling of disparity between clergy's perception of ministry and real-life experience in the ministry. Thus, the clergy's level of political skill may affect the presence and intensity of the vision conflict dimension. In other words, the clergy's ability to apply the most situationally appropriate tactics within a given environmental context exemplifies a certain level of leadership effectiveness that may lead to the accomplishment of organizational goals, greater satisfaction, and diminished vision conflict.

SCALE DEVELOPMENT, CONTENT VALIDITY, AND FACE VALIDITY

Developing the VCS required a variety of research activities in a proven methodical approach (DeVellis, 2003). Table 1 shows Spencer et al.'s (2009) factor analysis of Wickman's PaRI instrument that provides the initial emergence of vision conflict as a viable research topic. Content validity was established through a two-step refinement process using qualitative and quantitative procedures that, as Netemeyer et al. (2003) stated, "can help identify elements of the items that need to be refined, changed, or deleted" (p. 103).

The qualitative refinement involved interviews with clergy who have served in ministry for a minimum of five years to confirm, modify, add, or invalidate the items associated with the phenomenon referred to as vision conflict (DeVellis, 2003). Although there were no minimum number of subjects or interviews required, a sample size of 30 was originally proposed, but after 19 interviews, it became clear that redundancy had been reached (Lincoln & Guba, 1985). After the interviews, the data were reviewed and categorized to develop themes within the interviews. This process allowed for convergence and divergence to be determined, and it ensured that internal and external homogeneity were met (Patton, 2002). The interviews produced 45 items containing a level of redundancy as described by DeVellis (2003).

The quantitative phase of development involved forming a group of five experts from the representative population who would evaluate 55 items associated with the project (i.e., 45 items collected via interviews plus the ten original items from Spencer et al.'s [2009, 2012] study in Table 1). According to Netemeyer et al. (2003), a mixture of scholar–judges (i.e., experts in research who will check for content validity) and judges from the target population (i.e., to check for face validity) can help to "identify elements of the items that need to be refined, changed, or deleted" (p. 103). In this case, two scholar-experts and three ministers who were representative of the target population were selected as judges. They used a 5-point scale to evaluate the strength and type of recommendation for each of the 55 items. The judges' responses were assessed using a reflective process to determine the outcome of the expert opinion and confirm which items are most appropriate to include in the scale. The items that comprise the 21-item revised VCS are in Table 2.

The final items in the VCS instrument included the revised vision conflict items from Table 2 and the validated Likert-type scales that assess the variables associated with each of the four theoretical areas observed (e.g., role stress, motivation, person-organization fit, and environmental determinism). The items from the various scales were assembled into a single survey of 68 items and 16 demographic questions and administered to a cross-section of evangelical clergy. Of the 68 survey items, 21 items are related to vision conflict (Table 2). The minimum number of clergy needed as subjects for the survey was 210, based on a preferred sample size of ten subjects per scale item for conducting a principal components analysis as described in Hair, Black, Babin, Anderson, and Tatham (2006). The 16 demographic questions included items focusing on ministry tenure, the ministry organization–clergy relationship, and whether the clergy has experienced forced or unforced termination in a ministry context. Additional items were also requested, such as age, gender, ministry role, remuneration level, whether employment is full-time or part-time, and denominational affiliation. The survey was administered via written and online for-

Table 2. Revised vision conflict survey items

Item #	Item
1.	I am confused about my major role in the church.
2.	I have lost the sense of meaning in my work.
3.	I feel my work is futile.
4.	I wonder about my calling as a pastor.
5.	Ministry doesn't bring me satisfaction.
6.	I find little joy in my work.
7.	I feel I would like to leave the church I now serve.
8.	I seriously consider leaving the ministry entirely.
9.	I feel my hope for success has not developed.
10.	I feel my personal relationship with Christ is a real problem.
11.	The requirements of the ministry seem different from what I am able to do.
12.	I wonder if I am the right person for this ministry.
13.	My original calling versus where I am and what I am doing does not match.
14.	Ministry results are not what I expect.
15.	Ministry is not like I originally envisioned it.
16.	I feel ill-prepared for what I now face.
17.	I expected ministry to be more fulfilling.
18.	Ministry is not working out the way I expected.
19.	I feel that I lack effectiveness as a minister.
20.	I am losing my desire to carry out ministry responsibilities.
21.	My passion for ministry is decreasing.

mats with the option for subjects to answer anonymously. Surveys were completed by 224 respondents. To consider the differences in survey types (i.e., in-person and online), an independent samples t-test was conducted and revealed that there were no significant differences between the in-person written responses and the online responses.

Reliability

The 21 vision conflict items were refined using a principal component analysis (PCA). The resulting correlation matrix was inspected to ensure coefficients were at least .5 or higher. The Kaiser-Meyer-Oklin Measure of Sampling Accuracy was .92, which exceeds the recommended value of .6 or higher (Pallant, 2006). Bartlett's Test of Sphericity reached statistical significance, which supports the factorability in the correlation matrix. The results of the PCA initially revealed the presence of three potential components with eigenvalues exceeding 1, but an inspection of the scree plot showed a clear break after the first component (i.e., vision conflict), indicating that it should be retained. Four of the original ten items from Table 1 (the initial research) were retained in the final 9-item composite VCS with a reliability alpha coefficient of .90, as shown in Table 3.

Table 3. (Final) Vision conflict scale items

Item #	Item statement	Load
01	I am confused about my major role in the church.	0.68
03	I feel my work is futile.	0.59
07	I feel I would like to leave the church I now serve.	0.60
09	I feel my hope for success has not developed.	0.63
13	My original calling versus where I am and what I am doing do not match.	0.63
14	Ministry results are not what I expect.	0.69
15	Ministry is not like I originally envisioned it.	0.75
17	I expected ministry to be more fulfilling.	0.66
18	Ministry is not working out the way I expected.	0.83

Note. Extraction method: Principal Component Analysis. Rotation method: Varimax with Kaiser Normalization. A Rotation converged in seven iterations.

The importance of the nine scale items in Table 3 is further understood by examining the results of the reliability scores of the composite variables drawn from the four associated theoretical areas, which are shown in Table 4. Of the various scales incorporated in this research, the reliability of the role conflict scale, although internally consistent, shows the greatest disparity with the reliability score of previous research.

Table 4. Reliability of scales used

Theoretical area	Scale(s)	Previous Reliability	Present Reliability
Vision conflict	New vision conflict	–	.90
Role stressors	Role conflict	.93	.73
	Role ambiguity	.87	.89
	Role overload	.93	.91
Motivation	Job satisfaction	.88	.90
	Career commitment	.76-.88	.74
P–O fit	Values congruence	.87	.86
	Ability–job fit	.73-.80	.82
Environmental determinism	Political skill	.71	.80

Note. The reliability of the eight-item interval scale drawn from the literature and expertise of the researcher to examine specific environmental determinants is not applicable.

Validity

The initial content and face validity were achieved using a two-step process to finalize the survey items. The Pearson correlation for the final VCS (Table 3) shows convergent validity (i.e., the extent of the relationship) between vision conflict and each of the other variables in the study (Ferris et al., 2005).

The correlations in Table 5 show concurrent validity, meaning that the scales used in the research are measuring the extent of a similar phenomenon between vision conflict and the variables listed.

Table 5. Correlation analysis

Variable	1	2	3	4	5	6	7	8	9	10	11	12	13	14	15	16
1 Vision conflict	—															
2 Role conflict	.41**	—														
3 Role ambiguity	.67**	.39**	—													
4 Role overload	.29**	.44**	.28**	—												
5 Job satisfaction	-.67**	-.36**	-.59**	-.26**	—											
6 Career commit	-.41**	-.11	-.31**	-.21**	.32**	—										
7 Values congru	-.52**	-.37**	-.44**	-.22**	.54**	.29**	—									
8 Ability-job fit	-.55**	-.34**	-.52**	-.26**	.58**	.33**	.41**	—								
9 Political skill	-.27**	-.14*	-.26**	-.09	.21**	.20**	.21**	.43**	—							
10 Church divrsty	.08	.17*	.01	-.18**	.04**	.04	.04	.03	.03	—						
11 Comun. divrsty	.27**	.12	.15*	.04	-.19**	-.15*	-.15*	-.05	-.08	.35**	—					
12 Location	.25**	.11	.12	.11	-.16**	-.09	-.08	-.12	-.13*	.12	.22**	—				
13 Climate/geog	.05	.06	.12	.17*	-.03	-.08	-.08	-.06	-.07	.11	.13	.19	—			
14 Money	.34**	.28**	.34**	.27	-.20**	-.20**	-.15*	-.15*	-.08	.10	.22**	.32**	.17*	—		
15 Facilities	.02	-.11	.02	-.14*	.10	.02	.03	.16*	.10	-.05	.03	-.27**	-.08	-.09	—	
16 Denom support	-.24**	-.12	-.07	-.12	.25**	.16*	.29**	.17*	.14*	-.01	-.11	-.19**	-.01	-.18**	.18**	—
17 Loc chrch gov	-.14**	-.11	-.19**	-.04	.32**	.08	.26**	.20**	.08	-.08	-.13	-.10	-.05	.09	.25**	.54**

*p < .05. **p < .01.

Source: (Spencer, 2010)

RESULTS

The immediate benefit of the VCS is having a tool to identify the degree to which a minister is experiencing vision conflict (i.e., the level of disparity between what they expected to experience in the ministry versus what is actually experienced in the ministry). The correlations showed that vision conflict is related to each of the composite variables and to five of the environmental determinants. However, the strongest correlations involving vision conflict, negative or positive, are seen between vision conflict and role ambiguity, job satisfaction, values congruence, and ability-job fit. The strength of correlation between vision conflict and other composite variables was considered medium or small. Finally, the strongest correlation between vision conflict and individual item-level environmental determinants was with money.

Commentary

The VCS measures the disparity ministers feel the ministry should be like to how it actually is. The VCS began as a practitioner's observations of repeated causes of pastoral exits from the ministry (Wickman, 2004) and developed into a Pastor's at Risk Inventory (PaRI) using a grounded theory approach (Creswell, 2014). Then, a factor analysis determined an initial recognition of vision conflict as a dimension associated with forced and unforced pastoral termination and then underwent qualitative and quantitative scale development resulting in 21 items (Spencer et al., 2009, 2012). These were finally revised through principal components analysis resulting in a 9-item VCS (Spencer, 2010). The correlation between vision conflict and each of the four theoretical areas examined in the study was confirmed, but the shared variance fluctuates, with the strongest correlations existing between vision conflict and role ambiguity (one of three role stressor variables in the study), vision conflict and negative job satisfaction (one of the two motivational variables in the study), and vision conflict and negative values congruence and negative ability-job fit (both P-O fit variables used in the study). The variables connected with environmental determinism, although present in the correlation analysis, were only slightly significant.

As a consequence of the VCS, there are at least four significant phenomena that are likely to occur concurrently with vision conflict. Those four phenomena—role ambiguity, negative job satisfaction, negative values congruence, and negative ability-job fit—also show significant correlations with all other variables associated with the validated scales used in this research. The benefit of confirming the relationship between these similar phenomena along with vision conflict is to better understand what ministers typically experience in ministry. The correlation analysis between vision conflict and the other study variables represents an important step in recognizing vision conflict as a distinct dimension since those results provide similar empirical findings that align with the literature and with similar research (Joynt, 2018; Rosendahl, 2019).

Perhaps it becomes an overstatement to conclude that every member of the clergy possesses some level of vision conflict, but the likelihood of some type of an encounter with the experience may be viewed as a normal part of ministry life. A recognition of the normative presence of vision conflict (and accompanying variables mentioned in the study) is not so much about why ministers leave the ministry but about what can be done to strengthen their effectiveness where they serve and create a stronger resilience to the likelihood of exiting the ministry. Since the strongest correlations between vision conflict and associated variables result in negative experiences that are typical of the ministry, ministerial training curriculum should present the reality of these phenomena along with a focused educational emphasis on dealing with them. Such an emphasis ought to be part of the preparation, training, and continuing education of clergy. Ministers who understand vision conflict and its effects will be more prepared to deal with the difficulties of it and will be able to more effectively navigate the challenging terrain their service if they experience it.

The VCS can be applied in the coaching and mentoring of pastors. At some point, the VCS and correlated variables (role ambiguity, negative job satisfaction, negative values congruence, and negative ability-job fit) could become the basis for a tool to assist coaches and mentors in working with pastoral clients who are considering an exit from the ministry. A coach or mentor could discuss and assess the degree to which any of the nine items in the VCS or any of the four most correlated variables are significant issues in their life so that appropriate actions may be determined.

FUTURE RESEARCH

The VCS may be further developed to integrate continuing pastoral research to uncover and clarify theoretical streams beyond what is included in the present revised scale (Speight & Speight, 2017; Tanner, 2016). One notable area for further study is the connection between pastoral calling and pastoral exiting. Joynt's (2017) study of the exodus of clergy from the ministry identifies calling as a significant antecedent forcing the exit of full-time clergy, particularly from within a megachurch setting. Shehan et al. (2007) found that a sacred calling by God may be a source of strength to overcome negative factors associated with the ministry and may lead people to continue their service in the ministry because they commit to altruistic purposes beyond their initial intent and understanding. Vision conflict research may help clarify the typical negative elements that calling addresses and overcomes, which may contribute to a better understanding of both calling and vision conflict (Markow & Klenke, 2005). Since this research was first presented, vision conflict has begun to be considered as a dynamic theoretical dimension that will continue to be examined and used within the academic community (Frederick et al., 2018; Joynt, 2018; Rosendahl, 2019).

Pastoral ministry is not the only sector where a phenomenon similar to vision conflict may be seen. To advance research for other related areas, a process of scale development similar to what is described herein will need to be applied because of the distinctive nature of what vision conflict may look like in other sectors. Although the similarity of vision conflict elements may seem to suggest a certain degree of a shared experience for leaders across sectors, the unique contexts from one sector to another will likely require developing individual instruments for each unique context that considers those unique realities. Such a process would likely involve sector-specific literature considerations and research. However, the development of such research tools will further the overall advancement of understanding leaders and what they typically encounter (and must learn to overcome) in their particular contexts.

Cost of the Vision Conflict Scale

The revised VCS is available for free and is located in Table 3 of this chapter.

REFERENCES

Abdel-Halim, A. A. (1981). A reexamination of ability as a moderator of role perception–satisfaction relationship. *Personnel Psychology*, *34*(3), 549–561. doi:10.1111/j.1744-6570.1981.tb00495.x

Addae, H. M., Parboteeah, K. P., & Velinor, N. (2008). Role stressors and organizational commitment: Public sector employment in St Lucia. *International Journal of Manpower*, *29*(6), 567–582. doi:10.1108/01437720810904220

Bacharach, S., Bamberger, P., & Conley, S. (1991). Work–home conflict among nurses and engineers: Mediating the impact of role stress on burnout and satisfaction with work. *Journal of Organizational Behavior*, *12*(1), 39–53. doi:10.1002/job.4030120104

Barfoot, D. S., Winston, B. E., & Wickman, C. (2005). *Forced pastoral exits: An exploratory study* [Unpublished manuscript]. School of Global Leadership and Entrepreneurship, Regent University.

Bartram, T., & Casimir, G. (2007). The relationship between leadership and follower in-role performance and satisfaction with the leader: The mediating effects of empowerment and trust in the leader. *Leadership and Organization Development Journal*, *28*(1), 4–19. doi:10.1108/01437730710718218

Bauer, J. C. (2002). *A longitudinal evaluation of the impact of organizational structure on role ambiguity and work group performance* (Publication No. 3086349) [Doctoral dissertation, University of Sarasota]. Proquest Dissertation Abstracts and Theses.

Beebe, R. S. (2007). Predicting burnout, conflict management style, and turnover among clergy. *Journal of Career Assessment*, *15*(2), 257–275. doi:10.1177/1069072706298157

Blau, G. (1989). Testing generalizability of a career commitment measure and its impact on employee turnover. *Journal of Vocational Behavior*, *35*(1), 88–103. doi:10.1016/0001-8791(89)90050-X

Bray, S. R., & Brawley, L. R. (2002). Role efficacy, role clarity, and role performance effectiveness. *Small Group Research, 33*(2), 233–253. doi:10.1177/104649640203300204

Caykoylu, S., Egri, C. P., & Havlovic, S. (2007). Organizational commitment across different employee groups. *Business Review (Federal Reserve Bank of Philadelphia), 8*(1), 191–197.

Chan, D. (1996). Cognitive misfit of problem-solving style at work: A facet of person-organization fit. *Organizational Behavior and Human Decision Processes, 68*(3), 194–207. doi:10.1006/obhd.1996.0099

Chang, P. M. Y. (2000). The effects of organizational variation in the employment relationship on gender discrimination in denominational labor markets. *Unusual Occupations, 11*, 213–240.

Chatman, J. A. (1989). Improving interactional organizational research: A model of person-organization fit. *Academy of Management Review, 14*(3), 333–349. doi:10.5465/amr.1989.4279063

Chatman, J. A. (1991). Matching people and organizations: Selection and socialization in public accounting firms. *Administrative Science Quarterly, 36*(3), 459–484. doi:10.2307/2393204

Creswell, J. W. (1998). Qualitative inquiry and research design: Choosing among five traditions. *Sage (Atlanta, Ga.).*

Creswell, J. W. (2014). *Research design: Qualitative, quantitative, and mixed methods approaches* (4th ed.). Sage.

Croucher, R. (2002). *Forced terminations: When a church asks a pastor to leave.* Priscilla's Friends. https://www.priscillasfriends.org/studies/terminations.html

DeVellis, R. F. (2003). *Scale development: Theory and application* (2nd ed.). Sage.

Elkington, R. (2013). Adversity in pastoral leadership: Are pastors leaving the ministry in record numbers, and if so, why? *Verbum et Ecclesia, 34*(1), 1–13. doi:10.4102/ve.v34i1.821

Farley, H. (2016, April 28). Low pay, no savings and financial stress: The reality for evangelical pastors. *Christianity Today.* http://www.christiantoday.com/article/low.pay.no.savings.and.financial.stress.the.reality.for.evangelical.pastors/84984.htm

Francis, L. J., & Rodger, R. (1994). The influence of personality on clergy role prioritization, role influences, conflict, and dissatisfaction with ministry. *Personality and Individual Differences, 16*(6), 947–957. doi:10.1016/0191-8869(94)90237-2

Frederick, T. V., Dunbar, S., & Thai, Y. (2018). Burnout in Christian perspective. *Pastoral Psychology, 67*(3), 267–276. doi:10.100711089-017-0799-4

Greenfield, G. (2001). *The wounded minister: Healing from and preventing personal attacks.* Baker Books.

Hair, J. F., Black, W. C., Babin, B. J., Anderson, R. E., & Tatham, R. L. (2006). *Multivariate data analysis* (6th ed.). Pearson-Prentice Hall.

Hall, D. T., & Moss, J. E. (1998). The new protean career contract: Helping organizations and employees adapt. *Organizational Dynamics, 26*(3), 22–37. doi:10.1016/S0090-2616(98)90012-2

Hang-yue, N., Foley, S., & Loi, R. (2005). Work role stressors and turnover intentions: A study of professional clergy in Hong Kong. *International Journal of Human Resource Management, 16*(11), 2133–2146. doi:10.1080/09585190500315141

Hoge, D. R., & Wenger, J. E. (2005). *Pastors in transition: Why clergy leave local church ministry.* Wm. B. Eerdmans.

Ivancevich, J. M., Konopaske, R., & Matteson, M. T. (2005). *Organizational behavior and management* (7th ed.). McGraw-Hill Higher Education.

Joynt, S. (2017). Exodus of clergy: Responding to, reinterpreting or relinquishing the call. *Verbum et Ecclesia, 38*(1), 1–6. doi:10.4102/ve.v38i1.1664

Joynt, S. (2018). Exodus of clergy: "When the fight is just not worth it anymore" – The role of conflict in responding to the call. *Die Skriflig, 52*(1). Advance online publication. doi:10.4102/ids.v52i1.2331

Kahn, R. L., Wolfe, D. M., Quinn, R. P., Snoek, J. E., & Rosenthal, R. A. (1964). *Organizational stress: Studies in role conflict and ambiguity.* John Wiley.

Kay, W. K. (2000). Role conflict and British Pentecostal ministers. *Journal of Psychology and Theology, 28*(2), 119–124. doi:10.1177/009164710002800204

Kisslinger, S. A. (2007). *Burnout in Presbyterian clergy of southwestern Pennsylvania* (Publication No. 3252060) [Doctoral dissertation, Indiana University of Pennsylvania]. Proquest Dissertation Abstracts and Theses.

Krejcir, R. J. (2016). *Statistics on pastors: 2016 update.* Francis L. Schaeffer Institute of Church Leadership Development. https://files.stablerack.com/webfiles/71795/pastorsstatWP2016.pdf

Kristof, A. L. (1996). Person-organization fit: An integrative review of its conceptualizations, measurement, and implications. *Personnel Psychology, 49*(1), 1–49. doi:10.1111/j.1744-6570.1996.tb01790.x

Lee, A. A. (2017). *Ministry longevity, family contentment, and the male clergy family: A phenomenological study of the experience of ministry* (Publication No. 10599056) [Doctoral dissertation, Liberty University]. Proquest Dissertations.

Lincoln, Y. S., & Guba, E. G. (1985). Naturalistic inquiry. *Sage (Atlanta, Ga.).*

Locke, E. A., & Latham, G. P. (1990). Work motivation and satisfaction: Light at the end of the tunnel. *Psychological Science, 1*(4), 240–246. doi:10.1111/j.1467-9280.1990.tb00207.x

Locke, E. A., & Latham, G. P. (2002). Building a practically useful theory of goal setting and task motivation: A 35-year odyssey. *The American Psychologist, 57*(9), 705–717. doi:10.1037/0003-066X.57.9.705 PMID:12237980

London, H. B., & Wiseman, N. B. (2011). *Pastors at greater risk.* Baker.

Malony, H. N., & Hunt, R. A. (1991). *The psychology of clergy.* Morehouse.

Markow, F., & Klenke, K. (2005). The effects of personal meaning and calling on organizational commitment: An empirical investigation of spiritual leadership. *The International Journal of Organizational Analysis, 13*(1), 8–27. doi:10.1108/eb028995

McDuff, E. M., & Mueller, C. W. (2000). The ministry as an occupational labor market: Intentions to leave an employer (church) versus intentions to leave a profession (ministry). *Work and Occupations, 27*(1), 89–116. doi:10.1177/0730888400027001005

Ministry retrains 'exited' pastors. (1997). *Christianity Today, 41*(7), 67. https://www.christianitytoday.com/ct/1997/june16/7t767b.html

Mohr, A. T., & Puck, J. F. (2007). Role conflict, general manager job satisfaction and stress and the performance of IJVs. *European Management Journal, 25*(1), 25–35. doi:10.1016/j.emj.2006.11.003

Mueller, C. W., & McDuff, E. (2004). Clergy–congregation mismatches and clergy job satisfaction. *Journal for the Scientific Study of Religion, 43*(2), 261–273. doi:10.1111/j.1468-5906.2004.00231.x

Netemeyer, R. G., Bearden, W. O., & Sharma, S. (2003). Scaling procedures: Issues and applications. *Sage (Atlanta, Ga.).*

Northouse, P. G. (2007). *Leadership: Theory and practice* (4th ed.). Sage.

Pallant, J. (2006). *SPSS survival manual* (2nd ed.). Open University Press.

Palser, S. J. (2005). *The relationship between occupational burnout and emotional intelligence among clergy or professional ministry workers* (Publication No. 3162679) [Doctoral dissertation, Regent University]. Proquest Dissertation Abstracts and Theses.

Patton, M. Q. (2002). *Qualitative research & evaluation methods* (3rd ed.). Sage.

Perrewé, P. L., Zellars, K. L., Ferris, G. R., Rossi, A. M., Kacmar, C. J., & Ralston, D. A. (2004). Neutralizing job stressors: Political skill as an antidote to the dysfunctional consequences of role conflict stressors. *Academy of Management Journal, 47*(1), 141–152. doi:10.2307/20159566

Peterson, M. F., Smith, P. B., Akande, A., Ayestaran, S., Bochner, S., Callan, V., Jesuino, J. C., D'Amorim, M., Francois, P.-H., Hofmann, K., Koopman, P. L., Mortazavi, S., Munene, J., Radford, M., Ropo, A., Savage, G., & Setiadi, B. (1995). Role conflict, ambiguity, and overload: A 21-nation study. *Academy of Management Journal, 38*(2), 429–452. doi:10.2307/256687

Rediger, G. L. (2003). Managing depression. *The Clergy Journal, 79*(9), 15-16. https://www-proquest-com.ezproxy2.apus.edu/trade-journals/managing-depression/docview/230520595/se-2?accountid=8289

Reed, A. (2016). Rooted in relationship: Longevity in congregational ministry. *Review & Expositor, 113*(3), 303–314. doi:10.1177/0034637316659304

Reilly, N. P., & Orsak, C. L. (1991). A career stage analysis of career and organizational commitment in nursing. *Journal of Vocational Behavior, 39*(3), 311–330. doi:10.1016/0001-8791(91)90041-J

Rosendahl, D. K. (2019). *Causes, consequences and cures of role stress among Swedish Free-Church pastors* [Unpublished doctoral dissertation]. Trinity College of the Bible and Trinity Theological Seminary.

Schmidt, J. E. (1993). *Transformational leadership: The relationship between consciousness, values and skills* (Publication No. 9412221) [Doctoral dissertation, Western Michigan University]. Proquest Dissertation Abstracts and Theses. https://scholarworks.wmich.edu/cgi/viewcontent.cgi?article=2902 &context=dissertations

Sheffield, B. (2008, July). *Avoid the top 5 reasons for pastoral termination, Part 5, Who runs the church?* LifeWay Christian Resources. http://www.lifeway.com/lwc/article_main_page/0%2C1703%2CA %25 253D167900%252526M%25253D200829%2C00.html

Shehan, C., Wiggins, M., & Cody-Rydzewski, S. (2007). Responding to and retreating from the call: Career salience, work satisfaction, and depression among clergywomen. *Pastoral Psychology*, *55*(5), 637–643. doi:10.100711089-006-0064-8

Snyder, H. (1979). *The problem of wineskins: The church in a technological age*. InterVarsity Press.

Somers, M. J., & Birnbaum, D. (1998). Work-related commitment and job performance: It's also the nature of the performance that counts. *Journal of Organizational Behavior*, *19*(6), 621–634. doi:10.1002/ (SICI)1099-1379(1998110)19:6<621::AID-JOB853>3.0.CO;2-B

Speight, D. E., & Speight, S. W. (2017). Exploring the lived experience of forced termination among Southern Baptist clergy couples: A retrospective study. *Journal of Psychology and Christianity*, *36*(2), 149–160.

Spencer, J. L. (2010). *Vision conflict within pastoral ministry* (Publication No. 3425735) [Doctoral dissertation, Regent University]. Proquest Dissertation Abstracts and Theses.

Spencer, J. L., Winston, B. E., & Bocarnea, M. C. (2012). Predicting the level of pastors' risk of termination/exit from the church. *Pastoral Psychology*, *1*(61), 85–98. doi:10.100711089-011-0410-3

Spencer, J. L., Winston, B. E., Bocarnea, M. C., & Wickman, C. A. (2009). *Validating a practitioner's instrument measuring the level of pastors' risk of termination/exit from the church: Discovering vision conflict and compassion fatigue as key factors* [Unpublished manuscript]. School of Global Leadership and Entrepreneurship, Regent University.

Tanner, M. N. (2016). Learning from clergy who have been forcibly terminated. *Journal of Management, Spirituality & Religion*, *14*(3), 179–195. doi:10.1080/14766086.2016.1253496

The Barna Group. (2008, October 7). *American spirituality gives way to simplicity and the desire to make a difference.* http://www.barna.org/barna-update/article/12-faithspirituality/19-american-spirituality-gives-way-to-simplicity-and-the-desire-to-make-a-difference

Wheeler, B. G. (2001). Fit for ministry? *Christian Century (Chicago, Ill.)*, *118*(12), 16–23. https://www. christiancentury.org/article/fit-ministry

Wickman, C. A. (2004). *Pastor in residence: At-risk pastor profile*. Regent University, School of Global Leadership & Entrepreneurship. https://www.regent.edu/acad/global/pir/pir_section1.cfm

Wickman, C. A. (2014). *Pastors at risk: Protecting your future, guarding your present*. Morgan James.

Wildhagen, T., Mueller, C. W., & Wang, M. (2005). Factors leading to clergy job search in two Protestant denominations. *Review of Religious Research*, *46*(4), 380–403. doi:10.2307/3512168

Xie, J. L. (1996). Karasek's model in the People's Republic of China: Effects of job demands, control, and individual differences. *Academy of Management Journal*, *39*(6), 1594–1619. doi:10.5465/257070

Xie, J. L., & Johns, G. (1995). Job scope and stress: Can job scope be too high? *Academy of Management Journal*, *38*(5), 1288–1310. doi:10.5465/256858

Yukl, G. (2006). *Leadership in organizations* (6th ed.). Pearson Prentice Hall.

Zondag, H. J. (2004). Knowing you make a difference: Result awareness and satisfaction in the pastoral profession. *Review of Religious Research*, *45*(3), 254–269. doi:10.2307/3512263

KEY TERMS AND DEFINITIONS

Ability-Job Fit: The extent to which an individual's ability and competence is perceived to match a job.

Calling: The ongoing process by which an individual comes to terms with a personal sense of destiny and purpose in life, and may be viewed as a task set by God with a sense of obligation to work for purposes other than one's own.

Clergy: A term used interchangeably with minister and pastor. This term refers to someone whose primary vocation is serving in a church or Christian ministry.

Environmental Determinism: The manner and extent to which human activities within an organization are influenced by the environmental conditions of that organization.

Minister: A term used interchangeably with clergy and pastor.

Person-Organization Fit: The determination of compatibility between an individual's attributes, such as personality traits, beliefs, values, interests, and preferences, and those attributes representative of the work organization, such as culture, climate, values, goals, and norms.

Role Ambiguity: The perception of a vague or unspecified definition about job responsibilities, including information about what, when, and how work should be accomplished while exhibiting certain behaviors.

Role Stressors: A triad of variables, namely, role conflict, role ambiguity, and role overload.

Values Congruence (Values Alignment): The degree to which an individual's values, those enduring beliefs through which a specific mode of conduct or end- state is personally preferable, match those of the organization.

Vision Conflict: The disparity that exists between clergy's positive anticipation of what ministry will comprise and the actual experience of serving in the ministry.

Chapter 14
Organizational Arrogance and a Theory–Based Instrument

C. Victor Herbin III
Regent University, USA

ABSTRACT

Prior studies provided insight on arrogance at the individual level and how arrogant individuals express superiority through (1) overconfidence in capabilities, (2) dismissiveness, (3) and disparagement, and how these behaviors may negatively impact those employees in and around their work teams, yet did not indicate how these behaviors impact organizational culture. Organizational arrogance represents an emerging concept that describes arrogance at the organizational level. Organizational arrogance provides the body of knowledge with a comprehensive and inclusive definition that led to the development and validation of the Organizational Arrogance Scale with a Cronbach Alpha of .922 that accurately measures the presence of organizational arrogance.

INTRODUCTION

Organizational arrogance explains arrogance at the organizational level and how a leader's arrogant behavior shapes organizational culture and organizational members' acceptable behaviors. The theoretical and conceptual foundation consists of narcissistic leadership theory, Machiavellian leadership theory, psychopathy leadership theory, autocratic leadership theory, organizational identity, and arrogance. This chapter shows the origin of the organizational arrogance concept and demonstrates how it impacts organizational behavior and culture. Organizational arrogance introduces a comprehensive and inclusive definition that helps the reader recognize this phenomenon's intricacies. It also explains how organizational arrogance contains three behavioral components: Overconfidence in Organizational Capabilities, Dismissiveness Towards Internal and External Organizational Matters, and Disparagement Towards Intra-organizational and Interorganizational Members. Finally, this chapter presents the validation process for the 5-Item Organizational Arrogance Scale that measures organizational arrogance in the workplace.

DOI: 10.4018/978-1-7998-7665-6.ch014

Learning Objectives

After studying this chapter, one should be able to:

- Understand the historical evolution of studies on arrogance
- Recognize how leader behavior can influence arrogant behaviors in the workplace
- Theoretical and conceptual influences that build organizational arrogance
- Define organizational arrogance
- Understand the three organizational arrogance behavioral components
- Understand the development of the Organizational Arrogance Scale
- Recognize the five indicators that measure organizational arrogance
- Identify future research opportunities on organizational arrogance

BACKGROUND

Arrogance represents a collection of thoughts, attitudes, and behaviors that demonstrate an individual's superiority level. The term "sense of superiority" reflects a consistent theme identified throughout the literature and pertinent to the definition of arrogance. Whether one perceives "the sense of superiority" as realistic or not, it serves as the foundational premise for understanding arrogance. Tiberius and Walker (1998) claimed that arrogant people possess an actual or perceived belief in their considerable talents and abilities, creating opportunities for them to infer their above-average superiority to most other people. Arrogance also describes an essential human trait whereby individuals feel inclined to publicly convey their individual qualities and value over others (Lewis, 2000). Brown (2012) strengthens the definition as a "chronic belief of superiority and exaggerated self-importance that is demonstrated through excessive and presumptuous claims" (p. 555). Arrogance also describes a specific type of pride that leads one to believe that they hold power over other individuals (Poggi & D'Errico, 2011). Additionally, Tiberius and Walker (1998) submit a critical assertion that previous studies mistakenly focused arrogance on the person instead of recognizing arrogance as an interpersonal matter that illustrates how individuals engage with one another.

Before developing the organizational arrogance construct, arrogance was only evident at the individual level and described how an individual's self-perception of superiority manifests itself within the organizational environment. Arrogance harvests self-perceptions that an individual possesses invincibility and omnipotence (Ma & Karri, 2005). Maintaining this excessive belief in oneself establishes an attitude and behavior that distinguishes an arrogant individual from other individuals and contributes to a sense of overconfidence and overestimation of their capabilities. Similarly, arrogant people dismiss internal or external contributing factors and instead attribute their success to their high intellect and other noncontrollable, internal, stable, or desirable causes (Hareli & Weiner, 2000). Arrogance also depicts an extreme belief in an individual's superiority and exaggerated self-importance that reveals itself through excessive and presumptuous claims (Brown H., 2012). Most notably and more emotionally detrimental, arrogance describes an assortment of attitudes, behaviors, and thoughts that portrays one's exaggerated sense of superiority achieved through disparaging others (Johnson et al., 2010).

Johnson et al. (2010) further declared that organizational scholars rarely study arrogance due to the limited empirical evidence involving arrogance and the inability to measure how arrogant behaviors manifest in the workplace. Despite their findings, the researchers explored this phenomenon and developed the workplace arrogance construct, which the researchers defined as "behaviors that exaggerate actors' self-importance and that disparage their colleagues" (p.410). The workplace arrogance construct and subsequent Workplace Arrogance Scale provided relevant and purposeful insight that successfully targeted the existing knowledge gap. However, the body of knowledge still lacked a more exhaustive, inclusive, supportable definition and a means to measure arrogance on an organizational-wide scale. To this point, prior studies provided insight on arrogance at the individual level and how arrogant individuals express superiority through (a) overconfidence in capabilities, (b) dismissiveness, (c) and disparagement, and how these behaviors may negatively impact those employees in and around their work teams, yet did not indicate how these behaviors impact organizational culture.

Herbin (2018) filled the void in the body of knowledge and built upon Johnson et al.'s findings and posited that arrogant leaders could influence and shape a culture of arrogance and developed the organizational arrogance construct. Organizational arrogance defines an organizational environment where leaders shape a culture in which members behave with a sense of superiority, leading to overconfidence in organizational capabilities, dismissiveness toward internal and external organizational matters, and disparagement toward intra-organizational inter-organizational members (Herbin, 2018). Specifically, this definition focuses on arrogance at the organizational level, addresses organizational behavior, and how an organization treats its employees as a culture.

Organizational arrogance requires an understanding that organizational behavior exists at three distinct levels that include: (a) individual level that examines employees' motivation, personality, perception, and attitudes; (b) group level that investigates leadership, power, communication, politics, and work teams; and (c) organizational level that explores organizational culture, structure, conflict and change, cultural diversity, and inter-organizational cooperation (Robbins & Judge, 2012). Arrogance at the individual level primarily impacts members at the individual or group level but not at the organizational level. Hence the need for the Organizational Arrogance Scale that Herbin (2018) also developed to measure arrogant behaviors at the organizational level. Most specifically, arrogant behaviors, thoughts, and attitudes that represent overconfidence, dismissiveness, and disparagement. Again, organizational arrogance describes an organizational environment where leaders shape a culture in which these behavioral components manifest themselves. Issues arise when arrogant individuals assume leadership positions because their span of influence expands in width and depth, impacting organizational members.

Organizational arrogance denotes a culture. Leader-inspired and leader developed arrogant beliefs, customs, ideas, and behaviors that organizational members execute and encapsulate the organizational environment. Instances of rogue managers and leaders engaging in immoral and unethical conduct in the workplace indicate that this behavior contributes to incivility (Solas, 2016). Enron, Kodak, and IBM represent a sample of organizations that experienced organizational failure directly attributed to individual arrogance. A thorough review of these cases demonstrates a recurring theme whereby leaders within these organizations behaved with a sense of superiority that contributed to a level of overconfidence in business practices, disregard for organizational members' input and contributions, or some level of employee maltreatment or disparagement. Whether governmental, private, public, or non-profit, each industry remains susceptible to arrogant organizational members fostering a hostile work environment and low morale.

Organizations develop when leaders successfully convey values that employees accept as appropriate thinking and behavior (Sergiu, 2015). Arrogant behaviors can become acceptable behaviors that influence organizational members to replicate and mirror. Possibilities exist where a leader may inherit a culture of arrogance and, based on their level of influence, may reinforce, shape, or transform the existing arrogance culture. Yukl (2010) posited that "it takes considerable insight and skill for a leader to understand the current culture in an organization and implement changes successfully" (p. 309). Bolman and Deal (1997) discovered that a leader's ability to help shape the culture becomes challenged when uncertainty prompts organizational members to assign meaning to their current environment and how their interpretations contribute to develop a highly interwoven patchwork of culture. Bolman and Deal further presented the question, "do leaders shape culture, or are they shaped by it?" (p. 231). In which, Schein (2010) answered that "if leaders…do not become conscious of the culture in which they are embedded, cultures will manage them" (p. 22). Essentially, an organization can function as an arrogant organization without an arrogant leader when existing norms, values, and customs display and support arrogant behaviors. These arrogant behaviors lead to the existence of two underlying themes: arrogant leaders possess the capability to influence, foster, and shape an organizationally arrogant culture (leader arrogance), and that an arrogant culture can prevail independent from the leader (organizational arrogance).

Organizational arrogance illustrates how an organization as a culture behaves and treats organizational members. Most importantly, a culture where arrogance surpasses the individual level and settles at the organizational level. At this point, arrogant behaviors develop into cultural norms that shape an arrogant organizational culture. One cannot underestimate the influential nature arrogant leaders possess when developing an organizational culture and incorporating acceptable workplace behaviors, attitudes, and thoughts. Leadership and culture seamlessly work together. Directly or indirectly, a leaders' influence affects the direction of an organization because leaders "help to shape a culture, to transform. In turn, the organizational culture and the management will shape the attitudes and behaviours of managers and employees within the company" (Sergiu, 2015, p. 139). When organizational members at the individual or group level perceive certain arrogant leader behaviors as acceptable, these behaviors expand to the organizational level. They can create a culture of arrogance, creating the phenomenon of organizational arrogance.

Unlike prior attempts to formulate a consistent definition for arrogance, organizational arrogance encompasses a series of critical leadership theories and concepts that explore arrogant leader behavior and explains how leaders who demonstrate this aura of superiority impact the organizational environment. Narcissistic leadership theory, Machiavellian leadership theory, psychopathy leadership theory, autocratic leadership theory, and organizational identity provide the breadth necessary for explaining arrogant behaviors in the organizational environment and the width required to encapsulate the pervasive nature of culturally arrogant behaviors.

Narcissistic Leadership

Narcissist leaders endeavor for external affirmation. Narcissistic Leadership Theory represents a behavioral characteristic that indicates a leader's self-absorption and proclivity for exploiting opportunities that elevate their self-image and importance. Within the workforce, this leadership style promotes an environment that encourages an inflated ego and high-risk behavior. Zhu and Chen (2015) introduced the idea that narcissistic leaders display a self-absorbed behavioral characteristic and an innate desire for continual praise and belief that the organizational environment revolves around them. Zhu and Chen examined 292 CEOs from Fortune 500 companies that possessed narcissistic behaviors. They found they were more likely to hire directors that displayed an equal level of narcissism, which led to significant levels of risky spending. A narcissistic leader also possesses self-motivated actions and behaviors that support their egomaniacal needs and belief that supersedes an organization and its members' needs and interests (Rosenthal & Pittinsky, 2006).

Narcissistic leader behavior increases jealous behaviors that create a counterproductive organizational environment and negatively impact organizational citizenship (Braun, Aydin, Frey, & Peus, 2016). More alarming involves the narcissistic leaders increased level of insecurity that "any recognition of someone else's accomplishments or abilities are a threat to their self-importance and risks the loss of the exclusive admiration they crave from their followers" (McIntosh & Rima, 2007). When these leaders are no longer the center of attention, they not only perceive the slight as a threat, but their level of insecurity dramatically increases that can lead to a destructive nature, a ruthlessness that hinders their productivity and contributions to the overall team (Maccoby, 2000); (Lubit, 2002). Essentially, this leader functions with a superior attitude that suggests self-reliance, extreme confidence, and independence that significantly distances themselves from organizational members they deem inferior. Moreover, the narcissistic leader's inflated self-importance and perceived sense of superiority contribute towards faulty, damaging, and unstainable decision-making that places an organization and its employees' reputation at risk (Rijsenbilt & Commandeur, 2013). When these behaviors occur at the highest level of an organization, it impacts collaborative efforts, and the levels of insecurity and fractured personal relationships trickle down to lower levels of management (Braun, Aydin, Frey, & Peus, 2016); (Nevicka, De Hoogh, Van Vianen, Beersma, & McIlwain, 2011).

When leaders display these behaviors at the individual or group level, it may occur unbeknownst to upper management because it directly impacts members at an isolated level. However, when leaders exhibit these narcissistic leadership characteristics at the organizational level and assume higher levels of influence, they can foster an environment of prideful, self-destructive, and mistrustful behaviors that negatively impact the organization. Ultimately, these thoughts, attitudes, and behaviors directly threaten to build cohesive relationships, effective communication, empowerment, transparency, and a mutually respectable work environment organizational-wide.

Machiavellian Leadership

Machiavellian leadership theory represents another leadership style that leverages arrogant behavioral characteristics established on the premise of self-preservation. Specifically, a Machiavellian leader describes a self-interested leader singularly focused on their achievements. Motivated to maintain relevancy and importance, the Machiavellian leader exploits opportunities to accomplish tasks, objectives, or goals that reinforce their greatness and success even at the expense of others. Brown and Trevino (2006) contend, "Machiavellian leaders are motivated to manipulate others to accomplish their own goals. They have little trust in people and, in turn, tend not to be trusted by others" (p. 604). In turn, this mistrustful environment promotes apathetic leader behavior for both the interpersonal relationships with their subordinates and their feelings (Drory & Gluskinos, 1980); (Sakalaki, Richardson, & Thepaut, 2007). While the Machiavellian leader pursues greatness and mission accomplishment, they invariably possess a "willingness to utilize manipulative tactics and act amorally and endorse a cynical, untrustworthy view of human nature" (Dahling, Whitaker, & Levy, 2009, p. 220).

Notably, this leader disregards morals and maximizes guile or manipulation in conjunction with dishonesty to pursue and maintain power (Smith & Lilienfeld, 2013). Because retaining power serves the ultimate goal, these manipulative tactics can foster an organizational environment whereby counterproductive and harmful work behaviors such as apathy or callousness towards interpersonal relationships devalue subordinates' feelings, deceit, propensity to cheat, and abuse subordinates become prevalent (H. Brown, 2012; Drory & Gluskinos, 1980; (Lee & Ashton, 2005). Invariably, this leadership style conveys that when it operates at the individual, group, or organizational level, "Machiavellian leaders have a detrimental impact on employees' organizational cynicism and emotional exhaustion. Given that both outcomes negatively affect core attitudinal and behavioral outcomes…it is of utmost importance that organizations should avoid recruiting and nourishing Machiavellian leadership" (Gkorezis, Petridou, & Krouklidou, 2015). Leaders that display untrustworthiness, cynicism, and apathetic behaviors negatively impact the organizational environment. The Machiavellian leader's sense of superiority and self-preservation behaviors within a culture hinder organizational progress, degrade organizational commitment, threaten organizational health, decrease organizational cohesion and employee morale. Highlighting the Machiavellian leader behavior characteristics conveys how this leader can establish arrogant organizational culture conditions.

Psychopathy Leadership

Psychopathy leader also exhibits a sense of superiority and self-centeredness. Cleckley (1941) discovered that psychopathy leaders manifest 16 behavioral characteristics: a lack of anxiety, superficial charm, inadequate impulse control, empathy, egocentricity, absence of psychotic or neurotic symptoms, irresponsibility, inability to possess love, or maintain close relationships, and unmotivated antisocial deviance. When these behavioral characteristics appear in the work environment, it poses substantial risks that lead to others' emotional or physical harm. Invariably this sense of superiority contributes towards unnoticeable mistreatment that destroys a work environment. Similarly, Smith and Lilienfeld (2013) posit how psychopathic leaders' behavioral characteristics are well-established correlators and predictors of violence and aggression in other settings. Because this leader possesses a dual behavioral nature, recognizing and correcting unhealthy behaviors within the work environment presents significant challenges.

On the one hand, this leader operates under the cloak of normalcy and charm, while the other hand functions with manipulative or deceptive that destroy the organization's internal essence. Babiak, Neuman, and Hare (2010) observed that executives that possessed exceptional communication skills in conjunction with innovative and strategic mindsets also displayed ineffective management skills, unsatisfactory teamwork, and received low appraisals from their immediate bosses. A leader that demonstrates a psychopathy leadership style can shape an organizational culture with a sense of superiority that deems misleading kindness, incivility, irrational decision making, and harmful behaviors as acceptable.

Autocratic Leadership

Autocratic leaders demonstrate a sense of superiority and self-belief in their intellect to discount, ignore, and dismiss others' input and guidance. An autocratic leader operates autonomously to accomplish self-glorifying goals through maximum, authoritarian control over subordinates and displays the ability to "force favorable or unfavorable decisions upon others" (De Cremer, 2007, p. 1388). In turn, organizational members feel devalued because they lack the opportunity to participate in organizational decision-making, maintain limited to no direct influence on decisions, or execute decisions without considering their employees' opinions (Bhatti, Mura Maitlo, Shaikh, Hashmi, & Shaikh, 2012). Essentially, this leader's behavior conveys little concern regarding subordinates' ideas, inputs, or feelings related to decision-making. Most notably, this leader possesses a self-belief that others lack the intellectual capability to participate in organizational matters that shape an environment whereby subordinates display fear, insecurities, blame-shifting, demonstrate nervous behaviors of doubt, and immediacy to remain distant from the leader (Daft, 2005); (Siewiorek & Lehtinen, 2011). Without limits or balance, an autocratic leader tends to rely upon their intuition for decision making with a mission-focused approach that cannot display concern for organizational members' wellbeing. (Bhatti, Mura Maitlo, Shaikh, Hashmi, & Shaikh, 2012). Leaders who subscribe to this leadership style foster a workplace that reinforces the leader's perception of inferior subordinates and contributes to employee neglect, decreased morale, and job satisfaction.

To grasp the complexity of organizational arrogance, it remains imperative one recognizes how these leadership styles mentioned above contribute to the existence and development of organizational arrogance. In particular, a leader who demonstrates a leadership style from one of the "Dark Triad" characteristics impacts an organizational environment. However, these leadership styles alone are not solely responsible for forming organizational arrogance. Instead, one must also accept how a leader with a sense of superiority and their subsequent arrogant behaviors shape an organizational environment where these behaviors no longer exist at the individual or group level but expand to the organizational level and become accepted as an organizational identity.

Organizational Identity

When one considers that leaders' behavior shapes culture and affects members' behavior, it becomes noteworthy to understand how organizational members and organizations perceive themselves and develop their identity. Organizational identity represents the final pillar in constructing organizational arrogance. It explains how, like individual identities, organizations also hold unique qualities and identities that capture their internal essence and define them. Albert & Whetten (1985) asserts that organizational identity reflects a set of central (relevant and critical organizational descriptors), distinctive (exclusive and noticeable from other organizations), and enduring (continual and permanent towards organizational change) statements that organizational members believe accurately epitomize their organization. When organizational members develop a sense of belonging, it creates an organizational identity. Organizational identity introspectively poses the question of "Who are we? What are we? Where are we going?" Organizational identity describes the shared and collective work experiences that provide meaning for organizational members and professional groups operating at various hierarchical levels (Glynn, 2000); (Harrison, 2000); (Kjaergaard & Ravasi, 2011). Leaders that demonstrate arrogant behaviors can establish an organizational environment that reflects an organizational identity displaying these arrogant behaviors and experiences. When arrogant leaders develop an organization where organizational members adopt the central, distinctive, and enduring cultural characteristics of arrogance, their connection to the organization evolves to mirror these characteristics.

Arrogance represents the overarching theme that connects narcissistic, Machiavellian, psychopathy, and autocratic leadership styles. Recognizing how arrogance as a behavioral characteristic interacts with organizational identity helps understand the formation of the organizational arrogance construct. Organizational arrogance leverages the idea that leader behavior shapes the culture. A leader with any arrogance level, especially to the extreme degree of the "dark triad" characteristics, can influence the norms, beliefs, shared values, customs, and life within the organization that reflects an organizationally arrogant culture.

ORGANIZATIONAL ARROGANCE

While organizational arrogance recognizes a leaders' role in shaping an environment with a sense of superiority, it also presents behavioral components that describe how this phenomenon manifests itself in the workforce at the organizational level. Prior research indicated a lack of clear evidence that arrogance existed at the organizational level and, therefore, limited the discourse towards individual and leader arrogance operating at the individual or group level. However, Herbin (2018) leveraged the current literature that classified individuals exhibiting a sense of superiority as arrogance and developed the comprehensive definition that demonstrates how arrogance manifests itself at the organizational level, that describes how organizational members treat one another and become culturally acceptable norms, in three distinctive behavioral patterns: overconfidence in organizational capabilities, dismissiveness towards internal and external organizational matters, or disparagement towards intra-organizational and inter-organizational members.

Overconfidence in Organizational Capabilities

Overconfidence in organizational capabilities represents an organizational arrogant behavioral component that describes when organizational members exhibit self-absorbed behaviors and an overinflated ego in their abilities, thoughts, attitudes, and behaviors when performing organizational tasks or making organizational decisions. These behaviors promote a work environment that displays overconfidence and contributes to eventual organizational impediments at the organizational level. At the individual and group level, Pater (2013) found that arrogance epitomizes a dangerous flaw because it misguides individuals that they possess all-knowing powers, the inability to fail, or a superior intellect level than others that contributes to overestimating oneself, underestimating others, and a firm conviction that they can possess all the correct answers. When organizational members model this leader behavior at the organizational level, it promotes a culture whereby organizational members no longer display humility or receptive to openly evaluate and assess environmental threats and factors that potentially hinder organizational growth or even organizational survival. For example, Mui (2012) and Anthony (2016) demonstrate how Kodak represented an industry giant in photography for over a century. When Kodak invented the digital camera, many Kodak executives overconfidently believed that the digital camera would never surpass film camera popularity and failed to effectively expand their digital camera market's technological capabilities to remain relevant. As a result, Kodak's leadership mistakenly relied upon their past successes in the film camera industry and underestimated the emerging technologies that led to the once-industry giant declaring bankruptcy in 2012 and never returned to their once-prominent status.

Other research scholars indicated that highly overconfident individuals develop overconfidence and rely upon their tuition after experiencing success and exhibit a false sense of security that leads towards a form of apathy, reckless expansion into diverse markets, dismiss feedback tools, external data, commitment towards activities outside their expertise and discount purposeful strategizing that negatively impact the organization's success (Ma & Karri, 2005; (Harms, Spain, & Hannah, 2011). The Kodak example demonstrated how this false sense of security dissuaded organizational members from accepting their vulnerability towards an emerging market and displayed complacency and an attachment to outdated marketing strategies. Overconfidence in organizational capabilities promotes an organizational-wide attitude of unrealistic desires, organizational expectations, and hope. Organizational members also tend to exhaust opportunities that reinforce their superiority or others' inferiority in ways that may encompass a series of unethical behaviors such as deceit, the misrepresentation of data or self, and workplace sabotage that stagnates the work environment. When this organizational arrogant behavioral component manifests itself in the workforce, organizational members recklessly commit to activities and engagements that supersede their individual and organizational capabilities and threatens organizational survivability.

Overconfidence in Organizational Capabilities

- **Overconfidence in Organizational Capabilities:** Organizational members exhibit self-absorbed behaviors and an overinflated ego in their thoughts, attitudes, and capabilities that influence organizational decision-making.
- Individuals can recognize this behavior's presence when organizational members behave with a personal belief that their intellect supersedes personal and organizational limitations.
  Examples may include:
  - Organizational members exaggerate self-importance.
  - Organizational members engage in reckless decision-making.
  - Organizational members believe they are more intelligent than anyone else.
  - Organizational members underestimate others.
  - Organizational members behave like they possess all the correct answers.
  - Organizational members do not value lessons from past mistakes.
  - Organizational members overestimate who they are.
  - Organizational members overestimate what they can do.
  - Organizational members overestimate what they can do.
  - Organizational members make those around them feel inferior.

Dismissiveness Towards Internal and External Organizational Matters

Dismissiveness towards internal and external organizational matters is another organizational arrogant behavioral component that describes when organizational members overtly or covertly dismiss, quell, discourage, or disregard other organizational members' thoughts, input, creativity, innovation, and active participation towards organizational matters. Internal and external organizational matters refer to activities, events, opportunities, or threats that impact organizational growth, morale, and cohesion. Examples of internal organizational matters may include employee training, self-development opportunities, logistical, financial, human resources, or equal opportunity and diversity concerns. Examples of external organizational matters may consist of corporate social responsibility, marketing and branding, mergers and acquisitions, emerging markets and technological advancements, and even pandemics.

Dismissiveness that occurs at the organizational level impedes organizational progress, trust, respect, and effective organizational communication. Unfortunately, this behavioral component is so commonplace and prevalent in the work environment that one may overlook it as an arrogant organizational trait. Arrogant leaders that devalue or dismiss their subordinates' input towards internal and external organizational matters only reinforce their sense of superiority and prevent receiving critical insight, advice, and counsel from organizational members. Milyavsky, Krunglanski, Chemikova, & Schori-Eyal (2017) posited that arrogant leaders passively or actively dismiss organizational members' feelings, thoughts, counsel, or words self-justify their actions due to their self-perceived intellectual superiority.

This organizational arrogant behavioral component also demonstrates how organizational members that inflict harm on one another who desire more active workplace participation further hinder organizational progress. Organizational members with arrogant behaviors exhibit disdain, a lack of reciprocity, deference, hurtful and disrespectful behaviors, and conviction that organizational members do not possess the substance, competence, or value in their interactions and eventually discourages members from using their talents and capacities for future purposes (Tiberius & Walker, 1998). Examples of this behavior include disrespecting a colleague and their ideas, claiming to be more knowledgeable than others, discounting advice, dismissing organizational members', and even ignoring or punishing organizational members who provide negative feedback. (Johnson, 2010'; Pater, 2013; Milyavsky, Krunglanski, Chemikova, & Schori-Eyal, 2017). Leaders who encounter the stressors of internal or external organizational matters and exhibit a dismissive attitude toward other members' views and opinions inhibit their ability for self-awareness and shape a new cultural norm. A cultural norm whereby organizational members mirror this behavior discourages others from participating in the organization's decision-making process or feeling valued.

Dismissiveness towards internal and external organizational matters also demonstrates how individuals exhibit dismissive behavior when they remain fixated on past successes and refuse to accept the current technological environments to stay competitive (Ma & Karri, 2005). Tenured organizational members can possess an extreme attachment to outdated policies, processes, and procedures that once contributed towards organizational success. These same members now reject organizational members' input who recognize emerging markets and challenge the status quo by recommending new and evolving growth opportunities. Leaders that adopt this self-imposed limitation and commitment towards a nostalgic past resist change efforts that create complacency and ensures missed opportunities that risk organizational survival. In turn, these individuals dismiss pertinent and critical organizational needs required for succeeding in the current operating environment (Kane & Cunningham, 2013). This organizational arrogant behavioral component degrades organizational members' ability to maintain effective communication, stifles organizational members' creativity, engagement, and commitment to accomplishing organizational objectives, and impedes organizational growth. This stagnation leads to organizational failure based on complacency, inflexibility, and short-sightedness because arrogant individuals ignore organizational members' important input, wise counsel, environmental changes (such as changes in markets), and competitive threats (Rosenthal & Pittinsky, 2006).

As an example, Fusaro and Miller (2002), McLean and Elkind (2003), and Fox (2003) illustrate how the energy conglomerate Enron provides a good description of dismissiveness towards internal or external organizational matters. After experiencing a period of sustained success and publicly recognized as one of America's 100 best companies, Enron executives, attorneys, and accountants engaged in unethical business practices. These leaders created notional subsidiaries to sell and inflate assets, create false earnings, avoid taxes, and hide losses in an attempt to increase Enron's stock. As stocks continued to rise, arrogant organizational members dismissed existing policies and ethical conduct guidelines, encouraged improper accounting practices, failed to enforce conflict-of-interest rules, and even punished employees who attempted to report wrongdoing doing. The organizational members' arrogant and self-serving behaviors eventually led to Enron's bankruptcy in 2001. While some attribute the Enron organizational collapse to unethical behavior and leadership practices, a further examination into the case indicates how Enron leaders shaped an arrogant organizational culture where dismissiveness towards internal and external organizational matters became normal and acceptable practices. Enron dismissed and discouraged checks and balances that would provide organizational members the confidence in the ethical misconduct reporting process to ensure internal and external organizational matters remained a priority and protected. Instead, Spector & Lane (2007) indicated that Enron operated within a closed environment of dismissiveness, arrogance, complexity, no transparency, self-censorship towards existing problems, and organizational-wide deception.

Dismissiveness Towards Internal and External Organizational Matters

- **Dismissiveness Towards Internal and External Organizational Matters:** Organizational members overtly or covertly dismiss, quell, discourage, or disregard other organizational members' thoughts, input, creativity, innovation, and active participation in organizational matters.
  - Internal organizational matters may include employee training, self-development opportunities, logistical, financial, human resources, equal opportunity, and diversity concerns.
  - External organizational matters may include corporate social responsibility, marketing and branding, mergers and acquisitions, emerging markets and technological advancements, and even pandemics.
- Individuals can identify this behavior's existence when organizational members display the propensity to ignore or disregard information regarding organizational matters.
  Examples may include:
  - Organizational members prevent a close relationship with others.
  - Organizational members disregard the value of others.
  - Organizational members make others feel devalued.
  - Organizational members claim to be more knowledgeable than others.
  - Organizational members discourage the use of others' talents and capacities.
  - Organizational members ignore any instances where negative feedback occurs.
  - Organizational members display a lack of attention towards how others think.
  - Organizational members ignore or do not acknowledge others.

Disparagement Towards Intra-Organizational and Interorganizational Members

Disparagement towards intra-organizational and interorganizational members characterizes the third organizational arrogant behavioral component described when organizational members exhibit maltreatment, underappreciation, and disrespect towards internal or external organizational members. This particular component indicates the most aggressive, harmful, and damaging organizational arrogance characteristic compared to the other two organizational arrogance behavioral components. This behavioral component describes instances where arrogant members unjustly and publicly belittle their rivals, mock their presence, criticize and humiliate their staff members during meetings, display negative behavior toward staff, play staff members against each other, attack people and not issues, demonstrates a lack of self-awareness that contributes to insensitive behavior and failure to recognize how their behavior affects others (Hamlin & Hatton, 2013); (Ma & Karri 2005; Johnson, 2010, Pater, 2013). The psychological, emotional, and mental impact of this component significantly demoralizes the workforce, destroys employee self-confidence, creates a toxic environment, and can lead to high employee turnover.

In one example recounted by Wigglesworth (2018) and Wagner (2019), James B. Comey, Former FBI Director, oversaw an investigation into the possible linkage between Russia and Former President Donald Trump's 2016 election campaign. During the investigation, Trump fired Comey and publicly belittled

Comey with characterizations such as "a "nut job," "a showboat," "a grandstander," and a "weak and untruthful slime ball." Trump also publicly discredited Comey with statements that his leadership "was a disaster," with a nickname "Sanctimonious James Comey" and that Comey was "either very sick or very dumb." When Comey defended the FBI against Trump's criticism, Trump's Former Press Secretary, Kellyanne Conway, publicly attacked Comey also calling him, "a grandstander and a showboat" and referred to him as a liar. While Trump's disparaging comments towards Comey demonstrates arrogant leader characteristic at the individual level, Conway's disparagement and public criticism of Comey indicates that these mirrored behaviors now exist at the organizational level as an acceptable cultural practice supporting organizational arrogance.

An organization affected with disparagement towards intra-organizational and interorganizational members creates conditions where arrogant and distracted organizational members become aware of these problems and respond with anger and blame-filled reactions that discount their role in modeling the behavior. Within this component, organizational members exaggerate their self-importance and sense of mental superiority through disparaging others. These behaviors decrease productivity because individuals reluctantly share their ideas for fear of being attacked or seen as incompetent or discredited (Johnson et al., 2010; Tiberius & Walker, 1998). When organizational members in upper management, middle management, and lower management continually exhibit these disparaging behaviors throughout the organization, it reinforces these destructive arrogant characteristics as the cultural norm and acceptable behavior. Opportunities for cultivating a healthy work environment, organizational cohesion, information sharing, and employee commitment decreases and become replaced with maltreatment, condescension, neglect, and disrespect.

Disparagement Towards Intra-Organizational and Interorganizational Members

- **Disparagement Towards Intra-Organizational and Interorganizational Members:** Organizational members exhibit maltreatment, underappreciation, and disrespect towards internal or external organizational members.
- Individuals can identify this behavior's presence when organizational members' exhibit aggressive and hostile actions designed to belittle, degrade or discredit organizational members. Examples may include:
  - Organizational members mistreat others when they express their views.
  - Organizational members play staff members against each other.
  - Organizational members criticize staff in public areas.
  - Organizational members pass blame towards each other.
  - Organizational members attack each other and not the issues.
  - Organizational members discredit others.
  - Organizational members individuals appear incompetent during meetings.
  - Organizational members make jokes at the expense of others.

MEASURING ORGANIZATIONAL ARROGANCE

Organizational arrogance presents a new workplace complexity that illustrates how arrogance impacts organizational behavior and culture. Organizational members who exhibit arrogant behaviors reinforce cultural norms and present work environments with significant challenges that impede employee participation and organizational progress. Understanding organizational arrogance helps scholars, consultants, HR practitioners, and leaders describe these arrogant behaviors, recognize how they manifest within the workplace, and their enduring impact on organizational members and the organization. While acknowledging the existence of these arrogant organizational behaviors remain critical, possessing the ability to measure the presence of organizational arrogance remains just as important. Using existing literature on arrogant behaviors, Herbin (2018) developed and validated an Organizational Arrogance Scale designed to measure the three organizational arrogant behavioral components that appear in the organizational environment.

Construct and Instrument Development

Organizational arrogance builds upon theoretical domains that describe arrogance that include: individual arrogance, workplace arrogance, corporate arrogance, or consumer arrogance (Tiberius, 1998; Johnson et al., 2010; Brown, 2012; Gregg, 2014; Ruvio, 2016). The studies indicated that arrogance manifests itself in three distinct ways: a demonstrated sense of superiority that leads to overconfidence, dismissiveness, and disparaging behavior. Although limited to the individual level, these studies also signified construct validity for these three factors. Organizational arrogance uses these same constructs as elements for application at the organizational level. It includes a sense of superiority that leads to (a) overconfidence in organizational capabilities, defined as the organizational members' personal belief that their intellect supersedes any personal and organizational limitations; (b) dismissiveness towards internal and external organizational matters, described as the organizational members' propensity to ignore or disregard information regarding organizational matters; and (c) disparagement towards intra-organizational and interorganizational members, defined as the organizational members' actions that belittle, discredit, or degrade organizational members. These existing constructs prompted the need for a broad scale that measures arrogance at the organizational level.

Theoretically Based Item Pool

The literature displayed 75 illustrative examples that describe how arrogance manifested itself in the workplace and represent potential items to measure organizational members' attitudes, behavior, and thoughts to develop the organizational arrogance scale. The list of items extracted from the literature revealed 16 items related to a sense of superiority that leads to overconfidence in capabilities, and 34 items that address a sense of superiority that leads to dismissiveness towards internal and external organizational matters, and 27 items that relate to a sense of superiority that leads to disparagement towards intra-organizational and interorganizational members.

Expert Panelists

DeVellis (2017) indicates that selecting qualified panelists represents a critical step in developing a credible and reputable scale. To support their analysis of the 75-item measure, the panelists adhered to the following four guidelines: (1) confirm content validity, which required rating each item's relevancy between 0 to 6 and identify its effectiveness for measuring its assigned factor; (2) item evaluation, that required evaluating each survey item against the organizational arrogance definition and provide individual comments and recommended changes as necessary; (3) alternate means, whereby each panelist submits alternate perspectives to identify organizational arrogance; (4) conclusion, enabled panelists the opportunity to provide general comments, suggestions, or recommendations as required. This process reduced the items to 50 items.

Organizational Arrogance Scale Format

The organizational arrogance scale measures the frequency and intensity of behaviors that demonstrate a culture of superiority that leads to the overconfidence of organizational capabilities, dismissiveness towards internal and external organizational matters, and disparagement towards intra-organizational and interorganizational members. Each item captures organizational members' opinions, beliefs, and attitudes about arrogance within the organizational environment. The organizational arrogance scale uses a seven-point scale format because it provides the upper limits of a scale's reliability, decreases interpretive confusion and respondent fatigue (Allen & Seaman, 2007). The organizational arrogance instrument contains seven responses from left to right ranging from 1 to 7: 1- "never" (does not occur), 2 - "rarely" (occurs less than 10% of the time), 3 - "occasionally" (occurs about 30% of the time), 4 - "sometimes" (occurs 50% of the time), 5 - "frequently" (occurs about 70% of the time), 6 -"usually" (occurs about 90% of the time), and 7 - "always" (occurs all the time).

Population and Sample Size

According to DeVellis (2012), to achieve instrument validity and generalizability based on the 5:1 ratio of subjects to item, the 50-item pilot test was targeted to a population of at least three hundred participants. The test was administered to three-hundred twenty-two participants and collected demographic data to ensure participant validity that included the participants: (a) age, (b) gender, (c) ethnicity, (d) education, (e) job level, (f) and employer type. The participants represented a diverse group from various industries to validate the Organizational Arrogant Scale.

Analysis

Tabachnick and Fidell (2007) posited that correlation coefficients must achieve a score of .30 or greater because items that scored less indicate a weak relationship between variables. Based on this guidance and using SPSS Version 25, the pilot test underwent an exploratory principal component analysis (PCA) that indicated the existence of a five-factor solution that possessed eigenvalues over 1.0. Total Variance Explained table identified eigenvalues percentages reached a high of 50% for Component 1 to as low as 2% for Component 5. More specifically, Component 1 loaded 43 items that ranged in coefficient scores of .455 to .845.

Another principal component analysis was conducted that adjusted the fixed numbers of factors to extract to 3, with a Direct Oblimin rotation, and suppressed the coefficients with an absolute value below .600. The 50-item pilot test was further reduced to 43 items with all factors loading to Component 1 with new values that ranged from .604 to .846. An additional six items with an absolute value less than .650 were eliminated, reducing the items to 37. A reliability test on the 37 items produced a Cronbach Alpha of .955. According to DeVellis, a reliability test helps determine scale length because it provides insight on the strength of factor loads, redundant items, and items identified for retention or elimination that ensures optimal scale length. DeVellis asserts that shorter scales place less burden on participants and are more acceptable, while longer scales provide more reliability. For this reason, DeVellis recommends that scale developers must identify the balance between brevity and reliability.

To further optimize the scale length, coefficients with an absolute value below .818 were suppressed and revealed five top-loading items suggesting a unidimensional scale. The five items selected for the scale fit the brevity criteria and provide a broad umbrella encompassing the previously deleted items to create a more inclusive and restricted scale. A final reliability test performed on the 5-items resulted in a Cronbach Alpha of .922, signifying a highly reliable instrument that measures organizational arrogance.

Table 1. 5-item organizational arrogance component matrix

	Component
	1
Q15 (O13) Make those Feel Inferior	.879
Q22 (D6) Disregard the Value of Other	.884
Q27 (D11) Discourages Use of Talents and Capacities	.883
Q34 (B3) Demean Others	.884
Q50 (B15) Ignore Other Staff Members	.838

Table 2. 5-item organizational arrogance reliability statistics

Cronbach's Alpha	N of Items
.922	5

Indicators for Overconfidence in Organizational Capabilities

The Organizational Arrogance Scale at Table 3 contains one item entitled *"Organizational members exhibit behaviors that make those around them feel inferior,"* reflecting the behavioral component of Overconfidence in Organizational Capabilities. These arrogant thoughts, attitudes, and behaviors enable organizational members to overlook market trends, possess a false sense of security, display reckless decision-making, and underestimate others' strengths. When organizational members perceive a threat towards their superiority, it creates instances where organizational members engage in self-preserving behaviors, including deceit, misrepresentation of data or self, workplace sabotage, or theft aimed to protect their self-proclaimed reputation superiority and reinforce others inferiority.

Indicators for Dismissiveness Towards Internal and External Organizational Matters

The Organizational Arrogance Scale contains two items entitled *"Organizational members disregard the value of others' reactions, feelings, and thoughts"* and *"Organizational members' treatment towards coworkers discourages them from using their talents and capacities"* that reflect the behavioral component Dismissiveness Towards Internal and External Organizational Matters. These items demonstrate how organizational members behave in a manner that only their views, ideas, and perspectives matter and, as a result, limits information sharing with other organizational members. Incorporating these two items into the final 5-item scale denotes how organizational members can overtly or covertly display these pervasive behaviors in the work environment and their impact on others. Patterns of dismissiveness threaten opportunities to build synergy, collaboration, trust, sense of belonging, mutual respect, training, succession planning, job satisfaction, and morale.

Indicators for Disparagement Towards Intra-Organizational and Interorganizational Members

The Organizational Arrogance Scale contains two items entitled *"Organizational Members Demean Others"* and *"Ignore Other Staff Members,"* which reflect the behavioral component Disparagement Towards Intra-organizational and Interorganizational Members. These items measure organizational members' thoughts, attitudes, and behaviors that belittle, degrade, or discredit organizational members. In particular, organizational members exhibit more aggressive, hostile, intimidating, and threatening behaviors when interacting with internal or external organizational members. Disparaging behaviors range in intensity and manifests in various ways that inflict extreme psychological harm on others and the organization. When organizational members display these behaviors, it discourages participation levels, employee cohesion, job security, effective two-way communication, job satisfaction, and retention. It ostracizes certain members and discounts their value to the organization. These items reflect the breadth and depth necessary to capture this behavior accurately.

Organizational arrogance and the validated organizational arrogance scale represent significant steps in understanding this complex organizational phenomenon. The Organizational Arrogance Scale encapsulates this organizational behavioral characteristic's comprehensive, expansive, and exhaustive nature. The scale provides an effective means for evaluating the presence, frequency, and intensity of arrogant behaviors, attitudes, and thoughts that manifest within the organizational environment and threatens organizational effectiveness. The pilot test indicated that the participants across many industries, job experience, gender, and ethnic backgrounds encounter organizational arrogance in their respective work environments that pose risks to their long-term survival. The 5-item Organizational Arrogance Scale provides insight and awareness to organizational leaders that may not understand or witness the degree to which arrogant behaviors exist within their organizational culture.

Table 3. 5-item organizational arrogance scale

Behavioral Component	Item
Overconfidence in Organizational Capabilities	Organizational members exhibit behaviors that make those around them feel inferior.
Dismissiveness Towards Internal and External Organizational Matters	Organizational members disregard the value of others' reactions, feelings, and thoughts. Organizational members' treatment towards coworkers discourages them from using their talents and capacities.
Disparagement Towards Intra-organizational and Interorganizational Members	Organizational Members Demean Others Ignore Other Staff Members

SOLUTIONS AND RECOMMENDATIONS

Studies indicate countless examples that attempt to explain how organizational leaders engaged in unethical practices that contributed to poor employee morale, workplace stress, high turnover rates, abysmal organizational culture, and the eventual organizational collapse. However, organizational arrogance provides another perspective on the role leaders play in shaping organizational behavior and organizational culture, creating environmental conditions that threaten organizational survival. While this phenomenon poses significant risks to organizations, recognizing its existence provides the necessary awareness that should prompt organizational leaders to invest in training and develop mitigating strategies designed to counter the effects of organizational arrogance.

Organizational culture remains a leader's responsibility that requires keen attention, astute observations, and immediate action to eliminate any signs of organizational arrogance. Combatting organizational arrogance requires engaged leadership. Organizational leaders can dictate their strategic focus once they identify how severe and widespread organizational arrogance is within their organizational environment. Implement purposeful leadership efforts designed to eliminate any instances of institutional paranoia associated with transparent communication and knowledge sharing, increase job satisfaction, and incorporate a zero-tolerance policy. These strategies must remain focused on addressing individuals who display arrogant behaviors and maximize organizational efficiencies to reach optimal performance. Organizational arrogance and the Organizational Arrogance Scale provide opportunities to effectively diagnose organizations and implement strategies designed to improve organizational behavior, culture, and organizational productivity.

FUTURE RESEARCH DIRECTIONS

Limited studies examining arrogance at the organizational level indicate the endless research opportunities for furthering this phenomenon traditionally associated with arrogant leaders or arrogant individuals versus arrogant organizations. Organizational arrogance represents a construct that lends itself to applicability across many private and public sector organizations, academic disciplines, leadership training, and coaching. Conceptually, this construct provides the body of knowledge with a new insight that may better explain previous leadership or organizational failure findings. Exploring previous and current studies under the organizational arrogance auspice widens the research aperture, illuminating new areas for further research. A site may identify the relationship between workplace stress, job satisfaction, retention rates, and organizational arrogance. Researchers can also examine how organizational arrogance differs from each management level and what management level is more likely to exhibit this behavior. One can also investigate what careers or work environments are more susceptible to organizational arrogance. Phenomenological studies, narrative inquiry, ethnographic observations, or case studies represent a few recommended research methods that can capture organizational members' accounts that convey organizational arrogance's emotional, psychological, and mental impact. Exploring the behaviors, attitudes, thoughts, cultural norms, and customs within an organization will provide deeper insight into the phenomenon and further the body of knowledge. Overall, this chapter demonstrates how this emerging concept deems worthy of critique, examination, replication, and, most importantly, universal acceptance.

CONCLUSION

This chapter introduced a process whereby arrogant behaviors that no longer exist at the individual and group level manifest themselves at the organizational level evolving into an emerging concept called organizational arrogance. Organizational arrogance explains how organizational members interact with one another and how these arrogant behavioral characteristics impact a culture. Organizational arrogance defines an organizational environment whereby leaders shape a culture in which members behave with a sense of superiority, leading to overconfidence in organizational capabilities, dismissiveness towards internal and external organizational matters, and disparagement towards intra-organizational and interorganizational members. Organizational arrogance leveraged theoretical domains that described arrogance, narcissistic leadership theory, Machiavellian leadership theory, psychopathy leadership theory, autocratic leadership theory, and organizational identity to build a comprehensive and inclusive definition that describes arrogance at the organizational level.

Each domain provided insight in understanding the multiple ways arrogant behaviors manifested themselves in the workplace and served as a foundational premise for the three organizational arrogant behavioral characteristics. The first organizational arrogance behavioral component, Overconfidence in Organizational Capabilities, describes when organizational members exhibit self-absorbed behaviors and an overinflated ego in their thoughts, attitudes, and capabilities that influence organizational decision making. The second organizational arrogant behavioral component, Dismissiveness Towards Internal and External Organizational Members, denotes when organizational members overtly or covertly dismiss, quell, discourage, or disregard other organizational members' thoughts, input, creativity, innovation, and active participation towards organizational matters. Finally, the third and most psychologically damaging organizational arrogant behavioral component, Disparagement Towards Intra-Organizational and Interorganizational Members, represents instances where organizational members exhibit maltreatment, underappreciation, and disrespect towards internal or external organizational members.

This chapter also demonstrated the process of validating the 5-Item unidimensional Organizational Arrogance Scale. Existing literature that described arrogant behaviors contributed to the prospective pool of items that developed the Organizational Arrogance Scale. After extracting 50-items, Herbin (2018) administered the pilot test to a three-hundred twenty-two heterogeneous sample size representing various work experiences, management levels, age, race, and gender. Each respondent completed the scale based upon their workplace observations that indicated organizational arrogance. The 50-items were subjected to exploratory principal component analyses and suppressed coefficients with an absolute value below .818, revealing five top-loading items for inclusion on the unidimensional scale. The final 5-item Organizational Arrogance Scale produced an Alpha score of .922, indicating a reliable instrument that accurately measures the three organizational arrogance behavioral components, Overconfidence in Organizational Capabilities, Dismissiveness Towards Internal and External Organizational Matters, and Disparagement Towards Intra-organizational and Interorganizational members. Overall, this chapter indicates how organizational arrogance threatens employee engagement opportunities, cohesion and morale, and long-term organizational success worthy of the unlimited research opportunities that exist.

REFERENCES

Albert, S., & Whetten, D. (1985). Organizational Identity. In L. Cummings & M. Staw (Eds.), *Organizational Behavior* (Vol. 7, pp. 263–295). JAI Press.

Allen, E., & Seaman, C. (2007). Likert Scales and Data Analyses. *Quality Progress, 40*(7), 64–65.

Anthony, S. (2016, July 15). Kodak's Downfall Wasn't About Technology. *Harvard Business Review*. Retrieved from https://hbr.org/2016/07/kodaks-downfall-wasnt-about-technology

Babiak, P., Neumann, C., & Hare, R. (2010). Corporate Psychopathy: Talking the Walk. *Behavioral Sciences & the Law, 28*(2), 174–193. PMID:20422644

Bhatti, N., Mura Maitlo, G., Shaikh, N., Hashmi, M., & Shaikh, F. (2012). The Impact of Autocratic and Democratic Leaderships Style on Job Satisfaction. *International Business Research, 5*(2), 192–201. doi:10.5539/ibr.v5n2p192

Bolman, L. (1997). Reframing Organizations (2nd ed.) San Francisco, CA: Jossey-Bass.

Braun, S., Aydin, N., Frey, D., & Peus, C. (2016). Leader Narcissism Predicts Malicious Envy and Supervisor-targeted Counterproductive Behavior: Evidence from Field and Experimental Research. *Journal of Business Ethics, 135*, 1–17.

Brown, H. (2012, July/August). So What If I Don't Have An iPhone? The Unintended Consequences of Using Arrogance in Advertising. *Journal of Applied Business Research, 28*(4), 555–563. doi:10.19030/jabr.v28i4.7040

Brown, M., & Trevino, L. (2006). Ethical Leadership: A Review and Future Directions. *The Leadership Quarterly, 17*(6), 595–616. doi:10.1016/j.leaqua.2006.10.004

Cleckley, H. (1941). *The Mask of Sanity* (1st ed.). C.V. Mosby.

Daft, R. (2005). *The Leadership Experience*. Thomson Corporation.

Dahling, J., Whitaker, B., & Levy, P. (2009). The Development and Validation of a New Machiavellianism Scale. *Journal of Management, 35*(2), 219–257. doi:10.1177/0149206308318618

De Cremer, D. (2007). Emotional Effects of Distributive Justice as a Function of Autocratic Leader Behavior. *Journal of Applied Social Psychology, 37*(6), 1385–1404. doi:10.1111/j.1559-1816.2007.00217.x

DeVellis, R. (2012). *Scale Development: Theory and Applications* (3rd ed.). Sage.

Drory, A., & Gluskinos, U. (1980). Machiavellianism and Leadership. *The Journal of Applied Psychology, 65*(1), 81–86. doi:10.1037/0021-9010.65.1.81

Fox, L. (2003). *Enron: The rise and fall*. Wiley.

Fusaro, P., & Miller, R. (2002). *What went wrong at Enron: Everyone's guide to the largest bankruptcy in U.S.history*. Wiley.

Gkorezis, P., Petridou, E., & Krouklidou, T. (2015). Machiavellian Leadership, Organizational Cynicism and Emotional Exhaustion. *Europe's Journal of Psychology*, *11*(4), 619–631. doi:10.5964/ejop.v11i4.988 PMID:27247681

Glynn, M. (2000). When Cymbals become Symbols: Conflict over Organizational Identity within a Symphony Orchestra. *Organization Science*, *11*(3), 285–298. doi:10.1287/orsc.11.3.285.12496

Hamlin, R., & Hatton, A. (2013). Toward a British Taxonomy of Perceived Managerial and Leadership Effectiveness. *Human Resource Development Quarterly*, *24*(3), 365–406. doi:10.1002/hrdq.21163

Hareli, S., & Weiner, B. (2000). Accounts for Success as Determinants of Perceived Arrogance and Modesty. *Motivation and Emotion*, *24*(3), 215–236. doi:10.1023/A:1005666212320

Harms, P., Spain, S., & Hannah, S. (2011). Leader Development and the Dark Side of Personality. *The Leadership Quarterly*, *22*(3), 495–509. doi:10.1016/j.leaqua.2011.04.007

Harrison, J. (2000). Multiple Imaginings of Institutional Identity. *The Journal of Applied Behavioral Science*, *36*(4), 425–455. doi:10.1177/0021886300364003

Herbin, C. V., III. (2018). *Measuring Organizational Arrogance: Development and Validation of a Theory-Based Instrument* (Doctoral Dissertation). Regent University.

Johnson, R., Silverman, S., Shyamsunder, A., Swee, H., Rodopman, O., & Bauer, E. (2010). Acting Superior But Actually Inferior?: Correlates and Consequences of Workplace Arrogance. *Human Performance*, *23*(5), 403–427. doi:10.1080/08959285.2010.515279

Kane, C., & Cunningham, J. (2013). Leadership Changes and Approaches During Company Turnaround. *International Studies of Management & Organization*, *42*(4), 52–85. doi:10.2753/IMO0020-8825420403

Kjaergaard, M., & Ravasi, D. (2011). Mediating identity: A Study of Media Influence on Organizational Identity Construction in a Celebrity Firm. *Journal of Management Studies*, *48*(3), 514–543. doi:10.1111/j.1467-6486.2010.00954.x

Lee, K., & Ashton, M. (2005). Psychopathy, Machiavellianism, and Narcissism in the Five-Factor Model and the HEXACO Model of Personality Structure. *Personality and Individual Differences*, *38*(7), 1571–1582. doi:10.1016/j.paid.2004.09.016

Lewis, M. (2000). Self-conscious Emotions: Embarrassment, Pride, Shame, and Guilt. In *M. Lewis, & J. M. Haviland-Jones, Handbook of emotions* (pp. 623–636). Guilford.

Lubit, R. (2002). The Long-term Organizational Impact of Destructively Narcissistic Managers. *Academy of Management Review*, *16*, 127–138.

Ma, H., & Karri, R. (2005). Leaders Beware: Some Sure Ways to Lose Your Competitive Advantage. *Organizational Dynamics*, *34*(1), 63–76. doi:10.1016/j.orgdyn.2004.11.002

Maccoby, M. (2000). Narcissistic Leaders-The Incredible Pros, The Inevitable Cons. *Harvard Business Review*, *78*, 69–77.

McIntosh, G., & Rima, S. (2007). *Overcoming the Darkside of Leadership: How to Become an Effective Leader by Confronting Potential Failures*. Baker Books.

McLean, B., & Elkind, P. (2003). *Smartest guys in the room: The amazing rise and scandalous fall of Enron.* Portfolio/Penguin Group.

Milyavsky, M., Krunglanski, A., Chemikova, M., & Schori-Eyal, N. (2017). Evidence of Arrogance: On the Relative Importance of Expertise, Outcome, and Manner. *PLoS One, 12*(7), 1–31. doi:10.1371/journal.pone.0180420 PMID:28683114

Mui, C. (2012, January 18). How Kodak Failed. *Forbes.* Retrieved from https://www.forbes.com/sites/chunkamui/2012/01/18/how-kodak-failed/?sh=2941395a6f27

Nevicka, B., De Hoogh, A., Van Vianen, A., Beersma, B., & McIlwain, D. (2011). All I Need is a Stage to Shine: Narcissists' Leader Emergence and Performance. *The Leadership Quarterly, 22*(5), 910–925. doi:10.1016/j.leaqua.2011.07.011

Pater, R. (2013, November). Overcoming Leadership ADD: The Flaws of Arrogance, Distraction and Disconnection. *Professional Safety,* 30–34. www.asse.org

Poggi, I., & D'Errico, F. (2011). Types of Pride and their Expression. In A. Esposito, A. Vinciarelli, K. Vicsi, C. Pelachaud, & A. Nijholt (Eds.), *Analysis of Verbal and Nonverbal Communication and Enactment* (pp. 434–448). Springer-Verlag.

Rijsenbilt, A., & Commandeur, H. (2013). Narcissus Enters the Courtroom: CEO Narcissism and Fraud. *Journal of Business Ethics, 117*(2), 413–429. doi:10.100710551-012-1528-7

Robbins, S. P., & Judge, T. A. (2012). *Organizational Behavior* (15th ed.). Prentice Hall.

Sakalaki, M., Richardson, C., & Thepaut, Y. (2007). Machiavellianism and Economic Opportunism. *Journal of Applied Social Psychology, 37*(6), 1181–1190. doi:10.1111/j.1559-1816.2007.00208.x

Schein, E. (.-B. (2010). Organizational culture and leadership (4th ed.). San Francisco, CA: Jossey-Bass.

Sergiu, G. (2015, March). Developing the Organizational Culture. *Review of International Comparative Management, 16*(1), 137–143.

Siewiorek, A., & Lehtinen, E. (2011). Exploring Leadership Profiles from Collaborative Computer Gaming. *International Journal of Leadership Studies, 6*(3), 357–374.

Smith, S., & Lilienfeld, S. (2013, March-April). Psychopathy in the Workplace: The Knowns and Unknowns. *Aggression and Violent Behavior, 18*(2), 204–218. doi:10.1016/j.avb.2012.11.007

Solas, J. (2016). The Banality of Bad Leadership and Followership. *Society and Business Review, 11*(1), 12–23. doi:10.1108/SBR-09-2015-0049

Spector, B., & Lane, H. (2007). Exploring the Distinctions between a High Performance Culture and a Cult. *Strategy and Leadership, 35*(3), 18–24. doi:10.1108/10878570710745794

Tabachnick, B. G., & Fidell, L. S. (2007). *Using Multivariate Statistics* (5th ed.). Allyn & Bacon.

Tiberius, V., & Walker, J. (1998). Arrogance. *American Philosophical Quarterly, 35*(4), 379–390.

Wagner, J. (2019, May 29). 'A grandstander and a showboat': Kellyanne Conway attacks Comey for op-ed. *The Washington Post*. Retrieved from https://www.washingtonpost.com/politics/a-grandstander-and-a-show-boat-kellyanne-conway-attacks-comey-for-op-ed/2019/05/29/863b0594-8214-11e9-933d-7501070ee669_story.html

Wigglesworth, A. (2018, April 15). From 'nut job' to 'slimeball': A timeline of Trump's insults aimed at Comey. *Los Angeles Times*. Retrieved from https://www.latimes.com/politics/la-na-pol-trump-comey-insults-20180415-htmlstory.html

Yukl, G. (2010). *Leadership in Organizations*. Prentice Hall.

Zhu, D., & Chen, G. (2015). Narcissism, Director, Selection, and Risk-taking Spending. *Strategic Management Journal*, *36*(13), 2075–2098. doi:10.1002mj.2322

ADDITIONAL READING

Albert, S., & Whetten, D. (1985). Organizational Identity. In L. Cummings & M. Staw (Eds.), *Organizational Behavior* (Vol. 7, pp. 263–295). JAI Press.

Johnson, R., Silverman, S., Shyamsunder, A., Swee, H., Rodopman, O., & Bauer, E. (2010). Acting Superior But Actually Inferior?: Correlates and Consequences of Workplace Arrogance. *Human Performance*, *23*(5), 403–427. doi:10.1080/08959285.2010.515279

Lee, K., & Ashton, M. (2005). Psychopathy, Machiavellianism, and Narcissism in the Five-Factor Model and the HEXACO Model of Personality Structure. *Personality and Individual Differences*, *38*(7), 1571–1582. doi:10.1016/j.paid.2004.09.016

Ma, H., & Karri, R. (2005). Leaders Beware: Some Sure Ways to Lose Your Competitive Advantage. *Organizational Dynamics*, *34*(1), 63–76. doi:10.1016/j.orgdyn.2004.11.002

McIntosh, G., & Rima, S. (2007). *Overcoming the Darkside of Leadership: How to Become an Effective Leader by Confronting Potential Failures*. Baker Books.

Milyavsky, M., Krunglanski, A., Chemikova, M., & Schori-Eyal, N. (2017). Evidence of Arrogance: On the Relative Importance of Expertise, Outcome, and Manner. *PLoS One*, *12*(7), 1–31. doi:10.1371/journal.pone.0180420 PMID:28683114

Robbins, S. P., & Judge, T. A. (2012). *Organizational Behavior* (15th ed.). Prentice Hall.

Sergiu, G. (2015, March). Developing the Organizational Culture. *Review of International Comparative Management*, *16*(1), 137–143.

Solas, J. (2016). The Banality of Bad Leadership and Followership. *Society and Business Review*, *11*(1), 12–23. doi:10.1108/SBR-09-2015-0049

Tiberius, V., & Walker, J. (1998). Arrogance. *American Philosophical Quarterly*, *35*(4), 379–390.

KEY TERMS AND DEFINITIONS

Autocratic Leadership: Signifies a behavioral characteristic that indicates a leader with a sense of superiority and self-belief that they possess little concern regarding subordinates' ideas, inputs, or feelings related to decision-making.

Dismissiveness Towards Internal and External Organizational Matters: Organizational members tend to ignore or disregard information regarding internal and external organizational matters.

Disparagement Towards Intra-Organizational and Interorganizational Members: Organizational members' actions are designed to belittle, degrade, or discredit organizational members.

Internal and External Organizational Matters: Activities, events, opportunities, or threats that impact organizational growth, morale, and cohesion.

Machiavellian Leadership: Represents a behavioral characteristic that indicates a self-interested leader who behaves with a sense of superiority and engages in manipulative acts to accomplish tasks, objectives, or goals that reinforce their greatness and success even at others' expense.

Narcissistic Leadership: Denotes a behavioral characteristic that indicates a leader with self-absorbed behaviors and a perceived sense of superiority who exploits opportunities that elevate their self-image and importance.

Organizational Arrogance: An organizational environment whereby leaders shape a culture in which members behave with a sense of superiority, leading to overconfidence in organizational capabilities, dismissiveness towards internal and external organizational matters, and disparagement towards intra-organizational and interorganizational members.

Organizational Identity: An organizational theory construct explains how organizations are similar to individuals. They also hold unique qualities and identities that capture their internal essence and define them.

Overconfidence in Organizational Capabilities: Describes an organizational members' personal belief that their intellect supersedes any personal and organizational limitations.

Psychopathy Leadership: Characterizes a behavioral characteristic that indicates a self-centered leader with a sense of superiority who displays a dual behavior nature that can manipulatively inflict emotional or physical harm on others with unnoticeable mistreatment.

Chapter 15
Crisis Identification and Aversion Scale:
Crisis Leadership Competencies – Pre-Crisis Stages

Jamie Brownlee-Turgeon
Point Loma Nazarene University, USA

ABSTRACT

This chapter describes a new instrument that measures a leader's ability to identify and avert crisis in the pre-crisis stages. There is currently no other instrument that measures leadership ability pre-crisis but rather only leadership attributes during the crisis event. Based on the conceptual model developed by Wooten and James, the measurement focuses on the first two stages of the conceptual model, signal detection and prevention and preparation. This chapter covers multiple aspects of the measurement. First, it provides the framework for the development of the crisis identification and aversion tool. Secondly, it provides an analysis of the inclusive quartiles of the three-factor measurement, which includes the competencies of participatory management, sensemaking, and resourcefulness.

INTRODUCTION

This past year, the pandemic has forced organizational leaders into a crisis or series of crises. Organizations shifted to remote work, business continuity managers moved plans into action, human resource departments began investigations about COVID related cases, and leaders made decision after decision about reduction of force, options for balancing the budget, and what the future would look like in their industry in the short-term and the long-term. Mass layoffs and closures began to occur only a few weeks into the pandemic (Bartik et al., 2020). From a crisis leadership perspective, no leader was immune to the pandemic and the havoc it wreaked on the workplace. Pearson and Mitroff (1993) characterize a crisis as a high-impact event with high ambiguity in cause, effect, and resolution.

DOI: 10.4018/978-1-7998-7665-6.ch015

While this pandemic was not organizationally generated, it required a new set of competencies for leaders to succeed (Blythe, 2014). Bonvillian (2013) and DuBrin (2013) stated that leadership competencies during normal business operations differ from the competencies needed to lead through a crisis. Furthermore, leaders need to expect to lead through an organizational crisis within their professional careers (Klann, 2003). According to the Institute for Crisis Management, 50% of all crises occur due to management error or failure to take action. However, Klann (2013) also suggests that a leader can reduce the negative impact of the crisis. While it is common to bring in the public relations expert to manage the crisis, Blythe (2014) disagrees with this approach, arguing that the public relations expert be partnered with the leadership team navigating the crisis. Therefore, there is a great need to understand the competencies that create effective crisis leaders in the pre-crisis stages so that whenever possible, a crisis can be averted.

This chapter focuses on scale development to measure a leader's ability to identify and avert a crisis before the crisis event. It builds on Wooten and James' (2008) conceptual model, which identifies key competencies in each stage of a crisis. DeVellis (2012) provides an eight-step process for developing a scale: 1) determine what will be measured, 2) generate an item pool, 3) determine the format for measurement, 4) have initial item pool reviewed by experts, 5) consider the inclusion of validation items, 6) administer items to a development sample, 7) evaluate the items, and 8) optimize scale length.

BACKGROUND

Mitroff (2004), Fink (1986), and Wooten and James (2008) postulate that there are stages of crisis that expand beyond the actual event. Mitroff (2004) describes it as four stages, including signal detection, preparation and prevention, damage control and containment, and business recovery. Wooten and James (2008) add a fifth stage, called learning and redesign. Fink (1986) described four stages of a crisis, which he identifies as the anatomy of a crisis: the prodromal crisis stage, the acute crisis stage, the chronic crisis stage, and the crisis resolution stage. This literature supports that a crisis event is not the only aspect of a crisis, but rather there are pre-and post-crisis stages that must be considered.

Furthermore, Mitroff (2004) and Wooten and James (2008) postulate that crisis leaders focus on crisis identification and aversion, and when aversion is not possible, crisis leaders focus on developing an organization that is more resilient and stronger post-crisis. That said, the increase in organizational crises over the past couple of decades is human-induced, thus creating an opportunity for leaders to prevent a crisis from occurring (Pearson & Mitroff, 1993). A recent study showed that 50% of leaders believe their role in the crisis is to minimize damage and get back to business as usual (DuBrin, 2013). There has been little research on crisis leader competencies and even less on competencies needed to lead successfully through all stages of a crisis (Bonnvillian, 2013). There is currently no other instrument that measures leadership ability pre-crisis or post-crisis but rather only leadership attributes during the crisis event.

Leaders are often critiqued for how they led through a crisis because the expectation is that they will lead successfully (Bonvillian, 2013). However, when a leader does not lead effectively through a crisis, public reactions and brand management become increasingly important because the leader has not met the expectation placed on them (Bonvillian, 2013; James & Wooten, 2005; Pearson & Mitroff, 1993). The news highlights these leadership errors. Examples include Pennsylvania State University's football coach and the child molestation scandal, the Virginia Polytechnic Institute and State University mass shooting which led to 32 deaths, the delayed Ford and Firestone recall of the tires leading to deaths and injuries, the British Petroleum (BP) Gulf Oil Spill, or Texas A & M University bonfire disaster that led to multiple deaths of students (Wang & Hutchins, 2010; Nelson & Reierson, 2013). Wang and Hutchins (2010) postulate that with further examination of these incidents, all of them could have been averted had leaders seen the signals that showed a crisis was looming around the corner.

Wooten and James (2008) developed a conceptual model on the leadership attributes required to lead effectively during all five stages of the crisis; they conducted an archival qualitative research study and uncovered ten competencies. The study reviewed 20 cases representing the four types of human-induced crises: accidents, scandals, product safety and health incidents, and employee-centered (Wooten & James, 2008). The first stage is signal detection and includes sensemaking and perspective taking as competencies. Prevention and preparation is the second stage and includes issue selling, organizational agility, and creativity. Next, containment and damage control requires decision-making, communication, and risk-taking. This stage is often referred to as the crisis event. Business recovery requires a leader to promote organizational resilience and act with integrity. The final stage is learning and redesign, which requires a leader to have a learning orientation.

Sensemaking is a competency that answers three questions: how does something come to be an event, what does an event mean, and now what should one do (Weick et al., 2005)? Five subthemes further describe sensemaking. These subthemes are interpretation, mindfulness, retrospection, action, and implausibility (Weick, 1995). Sensemaking is a process that includes the ability to link patterns, interpretations, and events to form a conclusion about what they mean (Weick, 1995). Wooten and James (2008) connect sensemaking to crisis leadership in the signal detection stage due to the competency and focus on identifying what might be. A crisis is looming around every corner, and sensemaking provides an opportunity for a leader to identify the looming crisis before it becomes an event (Fink, 1986; Wooten & James, 2008)

Perspective-taking is the ability to take on another's perspective (Wooten & James, 2008). As part of the signal detection stage, this competency allows a crisis leader to see what might be implausible and the potential impact on different stakeholders if the looming crisis continues to approach (Brownlee-Turgeon, 2016). Davis (1983) connects perspective-taking with an ability to empathize. A leader that can take on other's perspective and empathize with the stakeholders is more likely to take action that can avert the crisis (Brownlee-Turgeon, 2016; Wooten & James, 2008). Many leaders are critiqued because they make decisions in the signal detection stage that do not demonstrate perspective-taking (James & Wooten, 2010). In the automobile industry, safety is a key factor; however, leaders depend on risk management, which is a mathematical formula, or a rules-based approach, to calculate whether the risk is worth it (Kapan & Mikes, 2012). Wooten and James (2010) identify Ford and Firestone leadership as waiting too long to recall the product, leading to several fatal victims. This example describes an inability to take on the perspective of the victims' families, and the leadership was highly critiqued for this lack of empathy (Wooten & James, 2010).

Issue selling is the ability to persuade leadership to take action on an imminent crisis (Wooten & James, 2008). Fink (1986) states that leaders must first identify that there is a potential crisis and have the ability to influence leaders toward action to avert the crisis. Issue selling requires two abilities: preparation and communication. Preparation refers to how to sell an issue to leadership, and communication refers to the actual communication of presenting the issue (Dutton et al., 2001). The Challenger explosion provides a well-known crisis event caused by an inability to issue-sell to decision-makers (Berkes, 2012). A NASA engineer identified that the o-ring used in the shuttle would likely not withstand the temperature conditions. However, there was a lot of pressure on decision-makers to move forward with the launch regardless of this information. The pressure to launch outweighed the information provided by the engineer; hence, the -ring did cause the explosion soon after launch (Berkes, 2012).

Organizational agility is the second competency in the prevention and preparation stage. In this stage, the focus is to prevent the crisis if possible; if not possible, then prepare in such a way for the crisis event to mitigate the damage (Wooten & James, 2008). A leader with organizational agility has a unique ability to understand all aspects of an organization instead of a narrow, tunnel vision perspective (Wooten & James, 2008). Flexibility and adaptability are two categories to describe organizational agility (Harraf et al., 2015). Crocitto and Youssef (2003) posit that participatory management is an aspect of organizational agility because it creates an opportunity for leaders to hear feedback from different levels and departments. Organizational agility is connected to organizational culture; as such, crisis leaders promote flexibility and adaptability while empowering employees to speak into decisions and situations (Crocitto & Youssef, 2003; Kidd, 1994).

Creativity is the final competency in the prevention and preparation stage (Wooten & James, 2008). With a crisis looming in the near future, leaders require an ability to think creatively about what can be done to avert or mitigate the crisis if it is not preventable (Mitroff, 2004; Wooten & James, 2008). Coman and Bonciu (2014) posit that leaders often are stuck with the mindset that it will not happen to them; yet, creativity removes this mindset as a viable option. Hence, creativity is included in the pre-crisis stage. Mitroff (2004) describes a crisis as an improbable event. Sensemaking is an ability to identify what is considered implausible (Weick, 1995). Therefore, Wooten and James (2008) posit that creativity helps shift a leader's thinking outside of the box to prevent the looming crisis or prepare in a way that mitigates damage. Furthermore, risk propensity is connected to this competency because creative thinking must occur without concern of failure or making a wrong decision (Coman & Bonciu, 2014; Weick, 1995).

There is currently one quantitative measurement that assesses a leader's ability to lead effectively during a crisis event. The C-LEAD (Crisis Leader Efficacy in Assessing and Deciding scale) focuses on a leader's ability to assess information and decision-making during an actual crisis (Noonan et al., 2011). C-LEAD is not connected to Wooten and James' (2008) conceptual model or the needed competencies suggested during the crisis event. The study is limited to leadership attributes during the crisis event and does not consider any aversion or resiliency competencies.

CRISIS IDENTIFICATION AND AVERSION SCALE

The crisis identification and aversion scale operationalizes Wooten and James' (2008) conceptual model for the first two stages: signal detection and prevention and preparation. The goal of the scale is to identify a leader's ability to identify and avert a crisis. The next section explains the methodology of the development of the scale, research on inclusive quartiles for each competency, and the full measurement.

Sample

The validation process had two stages and an additional study to identify inclusive quartiles. All three required different sample criterion. The Delphi panel required a group of experts to provide content validity. Using purposive sampling, 29 experts were identified from one of the following categories: educators in organizational leadership, educators in crisis leadership, emergency manager practitioners, or senior leaders who have dealt with a crisis. A total of 13 experts participated in the first iteration, and nine participated in the second iteration.

The second stage of the study required a large sample. The study used snowball sampling, and 205 participants were needed based on Pallant's (2010) recommendation of 5-10 respondents per item. There were 389 respondents; however, 111 respondents were eliminated due to a high number of responses missing. The analysis was based on the 278 remaining participants and used mean substitution for any missing items, with no more than two missing items per remaining participant. Mean substitution is an imputation approach for items with missing values. Since the items were reduced to no more than two items per participant, the imputation approach has little to no impact on the results of the study.

The third phase of the study required a large sample to assess for quartiles. The study used snowball sampling. There were 209 respondents with no more than four total missing items. Mean substitution was used for any missing items.

Measures

Wooten and James (2008) suggest five competencies in the pre-crisis stage. According to DeVellis (2012), the first step in scale development is to complete a literature review on each of the competencies. The second step is to identify an item pool supported by the literature. Brownlee-Turgeon (2016) identified validated scales for four out of the five competencies to begin the process of item development. Sense-making did not have a previously validated measure; therefore, 30 items emerged from the literature. Below is a list of the instruments and the number of items considered.

- Sensemaking, established from literature, 30 items
- Perspective Taking (Davis, 1983), seven items
- Issue Selling (Bishop et al., 2011), nine items
- Organizational Agility (Charbonnier-Voirin, 2011), 25 items
- Creativity (Gough, 1979), 30 items

Prior to sending to the Delphi panel, some items were eliminated due to duplication, and some were modified for language consistency. Modifications included rephrasing to reflect third person, using the present tense in lieu of present participle, and rewording from describing an organization to a leader. The Delphi panel reviewed two iterations of the item pool and ranked items on a 5-point Likert scale. Rating 1 indicated "Not at all important" to 5 "Very important." Items that scored 4 or higher and the scores with 80% or higher with scores of 4 or higher were retained.

The second stage of the study used a 7-point Likert scale. The anchors were "describes him/her very accurately" and "describes him/her very inaccurately. These items were used in the factor analysis.

Three additional scales were included in the development to assess for discriminant validity and predictive validity. Predictive validity supposes that a high score on one instrument would lead to a high score on another. Once factor analysis was conducted and final factors were determined, predictive validity used the correlation between the General Risk Propensity scale and the Leadership Effectiveness scale with the final factors. Discriminant validity assesses items loading on separate factors. Since the C-LEAD scale describes competencies needed during a crisis, it is supposed that the items will load separately from the pre-crisis factors.

- Discriminant Validity: C-LEAD (Noonan Hadley et al., 2011), nine items
- Predictive Validity: General Risk Propensity in Multifaceted Business Decisions (Hung & Tangpong, 2010), five items
- Predictive Validity: Leadership Effectiveness Scale (Ehrhart & Klein, 2001), six items

Table 1 identifies the remaining 41 items from the Delphi panel, the original item pool, and the 20 items for the additional validation.

Table 1. Delphi panel item pool reduced and validation scales

Measure	Items
Sensemaking	1. Willing to voice concern even when the concern seems unlikely 2. Able to identify something that does not fit with normal routines 3. Able to notice things that do not fit with the norm 4. Unable to see beyond normal patterns (R) 5. Able to see patterns well 6. Able to see when something does not fit a pattern more than most people 7. Shares concerns with supervisor even if the concerns do not make total sense 8. Able to see how events link together even when others do not 9. Spends time reflecting on events or behavior that does not seem to fit the norm to determine if there is a link 10. Able to provide meanings to events that others do not even notice 11. Assumes that things cannot go wrong (R) 12. Recognizes when something seems off 13. Does not dismiss things that do not seem normal but rather try to interpret it 14. Tells someone knows when something is not normal or routine 15. Spends time looking for discrepancies in a normal routine 16. Able to provide meaning to discrepancies in the normal routine 17. Looks for the unlikely to occur 18. Assumes that failure in the system is impossible (R) 19. Believes that the system will continue to function as it should (R) 20. Vocalizes concern 21. Follows appropriate channels of procedures when something seems off 22. Has no reason to believe that failure in the system will occur (R) 23. Reflects back on events as part of a normal routine 24. If nothing really bad occurs, does not spend time reflecting back on it (R) 25. Provides meanings for glitches in the system 26. Creates meanings for abnormal activity in order to understand it 27. Deciphers minute glitches in the system 28. Brings potential failures in the system to direct supervisor
Interpersonal Reactivity Index (Davis, 1980)	1. Sometimes finds it difficult to see things from the "other guy's" point of view (R) 2. Tries to look at everybody's side of a disagreement before making a decision 3. Sometimes tries to understand friends better by imagining how things look from their perspective 4. If he/she is sure he/she is right about something, doesn't waste much time listening to other people's arguments (R) 5. Believes there are two sides to every question and tries to look at them both 6. When upset at someone, I usually try to "put myself in his shoes" for a while 7. Before criticizing somebody, tries to imagine how he/she would feel if in their plac
Issue-selling Moves (Bishop et al., 2011)	Preparatory Moves 1. To what extent did he/she package the idea using a step-by-step process? 2. To what extent did he/she spend a great deal of time researching and investigating this idea before or during the selling process? 3. To what extent did he/she package this idea in terms of business plan logic? 4. To what extent did he/she continuously involve others outside of the organization in the selling of the idea? 5. To what extent did he/she identify and involve the best people during the beginning of the idea-selling process? 6. To what extent did he/she continuously involve others at the same level in the selling of this idea? Selling Moves 7. How much did he/she use multiple proposals for selling the idea? 8. To what extent did he/she believe he/she was fortunate to choose the correct time to start selling the idea? 9. To what extent did he/she continuously involve upper-level management in selling the idea?

continues on following page

Table 1. Continued

Measure	Items
Organizational Agility Scale (Charbonnier-Voirin, 2011)	Proactivity 1. Scans and examines the environment to anticipate and prevent risks 2. Creates and innovates continuously to keep ahead of competitors 3. Develops a culture of change among employees 4. Seizes new opportunities for development Reactivity 5. Able to make decisions quickly when circumstances change 6. Handles market information in real-time 7. Adapts very quickly to major market developments 8. Deploys resources easily to respond to opportunities and threats encountered 9. Able to identify and seize rapidly the best opportunities which come up in the environment Communication of the strategic vision 10. Clearly distributed strategy to all hierarchical levels 11. Communicates information about the organization and its action plans to all levels in terms easily understood by all 12. Informs employees about upcoming changes and their implementation Performance evaluation and recognition 13. Encourages employee participation in decision-making processes Skills development and knowledge sharing 14. Encourages employees to take initiatives to learn new things 15. Employees skills are developed with a view to the organization's future development 16. The firm organizes the management and sharing of knowledge and know-how among employees Creativity and continuous improvement 17. Encourages employees to suggest ideas and new solutions 18. Employees are called upon to act with a view to continuous improvement of products, processes, and/or working methods Delegation of responsibilities 19. Delegates the power of operational decision-making as low as possible Internal Cooperation 20. In order to reach objectives, works in teams 21. Implements solutions to facilitate internal cooperation 22. Encourages cooperation between people with different skills and profiles External cooperation 23. Functions on the basis of exchanges with external partners 24. Works with the employees of our external partners 25. Reinforces our partnerships
Creative Personality Scale (Gough, 1979)	Positive Items 1. Is capable 2. Is clever 3. Is confident 4. Is egotistical 5. Is humorous 6. Is individualistic 7. Is informal 8. Is insightful 9. Is intelligent 10. Has wide interests 11. Is inventive 12. Is original 13. Is reflective 14. Is resourceful 15. Is self-confident 16. Is unconventional Negative Items 17. Is affected 18. Is cautious 19. Is commonplace 20. Is conservative 21. Is conventional 22. Is dissatisfied 23. Is honest 24. Has narrow interests 25. Is mannerly 26. Is sincere 27. Is submissive 28. Is suspicious

continues on following page

Table 1. Continued

Measure	Items
Crisis Leader Efficacy in Assessing and Deciding (C-LEAD) Scale (Hadley et al., 2010)	1. Able to anticipate the political and interpersonal ramifications of my decisions and actions. 2. Able to summarize the key issues involved in a situation to others regardless of how much data I have. 3. Able to make decisions and recommendations even when I don't have as much information as I would like. 4. Able to assess how the members of the general public are being impacted by my unit's actions o inactions during times of adversity 5. Able to determine which information is critical to relay to other units in advance of them requesting it. 6. Able to keep others abreast of my work activities without over-informing or under-informing them. 7. Able to make decisions and recommendations even under extreme time pressure. 8. Able to estimate the potential deaths and injuries that may occur as a result of my decisions or recommendations at work. 9. Able to modify my regular work activities instantly to respond to an urgent need.
General Risk Propensity in Multifaceted Business Decisions (Hung & Tangpong, 2010)	1. Likes to take chances, although he/she may fail 2. Although a new thing has a high promise of reward, does not want to be the first one who tries it. Prefers to wait until it has been tested and proven before trying (R) 3. When a decision must be made for which the consequence is not clear, prefers to go with the safer option although it may yield limited rewards (R) 4. Likes to try new things, knowing well that some of them may end up to be disappointing 5. To earn greater rewards, willing to take higher risks.
Leadership Effectiveness, (Ehrhart & Klein, 2001)	1. To what extent did you work at a high level of performance under this leader? 2. To what extent did you enjoy working with this leader? 3. To what extent did you get along well with this leader? 4. To what extent did you admire this leader? 5. To what extent did you find this leader's style to be compatible with your leadership style? 6. To what extent did you find this leader to be an ideal leader?

Next, Brownlee-Turgeon conducted an additional research study with a new large sample to identify the inclusive quartiles. The study used snowball sampling and included a large sample with 209 participants. The survey included the remaining 35 items or three factors from the Crisis Identification and Aversion instrument. The survey used a 5-point Likert scale. The anchors were "Strongly Agree" and "Strongly Disagree." No surveys were eliminated as only four items had missing data. The mean substitution was the imputation approached used.

Analysis

In the second phase of the scale development, the sample size was reduced from 389 to 278 due to a large portion of the survey with incomplete responses. Mean substitution was used as the imputation approach for the 34 missing items from the 278 participants, with no more than two missing numbers per remaining participant.

Next, Kaiser-Meyer's (KMO) measure of sampling adequacy and Barlett's test of sphericity were examined to determine if factor analysis was the appropriate method of analysis. The study used principal component factor analysis. Because inter-item correlations were strong, Direct Oblimin was used for factor rotation and interpretation. The eigenvalue, the scree plot, and the communalities were evaluated, and factor analysis was used for further reduction of items and factor loadings. Cross-loaded items were removed with both iterations of factor analysis. After the second iteration, there were three distinct factors, and Cronbach's alpha was used to examine internal reliability.

Results

The Delphi panel included 13 in the first iteration and nine experts in the second iteration. The factor analysis and the quartile study, which required a large sample, included almost half of the respondents from the education industry and an almost even split between males and females. Respondents from both studies had 86% having been in the workplace for over ten years. The quartile study was more specific on work experience and showed that 67% of the respondents were in the workforce for over 20 years. The factor analysis had under ten years of experience ($n = 39$), and the quartile study had under ten years of experience ($n = 18$).

The panel reduced the items from 97 to 41 items by ranking how much each item described a crisis leader. The final rotation reduced the item pool to 35 items and supported three distinct factors. Table 2 identifies the final rotated pattern matrix.

Table 2. Final rotated patter matrix for the reduced set of 36 items

Items	Factor 1	Factor 2	Factor 3
Is sincere	**.959**	-.026	-.165
Encourages employees to suggest ideas and new solutions	**.899**	-.012	-.017
Is honest	**.834**	-.068	.015
Encourages cooperation between people with different skills and profiles	**.828**	.029	.034
Implements solutions to facilitate internal cooperation	**.826**	.121	-.049
Tries to look at everybody's side of a disagreement before making a decision	**.816**	-.195	.160
Encourages employee participation in the crisis identification process	**.780**	-.085	.148
Believes there are two sides to every question and tries to look at both sides	**.779**	-.160	.152
Encourages employees to act with a view to continuously improve products, processes, and/or working methods	**.775**	.179	-.041
Encourages employees to take initiative to learn new things	**.748**	.074	.046
Organizes the management and sharing of knowledge and know-how among employees	**.739**	.206	.029
Develops employees skills with a view to the organization's future development	**.738**	.185	.027
Informs employees about upcoming changes and their implementation	**.738**	.008	.142
Communicates information about the organization and its action plans to all levels in terms easily understood by all	**.647**	.169	.106
Clearly distributes strategy to all hierarchical levels	**.547**	.226	.165
Is insightful	**.510**	.235	.210
Is capable	**.413**	**.319**	.273
Is confident	-.020	**.757**	.075
Able to make decisions quickly when circumstances change	.206	**.693**	.083
Adapts very quickly to pending crisis developments	.236	**.545**	.268
Handles pending crisis information in real-time	.213	**.519**	.266
Deploys resources easily to respond to opportunities and threats encountered	.218	**.513**	.293
Able to identify and seize rapidly the best opportunities which come up in the environment	.325	**.485**	.222
Is inventive	**.383**	**.441**	.088
Is resourceful	.251	**.426**	.322
Does not dismiss things that do not seem normal but rather try to interpret them	.021	-.208	**.953**
Able to see how events link together when others do not	-.064	.193	**.807**
Able to see patterns well	-.038	.133	**.797**
Tells someone when something is not the normal routine	.066	-.074	**.781**
Spends time reflecting on events or behavior that does not fit the norm to determine if there is a link	.117	-.081	**.768**
Able to provide meaning to discrepancies in the normal routine	.099	.045	**.758**
Able to identify something that does not fit with normal routine	-.097	.182	**.728**
Recognizes when something seems off	.083	.124	**.715**
Brings potential failures in the system to direct supervisor	.111	.040	**.637**
Provides meaning for glitches in the system	.175	.152	**.559**
Scan and examines the environment to anticipate and prevent risks	.172	.312	**.450**

Note: Significant loadings are in bold.

Once the items were checked for cross-loading, there were 35 items and three distinct factors: participatory management, resourcefulness, and sensemaking. Table 3 shows the breakdown of each of these factors and the related items.

Table 3. Three-factor measure of crisis identification and aversion

Factors	Items
Participatory Management (17 items)	1. Tries to look at everybody's side of a disagreement before making a decision 2. Clearly distributed strategy to all hierarchical levels 3. Communicates information about the organization and its action plans to all levels in terms easily understood by all 4. Informs employees about upcoming changes and their implementation 5. Encourages employees to suggest ideas and new solutions 6. Encourages employee participation in crisis identification processes 7. Employees skills are developed with a view to the organization's future development 8. Organizes the management and sharing of knowledge and know-how among employees 9. Encourages employees to act with a view to continuous improvement of products, processes, and/or working methods 10. Implements solutions to facilitate internal cooperation 11. Encourages cooperation between people with different skills and profiles 12. Encourages employees to take initiative and learn new things 13. Believes there are two sides to every question and tries to look at both sides 14. Is capable 15. Is insightful 16. Is honest 17. Is sincere
Resourcefulness (7 items)	1. Able to make decisions quickly when circumstances change 2. Handles pending crisis information in real-time 3. Adapts very quickly to pending crisis developments 4. Deploys resources easily to respond to opportunities and threats encountered 5. Able to identify and seize rapidly the best opportunities which come up in the environment 6. Is confident 7. Is resourceful
Sensemaking (11 items)	1. Able to identify something that does not fit with normal routines 2. Able to see patterns well 3. Able to see how events link together even when others do not 4. Spends time reflecting on events or behavior that does not seem to fit the norm to determine if there is a link 5. Recognizes when something seems off 6. Does not dismiss things that do not seem normal but rather try to interpret it 7. Tells someone when something is not normal or routine 8. Able to provide meaning to discrepancies in the normal routine 9. Provides meanings for glitches in the system 10. Brings potential failures in the system to direct supervisor 11. Scans and examines the environment to anticipate and prevent risks

Scale Reliability and Validity

The scales for each dimension had high internal consistency: participatory management ($\alpha = .97$), resourcefulness ($\alpha = .950$), and sensemaking ($\alpha = .95$).

Construct validity was measured through the Delphi panel process. The Delphi panel consisted of experts in organizational leadership, crisis leadership, practitioners, and experienced senior leaders who have dealt with a crisis. The experts rated the items based on whether the items described the competencies. Only items with a rating of four or higher were kept.

There were two examples of predictive validity. The literature suggested that risk propensity correlates with crisis leadership abilities. Therefore, the risk propensity scale was used to examine predictive validity. Bivariate correlations support that all three scales are positively correlated to risk propensity. Pallant (2010) states that an *r*-value of .5 to 1.0 is a large correlation and that an *r*-value of .30 to .49 is a medium correlation. Using this scale, risk propensity has a medium correlation with participatory management ($r = .410$) and sensemaking ($r = .387$). Risk propensity has a large correlation with resourcefulness ($r = .852$).

Using Pallant's (2010) recommendation for correlation strength, leadership effectiveness was also used to determine predictive validity with the three scales. Leadership effectiveness had a strong correlation with participatory management ($r = .861$), resourcefulness ($r = .755$), and sensemaking ($r = .776$).

Discriminant validity was examined using the C-LEAD scale. Participatory management and sensemaking had minimal items cross-loaded and are therefore considered distinct from C-LEAD. Participatory management had four items cross-loaded; however, participatory management has a strong emphasis on the employee, and C-LEAD does not focus on the employee at all. Sensemaking had two items cross-loaded; however, the distinction between the two is that C-LEAD does not focus on warning signs pre-crisis whereas, sensemaking is focused on signal detection. Resourcefulness did not load separately from C-LEAD. Both scales focus on assessing and distributing information and resources. Because it did not load separately, resourcefulness is a competency that is needed in pre-crisis stages and during the actual crisis event.

Quartiles

The measurement allows a leader to know how they rank compared to other leaders. Table 4 identifies the inclusive quartiles for the three competencies and the complete measurement tool. Participatory management has seventeen items. With a 7-point Likert scale, this highest value possible was 119. Participatory management has a maximum value of 119 and a minimum value of 75. A leader with a score of 114 is classified within the top 75% of leaders in that category. Resourcefulness has seven items with a maximum value of 49 and a minimum value of 28. A leader with a score of 47 ranks in the top 75% of leaders. Sensemaking has 11 items with a maximum value of 77 and a minimum value of 42. A leader with a score of 72 ranks in the top 75% of leaders.

For the measurement tool with all three competencies, there were a total of 35 items. The maximum value was 245, and the minimum value was 157. Leaders with a score of 232 or higher were in the top 75% quartile.

There were some other nuances with the data as it was broken down by different demographics. Table 5 shows that males and females had the same maximum value of 245. However, the minimum values were quite different, with females scoring a 157 and males scoring a 178 value.

Furthermore, the quartiles were analyzed by the level of management the leader held. Table 6 shows that overall, senior managers report higher than all other levels within an organization. A senior manager has a minimum value of 187, whereas a first-line manager has a minimum value of 157. However, the maximum value aligns with all other levels of management. When analyzing the quartiles by management level and each competency individually, it is evident that the minimum value difference emerged from participatory management and sensemaking. The minimum value for resources was lowest for senior managers compared to all other management levels.

Table 4. Quartiles for crisis identification and aversion instrument and three factors

	Overall			
	Participatory Management	**Resourcefulness**	**Sensemaking**	**Total CIA**
Min Value	75	28	42	157
25%	104	41	65	212
50%	109	44	69	221
0.75	114	47	72	232
Max Value	119	49	77	245

Table 5. Quartiles by gender

	Total CIA	
	Female	**Male**
Min Value	157	178
25%	213.75	211
50%	222.5	220
75%	231	232.25
Max Value	245	245

The data were also reviewed from the years of experience for over 20 years ($n = 141$) and under four years ($n = 7$). Therefore, the data did not appropriately represent a strong representation for each category. Further research could be conducted to determine if years of experience impact a quartile value regardless of title.

SOLUTIONS AND RECOMMENDATIONS

The crisis identification and aversion instrument create an opportunity for practitioners, leadership development programs, and educators to assess an individual's current ability. In an organization with a leadership development program, assessing key leaders' abilities can help develop the training program. The quartile findings provide valuable information as well. It provides a means to understand the range for how leaders at different levels within the organization rate in each competency. If an organization finds that their middle management rank in the 25 percentile in any or all of the competencies, it would behoove the organization to train the middle management to enhance those competencies.

An interesting finding in the quartile data between first-line managers and senior managers is that first-line managers have the same maximum value as senior managers in resourcefulness and sensemaking and only one point difference in maximum value in participatory management. Additionally, first-line managers have a higher minimum value than senior managers in resourcefulness. This element requires additional research because it would typically be expected that a first-line manager has less experience using these competencies than senior management.

Table 6. Quartiles by level of management

Total CIA				
	First Line Manager	**Middle Manager**	**Upper Manager**	**Senior Manager**
Min Value	157	178	183	187
25%	207	209	211.5	217.5
50%	217	218.5	221	227
75%	230	230	228.5	235.75
Max Value	244	245	244	245
Total Participatory Management				
	First Line Manager	Middle Manager	Upper Manager	Senior Manager
Min Value	75	94	90	93
25%	99.75	102	105	107
50%	107.5	108	109	113
75%	113	112	112.5	115
Max Value	118	119	119	119
Total Resourcefulness				
	First Line Manager	Middle Manager	Upper Manager	Senior Manager
Min Value	31	34	35	28
25%	41	41	42	42
50%	42.5	43	44	46
75%	46.25	45.25	46.5	48
Max Value	49	49	49	49
Total Sensemaking				
	First Line Manager	Middle Manager	Upper Manager	Senior Manager
Min Value	42	48	53	59
25%	64.75	64.75	65	66.25
50%	66.5	69	69	70.5
75%	70.25	72	71.5	73.75
Max Value	77	77	76	77

Limitations

There were two limitations to the study that need to be considered upon review of the data. There was a limitation to the study in terms of directions about how to take the survey. Four respondents reached out to the author to ask for further clarification on three items. While the directions instructed the respondent to self-report and rate items based on their own leadership, there were three items that respondents seemed to want to evaluate the organizational leadership as opposed to themselves. It would behoove the author to review the directions and provide further clarification in any future deployment.

The sample on both studies, scale development and quartiles, was over 40% from the education industry. It would be beneficial to expand the sample outside of education by using a different sampling approach. Snowball sampling keeps a large portion of the sample skewed to the field of the researcher, which is education.

FUTURE RESEARCH DIRECTIONS

Turgeon (2019) conducted a Delphi panel study based on the competencies in the post-crisis stages identified in Wooten and James' (2008) conceptual model. The study provided content validity through a panel of experts in crisis leadership, educational professionals in leadership, or senior-level leaders within organizations. The item pool was established based on the literature for the following competencies: promoting resiliency, acting with integrity, and learning orientation. The Delphi panel identified connectivity as an additional competency needed in the post-crisis stage (Turgeon, 2019). Turgeon (2019) describes connectivity as a social exercise that cultivates, nurtures, and builds relational value with the goal of linking together objectives or patterns (Marcus et al., 2019).

This instrument presented in this chapter operationalizes the pre-crisis stages of Wooten and James' (2008) conceptual model. The next stage would be to operationalize the post-crisis stages of the conceptual model. Turgeon (2019) conducted the Delphi Panel, which is the first phase for operationalization. Distributing those results to a large sample and using factor analysis will provide new dimensions to operationalize a complete result of the conceptual model. Then, the crisis resilience and recovery tool could examine discriminant validity for the crisis identification and aversion instrument. After there is a complete operational instrument, it could be examined against other leadership theories such as transformational leadership or servant leadership. It is recommended to continue to examine quartiles after each deployment of the instrument.

CONCLUSION

Organizational crises are not going away. The past shows the negative impact on organizations when leaders do not lead through the crisis well. People's expectations of leaders are not changing, and people expect leaders to know how to lead through a crisis. The role of the leader is essential during a crisis; yet, there has not been a strong emphasis or empirical data about what it takes for leaders to lead well. The crisis identification and aversion instrument provides an opportunity to assess a leader's ability and build on those competencies through training. Leaders can be effective during times of crisis, and with the right skill set, they can avert, mitigate, and recover from a crisis to a point where an organization is stronger and more resilient because of their leadership.

REFERENCES

Bartik, A. W., Bertrand, M., Cullen, Z., Glaeser, E. L., Luca, M., & Stanton, C. (2020). The impact of COVID-19 on small business outcomes and expectations. *Proceedings of the National Academy of Sciences of the United States of America, 117*(30), 17656–17666. doi:10.1073/pnas.2006991117 PMID:32651281

Berkes, H. (2012). *Remembering Roger Boisjoly: He tried to stop shuttle Challenger launch*. NPR. https://www.npr.org/sections/thetwo-way/2012/02/06/146490064/remembering-roger-boisjoly-he-tried-to-stop-shuttle-challenger-launch%208/28/15

Bishop, K., Webber, S. S., & O'Neil, R. (2011). Preparation and prior experience in issue-selling success. *Journal of Managerial Issues, 23*(3), 323–340.

Blythe, B. T. (2014). *Blindsided: A manager's guide to crisis leadership* (2nd ed.). Rothstein Associates.

Bonvillian, B. (2013). Turnaround managers as crisis leaders. In A. Dubrin (Ed.), *Handbook of research on crisis leadership in organization* (pp. 92–109). Edward Elgar. doi:10.4337/9781781006405.00013

Brownlee-Turgeon, J. (2016). *Measuring leadership competencies to avert crisis: Development and validation of an instrument to operationalize a conceptual model* (UMI No. 10107445) [Doctoral dissertation, Regent University]. ProQuest Dissertations and Theses Global.

Coman, A., & Bonciu, C. (2014). Leadership and creativity. *Manager, 19*, 27–37.

Crocitto, M., & Youssef, M. (2003). The human side of organizational agility. *Industrial Management & Data Systems, 103*(5/6), 388–397. doi:10.1108/02635570310479963

Davis, M. H. (1983). Measuring individual differences in empathy: Evidence for a multidimensional approach. *Journal of Personality and Social Psychology, 44*(1), 113–126. doi:10.1037/0022-3514.44.1.113

DeVellis, R. F. (2012). *Scale development: Theory and application* (3rd ed.). Sage.

DuBrin, A. J. (2013). *Handbook of research on crisis leadership in organizations*. Edward Edgar Publishing. doi:10.4337/9781781006405

Dutton, J. E., Ashford, S. J., O'Neil, R. M., & Lawrence, K. A. (2001). Moves that matter: Issue selling and organizational change. *Academy of Management Journal, 44*(4), 716–736.

Ehrhart, M. G., & Klein, K. J. (2001). Predicting followers' preferences for charismatic leadership: The influence of follower values and personality. *The Leadership Quarterly, 12*(2), 153–179. doi:10.1016/S1048-9843(01)00074-1

Fink, S. (1986). *Crisis management: Planning for the inevitable*. AMACOM.

Gough, H. G. (1979). A creative personality scale for the adjective checklist. *Journal of Personality and Social Psychology, 37*(8), 1398–1405. doi:10.1037/0022-3514.37.8.1398

Harraf, A., Wanasika, I., Tate, K., & Talbott, K. (2015). Organizational agility. *Journal of Applied Business Research, 31*(2), 675–685. doi:10.19030/jabr.v31i2.9160

Hung, K., & Tangpong, C. (2010). General risk propensity in multifaceted business decisions: Scale development. *Journal of Managerial Issues, 22*(1), 88–106.

James, E. H., & Wooten, L. P. (2005). Leadership as (Un) usual: How to display competence in times of crisis. *Organizational Dynamics, 34*(2), 141–152. doi:10.1016/j.orgdyn.2005.03.005

James, E. H., & Wooten, L. P. (2010). *Leading under pressure: From surviving to thriving, before, during, and after a crisis.* Routledge.

Kaplan, R. S., & Mikes, A. (2012). *Managing risks: A new framework.* Harvard Business Review. https://hbr.org/2012/06/managing-risks-a-new-framework

Kidd, P. T. (1984). *A 21st century paradigm in agile manufacturing: Forging new frontiers.* Addison-Wesley.

Klann, G. (2003). *Crisis leadership: Using military lessons, organizational experiences, and the power of influence to lessen the impact of chaos on the people you lead.* Center for Creative Leadership.

Marcus, L. J., McNulty, E. J., Henderson, J. M., & Dorn, B. C. (2019). *You're it: Crisis, change, and how to lead when it matters most.* PublicAffairs.

Mitroff, I. I. (2004). *Crisis leadership: Planning for the unthinkable.* Wiley.

Mitroff, I. I. (2005). Crisis leadership: Seven strategies of strength. *Leadership Excellence, 22,* 11.

Nelson, S. J., & Reierson, J. L. (2013). New leader, new path: BP's redemption through a post-crisis shift in rhetorical strategies following the Deepwater Horizon oil rig explosion and spill. *Journal of the Communication. Speech & Theatre Association of North Dakota, 25,* 37–52.

Noonan Hadley, C., Pittinsky, T. L., Sommer, S. A., & Zhu, W. (2011). Measuring the efficacy of leaders to assess information and make decisions in a crisis: The C-LEAD scale. *The Leadership Quarterly, 22*(4), 633–648. doi:10.1016/j.leaqua.2011.05.005

Pallant, J. (2010). *SPSS survival manual: A step by step guide to data analysis using the SPS program* (4th ed.). McGraw-Hill.

Pearson, C. M., & Mitroff, I. I. (1993). From crisis prone to crisis prepared: A framework for crisis management. *The Academy of Management Executive, 7*(1), 48–59. doi:10.5465/ame.1993.9409142058

Turgeon, P. (2019). *Identifying the leadership skills needed to develop the competencies to lead in a postcrisis organization: A Delphi study* (Corpus ID: 212980785) [Doctoral dissertation, Brandman University]. ProQuest Dissertations and Theses Global.

Wang, J., & Hutchins, H. M. (2010). Crisis management in higher education: What have we learned from Virginia Tech? *Advances in Developing Human Resources, 12*(5), 552–572. doi:10.1177/1523422310394433

Weick, K. E. (1995). *Sensemaking in organizations.* Sage Publications.

Weick, K. E., Sutcliffe, K. M., & Obstfeld, D. (2005). Organizing and the process of sensemaking and organizing. *Organization Science, 16*(4), 409–421. doi:10.1287/orsc.1050.0133

Wooten, L. P., & James, E. H. (2008). Linking crisis management and leadership competencies: The role of human resource development. *Advances in Developing Human Resources, 10*(3), 352–379. doi:10.1177/1523422308316450

Chapter 16
Instrument to Measure the Impact of Hope in Strategic Plan Implementation

Sarah E. Walters
Evangel University, USA

ABSTRACT

This chapter addresses how Winston et al.'s "An Instrument to Measure the Impact of Hope in Strategic Plan Implementation" can be implemented within the workplace. Leaders should have a way to measure the impact of hope on strategic plans. Winston et al.'s instrument include three main theories: hope, expectancy, and value chain theories. This instrument is unlike any other tool to date in its conceptualization of employee hope in the organizational context. This chapter explains the validity, reliability, and practical application steps of Winston et al.'s instrument.

INTRODUCTION

Hope. There are songs, businesses, books, and movies about hope. Merriam Webster's (2021) dictionary closely relates hope to a wish. Hope is a word many people use and few indeed practice. What is hope? More importantly, what role does hope play in organizations? Do leaders use it to inspire followers to take action? Many have said they hope a particular event or thing will happen, but how many have thought about what they mean when they say they hope something will happen? Synonyms of hope include wish, dream, desire, expectation, ambition, craving, yearning; yet, none of these are action-oriented. None of these synonyms help the person move towards action to make their hope a reality. They imply the person will sit back and wait on the wish to come true. Charles Snyder was one of the first to truly begin to operationalize hope and provide an actionable definition to the word hope. Snyder defined hope as "goal-directed thinking" (Snyder & Lopez, 2007).

Thus, for the first time, establishing hope may have an action component. Since Snyder's definition of hope was first promoted in 2000, leaders of organizations have struggled to measure hope within their organizations (Winston et al., 2008), specifically related to strategic plan implementation. Hence

DOI: 10.4018/978-1-7998-7665-6.ch016

the development of "An Instrument to Measure the Impact of Hope in Strategic Plan Implementation." This was the first attempt to operationalize and measure the impact of hope during strategic plan implementation. Leaders in any organization should seek to understand the amount of hope an organization's employees have about the organization's strategic plan because of Snyder's concept of goal-directed thinking. Goal-directed thinking says if an individual believes they have the capabilities and resources to carry out the strategic plan, they are more likely to do so (Snyder, 2000). Snyder's hope theory says an individual must set a goal for themselves, then determine their path to achieve that goal, followed by the agency or positive thinking to carry it through (Snyder, 2000). This appears to work differently in organizations where leaders are setting the goals for employees. This removes employee autonomy to set goals and forces them to determine the path and agency to attain a plan given to them. This cognitive appraisal is what Winston et al. sought to measure. Winston et al. wanted to know to what extent employees' assessment of pathways and agency inform the amount of hope employees have in implementing a strategic plan.

Background

The word "hope" dates back as far as Biblical times in the early AD. The writer of the book of 1 Corinthians 13 states, "Three things will last forever faith, hope, and love- and the greatest of these is love" (1 Corinthians 13:13, NLT). Old English writers used "hope" to indicate expectation or anticipation (Merriam-Webster, 2021). Hope was also a name Puritan families used in the 16th and 17th centuries. Names in the 16th and 17th centuries often reflected how parents and families felt about the expectation of their baby (Ahlstrom, 2004). Over the centuries, the definition of "hope" has not changed in the dictionary but has undoubtedly changed in meaning. Snyder et al. (1991a) first began operationalizing a definition of hope that could be used in the clinical mental health field in the 1980s and 1990s. Snyder et al. (1991b) even suggested hope as the premise of positive thinking. If one hopes something will happen, their perspective shifts to a more positive outcome; thereby, focusing on the positive effect (Snyder et al., 1991b). Snyder's hope theory suggests, hope consists of two main components: agency and pathway. If someone is hopeful, they assess their ability to see the positive outcome happening to them (agency) and develop a path providing them the steps they need to take to see the hope come to fruition (pathway) (Snyder, 2000). However, Winston et al. suggested there is more to hope theory than agency and pathway. Winston et al. agreed hope includes agency and pathways but added components from value chain and expectancy theory. Porter (1998) first proposed value chain theory, which says that the number of actual or perceived available resources determines someone's self-efficacy. If someone has more human, physical, or monetary resources, they are more likely to believe they have the capabilities to accomplish a task. If someone lacks these resources, they are less likely to think they will complete the job. Expectancy theory is the link between the amount of effort one puts into a task and completing the job (Vroom, 1964). Vroom stated expectancy theory informs motivation which then influences valence, instrumentality, and force. Valence is one person's ability to influence the outcome of a task (van Eerde & Thierry, 1996). Instrumentality is the belief one has about the amount of input versus the reward that one receives after completing the task (Vroom, 1964). Force is the objective measure of engagement a person puts into the job (van Eerde & Thierry, 1996).

Thus, the complete list of components in Winston et al.'s "An Instrument to Measure the Impact of Hope on Strategic Plan Implementation" includes agency, pathway, valence instrumentality, force, and value chain. Winston et al.'s instrument designed to measure hope in strategic plan implementation had some action component. The action components include valence, force, instrumentality (expectancy), and value chain. The cognitive appraisal components of Winston et al.'s instrument include agency and pathway (hope). Winston et al. believed all of these components are necessary because of observations of leaders of organizations in different countries and each leader's organization's ability to implement a strategic plan successfully. Snyder (1991a), Porter, and Vroom examined components of hope, but none of them were combined until Winston et al.'s instrument. Winston et al. wanted to find a way for leaders in the organizational setting to measure hope to improve strategic plan implementation. Winston et al.'s observations became a topic of discussion amongst themselves and eventually the development of "An Instrument to Measure the Impact of Hope on Strategic Plan Implementation." Winston et al. knew leaders lead people, and Tangri (As cited by Winston et al., 2008) suggested strategic plans fail because organizations do not consider the human resource component in strategic plan implementation. Theoretically, all pieces of a plan work together well, but the unknown dependent variable is people. People are motivated or demotivated by their leaders (Winston et al., 2008).

MAIN FOCUS OF THE CHAPTER

The focus of this chapter is to present the usefulness of Winston et al.'s instrument in organizations to measure hope in strategic plan implementation. However, to understand its usefulness, it is necessary to understand the design of the instrument and previous research involving the use of this instrument.

Instrument Design

This instrument is a thirteen (13) item survey in which respondents are expected to rate prompts on a ten (10) point scale. Zero (0) is equal to None and Ten (10) is equal to Complete/Total. When this instrument was initially developed in 2008, the authors developed eighteen (18) prompts which represented each of these theories. Four prompts were related to expectancy theory, seven prompts were related to value chain theory, and seven prompts related to hope. See table 1 for a full break down of the categories and statements. For the initial development of "An Instrument to Measure the Impact of Hope on Strategic Plan Implementation" Winston et al. (2008) used Fry's (2003) definition of hope which is, "…a desire with expectation of fulfillment. Faith adds certainty to hope. It is a firm belief in something for which there is no proof" (p. 713).

The original eighteen (18) item survey was distributed to three different groups of participants. The first group included attendees of a symposium in South Africa. The survey was distributed in the preferred language of the individual taking the survey. The second group included faculty at a University in the United States. The third group included members of the US Coast Guard. All of these groups were considered convenience samples because of the relationships each author had with each group. Statistical analysis revealed equal variance within and between the means of each group. Thus, the authors were able to move forward with exploratory factor analysis. Each group's data was analyzed separately then collectively. Upon individual examination, several factors were removed due to low Eigenvalue scores. Cosby and Bates (2015) suggest Eigenvalue scores need to be at least 1 for a factor to be kept in a scale. Thus, any factor with an Eigenvalue below one even if it is responsible for a large percentage of variance must be removed. Once those component scores were removed from each group's data, Winston et al. combined the data into one group and retested the ANOVA. Winston et al. found five (5) statements needed to be removed to achieve optimal coefficient alpha scores which demonstrates correlation among the factors. This correlation is important because it is what tells researchers which items to keep (Cosby and Bates, 2015). The final survey is described in Table 2.

Table 1. Initial prompts categorized by theory in an instrument to measure the impact of hope on strategic plan implementation

Expectancy Theory	Value Chain Theory	Hope Theory
What level of hope did you have that the project or idea would be successful?	What level of faith did you have in the other people in the organization/family doing their share of the work?	While I worked on the project/ idea, I felt tired all of the time (reverse worded).
What level of hope did you have that when the project was completed, your efforts would be recognized?	What level of faith did you have in the organization/ family providing the necessary resources of time, money, and materials to complete the project/ idea?	While I worked on the project, I complained about the project/ idea to other people who worked on the project/ idea (reverse worded).
What level of satisfaction did you expect from completing the project/idea?	Other people in the organization/ family did not do what they said they would do.	While I worked on the project/ idea, I put every bit of my energy into the project-just as if it was my project/ idea alone.
What level of satisfaction did you actually get from completing the project?	The plan to complete the project/ idea was clearly presented to me.	While I worked on the project, other people complained to me about the project/ idea (reverse worded).
	What level of faith did you have in your leader to coordinate and lead you and/or your group to complete the project/ idea?	Would you want to work on the same project/ idea again?
	What level of faith did you have in the organization/ family's systems to provide the resources (the resources were available, but you could not get them)?	I want to work on other projects/ ideas with my leader.
	I believe that what my leader says will happen just as he/she says it will.	I have hope in the future of my organization/ family.

Previous Research

In 2021, Walters et al. conducted concurrent and discriminant validity testing along with a test-retest reliability analysis. Walters et al. chose to survey employees of higher education and examine the relationship between Winston et al.'s (2008) "An Instrument to Measure the Impact of Hope on Strategic Plan Implementation," Snyder et al.'s (1991a) "Hope Scale," and deJong et al.'s "Organizational Citizenship Behavior Scale-Adapted." Employees were solicited via e-mail through a convenience sampling of the primary researcher's relationships through their employer. Employees asked to voluntarily take a thirty-one (31) prompt survey and were solicited at the end of the thirty-one (31) prompt survey to provide their e-mail if they were willing to take only Winston et al.'s survey again two weeks later. One hundred and two (102) respondents participated in the initial thirty-one (31) response survey, and twenty-eight (28) respondents completed the follow-up survey of Winston et al.'s instrument. Walters, et al. initially tested the normality of the data to ensure there was an equal distribution on either side of the means. Testing normality involved testing the skewness and kurtosis of the data. Kim (2013) suggests acceptable kurtosis is < 7 and skewness is between -3 and 3. Both of these were within acceptable ranges.

Table 2. Final prompts categorized by theory in an instrument to measure the impact of hope on strategic plan implementation

Expectancy Theory	Value Chain Theory	Hope Theory
What level of hope did you have that the project or idea would be successful?	What level of faith did you have in the other people in the organization/family doing their share of the work?	Would you want to work on the same project/ idea again?
What level of hope did you have that when the project was completed, your efforts would be recognized?	What level of faith did you have in the organization/ family providing the necessary resources of time, money, and materials to complete the project/ idea?	I want to work on other projects/ ideas with my leader.
What level of satisfaction did you expect from completing the project/idea?	The plan to complete the project/ idea was clearly presented to me.	I have hope in the future of my organization/ family.
What level of satisfaction did you actually get from completing the project?	What level of faith did you have in your leader to coordinate and lead you and/or your group to complete the project/ idea?	
	What level of faith did you have in the organization/ family's systems to provide the resources (the resources were available, but you could not get them)?	
	I believe that what my leader says will happen just as he/she says it will.	

Note: α= 0.91

Walters et al. then examined the correlation between Winston et al.'s, Snyder et al.'s (1991a), and deJong et al.'s (2017) instruments. Winston et al.'s instrument had a statistically significant positive correlation with deJong et al.'s instrument and no correlation with Snyder et al.'s instrument. This is not what Walters et al. expected to find. Rather it was hypothesized Winston et al.'s instrument would demonstrate concurrent validity with Snyder et al.'s instrument and discriminant validity with deJong et al.'s instrument. Walters et al. also expected to find test-retest reliability of Winston et al.'s instrument which they did find. Table 3 shows the relationships. Table 4 shows test-retest reliability.

Table 3. Correlations 13 item scale

		M	SD	1	2	3
1	Winston et al. (2008)	7	1.88	1	.02	.39**
2	Snyder et al. (1991a)	2.9	0.23	.02	1	.06
3	deJong et al. (2017)	4	0.83	.39**	.06	1

Note. ** Correlation is significant at the 0.01 level (2-tailed), *M* = Mean, *SD* = Standard Deviation.

Table 4. Paired samples correlations 13 item scale

		N	Correlation	Sig.
Pair 1	PRE & POST	28	.53	.004

Note. N = Number.

Walters et al. (2021) then decided to test a reduced item scale. To do this, Walters et al. (2021) performed an exploratory factor analysis using the data from their research and 0.4 as the factor loading value to examine factor loading and if the scale could potentially be reduced to fewer prompts and still maintain correlation and test-retest reliability. Walters et al. (2021) found four factors cross-loaded and the top two factors accounted for 56% and 7%, respectively, of the variance for factors with eigenvalues at or higher than 1. The four cross-loaded factors were removed and each previously mentioned step was repeated. The removal of these four factors reduced the instrument to nine (9) items. Table 5 shows the exploratory factor analysis component loading in the original thirteen (13) item instrument.

Table 5. Component matrix 13 item instrument

	Component	
	1	2
Q4_1	.698	
Q4_2	.822	
Q4_3	.647	.439
Q4_4	.777	
Q4_5	.631	.423
Q4_6	.752	
Q4_7	.717	
Q4_8	.703	-.524
Q4_9	.721	-.440
Q4_10	.764	
Q4_11	.825	
Q4_12	.865	
Q4_13	.843	

Skewness and kurtosis were found to be within acceptable limits and correlation and test-retest analyses were performed. Walters et al. found while the correlation between Winston et al.'s and deJong et al.'s instrument remained, Winston et al.'s instrument was no longer reliable. Tables 6, 7, and 8 show the nine (9) item instrument component factor loading, correlation, and test-retest reliability scores.

Because coefficient alpha was above 0.9, Walters et al. (2021) chose to perform one final exploratory factor analysis reduction to examine if test-retest reliability returned with an even further reduced number of factors. Walters et al. removed the lowest four factors and performed one final correlation and test-retest analysis. Walters et al. found that the relationship between Winston et al.'s and deJong et al.'s instrument remained and the test-retest reliability was still absent. Tables 9 and 10 show these results.

Thus, it can be concluded, organizations should continue to use the full thirteen (13) item instrument when attempting to measure the impact of hope on strategic plan implementation.

Table 6. Component matrix- 9 item instrument

	Component
	1
Q4_1	.693
Q4_2	.837
Q4_4	.780
Q4_6	.769
Q4_7	.692
Q4_10	.757
Q4_11	.845
Q4_12	.881
Q4_13	.869

Table 7. Correlations 9 item instrument

		M	SD	α	1	2	3
1	Winston et al. (2008)	7.1	1.91	.92	1	.02	.36**
2	Snyder et al. (1991a)	2.9	0.23		.02	1	.07
3	deJong et al. (2017)	4	0.83		.36**	.07	1
Note. ** Correlation is significant at the 0.01 level (2-tailed), *M* = Mean, *N* = Number, *SD* = Standard Deviation, α = coefficient alpha.							

Table 8. Paired samples correlations 9 item instrument

		N	Correlation	Sig.
Pair 1	PRE & POST	28	.26	.188
Note. N = Number.				

Table 9. Correlations 5 item instrument

		M	SD	α	1	2	3
1	Winston et al. (2008)	7	2.17	.91	1	-.03	.34**
2	Snyder et al. (1991a)	2.9	0.23		-.03	1	.07
3	deJong et al. (2017)	4	0.83		.34**	.07	1
Note. ** Correlation is significant at the 0.01 level (2-tailed), *M* = Mean, *SD* = Standard Deviation, α = coefficient alpha.							

Table10. Paired samples correlations- 5 item scale

		N	Correlation	Sig.
Pair 1	PRE & POST	28	.26	.18
Note. N = Number.				

While the intent of Walters et al. (2021) research was to examine the validity and reliability of Winston et al.'s (2008) instrument, many notable findings emerged. First, one organization's total score was 7.0 on a 10-point scale. This was seemingly high until leaders began to examine the raw data and provide average scores for each question. Leaders found four of the questions/prompts received a score below 7. Table 11 shows the four questions the employees scored lowest. Leaders wanted to examine scores below the average of the survey. Examples of ways organizations begin to dig deeper into these concerns include focus groups and discussions with middle management.

Table 11. Example organization's low scores

Expectancy Theory	Value Chain Theory	Hope Theory
What level of hope did you have that when the project was completed, your efforts would be recognized?	What level of faith did you have in the organization/ family providing the necessary resources of time, money, and materials to complete the project/ idea?	Would you want to work on the same project/ idea again?
	What level of faith did you have in the organization/ family's systems to provide the resources (the resources were available, but you could not get them)?	

Based on the results, leaders noted in their organization, employee hope was lacking as it related to resources. Employees may have had a scarcity mindset or lacked knowledge about where their resources would come from. Leadership understood hope is developed through experience, thus leaders acknowledged the organization's previous budget restrictions and spending patterns, or lack of available funding was causing employees to lose hope in the organization's strategic plan implementation.

This organization's employees struggled to receive the recognition given to them by the organization for their hard work towards the strategic plan. The organization currently has many recognition processes in place, but these were not implemented until the last 3 -4 years, thus employees because of their experiences in the past, were skeptical of these newer recognition processes. This organization is actively working to celebrate employee wins and encourage all employees to do the same.

The last question in the hope theory category has proven to be the most difficult to nail down because it is hard to pinpoint exact reasons why employees may not want to work on the same project/idea again. There are many factors that have emerged that could influence this. Some that came to light for this organization were the lack of resources making the project extra difficult to complete, lack of leadership skills from the leader, and the general, expected fatigue brought on by larger projects.

This organization chose to examine their strategic plan and adjust it accordingly to meet the needs of its employees in the areas of lower scores. The organization is hopeful with the necessary changes to the strategic plan based on feedback from this instrument that the organization will see increased employee hope in strategic plan implementation.

RECOMMENDATIONS

In discussing strategic planning with colleagues and at professional conferences, it has become apparent strategic plan implementation is rarely successful. If it is successful, leaders often do not know why it was successful. Thus, measuring employee hope is an essential step to gauging the successful implementation of the organization's strategic plan. I recommend leaders use this instrument in one of two ways.

The way depends on the organization's situation. If an organization has a strategic plan, it can be immediately implemented. I recommend the entire 13 question instrument be distributed to gauge the impact of hope in strategic plan implementation at the current point in time, then be repeated a minimum of 3-6 months later. For strategic plans to have an impact, an organization must allow time, thus re-surveying an organization too soon may provide inaccurate results. Strategic plans are often difficult to understand and genuinely begin to act upon, which may be why some organizations with strategic plans may not be seeing the results they hoped for or expected. This instrument could inform leadership in an organization of a deeper issue, as it did with the example organization. For example, if the employees within the organization rate hope low, further discussion is needed to understand why fully. This then allows the opportunity for leadership to ask why the strategic plan is the way it is. It also allows leadership to determine if the roadblock is a planning, training, or operational error. In those discussions, more is brought to light about why the roadblock exists. When the roadblock is determined leaders can address the breakdown.

The second way this instrument could be used is in an organization that does not currently have a strategic plan. Because of the wording of the tool, I generally do not suggest administering the instrument before a strategic plan has been communicated and its implementation begun. However, suppose an organization has existed for a period, and its employees know each other well. It could provide feedback to the leaders about the level of hope the employees have in the organization's strategic plan initiative and the ones leading the plan. Questions such as "What level of faith did you have in your leader to coordinate and lead you and/or your group to complete the project/ idea?" or "Would you want to work on the same project/ idea again?" would be hard to answer if the employees did not work together in the past. Thus, the instrument should only be used with employees who work within the organization, spent enough time in the organization to have a working knowledge of its operations, and completed work tasks while employed at the organization. A failure to ensure employees are qualified to take the instrument may cause confusion, frustration and generally be a waste of time for leadership. It will not produce the desired results. Leaders of organizations who meet these criteria could administer the instrument immediately then repeat the administration 3-6 months later to examine pre- and post-testing of the organization. This may help leadership understand how their organization is growing and if their vision casting/ strategic plan efforts impact their employees.

No matter which category an organization finds itself in and how the instrument is used, this instrument affords leaders with the knowledge they need to be able to examine the impact hope has in their organization's ability to implement a strategic plan. It also allows organizations to begin to give their employees a voice. Many colleagues have expressed concerns about their ability to support their employees in the strategic plan implementation process because they do not feel that the employees are vested in the plan. Measuring the impact of hope on an employee's ability to implement a strategic plan helps place some control back in the employee's hands. Since strategic planning rarely includes all employees, there is an element of control missing for employees. Using this instrument to measure hope allows employees to see their opinion matters about the implementation process.

This instrument also provides employees the opportunity to reflect on their work. Employees can make a cognitive appraisal of their work and physical resources. This appraisal is precisely what Snyder (2000) referred to in their work on agency and pathways. This instrument may bring awareness to the employee that they have everything they need, including cognitive, self-efficacy, and physical resources, to carry out its strategic plan.

FUTURE RESEARCH DIRECTIONS

Interestingly, when Winston et al. (2008) first developed this instrument, the original definition of hope proposed by Fry (2003) included a faith component. However, in Winston et al.'s (2008) research, faith was not a variable correlated with hoping; hence, its removal from the scale. I propose there is still an element of faith in hope. Snyder (2000) proposed hope stems from intrinsic motivation. Faith is defined as the "complete confidence in something or someone" (Merriam-Webster, 2021). If someone is intrinsically motivated to do something, they must believe it is possible to do it. Motivation implies the action orientation of the individual. They intend to act on their beliefs. Thus, if someone is wholly convinced or confident about something or someone, they will work. This means faith is action oriented. Since researchers can now say hope, as operationally defined by Winston et al., is action-oriented, there is potentially a relationship that needs to be re-examined. Perhaps research may include other instruments which measure faith to determine the level of concurrent or discriminant validity.

Future research may also include testing concurrent and discriminant validity with other instruments that measure Porter's (1998) value chain and Vroom's (1964) expectancy theories. Since these two theories combined with Fry's (2003) hope theory-informed Winston et al.'s instrument, it would be beneficial to know the relationship Winston et al.'s instrument has with other tools measuring the same theories. A positive relationship between these instruments would further strengthen the argument Winston et al.'s instrument does, in fact, help measure action-oriented definitions of hope.

CONCLUSION

Winston et al.'s (2008) instrument is the first of its kind. It is a valid and reliable tool leaders can use to measure employee hope in strategic plan implementation. However, the survey must be administered as a full 13 item survey to maintain it's validity and reliability. While others such as Snyder have examined personal hope, I have not found a researcher who measured the impact of employee hope on a strategic plan's implementation. Only assessing an employee's personal hope does not provide a leader with the complete picture they need to make decisions during the strategic plan implementation process. As seen in the example organization, employee hope impacted how decisions were being made at the lowest and middle levels which were ultimately causing leadership to question why key performance indicators and goals were not being met. Without an objective metric to measure employee hope, leaders cannot capture what is happening in their organizations as the plan is being implemented and potentially causing major change within the organization. If leaders fail to measure hope, they will not accurately guide the change, and the implementation may ultimately fail. Successful leaders consider the needs of their employees and seek to give those needs a voice. The example organization did not complicate the employee hope assessment process, rather kept it simple and continued strategic plan implementation while taking time to ask why certain scores were lower than the total average. This employee voice can improve trust between leaders and followers. Improved trust may lead to improved organizational outcomes.

REFERENCES

Ahlstrom, S. E. (2004). *A Religious History of the American People* (2nd ed.). Yale University Press.

Cosby, P., & Bates, S. (2015). *Methods in behavioral research*. McGraw Hill.

de Jong, J., Rigotti, T., & Mulder, J. (2017b, February 23). One after the other: Effects of sequence patterns of breached and overfulfilled obligations. *European Journal of Work and Organizational Psychology*, *26*(3), 337–355. doi:10.1080/1359432X.2017.1287074

Fry, L. W. (2003). Toward a theory of spiritual leadership. *The Leadership Quarterly*, *14*(6), 693–727. doi:10.1016/j.leaqua.2003.09.001

Kim, H. Y. (2013). Statistical notes for clinical researchers: Assessing normal distribution (2) using skewness and kurtosis. *Restorative Dentistry & Endodontics*, *52-54*(1), 52. Advance online publication. doi:10.5395/rde.2013.38.1.52 PMID:23495371

Merriam Webster. (2021, April). https://www.merriam-webster.com/

Porter, M. (1998). *Competitive advantage*. The Free Press. doi:10.1007/978-1-349-14865-3

Snyder, C. R. (2000). Genesis: The birth and growth of hope. In C. R. Snyder (Ed.), *Handbook of hope, theories, measure and applications* (pp. 25–36). Academic Press.

Snyder, C. R., Harris, C., Anderson, J. R., Holleran, S. A., Irving, L. M., Sigmon, S. T., Yoshinobu, L., Gibb, J., Langelle, C., & Harney, P. (1991a). The will and the ways: Development and validation of an individual-differences measure of hope. *Journal of Personality and Social Psychology*, *60*(4), 570–585. doi:10.1037/0022-3514.60.4.570 PMID:2037968

Snyder, C. R., Irving, L., & Anderson, J. (1991b). Hope and health. In C. R. Snyder & D. Forsyth (Eds.), *Handbook of social and clinical psychology: The health perspective* (pp. 285–305). Pergamon.

Snyder, C. R., & Lopez, S. J. (2007). *Positive psychology: The scientific and practical explorations of human strengths*. Sage Publications.

van Eerde, W., & Thierry, H. (1996). Vroom's expectancy models and work-related criteria: A meta-analysis. *The Journal of Applied Psychology*, *81*(5), 575–586. doi:10.1037/0021-9010.81.5.575

Vroom, V. H. (1964). *Work and motivation*. Wiley.

Walters, S., Winston, B., Dean, D., & Winner, W. (2021). *Gauging the Validation of An Instrument To Measure the Impact of Hope in Strategic Plan Implementation* [Unpublished doctoral dissertation]. Regent University, Virginia Beach, VA, United States.

Winston, B.E., Cerf, K., Eames, D., Helland, M., & Garnes, D. (2008). An instrument to measure the impact of hope in strategic plan implementation. *International Leadership Journal*, 39-56.

ADDITIONAL READING

de Jong, J., Rigotti, T., & Mulder, J. (2017b, February 23). One after the other: Effects of sequence patterns of breached and overfulfilled obligations. *European Journal of Work and Organizational Psychology*, *26*(3), 337–355. doi:10.1080/1359432X.2017.1287074

Degn, L. (2015). Sensemaking, sensegiving and strategic management in danish higher education. *Higher Education*, *69*(6), 901–913. doi:10.100710734-014-9812-3

Mitchell, T. R. (1974). Expectancy models of job satisfaction, occupational preference and effort: A theoretical, methodological, and empirical appraisal. *Psychological Bulletin*, *81*(12), 1053–1077. doi:10.1037/h0037495

Snyder, C. R., Cheavens, J., & Sympson, S. C. (1997). Hope: An individual motive for social commerce. *Group Dynamics*, *1*(2), 107–118. doi:10.1037/1089-2699.1.2.107

Snyder, C. R., Harris, C., Anderson, J. R., Holleran, S. A., Irving, L. M., Sigmon, S. T., Yoshinobu, L., Gibb, J., Langelle, C., & Harney, P. (1991b). The will and the ways: Development and validation of an individual-differences measure of hope. *Journal of Personality and Social Psychology*, *60*(4), 570–585. doi:10.1037/0022-3514.60.4.570 PMID:2037968

Snyder, C. R., Irving, L., & Anderson, J. (1991c). Hope and health. In C. R. Snyder & D. Forsyth (Eds.), *Handbook of social and clinical psychology: The health perspective* (pp. 285–305). Pergamon.

Temple, P. (2018). Academic strategy: The management revolution in american higher education, by george keller (1983) can strategy work in higher education? *Higher Education Quarterly*, *72*(2), 170–177. doi:10.1111/hequ.12160

KEY TERMS AND DEFINITIONS

Expectancy Theory: Individuals who expect a specific outcome are more likely to achieve the result they expect.

Force: The effort an individual puts into bringing the expected outcome to fruition.

Hope: A cognitive appraisal of the combined physical and emotional resources an individual has available to expect a specific outcome.

Instrumentality: The amount of expectation an individual has about their ability to accomplish a task and the reward of performing said task.

Strategic Plan: The organized process employees of an organization follow to carry out collective actions to accomplish an organization's goals.

Valence: An individual's cognitive appraisal of their ability to accomplish an outcome.

Value Chain: Resources available to an individual inform their belief in their ability to accomplish the goal.

Chapter 17
Modified General Employee Well–Being Scale

Bruce E. Winston
Regent University, USA

ABSTRACT

Taylor et al. evaluated Dupuy's general employee well-being measurement instrument and pointed out two concerns: a combination of positive and negative item wording and two different measurement response methods. Taylor et al. collected new data, ran a principal component analysis, and found three of Dupuy's five reported scales. In this study, the author reworded Taylor et al.'s final 18 items so that all items were worded positively, used a common measurement response, and removed double-barreled wording, which Taylor et al. did not note. The author of this current chapter conducted two studies. The first study's analysis of the new data produced a single eight-item scale with Cronbach alpha of .96 that explained 77% of the variance. The second study used confirmatory factor analysis that showed a four-item scale with GFI = 0.98, AGFI = 0.89, RMSEA = 0.13, and Chi-square = 9.96, df = 9, p < 0.000. The four-item scale had a Cronbach alpha of 0.86.

INTRODUCTION

The purpose of this chapter is to follow up on Taylor et al.'s (2003) evaluation of Dupuy's (1978) General Employee Well-being (GWB). Taylor et al. noted two serious concerns about Dupuy's instrument: (a) the use of both positive and negative wording of the items and two different response methods. DeVellis (2017) also cautioned about avoiding negative wording. Taylor et al., though, did not report that the 18 items from the Dupuy's (1978) study used multiple concepts in several items, such as "Have you been in firm control of your behavior, thoughts, emotions, or feelings?" (Taylor, 2003, p. 34). DeVellis cautioned against using "double-barreled" (p. 116) items when creating scale development items. The current chapter author conducted two studies, one used an Exploratory Factor Analysis and the second study used both an Exploratory Factor Analysis and a Confirmatory Factor Analysis. The author reports the results of each study's analysis and a recommendation for a four-item scale to measure employees' self-perception of well-being.

DOI: 10.4018/978-1-7998-7665-6.ch017

EMPLOYEE WELL-BEING

Ryan and Deci (2001) posited that employee well-being emerged from two research streams: hedonic studies that examined well-being related to pleasure and the absence of pain; and eudaimonic studies that explored happiness as self-realization. Ryan and Deci considered employee well-being as a multi-dimensional concept including both hedonic and eudaimonic properties. According to Fisher (2003), higher levels of employees' perceptions of well-being positively correlate with employees' productivity. Grant et al. (2007), Baptiste (2008), and Zheng et al. (2015) concurred with Fisher and purported that employee well-being is important to organizations' performance as well as survival because of the positive relationship between employees' perception of well-being and employees' performance. Grant et al. defined employees' well-being as "the overall quality of an employee's experience and functioning at work" (p. 52). Page and Vella-Brodrick (2009) reported that employee well-being (EWB) consisted of "high-levels of positive impact, low levels of negative impact, and cognitive evaluation of one's satisfaction with their life as a whole" (p. 443) and that someone with positive well-being is said to be in a state of "positive psychological functioning" (p. 443). Poulsen and Ipsen (2017) added to the discussion of well-being by pointing out that managers' attitudes and behaviors contribute to perceived well-being by both on-site and distance-based employees.

Zheng et al. (2015) emphasized the importance of employee well-being in that the concept has interested scholars since the earliest of times, thus tying the concept to human flourishing, which is, according to Kleinig and Evans (2013), similar to Aristotle's concept of eudaimonia that includes both process and achievement and has, as it end goal, to achieve a high quality of life and well-being for themselves and others (p. 540-541). Hendrix et al. (1994) concluded that low levels of employee well-being contributed to absenteeism, which Hendrix et al. inferred to be an avoidance tactic by employees who were seeking to improve their short-term well-being.

TESTING DUPUY'S GENERAL WELL-BEING SCALE

Taylor et al. (2003) conducted a factor analysis study of "599 African–American women from four geographic regions of the United States" (p. 32) using Dupuy's (1978) instrument. Taylor et al.'s study focused on participants' two conditions that might contribute to the participants' perception of well-being: (a) all participants were overweight with (b) low to moderate physical activity. Taylor et al. used Dubuy's original items but did not find the six dimensions reported by Dupuy (1978). Taylor et al. found three highly correlated factors indicating a possibility that fewer factors might be useful. Taylor et al. also posited that using both positive and negative wording may have led to the creation of three factors in their study. Taylor et al. conducted another factor analysis using four of the highest correlated items of Dupuy's instrument with the 18-item total score. They found that the four items explained 85% of the variance.

Chitra and Karunanidhi (2013) used Dupuy's scale and reported a Cronbach's alpha of 0.94 and significant negative correlation with occupational stress, a positive correlation with resilience, and a positive correlation with job satisfaction. Salles et al. (2014) researched the relationship of employee well-being, using Dupuy's scale, with grit and burnout in medical residents. Salles et al. found a significant correlation between employee well-being and along with a significant correlation between employee well-being and the emotional exhaustion sub-scale of Maslach's Burnout Inventory.

Pedersen et al. (2002) used seven items from Dupuy's scale in for Pedersen et al.'s new instrument to create the General Life Functioning scale. The studies reported above support the notion that Dupuy's scale had content and convergent validity.

MODIFICATION OF THE GENERAL WELL-BEING INSTRUMENT

Although the focus of Taylor et al.'s (2003) study did not seem to lend itself to a study of employee well-being, the author found Dupuy's (1978) items to apply to employees, as supported in the prior section showing research by Chitra and Karunanidhi (2013) and Salles et al. (2014). This finding led the author to conduct a study with Taylor's eighteen items modified to positive wording, with a single focus, and only one response method – a semantic differential scale. DeVellis, (2017) suggested that the first steps in scale development are to determine what is to be measured using the theoretical literature, generate an item pool, and then to create an appropriate response method. Dupuy's items aligned with the theoretical literature but did not align with Taylor et al.'s or DeVellis' comments about the use of positive wording and the avoidance of double-barreled items

The 18 items from Dupuy's (1978) study relate to Page and Vella-Brodrick (2009) definition of positive well-being producing satisfaction "with their life as a whole" (p. 443) and in a state of "positive psychological functioning (p 443). The alignment of items with the literature conforms to DeVellis' (2017) first step in scale development. The modification of the items to be positively worded, single-barreled, and using a common response method conforms to DeVellis' second and third steps. Table 1 contains the modified items and response-method.

First Study to Use the Modified General Employee Well-Being Scale

According to DeVellis (2017), factor analysis is used to determine if there are one or more latent variables consisting of one or more scale items presented in the data collected from the participants. A secondary purpose of factor analysis is to determine the level of importance of each scale item to the latent factor. A rotation of the data might be required to accommodate for correlation or non-correlation of the items' scores. Brown (2009) suggested that for a data set with moderate to high levels of correlation an oblique rotation such as direct-oblimin or promax would help to better understand the latent variables. Brown suggested using an orthogonal rotation such as varimax, quartimax, or equimax if the data set is not correlated.

Winston (2020) conducted a study of 170 participants that included 113 females and 55 males (two participants did not provide their gender) with the following age breakdown: (a) 46 were 18-29 years old; 50 were 30-39 years old; 34 were 40-49 years old; 24 were 50-59 years old; 12 were 60-69 years old; 3 were 70+ years old, and one person did not report his/her age. Winston's study resulted in a non-published working paper currently included in Preprints 2020.

Because the data was moderately correlated, Winston (2020) used the direct-oblimin rotation suggested by Brown (2009). An initial principal component analysis using IBM's SPSS Version 27 resulted in a Kaiser-Meyer-Olkin Measure of Sampling Adequacy (KMO) of .951 and Bartlett's Test of Sphericity approximate X^2 of 2643.581 with $df = 153$ that was significant at p=.000, implying that the data might benefit from factor analysis. KMO analysis, according to Charalambous et al. (2016), is a comparison of partial correlations to the original correlations. KMO scores greater than .80 indicate that factor analysis may help understand the data. Bartlett's test of sphericity evaluates the likelihood of multiple variables (Tekin & Polat, 2016).

Table 1. Items from the original GWB and modified general employee well-being instrument

General Well-being Instrument	Modified General Employee Well-being Instrument
1. How have you been feeling in general? [a][c]	In general, I felt great for the past two months.
2. Have you been bothered by nervousness or your 'nerves'? [a]	I have felt calm rather than nervous for the past two months.
3. Have you been in firm control of your behavior, thoughts, emotions, or feelings? [a][c]	I have been in firm control of my emotions for the past two months.
4. Have you felt so sad, discouraged, hopeless, or had so many problems that you wondered if anything is worthwhile? [a]	I generally felt that my life was worthwhile for the past two months.
5. Have you been under or felt you were under any strain, stress, or pressure? [a]	I felt no strain during the past two months.
6. How happy, satisfied, or pleased have you been with your personal life? [a][c]	I felt pleased with my personal life for the past two months.
7. Have you had any reason to wonder if you were losing your mind, or losing control over the way you act, talk, think, feel, or of your memory? [a][c]	I felt confident in the quality of my memory for the past two months.
8. Have you been anxious, worried, or upset? [a]	I felt calm, rather than anxious, during the past two months.
9. Have you been waking up fresh and rested? [a][c]	I woke up feeling fresh and rested for the past two months.
10. Have you been bothered by any illness, bodily disorder, pains, or fears about your health? [a]	I have felt physically healthy during the past two months.
11. Has your daily life been full of things that were interesting to you? [a][c]	My daily life has been full of things that were interesting to me for the past two months.
12. Have you felt downhearted and blue? [a]	I felt up-beat for the past two months.
13. Have you been feeling emotionally stable and sure of yourself? [a]	I felt emotionally stable for the past two months.
14. Have you felt tired, worn out, used-up, or exhausted? [a]	I felt energized for the past two months.
15. How concerned or worried about your health have you been? [b][c]	I felt good about my health for the past two months.
16. How relaxed or tense have you been? [b][c]	I felt relaxed for the past two months.
17. How much energy, pep, or vitality have you felt? [b]	I felt energetic for the past two months.
18. How depressed or cheerful have you been? [b]	I felt cheerful for the past two months.

Notes: a = six-point rating scale; b = 11-point rating scale; c = reversed scored

Note: response scale for the Modified General Well-being instrument:

Never 1 2 3 4 5 6 7 8 9 10 Always.

All 18 items loaded on two factors with eigenvalues greater than one, but factor two consisted of only one item that cross-loaded on a factor one item. Cross-loading occurs when an item loads on two or more factors. Reinius et al. (2017) suggested removing cross-loaded items. After removing the cross-loading item, a new principal component analysis showed KMO of .951 and Bartlett's Test f Sphericity $X^2 = 2852.810$, implying that the data might benefit from factor analysis. The principal component analysis showed all 17 items loading on one factor with an eigenvalue of 10.886 that explained 64% of the data and had a Cronbach's alpha of 0.96. Cho and Kim (2015) explain that Cronbach's Alpha is a measure of a scale's internal consistency, sometimes referred to as item relatedness. According to DeVellis (2017), when Cronbach's alpha is above 0.90, the scale would benefit from optimization, which implies selecting the highest factor-loading items and running another principal component analysis.

Of the 17 items in the factor, eight had factor loads higher than 0.80, so Winston (2020) included just those eight items in an additional principal component analysis. The final principal component analysis of the eight highest-loading items showed KMO of .937 and Bartlett's Test of Sphericity $X^2 = 1359.921$ (p=.000) with a Cronbach's alpha of .956 that explained 76.6% of the variance. Factor loadings ranged from .706 to .808. DeVellis (2017) also suggested removing items as far down as one remaining item but also cautioned that too few items weaken the content validity of the scale; thus, Winston chose to keep the eight items listed below:

1. I felt calm, rather than anxious, during the past two months.
2. I have felt physically healthy during the past two months.
3. I felt emotionally stable for the past two months.
4. I felt energized for the past two months.
5. I felt good about my health for the past two months.
6. I felt relaxed for the past two months.
7. I felt energetic for the past two months.
8. I felt cheerful for the past two months.

Convergent Validity

Convergent validity is the notion that a scale measures what it is supposed to measure (Krabbe, 2017). Convergent validity can be measured by a correlation with one, or more, other scales that measure something related to the targeted scale. Regarding similar scales, servant leadership has been linked to employees' well-being (Greenleaf. 1977), who said described a that of servant leadership:

Do those served grow as persons? Do they, while being served, become healthier, wiser, freer, more autonomous, more likely themselves to become servants? And, what is the effect on the least privileged in society? Will they benefit or at least not be further deprived? (Kindle Locations 351-352).

Meyers et al. (2019) defined perceived organizational support as "the extent to which employees feel actively supported by their organization to employ their unique strengths at work" (p. 1826). Since both servant leadership and perceived organizational support relate to employee well-being, Winston (2020) tested for convergent validity by correlating the Modified General Employee *Well-being (MGEW) scale with Winston and Fields' (2015) essential servant leadership behavior (ESLB) scale, and Eisenberger et al.'s (1986) perceived organizational support (POS) scale. Table 2 shows the moderate correlations between MGEW, ESLB, and POS, thus showing the MGEW scale has convergent validity.*

The Second Study to Use the Modified General Employee Well-Being Scale

The author conducted a follow-up study that included 213 participants (112 men and 101 females). All participants were above the age of 18 and had one or more of the following in the home: roommate, (b) spouse, (c) parent, (d) grandparent, and (e) child. Participants provided their perception of the ten-item

ESLB scale (Winston & Fields, 2015), ESLB, the eight-item MGEW scale, the eight-item POS scale, and, Netemeyer et al's five-item work-family conflict scale (WFC). The second study looked at the relationship of ESLB, POS, and WFC as independent variables and MGEW as the dependent variable.

Table 2. Pearson-r of ESLB, POS, and modified GWB

	ESLB	POS	MGEWB
ESLB	--		
POS	.391**	--	
MGEW	.305**	.375**	--

Notes: ESLB = Essential Servant Leadership Behaviors; POS = Perceived Organizational Support; MGEWB = Modified General Well-being

Note: N = 170

Note: **p=.000

The second study included an exploratory factor analysis of the MGEW scale, a test-retest analysis, a correlation of the four variables, and a confirmatory factor analysis of the MGEW scale. The exploratory factor analysis found that the eight items of the MGEW loaded on one factor with an eigenvalue of 5.50 that explained 68.8% of the variance with factor loads ranging from .735 to .886. The Cronbach's alpha for MGEW was .933, which showed a high level of scale reliability.

Test-Retest Reliability

According to DeVellis (2017), "temporal stability" (p. 66) indicates the reliability of the scale over a short period of time. Scales should produce the same result over repeated testing of the same participants, barring any unanticipated major life or environmental changes (Lukat et al. (2016). Temporal stability can be measured using a paired t-test and a correlation of scale results in which a test was followed by a retest after a short period of time. (DeVellis, 2017)

For the second study, a test-retest analysis of the eight-item MGEW scale with the retest 14 days after the first test, using 54 participants showed a test-retest Pearson Correlation $r=.85$ significant at $p=.000$ and a t-test of the two data collection efforts $t=1.167$ that was not significant $p=.248$. Thus, the MGEW scale showed test-retest reliability.

Correlation of ESLB, POS, WFC, and MGEW

The author used correlation to test for convergent and discriminant validity of the MGEW scale with the other three variables (ESLB, POS, WFC). The correlations were similar to the correlation of ESLB, POS, and MGEW from the first study. Table 3 presents the results.

The MGEW's correlation between ESLB and POS supported convergent validity. Theoretically, WFC should have negatively correlated with MGEW since higher levels of WFC should contribute to lowered Well-being.

Table 3. Correlations of the continuous variables

	ESLB	POS	WFC	MGEW
ESLB	—			
POS	0.33**	—		
WFC	0.15*	-0.47**	—	
MGEW	0.28**	0.09	0.14*	—

* Correlation is significant at the 0.05 level (2-tailed).
** Correlation is significant at the 0.01 level (2-tailed).
Note. N = 213
ESLB = essential servant leadership behaviors
POS = perceived organizational support
WFC = work-family conflict
MGEW = modified general employee well-being

Confirmatory Factor Analysis

Structured equation modeling, used for confirmatory factor analysis, usually follows exploratory factor analysis (Byrne, 2016). Confirmatory factor analysis is the process of determining the fit between exogenous (independent) variables with endogenous (dependent) variables after there is an understanding of the variables, usually determined in the exploratory factor analysis process (Byrne, 2016) and, according to Harrington (2009) is useful for social science research where psychometric measurements are used. The quality of the model-fit can be determined using the Goodness of Fit Index (GFI), which is a measure of variance and covariance; and the Absolute Goodness of Fit index (AGFI). The AGFI differs from GFI in that AGFI considers the degrees of freedom. The GFI and AGFI test the model against not having a model at all. A good model has GFI and AGFI of 0.95 or higher but is considered acceptable ad 0.90-094. In addition, Root Mean Square Error of Approximation (RMSEA) measures the model's fit with the population covariance. A good fit is indicated by RMSEA at or below .06. (Byrne, 2016)

For this chapter, Confirmatory factor analysis was conducted using IBM's AMOS Version 27. Confirmatory factor analysis from the 213 respondents showed GFI = 0.856, AGFI = 0.75, RMSEA = 0.18 and. Chi-square = 174.9, df = 21, $p < 0.000$. These results do not indicate an acceptable fit. According to Harrington (2009) modifications to a model need to be consistent with the theoretical base of the model and be logically sound. AMOS modification output implied that there was a correlation between the second and fifth item. Rerunning the analysis with a correlation between item 2 and 5 did not achieve an acceptable fit, thus the researcher removed item 5 and reran the analysis that resulted in GFI = 0.91, AGFI = 0.83, RMSEA = 0.14 and. Chi-square = 82.27, df = 15, $p < 0.000$. The output from AMOS implied a possible better fit with item 8 removed. Rerunning the analysis after removing item 8 showed GFI = 0.92, AGFI = 0.82, RMSEA = 0.16 and. Chi-square = 59.34, df = 9, $p < 0.000$. One final analysis retaining items 1, 2, 3, and 4 showed GFI = 0.98, AGFI = 0.89, RMSEA = 0.13 and. Chi-square = 9.96, df = 9, $p < 0.000$.

The GFI implies that the last model with MGEW items 1, 2, 3, 4, produced a better fit than using items 1 through 8, thus, the researcher reduced the MGEW scale to the following four items:

1. I felt calm, rather than anxious, during the past two months.
2. I have felt physically healthy during the past two months.

3. I felt emotionally stable for the past two months.
4. I felt energized for the past two months.

Final Principal Component Analysis

A final principal component analysis of the four-item scale showed that the four items of the MGEW loaded on one factor with an eigenvalue of 2.84 that explained 71.00% of the variance with factor loads ranging from .772 to .872. The Cronbach's alpha for the MGEW scale was .86 that showed a high level of scale reliability. Thus, researchers could use the four-item scale to measure employees' self-report of employee well-being.

FUTURE RESEARCH

Future bounded-case research using in-depth interviews or focus groups might determine: (a) what managers do that contributes to high-levels or low-levels of employee well-being, (b) how the managers' attitudes and behaviors impact the employees' well-being, and (c) why the managers' attitudes and behavior impact employees. Additional research using new items based on the literature might lead to additional items that would strengthen the scale's validity and reliability.

REFERENCES

Baptiste, R. N. (2008). Tightening the link between employee well-being at work and performance: A new dimension for HRM. *Management Decision*, *46*(2), 284–309. doi:10.1108/00251740810854168

Brown, J. D. (2009). Choosing the Right Type of Rotation in PCA and EFA. *Shiken: JALT Testing & Evaluation SIG Newsletter*, *13*(3), 20–25.

Byrne, B. M. (2016). *Structural Equation Modeling With AMOS (Multivariate Applications Series)* Taylor and Francis.

Charalambous, A., Kaite, C., Constantinou, M., & Kouta, C. (2016). Translation and validation of the cancer-related fatigue scale in Greek in a sample of patients with advanced prostate cancer. *BMJ Open*, *6*(12), e011798–e011798. doi:10.1136/bmjopen-2016-011798 PMID:27913557

Chitra, T., & Karunanidhi, S. (2013). Influence of occupational stress, resilience, and job satisfaction on psychological well-being of policewomen. *Indian Journal of Health and Wellbeing*, *4*(4), 724–730. http://eres.regent.edu/login?url=https://www-proquest-com.ezproxy.regent.edu/scholarly-journals/influence-occupational-stress-resilience-job/docview/1511429053/se-2?accountid=13479

Cho, E., & Kim, S. (2015). Cronbach's coefficient alpha: Well known but poorly understood. *Organizational Research Methods*, *18*(2), 207–230. doi:10.1177/1094428114555994

Dupuy, H. J. (1978). *Self-representations of General Psychological Well-Being of American Adults*. Paper presented at the American Public Health Association Meeting, Los Angeles, CA.

DeVellis. (2017). *Scale Development Theory and Applications* (4th ed.). SAGE Publications.

Eisenberger, R., Huntington, R., Hutchison, S., & Sowa, D. (1986). Perceived organizational support. *The Journal of Applied Psychology, 71*(3), 500–507. doi:10.1037/0021-9010.71.3.500

Eisenberger, R., Stinglhamber, F., Vandenberg, C., Sucharski, I. L., & Rhoades, L. (2002). Perceived supervisor support: Contributions to perceived organizational support and employee retention. *The Journal of Applied Psychology, 87*(3), 565–573. doi:10.1037/0021-9010.87.3.565 PMID:12090614

Fisher, C. D. (2003). Why do lay people believe that satisfaction and performance are correlated? possible sources of a commonsense theory. *Journal of Organizational Behavior, 24*(6), 753–777. doi:10.1002/job.219

Grant, A. M., Christianson, M. K., & Price, R. H. (2007). Happiness, health, or relationships? managerial practices and employee well-being tradeoffs. *The Academy of Management Perspectives, 21*(3), 51–63. doi:10.5465/amp.2007.26421238

Greenleaf, R. (1977). *Servant leadership: A journey into the nature of legitimate power and greatness – 25th Anniversary Edition*. Paulist.

Harrington, D. (2009). *Confirmatory factor analysis*. Oxford University Press.

Hendrix, W. H., Spencer, B. A., & Gibson, G. S. (1994). Organizational and extraorganizational factors affecting stress, employee well-being, and absenteeism for males and females. *Journal of Business and Psychology, 9*(2), 103–128. doi:10.1007/BF02230631

Kleinig, J., & Evans, N. G. (2013). Human flourishing, human dignity, and human rights. *Law and Philosophy, 32*(5), 539–564. doi:10.100710982-012-9153-2

Krabbe, P. F. M. (2017). *The Measurement of Health and Health Status*. Elsevier. doi:10.1016/B978-0-12-801504-9.00006-4

Lukat, J., Margraf, J., & Lutz, R. (2016). Psychometric properties of the Positive Mental Health Scale (PMH-scale). *BMC Psychology, 4*. http://dx.doi.org.ezproxy.regent.edu/10.1186/s40359-016-0111-x

Meyers, M. C., Adams, B. G., Sekaja, L., Buzea, C., Cazan, A.-M., Gotea, M., Stefenel, D., & van Woerkom, M. (2019). Perceived Organizational Support for the Use of Employees' Strengths and Employee Well-Being: A Cross-Country Comparison. *Journal of Happiness Studies, 20*(6), 1825–1841. doi:10.100710902-018-0026-8

Page, K. M., & Vella-Brodrick, D. A. (2009). The 'What,' 'Why,' and 'How' of employee well-being: A new model. *Social Indicators Research, 90*(3), 441–458. doi:10.100711205-008-9270-3

Pedersen, R. D., Pallay, A. G., & Rudolph, R. L. (2002). Can improvement in well-being and functioning be distinguished from depression improvement in antidepressant clinical trials? *Quality of Life Research: An International Journal of Quality of Life Aspects of Treatment, Care and Rehabilitation, 11*(1), 9–17. doi:10.1023/A:1014441826855 PMID:12003058

Poulsen, S., & Ipsen, C. (2017). In times of change: How distance managers can ensure employees' well-being and organizational performance. *Safety Science, 100*, 37–45. doi:10.1016/j.ssci.2017.05.002

Reinius, M., Wettergren, L., Wiklander, M., Svedhem, V., Ekstrom, A., & Eriksson, L. E. (2017). Development of a 12-item short version of the HIV stigma scale. *Health and Quality of Life Outcomes*, *15*(1), 115. doi:10.118612955-017-0691-z PMID:28558805

Ryan, R. M., & Deci, E. L. (2001). On happiness and human potentials: A review of research on hedonic and eudaimonic well-being. *Annual Review of Psychology*, *52*(1), 141–166. doi:10.1146/annurev.psych.52.1.141 PMID:11148302

Salles, A., Cohen, G. L., & Mueller, C. M. (2014). The relationship between grit and resident well-being. *American Journal of Surgery*, *207*(2), 251–254. doi:10.1016/j.amjsurg.2013.09.006 PMID:24238604

Taylor, T. E., Poston, W. S. C., II, Haddock, C. K., Blackburn, G. I., Heber, D., Heymsfield, S. B., & Foreyt, J. P. (2003). Psychometric characteristics of the general well-being schedule (GWB) with African-American women. *Quality of Life Research, 12*(1), 31-39. doi:http://dx.doi.org.ezproxy.regent.edu:2048/10.1023/A:1022052804109

Tekin, A., & Polat, E. (2016). A scale for E-content preparation skills: Development, validity and reliability. *Eurasian Journal of Educational Research*, *16*(62), 143. doi:10.14689/ejer.2016.62.9

Winston, B. (2020). *Correlation of Essential Servant Leadership Behaviors*. Perceived Organizational Support, and Employee Well-Being., doi:10.20944/preprints202003.0222.v1

Winston, B. (n.d.). The *Relationship of Servant Leadership, Perceived Organizational Support and Work-family Conflict with Employee Well-being* (Working paper).

Winston, B., & Fields, D. (2015). Seeking and measuring the essential behaviors of servant leadership. *Leadership and Organization Development Journal*, *36*(4), 413–434. doi:10.1108/LODJ-10-2013-0135

Zheng, X., Zhu, W., Zhao, H., & Zhang, C. (2015). Employee well-being in organizations: Theoretical model, scale development, and cross-cultural validation. *Journal of Organizational Behavior*, *36*(5), 645–647. doi:10.1002/job.2033

Chapter 18
COVID-19 vs. Healthcare Information System Self-Efficacy Perception (HISSEP):
A Formidable Opponent

B. J. Weathersby-Holman
Rutland & Associates, LLC, USA

ABSTRACT

Coronavirus has emphasized the importance of nursing contributions and their integral participation in interdisciplinary leadership teams providing patient care in healthcare organizations. Workforce shortages of qualified nurses in healthcare with technology skills are necessary to maintain a high level of patient care and healthcare operations. A validated instrument, Healthcare Information System Self-Efficacy Perception, was created providing a self-assessment tool for measuring an older working nurse's perception of self-efficacy of healthcare information system training within a healthcare environment. The study was the first of its kind to recognize the salient training differences that existed for older workers in a healthcare setting. The instrument was developed using a focus group, pilot study, and validated with registered nurses (RN) in a single healthcare organization. The sample (N=162) was assessed using an online survey tool. After face validity was established for HISSEP, a principal component factor analysis was conducted to determine content validity.

INTRODUCTION

The introduction of this chapter will provide a background of the healthcare establishment workforce, nurses, and the importance of the training and education strategies used to inform programs for nurses who spend much of their time on patient care. The primary drivers of the instrument development process are focused on older working nurses however, the benefits of the instrument are realized due to its flexibility of use for all ages. A successful training strategy begins with a relevant instrument. COVID-19

DOI: 10.4018/978-1-7998-7665-6.ch018

highlighted a deficiency of nursing staff. The need for qualified nursing staff reverberated the airwaves with the expressed need for retired, older, nurses to return to the field of nursing. Older nurses were needed to support the current overwhelmed and overworked community of healthcare providers. The chapter will provide relevant issues faced by nurses in healthcare establishments typically and extraordinary requests due to COVID-19. The older nurses based on years of knowledge and experience are gaining increased responsibilities during the pandemic to alleviate shortages of healthcare providers. The healthcare environment-focused instrument is targeted for older working nurses, age forty and over, however, the training and development strategy applies to employees of all ages.

Two-thousand and twenty began much like any other for organizations and individuals identifying their goals and objectives to accomplish and predicting what innovative projects would become successful. Healthcare organizations are no different, they evaluate which departments require focused attention from system upgrades to equipment decommissioning. Leadership demands consist of balancing the diverse types of care necessary to support the different communities and aligning healthcare staff in the appropriate proportions to maximize the economic demand and supply. One of the critical areas in a healthcare organization is the training and development of the workforce to ensure staff. It is imperative healthcare workers have the requisite education and knowledge based on regulatory requirements; awareness of policy changes to provide more focused patient care; and new innovative insight into areas that can set their workforce apart from competing healthcare choices for prospective patients. The largest percentage of the workforce for healthcare establishments are nurses. In May 2019, nurses made up 30%, over 1.8 million, of all hospital positions (Statistics, 2020). In the background of all the new year planning and goal setting prepared to make a formidable entrance was the onset of Coronavirus 2019 (COVID-19), a global pandemic that would test every healthcare professional and supporter in a race for a cure while identifying proven methods to protect the citizens of the world.

Healthcare organizations have critical service and delivery metrics which include preventative, maintenance, and emergency services for individuals in all socio-economic levels (Mantzana et al., 2007). The services offered are based on the healthcare organization's purpose, the vision of leadership, and the capacity of its workers.

To enable the delivery of services to customers, many healthcare organizations rely on information technology from initial admission records to the preparation of surgical kits used in operating rooms (Holman, 2014). "Healthcare and computer science occupations [will] lead the way in terms of projected rates of employment growth" (Neumark et al., 2011, p. 10). To support the deluge of information processing needs within healthcare many organizations rely on Healthcare Information Systems (HIS) to harness the volumes of data. "The amount of health and medical knowledge is increasing at such a phenomenal rate that we cannot hope to organize and retrieve it without HIS" (Mantzana et al., 2010, p. 10). Changing workforce dynamics and access to skilled workers, including training those who are older workers should be targeted to ensure successful acquisition of necessary skills which contribute to healthcare operations (Holman, 2014). Despite the excessive amount of money and countless working hours spent on system modernization in the healthcare sector healthcare information system projects have failed worldwide (Heeks, 2006). One reason for project failures from an organizational perspective is the lack of skilled workers to operate the system.

The population of workers in society today is diverging from traditional to non-traditional with many choosing to remain employed beyond the traditional retirement age. Reasons for this change range from supplementing retirement income to social interaction and intellectual gains. The baby boomer cohort is expected to be the largest workforce in history. Due to the increasing demand for skilled healthcare nurse leaders who can operate healthcare information systems software, Human Resource Development (HRD) leaders should consider developing training interventions for older workers. Organizational leadership in collaboration with human resource development leaders should consider developing interventions for healthcare information system training for nurse leaders (Holman, 2012).

BACKGROUND

The 21st century has brought a deluge of opportunities never known before and will probably continue to expand into the future; creating new opportunities coupled with challenges for healthcare leadership to overcome specifically regarding the changing workforce demographics. One issue for leadership is the blurred relationship between age and work. The baby boomer cohort has changed the way organizations will define their workforce in the next century (DeLong, 2004). Realizing the definition, of the older workforce, is a hard concept to succinctly construct, many organizations constantly struggle to identify options to meet the competitive new environment. Organizations are guided by mission statements and objectives which leadership translate into policies, guidelines, and processes for the workforce. Each of these translated guidelines help transform the organization on an individual basis. To support the transference of principles leadership interaction is required for the workforce (Yukl, 2006).

Nurse as Leader

The healthcare industry is a growth area with nursing being one of the largest growing segments. The Bureau of Labor Statistics (BLS, 2012), 2008 special report indicated there were 595,800 healthcare establishments. About 76 percent of healthcare establishments are offices of physicians, dentists, or other health practitioners. Although hospitals constitute only 1 percent of all healthcare establishments, they employ 35 percent of all workers within the U.S., (Bureau of Labor Statistics, 2008). Healthcare organizations have critical service and delivery metrics that include preventative, maintenance, and emergency services for individuals in all socio-economic levels (Mantzana et al., 2007). To maintain proficient hospital operations, nurse leaders are identified as a critical part of the management interdisciplinary teams. Jones (2007) contends the nursing profession claims many true leaders. Furthermore, leaders express bold visions, invest enormous amounts of energy to realize those visions, effectively engaging followers in the quest; maintain passion about the future they hoped to create, and absorb criticism, setbacks, and opposition on the road to success (Jones, 2007). Tourangeau and McGilton (2004) elucidate one of the critical tasks for a nurse leader is caring for patients using technology. Health information systems enable nurse leaders to create and monitor documentation procedures and provide efficient care to patients. The multiplicity of tasks can elevate stress (Battisto et al., 2009). DeLucia et al. (2009) purport nurses engage in multiple tasks under cognitive load and frequent interruptions.

Nursing leadership faces multiple challenges within healthcare globally, ranging from reduced healthcare funding, competency development and an ageing workforce (Parker & Hyratus, 2011). There is a critical importance to cultivate a strong sense of self-efficacy through training for older nurse leaders from an organizational perspective. Healthcare organizations are supported by nursing leadership. Nurse leaders are intricate members of interdisciplinary teams and many provide a higher majority of patient to provider care. To precipitate the ongoing care for clients using advanced healthcare technology "...nurses need to be educated to be more efficient and competent...to meet the ever increasing health-care needs of the population" (Parker & Hyratus, 2011). The increased competency can lead to increased self-efficacy.

Self-Efficacy theory posits people develop domain-specific beliefs about their own abilities and characteristics that guide their behavior; Perceived Organizational Support theory contends that employees develop a personal relationship with the organization to fulfill a socio-emotional requirement; they further evaluate the organizations willingness to exchange reward for effort completed by the employee on the organizations behalf (Shore & Shore, 1995); and Industrial Gerontology theory is the study of aging and work, focusing on employment of middle-age and older workers (Sterns & Miklos, 1995). Aging affects everyone at the personal, organizational, and societal level. Aging refers to changes that occur in biological, psychological, and social functioning through time, and play a critical role in the aging process at work (Birren & Birren, 1990). HISSEP is not just an assessment to guide training decisions it should be used to address the human needs of nurses in healthcare establishments during COVID-19. Nurses are not only in need of training and education to help patients they need it much more to care for their own well-being as they transverse the pandemic as leaders in the fight. The theories provide timely relevance for the use of HISSEP, against COVID-19, which is needed to support the learning and development of nursing staff overall and older working nurses specifically as a cadre of retired nurses are pleaded to return to healthcare establishments.

Self-Efficacy

Bandura (1997) theory of self-efficacy posits that people develop domain-specific beliefs about their own abilities and characteristics that guide their behavior. Their behavior can determine personal achievement and the extent of effort they expend toward performance in a particular situation. Fundamentally, self-efficacy is the belief in one's ability to perform at a certain level and accomplish sought after goals. Maslow (1987) posits that "...healthy people are primarily motivated by their needs to develop and actualize their fullest potentialities and capacities" (p. 31). Bandura (1997) self-efficacy theory posits the underlying factor is human motivation. Using Maslow's (1987) basic hierarchy of needs and expanding on them the defined need of each individual, is to realize a feeling of accomplishment, and belonging. A person's ability is not solely based on meeting their needs, but additionally on personal outlook and their capabilities.

Fundamentally, self-efficacy theory is founded through four different sources: mastery experience, vicarious observation, verbal/social persuasion, and arousal/physiological (Bandura, 1986). While important clues for consideration regarding self-efficacy (Bandura, 1986), a component of, social cognitive theory; Gist (1987) posits "cognitive appraisal and integration...ultimately determine self-efficacy" (p. 473). Mastery is the ability to increase individual skill level through repetitive accomplishment. The expressed outcome from an organizational perspective results in increased employee technology skills from HIS training. One method to increase technological ability is through defined training exposure which can lead to realized mastery skill level. According to Bandura (1986) the absence of mastery requires an individual to resort to vicarious observation, a form of modeling to obtain a defined skill-set, or ability. Vicarious observation considered less influential for acquisition can still prove beneficial. Verbal or social persuasion is the process of verbally convincing an individual they can complete a task, akin to a facilitator during a training workshop. It is a form of verbal coaching for encouragement and assurance. Bandura (1982)asserts verbal or social persuasion less effective compared to modeling or mastery for gained self-efficacy. Arousal or physiological status is an individual's level of arousal when met with unfamiliar stimuli such as playing the piano in front of an audience. Arousal could convey fear or feelings of failure related to low self-efficacy. The identified sources contributing to self-efficacy may contribute to internalized beliefs of an individual's ability or inability to accomplish a task. While behaviorist contribute these sources to human behavior, Bandura (1982) relates them to an individual's cognitive functioning.

Self-Efficacy and Training

Self-efficacy has proven to be a determinant in many training studies providing insight on how individuals navigate through challenge in diverse situations. Life threatening challenges can be fraught with anxiety or a lack of anxiety based on the perceived self-efficacy of an individual (Bandura 1988). Studies indicate that self-efficacy is associated with learning and achievement (Campbell & Hackett, 1986; Wood & Locke, 1987), and adaptability to new technology (Hill et al., 1987). Studies have further indicated that self-efficacy is influenced by training methods (Gist, 1989; Gist et al., 1989). From an organizational perspective information is derived from the individual, the work task, and others in the work environment which may contribute to creating a comprehensive assessment of the individuals capability (Gist & Mitchell, 1992, p. 184). Similarly, Gist et al. (1989), conducted a study on self-efficacy of individuals and computer training techniques. Two training techniques were presented modeling vs. tutorial. Based on a behavioral perspective, modeling was identified as a method to produce training results. Using two popular financial software packages with similar training content the only distinguishable difference was the training method employed. Upon completion of training a timed test was given to each group evaluating their training without assistance during the test. Participants scoring high in self-efficacy, using modeling, scored significantly better than participants with low self-efficacy scores, using tutorial. Training objectives met from an organizational perspective define training success in economic means allowing organizations to thwart off competitive challenge. The former of positive modeling enabled participants to achieve stellar results whereas ladder non-contact tutorial methods produced negative outcomes. Self-efficacy was identified as a main proposition by Earley (1994) who conducted a study on training interventions of individualism and collectivism. The basis of the study identified an individual's perceptions and attitudes toward him or herself and others in social relationships and training. Gudykunst et al. (1996) conclude in both individualistic and collectivistic cultures self-efficacy was shown to be a foundational determinate that allowed individuals to succeed in training endeavors. Additionally, self-efficacy beliefs contributed to motivation which manifests in several ways: determining the goals people set, the amount of effort they expend, length of time they persevere when faced with difficulties, and their resilience to failures (Bandura 1997). This ability to strengthen one's self-efficacy can propel them toward success in training endeavors. Some educational practices may validate a sense of efficacy by clearly conveying that students are becoming more capable, which should sustain task motivation and lead to further increases in self-efficacy and skills (Schunk, 1984). The capability of the individual's self-efficacy can be combined with facilitated training to provide synergy between intervention and human ability.

To amplify the point of synergy a study conducted by McNaught and Barth (1992) on older workers and customer service representative training for Days Inn of America was examined for further clarification. The study identified a significant difference in training time between older and younger workers. Training records revealed older workers required one week longer than younger counterparts who only required two weeks. This was normalized for both groups with curriculum adjustments to training focusing on increased repetition and self study producing increased capability and confidence. Training adjustments enhanced older workers self-perception to combat negative thoughts of inability when compared to the younger workers. More importantly, from an organizational perspective, final estimated training costs were normalized to $1,350 per training period for both workers with training intervention changes. Training has been identified as a conduit to improve current job skills, prepare for career advancement, retool for new or changing job requirements and commonly viewed as a point of entry into the organization (Goldstein, 1980). Lee et al. (2009), employing a focus group design, conducted a study of thirty-seven participants in the Greater Miami area of older workers seeking employment with limited technological skills. The sample population understood the value of technological skills for an organization and was willing to learn new skills necessary but found their lack of self-efficacy limited their personal capability. The most relevant obstacles for participants were "their lack of confidence… (95%) [and]…limited skills (49%)…" (p. 24). The ability to increase an individual's self-efficacy is directly tied to their outlook in meeting challenges successfully (Moos & Azevedo, 2009, p. 578). Liu et al. (2011) conducted a literature review on education and training motivations of older workers to participate in training found self-efficacy as the motivator for success during training. Success within a company sponsored training program may hinge on the ability to increase the participants self-efficacy; but self-efficacy may become a more salient issue when the individual is an older worker. HISSEP specifically addressed attributes of self-efficacy related to industrial gerontology when evaluating HIS training.

Perceived Organizational Support

Perceived organizational support (POS) theory contends that employees develop a personal relationship with the organization to fulfill a socio-emotional requirement; they further evaluate the organizations willingness to exchange reward for effort completed by the employee on the organizations behalf (Shore & Shore, 1995). Ali, Ahmad-Ur- Rehman, Ul Haq, Jam, Ghafoor, and Azeem (2010) conducted a correlational study of the relationships of perceived organizational support and employee psychological empowerment. Ali et al. (2010) posits when employees perceive organizational support of their financial and physical resources and workplace support from consequences of actions performed on behalf of the organization "their feeling of self-efficacy, impact, and self-determination would be increased" (p. 189). The impact of organizational messaging and actions contribute to an employee's self-efficacy. Bartholomew et al. (1993) support self-efficacy within communication identifying findings that support a multidimensional structure for self-efficacy consistent with multiple types of behavior required for management of a chronic illness. Ali et al., (2010) further posits when organizational environments portray support through its symbols, physical environment, and interactive methods between employees it can help them develop positive and supportive perceptions about the organization (p. 189). In opposition, Bunch (2007) portends mixed messages result in perceived lack of organizational support for employees. Organizations conveying transparent messaging can lead to positive perception of organizational support. Juxtaposed to the fact that it is reported that nearly $200 billion dollars annually is spent on training with poorly constructed, implemented, and executed training initiatives which convey negative organizational support and wasted resources (Bunch, 2007). A higher level of negative messaging becomes apparent when organizations verbally professes a high premium on training yet initiate immediate termination of corporate trainers when the economy begins to decline representing a dichotomy (Ruona et al., 2003). Another disconnecting message of organizational support is the use of inappropriate training that negates a connection between training objective and the participant's tasks. Direct linkage to a task allows individuals to adequately assess required skills to successfully perform their required duties for future evaluations by the organization. Chen and Scannapieco (2010) identified an opposing relationship of organizational support by child welfare workers who experienced an increased level of self-efficacy due to supervisor support on work related activities. Supervisors and managers are viewed as direct organizational representatives for employees when evaluating organizational support. It was Zellars et al. (2001) who further related high self-efficacy to higher job satisfaction and lower turnover intentions among nurses. Chuo et al. (2011) found that organizational support, self-efficacy, and computer anxiety all have indirect influences on usage intention of new technology. Armstrong-Stassen and Ursel (2009) suggest that training is a mediator between organizational support identifying that targeted training and development practices led to the retention of older workers. Perceived organizational support can be a major contributor of worker self-efficacy. When reviewing the contributory factors of worker self-efficacy age should be evaluated for cognitive related factors when developing training initiatives. According to Bandura (1977) the physiological ability of an individual leads to an increase or decrease of self-efficacy, mastery experience, when related to facets of cognitive conditioning within the older worker. Allison and Keller (2004) identified self-efficacy interventions consisting of all four self-efficacy sources led to greater improvements in physical-activity performance in older adults. Contributory components related to self-efficacy of the older worker reviewed in relation to Industrial Gerontology were cognition, chronological age, and technology.

Industrial Gerontology

Industrial gerontology is the study of aging and work, focusing on employment of middle-age and older workers (Sterns & Miklos, 1995). Aging affects everyone at the personal, organizational, and societal level. Aging refers to changes that occur in biological, psychological, and social functioning through time, and play a critical role in the aging process at work (Birren & Birren, 1990). There are societal prejudices and stereotypes that are perpetuated against the aged in organizations such as "healthcare" (Butler, 1969) that sometimes prohibit them from full participation (Butler, 2002). One of the more prevalent organizational events is training. Despite the importance of updating and maintaining competence for all workers, there is evidence that older workers are not treated comparably to younger workers in gaining access to training (Barth et al., 1993). Allen and Hart (1998) posit competencies needed for workers are "acquiring and evaluating information...using computers to process information...[and] applying technology to tasks" (p. 94). Allen and Hart (1998) further assert that "one assumption about older workers is that they are afraid of technology or cannot learn quickly in this area....yet the dominate role of technology requires all workers to be lifelong learners in order to keep up with technological innovations" (p. 95).

Cognition

Alley et al. (2007) conducted a study to assess the relationship between higher education and change across multiple domains of cognitive function in a representative sample of older Americans aged 70 and older. One conclusion drawn from Alley et al., (2007) identified continued training as an intervention to reduce the rate of cognitive decline, elucidating the importance of training to build self-efficacy for the older worker. Shultz et al. (2010) conducted an empirical study reviewing the Karasek (1979) model of demand control work stress which conceptualized job demands as a mental workload emphasizing the potential role of cognitive changes associated with age. They conclude that organizations have the opportunity to enhance the perception of work life for older workers with increase job skill level training. Ganster and Murphy (2000) propose the work environment may influence positive outcomes for workers. Individuals mastering high levels of self-efficacy have been identified to be more equipped to handle challenging demands (Bandura 1997) within the work environment including technology training.

Chronological Age

Peeters and van Emmerik (2008) wrote an article focusing on the portrayal of the older workers well-being, highlighting the static chronological age of workers and the continuity of the aging process. The aging process does not change a worker's desire or motivation, or their desire for development or a need for training and continual socialization and support from their managers and organizations. They have a continued desire to feel impactful making the organization a determined linkage in providing necessary support for this segment of worker. The study further identified perceptual age factors based on chronological, biological, or social factors contributing to how older individuals are viewed. Someone's age may be old in one context, due to lifestyle and lack of exercise, but young in another context, vibrancy, willingness to try new things, outlook, etc. "Not all the cognitive abilities appear to deteriorate over the years....intelligence remains stable until on average the age of 80" (p. 356). Song and Erdem (2011) conducted a qualitative study within the hospitality industry of older workers, over the age of 40, to understand the challenges of implementing a mobile learning (m-learning) program. Their study identified environmental accommodations as relevant for generational learning to increase capability. The researchers found related benefits to building generation specific training based on current skill set to induce plasticity. Plasticity is the ability for an individual to acquire new cognitive skills through training that engage cognitive functioning. Song and Erdem (2011) further postulate "training...[and] needs assessment...should be established to facilitate the learning styles of older workers" (p. 3). Additionally, Rothwell et al. (2008) portend training should be modified according to different generational characteristics of employees, their respective expectations, attitudes, and level of satisfaction in current work environment to realize positive results.

Technology

Cau-Bareille et al. (2012) posit that the rapid change in technology prohibits any worker from remaining stagnate of new learning. They further recognize that "older people are just as capable of learning as young people, provided they are allowed favorable conditions for their learning to take place" (p. 128). Bandura (1997) summarized:

The "rapid pace of technological change and the accelerated growth of knowledge require continual upgrading of competencies if people are to survive and prosper under increasingly competitive conditions....people are now living much longer than previous generations did. Self-development with age partly determines whether the expanded life span is lived self-fulfillingly or apathetically...." (p. 227).

Training should not be regulated on age using economic theory due to varying cognitive factors and "all studies agree that the scale and timing of ...changes in learning...are very unpredictable from one person to another" (p. 128). Prensky (2001) wrote an article summating differences of generational learning and proposed recommendations to reduce the glacier divide. HISSEP has taken each of the supporting theories into consideration during development. The overview of the methodological framework including the results are outlined.

METHODOLOGY FRAMEWORK

This section will provide an abbreviated overview of the methods, hospital operations and limitations identified during development. It will provide the findings from instrument, HISSEP, and identify how it can be strengthened, using a multi-facility healthcare establishment in future research. The methodology used by the researcher to validate the Healthcare Information System Self-efficacy Perception (HISSEP); survey instrument was a three phased approach. The phases were survey development and creation, pilot survey, and validation of the survey. The following provides a high level review of the HISSEP development process.

Phase One: Survey Development

The researcher developed a study plan used to generate steps necessary to create, develop, and validate the HISSEP instrument. The validation study was based on the phased approach in Figure 1.

Phase One

Focus Group

To facilitate this process the researcher reached out to a professional contact and the director of nursing at a large hospital located in Reston Virginia regarding the proposal of the HISSEP tool. The researcher requested and was provided a recommended listing of nurses willing to participate in a focus group discussion. The guiding criteria for participants were simple, each had participated in a healthcare information system training course within the prior 24 months and used a healthcare information system to carry out the essential duties in their position caring for patients. Three nurses, two female and one male, participated in the focus group. Each participant held a minimum of a Baccalaureate degree in Nursing with one having a Master's degree in Nursing. Each nurse had over 15 years of experience in patient care and over the age of 40. Each participant was presented with study background and researcher interest in the topic.

Each respondent was requested to respond fully based on their understanding of the question presented. In addition, they were informed that follow up questions may be asked to probe for a full understanding of the response given. The four part question identified provided further input into one of the three dimensions in the study: self-efficacy, perceived organizational support, and industrial gerontology. The four part question presented was as follows:

"What are your thoughts or insights on prior Healthcare Information System (HIS) training that you have participated in? What is your current comfort level with using HIS and related technology (i.e., computers, applications, monitors, etc.) necessary to complete your job (i.e., essential tasks) in your working environment? Do you feel capable of effectively completing your job (i.e., essential tasks and duties) with your knowledge and abilities, with or without additional training? Please explain your response by giving details. Do you feel your organization supports your learning needs? Please explain your response by giving details. The responses were recorded and later used as additional input during item generation.

Figure 1. Holman's methodology of HISSEP development
Note. The phased development and output of the HISSEP instrument (Holman, 2014)

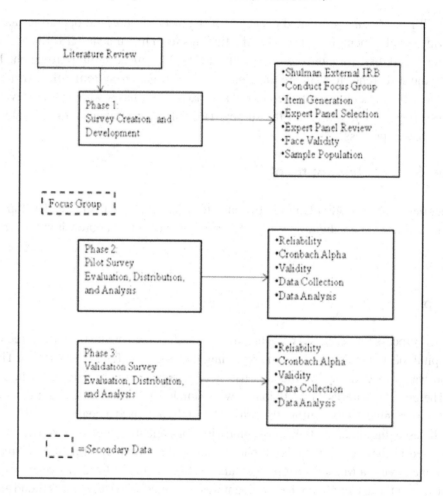

Phase Two: Pilot Survey, Distribution, and Analysis

The second phase provided an opportunity for the researcher to evaluate the confidence level of the defined item pool generated for HISSEP in phase one. To complete this part of the process a pilot survey is required using a sample population from the intended audience. Comrey and Lee (1992) posit a sample of 300 participants is recommended for a "good" sample size to elucidate the factors of interest and attain statistical significance (Pett et al., 2003). Conversely, Barrett and Kline (1981), conclude that "...*N* of 50 was the minimum needed to reproduce the pattern" in factor analysis. While many suggestions were given to obtain a 'good' assessment for factor analysis a sample equaling one tenth the 300 cases suggested was deemed applicable as an initial pilot test of the survey instrument (Pallant, 2007). Therefore, a target achieving a minimum of thirty participants for the pilot study was identified as acceptable.

A Cronbach's alpha coefficient was used to assess the internal consistency of HISSEP. Devellis (2003) posits the alpha measurement represents the amount of total variance within any of the scales that could be attributed to a common source. The Cronbach alpha for the entire HISSEP scale was $\alpha = .86$ and $\alpha = .87$ on standardized items. The coefficient values suggested the initial version of HISSEP demonstrated adequate internal consistency. Hair et al. (2010) posit that a level of consistency among variables on a summated scale indicate items measure the same construct. Hair et al. (2010) further recommends an interitem correlation to exceed .30 and item-total correlations exceed .50 as a diagnostic measure of internal consistency. A final reduction of 10-item statement in Table 1 excluding the informed consent and demographic questions, for the entire HISSEP scale with $\alpha = .95$ and $\alpha = .94$ on standardized items. Evaluating the interitem correlations HISSEP revealed all items correlated at or exceeded .30. Additionally, the summated scale was considered good and HISSEP subscales indicated strong reliability. While sample size can be viewed as a consideration for interpreting results another important issue is redundancy. Based on the evaluation HISSEP indicated a reliable measure of perceived self-efficacy and perceived organizational support within a healthcare environment, evidenced through data collection.

Table 1. 10-item statement HISSEP

Item Number	Item Detail
Q1	I value the Healthcare information system (HIS) documentation training offered by my organization
Q2	I value all type of technology training offered by my organization
Q3	I feel my organization supports my participation in Healthcare information system (HIS) documentation training
Q4	I feel the leadership in my organization conveys positive messages regarding Healthcare information system (HIS) documentation training
Q5	I feel my direct supervisor supports my participation in Healthcare information system (HIS) documentation training
Q6	I feel my organization supports my Healthcare information system (HIS) documentation training needs
Q7	I feel that my direct supervisor follows organizational policies regarding Healthcare information system (HIS) training opportunities
Q8	I feel my organization supports the participation of every employee in Healthcare information system (HIS) documentation training
Q9	I feel my organization is supportive of all employees regardless of age to obtain Healthcare information system (HIS) documentation training
Q10	My supervisor is always helpful in providing Healthcare information system (HIS) guidance on documentation procedures when I ask for help

Source: (Holman, 2014)

It is important for a researcher to use a data collection method conducive to the audience being surveyed. HISSEP employed an online survey for the hospital nursing audience. As healthcare workers email access is usually limited to a kiosk type of setup because most of the nursing duties are performed at the patient bedside. For ease of access the survey was distributed via email to participants meeting the identified qualifications as a healthcare nurse leader. Defined criteria: participated in healthcare information system training within the prior 36 months, a licensed Registered Nurse, and works within a healthcare environment providing patient care in the United States. Preceding data collection, expert reviewers were given detailed instructions to evaluate the HISSEP instrument. Response period for the pilot study extended for two weeks. Healthcare workers are highly engaged therefore minimal distractions are needed for any activities that take them away from primary patient care. To accommodate this, it was estimated that completion of the instrument for each participant would take approximately 10 minutes. Respondent completion time was identified using the online survey program. The data analysis of a survey is determined by the completed assessments. Since a researcher cannot read minds or make subjective judgements only completed surveys are relevant to a final product. In addition, the response rate is based on completed surveys returned and HISSEP received over 70%. Descriptive demographic statistics were used to analyze the personal characteristics of respondents that included age, gender, ethnicity, number of years nursing experience, and education. The primary goal of a Principal Component Analysis (PCA) is to synthesize interrelationships among initial variables into a smaller set of orthogonal principal components (Field, 2010; Pett et al., 2003). Eigenvalues provide another technique to evaluate the amount of variance that resides in a component for extraction for the factor model (Pett et al., 2003). To aid in the interpretation of these two components, oblimin rotation was performed. The rotation solution revealed the presence of simple structure (Thurstone, 1947), with both components showing a number of strong loadings and all variables loading substantially on only one component. The results supported the use of the Healthcare Information System Self-efficacy Perception (HISSEP) scale to provide interpretation of results (Revelle & Rocklin, 1979).

Phase Three: Validation Study

Validation completed in the third phase was conducted at Virginia Hospital Center (VHC) located in Northern Virginia. VHC was named one of the Nation's 100 Top Hospitals by Truven Health Analytics as a leading provider of information and solutions to improve the cost and quality of healthcare. In addition, VHC was the only hospital in the area at the time of the survey to be named an Everest Award winner based on metrics that evaluate the quality of care delivered to patients. The leadership, employees, and partnerships helped designate VHC as one of the leading healthcare facilities in the Washington Metropolitan area.

The HISSEP validation process invited a random sample from 742 nurse leaders to participate. Polit and Beck (2010) posit that a study begins by identifying the population researchers wish to generalize their results. The population is the totality of elements or people that have commonality, defined characteristics, and about whom the study results are relevant. The HISSEP validation study evaluated participants based on required criteria. Criteria included possessing a valid RN license, having participated in Healthcare Information Systems (HIS) training within prior 36 months, and use HIS in primary duties. The validation study only included nurse leaders.

A nurse leader is defined as an individual who actively participates on an interdisciplinary patient care team. The hospital operates using an interdisciplinary leadership patient care team framework where each team consists of a physician, nurse, social worker, psychologist, and nutritionist. The current landscape with COVID-19 includes necessary team participants as needed such as a radiologist, immunology specialist, spiritual counselors, or chaplain (Care, 2020). The leadership teams are responsible for professional collaboration on all aspects of patient care and maintenance. Members provide leadership and competent skill sets based on their individual area of expertise (e.g., clinical, care, nutrition, etc.) essential to team success of quality care for patients. Nurse leaders are seen as the major contributor of the leadership team based on time, up to 50%, spent with the patient (DeLucia et al., 2009). Nurse leaders are responsible for dividing their time between multiple duties while providing reliable information relating to patient care. It is critical for nurse leaders to be a reliable communicator, messenger, and multi-tasker to maintain hectic schedules and conflicting deadlines necessary for patient care. Each participant met the criteria. Participants ranged from age 21 and older dependent on matriculation from nursing school. Healthcare information system training is defined as a course that introduces or enhances a nurse leader understanding and functionality of a software application system to enable clinical and non-clinical information workflow within a healthcare organization. To ensure the study provided applicable results the sample size was considered. Many researchers (MacCallum et al., 1999) suggest that sample size is difficult to define. Devellis (2003) suggests that larger sample factor analysis produce more stability than smaller samples. According to Kline (1993) a minimum subject-to-item ratio necessary for a good factor analysis is 2 to 1 (p. 121) moreover, it will elucidate the factors of interest and attain statistical significance (Pett et al., 2003). Kline (1993) further states there are large disagreements among researchers regarding this number. Based on Kline's (1993) recommendation a minimum of 114 respondents provided a good factor analysis in the HISSEP study. Each study must evaluate the most expedient method of data collection without introducing unnecessary stress on the participant or into the environment. To ensure all the ethical considerations were followed this researcher completed an extensive Internal Review Board (IRB) at VHC, a university Human Subjects Review Board (HSRB) and finally a 3rd party external IRB. The project was approved in accordance with the ethical principles governing research with human subjects as specified by the American Psychology Association, VHC hospital research guidelines, and Shulman IRB. Since the researcher was not a hospital employee a research leader, a hospital employee, was assigned to navigate the internal communication, email distributions, and provide project oversight and leadership status reports.

COVID-19

The COVID-19 pandemic has led to a dramatic loss of human life worldwide and presents an unprecedented challenge to public health and the world of work (Chriscaden, 2020) requiring healthcare workers to face the most exposure. According to John's Hopkins Coronavirus Research Center (2021), the current global totals at the time of this writing were 90 million cases, 1.9 million deaths and within the US contributing to the totals are the current 'hot spots' of California and Florida where the virus is raging through the populations and stressing the healthcare systems capacity. "Nurses all around the country are being cross-trained to work in higher acuity or critical care patient areas as fast as possible to maximize efforts against COVID-19....[however] as nurses step out of their comfort zones, there have been concerns that many nurses feel unprepared (Jividen, 2020)". "When COVID-19 first hit the US, there were stories of nurses having to take care of patients without proper training or best practices to follow (Jividen, 2020)". Healthcare establishments are identified as treatment facilities assisting individuals to regain their health. However, the current pandemic has made even the slightest injury a potential danger due to increased exposure while in the healthcare facilities. To alleviate this risk most healthcare establishments have moved to telehealth, voice or video calls between provider and patient. While the movement of some of the less critical services have been diverted nurses are under extreme pressure to provide care for the sickness of our nation. There are currently two FDA, emergency use authorization approved (EUA) vaccines: Pfizer-BioNTech and Moderna COVID-19 Vaccines. To help combat the infection rate healthcare workers and first responders are among the first to receive the vaccine. COVID-19 is taking the foreground of the focus however, in the background is the perpetual need for efficient training for nurses as they fulfill the duties of care. We may never return to the pre-COVID-19 state but the ability to indoctrinate confidence into older working nurses standing daily to ensure patient safety and wellness requires an equally formattable assessment. HISSEP has been proven to evaluate and identify a nurses self-efficacy while providing insight of organizational support. It is surmised that HISSEP if used as a pre, pulse, and post assessment can help inform and align training methods ensuring nurses are trained and supported. Nurses are the primary attendant of care and one of the leading factors in positive outcomes of patient well-being (Cheung et al., 2008). COVID-19 probably will not be our last pandemic, however, with the fortitude and training of nurses, such as Mary Seacole over 150 years ago, patients will continue to heal and return to regular life.

RECOMMENDATION

The HISSEP instrument was validated in a single and a starting point to measure healthcare information system training perception for older workers based on self-efficacy. The HISSEP instrument offers advantages for organizational diagnosis and usage in developing HIS training curriculum within a healthcare environment. The analysis generates an opportunity to begin using HISSEP to develop cross organizational perception levels of nurse leaders. However, to allow the results to be extrapolated it should be evaluated using multiple healthcare establishments.

CONCLUSION

The instrument, HISSEP, was developed based upon research to identify dimensional characteristics of self-efficacy, perceived organizational support, and industrial gerontology. Self-efficacy summarily describes the tenets of an individual's belief in their ability to overcome challenges and maintain focus to excel in accomplishing defined goals. Goal attainment while a personal motivation is enhanced with external supports. This is the premise of healthcare organizations; their charter is to help individuals overcome diverse challenges while adding supports to their rehabilitation of health in coordination with their personal motivation to collaboratively meet a defined goal of better health. The health of an organization has fortuitous volumes regarding a multiplicity of diagnosis predicting recovery. Using medical terminology, within the connotations of prescribed ointments lay the primal focus in patient zero. An organization's resources comparably are not as important as healthcare providers within a hospital environment. Specifically, nursing whose support provide a direct linkage between hospital operations and patient recovery. One of the major supports provided to nurses is the healthcare information system to document, communicate, and track patient progress and inculcate an organizations economic well-being. Bandura (1997) contends that an individual's behavior can determine personal achievement and the extent of effort they expend toward performance in a particular situation. Overwhelmingly, those that enter the field of nursing have a strong desire to help those in a time of great need. Their ability to maintain a personal efficacy in their professional environment can help translate into enhanced care for themselves and the patient. Based on the data evaluated in the HISSEP findings a system can provide a measure of efficacy that can be translated into a specific value. As robust as some HIS systems can be it is more important to provide understanding on how to use this valuable tool that will add a benefit to nurses and been an extension of their personal care. HISSEP reported high measures for identifying the salient factors important to nurse leaders. The instrument and Holman model of HISSEP Training can be integrated into a workshop program considering self-efficacy and perceived organizational support informed by industrial gerontology characteristics in Figure 2 to support the learning of nursing leaders.

Figure 2. Holman model of HISSEP training
Note. HISSEP model to identify the intersection of optimal healthcare information system (HIS) curriculum development, facilitated training, and training delivery for nurses over forty in a healthcare environment (Holman, 2014)

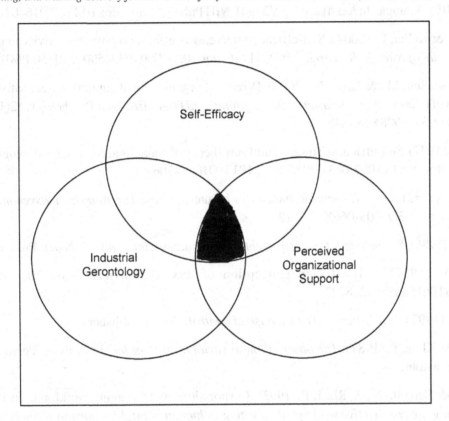

Nursing is a profession that individuals enter because of their compassion and desire to help others and leave for multiple reasons including burnout (Leiter et al., 2010). To enable nurses to reduce the stress of task multiplicity a training program that can cultivate their personal efficacy of HIS system training could potentially benefit the organization also. McNaught and Barth (1992) proved this correlation when older worker efficacy increased there was a direct correlation to organizational profits based on changes in training curriculum and facilitation. Potentially, HISSEP, as validated has the same opportunity to change the healthcare environment for training leadership.

REFERENCES

Ali, A., Ahmad-Ur-Rehman, M., Ul Haq, I., Jam, F. A., Ghafoor, M. B., & Azeem, M. U. (2010). Perceived organizational support and psychological empowerment. *European Journal of Soil Science, 17*(2), 186–192.

Allen & Hart. (1998). Training Older workers: Implications for HRD/HPT Professionals. *Performance Improvement Quarterly, 11*(4), 91-102.

Alley, D., Suthers, K., & Crimmins, E. (2007). Education and cognitive decline in older Americans: Results from the AHEAD sample. In *Res Aging* (pp. 73–94). NIH Public Access. doi:10.1177/0164027506294245

Allison, M., & Keller, C. (2004). Self-efficacy intervention effects on physical activity in older adults. *Western Journal of Nursing Research, 26*(1), 31–46. doi:10.1177/0193945903259350 PMID:14984643

Armstrong-Stassen, M., & Ursel, N. (2009). Perceived organizational support, career satisfaction, and the retention of older workers. *Journal of Occupational and Organizational Psychology, 82*(1), 201–220. doi:10.1348/096317908X288838

Bandura, A. (1977). Self-efficacy: Toward a unifying theory of behavioral change. *Psychological Review, 84*(2), 191–215. doi:10.1037/0033-295X.84.2.191 PMID:847061

Bandura, A. (1982). Self-efficacy mechanism in human agency. *The American Psychologist, 37*(2), 122–147. doi:10.1037/0003-066X.37.2.122

Bandura, A. (1986). *Social foundations of thought and action: A social cognitive theory.* Prentice-Hall, Inc.

Bandura, A. (1988). Self-efficacy conception of anxiety. *Anxiety Research, 1*(2), 77–98. doi:10.1080/10615808808248222

Bandura, A. (1997). *Self-Efficacy: The exercise of control.* Worth Publishers.

Barrett, P., & Kline, P. (1981). *The observation to variable ratio in factor analysis.* Personality Study & Group Behaviour.

Barth, M., McNaught, W., & Rizzi, P. (1993). Corporations and the aging workforce. In P. H. Mirvis (Ed.), *Building the competetive workforce: Investing in human capital for corporate success.* Wiley.

Bartholomew, L., Parcel, G., Swank, P., & Czyzewski, D. (1993). Measuring self-efficacy expectations for the self-management of cystic fibrosis. *CHEST Journal, 103*(5), 1524–1530. doi:10.1378/chest.103.5.1524 PMID:8486038

Battisto, D., Pak, R., Vander Wood, M., & Pilcher, J. (2009). Using a task analysis to describe nursing work in acute care patient environments. *The Journal of Nursing Administration, 39*(12), 537–547. doi:10.1097/NNA.0b013e3181c1806d PMID:19955968

Birren, J., & Birren, B. (1990). The concepts, models and history of the psychology of aging. In J. Birren & K. Schaie (Eds.), *Handbook of the psychology of aging* (pp. 3–18). Academic Press. doi:10.1016/B978-0-12-101280-9.50007-3

Bunch, K. (2007). Training Failure as a Consequence of Organizational Culture. *Human Resource Development Review*, *6*(2), 142–163. doi:10.1177/1534484307299273

Bureau of Labor Statistics. (2008). *Career Guide to Industries, 2010-11 Edition*. Bureau of Labor Statistics. https://www.bls.gov/oco/cg/cgs035.htm

Butler, R. (1969). Age-ism: Another form of bigotry. *The Gerontologist*, *9*(4 Part 1), 243–246. doi:10.1093/geront/9.4_Part_1.243 PMID:5366225

Butler, R. (2002). Guest Editorial The Study of Productive Aging. *The Journals of Gerontology. Series B, Psychological Sciences and Social Sciences*, *57*(6), S323–S323. doi:10.1093/geronb/57.6.S323 PMID:12426440

Campbell, N., & Hackett, G. (1986). The effects of mathematics task performance on math self-efficacy and task interest. *Journal of Vocational Behavior*, *28*(2), 149–162. doi:10.1016/0001-8791(86)90048-5

Care, C. A. P. (2020). *Using the Full Interdisciplinary Team During Crisis*. https://www.capc.org/covid-19/using-full-interdisciplinary-team-during-crisis/

Cau-Bareille, D., Caudart, C., & Delgoulet, C. (2012). Training, age and technological change: Difficulties assoicated with age, the design of tools, and the organization of work. *Workforce Management*, *41*(2), 127–141. doi:10.3233/WOR-2012-1278 PMID:22297777

Chen, S.-Y., & Scannapieco, M. (2010). The influence of job satisfaction on child welfare worker's desire to stay: An examination of the interaction effect of self-efficacy and supportive supervision. *Children and Youth Services Review*, *32*(4), 482–486. doi:10.1016/j.childyouth.2009.10.014

Cheung, R. B., Aiken, L. H., Clarke, S. P., & Sloane, D. M. (2008). Nursing care and patient outcomes: International evidence. *Enfermeria Clinica*, *18*(1), 35–40. doi:10.1016/S1130-8621(08)70691-0 PMID:18218265

Chriscaden, K. (2020). *Impact of COVID-19 on people's livelihoods, their health and our food systems*. World Health Organization. https://www.who.int/news/item/13-10-2020-impact-of-covid-19-on-people's-livelihoods-their-health-and-our-food-systems#:~:text=The%20economic%20and%20social%20disruption,the%20end%20of%20the%20year

Chuo, Y.-H., Tsai, C.-H., Lan, Y.-L., & Tsai, C.-S. (2011). The effect of organizational support, self efficacy, and computer anxiety on the usage intention of e-learning system in hospital. *African Journal of Business Management*, *5*(14), 5518–5523.

Comrey, A., & Lee, H. (1992). *A first course in factor analysis*. Lawrence Earlbaum.

DeLong, D. (2004). *Lost knowledge: Confronting the threat of an aging workforce*. Oxford University Press. doi:10.1093/acprof:oso/9780195170979.001.0001

DeLucia, P., Ott, T., & Palmieri, P. (2009). Performance in Nursing. *Review of Human Factors and Ergonomics*, *5*(1), 1–40. doi:10.1518/155723409X448008 PMID:19544931

Devellis, R. (2003). *Scale development: Theory and application* (2nd ed.). Sage Publications.

Earley, P. (1994). Self or Group? Cultural Effects of Training on Self-Efficacy and Performance. *Administrative Science Quarterly, 39*(1), 89–117. doi:10.2307/2393495

Field, A. (2010). *Discovering Statistics Using SPSS* (3rd ed.). Sage Publications.

Ganster, D., & Murphy, L. (2000). Workplace interventions to prevent stress-related illness: Lessons from research and practice. In I/O psychology: What we know about theory and practice (pp. 34–51). Basil Blackwell.

Gist, M. (1987). Self-Efficacy: Implications for Organizational Behavior and Human Resource Management. *Academy of Management Review, 12*(3), 472–485. doi:10.5465/amr.1987.4306562

Gist, M. (1989). The influence of training method on self-efficacy and idea generation among managers. *Personnel Psychology, 42*(4), 787–805. doi:10.1111/j.1744-6570.1989.tb00675.x

Gist, M., & Mitchell, T. (1992). Self-Efficacy: A Theoretical Analysis of Its Determinants and Malleability. *Academy of Management Review, 17*(2), 183–211. doi:10.5465/amr.1992.4279530

Gist, M., Schwoerer, C., & Rosen, B. (1989). Effects of alternative training methods on self-efficacy and performance in computer software training. *The Journal of Applied Psychology, 74*(6), 884–891. doi:10.1037/0021-9010.74.6.884

Goldstein, I. (1980). Training and organizational psychology. *Professional Psychology, 11*(3), 421–427. doi:10.1037/0735-7028.11.3.421

Gudykunst, W., Guzley, R., & Hammer, M. (1996). Designing Intercultural Training. In *Handbook of intercultural training*. Sage Publications, Inc.

Hair, Babin, & Anderson. (2010). Multivariate Data Analysis (7th ed.). Prentice Hall.

Hill, T., Smith, N., & Mann, M. (1987). Role of efficacy expectations in predicting the decision to use advanced technologies. *The Journal of Applied Psychology, 72*(2), 307–314. doi:10.1037/0021-9010.72.2.307

Jividen, S. (2020). *5 Online COVID-19 Courses For Nurses.* https://nurse.org/articles/online-nurse-training-courses-covid-19-coronavirus/

Jones. (2007). *Nursing Leadership and Management: Theories, Processes, and Practice.* F.A. Davis Co. http://0-search.ebscohost.com.library.regent.edu/login.aspx?direct=true&db=nlebk&AN=188356&site=eds-live

Karasek, R. (1979). Job demands, job decision latitude, and mental strain: Implications for job re-design. *Administrative Science Quarterly, 24*(2), 285–306. doi:10.2307/2392498

Lee, C., Czaja, S. J., & Sharit, J. (2009). Training Older Workers for Technology-Based Employment. *Educational Gerontology, 35*(1), 15–31. doi:10.1080/03601270802300091 PMID:20351795

Leiter, M., Price, S., & Spence Laschinger, H. (2010). Generational differences in distress, attitudes and incivility among nurses. *Journal of Nursing Management, 18*(8), 970–980. doi:10.1111/j.1365-2834.2010.01168.x PMID:21073569

Liu, S.-F., Courtenay, B., & Valentine, T. (2011). Managing Older Worker Training: A Literature Review and Conceptual Framework. *Educational Gerontology, 37*(12), 1040–1062. doi:10.1080/03601277.2010.500576

MacCallum, R., Widaman, K., Zhang, S., & Hong, S. (1999). Sample size in factor analysis. *Psychological Methods, 4*(1), 84–99. doi:10.1037/1082-989X.4.1.84

Mantzana, V., Themistocleous, M., Irani, Z., & Morabito, V. (2007). Identifying healthcare actors involved in the adoption of information systems. *European Journal of Information Systems, 16*(1), 91–102. doi:10.1057/palgrave.ejis.3000660

Maslow, A. (1987). A theory of human motivation. In *Motivation and personality* (pp. 15–34). Harper & Rob Publishers.

McNaught, W., & Barth, M. (1992). Are older workers good buys? A case study of Days Inn of America. *Sloan Management Review, 33*(3), 1–17.

Medicine, J. H. U. o. (2021). *Coronavirus Resource Center*. https://coronavirus.jhu.edu/map.html

Moos, D., & Azevedo, R. (2009). Learning With Computer-Based Learning Environments: A Literature Review of Computer Self-Efficacy. *Review of Educational Research, 79*(2), 576–600. doi:10.3102/0034654308326083

Pallant, J. (2007). *SPSS survival manual*. Open University Press.

Parker, S., & Hyratus, K. (2011). Priorities in nursing management. *Journal of Nursing Management, 19*(5), 567–571. doi:10.1111/j.1365-2834.2011.01285.x PMID:21749530

Peeters, M., & van Emmerik, H. (2008). An introduction to the work and well-being of older workers. *Journal of Managerial Psychology, 23*(4), 353–363. doi:10.1108/02683940810869006

Pett, M., Lackey, N., & Sullivan, J. (2003). Making sense of factor analysis: The use of factor analysis for instrument development in health care research. *Sage (Atlanta, Ga.).*

Polit & Beck. (2010). Generalization in quantitative and qualitative research: Myths and strategies. *International Journal of Nursing Studies, 47*(11), 1451-1458.

Prensky, M. (2001). Digital Natives, Digital Immigrants Part 1. *On the Horizon, 9*(5), 1–6. doi:10.1108/10748120110424816

Revelle, W., & Rocklin, T. (1979). Very simple structure: An alternative procedure for estimating the optimal number of interpretable factors. *Multivariate Behavioral Research, 14*(4), 403–414. doi:10.120715327906mbr1404_2 PMID:26804437

Rothwell, W., Sterns, H., Spokus, D., & Reaser, J. (2008). *Working longer: New strategies for managing, training, and retaining older employees*. American Management Association.

Ruona, W., Lynham, S., & Chermack, T. (2003). Insights on emerging trends and the future of human resource development. *Advances in Developing Human Resources, 5*(3), 272–282. doi:10.1177/1523422303254667

Schunk, D. (1984). Self-efficacy perspective on achievement behavior. *Educational Psychologist, 19*(1), 48–58. doi:10.1080/00461528409529281

Shore, L., & Shore, T. (1995). Perceived organizational support and organizational justice. In R. S. Cropanzano & K. M. Kacmar (Eds.), *Organizational politics, justice, and support: Managing the social climateof the workplace* (pp. 149–164). Quorum.

Shultz, K., Wang, M., Crimmins, E., & Fisher, G. (2010). Age differences in the demand–control model of work stress: An examination of data from 15 European countries. In *Journal of applicced Gerontology* (pp. 21–47). NIH Public Access. doi:10.1177/0733464809334286

Song, J., & Erdem, M. (2011). *M-learning in hospitality: An exploration of older workers needs and attitudes*. http://scholarworks.umass.edu/cgi/viewcontent.cgi?article=1273&context=gradconf_hospitality&sei-redir=1&referer=http%3A%2F%2F0-scholar.google.com.library.regent.edu%2Fscholar%3Fhl%3Den%2 6q%3DSong%2Band%2BM-learning%2Bin%2Bhospitality%253A%2BAn%2Bexploration%2Bof%2Bol der%2Bworkers%2Bneeds%2Band%2Battitudes%26btnG%3DSearch%26as_sdt%3D0%252C47%26as_ ylo%3D%26as_vis%3D0#search=%22Song%20M-learning%20hospitality%3A%20An%20explora-tion%20older%20workers%20needs%20attitudes%22

Sterns, H., & Miklos, S. (1995). The aging worker in a changing environment: Organizational and indi-vidual issues. *Journal of Vocational Behavior, 47*(3), 248–268. doi:10.1006/jvbe.1995.0003

Thurstone, L. (1947). *Multiple factor analysis*. University of Chicago Press.

Tourangeau, A., & McGilton, K. (2004). Measuring Leadership Practices of Nurses Using the Leader-ship Practices Inventory. *Nursing Research, 53*(3), 182–189. doi:10.1097/00006199-200405000-00005 PMID:15167506

Wood, R., & Locke, E. (1987). The relation of self-efficacy and grade goals to academic performance. *Educational and Psychological Measurement, 47*(4), 1013–1024. doi:10.1177/0013164487474017

Yukl. (2006). *Leadership in organizations* (6th ed.). Prentice Hall.

Zellars, K., Hochwarter, W., Perrewe, P., Miles, A., & Kiewitz, C. (2001). Beyond self-efficacy: Interac-tive effects of role conflict and perceived collective efficacy. *Journal of Managerial Issues, 13*, 483–499.

ADDITIONAL READING

Cheung, R. B., Aiken, L. H., Clarke, S. P., & Sloane, D. M. (2008). Nursing care and patient outcomes: International evidence. *Enfermeria Clinica, 18*(1), 35–40. doi:10.1016/S1130-8621(08)70691-0 PMID:18218265

Chriscaden, K. (2020). *Impact of COVID-19 on people's livelihoods, their health and our food systems*. https://www.who.int/news/item/13-10-2020-impact-of-covid-19-on-people's-livelihoods-their-health-and-our-food-systems#:~:text=The%20economic%20and%20social%20disruption,the%20end%20of%20 the%20year

De Avila, J., & Chen, T.-P. (2020). To Fight Coronavirus, States Call on Retired Medical Staff and New Graduates. *Wall Street Journal*. https://www.wsj.com/articles/to-fight-coronavirus-states-call-on-retired-medical-staff-and-new-graduates-11585647003

Huang, L., Lin, G., Tang, L., Yu, L., & Zhou, Z. (2020). Special attention to nurses' protection during the COVID-19 epidemic. *Critical Care (London, England)*, *24*(1), 120. doi:10.118613054-020-2841-7 PMID:32220243

Labrague, L. J., & De los Santos, J. A. A. (2020). COVID-19 anxiety among front-line nurses: Predictive role of organisational support, personal resilience and social support. *Journal of Nursing Management*, *28*(7), 1653–1661. doi:10.1111/jonm.13121 PMID:32770780

Marks, S., Edwards, S., & Jerge, E. H. (2020). Rapid Deployment of Critical Care Nurse Education During the COVID-19 Pandemic. *Nurse Leader*. Advance online publication. doi:10.1016/j.mnl.2020.07.008 PMID:32837354

Reed, K. (1998). *New age technology and new "aged" workers: The impact of age on computer technology skill acquisition and the influence of computer self-efficacy, age-related beliefs, and change attitudes* (Publication Number 9903783) [Dissertation, University of Nebraska]. Lincoln, Nebraska, United States.

Staff, A. C. (2019). *2020 Census Will Help Policymakers Prepare for the Incoming Wave of Aging Boomers*. https://www.census.gov/library/stories/2019/12/by-2030-all-baby-boomers-will-be-age-65-or-older.html#:~:text=Enter%20the%20Baby%20Boomers,born%20from%201982%20to%202000.&text=In%20 2018%2C%20there%20were%2052,Census%20Bureau's%20Vintage%20Population%20Estimates

KEY TERMS AND DEFINITIONS

Healthcare Information System (HIS): Health Information System, a software processing system enabling shared processing of clinical and non-clinical information across a healthcare establishment to facilitate patient care using software modules (e.g., documentation management, and financial functions) to process patient encounters.

Healthcare Information System Self-Efficacy Perception (HISSEP): Health information system self-efficacy scale measures an individuals' self-perception of ability and accomplishments integral to Health Information System (HIS) software application knowledge, skills, and ability for older working nurses within a healthcare environment.

Holman Model of HISSEP Training: A model informed by perceived self-efficacy, perceived organizational support and industrial gerontology used to create training interventions and programs geared to optimally support older working nurse leaders.

Industrial Gerontology (IG): The workplace environment attributes, or tasks that are transformed using lighting, seating, technical equipment, and training skills to accommodate older workers.

Interdisciplinary Leadership Team Member (ILTM): A leadership team framework where each team consists of a physician, nurse, social worker, psychologist, and nutritionist. The leadership teams are responsible for professional collaboration on all aspects of patient care and maintenance. The ability for each member to provide highly competent skill sets based on their individual area of background (e.g., clinical, care, nutrition, etc.) is essential to team success and effectiveness. Nurses are seen as the major contributor of the leadership team due to time spent with patient, more than 50%, in relation to other members (DeLucia et al., 2009).

Perceived Organizational Support (POS): An individual's perception that their employer has a vested interest in their well-being, both professionally and personally, through communication messages, actions conveyed through policies and regulations, and providing required resources. The employee perceives a feeling of involvement by the organization which produces increased confidence in skills and ability (self-efficacy) to complete organizational tasks.

Self-Efficacy (SE): An individual's internal belief in their capability to be successful in their ability to succeed in tasks pursued (e.g., training endeavors). A strong internal belief that the successful accomplishment of pursuits is realizable regardless of the adverse conditions.

Chapter 19
Measuring Clergy Effectiveness:
The Development of the Clergy Effectiveness Scale

Samuel P. Dobrotka

(iD) https://orcid.org/0000-0002-6761-6489

Grace Covenant Church, USA

ABSTRACT

A review of the current literature showed that clergy effectiveness (CE) instruments were inadequate due to age, insufficient content validity, and/or based on secondary criteria. The premise of this study was that an instrument built upon qualitative data reflective of 21st-century ministry paradigms is needed. Such data did not exist until DeShon identified 64 personal and behavioral characteristics of clergy deemed to enhance effectiveness. The purpose of this study was to operationalize the characteristics identified by DeShon. Staff and lay leaders in churches of various sizes from five different denominations were selected using a snowball technique (N = 397). Scale optimization resulted in a final three-factor instrument consisting of 14 items: professional competence (five items), socially adept (five items), and inclination to lead (four items). Scale reliability was substantiated by Cronbach's alpha scores of .89 (professional competence), .94 (socially adept), and .73 (inclination to lead).

INTRODUCTION

The act of empirically assessing clergy effectiveness (CE) gained prominence with the development of the Ministerial Activities Scale (MAS) by Kling (1958). However, in more than 60 years since Kling, only six instruments have been created that demonstrate proper construct and content validity in published empirical studies (Nauss 1996). In addition to the MAS, the instruments identified by Nauss (1996) were the Presbyterian Inventory (PI; Klever & Dyble 1972), Ten Faces of Ministry (TFM; Brekke, Strommen & Williams 1979), Profiles of Ministry (POM; Schuller, Strommen, & Brekke 1980), Ministerial Effectiveness Inventory (MEI; Majovski 1982), and the Clergy Evaluation Instrument (CEI; Nauss, Schmiel & Sohns 1992). A few additional validated instruments have been developed since Nauss but

DOI: 10.4018/978-1-7998-7665-6.ch019

are adaptations of one of the just-referenced instruments. For example, Nauss (1989, 1994) and Bunn (1998) developed adaptations of the MAS.

Critical to the development of any scale is the criteria used to select the specific scale items (Haight 1980). Within the context of CE, one must first determine the appropriate clergy behaviors and characteristics that are representative of effectiveness. Such criteria are usually identified through in-depth qualitative research. Such was the case with the above-referenced instruments. Nauss (1996) pointed out that all six were built upon the research from only two qualitative studies; the Ministry Study (MS) in 1957 was the basis for the MAS and PI, and the Readiness for Ministry Study (RMS) conducted by the Association of Theological Schools (ATS) in the mid-1970s was the basis for the development of the POM, TFM, and MEI. The CEI utilized both the MS and RMS studies in its development.

One concern with the above referenced instruments is the age of the qualitative data used in their development. As previously stated, the validated instruments being used to measure CE were developed from the qualitative research conducted for the MS as reported in Kling (1958) and the RMS as reported in Schuller, Strommen, and Brekke (1980). The social, cultural, and technological changes that have occurred since these studies were conducted have significantly altered clergy behaviors. For example, when the MS and RMS studies were conducted, communication from clergy consisted primarily of live preaching, print media, and phone calls. More than 40 years later, the ubiquitous presence of the Internet necessitates an online presence, as well as the utilization of social media by clergy members (Waters & Tindall 2010). Furthermore, these studies were conducted at a time when globalization was primarily an academic concept, rarely considered by the general public (James & Steger 2014). Today, globalization affects not just worldview paradigms, but also ecclesial organizational values. Most significant, it is reasonable to think the technological advancements and changing worldview paradigms that have occurred since the MS and RMS were conducted have also altered congregant perceptions of the behaviors and characteristics that contribute to CE. In other words, congregant perceptions of CE would be expected to be different in the early 21st century than they were in the middle to late 20th century. While it is true that some of the instruments developed from the MS (Nauss 1989, 1994) and RMS (Aleshire 1990) have been updated, the qualitative data that support these instruments is unchanged.

A second concern with the above referenced instruments is the sample used in the qualitative research to identify effective clergy behavior. Although the RMS continues to be the most extensive qualitative study of CE ever conducted (47 denominations), its sample was not truly representative of the clergy spectrum within the United States. Specifically, as described by Schuller, Strommen and Brekke (1980), the RMS was conducted through 200 seminaries that were part of the ATS. This eliminated denominational clergy/lay respondents not linked with such a seminary (e.g., almost one-half of those associated with the Southern Baptist Convention; Schuller, Strommen and Brekke 1980). Furthermore, only 16% (801 of 4,995) of the RMS respondents were part of what could be considered an evangelical denomination. There was no representation from a Pentecostal denomination. In contrast, the RMS contained significant representation from what are often referred to as mainline denominations and even included representation from groups that do not possess a Christian orthodoxy—Universalist and Jewish. Such a sample appears to have skewed the data in such a way that it reflected a traditionally liberal theology with an emphasis on social action behaviors on the part of clergy. Indeed, one of the eleven themes, *ministry to community and world*, emphasizes *aggressive political leadership* (cluster 18), *ecumenical pluralism* (cluster 8), and *development of community services* (cluster 13). Furthermore, clergy behaviors that prioritize evangelism (cluster 19) were viewed as *undesirable*. In short, the sample used to determine CE in the RMS did not accurately reflect the perceptions of those from more conservative faith traditions.

Based upon inadequacies in the above referenced CE instruments, the premise of this study was that an instrument built upon qualitative data reflective of 21st century ministry paradigms is needed. Such data did not exist until DeShon (2010) identified 64 personal and behavioral characteristics of clergy deemed to enhance effectiveness. The purpose of this study was to operationalize the characteristics identified by DeShon.

BACKGROUND

The idea of assessing clergy can be traced back to the 1st-century church (1 Tim. 3:1-7; Titus 1:7-9). By the end of the 1st century, the idea was fairly established that primary leadership at the local church level was being conducted by individual appointment to a permanent office (Guy 2004). This development was born more out of pragmatic response than intentional design. As the years passed and the church continued to expand into regions far from Jerusalem, some formal mechanism was needed to keep the church united in both relationship and doctrine. As stated by Guy, "Institutional containers were needed for the heady wine of the Spirit" (p. 21). With this development came an organizational component to the role of clergy that has remained to this day. While other lay leaders (e.g., deacons, elders) continued to serve within the churches, overall responsibility for a local congregation increasingly fell to appointed members of the clergy.

The position that the dichotomy between lay and clergy leaders diverged from the biblical standard may be valid. However, the rightness or wrongness of that divergence is not central to this study. The separation did occur and remains present in most forms of ecclesial organizational life today. Thus, the concept of CE as discussed in this study relates specifically to the senior leader of a local congregation. It should be noted that when referencing the senior leader of a local church, the terms *clergy*, *minister*, and *pastor* are treated as synonymous terms throughout this study.

Some of the earliest attempts to objectively understand CE in the modern era can be seen in Moxcey (1922). Articles published at the end of the 19th century and early 20th century described the fast-changing functions of the pastorate and discussed the need for a renewed training emphasis to enhance "executive ability" among clergy members (Moxcey 1922, p. 5). Standards for clergy behaviors focused on various abilities: sermon, pastoral (e.g., visitation), executive (e.g., administration, fundraising), and evangelistic.

Kolarik (1954) solicited qualitative data from 340 laypeople (both men and women) and 59 clergy, which resulted in the identification of more than 1,000 clergy behaviors considered to be related to CE. Later research consolidated these behaviors into 199 categories in 13 major areas. Nauss (1974) used this data to develop the Ministerial Function Scale (MFS), which consisted of 36 statements measuring pastoral care, counseling, interpersonal relationships, evangelism, religious education, preaching, the conduct of worship, and administrative activity. No other instruments were found that were developed using data from Kolarik. Similarly, no additional empirical studies were found that used this version of the MFS.

In the Ministry Study (MS), Kling (1958) collected qualitative data from 17 seminary faculty, 545 ministers, and 570 laymen that resulted in the identification of six dimensions of CE within the categories of organizational goals (internal and external) and activities (solitary, one-on-one, group, and administrative) of clergy. The specific dimensions of CE identified by Kling were priest/preacher, community/social involvement, administrator, personal/spiritual development, visitor/counselor, and teacher. Kling used this data to create the 30-item MAS, which was used by Nauss (1983). Nauss (1989) later added the dimension of evangelist based upon a study of 310 parish pastors in three districts of the Lutheran Church–Missouri Synod (LCMS). Nauss (1994) subsequently added the dimensions of teaching adults, working with children, and equipping members based upon a study of 421 pastors and congregations of the LCMS. The adapted MAS had 46 items that measured 10 dimensions. Bunn (1998) further adapted the MAS by expanding the instrument to 56 items measuring the same 10 dimensions. As reported by Nauss (1996), Klever and Dyble (1972) also revised the original MAS by adding an additional 15 statements deemed to be meaningful for ministry in order to create the PI. To date, no additional empirically validated instruments have been found that were developed using the MS.

The Readiness for Ministry Study (RMS) consisted of collecting qualitative data from pastors and church leaders from more than 200 seminaries with ties to the Association of Theological Schools (ATS). The final sample consisted of 4,995 participants who rated clergy on 444 criterion statements (Schuller, Strommen, & Brekke 1980). From this data, the original Profiles of Ministry (POM) instrument was created. It identified 64 characteristics within 11 themes. Probably the most significant aspect of the RMS was that, for the first time, personal characteristics of clergy were considered as appropriate measures of CE. Both Kolarik (1954) and Kling (1958) gave attention only to observable clergy behaviors.

In addition to the POM, the RMS has been used as the basis to develop three empirically validated instruments—the Ten Faces of Ministry (TFM), the Ministerial Effectiveness Inventory (MEI), and the Clergy Evaluation Instrument (CEI). In their survey of 5,000 Lutheran clergy and laity, Brekke, Strommen and Williams (1979) revised the POM to suit a Lutheran context. The resultant TFM used 461 items to identify 77 characteristics within 10 themes—five personal characteristics and five ministry skills. Majovski (1982) used eight of the 11 POM themes to develop the MEI (open affirming style, caring for persons, congregational leadership, theologian, personal faith, developing fellowship and worship, denominational awareness, and disqualifying characteristics). In addition to the 24 items associated with the eight themes, Majovski also added 35 items derived from United Methodist responses in the POM. The resultant 59 items in the MEI produce only a single score and do not identify individual behaviors or characteristics. The CEI was developed from a set of 431 items obtained from the POM, TFM, and MAS (Nauss, Schmiel & Sohns 1992). It was later reduced to 98 items that identified 20 themes—13 related to personal characteristics and ministry skills and 7 related to personal traits that diminish effectiveness.

Since Majovski (1982) developed the MEI, there have been 34 theses and dissertations written that sought to empirically assess CE through quantitative means. Table 1 identifies each study and the means utilized to measure CE. Of those, 11 (32%) used one of the validated instruments identified above—MEI (8), MAS (2), and POM (1). The challenges with these instruments have already been discussed. Four dissertations (12%) assessed leadership effectiveness among clergy using Bass and Avolio's (1995) Multifactor Leadership Questionnaire (MLQ). While the MLQ is quite appropriate for assessing leadership effectiveness as described within the context of transformational leadership theory, it does not adequately cover the unique role requirements for clergy members. Of the remaining 19 dissertations written since 1982, two (6%) used a non-validated scale, six (18%) were simply *rated* as effective with no quantifiable justification, and 11 (32%) used secondary criteria to assess CE (e.g., attendance, conversions, offerings, etc.). While primary criteria are specific observable *behaviors* on the part of the leader, secondary criteria are specific observable *consequences* of what the leader does. The challenge with secondary criteria is their diminished validity and reliability. For instance, is church size directly related to CE? In short, all dissertations written since 1982 have used questionable criteria for assessing CE.

Table 1. Theses and dissertations (34) written since the development of the MEI and the means utilized to measure clergy effectiveness

Validated scale (11)	MLQ (4)	Non-validated scale (2)	Rated (6)	Secondary criteria (11)
Barnett 2003 (MEI)				Adams 2013
Bunn 1998 (MAS)				Atchison 2009
Belcher 2002 (MEI)				Church 2012
Cardoza 2005 (MEI)				Drake 2003
Eaton 2002 (MEI)	Fulks 1994		Lichtman 1989	Ford 2015
Feaster 2015 (MEI)	Scuderi 2010	Corbett 2006	Pense 1996	Hagiya 2011
Hammond 2016 (MEI)	Vardaman 2013	Olbrych 2012	Rieder 1991	Jones 2005
Moy 1985 (MAS)	Wasberg 2013		Ross 1987	Oney 2009
Puls 2011 (MEI)			Swanson 1999	Pontius 1992
Wesemann 1995 (POM)			York 2016	Roth 2011
Wright 2004 (MEI)				Sandstrom 1991

With regard to peer-reviewed journal articles, only three empirical studies were found within the past 25 years that sought to assess CE through quantitative means. Butler and Herman (1999) and Puls, Ludden and Freemyer (2014) measured CE using the MEI. Carter (2009) developed the Pastoral Leadership Effectiveness Survey—a 23-item scale "generated from literature regarding pastoral leader effectiveness" (p. 266). Scale development in this manner is inconsistent with the *consensual approach*, which relies on qualitative data covering a wide range of behaviors associated with CE (Nauss 1996). While the quantity of empirical studies that assess CE in journal articles is lacking, the little that does exist is based upon CE instruments with particular shortcomings.

Relevant to this study, DeShon (2010) identified 64 characteristics within the domains of knowledge, skills, abilities, and personal characteristics (KSAPs) considered to be effectiveness enablers for clergy members from focus group interviews conducted with Michigan clergy belonging to the United Methodist Church (UMC). Table 2 identifies the sixty-four characteristics that were identified within the four domains. The KSAPs were subsequently generalized to a national sample of local church pastors that represented the diversity of pastors and churches existing in the UMC. To maximize the representativeness of the sample, a stratified sampling plan was developed where 15 local church pastors were randomly selected within each of the 63 conferences in the UMC. The final sample contained 935 local church pastors. After removing substantially incomplete or invalid responses from the data set, 341 local church pastors provided survey responses resulting in a 37% response rate. As reported by DeShon, this rate compares favorably with recent reviews of web-based survey response rates indicating a median response rate of 29%.

METHODOLOGY

The methodology used in this study closely followed the widely accepted steps of scale development outlined by DeVellis (2017). Those steps are (a) determine clearly what it is you want to measure, (b) generate an item pool, (c) determine the format for measurement, (d) have the initial item pool reviewed by experts, (e) consider inclusion of validation items, (f) administer items to a development sample, (g) evaluate the items, and (h) optimize scale length. Steps a-f will be discussed in this Methodology section. Steps g-h will be discussed in the following Results section.

Table 2. Knowledge, skills, abilities, and personal characteristics that contribute to clergy effectiveness identified by DeShon (2010)

Knowledge (12)	Skills (19)	Abilities (10)	Personal characteristics (22)
Administration Clerical Community demographics Community history Counseling principles Local church history Management principles Psychology Sociology Theology and scripture Training principles UMC doctrine	Active learning Active listening Conflict management Decision making Discernment Exegetical skills Goal setting and feedback Motivating others Multitasking Negotiation Oral communication Problem solving Public speaking Social perceptiveness Spiritual disciplines Teaching Teamwork Time management Written communication	Adaptability Attentional focus Creativity Idea fluency Inductive reasoning Intelligence Memorization Oral comprehension Reading comprehension Trust in God	Achievement orientation Attention to detail Authenticity Autonomy Balance Cooperation Dependability Empathy Initiative Integrity Leadership Learning orientation Openness Passion Patience Persistence Risk taking Self-awareness Self-control Social orientation Stress tolerance Willingness to seek help

Note: *Calling to ministry* was deemed to be relevant in each of the four domains and undergirds all of them.

While the construct of CE has varied dimensions, the focus of this study was quite specific (step a). Namely, the behaviors and characteristics of CE to be measured were the 64 characteristics that enhance CE as determined by DeShon (2010). As such, one to two items were developed for each characteristic (step b). Attention was given to item clarity, item length, reading level, semantics, and syntax. Only positive characteristics were used in order to avoid confusing respondents about the difference between the strength of their agreement with a statement and the strength of the attribute being measured.

A semantic differential scaling method was used to collect responses from the participants to their perceptions of the behaviors and characteristics of their senior pastor (step c). As described by DeVellis (2017), scales that consist of items that can be scored on a continuum are very compatible with a theoretical orientation like the one in this study. Study participants were asked to rank their pastor on the basis of observed behaviors. The ranking was based on a continuum from 1 (*never*) to 7 (*always*). Two examples of scale items follow:

My pastor is attentive and fully engaged when talking with other people.
    never— 1 2 3 4 5 6 7 —*always*
My pastor demonstrates a deep knowledge of the needs within our community.
    never— 1 2 3 4 5 6 7 —*always*

DeVellis (2017) provided three purposes for submitting the list of items for review by an expert panel (step d). First, the experts are able to rank the relevancy of each item to the construct being measured. Second, the experts can point to other aspects of the construct being measured that may have been missed. And third, the experts can evaluate the clarity and conciseness of the items. With regard to the relevancy of the items in this study, DeShon (2010) utilized focus groups and denominational leaders and collected data from pastors to establish the relevancy of the 64 characteristics related to CE. With regard to other aspects of CE that might have been missed, the focus of this study was solely on the 64 characteristics in DeShon's research. As such, an expert panel was used to assess the relevancy of just those items related to DeShon. The expert panel was also used to evaluate the clarity and conciseness of the items in the scale. The use of experts in this manner reduced item ambiguity, which, in turn, increased item reliability (DeVellis 2017). The expert panelists were asked to score each item on a scale of 1 (*least important*) to 5 (*most important*) as they deemed it relevant to CE. The combined scores for each item were then averaged, with scores below 3.5 deemed suitable for elimination. The panelists were also asked to identify items that were unclear, confusing, or awkwardly written and to propose alternatives. From the original list of 89 items, 15 items were eliminated leaving 74 items in the scale used in this study.

Under some circumstances, DeVellis (2017) recommended the use of validation items in scales (step e). The inclusion of such items is particularly relevant when scale respondents are self-rating or if "the phenomenon you are setting out to measure relates to other constructs" (DeVellis 2017, p. 137). The need for validation items in this scale did not apply in either circumstance. The scale was other-rated, and the construct of CE was not related to other constructs. As such, validation items were not included in the scale developed in this study.

A snowball sampling technique was used to obtain study participants (step f). Through numerous personal contacts, a total of 128 senior pastors were contacted by email with an invitation to participate in this study. Thirty pastors responded positively to the invitation and committed to sending their leaders a church-specific link to the 74-item survey. In fact, only 26 pastors actually sent the link to their leaders. From these 26 pastors, 953 church leaders (both staff and lay) were invited to participate in the anonymous study on a voluntary basis. Of these, 424 leaders submitted online responses (45% response rate). These leaders represented five different denominations: Assembly of God, Foursquare, Missionary Church, United Methodist Church (UMC), and Wesleyan. In order to minimize the possibility of a *halo effect*, responses from leaders who had been in a leadership position for less than 1 year were removed from the data sample. Twenty-seven participants were removed, leaving a final sample size of 397 participants ($N = 397$). This number exceeds the required minimum ratio of five participants for each item as described by DeVellis (2017).

When a sufficient number of responses had been obtained, the responses were downloaded to an Excel spreadsheet where the 27 participant responses described above were removed and demographic data related to the pastor and church was added. The following information was then converted to nominal data: pastor name, denominational affiliation, gender, age, race, ethnicity, level of income, ministry role, and number of years in leadership role. The responses were then uploaded into SPSS V23.0 for further analysis. Table 3 describes the study participants.

RESULTS

As discussed by DeVellis (2017), the next step (g) in the process of scale development was to "evaluate the performance of the individual items so that appropriate ones can be identified to constitute the scale" (p. 139). Ideally, an item has a high correlation with the true score of the latent variable. A reflection of the relationship to the true score can be observed in the relationship among items. The higher the correlation among items, the higher the reliability of the individual items. The higher the reliability of the individual items, the higher reliability of the scale as a whole.

Table 3. Demographic profile of participants (N = 397)

Table 3. Continued

Demographics	n	%
Gender		
Female	213	53.7
Male	184	46.3
Age		
18-29	26	6.5
30-39	42	10.6
40-49	80	20.2
50-59	110	27.7
60-69	87	21.9
70+	52	13.1
Annual household income		
< $20,000	14	3.5
$20,000 to $34,999	32	8.1
$35,000 to $49,999	38	9.6
$50,000 to $74,999	97	24.4
$75,000 to $99,999	82	20.7
$100,000 to $149,999	65	16.4
> $150,000	69	17.4
Race (Hispanic, Latino, or Spanish?)		
No	382	96.2
Yes	15	3.8
Ethnicity		
White	344	86.6
Black or African American	33	8.3
Asian Pacific Islander	8	2.0
American Indian or Alaskan native	3	0.8
Mexican American	3	0.8
American	1	0.3

continues in next column

Demographics	n	%
Asian Pacific Islander, Black or African American, White	1	0.3
Asian Pacific Islander, White	1	0.3
Blended	1	0.3
Human	1	0.3
Puerto Rican	1	0.3
Current leadership role		
Ministry lay leader (e.g., youth)	107	27.0
Lay leader without a specific role	96	24.2
Part-time volunteer staff member	65	16.4
Full-time paid staff member	51	12.8
Part-time paid staff member	31	7.8
Other (various designations)	21	5.3
Full-time volunteer staff member	12	3.0
Member of governing body (e.g., board, elder)	11	2.8
Small group leader	3	0.8
Total number of years in leadership role		
1 year up to 3 years	74	18.6
3 years up to 5 years	82	20.7
5 years up to 7 years	49	12.3
7 years up to 10 years	48	12.1
10 years up to 15 years	48	12.1
> 15 years	96	24.2
Denominational representation of participants		
Foursquare	233	58.7
Missionary Church	89	22.4
Assembly of God	55	13.9
UMC	10	2.5
Wesleyan	10	2.5

A review of the correlation matrix revealed a large number of high correlations between the items, most of them greater than .50. In such a situation, Brown (2009) suggested using an oblique rotation because it assumes the factors are also correlated. Thus, a factor analysis was performed on the data using an oblique rotation (direct oblimin). However, a review of the subsequent correlation matrix showed that only one of the correlations had a score higher than .32. Brown posited that such scores were an indication that the factors had not achieved *simple structure*. Thus, an orthogonal rotation (varimax) should be performed to determine if it achieved a more interpretable form of simple structure. Hair, Black, Babin, and Anderson (2010) substantiated this assessment by adding that an orthogonal method was preferred "when the research goal is data reduction" (p. 116). As such, a varimax rotation was chosen because it minimizes the number of variables that have high loadings on each factor. In short, it simplifies the interpretation of the factors (Brown 2009).

In addition to item correlation, the data were deemed suitable for factor analysis through two other measures. First, the Kaiser–Meyer–Olkin (KMO) measure of sampling adequacy was .967, exceeding the score of .6, which is deemed to indicate a sufficient sample size for factor analysis (Hair, Black, Babin and Anderson 2010). Second, Bartlett's test of sphericity is significant at .000. Hair, Black, Babin and Anderson (2010) maintained that a score of $p < .05$ indicates that sufficient correlations exist among the variables to proceed with factor analysis.

Principal Component Analysis (PCA) was performed on the data with varimax rotation. Small coefficients below .40 were suppressed in order to eliminate borderline factor loading. Results showed 10 factors having total eigenvalues greater than 1.0, the minimum value for seeing the number of factors identified in the factor analysis (DeVellis 2017). However, the rotated component matrix revealed that Item 2 did not load on any factor and that 19 items cross-loaded on at least two factors (3, 4, 6, 23, 26, 27, 32, 39, 44, 45, 54, 55, 57, 60, 63, 65, 66, 70, and 72). As stated by Hair, Black, Babin and Anderson (2010), such an item is a "candidate for deletion" (p. 119) in order to achieve simple structure.

Following the removal of the 20 items identified above, a second factor analysis was performed on the remaining 54 items using the same criteria as before. Results showed seven factors having total eigenvalues greater than 1.0, suggesting a seven-factor model. However, similar to the first factor analysis, four items cross-loaded on at least two factors (39, 42, 49, and 54), and Items 27 and 35 did not load on any factor.

Following the removal of the six items identified above, a third factor analysis was performed on the remaining 48 items using the same criteria as before. Results showed six factors having total eigenvalues greater than 1.0, suggesting a six-factor model. However, similar to the previous two factor analyses, Item 37 cross-loaded on two factors, and Item 44 did not load on any factors.

Following the removal of the two items identified above, a fourth factor analysis was performed on the remaining 46 items using the same criteria as before. Results showed six factors having eigenvalues greater than 1.0, again suggesting a six-factor model. Additionally, all of the items were significantly loaded on at least one factor (> .4), and none of the items cross-loaded on two or more factors.

Based on the elimination of no-load and cross-load items, one might decide to move forward with a six-factor model. However, a closer look at Factors 4 and 5 showed that both factors loaded only two items, and Factor 6 loaded only one item. As stated by DeVellis (2017), one of the goals of factor analysis is to "define the substantive content or meaning of the factors" (p. 155). Thus, the question arises as to the number of items needed to provide substantive content to each factor. Hair, Black, Babin and Anderson (2010) acknowledged that some studies are conducted with just one item representing a single factor. However, "good practice dictates a minimum of three items per factor" (Hair, Black, Babin and Anderson 2010, p. 676). In such a scenario, Factors 4, 5, and 6 would be removed. The scree plot in Figure 1 appeared to substantiate the idea that this model was best served with three factors, not six. As such, Factor 4 (Items 42, 43), Factor 5 (Items 44, 45), and Factor 6 (Item 46) were removed.

Figure 1. Scree plot showing a three-factor model

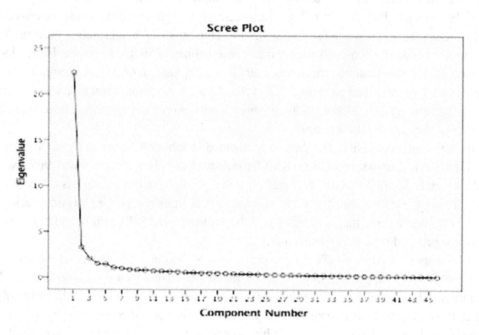

Final factor analysis revealed a three-factor model for assessing CE consisting of 41 total items. Factor 1 had 31 items, Factor 2 had six items, and Factor 3 had four items. The corresponding Cronbach's alpha scores for each of the factors was sufficient (see Table 4). As described by DeVellis (2017), a Cronbach's alpha score between .70 and .80 is respectable, and a score between .80 and .90 is very good. DeVellis added that a score above .90 might make the factor a candidate for shortening.

Table 4. Cronbach's alpha scores for three-factor model

Factor	Cronbach's alpha	n
1	0.98	31
2	0.88	6
3	0.73	4

Table 5. Reliability of final three scales

Scales	Cronbach's alpha	n
Socially adept	0.94	5
Professional competence	0.89	5
Inclination to lead	0.73	4

The final step in scale development is the optimization of the scale's length (step h). As discussed by DeVellis (2017), a tension exists between minimizing the length of the scale in consideration of respondents (i.e., remove items) and increasing the length of the scale in order to increase reliability (i.e., add items). The Cronbach's alpha for Factor 1 was very high at .98, making it a candidate for item reduction. This premise was supported by the significantly larger number of items that loaded on the factor compared to Factors 2 and 3.

In order to optimize Factor 1, a reliability test was run on the items with the 10 highest factor loadings. The 10-item scale had a Cronbach's alpha score of .96. If Item Deleted scores were the same for each item, the Cronbach's alpha was .96. Since the reliability of Factor 1 remained very high even when reduced to 10 items, the same reliability test was applied to the items with the five highest factor loadings. The five-item scale had a Cronbach's alpha score of .94. If Item Deleted scores varied, the Cronbach's alpha varied between .91 to .93. Although the Cronbach's alpha score remained greater than .90, it was determined to stop the optimizing process for Factor 1 at five items given the similarity in size to Factor 2 and Factor 3.

Factor 2 had a Cronbach's alpha score of .88, which is "very good" (DeVellis 2017, p. 145). However, Item 37 had a factor loading of only .43, significantly lower than the other five items and barely surpassing the .40 minimum established in the analysis. Furthermore, the Cronbach's alpha of If Item Deleted increased the scale's reliability to .89 if this item was deleted. As such, Item 37 was removed from this factor, making Factor 2 a five-item scale. All four items were retained for Factor 3.

FINAL CLERGY EFFECTIVENESS SCALE

Upon completing the optimization of Factors 1 and 2, the resulting 14-item CE scale had three factors—Factor 1 had five items, Factor 2 had five items, and Factor 3 had four items. The 14-item scale, as a whole, had a KMO measure of sampling adequacy of .872, exceeding the score of .6. Bartlett's test of sphericity was significant at .000 ($p < .05$; Hair, Black, Babin and Anderson 2010). The final three factors can each be considered as individual scales. All three scales represent an observable *variable*—together constituting the latent variable of CE. In other words, one can measure the three observable factors and infer their effect upon the latent variable of CE.

Together, the five items in Factor 1 are reflective of the leader's ability to be socially adept, the five items in Factor 2 are reflective of the leader's professional competence, and the four items in Factor 3 are reflective of the leader's inclination to lead. As seen in Table 5, the Cronbach's alpha for inclination to lead fell within the *respectable* category (between .70 and .80) as described by DeVellis (2017), professional competence fell within the *very good* category (between .80 and .90), and socially adept scored even higher. In short, all three scales can be deemed reliable as defined by both DeVellis (2017) and Hair, Black, Babin and Anderson (2010). Table 6 shows the final 14-item scale.

DISCUSSION

This study was predicated on the premise that a new instrument is needed to measure clergy effectiveness (CE)—one that provided content validity and reliability for empirical research. Existing instruments are significantly outdated and are no longer representative of the characteristics of CE in the 21st century. Furthermore, these same existing instruments were developed with qualitative data sorely lacking representation from those with an evangelical paradigm. Thus, the purpose of this study was to develop an instrument to measure CE by operationalizing the 64 characteristics deemed to enhance CE identified by DeShon (2010).

Table 6. Clergy effectiveness scale

Construct	Item
Socially Adept	In social settings, my pastor is aware of the emotions and behaviors of others. My pastor is socially perceptive. My pastor is adaptable. My pastor motivates others by relating to people in a way that inspires them to do their best. My pastor functions well as a member of a team.
Professional Competence	To what extent do you believe your pastor has knowledge of theology? To what extent do you believe your pastor has knowledge of the biblical text? To what extent do you believe your pastor has knowledge of the principles of teaching? To what extent do you believe your pastor has knowledge of church doctrine? My pastor communicates the meaning of Scripture and other religious documents in a manner that is comprehensible to others.
Inclination to Lead	My pastor is goal oriented. My pastor shows initiative in taking on challenges and accomplishing goals. My pastor is willing to assume a leadership role when necessary. My pastor will take risks if the situation requires it.

This study builds upon the work of DeShon (2010), who identified 64 characteristics deemed to enhance CE that fell within the four categories of knowledge, skills, abilities, and personal characteristics. When comparing the final 14 items in the Clergy Effectiveness Scale (CES) developed in this study to DeShon's characteristics, similar groupings were observed. Four of the five items in socially adept have their basis in DeShon's category of skills (the remaining item from abilities), four of the five items in professional competence have their basis in DeShon's category of knowledge (the remaining item from skills), and all four of the items in inclination to lead have their basis in DeShon's category of personal characteristics. These associations suggest that the instrument developed in this study has remained consistent with the results originally determined by DeShon.

One of the critiques of the extensive Readiness for Ministry Study (RMS) was that it was not "geared to investigate a style of leadership that contributes to the growth of congregations numerically and spiritually" (Hubbard and McLemore 1980, p. 393). This criticism is supported when one considers the items used in the Ministerial Effectiveness Inventory (MEI) (Majovski 1982). Within the MEI, leadership is positioned more as a *posture* toward people (e.g., open, flexible) rather than one's capacity to influence people toward the fulfillment of a missional mandate. In contrast, the construct *Inclination to Lead* gives attention to goal orientation, taking initiative, willingness to lead, and risk-taking—all necessary for CE in the 21st century (Butler and Herman 1999; Scholl 2009). Similarly, the concept of teamwork is nonexistent in the MEI, as is the concept of emotional intelligence, both contributors toward CE today (Higley 2007; Oney 2009). In contrast, the construct *Socially Adept* gives consideration to emotional intelligence, social awareness, adaptability, ability to motivate others, and working in a team environment. The one area where overlap can be found is related to the construct *Professional Competence*. Professional Competence and the MEI both give attention to concepts like biblical knowledge, doctrine, denominational knowledge, and effective communication.

When the fourth and final factor analysis was conducted, the result was a six-factor model consisting of 46 items. Of those items, 31 (67%) were loaded on one factor. Consideration was given to the idea that this scale might be best served as a single-factor model, especially since the first factor accounted for 48.51% of the total variance. From a conceptual standpoint, this option had statistical merit (Fuchs and Diamantopoulos 2009). However, this consideration was dismissed for both pragmatic and empirical reasons. From a pragmatic standpoint, the complexities within the role of clergy are such that one would be hard-pressed to conceptualize the role within a single factor. With regard to this study, the constructs of *Professional Competence* and *Inclination to Lead* would be lost. This reality is at the heart of the empirical reason for not pursuing a single-factor model. As stated by Hair, Black, Babin and Anderson (2010), "If too few factors are used, then the correct structure is not revealed, and important dimensions may be omitted" (p. 111). Ultimately, a three-factor model was pursued because the data did not support a single-factor model.

Of some concern is the low reliability of the scale *Inclination to Lead*. The Cronbach's alpha for the scale is .73, which is on the low end of *respectable* (.70 to .80) as described by DeVellis (2017). The reliability of this scale is significantly lower than both socially adept (.94) and professional competence (.89). Additional research is needed to strengthen this scale.

SIGNIFICANCE OF THE STUDY

The results of this study are significant for several reasons. First, from the perspective of scholarly research, a valid, reliable, and contemporary instrument is now available for CE research. The CES developed in this study is much shorter (14 items) than the MEI used most frequently in empirical research to date (59 items). As discussed by DeVellis (2017), fewer items may be an inducement to increase participant responses. Similarly, it is hoped the shortness of the CES will appeal to future researchers such that they will refrain from using secondary criteria to measure CE. Of even more potential significance to researchers is that a valid and reliable scale is now available that is specific to CE. Because such an option had not been available in the recent past, some researchers measured *leadership* effectiveness among clergy. In other words, some have measured transformational leadership behaviors (Carter 2009; Fulks 1994; Manners 2008), authentic leadership behaviors (Puls 2011), or servant leadership behaviors (Scuderi 2010) as they relate to the effectiveness of clergy. The CES will now allow researchers to give exclusive attention to those behaviors and characteristics deemed to be important specifically to clergy.

This study has less immediate significance to the practitioner. DeVellis (2017) maintained that a statistical difference exists between an instrument that will be used in *group data* and one that will be used for *individual assessment*. Specifically, "Individual assessment, especially when important decisions rest on that assessment, demand a much higher standard. Instruments that are intended for individual diagnostic, employment, academic placement, or other important purposes should probably have considerably higher reliabilities" (DeVellis 2017, p. 146). Cronbach's alpha scores in the mid-.90s were recommended. Within this context, only one of the CES scales, *Socially Adept* (.94), would qualify for such a high standard. Both *Professional Competence* (.89) and *Inclination to Lead* (.73) fall below the desired threshold. As such, while this instrument may not be helpful for individual assessment, it is ideal for group research. The fulfillment of the initial intended goal will need to come from subsequent research.

It is hoped that the instrument developed in this study will ultimately serve senior pastors and church leadership by providing an objective tool for substantive conversations about expectations of clergy performance. Personal experience has shown that both pastors and church leaders often have divergent views of the roles and duties of the senior pastor. The opportunity for healthy discussions can be greatly enhanced through the use of an objective instrument that gives attention to the various behaviors and characteristics of an effective senior pastor. The pastor and church leadership are then able to discuss the priority of these behaviors and characteristics in order to confirm (or gain) both clarity and unity of the appropriate leadership for the church.

LIMITATIONS OF THE STUDY

There are four general limitations to this study: (a) the qualitative research upon which this study was based came from a single denomination; (b) the instrument developed in this study was to assess clergy *in-ministry*, as opposed to predicting effectiveness of those just entering into pastoral ministry; (c) the instrument developed in this study could only identify the characteristics and behaviors of clergy, not determine the subjective aspects of assessment; and (d) in general, all instruments and/or scales have limitations. Upon completion of the study, a few other limitations have also been identified.

First, there were subjective aspects to the optimization of the scales, specifically the removal of Factors 4, 5, and 6. While their removal was statistically justifiable, they did represent two additional dimensions of perceived CE. Of particular note was Factor 6, which contained the single item, *To what extent do you believe your pastor feels called to pastoral ministry?* DeShon (2010) maintained that of the 64 characteristics of CE, this one was deemed most important in the qualitative research. The CES does not account for this characteristic.

Second, while participants in this study represented 13 states from across the country, the data sample came entirely from within the United States. The CES would have benefitted from a broader representation of cultures, specifically non-Western cultures. This is an area for future research.

Third, significant efforts were made to obtain responses from racially diverse participants. Even so, almost 87% of the respondents described themselves as White. Some of the lack of representation may be due to the snowball methodology used to identify pastors willing to participate. Since the researcher is White, many denominational associations are also White. A willingness to participate in the study from a group representing a large number of African American pastors came after the data collection process had been completed.

Fourth, of even more concern is the lack of gender diversity among participating pastors. Here, too, some of the lack of representation may be due to the snowball methodology used to identify pastors willing to participate in the study as described above. Only one female senior pastor was known to the researcher. She, too, agreed to participate only after data collection had been completed. Even so, the simple fact is that there are too few female senior pastors, especially within many evangelical groups. For some, it is a matter of theological understanding, and, for others, it is a matter of cultural preference. Regardless, this too is an area for future research.

Finally, this study is predicated on the idea that a difference exists between a *good* pastor and an *effective* pastor. A good pastor is one who manifests the behaviors and characteristics generally expected of a pastor. An effective pastor is one who is able to facilitate the movement of the organization toward agreed upon goals and objectives. However, as pointed out by Nauss (1996), the perception of CE will vary from one congregation to the next. In other words, the perception of clergy behaviors and characteristics that enhance effectiveness will be different in a church with 100 attendees than they will be in a church with 1,000 attendees. In addition, an instrument to measure CE can only *identify* the extent of behaviors and characteristics exhibited by a pastor at the time of the assessment. The key to an assessment of CE rests in the *analysis* of the assessment results by the pastor and church leadership. The intent of this study was to develop an instrument that will measure the perceived behaviors and characteristics that are deemed to enhance a pastor's ability to positively affect the organization. It would then be up to the pastor and church leadership to assess whether those behaviors and characteristics are aligned with the needs and expectations of the congregation.

IMPLICATIONS FOR FUTURE RESEARCH

As has already been mentioned, future research should include the potential strengthening of the scale *Inclination to Lead*. It is quite probable that additional and/or different items will improve its reliability. Also, the idea of expanding research into other cultures, racial groups, and female senior pastors has also been suggested in order to better improve the validity and reliability of the CES instrument.

The greatest need for future research identified in this study is the development of an instrument suitable for individual assessment. Almost without exception, the participating pastors in this study expressed their hope for objective feedback from this study. While they were informed that such feedback would not be available due to the factor analysis process, their comments clearly demonstrated a significant unmet need among many pastors today. They want objective feedback—information that will help them improve the quality and expand the capacity of their effectiveness as pastors. Future research should include the utilization of the 64 characteristics of CE enhancers identified by DeShon (2010) in the development of an instrument suitable for individual assessment.

CONCLUSION

This study was designed to develop an instrument to measure CE by operationalizing the 64 characteristics deemed to enhance CE identified by DeShon (2010). Four hundred twenty-four church leaders, both staff and lay, submitted responses via a 74-item online survey. Twenty-seven responses were eliminated to minimize a halo effect ($N = 397$). Factor analysis (principal component analysis [PCA]) was performed, and a six-factor model was observed, accounting for almost 69% of the variance. However, factor optimization resulted in a final three-factor model that accounted for 71% of the variance. The three factors were labeled *Socially Adept*, *Professional Competence*, and *Inclination to Lead* and were shown to have high reliability. The 14-item, three-factor CES provides researchers with a relatively short, contemporary, valid, and reliable tool for future research related to clergy effectiveness.

ACKNOWLEDGMENT

This research received no specific grant from any funding agency in the public, commercial, or not-for-profit sectors.

REFERENCES

Adams, A. W. (2014). *Shepherd leadership of Church of God pastors and how this relates to ministerial effectiveness* (Doctoral dissertation). Available from ProQuest Dissertations and Theses database. (UMI No. 3570373)

Aleshire, D. (1990). ATS profiles of ministry project. In R. A. Hunt, J. Hinkle, Jr., & H. N. Malony (Eds.), Clergy assessment and career development (pp. 97–103). Academic Press.

Atchison, B. J. G. (2009). *A study of African American pastors' method of entry into the ministry and pastoral success* (Doctoral dissertation). Available from ProQuest Dissertations and Theses database. (ProQuest No. 10258492)

Barnett, D. C. (2003). *A comparative analysis of critical competencies of the assessment of ministry effectiveness* (Doctoral dissertation). Available from ProQuest Dissertations and Theses database. (UMI No. 3102040)

Bass, B. M., & Avolio, B. J. (1995). *MLQ Multifactor leadership questionnaire for research*. Mindgarden.

Belcher, G. D. (2002). *The relationship of mentoring to ministerial effectiveness among pastors of the Southern Baptist Convention* (Doctoral dissertation). Available from ProQuest Dissertations and Theses database. (UMI No. 3048643)

Brekke, M. L., Strommen, M. P., & Williams, D. (1979). *Ten faces of ministry*. Augsburg Press.

Brown, J. D. (2009). Choosing the right type of rotation in PCA and EFA. *Shiken: JALT Testing and Evaluation SIG Newsletter, 13*(3), 20–25.

Bunn, T. P. E. (1998). *A study of the difference between senior pastors and laity perceptions of senior pastoral effectiveness* (Doctoral dissertation). Available from ProQuest Dissertations and Theses database. (UMI No. 304451491)

Butler, D. M., & Herman, R. D. (1999). Effective ministerial leadership. *Nonprofit Management & Leadership, 9*(3), 229–239. doi:10.1002/nml.9302

Cardoza, F. I. I. (2005). *Perceptions of ministerial effectiveness by leaders of urban churches in the Southern Baptist Convention* (Doctoral dissertation). Available from ProQuest Dissertations and Theses database. (UMI No. 3167902)

Carter, J. (2009). Transformational leadership and pastoral leader effectiveness. *Pastoral Psychology, 58*(3), 261–271. doi:10.100711089-008-0182-6

Church, D. M. (2012). *Leadership style and organizational growth: A correlational study* (Doctoral dissertation). Available from ProQuest Dissertations and Theses database. (UMI No. 3507222)

Corbett, J. C. (2006). *The personal and spiritual characteristics of effective pastoral leaders* (Doctoral dissertation). Available from ProQuest Dissertations and Theses database. (UMI No. 3437177)

DeShon, R. P. (2010). *Clergy effectiveness: National survey results*. Unpublished internal report, General Board of Higher Education and Ministry: The United Methodist Church. Retrieved from https://www.gbhem.org/clergy/boards-ordained-ministry

DeVellis, R. F. (2017). *Scale development: Theory and applications* (4th ed.). Sage.

Drake, T. G. (2003). *The impact of leadership development training experiences on the development of senior pastors' effectiveness as leaders of member churches in an American, evangelical denomination* (Doctoral dissertation). Available from ProQuest Dissertations and Theses database. (UMI No. 3082717)

Eaton, K. J. (2002). *A study of the relationship between 16PF personality factors and ministerial effectiveness in a sample of Anglican clergy* (Masters thesis). Available from ProQuest Dissertations and Theses database. (UMI No. MQ72148)

Feaster, W. B. (2015). *The relationship between time management behaviors and ministerial effectiveness among ministers of education in the state of Texas* (Doctoral dissertation). Available from ProQuest Dissertations and Theses database. (UMI No. 3716280)

Ford, R. (2015). *Factors influencing clergy leadership effectiveness* (Doctoral dissertation). Available from ProQuest Dissertations and Theses database. (UMI No. 3715502)

Fuchs, C., & Diamantopoulos, A. (2009). Using single-item measures for construct measurement in management research: Conceptual issues and application guidelines. *Betriebswirtschaft, 69*(2), 195–210.

Fulks, J. L. (1994). *Transformational leadership and its relationship to success in developing new churches* (Doctoral dissertation). Available from ProQuest Dissertations and Theses database. (UMI No. 9505499)

Guy, L. (2004). *Introducing early Christianity: A topical survey of its life, beliefs and practices*. Inter-Varsity Press.

Hagiya, G. J. (2011). *Significant traits, characteristics, and qualities of high effective United Methodist Church clergy* (Doctoral dissertation). Available from ProQuest Dissertations and Theses database. (UMI No. 3468837)

Haight, E. S. D. (1980). *Psychological criteria for the selection of ministerial candidates* (Doctoral dissertation). Available from ProQuest Dissertations and Theses database. (UMI No. 8026819)

Hair, J. F. Jr, Black, W. C., Babin, B. J., & Anderson, R. E. (2010). *Multivariate data analysis* (7th ed.). Prentice Hall.

Hammond, P. B. (2016). *Wesleyan ministerial study programs' relationship to ministerial effectiveness of Wesleyan pastoral leaders* (Doctoral dissertation). Available from ProQuest Dissertations and Theses database. (ProQuest No. 10129765)

Higley, W. J. (2007). *The relationship between the lead pastor's emotional intelligence and pastoral leadership team effectiveness* (Doctoral dissertation). Available from ProQuest Dissertations and Theses database. (UMI No. 3264648)

Hubbard, D. A., & McLemore, C. W. (1980). Evangelical churches. In D. S. Schuller, M. P. Strommen, & M. L. Brekke (Eds.), *Ministry in America: A report and analysis, based on an in-depth survey of 47 denominations in the United States and Canada, with interpretations by 18 experts*. Harper and Row.

James, P., & Steger, M. B. (2014). A genealogy of "globalization": The career of a concept. *Globalizations, 11*(4), 417–434. doi:10.1080/14747731.2014.951186

Jones, K. E. (2005). *A quantitative study: Leadership attributes of effective ministers* (Doctoral dissertation). Available from ProQuest Dissertations and Theses database. (UMI No. 3194292)

Klever, G., & Dyble, J. (1972). *Report to ad hoc ministry study committee*. Unpublished manuscript, Office of Research, Board of Christian Education, United Presbyterian Church in the U.S.A., Philadelphia, PA.

Kling, F. R. (1958). A study of testing as related to the ministry. *Religious Education (Chicago, Ill.), 53*(3), 243–248. doi:10.1080/0034408580530301

Kolarik, J. M. (1954). *A study of the critical requirements of the Lutheran ministry* (Doctoral dissertation). Available from ProQuest Dissertations and Theses database. (UMI No. 302015094)

Lichtman. (1989). *Ministerial effectiveness as a function of personal preferences and job expectancies* (Doctoral dissertation). Fuller Theological Seminary.

Majovski, L. F. (1982). *The role of psychological assessment in ministerial selection* (Doctoral dissertation). Available from ProQuest Dissertations and Theses database. (UMI No. 8223416)

Manners, A. T. (2008). *Influence of transformational, autocratic, democratic, and laissez-faire leadership principles on the effectiveness of religious leaders* (Doctoral dissertation). Available from ProQuest Dissertations and Theses database. (UMI No. 3370948)

Moxcey, M. E. (1922). *Some qualities associated with success in the Christian ministry*. Teachers College, Columbia University.

Moy, A. C. (1985). *The relationship between leadership and ministerial effectiveness* (Doctoral dissertation). Fuller Theological Seminary.

Nauss, A. H. (1972). Problems in measuring ministerial effectiveness. *Journal for the Scientific Study of Religion, 11*(2), 141–151. doi:10.2307/1384926

Nauss, A. H. (1974). The relation of pastoral mobility to effectiveness. *Review of Religious Research, 15*(2), 80–86. doi:10.2307/3510237

Nauss, A. H. (1983). Seven profiles of effective ministers. *Review of Religious Research, 24*(4), 334–346. doi:10.2307/3511012

Nauss, A. H. (1989). Leadership styles of effective ministry. *Journal of Psychology and Theology, 17*(1), 59–67. doi:10.1177/009164718901700109

Nauss, A. H. (1994). Ministerial effectiveness in ten functions. *Religious Research Association, 36*(1), 58–69. doi:10.2307/3511652

Nauss, A. H. (1996). Assessing ministerial effectiveness: A review of measures and their use. In J. M. Greer, D. O. Moberg, & M. L. Lynn (Eds.), *Research in the social scientific study of religion* (Vol. 7, pp. 221–252). JAI Press.

Nauss, A. H., Schmiel, D., & Sohns, W. (1992). *Clergy evaluation instrument*. Board for Higher Education Services, The Lutheran Church-Missouri Synod.

Olbrych, J. C. (2012). *The bonds of affection: Assessing clergy leadership effectiveness using adult attachment theory* (Doctoral dissertation). Available from ProQuest Dissertations and Theses database. (UMI No. 3529297)

Oney, R. M. (2009). *Exploring the causal relationship of emotional intelligence to clergy leadership effectiveness* (Doctoral dissertation). Retrieved from Regent University database. (UMI No. 3392554)

Pense, B. C. (1996). *Leadership styles and pastoral effectiveness* (Masters thesis). Available from ProQuest Dissertations and Theses database. (ProQuest No. 1380374)

Pontius, K. D. (1992). *A descriptive study of motivational and personality characteristics in evangelical pastors* (Doctoral dissertation). Available from ProQuest Dissertations and Theses database. (UMI No. 9307480)

Puls, T. R. (2011). *Authentic leadership and its relationship to ministerial effectiveness* (Doctoral dissertation). Available from ProQuest Dissertations and Theses database. (UMI No. 3498652)

Puls, T. R., Ludden, L. L., & Freemyer, J. (2014). Authentic leadership and its relationship to ministerial effectiveness. *The Journal of Applied Christian Leadership*, 8(1), 55–75.

Rieder, K. L. (1991). *Vocational interests as predictors of effectiveness in the ministry* (Doctoral dissertation). Available from ProQuest Dissertations and Theses database. (UMI No. 9217952)

Ross, D. L. (1987). *Similarity among ratings of ministerial effectiveness and its relationship to interpersonal responsiveness* (Doctoral dissertation). Available from ProQuest Dissertations and Theses database. (UMI No. 8801949)

Roth, J. (2011). *The relationship between emotional intelligence and pastor leadership in turnaround churches* (Doctoral dissertation). Available from ProQuest Dissertations and Theses database. (UMI No. 3487845)

Sandstrom, C. R. (1991). *The components of empowerment and personality of effective clergy leaders* (Doctoral dissertation). Available from ProQuest Dissertations and Theses database. (UMI No. 9129207)

Scholl, M. L. (2009). *The relationship between church effectiveness and pastoral management behavior* (Doctoral dissertation). Available from ProQuest Dissertations and Theses database. (UMI No. 3385075)

Schuller, D. S., Strommen, M. P., & Brekke, M. L. (Eds.). (1980). *Ministry in America: A report and analysis, based on an in-depth survey of 47 denominations in the United States and Canada, with interpretations by 18 experts*. Harper and Row.

Scuderi, N. F. (2010). *Servant leadership and transformational leadership in church organizations* (Doctoral dissertation). Available from ProQuest Dissertations and Theses database. (UMI No. 3413541)

Swanson, H. P. (1999). *Pastoral effectiveness: A study of differences among comparison groups of Seventh-day Adventist clergy* (Doctoral dissertation). Available from ProQuest Dissertations and Theses database. (UMI No. 9937628)

Vardaman, D. L. (2013). *Leading change: Exploring the relationship between transformational, transactional, and change-oriented leadership and their impact on leadership effectiveness among pastors in a protestant denomination in the mid-western United States* (Doctoral dissertation). Available from ProQuest Dissertations and Theses database. (UMI No. 3613541)

Wasberg, G. D. (2013). *Differentiation of self and leadership effectiveness in Christian clergy: A mixed methods study* (Doctoral dissertation). Available from ProQuest Dissertations and Theses database. (UMI No. 3602885)

Waters, R. D., & Tindall, N. T. J. (2010). Marketing churches on the Internet: An analysis of the dialogic potential of Christian web sites. *Journal of Philanthropy and Marketing*, *15*(4), 369–381. doi:10.1002/nvsm.400

Wesemann, K. R. (1995). *Predicting ministerial effectiveness* (Doctoral dissertation). Available from ProQuest Dissertations and Theses database. (UMI No. 9536609)

Wright, S. D. (2004). *The social phenomenon of transformational leadership among clergy* (Doctoral dissertation). Available from ProQuest Dissertations and Theses database. (UMI No. 3111407)

York, D. E. (2016). *Not Saul's armor: Introversion and effective pastoral leadership* (Doctoral dissertation). Available from ProQuest Dissertations and Theses database. (ProQuest No. 10156648)

ADDITIONAL READING

Bergquist, K. E. (2014). *Finding the right fit: Using organizational culture and emotional intelligence in the lead pastor search process* [Unpublished doctoral dissertation]. Assemblies of God Theological Seminary, Springfield, MO, United States.

Lancaster, J. T. (2020). *Effective church leadership through emotional intelligence* [Unpublished doctoral dissertation]. Liberty University, Lynchburg, VA, United States.

Malphurs, A. (1995). *Maximizing your effectiveness: How to discover and develop your divine design.* Baker Books.

Mueller, C. W., & McDuff, E. (2004). Clergy-congregation mismatches and clergy job satisfaction. *Journal for the Scientific Study of Religion*, *43*(2), 261–273. doi:10.1111/j.1468-5906.2004.00231.x

Nathan, M. (2012). *Pastoral leadership: A guide to improving your management skills.* Taylor & Francis.

Oswald, R. M., West, J. L., & Guzmán, N. (2018). *Emotional intelligence for religious leaders.* Rowman & Littlefield.

Owens, B. F. (1992). *Ministerial effectiveness in multi-church charges* [Unpublished doctoral dissertation]. Fuller Theological Seminary, Pasadena, CA, United States.

KEY TERMS AND DEFINITIONS

Clergy Behavior: The observable actions and tasks carried out by clergy in the preformance of their duties.

Clergy Characteristics: The observable attitudes, mannerisms, and personality demonstrated by clergy in the performance of their duties.

Clergy Effectiveness: The perceived ability of the senior leader of a local congregation to lead his/her congregation to agreed upon goals and objectives of the organization.

Factor Analysis: The statistical process of condensing multiple variables (items) into a smaller set of common factors.

Qualitative Data: Descriptive information gathered through interviews and surveys that is non-numerical in nature.

Quantitative Data: Numerical information that can be used for mathematical calculation or statistical analysis.

Scale Optimization: A process related to the length of a scale (total number of items) that seeks to find the right balance between scale reliability (more items) and convenience to respondents (less items).

Secondary Criteria: Criteria (e.g., attendance) used to measure clergy effectiveness which, while related to clergy effectiveness, may also also be directly influenced by factors other than the senior leader.

Chapter 20
Developing a Measurement Plan for Monitoring Diverse Friendships in the Workplace

Janet L. Reynolds

Reynolds & Reynolds Consulting, USA

ABSTRACT

Corporations have failed to charge human resource officers with the responsibility of facilitating the unique diverse relationships needed for enriching their own workforce. Often, at best, training programs introduce intercultural sensitivity and only suggest the actual need for employee connections with diverse others. The trainers hesitate to discuss how to monitor and facilitate accountability for forming the diverse relationships that make others feel a sense of inclusion and create safe places for voices to be asserted. This chapter calls for a human resources plan for raising the awareness for engaging in the actual networking, accountability, and the building of the human relationships that enrich the vitality of the workplace. This plan sees the corporate diversity mission as a persuasive message and thus looks at how employees may become involved in the mission in different ways related to their values, their relevant impressions, and possible outcomes.

INTRODUCTION

Altman (2017) and Zojceska (2018) argue that diversity is good for businesses and organizations. Diversity: Ensures a variety of Different Perspectives, Increases creativity; Increases Profits; Speeds-up Problem-Solving; Fosters Innovation; Produces Higher Employee Engagement; Improves Understanding of Clients, Markets, and Constituents; Reduces Employee Turnover; Enhances Brainstorming; Improves the Organization's Reputation; Attracts New Employees; and Leads to Better Decision Making.

Corporate reports show that 76% of companies are wanting a more inclusive culture but only 11% of companies have achieved inclusion (Emelo, 2014, p. 48.). Law (2000) reports that developing a discipline of extending our boundaries is one way to reach a higher level of inclusion (see also Toosi, Sommers, & Ambady, 2012). Many organizations have created diversity officers or diversity com-

DOI: 10.4018/978-1-7998-7665-6.ch020

mittees within their Human Resources office to encourage diversity. The theme is often that diverse personnel can bring desirable innovations to the creative process within corporations as well as add needed cohesion. Unfortunately, the trainers have generally failed to develop accountability plans that employees can embrace and lack the data to talk about how true diversity and interdependence might look in the future as the corporation grows and changes. Organizations should know that they need to go beyond the appreciation of diversity and progress toward preparing worker-centered adoption of diverse relationships. This allows new employees to realize that a flow of diverse ideas from communication networks, stimulated by Human Resources, will contribute to the bottom-line and stimulate employee satisfaction (See Chamberlain, Stansell, & Zhao, 2021; Darling-Hammond, Lee, & Mendoza-Denton, 2020; Fay, & Kline, 2011; Gündemir, Homan, Usova, & Galinsky, 2017; Mortensen & Neeley, 2012; Payne, McDonald, & Hamm, 2013).

Regrettably, with all the legal red tape that Human Resources must oversee, little time is left to assure that corporate training includes relationship building over time across the demographics of the corporation. Hersey and Blanchard (1982, p. 6) quote John D. Rockefeller as saying, "I will pay more for the ability to deal with people than any other ability under the sun." Hersey and Blanchard stress the idea that most managers want employees that have strong interpersonal skills more than just job skills. This chapter calls for Human Resource officers to incorporate interpersonal diversity activities, skills, and accountability into their training to encourage employees to embrace their associations with diverse others which in turn will improve the vitality and overall synergy of the company.

There is considerable controversy surrounding the means, methods, practices, or results from diversity training and recruiting. This chapter is not the place to address those issues in depth. What is clear is that the current diversity training programs are generally failing (Lai, et al, 2016) to produce the synergies of diversity that can improve needed productivity and innovation. There clearly needs to be a new focus on measuring what matters (Doerr, 2018) on how diversity can add to the productivity, success, and longevity of the organization (Kirkpatrick, 1998; Reynolds, 2017). Doer (2018) makes it clear that organizations must have objectives and know what would count as key results. Kirkpatrick (1998) argues that training untethered from data on how they contribute to organizational goals and bottom-line outcomes (productivity and profit) is useless.

The charge for diversity should stem from the corporate mission that comes from the CEO and the Board of Directors. The following overview allows the reader to understand the task that H. R. is being called to perform, to foster the development of a genuine diverse corporate culture climate. Human Resource staff need to collect data to monitor the progress that is made on developing contact and relationships with diverse others. These accountability measures of diversity imperatives will remind employees that the company sees the building of diverse relationships as essential to the health of the company. As this plan is incorporated into the corporate mission, the organization will follow the leadership of many companies in Silicon Valley and beyond who have received recognition for innovative organizations. Employees should be informed during the hiring process that summaries of such measures will appear on corporate websites, and in corporate reports to all employees, investors, and potential clients concerning the progress of fulfilling the company's mission. The CEOs of the corporation should lead with the idea that diversity is important to the fabric of the company and not just an addon that results in merely a grand total of diverse new hires.

Different methods of data collection and different modes of contact would allow employees to find their own comfort zone for data participation. Open conversations at the initial orientation should allow for focus groups to form so there is clarity about opportunities for repeated interaction with others concerning topics and timing. The more practice the employees have from the very start in conversing with diverse others, the greater their deep learning and insight about how the corporate mission requires them to engage with and adopt the strong advantages of working within a diverse and inclusive company. The ways that these groups are formed should be custom-designed by the human resource office for the multiple specific teams that the new hires will likely move and work in as they advance in their employment. Appropriate data collection taken at six months into employment could be custom designed into items gleaned from the initial focus group transcripts. In addition, the initial focus group themes and conclusions should stimulate six-month focus group discussion follow-up. Data from initial and six-month focus groups could later be formulated into email messages designed to further stimulate interaction within integrated team members as they develop true interdependence. Examples topics can also be gathered from survey items given below in the measurement instruments cited. Data collection toward the end of the first year would include self-reflection on interactions and relationships with diverse team members and supervisors. These self-reflection reports of interactions can be tabulated to create pictures of actual diversity development in the organizational networks that have formed over the year of interactions.

BALANCING INDIVIDUAL DIFFERENCES

In the United States our individualistic culture may cause people to withdraw from some conversations and they may not reach out to the needs of others because of their innate need for being autonomous (Triandis, Bontempo & Villareal, 1988). Collectivistic cultures understand that there are values to small groups of friends that become in-group members for intellectual and relational insight where opportunities for intellectual and relational insight can occur. Some Eastern cultures socialize their population to not be a star or the nail that sticks up and, so, blending as a cohesive group is second nature. An expressed appreciation of the perspectives and interests of (diverse) others is just the quality that is so often missed in some individual workplace associations (Ehrhardt & Ragins, 2019).

Idioms and perspectives create sharing opportunities that break down boundaries. Petronio (1991; 2002; 2013; Communication Privacy Management Center, 2019) provides a strong theoretical foundation for these ideas. Much of the thinking in this chapter relies on Petronio's notion of boundary management. As individualistic people exert effort and time and patience, they begin to appreciate the cultural ideas embedded in the collective groups. The breaking down of the boundaries of "secret codes" within cultures starts to build cohesiveness and cooperativeness.

DATA COLLECTION ACROSS THE GROUPS

First, at the new employee orientation, accountability partners would be alerted in advance of times where they will be expected to report the progress they have made in their communication with diverse others. A life example for the need for this type of accountability can be realized by reading the following example from the author's professional experience:

An educational institution spent ten years building a group of students from Korea and bringing them to California for a specific curriculum. They finished a Master's Degree in three years and most of the students returned to their home country. The institution was proud to count them in their "diversity" numbers and pat themselves on the back for doing a good job with a diverse student body. But the cohorts never met other students on campus. Their cohorts met and lived together and their class instruction was segregated from the other parts of the campus. One Human Resource officer asked a current student not in the Korean Studies program: How many friends do you have in the Korean Studies program? Answer: none -- "They are in their own ivory tower. I have never even had a conversation with any of those students!"

This story is reminiscent of the stories from the early failings to recognize and address segregation in the USA (Aronson, Stephan, Sikes, Blaney, & Snapp, 1978). Employees need to understand that allowing this type of self-segregation in organizations is not desirable. If corporations collect data about such things as sexual harassment, recruitment, and terminations, they should also collect data on the development of diversity in interpersonal networks. Data is also needed on the shared sense of interdependence. If these data have not been previously gathered, then work-related networks can be a new area of exploration that can enrich the texture of the company.

Content analysis of focus group sharing could be done by transcript coding of topics introduced in the orientation groups. Personal sharing is a sensitive issue that has been the topic of numerous communication articles (see Petronio, 2015; see also Communication Privacy Management Center, 2019, webpage). Many employees may be too reserved to share personal disclosures and, so, this may inhibit the sharing of information with diverse others. It takes relationship building overtime for shared idioms and cultural perspectives to emerge. It is as simple as understanding and appreciating common statements like, "Are you are pulling my leg?" Personal sharing varies from context to context. As employees lean in toward understanding the cultural aspects of others, they start to understand their own responsibility for the inclusion of others who might want decoding explanations. The idea of boundary management is especially important in overlapping social networks because there is such a high need for common meaning systems. Research on privacy invasion (Petronio, 1994) emphasizes that when done properly appropriate sharing builds bonding for nested social networks.

The personnel administrator would begin by organizing a plan for the training sessions. In the initial training session employee cohorts would be given time for round-robin brainstorming to encourage their desire for reaching out to others. Second, in the training, it would be very important to include diversity topics that might speak to differences in age, gender, sexual orientation, race, or specialization. Demographic variables such as date of hire, completion of HR. training, relational supervisor connections and ethnic background would enable researchers to plan for how data collection could be tabulated. A human resources staff person would be responsible for drawing accountability pairings within the new hire cohorts. Each new hire would have an opportunity to give personal background and the dyads would be given time to find commonality so that they can realize a basis for extending their shared workplace relationships. The session may be the only time the new cohort is allowed the luxury of time to be able to know the full range of diversity (or potential need for diversity) where they work. These bonding sessions should cause the participants to remember this time later when they fully realize the positive attributes of these individuals for work insight on projects that appear in the course of employment and the participation in work teams. The primary goal would be to build mindfulness about how cultural biases can cause people to dismiss possible connections and thus lose the insights diverse others can help them each be more creative and develop enhanced decision making.

ONLINE SESSION AT SIX MONTHS

A personal network analysis looks at the direct and indirect connections within the organization. As workers articulate their roles there are pictures of density that emerge and central connections can be pointed out. Eventually emergent networks appear where the computation of network metrics can be done. Both weak and strong ties will emerge.

There is a technique called cluster analysis to enhance where people's views of the corporate climate emerge over and above their formal roles at work. Joyce and Slocum (1984) called this view the collective climate. Every corporation develops a corporate personality. An example of that is to go back in time to the early 1980s when employees of Apple Corporation could be recognized at deli lunch tables by their Aloha shirts. They were making a statement that their culture was not like the IBM culture with their white shirt and black tie. Their mode of dress signaled to all who would notice that the culture at Apple was as innovative as their corporate shirts.

The corporate change can be explained by how individuals slowly come to be involved in issues. Agreement, however, will not come automatically and connections found through network analysis will show the frequency of connections but not the quality of mission acceptance. Many new hires will not swallow the cultural diversity mantra immediately. They will give lip service to the idea of contact with others but will be hesitant to believe that ideas from diverse others are important for building inclusivity. The bias that everyone brings into the workplace is hard to break down and this process can be explained for greater understanding by the communication literature on involvement in persuasion (see below). With practice in communication with other dyads and small groups, slowly the company will start to change. Continuity will come much later.

At the end of six months the cohort would be sent an email survey that can assess their frequency of contact with others. It is probably only at this point that some new hires will discover that the accountability that was mentioned in orientation is indeed going to happen. Network analysis is an important part of understanding how involved the employees are and how active their connections with others have become. Such data can reveal to the individual the amount of time and effort expended to developing friendly conversations with diverse others about work and nonwork topics. For some of them, they may realize that they have dropped the ball on the admonition at the new hire session to develop a friendship among the cohort. The purpose of this network survey would also remind the participants that the company is serious about exchanges of communication in both dyads and small groups that include diverse others. This step would reveal who serves as a bridge to other dyads and show the social isolates. This data will tell the researchers much about the texture of the budding corporate climate. Often the employees themselves do not understand how the networks around them are operating. It is different to realize that a person who is not perceived as a leader per se is a bridge connecting two networks because of the frequency of their communication. This survey would ask for frequency of contacts over the last six months. Plans could be made by H.R. for follow-up surveys on the employee's company anniversaries. The questions could reveal the beginning of involvement with others. It would also reveal those who have become apathetic about the serious value of diverse connections. Examples might include:

How many times have you called [specific cohort member]?

How many times have you emailed [specific cohort member]?

How many times have you invited the [specific cohort member] to coffee or lunch?

How many times have you inquired about this person's expertise in a project?How often have you gone out of your way to include this person?

(Various questions such as these can be expanded depending on corporation type.)

SESSION AT CLOSE OF YEAR ONE

At end of year one, cohorts could be brought together for a round-robin of sharing. In addition, there should be an end-of-the-year diversity evaluation survey to help the Human Resources staff monitor progress. How supervisors and subordinates maintain their relationships impacts the cohesion of the corporate diversity mission. If the relationships are escalating then subordinates learn to adapt their communication as they maintain these relationships and the relationships become both hierarchical and personal. This leads to more complex discussions where in-groups are developed. This provides a sense of equality and balance and raises their self-esteem. These in-groups develop higher-quality work experiences and a greater desire to adapt to shared values.

Suggested items listed here are from the Organizational Communication Relationship questions from the International Communication Association Audit (Rubin, Palmgreen, & Sypher, 1994). Since these items are quite dated, they are listed here at suggestions for review of original items that each organization would customize for their purposes. These are Likert-type scales with a range of 1 to 5 including very little, little, some, great, and very great. The items are:

1. I trust my coworkers.
2. My coworkers get along with each other.
3. My relationship with my coworkers is satisfying.
4. I trust my immediate supervisor.
5. My immediate supervisor is honest with me.
6. My immediate supervisor listens to me.
7. I am free to disagree with my immediate supervisor.
8. I can tell my immediate supervisor when things are going wrong.
9. My immediate supervisor praises me for a good job.
10. My immediate supervisor is friendly with his/her subordinates.
11. My immediate supervisor understands my job needs.
12. My relationship with my immediate supervisor is satisfying

The reliability alpha averages are reported at .90 (Dewine & Person, 1985). Filling out items such as these forces the employee to realize that the company cares about how the employee feels about their team and the act of participating in this process with be improving their overall job satisfaction as they start to realize that practicing communication with their co-workers has influenced their overall feelings about their workplace. Retention and job satisfaction are only two of the things that would be improved if more organizations reinforced this type of data collection.

ASSESSMENT AND UNDERSTANDING EFFECTIVENESS FOR THE FUTURE

Following one year of participation in diversity encounter relationships, employees should be able to give feedback on how they learned from diverse others about new types of life skills they can use in their second year. They should each be able to explain how relationships with diverse colleagues contribute to their personal potential for contribution to the corporate mission. In short, there needs to be self-reports on how relationships with diverse others became a greater priority in their minds. Unfortunately, the record of training sessions that increase inclusion and reduce discrimination has many reasons why the effectiveness falls far short

INVITING CHANGE WITH POSITIVE DEVIANCE

As outlined above, HR professionals face a complex multi-edged diversity sword as they assist employees in improving life skills and embracing corporate diversity missions. They are to guide the organization away from explicit racism and discrimination while simultaneously raising employee awareness about racism and discrimination. At the same time there is the task of making employees aware of their own race-based implicit biases. Lai, et al (2016) document, sadly, that most discrimination training efforts are not successful. Often diversity training fails because of an over reliance on 'learning' knowledge about racial injustices, instilling guilt, and a suggesting a weak sense of being an ally for those facing discrimination. What is needed instead are efforts based on positive deviance (see Dearing and Singhal, 2020). Positive Deviance is the unique and unexpectantly successful atypical practices of individuals who overcome obstacles where others fail. For example, in Viet Nam there was a set of people who faced overwhelming obstacles of providing nutrition for family groups who were seriously malnourished. This serious problem was solved as small little crabs were incorporated into a diet that was deprived of protein. The solution merely involved doing a positive change of adding organisms that were going unnoticed and unused and incorporating them into the overall cooking process for the community. The change was overwhelming and the families learned the importance of adding protein as an ingredient to the diet and learned to watch thriving children grow strong.

A useful example of the potential use is offered by Jain, Sachdev, Singhal, Svenkerud, and Agrawal (2019). They report learning that women entrepreneurs were able to overcome gender biases by micro interpersonal behaviors, connecting with customers, doing personalized branding of their businesses, using novel strategies to monitor sales and profits, and the influencing of partners and clients with value-reframing tactics. These insights led to completely new training strategies (and trainers). The key after learning novel positive deviance strategies is for HR professionals to develop the needed change toward increased diversity by allowing employees to 'self-learn' new behaviors by adopting a practice first, attitude change second, and learning knowledge last strategy (Singhal & Svenkerud, 2018).

INVOLVEMENT WITH DIVERSITY

It should be noted that the extensive pattern given at the beginning of the chapter would take considerable ground work and effort. However, a diversity officer who researched ways to get people involved in the organization's diversity mission would be amiss if they overlooked the process of building and creating involvement (see instrument in Cho and Boster, 2005).

The concept of involvement was originally tied to the concept of 'ego' in the sense that involvement is personal (and not at all tied to old view of the ego). In addition, various authors have adopted alternative terminology and unique versions of involvement or involvement objects (see Johnson & Eagly, 1989; Petty and Cacioppo, 1990). For the purposes here, Johnson and Eagly's (1989; 1990) conceptions of Value Involvement (core to your values), Outcome Involvement (direct benefits), and Impression Involvement (being seen and assessed by others) are pragmatically useful.

Often organizational change is assumed to be automatic and the source, such as the H.R. officer, believe that the employee will swallow the corporate rhetoric simply and completely. Unfortunately, that induction of mission and objectives does not happen without building involvement that becomes relevant to the individual. Impression involvement is the degree to which one cares about having opinions that other people find acceptable (Johnson & Eagly, 1989). As an example, a person with high impression involvement would be less likely to take a position against a person with a lower involvement because denying the message would be unacceptable behavior considering the entire corporate view. This appealing to employee impression involvement, over time, would raise the level of corporate acceptance of the need for diverse relationships as stated in the corporate mission. The suggestion here is that Impression Involvement precedes and leads to Value and Outcome Involvement. The instillation of Value involvement and Outcome involvement, in turn, would slowly change the organizational climate. Embracing the corporate value for an eventual outcome of a realized corporate mission becomes innately exciting for all involved in the mission.

The seven-point Likert-type Impression Involvement scale would have responses ranging from strongly disagree to strongly agree. The instrument could incorporate such things as:

1. Talking about my beliefs concerning diversity has little effect on what others think of me.
2. The impressions that others have of me are very much affected when I talk with them about my position on diversity.
3. The kind of opinion I express at work about a need for diversity has little effect on what others think of me.
4. People may judge me on the opinion that I express at work about the need for diversity.
5. If I express the right kind of opinion on diversity people will find me more task attractive.

In the beginning of corporate involvement there would be a desire to manage the positive impression for assimilation into the organizational values. Newer employees would come to realize that they eventually become the seasoned example of involvement into this vibrant, reflective organizational whole that they are part of now. Cho and Boster (2005) also provide Value Involvement and Outcome Involvement items.

The measurement of impression-relevant involvement is a unique way to create a picture of how employees are incorporating incoming persuasive messages into their work persona. The measure has good factor loadings, good fit indices, and acceptable reliability. Different personnel will react to messages in alternative ways. The ability to embrace the diversity message at a high level can be captured by measurement. Embracing the message as a high value may need coaching for some but longevity with the company and exposure to attitudes of others will contribute to the incorporation of the desired value into the employee's persona. Workshops on such things as power distance, friendliness, stereotyping and prejudicial bias can help start the process but the first cohorts would be able to testify at the level of job satisfaction that is magnified as they move beyond topics and move on to practicing relationships. Practicing their communication with others is a hidden bonus that they will eventually appreciate.

CONCLUSION

The strategies, tactics, and measures mentioned here can inspire HR offices with meaningful and practical approaches to encouraging and monitor the progress of building organizational diversity. The informed reader may wonder about other popular measures and programs for addressing diversity issues. Most address past dispositions or learned cultural biases or perspectives and do not offer generative forces for building diversity. Please be sure to weigh alternative measures and programs for the capacity to actually encourage or assess communication between organizational members from diverse backgrounds.

Corporations may give lip service to the ideas given in this chapter but a budget for the cost of running such a program should be drawn up before the initiation of the cohort year. The goal is to develop a cohesive, inclusive workforce (Reynolds & Lawrence, 2018). Human Resource officers that do not feel qualified to come to the plate on the ideas presented here should be brave enough to hand-off diversity network development to a qualified consultant.

Failing to improve the overall cohesiveness of the organization should not be a lost opportunity. The view of the company that the satisfied employee shares with their interpersonal networks outside of work enables the reputation of the company to be magnified beyond the service or product that they produce. This gives the company a reputation in social networks of the employee as being a desirable company to have in the area and in the whole society. The rising tide of diversity in a corporate mission raises the quality of life in society itself.

REFERENCES

Altman, Z. (2017, March 5). *5 Reasons Why Workplace Diversity Is Good For Business: Why one polling expert sees lack of diversity as the most dangerous blind spot affecting corporate America today.* https://www.inc.com/ian-altman/5-reasons-why-workplace-diversity-is-good-for-business.html

Aronson, E., Stephan, C., Sikes, J., Blaney, N., & Snapp, M. (1978). *The Jigsaw Classroom.* Sage.

Chamberlain, A., Stansell, A., & Zhao, D. (2021). *America's workplace diversity crisis: Measuring gaps in diversity & inclusion satisfaction by employee race and ethnicity.* https://www.glassdoor.com/research/app/uploads/sites/2/2021/04/DEI-:10.11._2021-Final.pdf

Cho, H., & Boster, F. J. (2005). Development and validation of value-, outcome-, and impression-relevant involvement scales. *Communication Research, 32*(2), 235–264. doi:10.1177/0093650204273764

Communication Privacy Management Center. (2019, May 4). https://cpmcenter.iupui.edu/

Darling-Hammond, S., Lee, R. T., & Mendoza-Denton, R. (2020). Interracial contact at work: Does workplace diversity reduce bias? *Group Processes & Intergroup Relations, 1.* Advance online publication. doi:10.1177/1368430220932636

Dearing, J. W., & Singhal, A. (2020). New directions for diffusion of innovations research: Dissemination, implementation, and positive deviance. *Human Behavior and Emerging Technologies*, *2020*(4), 1–7. doi:10.1002/hbe2.216

Dewine, S., & Pearson, J. C. (1985, May). *The most frequently used self-report instruments in communication*. Paper presented at the ICA, Honolulu, HI. https://files.eric.ed.gov/fulltext/ED260479.pdf

Doerr, J. (2018). *Measure What Matters: How Google, Bono, and the Gates Foundation Rock the World with OKRs*. Penguin Random House.

Ehrhardt, K., & Ragins, B. R. (2019). Relational attachment at work: A complementary fit perspective on the role of relationships in organizational life. *Academy of Management Journal*, *62*(1), 248–282. doi:10.5465/amj.2016.0245

Emelo, R. (2014). Peer collaboration enhances diversity and inclusion. *TD: Talent Development*, *68*(12), 48–52.

Fay, M., & Kline, S. (2011). Coworker relationships and informed communication in high-intensity telecommuting. *Journal of Applied Communication Research*, *39*(2), 144–163. doi:10.1080/00909882.2011.556136

Gündemir, S., Homan, A. C., Usova, A., & Galinsky, A. D. (2017). Multicultural meritocracy: The synergistic benefits of valuing diversity and merit. *Journal of Experimental Social Psychology*, *73*, 34–41. doi:10.1016/j.jesp.2017.06.002

Hersey, P., & Blanchard, K. H. (1982). *Management of Organizational Behavior: Utilizing Human Resources*. Prentice-Hall, Inc.

Jain, P., Sachdev, A., Singhal, A., Svenkerud, P. J., & Agrawal, S. (2019). A positive deviance inquiry on effective communicative practices of rural Indian women entrepreneurs. *The Journal of Development Communication*, *30*(1), 10–22. http://jdc.journals.unisel.edu.my/ojs/index.php/jdc/article/view/137

Johnson, B. T., & Eagly, A. H. (1989). Effects of involvement on persuasion: A meta-analysis. *Psychological Bulletin*, *106*(2), 290–314. doi:10.1037/0033-2909.106.2.290

Johnson, B. T., & Eagly, A. H. (1990). Involvement and persuasion: Types, traditions, and the evidence. *Psychological Bulletin*, *107*(3), 375–384. doi:10.1037/0033-2909.107.3.375

Joyce, W. F., & Slocum, J. W. Jr. (1984). Collective climate; Agreement as bases for defining aggregated climates in organizations. *Academy of Management Journal*, *27*, 721–742.

Joyce, W. F., & Slocum, J. W. Jr. (1984). Collective climate; Agreement as bases for defining aggregated climates in organizations. *Academy of Management Journal*, *27*, 721–742.

Kirkpatrick, D. L. (1998). *Evaluating training programs: The four levels* (2nd ed.). Berrett-Koehler Publishers.

Lai, C. K., Skinner, A. L., Cooley, E., Murrar, S., Brauer, M., Devos, T., Calanchini, J., Xiao, Y. J., Pedram, C., Marshburn, C. K., Simon, S., Blanchar, J. C., Joy-Gaba, J. A., Conway, J., Redford, L., Klein, R. A., Roussos, G., Schellhaas, F. M. H., Burns, M., ... Nosek, B. A. (2016). Reducing implicit racial preferences: II. Intervention effectiveness across time. *Journal of Experimental Psychology. General*, *145*(8), 1001–1016. doi:10.1037/xge0000179 PMID:27454041

Law, E. H. F. (2000). *Inclusion: Making Room for Grace*. Chalice Press.

Mortensen, M., & Neeley, T. B. (2012). Reflected knowledge and trust in global collaboration. *Management Science*, *58*(12), 2207–2224. doi:10.1287/mnsc.1120.1546

Payne, J., McDonald, S., & Hamm, L. (2013). Production teams and producing racial diversity in workplace relationships. *Sociological Forum, 28*(2), 326–349. doi:10.1111ocf.12021

Petronio, S. (1991). Communication boundary management: A theoretical model of managing disclosure of private information between martial couples. *Communication Theory, 1*(4), 311–335. doi:10.1111/j.1468-2885.1991.tb00023.x

Petronio, S. (1994). Privacy binds in family interactions the case of parental privacy invasion. In W. R. Cupach & B. H. Spitzberg (Eds.), *The Dark Side of interpersonal communication* (pp. 241–258). Lawrence Erlbaum. doi:10.4324/9781315807010-10

Petronio, S. (2002). *Boundaries of privacy: Dialectics of disclosure*. SUNY Press.

Petronio, S. (2013). Brief status report on communication privacy management theory. *Journal of Family Communication*, *13*(1), 6–14. doi:10.1080/15267431.2013.743426

Petronio, S. (2015). Communication privacy management theory. In C. R. Berger, M. E. Roloff, S. R. Wilson, J. P. Dillard, J. Caughlin, & D. Solomon (Eds.), *The International Encyclopedia of Interpersonal Communication*. doi:10.1002/9781118540190.wbeic132

Reynolds, J. L., & Lawrence, D. (2018). Is diversity & inclusion training really training? Rethinking New Models. In S. K. Camara, M. P. Orbe, K. S. Makai, & L. Gilinets (Eds.), *Communication & Training & Development: Exploring the Cutting Edge*. Kendall Hunt.

Reynolds, R. A. (2017). Begin with the end in mind: Conducting post training evaluations. In S. K. Camara (Ed.), *Communication training and development: Exploring the cutting edge*. Kendall/Hunt Publishing Co.

Rubin, R. B., Palmgreen, P., & Sypher, H. E. (Eds.). (1994). *Communication Research Measures: A Sourcebook*. The Guilford Press.

Singhal, A., & Svenkerud, P. J. (2018). Diffusion of evidence-based interventions or practice-based positive deviations. *The Journal of Development Communication*, *29*(2), 54–64. http://jdc.journals.unisel.edu.my/ojs/index.php/jdc/article/view/134

Toosi, N. R., Sommers, S. R., & Ambady, N. (2012). Getting a word in group-wise: Effects of racial diversity on gender dynamics. *Journal of Experimental Social Psychology*, *48*(5), 1150–1155. doi:10.1016/j.jesp.2012.04.015

Triandis, H. C., Bontempo, R., Villareal, M. J., Asai, M., & Lucca, N. (1988). Individualism and collectivism: Cross-cultural perspectives on self-ingroup relationships. *Journal of Personality and Social Psychology, 54*(2), 323–338. doi:10.1037/0022-3514.54.2.323

Zojceska, A. (2018, December 19). Top 10 Benefits of Diversity in the Workplace. *Talent Lyft.* https://www.talentlyft.com/en/blog/article/244/top-10-benefits-of-diversity-in-the-workplace#:~:text=What%20are%20the%20benefits%3F%201%20Variety%20of%20different,5%20Better%20decision%20making.%20...%20More%20items...%20

Chapter 21
Introduction to Machine Learning as a New Methodological Framework for Performance Assessment

Jason D. Baker
Regent University, USA

ABSTRACT

Machine learning enables organizations to leverage data strategically to improve employee performance, promote continuous improvement, and better fulfill the mission. Opportunities for leveraging machine learning within organizations exist throughout the employee lifecycle but should be pursued with a clear understanding of the strengths and limitations of the methodology. This chapter will review traditional performance management processes, introduce machine learning as a methodology, highlight how machine learning methods could be used in new performance assessment models, and note future research directions to improve the use of machine learning within organizations.

INTRODUCTION

According to a 2020 report from Paycor (2020), a human resources software and payroll service provider, labor costs account for as much as 70% of all business costs. If human capital is one of the costliest aspects of businesses and organizations, it follows that they would create processes and structures to ensure a strong return on investment of employee labor. Traditionally, this has been pursued via a regular performance planning and review process. Additionally, the influence of quality metrics used within manufacturing, supply chain management, and other industrialized sectors provoked the application of key performance indicators to human resource evaluation. The emergence of big data, data science, and business analytics has opened a new opportunity that organizations can consider as yet another means of improving employee productivity. This chapter will introduce machine learning as a new methodological framework for performance assessment. It will briefly review traditional performance management

DOI: 10.4018/978-1-7998-7665-6.ch021

processes, introduce machine learning as a methodology, highlight how machine learning methods could be used in new performance assessment models, discuss threats associated with machine learning approaches, and conclude with future research directions.

TRADITIONAL PERFORMANCE MANAGEMENT

One of the most common approaches to employee performance assessment is an annual planning and review model. Unsurprisingly, this approach follows from a common organizational financial approach in which the annual budget drives much of the decision-making over the subsequent year. As Hope and Fraser (2003) describe in *Beyond Budgeting: How Managers Can Break Free from the Annual Performance Trap*:

For most participants, the budgeting process is an annual ritual that is deeply embedded in the corporate calendar.... It typically begins at least four months prior to the year to which it relates...it starts with a mission statement that sets out some of the aims of the business. This is followed by a group strategic plan that sets the direction and high-level goals of the firm. These form the framework for a budgeting process that grinds its way through countless meetings at which points are traded as targets are negotiated and resources agreed upon. (p. 3)

They note that these targets then form the basis of "budget packs" that are distributed to various departments and units which subsequently define how success will be measured in the coming year. With such metrics in mind, departments can then incorporate such priorities and direction in determining employee priorities and ultimately how they would contribute to the organizational success.

The process for employees often follows analogously to the aforementioned budgetary one. Similar to how the budget process first involves an evaluation of how the organization did compared to the fiscal year plan, employee prior performance plans or goals are unearthed and they're typically tasked to document specific achievements, deliverables, and activities as they relate to the plan. Supervisors then combine those materials with their own internal assessments, to determine how employees performed in year passed. Then, either individually or collaboratively, new goals are established for the upcoming year and documented in a manner to be revisited in the next annum. This too follows the budget planning cycle in that the planning is intended to flow from the organizational mission, down to the departmental level, and ultimately to the individual employee, thus providing a framework to ensure that every employee is proverbially rowing in the same direction and contributing to the overall effectiveness of the organization.

In concept, it would appear to be an elegant and constructive means of not only evaluating employee performance for promotions, raises, and constructive placement. Ideally it would also provide a regular means of reinforcing the inherent value of employees to the success of the institution and provide structure to determine how to reward, support, and equip employees in the year to come to make an even greater impact. Such activities should increase employee effectiveness and satisfaction, while also strengthening the human capital contribution to the mission and make the organization stronger and more capable of fulfilling its mission. As Pulakos (2004) noted in a review of performance management systems, "In fact, if developed and implemented properly, performance management systems drive employees to engage in behaviors and achieve results that facilitate meeting organizational objectives" (p. 5).

Ironically, while the rhythm of annual performance reviews and planning occurring during or shortly after budget reviews and planning often occurs chronologically, there's frequently a disconnect between the practice and its effectiveness. While budgets and financial analyses tend to be fairly objective assessments which provide industry-accepted points of comparison across industries and time, corresponding reviews of humans aren't as uniformly defined or accepted. And if the budget ritual "absorbs huge amounts of time for an uncertain benefit" as Hope and Fraser (2003) claim, the annual employee performance review provokes downright hostility.

A 1972 article in *Harvard Business Review* entitled "An Uneasy Look at Performance Appraisal" revisited a famous 1957 assessment by Douglas McGregor in which he declared, "Managers are uncomfortable when they are put in the position of 'playing God'" (p. 27). McGregor, who subsequently developed his Theory X and Theory Y managerial framework, highlighted the frequent discomfort experienced by both supervisors and subordinates over the annual performance review process. As Pulakos (2004) summarized:

Managers are reluctant to provide candid feedback and have honest discussions with employees for fear of reprisal or damaging relationships with the very individuals they count on to get work done. Employees feel that their managers are unskilled at discussing their performance and ineffective at coaching them on how to develop their skills. Many complain that performance management systems are cumbersome, bureaucratic and too time consuming for the value added. This leads both managers and employees to treat performance management as a necessary evil of work life that should be minimized rather than an important process that achieves key individual and organizational outcomes. (p. 1)

One response to such concerns has been to make the performance management process more robust. Rather than reducing the experience to an annual review and planning session, many human resource management experts recommend an ongoing process that occurs throughout the year. For example, Pulakos (2004) describes a five-phase cycle of performance planning, ongoing feedback, employee input, performance evaluation, and performance review. The inclusion of ongoing feedback and employee input, in particular, offer both structural and cultural approaches to transform performance assessment from an annual event to an ongoing process. Similarly, Armstrong (2017) in *Armstrong on Reinventing Performance Management* promotes the development of a culture of continuous improvement. In a chapter entitled "Replace the annual performance review," Armstrong argues that the tradition of a yearly performance review and planning session should instead be transformed into more frequent but less formal, lower-stakes, discussion and feedback sessions with a greater emphasis on forward-facing planning rather than backward-facing analysis. Furthermore, Armstrong advocates for the decoupling of performance ratings and reviews and pay scale decisions, in part to emphasize the priority of continuous improvement.

QUANTIFIED PERFORMANCE MANAGEMENT

A more quantiatively-oriented approach to help drive corporate performance has been the balanced scorecard (BSC). Kaplan and Norton (1992) evaluated a dozen companies known to excel in performance management and developed what they called a balanced scorecard to serve as a master corporate performance dashboard. Specifically, their balanced scorecard is designed to evaluate four important performance measures: financial, customer, internal, innovation and learning. Each of these helps the organization to evaluation and answer critical questions, namely "How do customers see us? (customer perspective); What must we excel at? (internal perspective); Can we continue to improve and create value? (innovation and learning perspective); How do we look to shareholders? (financial perspective)" (Kaplan & Norton, 1992, p. 74.) The balanced scorecard is focused more on business strategy rather than employee performance, but it is not uncommon for organizations to start with a balanced score-card at a high level and then drill down to more localized performance drivers, often by leveraging key performance indicators.

This approach to quantifying the performance management process, designed to remove some of the concern associated with subjective assessments but also to more tightly couple the human performance assessment with the financial and organizational assessment, is most frequently implemented by incorporating key performance indicators (KPIs) into the process. Parmenter (2020) defines a key performance indicator as "an indicator that focuses on the aspects of organizational performance that are the most critical for the current and future success of the organization" (para. 1). In *Key Performance Indicators: Developing, Implementing, and Using Winning KPIs* Parmenter (2015) defines seven characteristics that define KPIs:

- Nonfinancial measures (that is, not expressed in dollars, yen, euros, etc.)
- Measured frequently (e.g., 24/7, daily, or weekly)
- Acted on by CEO and senior management team
- Clear indications of what action is required by staff (e.g., staff can understand the measures and know what to fix)
- Measures that tie responsibility down to a team or a group of teams that work closely together
- Significant impact (e.g., it impacts most of the core CSFs and more than one BSC perspective)
- Encouragement for appropriate action (e.g., have been tested to ensure they have a positive impact on performance, a minimal dark side) (p. 206)

Despite these guidelines, many KPI-based approaches to performance planning, review, and assessment start with financial measures. As Janakova et al. (2020) declares, "The first idea for CRM is that the sales quota (a minimum volume of sales to meet in a given period) and customer satisfaction is the starting point for monitoring customer relationships and their needs" (p. 265). Similarly, in "7 Sales KPIs (Key Performance Indicators) You Should Measure in 2021", Neely (2021) lists gross/net profit margins, sales revenue, prospecting activity, funnel flow, customer retention, churn rate, and year-to-date sales growth. Others use a numerical approach that identifies metrics that are weighed and measured on an individual basis from the bottom up rather than from the top down. For example, in "KPIs Every Field Sales Leader Should Be Measuring," eight initial KPIs are proposed: "Sales Volume by Location; Competitor Pricing; Existing Client Engagement; Employee Satisfaction; Upsell and Cross-Sell Rates; Net Promoter Score (NPS); Sales Cycle Length; Customer Lifetime Value (CLV)" (April, 2020, para. 4).

Parmenter (2015) critiques such approaches in his discussion of winning KPIs. First, he declares, that, "I do not believe performance measures are on this planet to implement strategies. Performance measures are here to ensure that staff members spend their working hours focused primarily on the organization's critical success factors" (p. 40). He then defines the winning KPI process as one in which "Measures are derived from the critical success factors first and then the success factors; There is no cascading down of measures; Monthly measures will never be important to management as they report progress too late; It is the critical success factors that influence the day" (p. 41).

Key performance indicators are often used in concert with balanced scorecards, organizational dashboards, or critical success factors (CSFs). As Marr (2020) delineated:

The difference between KPIs and CSFs is the difference between cause and effect:

- CSFs are the cause of success, i.e. they set out what you need to do to be successful. These are often quite universal across the business world, and include things like good leadership, engaged employees, strong profits and so on.
- KPIs are the effects of your actions, i.e. they measure whether you are successful or not. KPIs typically differ from company to company, depending on the business's strategic priorities and goals. (para. 3-4)

While there are multiple approaches to KPIs, they reflect an effort to infuse timely, impactful, mission-centric metrics into the employee performance process. As Lazarova (2017) noted, while the traditional approach to KPIs has been a top-down effort, the emergence of business analytics and accessible data analytics tools has resulted in a concurrent bottom-up approach to performance metrics (p. 90). In such cases, various performance dashboards are developed at the individual or departmental level based on the associated tasks and available data. Such dashboards are used not only to evaluate ground-level performance but are often then rolled-up to create broader, organizational-level views. This bottom-up approach represents an inversion of the original scorecard or key performance indicator models which worked from a top-down organizational and strategic view. After evaluating the benefits of both approaches, Lazarova concludes, "A good performance management strategy incorporates both top-down and bottom-up approaches" (p. 95).

PERFORMANCE MANAGEMENT LIMITATIONS

Limitations associated with traditional and quantified performance management approaches have emerged from both the bottom-up and top-down perspectives within organizations. From the bottom-up vantage point, employees often report dissatisfaction with the performance review or indicator approaches. From the top-down perspective, organizations are coping with rapidly-changing geographic and physical presence dynamics associated with remote work which only accelerated in 2020-2021 due to the COVID-19 global pandemic. Furthermore, it seems that many of the labor-intensive approaches to performance management receive limited attention from human resources professionals when businesses face financial challenges.

Shmailan (2016) examined the relationship between job satisfaction, job performance, and employee engagement under the premise that such dynamics will contribute to a successful organization. A key finding from this literature-based study was that high levels of employee engagement not only contributed to increased levels of employee satisfaction, but materially affected employee performance in their operational tasks. Additionally, engaged employees were more likely to invest more time and effort into the success of the organization and are less likely to leave. Shmailan reported that effective two-way communication between the organization and the employee was an important ingredient for promoting employee engagement. As such, the design of the performance management system affects employee perception of employers, as evidenced in a 2015 study from Abdelhadi, Jamal, and Leclerc. They examined the relationship between employee perceptions performance appraisal systems and employee satisfaction and found a significant positive correlation between these variables. They also found that that employee trust toward supervisors affected both employee satisfaction but also their attitudes toward the performance appraisal itself.

Additionally, research into performance reviews has shown a tendency to reinforce gender bias within organizations. As Cecchi-Dimeglio (2017) flatly stated, "The annual performance review already has many strikes against it. Harried managers end up recalling high and low points on the fly; employees often get unclear direction. Here's another flaw: Women are shortchanged by these reviews" (para. 1). Cecchi-Dimeglio found that women were 1.4 times more likely than men to receive negative subjective feedback and were also less likely to get constructively critical feedback. Such patterns are not only harmful to the women who receive such unbalanced performance feedback, but undermine the development of a healthy and productive organizational culture.

If it weren't challenging enough for employees in traditionally-structured organizations, the ubiquity of networking technology has enabled many organizations to leverage remote work for full-time and contract employees. The sudden shutdowns prompted by the COVID-19 pandemic significantly accelerated this dynamic. According to a February 2021 McKinsey report on the future of work, executives plan to reduce physical office space by 30 percent and 20-25 percent of workforces in advanced countries could transition to a work from home model for 3-5 days per week. "This represents four to five times more remote work than before the pandemic and could prompt a large change in the geography of work, as individuals and companies shift out of large cities into suburbs and small cities" (Lund et al., 2021, para. 12). Wang et al. (2021) examined work from home employee dynamics during the early days of the COVID-19 pandemic and found four major psychological challenges: work-home interference, ineffective communication, procrastination, and loneliness (p. 16). Additionally, they found that social support, job autonomy, monitoring, and workload dynamics could affect these psychological challenges, and offered recommendations for how to structure remote work environments to compensate. Specifically, employers who provided greater levels of social support to remote workers reduced employee work-home interference, procrastination, and loneliness (p. 44). Given the likelihood that remote work will continue to grow for many employees, whether in whole or in part, organizations need to consider how to reframe the performance assessment process to serve a growing population of off-site workers.

Perhaps most disconcertingly, much activity associated with traditional and quantified performance management approaches has simply been outmatched by the financial needs of businesses. The U.S. Bureau of Labor Statistics (2020) reported that employee compensation averaged $35.95 per hour for private industry workers, $38.26 per hour for civilian workers, and $52.94 per hour for state and local government workers. Even so, a Paycor (2020) report found that while labor accounts for 70% of business costs, human resource professionals spent only 15% of their time managing labor costs, much of which went toward streamlining and reducing benefits costs, particularly regarding health care. One of the reasons that many employers transitioned from traditional medical provider options (e.g., Fee-for-Service plans, Health Maintenance Organizations, Preferred Provider Organizations, etc.) to High Deductible Health Plans, frequently coupled with Health Savings Accounts, is because the latter is frequently a lower-cost solution for the employer (Knowledge@Wharton, 2019). Such efforts are one means by which employers can cut costs while still providing employees with expected benefits. Similarly, employers have largely replaced defined benefit retirement plans such as pensions with defined contribution plans such as 401(k) and 403(b) retirement accounts (Fadlon et al., 2016). Such activities avoid situations where employers have to cut the compensation packages more overtly by freezing salaries, reducing retirement contributions, decreasing paid time off, restricting tuition remission, or cutting back on professional development training. Even these are generally seen as preferable to workforce reductions through attrition or layoffs but they still represent a fundamental lack of creativity when seeking to optimize the most costly component of businesses. Rather than reducing those costs through layoffs or benefit cuts, can organizations not reinvent the performance management process to enhance the value and productivity of labor and thus turn people into a competitive advantage?

INTRODUCTION TO MACHINE LEARNING

In the digital era, data have become ubiquitous and voluminous. In 2013 it was estimated that over 90% of all data in the world was created within the previous two years (ScienceDaily, 2013). When combined with the growth in computing power, particularly the orders of magnitude leaps in computing power enabled by parallelization and cloud computing, new approaches to data analysis have emerged in mainstream practice that were previously limited to specialized high performance computing applications. One of these approaches that is rapidly being applied in a variety of business and organizational contexts is machine learning. Before considering how machine learning can support new approaches to performance management it is useful to first gain an understanding of what machine learning is and how it differs from traditional descriptive and inferential statistical approaches.

Put simply, machine learning is "the automated detection of meaningful patterns in data" (Shalev-Swartz & Ben-David, 2014, p. xv). What distinguishes machine learning from other statistical procedures is this concept of automated detection of patterns. Traditional statistics, at least within business and organizational applications, tends to focus on either descriptive or inferential methods. In descriptive statistics, data are analyzed for measures of central tendency and then are reported in summary fashion to help people make sense of the numbers. For example, a large dataset of employee demographic information might be presented with descriptive statistics such as the mean (average) age of the employee, the frequency counts of how many employees are male versus female, the percentile distribution of employee ages across the company, and the salaries grouped by quartile or quintile ranges, perhaps with both mean and median salaries reported for comparison. Such statistics are being use to describe the "shape" of the data, so someone can distill hundreds or thousands of data points into something visually or cognitively comprehensible. Charts and graphs are often employed to further bridge the gap between the underlying numbers and the humans comprehending them.

Beyond mere descriptive statistics, researchers and analysts may also venture into the realm of inferential statistics. In such circumstances, a research question is typically posed, such as "Are male and female employees paid the same?" or "Can we predict sales based on our advertising expenditures?" Data are then gathered that include information about these variables. So, for example, an internal auditor might have access to the payroll system which would include employee salaries along with the corresponding employee gender. Using a difference inferential test, such as a t-test, such data could be compared to determine whether there was a difference between the salary means across the two groups to a level of statistical significance that it was highly unlikely to be caused by mere chance. Similarly, if the desire was to predict sales based on ad spending, then a business analyst might gather marketing budget information and align that with corresponding sales of various product lines and then use a relationship inferential test such as a linear regression to see if advertising could reliably predict sales. In both cases, the human researchers selected the variables that they wanted to evaluate, made a priori assumptions about justifiable relationships, and then choose suitable statistical procedures to perform the evaluation.

In the realm of machine learning, however, computer algorithms determine which variables contribute to the predictive capability based on various mathematical analyses that may or may not have human-interpretable analogs. For example, suppose analysts wanted to differentiate between male and female employees. They might gather as much data on the employees as was feasible – demographic, personnel, performance, tracking, social media, and so on – and then use a machine learning algorithm such as a random forest to differentiate them. In this case, all of the data would be fed into a random forest algorithm, with each of the underlying variables (e.g., salary, years of service, prior employer, Twitter usage, last performance score, etc.) included and tagged by employee with a group label (i.e., female, male) as the classification variable. The system would then seek to determine the best combination of variables and pivot points to best categorize the employees into female and male categories. In this algorithm, the machine learning system creates multiple decision trees which function like a Plinko game such that an inverted tree or pyramid structure causes each employee entry to cascade through a series of dividing metrics (e.g., years of service <10 flows down to the left, while >=10 flows down to the right) until it reaches the bottom. Myriad such trees are built, tested, and evaluated, until ultimately a complex combination is reached that optimizes the classification based on the specified hyperparameters set by the researcher. While it may be that the result is some interpretable combination of variables, often that is not the case.

The aforementioned approach is an example of supervised learning, in that the human analyst specified the grouping variable (in this case, gender) up front and then used the random forest algorithm to develop a classification model. However, neither classification in particular nor machine learning in general needs to be supervised; unsupervised algorithms also exist. In these cases, not only are the various variables and weights used in classification not initially specified by the analyst, but neither is the grouping variable. For example, a company might gather similar levels of detailed data on customers (e.g., number of purchases, average purchase value, days since most recent purchase, total money spent, zip code, cell phone area code, etc.) and feed it into an unsupervised machine learning algorithm like k-means clustering. In this case, all of the data would be fed into the k-means clustering machine learning algorithm, with each of the underlying variables included, but then the system would be tasked with grouping them into k different clusters. The system would then seek to determine the best combination of variables, weights, and vectors that maximize the distance between that maximize the distances between the clusters in n-dimensional space. Once again, while the result may map to some human-interpretable dimension, frequently it does not.

There are numerous other supervised and unsupervised algorithms, as well as other categories such as reinforcement learning (which might be used to train an autonomous vehicle to navigate an unknown track based on positive and negative feedback from sensor data), within the machine learning space. But why would an organization be interested in analytical algorithms that often don't generate traditional human-interpretable results? There are multiple reasons that such machine learning algorithms have utility. One is that such machine learning models are frequently able to find patterns in data that people miss or would never find through traditional means. There may be underlying combinations of variables that can predict membership in different groups, for example, that can only be discovered when the groups are plotted in n-dimensional space rather than in the two or three dimensional space more frequently evaluated by traditional analytics. Prediction models in particular may be developed using neural networks in which even the evaluative layers themselves are largely hidden from view. In such neural networks, even these hidden layers are automatically adjusted using a process called backpropagation in which partial derivatives are calculated in order to reduce the error rate and thus enable the system to automatically tune the weights within the artificial neural network to produce an optimal result.

Similarly, machine learning algorithms are not only capable of handling voluminous census data (or big data) rather than relying on selective sampling more often used in traditional inferential statistics, but such algorithms are strengthened by such data. While traditional approaches use sampling and a priori selection of variables to reduce an abundance of data to something more manageable, both conceptually and procedurally, machine learning algorithms work better when they're fed more data.

MACHINE LEARNING PERFORMANCE ASSESSMENT

Machine learning models have the ability to create ongoing classification and prediction systems that can be used in real time. Unlike traditional data analysis which tends to be backwards looking, machine learning models can be put into the pipeline of a production system and be forward facing. Procedurally, researchers gather the data to be used for the development of such a production model and spend time cleaning it and otherwise readying the data for analysis. According to Anaconda's *2020 State of Data Science* report, data scientists spend nearly half of their time locating and preparing data for analysis (Anaconda, 2020). Once the data are ready, researchers typically divide the data into at least two distinct subsets: a training set used to build the machine learning model and a testing set used to evaluate the model. The idea is to use as much data as possible to build the model but then to evaluate it against data that wasn't used in the construction of the model. This helps to determine how useful the model would be when used with previously unseen data. After all, it's possible to overfit a model, such that it fits the existing data exceedingly well thanks to mathematical hindsight but has little predictive power going forward.

Suppose a company runs a call center and wants to optimize employee phone time in order to secure a sale. Specifically, they want the sales person to spend time more time on the phone pitching to a likely buyer and less time when it seems that they're not likely to make a sale. Based on history, suppose the know that on average 50% of callers end up buying their products. How do they know which half of the callers is worth the extra time to close the deal and which half should be released more quickly? One approach is to take all of the data they have on all of their previous callers, along with anything else they can gather and combine with the data (e.g., public data sets based on caller id, geography, or other such data that could be captured based on where the person is calling from), and feed it into a supervised machine learning classification system in order to classify them into buyer and non-buyer groups. Once the model is trained, which means that it's been developed using a subset of this data, it's then tested to see how well it works by running the remaining subset of the data through the trained model. Suppose that the result is a system that correctly classifies the test set of data 60% of the time into buyers and non-buyers. While that may not sound like much of an improvement over the 50-50 ratio, it can add up to significant financial benefit over time.

A typical implementation of such an approach would be for that machine learning model to be put into the workflow of the call center such that when a new call comes into the call center, everything known about the caller (area code, zip code, phone type, etc.) is fed into the model, and the system produces a lead score which indicates the percentage probability that the caller will be a buyer. In this case, rather than answering the call blindly with a 50% chance of the person on the other end being a likely buyer, the call center employee would see a lead score on the screen indicating that the caller has, say, a 91% chance of being a buyer. The phone worker may have no idea which combination of variables was used to make this calculation, but if it's a viable model that's working better than the default (50-50 chance), then the sales person can invest more time into the caller with the high lead score and be more quick to end the call with someone having a lower lead score. Such systems can even be configured to use the ongoing call center activity to regularly tune the machine learning model so that it remains current, even if calling and buying patterns change over time. This is yet another difference compared to most traditional statistical analyses in which historic data is used to evaluate relationships but which rarely are then revised with new data to determine whether those findings hold up over time when applied in the real world.

This is one of the truly impressive aspects about machine learning. It's possible to feed enormous amounts of data into a system, develop, train, test, and tune machine learning models for classification or prediction based on either supervised or unsupervised algorithms, and then put them into the workflow in order to support business practices and improve performance. As seen with the call center example, such models can work hand-in-hand with human processes such that the machine learning systems don't replace people but rather give people insights that they wouldn't otherwise have when conducting business.

Such approaches can also be used throughout the employee management cycle, from hiring to performance assessment to retention. For example, one could build a machine learning hiring model based around successful employees. Essentially, myriad attributes of employees (whether all current employees or a subset of those deemed to be particularly successful) could be used to fit a model, and then new applicants could have their corresponding application data entered into the system in order to generate a success score. Similar to call center lead scoring, such an approach could produce a percentage score that predicts, say, a 71% probability of the applicant matching the successful employee profile. Again, because such a model would be developed via machine learning, the hiring manager may not have insight into the specific set of variables and weights that were used to calculate the score because they aren't typically developed with such variable-level human-readability in mind and any attempt to do so would likely result in a weaker model than the one generated by the algorithm. Such a scoring system could make the hiring process much more effective by reducing the need for cumbersome manual evaluation of resumes and unproductive interviews that only serve to highlight the mismatch between applicant and organization.

This hiring example raising the very real concern of how such opaque algorithms when used for high-stakes decisions like hiring can inadvertently serve to reinforce discriminatory practices. If, for example, a company is overrepresented by a particular demographic such as white males with Ivy League degrees, then the machine learning model is likely to generate success profiles that prioritize whiteness, maleness, and Ivy League degrees. It's not that the system is attempting to a priori focus on any particular variable, but when certain attributes are overrepresented in the training data, any mathematical models that maximize classification rates or minimize errors will be necessarily affected by such disproportionate inclusion. As a result, in an attempt to reduce conscious or unconscious human bias in the hiring process or to identify latent attributes that contribute to success, such a machine learning algorithm could actually reinforce historic discriminatory hiring patterns that lead to such disproportionate demographics currently in the company.

Machine learning can also be used to reinvent the performance assessment process. Just as KPIs and other business-centric metrics can be used to transform annual performance review cycles into a system of continuous improvement, machine learning algorithms can be used to enhance employee performance as an ongoing activity as well as serve as an evaluative tool. In other words, they're less useful for the retrospective aspect of the traditional performance assessment process. Replacing an annual qualitative or narrative summary of employee performance with an annual quantitative metric-based assessment is useful but isn't dependent upon machine learning to accomplish as those can be done via KPIs or other metrics. Where the machine learning system can be most effective is to enhance ongoing employee performance. Brynjolfsson and Mitchel (2017) describes one such strategy:

One approach that is particularly relevant to gauging the rate of future automation is the "learning apprentice" (sometimes called the "human in the loop") approach…in which the artificial intelligence (AI) program acts as an apprentice to assist the human worker, while also learning by observing the human's decisions and capturing these as additional training examples…Training a learning apprentice to mimic human-generated decisions offers the potential for machines to learn from the combined data of multiple people it assists, perhaps leading to outperforming each individual on the team that trains it…in cases where the computer can also access independent data to determine the optimal decision (ground truth), it may be possible to improve on human decisions and then to help the human improve their own performance. (pp. 1531-1532)

Additionally, machine learning can be considered organizationally when determining the optimal mix of employees on the basis of performance. Chalfin et al. (2016) described a scenario in which machine learning could be used to determine teacher tenure decisions. Specifically, they leveraged a variety of teaching quality indicators (e.g., surveys, classroom observations, student test scores, principal evaluations, etc.) and then measured the effect of replacing the bottom 10% of teachers with the average performing teacher. They found that using a machine learning algorithm to determine the replacements rather than relying solely on principal ratings of teachers produced significant learning benefits to the students (up to ten times that of leaving the low performing teachers in place) and also in a cost effective manner. "Our back-of-the-envelope calculations suggest that using ML rather than the current system to promote teachers may be on the order of two or three times as cost-effective as reducing class size by one-third during the first few years of elementary school" (p. 126).

Finally, employee attrition is another area in which machine learning is increasingly being implemented. Zhao et al. (2018) evaluated ten different supervised machine learning methods and found various levels of predictive performance. What was particularly useful in their analysis was not only the comparison of different algorithms based on effectiveness, but the steps to bring transparency to the algorithms themselves by extracting the most important features that emerged from the various models. While not all machine learning algorithms allow for human-interpretable findings, their comparative work enabled them to extract and rank order features that had the strongest predictive power in terms of employee attrition. They found, for example, that the most important feature was days since last pay raise, followed by job tenure (days), then age, then compensation with title, gender, management level, and client-facing role being the least predictive (p. 754). While such extraction and ranking isn't always feasible with machine learning, it provided useful in this circumstance and could affect employer efforts to retain quality employees over time.

MACHINE LEARNING THREATS

The benefits of machine learning in performance management cannot be considered without also giving attention to the challenges and threats associated with the design and implementation of machine learning systems. These include concerns about the machine learning models themselves, the potential for dehumanizing what is supposed to be a process for improving human resources, and the insidious nature of bias in applied machine learning.

In a 2017 analysis of machine learning and artificial intelligence trends, Accenture Consulting highlighted that one of the significant challenges in machine learning model validation relating to the conceptual soundness of the resulting models. Given the relative newness of the field, they noted that many practitioners didn't understand differences between various methodologies, or nuances associated with different approaches, or even how to fit the best algorithmic approach to the use case in question. "That means it is going to be harder for model developers to demonstrate the suitability of the framework or theory with respect to the modeling or business context at hand" (Accenture, 2017, p. 10). Similarly, they noted that the rise of off-the-shelf vendor models meant that organizations could have even greater distance from the underlying algorithms, as the vendors may use proprietary models which could be difficult for organizations to effectively analyze and audit (p. 11). While explainable AI (XAI) could use artificial intelligence to help provide human-interpretable explanations of otherwise opaque model outcomes, the Accenture report notes that such technology is nascent and not yet ready for commercial usage (p. 15).

Another area of concern, particularly when considering the use of machine learning in performance assessment and management, is the dehumanizing potential of the approach. Managing human resources is, by the very term, supposed to be human centric. Unlike other organizational resources, human resources are living, breathing people. To give over large parts of the performance planning, review, and management process to non-human entities and then using the results to direct the work of people has the potential of not only removing the human dimension but causing increased levels of stress and anxiety. Wang et al. (2021) found that higher levels of monitoring served as a burden to remote workers and could negatively affect employee well-being (p. 45). Similarly, Rosanas (2020) found that even pre-machine learning quantitative models such as the Balanced Scorecard were dehumanizing and demoralizing and were better used as a personal diagnostic tool rather than a performance management system (p. 56). If this concern exists for classical approaches to performance management, how much more could machine learning models contribute to the dehumanization of the workforce?

Bias in machine learning models is perhaps the most significant of the threats. Most commonly, this is conceptualized as inadvertent outcomes resulting from limited or skewed input data. For example, Buolamwini and Gebru (2018) famously found that commercial facial recognition systems misclassified darker-skinned females up to 34.7% of the time compared to a maximum error rate of 0.8% for lighter-skinned males (p. 1). In their analysis, the underlying cause was largely due to the unbalanced datasets used to train the machine learning models, with the datasets being overwhelmingly composed of lighter-skinned subjects (p. 1). This is a variation of the famous garbage in, garbage out concept, in that machine learning models can only work with the data they're fed. If the input data are skewed then the predictive output models will also be skewed.

Machine learning bias extends beyond garbage in, garbage out. In the article "A survey on bias and fairness in machine learning" Mehrabi et al. (2019) identified 23 different types of bias that could affect machine learning models. Many of these types can be broadly classified into biases associated with the underlying data, the algorithm itself, or with user interaction. What's particularly challenging about using machine learning is that it's difficult to cleanly separate and isolate these bias-inducing dynamics. As Mehrabi et al. note:

Existing work tried to categorize these bias definitions into groups, such as definitions falling solely under data or user interaction. However, due to the existence of the feedback loop phenomenon, which is a situation in which the trained machine learning model makes decisions that produce outcomes, and these very outcomes affect future data that will be collected for subsequent training rounds or models, these definitions are intertwined, and we need a categorization which closely models this situation. (p. 7)

As Hutson (2021) observed, "The opacity of artificial intelligence makes it hard to tell when decision-making is biased" (p. 40). Any effort to automate personnel efforts or to leverage machine learning algorithms as a supplemental evaluative source must keep these dynamics in mind, lest the computers become the cause of increased workplace discrimination.

FUTURE RESEARCH DIRECTIONS

The issue of biased algorithms warrants significant research. Given that any data-driven models are so dependent on the quality of the data, it's critical to understand how machine learning can inadvertently reinforce and promote discriminatory practices. Furthermore, research should be conducted to produce standard practices, markers, and metrics that can be applied to existing algorithms to uncover such underlying concerns. Similarly, further research to promote ethical use of machine learning algorithms would benefit the entire community.

The learning apprentice, or human in the loop, approach offers the possibility of using machine learning to enhance the performance and effectiveness of employees toward a more robust outcome than could be achieved by either working independently. Determining what types of employee functions are best suited to reconfiguration using a learning apprentice approach is an area that warrants additional research. Because machine learning is generally understood to be a subset of artificial intelligence, and artificial intelligence has not yet reached a level of generalized intelligence, ML-based refinements are necessarily limited to those tasks where existing data can be used to create models for functions such as classification and regression.

In their assessment of what machine learning can do in the workforce, Brynjolfsson and Mitchell (2017) outline characteristics of the types of activities that are well-suited for machine learning. For example, they include functions that map well-defined inputs to well-defined outputs, where large digital data sets exist, and where there are clearly definable goals and metrics with corresponding feedback (p. 1532). Further research into business processes to determine what types of functions, disciplines, corporate structures, and other aspects are suitable for machine learning enhancement will enable organizations to focus their energies and limited resources on worthwhile initiatives rather than scattershot efforts.

Finally, whether through an automated explainable AI (XAI) framework or just a more elaborate effort of involving humans in the evaluation and presentation of findings, it's critically important to engage in additional research into interpretable machine learning models when considering the use of such technology in human resources performance management. Beyond improvements in productivity, the organizational performance management process has significant material effects on employees, their personal well-being, and even their own health and welfare as well as that of family members. Entrusting one's career to an opaque performance evaluation process such employee hiring, salary, promotion, and termination could be determined primarily, or even solely, by so-called black box algorithms and machine learning models is potentially discriminatory, dangerous, and dehumanizing.

CONCLUSION

Machine learning enables organizations to leverage data strategically to improve employee performance, promote continuous improvement, and better fulfill the mission. Opportunities for leveraging machine learning within organizations exist throughout the employee lifecycle, but such approaches should be pursued with a clear understanding of the strengths and limitations of the methodology. It's incumbent upon human resources professionals to partner with data scientists and researchers in the field to make the algorithms and models more transparent and human-interpretable so that people can effectively and ethically direct the use of such technological systems within organizations. Uncritical use of machine learning algorithms can prove to be counterproductive if the wisdom of humans gets fully replaced by the mathematics of computers.

REFERENCES

Abdelhadi, N., Jamal, B. M., & Leclerc, A. (2015). Performance appraisal system and employee satisfaction: The role of trust towards supervisors. *Journal of Human Resources Management and Labor Studies*, *3*(1), 40–53.

Accenture Consulting. (2017). *Emerging trends in the validation of machine learning and artificial intelligence models*. https://www.accenture.com/_acnmedia/PDF-114/Accenture-Emerging-Trends-in-the-Validation-of-ML-and-AI-Models.pdf

Anaconda. (2020). *The state of data science 2020: Moving from hype toward maturity*. https://know.anaconda.com/rs/387-XNW-688/images/Anaconda-SODS-Report-2020-Final.pdf

April, R. (2020). *24 KPIs every sales manager should measure in 2020*. https://blog.hubspot.com/sales/kpis-every-field-sales-leader-should-be-measuring

Armstrong, M. (2017). *Armstrong on reinventing performance management: Building a culture of continuous improvement*. Kogan Page.

Brynjolfsson, E., & Mitchell, T. (2017). What can machine learning do? Workforce implications. *Science*, *358*(6370), 1530–1534. doi:10.1126cience.aap8062 PMID:29269459

Buolamwini, J., & Gebru, T. (2018). Gender shades: Intersectional accuracy disparities in commercial gender classification. *Proceedings of Machine Learning Research*, *81*, 1–15.

Cecchi-Dimeglio, P. (2017, April 12). How gender bias corrupts performance reviews, and what to do about it. *Harvard Business Review*. https://hbr.org/2017/04/how-gender-bias-corrupts-performance-reviews-and-what-to-do-about-it

Chalfin, A., Danieli, O., Hillis, A., Jelveh, Z., Luca, M., Ludwig, J., & Mullainathan, S. (2016). Productivity and selection of human capital with machine learning. *The American Economic Review*, *106*(5), 124–127. doi:10.1257/aer.p20161029

Fadlon, I., Laird, J., & Nielsen, T. H. (2016). Do employer pension contributions reflect employee preferences? Evidence from a retirement savings reform in Denmark. *American Economic Journal. Applied Economics*, *8*(3), 196–216. doi:10.1257/app.20150015 PMID:27917259

Hope, J., & Fraser, R. (2003). *Beyond budgeting: How managers can break free from the annual performance trap*. Harvard Business School Publishing Corporation.

Hutson, M. (2021, February). Lyin' AIs. *IEEE Spectrum*, 40–45. doi:10.1109/MSPEC.2021.9340114

Janakova, M., Suchanek, P., Padysak, P., & Botlik, J. (2020). The KPI hierarchy for CRM and marketing. *GIS Business*, *15*(1), 263–277. doi:10.26643/gis.v15i1.18378

Kaplan, R. S., & Norton, D. P. (1992). The balanced scorecard: Measures that drive performance. *Harvard Business Review*, *70*(1), 71–79. PMID:10119714

Knowledge@Wharton. (2019, June 17). *With high-deductible employer health plans, who wins?* https://knowledge.wharton.upenn.edu/article/high-deductible-health-plans-pros-and-cons/

Lazarova, S. (2017). Business intelligence approaches to the design of key performance indicators. In *Proceedings of the 2nd Conference on Innovative Teaching Methods* (ITM 2017, pp. 90-96). University of Economics – Varna.

Lund, S., Madgavkar, A., Manyika, J., Smit, S., Ellingrud, K., Meaney, M., & Robinson, O. (2021). *The future of work after COVID-19*. https://www.mckinsey.com/featured-insights/future-of-work/the-future-of-work-after-covid-19

Marr, B. (2020). *What is the difference between key performance indicators (KPIs) and critical success factors (CSFs)?* https://www.bernardmarr.com/default.asp?contentID=1406

McGregor, D. (1975). An uneasy look at performance appraisal. *Harvard Business Review*, *5*(7), 27–31.

Mehrabi, N., Morstatter, F., Saxena, N., Lerman, K., & Galstyan, A. (2019, September). *A survey on bias and fairness in machine learning*. https://arxiv.org/pdf/1908.09635.pdf

Neely, J. (2021). *7 sales KPIs (key performance indicators) you should measure in 2021*. https://toggl.com/blog/sales-kpi

Parmenter, D. (2015). *Key performance indicators: Developing, implementing, and using winning KPIs* (3rd ed.). John Wiley and Sons.

Parmenter, D. (2019). *What is a KPI (introduction to key performance indicators)?* https://kpi.davidparmenter.com/defining-kpis/

Paycor. (2020, December 24). *The biggest cost of doing business: A closer look at labor costs*. https://www.paycor.com/resource-center/a-closer-look-at-labor-costs

Pulakos, E. D. (2004). *Performance management: A roadmap for developing, implementing and evaluating performance management systems*. Society for Human Resource Management Foundation.

Rosanas, J. M. (2020). The dehumanization and demoralization of management control systems: Can we possibly re-humanize and re-moralize them? *European Accounting and Management Review*, 6(2), 56–80.

ScienceDaily. (2013). *Big data, for better or worse: 90% of world's data generated over last two years*. https://www.sciencedaily.com/releases/2013/05/130522085217.htm

Shalev-Shwartz, S., & Ben-David, S. (2014). *Understanding machine learning: From theory to algorithms*. Cambridge University Press.

Shmailan, A. S. B. (2016). The relationship between job satisfaction, job performance and employee engagement: An explorative study. *Issues in Business Management and Economics*, 4(1), 1–8.

U.S. Bureau of Labor Statistics. (2020, December 17). *Employer costs for employee compensation summary*. https://www.bls.gov/news.release/ecec.nr0.htm

Wang, B., Liu, Y., Qian, J., & Parker, S. K. (2020). Achieving effective remote working during the COVID-19 pandemic: A work design perspective. *Applied Psychology*, 70(1), 16–59.

Zhao, Y., Hryniewicki, M. K., Cheng, F., Fu, B., & Zhu, X. (2018). Employee turnover prediction with machine learning: A reliable approach. In *Proceedings of SAI Intelligent Systems Conference* (pp. 737-758). Academic Press.

ADDITIONAL READING

Baer, T. (2019). *Understand, manage, and prevent algorithmic bias: A guide for business users and data scientists*. Springer. doi:10.1007/978-1-4842-4885-0

Garg, S., Sinha, S., Kar, A. K., & Mani, M. (2021). A review of machine learning applications in human resource management. *International Journal of Productivity and Performance Management*. Advance online publication. doi:10.1108/IJPPM-08-2020-0427

Hastie, T., Tibshirani, R., & Friedman, J. (2016). *The elements of statistical learning: Data mining, inference, and prediction* (2nd ed.). Springer.

Parmenter, D. (2019). *Key performance indicators: Developing, implementing, and using winning KPIs* (4th ed.). John Wiley and Sons. doi:10.1002/9781119620785

Schelter, S., Biessmann, F., Januschowski, T., Salinas, D., Seufert, S., & Szarvas, G. (2018). On challenges in machine learning model management. *Bulletin of the IEEE Computer Society Technical Committee on Data Engineering*. http://sites.computer.org/debull/A18dec/p5.pdf

Shalev-Shwartz, S., & Ben-David, S. (2014). *Understanding machine learning: From theory to algorithms*. Cambridge University Press. doi:10.1017/CBO9781107298019

Trost, A. (2017). *The end of performance appraisal: A practitioners' guide to alternatives in agile organisations*. Springer. doi:10.1007/978-3-319-54235-5

Watt, J., Borhani, R., & Katsaggelos, K. (2020). *Machine learning refined: Foundations, algorithms, and applications* (2nd ed.). Cambridge University Press. doi:10.1017/9781108690935

KEY TERMS AND DEFINITIONS

Algorithmic Bias: The phenomenon when a machine learning algorithm produces biased output based on the biased input data.

Decision Tree: A machine learning algorithm that cascades data through a series of sequential decisions to determine classification or regression outcomes.

Explainable AI (XAI): An emerging approach where one artificial intelligence system evaluates the underlying code of another artificial intelligence or machine learning model and generates a human-interpretable explanation of the outcomes.

Machine Learning: Use of computer algorithms to automatically discover patterns in data based on mathematical processes.

Performance Management: A process of planning, tracking, and evaluating goals and performance in order to ensure that employees are effectively contributing to the organizational mission.

Random Forest: A machine learning methodology in which multiple decision trees are created and combined to produce a more robust model.

Supervised Learning: A type of machine learning which uses a labeled dataset, such that the algorithm attempts to match the output labels based on input data.

Testing Dataset: The portion of the input dataset used to test the effectiveness of the trained model against previously unseen data.

Training a Model: The process of processing input data using a machine learning algorithm in order to generate a model that minimizes error.

Training Dataset: The portion of the input dataset used to train the machine learning model.

Unsupervised Learning: A type of machine learning in which the algorithm attempts to find patterns in the data without predefined outputs.

Compilation of References

Abdelhadi, N., Jamal, B. M., & Leclerc, A. (2015). Performance appraisal system and employee satisfaction: The role of trust towards supervisors. *Journal of Human Resources Management and Labor Studies*, *3*(1), 40–53.

Abdel-Halim, A. A. (1981). A reexamination of ability as a moderator of role perception–satisfaction relationship. *Personnel Psychology*, *34*(3), 549–561. doi:10.1111/j.1744-6570.1981.tb00495.x

Accenture Consulting. (2017). *Emerging trends in the validation of machine learning and artificial intelligence models.* https://www.accenture.com/_acnmedia/PDF-114/Accenture-Emerging-Trends-in-the-Validation-of-ML-and-AI-Models.pdf

Adadevoh, D. (2006). *Leading transformation in Africa.* International Leadership Foundation.

Adams, A. W. (2014). *Shepherd leadership of Church of God pastors and how this relates to ministerial effectiveness* (Doctoral dissertation). Available from ProQuest Dissertations and Theses database. (UMI No. 3570373)

Addae, H. M., Parboteeah, K. P., & Velinor, N. (2008). Role stressors and organizational commitment: Public sector employment in St Lucia. *International Journal of Manpower*, *29*(6), 567–582. doi:10.1108/01437720810904220

Ahlstrom, S. E. (2004). *A Religious History of the American People* (2nd ed.). Yale University Press.

Ahrens, T., & Ferry, L. (2015). Newcastle City Council and the grassroots: Accountability and budgeting under austerity. *Accounting, Auditing & Accountability Journal*, *28*(6), 909–933. doi:10.1108/AAAJ-03-2014-1658

Ai, A. L., Peterson, C., Bolling, S. F., & Koenig, H. (2002). Private prayer and optimism in middle-aged and older patients awaiting cardiac surgery. *The Gerontologist*, *42*(1), 70–81. doi:10.1093/geront/42.1.70 PMID:11815701

Albert, S., & Whetten, D. (1985). Organizational Identity. In L. Cummings & M. Staw (Eds.), *Organizational Behavior* (Vol. 7, pp. 263–295). JAI Press.

Aleshire, D. (1990). ATS profiles of ministry project. In R. A. Hunt, J. Hinkle, Jr., & H. N. Malony (Eds.), Clergy assessment and career development (pp. 97–103). Academic Press.

Ali, A., Ahmad-Ur-Rehman, M., Ul Haq, I., Jam, F. A., Ghafoor, M. B., & Azeem, M. U. (2010). Perceived organizational support and psychological empowerment. *European Journal of Soil Science*, *17*(2), 186–192.

Aliyu, A., Bello, M., Kasim, R., & Martin, D. (2014). Positivist and non-positivist paradigm in social science research: Conflicting paradigms or perfect partners. *Journal of Management and Sustainability*, *4*(3), 79–95. doi:10.5539/jms.v4n3p79

Allen & Hart. (1998). Training Older workers: Implications for HRD/HPT Professionals. *Performance Improvement Quarterly*, *11*(4), 91-102.

Allen, E., & Seaman, C. (2007). Likert Scales and Data Analyses. *Quality Progress*, *40*(7), 64–65.

Alley, D., Suthers, K., & Crimmins, E. (2007). Education and cognitive decline in older Americans: Results from the AHEAD sample. In *Res Aging* (pp. 73–94). NIH Public Access. doi:10.1177/0164027506294245

Alliger, G. M., & Janak, E. A. (1989). Kirkpatrick's levels of training criteria: Thirty years later. *Personnel Psychology, 41*, 331-342. doi:10.1111/j.1744-6570.1989.tb00661.x

Allison, M., & Keller, C. (2004). Self-efficacy intervention effects on physical activity in older adults. *Western Journal of Nursing Research, 26*(1), 31–46. doi:10.1177/0193945903259350 PMID:14984643

Altman, Z. (2017, March 5). *5 Reasons Why Workplace Diversity Is Good For Business: Why one polling expert sees lack of diversity as the most dangerous blind spot affecting corporate America today.* https://www.inc.com/ian-altman/5-reasons-why-workplace-diversity-is-good-for-business.html

Amit, K., Lisak, A., Popper, M., & Gal, R. (2007). Motivation to lead: Research on the motives for undertaking leadership roles in the Israel Defense Forces (IDF). *Military Psychology, 19*(3), 137–160. doi:10.1080/08995600701386317

Anaconda. (2020). *The state of data science 2020: Moving from hype toward maturity.* https://know.anaconda.com/rs/387-XNW-688/images/Anaconda-SODS-Report-2020-Final.pdf

Andersen, J. A. (2009). When a servant-leader comes knocking. *Leadership and Organization Development Journal, 30*(1), 4–15. doi:10.1108/01437730910927070

Anderson, L. W., & Krathwohl, D. R. (2001). *A taxonomy for learning, teaching, and assessing: A revision of Bloom's taxonomy of educational objectives.* Longman.

Andersson, J., & Wikström, E. (2014). Constructing accountability in inter-organisational collaboration. *Journal of Health Organization and Management, 28*(5), 619–634. doi:10.1108/JHOM-10-2013-0220 PMID:25735421

Anthony, S. (2016, July 15). Kodak's Downfall Wasn't About Technology. *Harvard Business Review.* Retrieved from https://hbr.org/2016/07/kodaks-downfall-wasnt-about-technology

April, R. (2020). *24 KPIs every sales manager should measure in 2020.* https://blog.hubspot.com/sales/kpis-every-field-sales-leader-should-be-measuring

Armstrong, M. (2017). *Armstrong on reinventing performance management: Building a culture of continuous improvement.* Kogan Page.

Armstrong-Stassen, M., & Ursel, N. (2009). Perceived organizational support, career satisfaction, and the retention of older workers. *Journal of Occupational and Organizational Psychology, 82*(1), 201–220. doi:10.1348/096317908X288838

Arnold, J. A., Arad, S., Rhoades, J. A., & Drasgow, F. (2000). The empowering leadership questionnaire: The construction and validation of a new scale for measuring leader behaviors. *Journal of Organizational Behavior, 21*(3), 249–269. doi:10.1002/(SICI)1099-1379(200005)21:3<249::AID-JOB10>3.0.CO;2-#

Aronson, E., Stephan, C., Sikes, J., Blaney, N., & Snapp, M. (1978). *The Jigsaw Classroom.* Sage.

Ashmos, D. P., & Duchon, D. (2000). Spirituality at work. *Journal of Management Inquiry, 9*(2), 134–145. doi:10.1177/105649260092008

Assael, H., & Keon, J.Sampling Errors in Survey Research. (1982). Nonsampling vs. sampling errors in survey research. *Journal of Marketing, 46*(2), 114–123. doi:10.1177/002224298204600212

Atchison, B. J. G. (2009). *A study of African American pastors' method of entry into the ministry and pastoral success* (Doctoral dissertation). Available from ProQuest Dissertations and Theses database. (ProQuest No. 10258492)

Atkinson, T. M., Rosenfeld, B. D., Sit, L., Mendoza, T. R., Fruscione, M., Lavene, D., Shaw, M., Li, Y., Hay, J., Cleeland, C. S., Scher, H. I., Breitbart, W. S., & Basch, E. (2011). Using confirmatory factor analysis to evaluate construct validity of the Brief Pain Inventory (BPI). *Journal of Pain and Symptom Management*, *41*(3), 558–565. doi:10.1016/j.jpainsymman.2010.05.008 PMID:21131166

Auyang, S. Y. (1999). *Foundations of complex-system theories: in economics, evolutionary biology, and statistical physics*. Cambridge University.

Avolio, B. J., Bass, B. M., & Jung, D. I. (1999). Re-examining the components of transformational and transactional leadership using the Multifactor Leadership Questionnaire. *Journal of Occupational and Organizational Psychology*, *72*(4), 441–462. doi:10.1348/096317999166789

Avolio, B. J., & Gardner, W. L. (2005). Authentic leadership development: Getting to the root of positive forms of leadership. *The Leadership Quarterly*, *16*(3), 315–338. doi:10.1016/j.leaqua.2005.03.001

Babiak, P., Neumann, C., & Hare, R. (2010). Corporate Psychopathy: Talking the Walk. *Behavioral Sciences & the Law*, *28*(2), 174–193. PMID:20422644

Bacharach, S., Bamberger, P., & Conley, S. (1991). Work–home conflict among nurses and engineers: Mediating the impact of role stress on burnout and satisfaction with work. *Journal of Organizational Behavior*, *12*(1), 39–53. doi:10.1002/job.4030120104

Badura, K. L., Grijalva, E., Galvin, B. M., Owen, B. P., & Joseph, D. L. (2020). Motivation to lead: A meta-analysis and distal-proximal model of motivation and leadership. *The Journal of Applied Psychology*, *105*(4), 331–354. doi:10.1037/apl0000439 PMID:31393147

Ballou, D. (2009). Test scaling and value-added measurement. *Education Finance and Policy*, *4*(4), 351–383. doi:10.1162/edfp.2009.4.4.351

Bandura, A. (2006). Guide for constructing self-efficacy scales. In F. Pajares & T. Urdan (Eds.), Adolescence and education: Vol. 5. Self efficacy and adolescence (pp. 307-337). Greenwich, CT: Information Age.

Bandura, A. (1977). Self-efficacy: Toward a unifying theory of behavioral change. *Psychological Review*, *84*(2), 191–215. doi:10.1037/0033-295X.84.2.191 PMID:847061

Bandura, A. (1982). Self-efficacy mechanism in human agency. *The American Psychologist*, *37*(2), 122–147. doi:10.1037/0003-066X.37.2.122

Bandura, A. (1986). *Social foundations of thought & action: A social cognitive theory*. Prentice-Hall.

Bandura, A. (1986). *Social foundations of thought & action: Social cognitive theory*. Prentice Hall.

Bandura, A. (1986). *Social foundations of thought and action: A social cognitive theory*. Prentice-Hall, Inc.

Bandura, A. (1988). Self-efficacy conception of anxiety. *Anxiety Research*, *1*(2), 77–98. doi:10.1080/10615808808248222

Bandura, A. (1997). *Self-efficacy: The exercise of control*. Freeman and Company.

Bandura, A. (1997). *Self-Efficacy: The exercise of control*. Worth Publishers.

Baptiste, R. N. (2008). Tightening the link between employee well-being at work and performance: A new dimension for HRM. *Management Decision*, *46*(2), 284–309. doi:10.1108/00251740810854168

Barbuto, J. E. Jr, & Wheeler, D. W. (2006). Scale development and construct clarification of servant leadership. *Group & Organization Management*, *31*(3), 300–326. doi:10.1177/1059601106287091

Barfoot, D. S., Winston, B. E., & Wickman, C. (2005). *Forced pastoral exits: An exploratory study* [Unpublished manuscript]. School of Global Leadership and Entrepreneurship, Regent University.

Barnett, D. C. (2003). *A comparative analysis of critical competencies of the assessment of ministry effectiveness* (Doctoral dissertation). Available from ProQuest Dissertations and Theses database. (UMI No. 3102040)

Barrett, P., & Kline, P. (1981). *The observation to variable ratio in factor analysis*. Personality Study & Group Behaviour.

Barth, M., McNaught, W., & Rizzi, P. (1993). Corporations and the aging workforce. In P. H. Mirvis (Ed.), *Building the competetive workforce: Investing in human capital for corporate success*. Wiley.

Bartholomew, L., Parcel, G., Swank, P., & Czyzewski, D. (1993). Measuring self-efficacy expectations for the self-management of cystic fibrosis. *CHEST Journal, 103*(5), 1524–1530. doi:10.1378/chest.103.5.1524 PMID:8486038

Bartik, A. W., Bertrand, M., Cullen, Z., Glaeser, E. L., Luca, M., & Stanton, C. (2020). The impact of COVID-19 on small business outcomes and expectations. *Proceedings of the National Academy of Sciences of the United States of America, 117*(30), 17656–17666. doi:10.1073/pnas.2006991117 PMID:32651281

Bartram, T., & Casimir, G. (2007). The relationship between leadership and follower in-role performance and satisfaction with the leader: The mediating effects of empowerment and trust in the leader. *Leadership and Organization Development Journal, 28*(1), 4–19. doi:10.1108/01437730710718218

Bass, B. M. (1990). *Bass and Stogdill's handbook of leadership: Theory, research, and managerial applications* (3rd ed.). Free Press.

Bass, B. M., & Avolio, B. J. (1993). Transformational leadership and organizational culture. *Public Administration Quarterly, 17*(1), 112–121.

Bass, B. M., & Avolio, B. J. (1995). *MLQ Multifactor leadership questionnaire for research*. Mindgarden.

Battisto, D., Pak, R., Vander Wood, M., & Pilcher, J. (2009). Using a task analysis to describe nursing work in acute care patient environments. *The Journal of Nursing Administration, 39*(12), 537–547. doi:10.1097/NNA.0b013e3181c1806d PMID:19955968

Bauer, J. C. (2002). *A longitudinal evaluation of the impact of organizational structure on role ambiguity and work group performance* (Publication No. 3086349) [Doctoral dissertation, University of Sarasota]. Proquest Dissertation Abstracts and Theses.

Beatty, P., & Willis, G. (2007). Research synthesis: The practice of cognitive interviewing. *Public Opinion Quarterly, 71*(2), 287–311. doi:10.1093/poq/nfm006

Becker, J., Schwartz, C., Saris-Baglama, R., Kosinski, M., & Bjorner, J. (2007). Using item response theory (IRT) for developing and evaluating the pain impact questionnaire (PIQ-6™). *Pain Medicine, 8*(s3), 129–144. doi:10.1111/j.1526-4637.2007.00377.x

Beebe, R. S. (2007). Predicting burnout, conflict management style, and turnover among clergy. *Journal of Career Assessment, 15*(2), 257–275. doi:10.1177/1069072706298157

Belcher, G. D. (2002). *The relationship of mentoring to ministerial effectiveness among pastors of the Southern Baptist Convention* (Doctoral dissertation). Available from ProQuest Dissertations and Theses database. (UMI No. 3048643)

Berkes, H. (2012). *Remembering Roger Boisjoly: He tried to stop shuttle Challenger launch*. NPR. https://www.npr.org/sections/thetwo-way/2012/02/06/146490064/remembering-roger-boisjoly-he-tried-to-stop-shuttle-challenger-launch%20 8/28/15

Berry, A. J., & Cartwright, S. (2000). Leadership: A critical construction. *Leadership and Organization Development Journal, 21*(7), 342–349. doi:10.1108/01437730010377881

Best, K. C. (2011). Holistic Leadership: A Model for Leader-Member Engagement and Development. *Journal of JVBL, 4*(1).

Bethlehem, J., & Schouten, B. (2016). Nonresponse error: detection and correction. In *The SAGE handbook of survey methodology* (pp. 558–578). Sage Publications Ltd. doi:10.4135/9781473957893.n35

Beverly, T., & McCoach, D. B. (2015). *Perceptions of standardized test-taking ability survey (PTTAS): Development, validation, and replication* [Paper presentation]. American Educational Research Association.

Bhatti, N., Mura Maitlo, G., Shaikh, N., Hashmi, M., & Shaikh, F. (2012). The Impact of Autocratic and Democratic Leaderships Style on Job Satisfaction. *International Business Research, 5*(2), 192–201. doi:10.5539/ibr.v5n2p192

Birren, J., & Birren, B. (1990). The concepts, models and history of the psychology of aging. In J. Birren & K. Schaie (Eds.), *Handbook of the psychology of aging* (pp. 3–18). Academic Press. doi:10.1016/B978-0-12-101280-9.50007-3

Bishop, K., Webber, S. S., & O'Neil, R. (2011). Preparation and prior experience in issue-selling success. *Journal of Managerial Issues, 23*(3), 323–340.

Blackmon, V. Y. (2008). *Strategic planning and organizational performance: An investigation using the balanced scorecard in non-profit organizations* (Publication No. 3311386) [Doctoral Dissertation, Capella University]. ProQuest Dissertations and Theses Global.

Blau, G. (1989). Testing generalizability of a career commitment measure and its impact on employee turnover. *Journal of Vocational Behavior, 35*(1), 88–103. doi:10.1016/0001-8791(89)90050-X

Bloom, B. S., Engelhart, M. D., Furst, E. J., Hill, W. H., & Krathwohl, D. R. (1956). *Taxonomy of educational objectives: The classification of educational goals. Handbook I: Cognitive domain.* David McKay Company.

Blythe, B. T. (2014). *Blindsided: A manager's guide to crisis leadership* (2nd ed.). Rothstein Associates.

Bobbio, A., & Manganelli Rattazzi, A. M. (2006). A contribution to the Validation of the Motivation to Lead Scale (MTL): A research in the Italian context. *Leadership, 2*(1), 117–129. doi:10.1177/1742715006057240

Bocarnea, M. C., & Brown, W. J. (2007). Celebrity-Persona Parasocial Interaction Scale. In R. A. Reynolds, R. Woods, & J. D. Baker (Eds.), *Handbook of research on electronic surveys and measurements* (pp. 309–312). Idea Group Reference. doi:10.4018/978-1-59140-792-8.ch039

Böckenholt, U. (2017). Measuring response styles in Likert items. *Psychological Methods, 22*(1), 69–83. doi:10.1037/met0000106 PMID:27893218

Bodenmiller, J. J. (2015). *A Quantitative relational analysis of leadership style and leader accountability in non-profit organizations* (Publication No. 3714860) [Doctoral Dissertation, University of Phoenix]. Proquest Dissertations and Theses Global.

Bollen, K. A. (1989). *Structural equations with latent variables.* John Wiley. doi:10.1002/9781118619179

Bolman, L. (1997). Reframing Organizations (2nd ed.) San Francisco, CA: Jossey-Bass.

Boloka, G. M. (1999). African Renaissance: A quest for (un)attainable past. *Critical Arts, 13*(2), 92–103. doi:10.1080/02560049985310151

Bonvillian, B. (2013). Turnaround managers as crisis leaders. In A. Dubrin (Ed.), *Handbook of research on crisis leadership in organization* (pp. 92–109). Edward Elgar. doi:10.4337/9781781006405.00013

Borsboom, D. (2006). When does measurement invariance matter? *Medical Care*, *44*(11, Suppl 3), S176–S181. doi:10.1097/01.mlr.0000245143.08679.cc PMID:17060825

Bourgeois Iii, L. J. (1979). Toward a method of middle-range theorizing. *Academy of Management Review*, *4*(3), 443–447. doi:10.5465/amr.1979.4289127

Bowlby, J. (1969). Attachment and loss, Vol. 1, attachment. Holgarth.

Bowman, N. A., & Schuldt, J. P. (2014). Effects of item order and response options in college student surveys. *New Directions for Institutional Research*, *2014*(161), 99–109. doi:10.1002/ir.20070

BRANDfog. (2013). *CEO, Social media and leadership survey.* Retrieved Feb. 7, 2021, from https://brandfog.com/resource/2013-ceo-social-media-and-leadership-survey/

Braun, S., Aydin, N., Frey, D., & Peus, C. (2016). Leader Narcissism Predicts Malicious Envy and Supervisor-targeted Counterproductive Behavior: Evidence from Field and Experimental Research. *Journal of Business Ethics*, *135*, 1–17.

Bray, S. R., & Brawley, L. R. (2002). Role efficacy, role clarity, and role performance effectiveness. *Small Group Research*, *33*(2), 233–253. doi:10.1177/104649640203300204

Brekke, M. L., Strommen, M. P., & Williams, D. (1979). *Ten faces of ministry.* Augsburg Press.

Brick, J. M., & Tourangeau, R. (2017). Responsive survey designs for reducing nonresponse bias. *Journal of Official Statistics*, *33*(3), 735–752. doi:10.1515/jos-2017-0034

Briggs, D. C. (2013). Measuring growth with vertical scales. *Journal of Educational Measurement*, *50*(2), 204–226. doi:10.1111/jedm.12011

Broom, G. M., Casey, S., & Ritchey, J. (1997). Toward a concept and theory of organization-public relationships. *Journal of Public Relations Research*, *9*(2), 83–98. doi:10.12071532754xjprr0902_01

Broom, G. M., & Dozier, D. M. (1990). *Using research in public relations: Applications to program management.* Prentice-Hall.

Brown, W. J., Barker, G., & Presnell, K. K. (2008). *The social impact of mediated celebrities: Cognitive and emotional responses to the death of Dale Earnhardt.* Paper presented to the National Communication Association, San Diego, CA.

Brown, H. (2012, July/August). So What If I Don't Have An iPhone? The Unintended Consequences of Using Arrogance in Advertising. *Journal of Applied Business Research*, *28*(4), 555–563. doi:10.19030/jabr.v28i4.7040

Brown, J. D. (2009). Choosing the right type of rotation in PCA and EFA. Shiken. *JALT Testing & Evaluation SIG Newsletter*, *13*(3), 20–25.

Brown, J. D. (2009). Choosing the Right Type of Rotation in PCA and EFA. *Shiken: JALT Testing & Evaluation SIG Newsletter*, *13*(3), 20–25.

Brown, J. D. (2009). Choosing the right type of rotation in PCA and EFA. *Shiken: JALT Testing and Evaluation SIG Newsletter*, *13*(3), 20–25.

Brownlee-Turgeon, J. (2016). *Measuring leadership competencies to avert crisis: Development and validation of an instrument to operationalize a conceptual model* (UMI No. 10107445) [Doctoral dissertation, Regent University]. ProQuest Dissertations and Theses Global.

Brown, M., & Trevino, L. (2006). Ethical Leadership: A Review and Future Directions. *The Leadership Quarterly*, *17*(6), 595–616. doi:10.1016/j.leaqua.2006.10.004

Brown, W. J. (2010). Steve Irwin's influence on wildlife conservation. *Journal of Communication, 60*(1), 73–93. doi:10.1111/j.1460-2466.2009.01458.x

Brown, W. J. (2015). Examining four processes of audience involvement with media personae: Transportation, parasocial interaction, identification and worship. *Communication Theory, 25*(3), 259–283. doi:10.1111/comt.12053

Brown, W. J., Basil, M. D., & Bocarnea, M. C. (2003). Social influence of an international celebrity: Responses to the death of Princess Diana. *Journal of Communication, 53*(4), 587–605. doi:10.1111/j.1460-2466.2003.tb02912.x

Brown, W. J., & Cody, M. J. (1991). Effects of an Indian television soap opera in promoting women's status. *Human Communication Research, 18*(1), 114–142. doi:10.1111/j.1468-2958.1991.tb00531.x PMID:12319295

Brown, W. J., & de Matviuk, M. A. C. (2010). Sports celebrities and public health: Diego Maradona's influence on drug use prevention. *Journal of Health Communication, 15*(4), 358–373. doi:10.1080/10810730903460575 PMID:20574875

Brynjolfsson, E., & Mitchell, T. (2017). What can machine learning do? Workforce implications. *Science, 358*(6370), 1530–1534. doi:10.1126cience.aap8062 PMID:29269459

Bunch, K. (2007). Training Failure as a Consequence of Organizational Culture. *Human Resource Development Review, 6*(2), 142–163. doi:10.1177/1534484307299273

Bunn, T. P. E. (1998). *A study of the difference between senior pastors and laity perceptions of senior pastoral effectiveness* (Doctoral dissertation). Available from ProQuest Dissertations and Theses database. (UMI No. 304451491)

Buolamwini, J., & Gebru, T. (2018). Gender shades: Intersectional accuracy disparities in commercial gender classification. *Proceedings of Machine Learning Research, 81*, 1–15.

Bureau of Labor Statistics. (2008). *Career Guide to Industries, 2010-11 Edition*. Bureau of Labor Statistics. https://www.bls.gov/oco/cg/cgs035.htm

Burke, K. (1969). *A rhetoric of motives*. University of California Press.

Burns, J. M. (1978). *Leadership*. Harper & Row.

Burns, J. M. (1998). Foreword. In J. B. Ciulla (Ed.), *Ethics: The heart of leadership* (pp. x–xii). Praeger.

Burns, J. M. (2003). *Transforming leadership*. Atlantic Monthly Press.

Bussing, A., Matthiessen, P. F., & Ostermann, T. (2005). Engagement of patients in religious and spiritual practices: Confirmatory results with the SpREUK-P 1.1 questionnaire as a tool of quality of life research. *Health and Quality of Life Outcomes, 3*(53). PMID:16144546

Butler, D. M., & Herman, R. D. (1999). Effective ministerial leadership. *Nonprofit Management & Leadership, 9*(3), 229–239. doi:10.1002/nml.9302

Butler, R. (1969). Age-ism: Another form of bigotry. *The Gerontologist, 9*(4 Part 1), 243–246. doi:10.1093/geront/9.4_Part_1.243 PMID:5366225

Butler, R. (2002). Guest Editorial The Study of Productive Aging. *The Journals of Gerontology. Series B, Psychological Sciences and Social Sciences, 57*(6), S323–S323. doi:10.1093/geronb/57.6.S323 PMID:12426440

Byrne, B. M. (2016). Structural Equation Modeling With AMOS (3rd ed.). Taylor and Francis. doi:10.4324/9781315757421

Byrne, B. M. (2016). *Structural Equation Modeling With AMOS (Multivariate Applications Series)* Taylor and Francis.

Byrne, A., Dionisi, A. M., Barling, J., Akers, A., Robertson, J., Lys, R., Wylie, J., & Dupré, K. (2014). The depleted leader: The influence of leaders' diminished psychological resources on leadership behaviors. *The Leadership Quarterly, 25*(2), 344–357. doi:10.1016/j.leaqua.2013.09.003

Byrne, B. M., Shavelson, R. J., & Muthén, B. (1989). Testing for the equivalence of factor covariance and mean structures: The Issue of partial measurement invariance. *Psychological Bulletin, 105*(3), 456–466. doi:10.1037/0033-2909.105.3.456

Byrne, T. P. (2014). Ethical dilemmas in a California city: Lessons in leadership transparency and accountability. *California Journal of Politics and Policy, 6*(4), 577–598. doi:10.5070/P26K5N

Caldwell, S. D., Herold, D. M., & Fedor, D. B. (2004). Toward an understanding of the relationships among organizational change, individual differences, and changes in person-environment fit: A cross-level study. *The Journal of Applied Psychology, 89*(5), 868–882. doi:10.1037/0021-9010.89.5.868 PMID:15506866

Campbell, D. T., & Fiske, D. W. (1959). Convergent and discriminant validation by the multitrait-multimethod matrix. *Psychological Bulletin, 56*(2), 81–105. doi:10.1037/h0046016 PMID:13634291

Campbell, D., & Stanley, J. (1963). *Experimental and quasi-experimental designs for research*. Houghton Mifflin Company.

Campbell, N., & Hackett, G. (1986). The effects of mathematics task performance on math self-efficacy and task interest. *Journal of Vocational Behavior, 28*(2), 149–162. doi:10.1016/0001-8791(86)90048-5

Cardoza, F. I. I. (2005). *Perceptions of ministerial effectiveness by leaders of urban churches in the Southern Baptist Convention* (Doctoral dissertation). Available from ProQuest Dissertations and Theses database. (UMI No. 3167902)

Care, C. A. P. (2020). *Using the Full Interdisciplinary Team During Crisis*. https://www.capc.org/covid-19/using-full-interdisciplinary-team-during-crisis/

Carter, J. (2009). Transformational leadership and pastoral leader effectiveness. *Pastoral Psychology, 58*(3), 261–271. doi:10.100711089-008-0182-6

Cashman, D. (2008). *The effects of vertical leadership, team demographics, and group potency upon shared leadership emergence within technical organizations* [Unpublished doctoral dissertation]. Available from ProQuest Dissertations and Theses database. (UMI No. 3320543)

Cau-Bareille, D., Caudart, C., & Delgoulet, C. (2012). Training, age and technological change: Difficulties assoicated with age, the design of tools, and the organization of work. *Workforce Management, 41*(2), 127–141. doi:10.3233/WOR-2012-1278 PMID:22297777

Caykoylu, S., Egri, C. P., & Havlovic, S. (2007). Organizational commitment across different employee groups. *Business Review (Federal Reserve Bank of Philadelphia), 8*(1), 191–197.

Cecchi-Dimeglio, P. (2017, April 12). How gender bias corrupts performance reviews, and what to do about it. *Harvard Business Review*. https://hbr.org/2017/04/how-gender-bias-corrupts-performance-reviews-and-what-to-do-about-it

Cerff, K. (2004). Exploring Ubuntu and the African Renaissance: A conceptual study of servant leadership from an African perspective. In *Proceedings of the Servant Leadership Research Roundtable*. Retrieved October 5, 2004, from https://www.regent.edu/acad/sls/publications/journals_and_proceedings/proceeding/servant_leadership_roundtable/pdf/Cerff-2004SL.pdf

Cerff, K. (2006). *The role of hope, self-efficacy and Motivation to Lead in the development of leaders in the South African college student context* [Unpublished doctoral dissertation]. Regent University, Virginia Beach, VA.

Cerff, K., & Bocarnea, M. C. (2007). Group-centered leading factor as a scale for measuring altruism. In *Proceedings of the Servant Leadership Roundtable*. Retrieved December 7, 2007 from https://www.regent.edu/acad/global/publications/sl_proceedings/2007/cerff-bocarnea.pdf

Chalfin, A., Danieli, O., Hillis, A., Jelveh, Z., Luca, M., Ludwig, J., & Mullainathan, S. (2016). Productivity and selection of human capital with machine learning. *The American Economic Review*, *106*(5), 124–127. doi:10.1257/aer.p20161029

Chamberlain, A., Stansell, A., & Zhao, D. (2021). *America's workplace diversity crisis: Measuring gaps in diversity & inclusion satisfaction by employee race and ethnicity*. https://www.glassdoor.com/research/app/uploads/sites/2/2021/04/DEI-:10.11._2021-Final.pdf

Chan, K. (1999). *Toward a theory of individual differences and leadership: Understanding the motivation to lead* [Unpublished doctoral dissertation]. University of Illinois, Urbana, IL.

Chan, D. (1996). Cognitive misfit of problem-solving style at work: A facet of person-organization fit. *Organizational Behavior and Human Decision Processes*, *68*(3), 194–207. doi:10.1006/obhd.1996.0099

Chandler, D. J. (2008). Pastoral burnout and the impact of personal spiritual renewal, rest-taking, and support system practices. *Pastoral Psychology*, *58*(3), 273–287. doi:10.100711089-008-0184-4

Chang, P. M. Y. (2000). The effects of organizational variation in the employment relationship on gender discrimination in denominational labor markets. *Unusual Occupations*, *11*, 213–240.

Chan, K., & Drasgow, F. (2001). Toward a theory of individual differences and leadership: Understanding the motivation to lead. *The Journal of Applied Psychology*, *86*(3), 481–498. doi:10.1037/0021-9010.86.3.481 PMID:11419808

Chan, K., Rounds, J., & Drasgow, F. (2001). The relation between vocational interests and the motivation to lead. *Journal of Vocational Behavior*, *57*(2), 226–245. doi:10.1006/jvbe.1999.1728

Chapman, K. (2019). Accountability-based leadership. *Plumbing & Mechanical*, *4*(37), 22–26.

Charalambous, A., Kaite, C., Constantinou, M., & Kouta, C. (2016). Translation and validation of the cancer-related fatigue scale in Greek in a sample of patients with advanced prostate cancer. *BMJ Open*, *6*(12), e011798–e011798. doi:10.1136/bmjopen-2016-011798 PMID:27913557

Chatman, J. A. (1989). Improving interactional organizational research: A model of person-organization fit. *Academy of Management Review*, *14*(3), 333–349. doi:10.5465/amr.1989.4279063

Chatman, J. A. (1991). Matching people and organizations: Selection and socialization in public accounting firms. *Administrative Science Quarterly*, *36*(3), 459–484. doi:10.2307/2393204

Chen, P. H. (2010). *Item order effects on attitude measures* (Dissertation thesis). University of Denver.

Chen, C. H. (2011). The major components of corporate social responsibility. *Journal of Global Responsibility*, *2*(1), 85–99. doi:10.1108/20412561111128546

Chen, F. F. (2008). What happens if we compare chopsticks with forks? The impact of making inappropriate comparisons in cross-cultural research. *Journal of Personality and Social Psychology*, *95*(5), 1005–1018. doi:10.1037/a0013193 PMID:18954190

Chen, G., Gully, S., & Eden, D. (2001). Validation of a new general self-efficacy scale. *Organizational Research Methods*, *4*(1), 62–83. doi:10.1177/109442810141004

Chen, S.-Y., & Scannapieco, M. (2010). The influence of job satisfaction on child welfare worker's desire to stay: An examination of the interaction effect of self-efficacy and supportive supervision. *Children and Youth Services Review*, *32*(4), 482–486. doi:10.1016/j.childyouth.2009.10.014

Cheung, G. W., & Rensvold, R. B. (1998). Cross-cultural comparisons using noninvariant measurement items. *Applied Behavioral Science Review*, *6*(1), 93–110. doi:10.1016/S1068-8595(99)80006-3

Cheung, R. B., Aiken, L. H., Clarke, S. P., & Sloane, D. M. (2008). Nursing care and patient outcomes: International evidence. *Enfermeria Clinica*, *18*(1), 35–40. doi:10.1016/S1130-8621(08)70691-0 PMID:18218265

Chia, S. C., & Poo, Y. L. (2009). Media, celebrities, and fans: An examination of adolescents' media usage and involvement with entertainment celebrities. *Journalism & Mass Communication Quarterly*, *86*(1), 23–44. doi:10.1177/107769900908600103

Chiavenato, I. (2001). Advances and Challenges in Human Resource Management in The New Millennium. *Public Personnel Management*, *30*(1), 17–26. doi:10.1177/009102600103000102

Childs, J., & McGrath, R. (2001). Organizations unfettered: Organizational forming an information-intensive company. *Academy of Management Journal*, *44*(6), 1134–1148.

Chimi, C. J., & Russell, D. L. (2009, November). *The Likert scale: A proposal for improvement using quasi-continuous variables*. Paper presented at the ISECON 2009, Washington, DC.

Chitra, T., & Karunanidhi, S. (2013). Influence of occupational stress, resilience, and job satisfaction on psychological well-being of policewomen. *Indian Journal of Health and Wellbeing*, *4*(4), 724–730. http://eres.regent.edu/login?url=https://www-proquest-com.ezproxy.regent.edu/scholarly-journals/influence-occupational-stress-resilience-job/docview/1511429053/se-2?accountid=13479

Cho, E., & Kim, S. (2015). Cronbach's coefficient alpha: Well-known but poorly understood. *Organizational Research Methods*, *18*(2), 207–230. doi:10.1177/1094428114555994

Cho, H., & Boster, F. J. (2005). Development and validation of value-, outcome-, and impression-relevant involvement scales. *Communication Research*, *32*(2), 235–264. doi:10.1177/0093650204273764

Chriscaden, K. (2020). *Impact of COVID-19 on people's livelihoods, their health and our food systems*. World Health Organization. https://www.who.int/news/item/13-10-2020-impact-of-covid-19-on-people's-livelihoods-their-health-and-our-food-systems#:~:text=The%20economic%20and%20social%20disruption,the%20end%20of%20the%20year

Chuang, A., Shen, C., & Judge, T. A. (2016). Development of a Multidimensional Instrument of Person–Environment Fit: The Perceived Person–Environment Fit Scale (PPEFS). *Applied Psychology*, *65*(1), 66–98. doi:10.1111/apps.12036

Chuo, Y.-H., Tsai, C.-H., Lan, Y.-L., & Tsai, C.-S. (2011). The effect of organizational support, self efficacy, and computer anxiety on the usage intention of e-learning system in hospital. *African Journal of Business Management*, *5*(14), 5518–5523.

Church, D. M. (2012). *Leadership style and organizational growth: A correlational study* (Doctoral dissertation). Available from ProQuest Dissertations and Theses database. (UMI No. 3507222)

Chyung, S. Y., Roberts, K., Swanson, I., & Hankinson, A. (2017). Evidence-Based survey design: The use of a midpoint on the Likert scale. *Performance Improvement*, *56*(10), 15–23. doi:10.1002/pfi.21727

Ciulla, J. B. (2009). Leadership ethics: Mapping the Territory. *Business Ethics Quarterly*, *5*(1), 5–28. doi:10.2307/3857269

Ciulla, J. B. (2014). *Ethics, the heart of leadership* (2nd ed.). Praeger.

Cleckley, H. (1941). *The Mask of Sanity* (1st ed.). C.V. Mosby.

Click, M. A., Lee, H., & Holladay, H. W. (2013). Making monsters: Lady Gaga, fan identification, and social media. *Popular Music and Society, 36*(3), 360–379. doi:10.1080/03007766.2013.798546

Cohen, J. (2003). Parasocial breakups: Measuring individual differences in responses to the dissolution of parasocial relationships. *Mass Communication & Society, 6*(2), 191–202. doi:10.1207/S15327825MCS0602_5

Coker, K., Howie, K., Syrdal, H., Vanmeter, R., & Woodroof, P. (2017, May). The truth about transparency and authenticity on social media: how brands communicate and how customers respond: an abstract. In *Academy of Marketing Science Annual Conference* (pp. 659-660). Springer.

Collins, J. C. (2001). *Good to great: Why some companies make the leap—and others don't* (1st ed.). HarperBusiness.

Colton, D., & Covert, R. W. (2007). *Designing and constructing instruments for social research and evaluation.* Jossey-Bass.

Coman, A., & Bonciu, C. (2014). Leadership and creativity. *Manager, 19*, 27–37.

Communication Privacy Management Center. (2019, May 4). https://cpmcenter.iupui.edu/

Comrey, A. L., & Lee, H. B. (1992). *A first course in factor analysis*. Erlbaum.

Conger, J. A. (1994). *Spirit at work: Discovering the spirituality in leadership*. Jossey-Bass.

Conte, F. (2018). Understanding the influence of CEO tenure and CEO reputation on corporate reputation: An exploratory study in Italy. *International Journal of Business and Management, 13*(3), 54–66. doi:10.5539/ijbm.v13n3p54

Conway, J. M., & Lance, C. E. (2010). What reviewers should expect from suthors regarding common method bias in organizational research. *Journal of Business and Psychology, 25*(3), 325–334. doi:10.100710869-010-9181-6

Cook, J. D., Hepworth, S. J., Wall, T. D., & Warr, P. B. (1981). *The experience of work: A compendium of 249 measures and their use*. Academic Press.

Corbett, J. C. (2006). *The personal and spiritual characteristics of effective pastoral leaders* (Doctoral dissertation). Available from ProQuest Dissertations and Theses database. (UMI No. 3437177)

Cortina, J. M. (1993). What is coefficient alpha? An examinationof theory and applications. *The Journal of Applied Psychology, 78*(1), 98–104. doi:10.1037/0021-9010.78.1.98

Cozby, P., & Bates, S. (2020). *Methods in behavioral research*. McGraw-Hill Education.

Creswell, J. (2009). *Research design: Qualitative, quantitative, and mixed methods approaches*. Sage.

Creswell, J. W. (1998). Qualitative inquiry and research design: Choosing among five traditions. *Sage (Atlanta, Ga.)*.

Croasmun, J. T., & Ostrom, L. (2011). Using Likert-type scales in the social sciences. *Journal of Adult Education, 40*(1), 19–22.

Crocitto, M., & Youssef, M. (2003). The human side of organizational agility. *Industrial Management & Data Systems, 103*(5/6), 388–397. doi:10.1108/02635570310479963

Cronbach, L. (1951). Coefficient alpha and the internal structure of tests. *Pschometrika, 16*(3), 297–334. doi:10.1007/BF02310555

Cronbach, L. J., & Shavelson, R. J. (2004). My current thoughts on coefficient alpha and successor procedures. *Educational and Psychological Measurement, 64*(3), 391–418. doi:10.1177/0013164404266386

Crossan, F. (2003). Research philosophy: Towards an understanding. *Nurse Researcher, 11*(1), 46–55. doi:10.7748/nr2003.10.11.1.46.c5914 PMID:14533474

Crossman, J. (2010). Conceptualising spiritual leadership in secular organizational contexts and its relation to transformational, servant and environmental leadership. *Leadership and Organization Development Journal, 31*(7), 596–608. doi:10.1108/01437731011079646

Croucher, R. (2002). *Forced terminations: When a church asks a pastor to leave.* Priscilla's Friends. https://www.priscillasfriends.org/studies/terminations.html

Cuilla, J. B. (1998). *Ethics: The heart of leadership.* Praeger.

Cycyota, C., & Harrison, D. (2018). What (not) to expect when surveying executives: A meta-analysis of top manager response rates and techniques over time. *Organizational Research Methods, 9*(2), 133–160. doi:10.1177/1094428105280770

Czajka, J. L., & Beyler, A. (2016). *Declining response rates in federal surveys: Trends and implications (background paper).* Mathematica Policy Research. https://mathematica.org/publications/declining-response-rates-in-federal-surveys-trends-and-implications-background-paper

Daft, R. (2005). *The Leadership Experience.* Thomson Corporation.

Dahling, J., Whitaker, B., & Levy, P. (2009). The Development and Validation of a New Machiavellianism Scale. *Journal of Management, 35*(2), 219–257. doi:10.1177/0149206308318618

Daniel, L. G., & Siders, J. A. (1994). Validation of teacher assessment instruments: A confirmatory factor analytic approach. *Journal of Personnel Evaluation in Education, 8*(1), 29–40. doi:10.1007/BF00972707

Darling-Hammond, S., Lee, R. T., & Mendoza-Denton, R. (2020). Interracial contact at work: Does workplace diversity reduce bias? *Group Processes & Intergroup Relations, 1.* Advance online publication. doi:10.1177/1368430220932636

Davern, M. (2013). Nonresponse rates are a problematic indicator of nonresponse bias in survey research. *Health Services Research, 48*(3), 905–912. doi:10.1111/1475-6773.12070 PMID:23656501

Davis, A., & Blass, E. (2006). The future workplace: Views from the floor. *Futures, 39*(1), 38–52. doi:10.1016/j.futures.2006.03.003

Davis, M. H. (1983). Measuring individual differences in empathy: Evidence for a multidimensional approach. *Journal of Personality and Social Psychology, 44*(1), 113–126. doi:10.1037/0022-3514.44.1.113

Day, D. V., Harrison, M. M., & Halpin, S. M. (2009). *An integrative approach to leader development.* Routledge.

De Cremer, D. (2007). Emotional Effects of Distributive Justice as a Function of Autocratic Leader Behavior. *Journal of Applied Social Psychology, 37*(6), 1385–1404. doi:10.1111/j.1559-1816.2007.00217.x

de Jong, J., Rigotti, T., & Mulder, J. (2017b, February 23). One after the other: Effects of sequence patterns of breached and overfulfilled obligations. *European Journal of Work and Organizational Psychology, 26*(3), 337–355. doi:10.1080/1359432X.2017.1287074

de Winter, J., & Dodou, D. (2012). Five-point Likert items: T test versus Mann-Whitney-Wilcox on. *Practical Assessment, Research & Evaluation, 15*(11), 1–16. doi:10.7275/bj1p-ts64

Dearing, J. W., & Singhal, A. (2020). New directions for diffusion of innovations research: Dissemination, implementation, and positive deviance. *Human Behavior and Emerging Technologies, 2020*(4), 1–7. doi:10.1002/hbe2.216

DeLong, D. (2004). *Lost knowledge: Confronting the threat of an aging workforce.* Oxford University Press. doi:10.1093/acprof:oso/9780195170979.001.0001

DeLucia, P., Ott, T., & Palmieri, P. (2009). Performance in Nursing. *Review of Human Factors and Ergonomics, 5*(1), 1–40. doi:10.1518/155723409X448008 PMID:19544931

Dennis, R. S., & Bocarnea, M. (2005). Development of the servant leadership assessment instrument. *Leadership and Organization Development Journal, 26*(8), 600–615. doi:10.1108/01437730510633692

Derrick, J. L., Gabriel, S., & Tippin, B. (2008). Parasocial relationships and self-discrepancies: Faux relationships have benefits for low self-esteem individuals. *Personal Relationships, 15*(2), 261–280. doi:10.1111/j.1475-6811.2008.00197.x

DeShon, R. P. (2010). *Clergy effectiveness: National survey results.* Unpublished internal report, General Board of Higher Education and Ministry: The United Methodist Church. Retrieved from https://www.gbhem.org/clergy/boards-ordained-ministry

Desimone, J., & Harms, P. (2018). Dirty data: The effects of screening respondents who provide low-quality data in survey research. *Journal of Business and Psychology, 33*(5), 559–557. doi:10.100710869-017-9514-9

Desimone, L. M., & Kerstin Carlson, L. F. (2004). Are we asking the right questions? Using cognitive interviews to improve surveys in education research. *Educational Evaluation and Policy Analysis, 26*(1), 1–22. doi:10.3102/01623737026001001

DeVellis, R. F. (2016). Scale development: Theory and applications (4th ed.). Thousand Oaks, CA: Sage.

DeVellis. (2017). *Scale Development Theory and Applications* (4th ed.). SAGE Publications.

DeVellis, R. (2012). *Scale Development: Theory and Applications* (3rd ed.). Sage.

DeVellis, R. F. (1991). *Scale development: Theory and practice.* Sage.

DeVellis, R. F. (2006). Classical test theory. *Medical Care, 44*(11, Suppl 3), S50–S59. doi:10.1097/01.mlr.0000245426.10853.30 PMID:17060836

DeVellis, R. F. (2017). *Scale development: Theory and application* (4th ed.). SAGE.

DeVellis, R. F. (2017). *Scale development: Theory and applications.* SAGE.

Dewine, S., & Pearson, J. C. (1985, May). *The most frequently used self-report instruments in communication.* Paper presented at the ICA, Honolulu, HI. https://files.eric.ed.gov/fulltext/ED260479.pdf

DeYoung, R. (2000). Expanding and evaluating motives for environmentally responsible behavior. *The Journal of Social Issues, 56*(3), 509–526. doi:10.1111/0022-4537.00181

Dhiman, S. (2017). *Holistic leadership: A new paradigm for today's leaders.* Palgrave Macmillan US. doi:10.1057/978-1-137-55571-7

Dibble, J. L., Hartmann, T., & Rosaen, S. F. (2016). Parasocial interaction and parasocial relationship: Conceptual clarification and a critical assessment of measures. *Human Communication Research, 42*(1), 21–44. doi:10.1111/hcre.12063

Dillman, D. A. (1978). *Mail and telephone surveys: The total design method.* John Wiley & Sons, Inc.

Dimitrov, D. M. (2010). Testing for factorial invariance in the context of construct validation. *Measurement & Evaluation in Counseling & Development, 43*(2), 121–149. doi:10.1177/0748175610373459

Ding, Z., & Ng, F. (2008). A new way of developing semantic differential scales with personal construct theory. *Construction Management and Economics, 26*(11), 1213–1226. doi:10.1080/01446190802527522

Doerr, J. (2018). *Measure What Matters: How Google, Bono, and the Gates Foundation Rock the World with OKRs.* Penguin Random House.

Drach-Zahavy, A., Leonenko, M., & Sruloviet, E. (2018). Towards a measure of accountability in nursing: A three-stage validation study. *Journal of Advanced Nursing, 74*(10), 2450–2464. doi:10.1111/jan.13735 PMID:29869349

Drake, T. G. (2003). *The impact of leadership development training experiences on the development of senior pastors' effectiveness as leaders of member churches in an American, evangelical denomination* (Doctoral dissertation). Available from ProQuest Dissertations and Theses database. (UMI No. 3082717)

Draugalis, J., Coons, S., & Plaza, C. (2008). Best practice for survey research reports: A synopsis for authors and reviewers. *American Journal of Pharmaceutical Education, 72*(1), 1–6. doi:10.5688/aj720111 PMID:18322573

Drennan, J. (2003). Cognitive interviewing: Verbal data in the design and pretesting of questionnaires. *Journal of Advanced Nursing, 42*(1), 57–63. doi:10.1046/j.1365-2648.2003.02579.x PMID:12641812

Drory, A., & Gluskinos, U. (1980). Machiavellianism and Leadership. *The Journal of Applied Psychology, 65*(1), 81–86. doi:10.1037/0021-9010.65.1.81

Druckman, D. (2005). *Doing research: Methods of inquiry for conflict analysis.* Sage Publication., doi:10.4135/9781412983969

DuBrin, A. J. (2013). *Handbook of research on crisis leadership in organizations.* Edward Edgar Publishing. doi:10.4337/9781781006405

Dupuy, H. J. (1978). *Self-representations of General Psychological Well-Being of American Adults.* Paper presented at the American Public Health Association Meeting, Los Angeles, CA.

Dutton, J. E., Ashford, S. J., O'Neil, R. M., & Lawrence, K. A. (2001). Moves that matter: Issue selling and organizational change. *Academy of Management Journal, 44*(4), 716–736.

Earley, P. (1994). Self or Group? Cultural Effects of Training on Self-Efficacy and Performance. *Administrative Science Quarterly, 39*(1), 89–117. doi:10.2307/2393495

Eaton, K. J. (2002). *A study of the relationship between 16PF personality factors and ministerial effectiveness in a sample of Anglican clergy* (Masters thesis). Available from ProQuest Dissertations and Theses database. (UMI No. MQ72148)

Eck, B. E. (2002). An exploration of the therapeutic use of spiritual disciplines in clinical practice. *Journal of Psychology and Christianity, 21*(3), 266–280.

Edelen, M., & Reeve, B. (2007). Applying Item Response Theory (IRT) modeling to questionnaire development, evaluation, and refinement. *Quality of Life Research: An International Journal of Quality of Life Aspects of Treatment, Care and Rehabilitation, 16*(5), 5–18. doi:10.100711136-007-9198-0 PMID:17375372

Ehrhardt, K., & Ragins, B. R. (2019). Relational attachment at work: A complementary fit perspective on the role of relationships in organizational life. *Academy of Management Journal, 62*(1), 248–282. doi:10.5465/amj.2016.0245

Ehrhart, M. G., & Klein, K. J. (2001). Predicting Followers' Preferences for Charismatic Leadership: The Influence of Follower Values and Personality. *The Leadership Quarterly, 12*(2), 155–179. doi:10.1016/S1048-9843(01)00074-1

Eisenbeiß, S., & Brodbeck, F. (2014). Ethical and unethical leadership: A cross-cultural and cross-sectoral analysis. *Journal of Business Ethics, 122*(2), 343–359. doi:10.100710551-013-1740-0

Eisenberger, R., Huntington, R., Hutchison, S., & Sowa, D. (1986). Perceived organizational support. *The Journal of Applied Psychology, 71*(3), 500–507. doi:10.1037/0021-9010.71.3.500

Eisenberger, R., Stinglhamber, F., Vandenberg, C., Sucharski, I. L., & Rhoades, L. (2002). Perceived supervisor support: Contributions to perceived organizational support and employee retention. *The Journal of Applied Psychology, 87*(3), 565–573. doi:10.1037/0021-9010.87.3.565 PMID:12090614

Eliya, Y., & Bibu, N. (2019). The relation between accountability and the climate of service in Israeli Public organisations. *Review of International Comparative Management, 1*(20), 31–51. doi:10.24818/RMCI.2019.1.30

El-Kasim, M., & Idid, S. A. (2017). PR practitioners' use of social media: validation of an online relationship management model applying structural equation modeling. *Jurnal Komunikasi: Malaysian Journal of Communication, 33*(1). doi:10.17576/JKMJC-2017-3301-15

Elkington, R. (2013). Adversity in pastoral leadership: Are pastors leaving the ministry in record numbers, and if so, why? *Verbum et Ecclesia, 34*(1), 1–13. doi:10.4102/ve.v34i1.821

Emelo, R. (2014). Peer collaboration enhances diversity and inclusion. *TD: Talent Development, 68*(12), 48–52.

Ericksen, R. W. (2005). *Exploring the antecedents of motivation to lead and the affects of collective efficacy* [Unpublished doctoral dissertation]. Regent University, Virginia Beach, VA.

Evans, J. R. (2013). *Statistics, data analysis, and decision modeling*. Pearson Education.

Eyal, K., & Rubin, A. M. (2003). Viewer aggression and homophily, identification, and parasocial relationships with television characters. *Journal of Broadcasting & Electronic Media, 47*(1), 77–98. doi:10.120715506878jobem4701_5

Fadlon, I., Laird, J., & Nielsen, T. H. (2016). Do employer pension contributions reflect employee preferences? Evidence from a retirement savings reform in Denmark. *American Economic Journal. Applied Economics, 8*(3), 196–216. doi:10.1257/app.20150015 PMID:27917259

Famule, F. D. (2010). Assessing and reducing survey error in mail surveys. *Pacific Journal of Science and Technology, 11*(2), 422–428.

Farley, H. (2016, April 28). Low pay, no savings and financial stress: The reality for evangelical pastors. *Christianity Today*. http://www.christiantoday.com/article/low.pay.no.savings.and.financial.stress.the.reality.for.evangelical.pastors/84984.htm

Fay, M., & Kline, S. (2011). Coworker relationships and informed communication in high-intensity telecommuting. *Journal of Applied Communication Research, 39*(2), 144–163. doi:10.1080/00909882.2011.556136

Feaster, W. B. (2015). *The relationship between time management behaviors and ministerial effectiveness among ministers of education in the state of Texas* (Doctoral dissertation). Available from ProQuest Dissertations and Theses database. (UMI No. 3716280)

Felfe, J., & Schyns, B. (2014). Romance of leadership and motivation to lead. *Journal of Managerial Psychology, 29*(7), 850–865. doi:10.1108/JMP-03-2012-0076

Felt, J., Castaneda, R., Tiemensma, J., & Depaoli, S. (2017). Using person fit statistics to detect outliers in survey research. *Frontiers in Psychology, 8*, 863. doi:10.3389/fpsyg.2017.00863 PMID:28603512

Ferguson, L. (2004). External validity, generalizability, and knowledge utilization. *Journal of Nursing Scholarship, 36*(1), 16-22. http://dx.doi.org.ezproxy.regent.edu/10.1111/j.1547-5069.2004.04006.x

Ferketic, S. (1991). Focus on psychometrics: Aspects of item analysis. *Research in Nursing & Health, 14*(2), 165–168. doi:10.1002/nur.4770140211 PMID:2047538

Fetzer Institute on Aging. (n.d.). *Multidimensional measurement of religiousness/spirituality for use in health research*. Retrieved July 25, 2014, from http://www.fetzer.org/resources/multidimensional-measurement-religiousnessspirituality-use-health-research

Field, A. (2010). *Discovering Statistics Using SPSS* (3rd ed.). Sage Publications.

Field, A. (2015). *Discovering Statistics Using IBM SPSS Statistics*. SAGE Publications.

Fields, D. L. (2002). *Taking the Measure of Work*. Sage Publications.

Fields, D. L. (2007). Determinants of follower perceptions of a leader's authenticity and integrity. *European Management Journal*, *25*(3), 195–206. doi:10.1016/j.emj.2007.04.005

Fincham, J. E. (2008). Response rates and responsiveness for surveys, standards, and the journal. *American Journal of Pharmaceutical Education*, *72*(2), 1–3. doi:10.5688/aj720243 PMID:18483608

Fink, S. (1986). *Crisis management: Planning for the inevitable*. AMACOM.

Finn, B. (2015). *Measuring motivation in low-stakes assessments*. ETS Research Report Series No. RR-15-19. Available from https://onlinelibrary.wiley.com/ doi:10.1002/ets2.12067

Finsted, K. (2010). Response Interpolation and Scale Sensitivity: Evidence Against 5-Point Scales. *Journal of Usability Studies*, *5*(3), 104–110.

Fishbein, M., & Ajzen, I. (1975). *Belief, attitude, intention and behavior: An introduction to theory and research*. Adisson-Wesley.

Fishbein, M., & Ajzen, I. (2010). *Predicting and changing behavior: The reasoned action approach*. Psychology Press.

Fisher, C. D. (2003). Why do lay people believe that satisfaction and performance are correlated? possible sources of a commonsense theory. *Journal of Organizational Behavior*, *24*(6), 753–777. doi:10.1002/job.219

Ford, R. (2015). *Factors influencing clergy leadership effectiveness* (Doctoral dissertation). Available from ProQuest Dissertations and Theses database. (UMI No. 3715502)

Fosnacht, K., Sarraf, S., Howe, E., & Peck, L. K. (2017). How important are high response rates for college Surveys? *Review of Higher Education*, *40*(2), 245–265. doi:10.1353/rhe.2017.0003

Foster, R. J., & Griffin, E. (Eds.). (2000). *Spiritual classics: Selected readings on the twelve spiritual disciplines*. HarperOne.

Fowler, F. J. (2014). *Survey Research Methods* (5th ed.). Sage.

Fox, L. (2003). *Enron: The rise and fall*. Wiley.

Francis, L. J., & Rodger, R. (1994). The influence of personality on clergy role prioritization, role influences, conflict, and dissatisfaction with ministry. *Personality and Individual Differences*, *16*(6), 947–957. doi:10.1016/0191-8869(94)90237-2

Fraser, B. J., McLure, F. I., & Koul, R. B. (2021). Assessing classroom emotional climate in STEM classrooms: Developing and validating a questionnaire. *Learning Environments Research*, *24*(1), 1–21. doi:10.100710984-020-09316-z

Frederick, H. R. (2015). *The Effect of the Accountability Variables of Responsibility, Openness, and Answerability on Authentic Leadership* (Publication No. 3671894) [Doctoral Dissertation, Regent University], ProQuest Dissertations Publishing.

Frederick, H., West, G., Winston, B. E., & Wood, J. A. (2016). The Effects of Accountability Variables on Authentic Leadership. *Journal of Research on Christian Education*, *25*(3). Advance online publication. doi:10.1080/10656219.2016.1237907

Frederick, T. V., Dunbar, S., & Thai, Y. (2018). Burnout in Christian perspective. *Pastoral Psychology*, *67*(3), 267–276. doi:10.100711089-017-0799-4

Frese, M. (1997). Dynamic self-reliance: An important concept for work in the twenty-first century. In C. L. Cooper & S. E. Jackson (Eds.), *Creating tomorrow's organizations: A handbook for future research in organizational behavior* (pp. 399–416). John Wiley & Sons.

Freud, S. (1922). *Group psychology and the analysis of ego.* Norton. doi:10.1037/11327-000

Freud, S. (1989). *An outline of psychoanalysis* (J. Strachey, Trans.). Norton. (Original work published 1940)

Fry, L. W. (2003). Toward a theory of spiritual leadership. *The Leadership Quarterly, 14*(6), 693–727. doi:10.1016/j.leaqua.2003.09.001

Fuchs, C., & Diamantopoulos, A. (2009). Using single-item measures for construct measurement in management research: Conceptual issues and application guidelines. *Betriebswirtschaft, 69*(2), 195–210.

Fulks, J. L. (1994). *Transformational leadership and its relationship to success in developing new churches* (Doctoral dissertation). Available from ProQuest Dissertations and Theses database. (UMI No. 9505499)

Fulton, B. (2018). Organizations and survey research: Implementing response enhancing strategies and conducting nonresponse analyses. *Sociological Methods & Research, 47*(2), 240–276. doi:10.1177/0049124115626169

Fusaro, P., & Miller, R. (2002). *What went wrong at Enron: Everyone's guide to the largest bankruptcy in U.S.history.* Wiley.

Ganster, D., & Murphy, L. (2000). Workplace interventions to prevent stress-related illness: Lessons from research and practice. In I/O psychology: What we know about theory and practice (pp. 34–51). Basil Blackwell.

Garcia-Zamor, J.-C. (2003). Workplace spirituality and organizational performance. *Public Administration Review, 63*(3), 355–363. doi:10.1111/1540-6210.00295

Gardner, W. L., Cogliser, C. C., Davis, K. M., & Dickens, M. P. (2011). Authentic leadership: A review of the literature and research agenda. *The Leadership Quarterly, 22*(6), 1120–1145. doi:10.1016/j.leaqua.2011.09.007

Geer, B. W., Maher, J. K., & Cole, M. T. (2008). Managing non-profit organizations: The importance of transformational leadership and commitment to operating standards for non-profit accountability. *Public Performance & Management Review, 32*(1), 51–75. doi:10.2753/PMR1530-9576320103

Gehlbach, H., & Brinkworth, M. (2011). Measure twice, cut down error: A process for enhancing the validity of survey scales. *Review of General Psychology, 15*(4), 380–387. doi:10.1037/a0025704

Gemechu, T. F. (2019). *Creating an instrument to measure holistic ethical leadership* (Order No. 13805441). Available from Dissertations & Theses @ Regent University. (2193421074). Retrieved from http://eres.regent.edu/login?url=https://www-proquest-com.ezproxy.regent.edu/dissertations-theses/creating-instrument-measure-holistic-ethical/docview/2193421074/se-2?accountid=13479

Gemechu, T. F., West, G., Winner, W. D., & Winston, B. E. (2020). Creating an Instrument to Measure Holistic Ethical Leadership. *International Leadership Journal, 12*(4). http://internationalleadershipjournal.com/

George, D., & Mallery, P. (2003). *SPSS for Windows step by step: A simple guide and reference: 11.0 update* (4th ed.). Allyn and Bacon.

Ghela, K. G., & Bhanderi, R. (2016). Leadership practices in NGOs: Issues of accountability. *Sankalpa: Journal of Management & Research, 6*(1), 1–8.

Giacalone, R. A., & Jurkiewicz, C. L. (2003). *Handbook of workplace spirituality and organizational performance.* M.E. Sharpe., doi:10.4324/9781315703817

Gignac, G. (2015). *What is Cronbach's Alpha*. Retrieved February 18, 2021, from https://youtu.be/PCztXEfNJLM

Giles, D. C. (2002). Parasocial interaction: A review of the literature and a model for future research. *Media Psychology*, *4*(3), 279–305. doi:10.1207/S1532785XMEP0403_04

Giles, D. C., & Maltby, J. (2004). The role of media figures in adolescent development: Relations between autonomy, attachment, and interest in celebrities. *Personality and Individual Differences*, *36*(4), 813–822. doi:10.1016/S0191-8869(03)00154-5

Gilley, J. W., Eggland, S. A., & Gilley, A. M. (2002). *Principles of human resource development* (2nd ed.). Basic Books.

Girden, E. R. (2011). *Evaluating research articles from start to finish* (3rd ed.). Sage Publications, Inc.

Gist, M. (1987). Self-Efficacy: Implications for Organizational Behavior and Human Resource Management. *Academy of Management Review*, *12*(3), 472–485. doi:10.5465/amr.1987.4306562

Gist, M. (1989). The influence of training method on self-efficacy and idea generation among managers. *Personnel Psychology*, *42*(4), 787–805. doi:10.1111/j.1744-6570.1989.tb00675.x

Gist, M., & Mitchell, T. (1992). Self-Efficacy: A Theoretical Analysis of Its Determinants and Malleability. *Academy of Management Review*, *17*(2), 183–211. doi:10.5465/amr.1992.4279530

Gist, M., Schwoerer, C., & Rosen, B. (1989). Effects of alternative training methods on self-efficacy and performance in computer software training. *The Journal of Applied Psychology*, *74*(6), 884–891. doi:10.1037/0021-9010.74.6.884

Gkorezis, P., Petridou, E., & Krouklidou, T. (2015). Machiavellian Leadership, Organizational Cynicism and Emotional Exhaustion. *Europe's Journal of Psychology*, *11*(4), 619–631. doi:10.5964/ejop.v11i4.988 PMID:27247681

Glynn, M. (2000). When Cymbals become Symbols: Conflict over Organizational Identity within a Symphony Orchestra. *Organization Science*, *11*(3), 285–298. doi:10.1287/orsc.11.3.285.12496

Goethals, G., & Sorenson, G. (2006). *The quest for a general theory of leadership*. Edward Elgar. doi:10.4337/9781847202932

Goldstein, I. (1980). Training and organizational psychology. *Professional Psychology*, *11*(3), 421–427. doi:10.1037/0735-7028.11.3.421

Goodwin, B., Cameron, G., & Hein, H. (2015). *Balanced leadership for powerful learning*. Association for Supervision & Curriculum Development.

Gough, H. G. (1979). A creative personality scale for the adjective checklist. *Journal of Personality and Social Psychology*, *37*(8), 1398–1405. doi:10.1037/0022-3514.37.8.1398

Gould, J. (2005). Becoming good: The role of spiritual practice. *Philosophical Practice: Journal of the American Philosophical Practitioners Association*, *1*(3), 135–147. doi:10.1080/17428170600595846

Grant, A. M., Christianson, M. K., & Price, R. H. (2007). Happiness, health, or relationships? managerial practices and employee well-being tradeoffs. *The Academy of Management Perspectives*, *21*(3), 51–63. doi:10.5465/amp.2007.26421238

Gravetter, F. J., & Wallnau, L. B. (2017). *Statistics for the Behavioral Sciences* (10th ed.). Thomson/Wadsworth.

Greenfield, G. (2001). *The wounded minister: Healing from and preventing personal attacks*. Baker Books.

Greenleaf, R. (1977). *Servant leadership: A journey into the nature of legitimate power and greatness – 25th Anniversary Edition*. Paulist.

Greenleaf, R. K. (1977). *Servant leadership*. Paulist Press.

Greenleaf, R. K. (1977). *Servant leadership: A journey into the nature of legitimate power and greatness.* Paulist Press.

Greenleaf, R. K. (1998). *The power of servant-leadership.* Berrett-Koehler.

Groves, R. M. (2006). Nonresponse rates and nonresponse bias in household surveys. *Public Opinion Quarterly, 70*(5), 646–675. doi:10.1093/poq/nfl033

Groves, R. M., & Peytcheva, E. (2008). The impact of nonresponse rates on nonresponse bias: A meta-analysis. *Public Opinion Quarterly, 72*(2), 167–189. doi:10.1093/poq/nfn011

Gudykunst, W., Guzley, R., & Hammer, M. (1996). Designing Intercultural Training. In *Handbook of intercultural training.* Sage Publications, Inc.

Gumpert, G., & Cathcart, R. (1986). The interpersonal and media connection. In G. Gumpert & R. Cathcart (Eds.), *Inter/Media: Interpersonal communication in a media world* (3rd ed., pp. 17–25). Oxford University Press.

Gündemir, S., Homan, A. C., Usova, A., & Galinsky, A. D. (2017). Multicultural meritocracy: The synergistic benefits of valuing diversity and merit. *Journal of Experimental Social Psychology, 73*, 34–41. doi:10.1016/j.jesp.2017.06.002

Guy, L. (2004). *Introducing early Christianity: A topical survey of its life, beliefs and practices.* InterVarsity Press.

Hagger, M. S., Gucciardi, D. F., & Chatzisarantis, N. L. D. (2017). On nomological validity and auxiliary assumptions: The importance of simultaneously testing effects in social cognitive theories applied to health behavior and some guidelines. *Frontiers in Psychology, 8*, 1933–1933. doi:10.3389/fpsyg.2017.01933 PMID:29163307

Hagiya, G. J. (2011). *Significant traits, characteristics, and qualities of high effective United Methodist Church clergy* (Doctoral dissertation). Available from ProQuest Dissertations and Theses database. (UMI No. 3468837)

Haight, E. S. D. (1980). *Psychological criteria for the selection of ministerial candidates* (Doctoral dissertation). Available from ProQuest Dissertations and Theses database. (UMI No. 8026819)

Hair, Babin, & Anderson. (2010). Multivariate Data Analysis (7th ed.). Prentice Hall.

Hair, J., Anderson, R., Tatham, R., & Black, W. (1995). *Multivariate data analysis.* Prentice-Hall.

Hair, J., Black, W., Babin, B. J., & Anderson, R. E. (2010). *Multivariate Data Analysis.* Prentice Hall.

Haladyna, T. M., & Rodriguez, M. C. (2013). *Developing and validating test items.* Taylor & Francis. doi:10.4324/9780203850381

Halbesleben, J. R. B., & Whitman, M. V. (2013). Evaluating survey quality in health services research: A decision framework for assessing nonresponse bias. *Health Services Research, 48*(3), 913–930. doi:10.1111/1475-6773.12002 PMID:23046097

Hale, J. R., & Fields, D. L. (2007). Exploring servant leadership across cultures: A study of followers in Ghana and the USA. *Leadership, 3*(4), 397–417. doi:10.1177/1742715007082964

Hall, D. T., & Moss, J. E. (1998). The new protean career contract: Helping organizations and employees adapt. *Organizational Dynamics, 26*(3), 22–37. doi:10.1016/S0090-2616(98)90012-2

Hambleton, R. K., Swaminathan, H., & Rogers, H. J. (1991). Fundamentals of Item Response Theory. *Sage (Atlanta, Ga.).*

Hamlin, R., & Hatton, A. (2013). Toward a British Taxonomy of Perceived Managerial and Leadership Effectiveness. *Human Resource Development Quarterly, 24*(3), 365–406. doi:10.1002/hrdq.21163

Hammond, P. B. (2016). *Wesleyan ministerial study programs' relationship to ministerial effectiveness of Wesleyan pastoral leaders* (Doctoral dissertation). Available from ProQuest Dissertations and Theses database. (ProQuest No. 10129765)

Hang-yue, N., Foley, S., & Loi, R. (2005). Work role stressors and turnover intentions: A study of professional clergy in Hong Kong. *International Journal of Human Resource Management, 16*(11), 2133–2146. doi:10.1080/09585190500315141

Hareli, S., & Weiner, B. (2000). Accounts for Success as Determinants of Perceived Arrogance and Modesty. *Motivation and Emotion, 24*(3), 215–236. doi:10.1023/A:1005666212320

Harms, P., Spain, S., & Hannah, S. (2011). Leader Development and the Dark Side of Personality. *The Leadership Quarterly, 22*(3), 495–509. doi:10.1016/j.leaqua.2011.04.007

Harraf, A., Wanasika, I., Tate, K., & Talbott, K. (2015). Organizational agility. *Journal of Applied Business Research, 31*(2), 675–685. doi:10.19030/jabr.v31i2.9160

Harrington, D. (2009). *Confirmatory factor analysis*. Oxford University Press.

Harrison, J. (2000). Multiple Imaginings of Institutional Identity. *The Journal of Applied Behavioral Science, 36*(4), 425–455. doi:10.1177/0021886300364003

Harter, N. (2006). *Clearings in the forest: On the study of leadership*. Purdue University Press.

Hasson, F., Keeney, S., & McKenna, H. (2000). Research guidelines for the Delphi survey technique. *Journal of Advanced Nursing, 32*(4), 1008–1015. doi:10.1046/j.1365-2648.2000.t01-1-01567.x PMID:11095242

Hattie, J. (1985). *Methodology review: Assessing unidimensionality of tests and items*. doi:10.1177/014662168500900204

Hays, R. D., Hayashi, T., & Stewart, A. L. (1989). A five-item measure of socially desirable response set. *Educational and Psychological Measurement, 49*(3), 629–636. doi:10.1177/001316448904900315

Head, A. J. (2003). Personas: Setting the stage for building usable information sites. *Online (Bergheim), 27*(4), 1–7.

Heifetz, R. A. (1994). *Leadership without easy answers*. Harvard University Press.

Hendra, R., & Hill, A. (2019). Rethinking response rates: New evidence of little relationship between survey response rates and nonresponse bias. *Evaluation Review, 43*(5), 307–330. doi:10.1177/0193841X18807719 PMID:30580577

Hendrix, W. H., Spencer, B. A., & Gibson, G. S. (1994). Organizational and extraorganizational factors affecting stress, employee well-being, and absenteeism for males and females. *Journal of Business and Psychology, 9*(2), 103–128. doi:10.1007/BF02230631

Herbert, J. T., Ward, T. J., & Hemlick, L. M. (1995). Confirmatory factor analysis of the supervisory style inventory and the revised supervision questionnaire. *Rehabilitation Counseling Bulletin, 38*(4), 334–349.

Herbin, C. V., III. (2018). *Measuring Organizational Arrogance: Development and Validation of a Theory-Based Instrument* (Doctoral Dissertation). Regent University.

Hersey, P., & Blanchard, K. H. (1982). *Management of Organizational Behavior: Utilizing Human Resources*. Prentice-Hall, Inc.

Hickman, G. R. (Ed.). (1998). *Leading organizations: Perspectives for a new era*. Sage.

Higley, W. J. (2007). *The relationship between the lead pastor's emotional intelligence and pastoral leadership team effectiveness* (Doctoral dissertation). Available from ProQuest Dissertations and Theses database. (UMI No. 3264648)

Hill, T., Smith, N., & Mann, M. (1987). Role of efficacy expectations in predicting the decision to use advanced technologies. *The Journal of Applied Psychology*, *72*(2), 307–314. doi:10.1037/0021-9010.72.2.307

Hogan, R., Curphy, G. J., & Hogan, J. (1994). What we know about leadership. *The American Psychologist*, *49*(6), 493–504. doi:10.1037/0003-066X.49.6.493 PMID:8042818

Hoge, D. R., & Wenger, J. E. (2005). *Pastors in transition: Why clergy leave local church ministry*. Wm. B. Eerdmans.

Hollander, E. P. (1992). The essential interdependence of leadership and followership. *Current Directions in Psychological Science*, *1*(2), 71–75. doi:10.1111/1467-8721.ep11509752

Hope, J., & Fraser, R. (2003). *Beyond budgeting: How managers can break free from the annual performance trap*. Harvard Business School Publishing Corporation.

Hoppe, S. L. (2005). Spirituality and leadership. *New Directions for Teaching and Learning*, *104*(104), 83–92. doi:10.1002/tl.217

Horn, J. L., & Mcardle, J. J. (1992). A practical and theoretical guide to measurement invariance in aging research. *Experimental Aging Research*, *18*(3), 117–144. doi:10.1080/03610739208253916 PMID:1459160

Horton, D., & Wohl, R. R. (1956). Mass communication and parasocial interaction: Observations on intimacy at a distance. *Psychiatry*, *19*, 215–229. doi:10.1080/00332747.1956.11023049 PMID:13359569

House, R. J., & Aditya, R. N. (1997). The social scientific study of leadership: Quo vadis? *Journal of Management*, *23*(3), 409–473. doi:10.1177/014920639702300306

Hsu, C., & Sandford, B. A. (2007). The Delphi technique: Making sense of consensus. *Practical Assessment, Research & Evaluation*, *12*(10), 1–8. http://pareonline.net/pdf/v12n10.pdf

Hsu, T. (2005). Research methods and data analysis procedures used by educational researchers. *International Journal of Research & Method in Education*, *28*(2), 109–133. doi:10.1080/01406720500256194

Hubbard, D. A., & McLemore, C. W. (1980). Evangelical churches. In D. S. Schuller, M. P. Strommen, & M. L. Brekke (Eds.), *Ministry in America: A report and analysis, based on an in-depth survey of 47 denominations in the United States and Canada, with interpretations by 18 experts*. Harper and Row.

Hung, K., & Tangpong, C. (2010). General risk propensity in multifaceted business decisions: Scale development. *Journal of Managerial Issues*, *22*(1), 88–106.

Hunter, S. T., Bedell-Avers, K., & Mumford, M. D. (2007). The typical leadership study: Assumptions, implications, and potential remedies. *The Leadership Quarterly*, *18*(5), 435–446. doi:10.1016/j.leaqua.2007.07.001

Hutson, M. (2021, February). Lyin' AIs. *IEEE Spectrum*, 40–45. doi:10.1109/MSPEC.2021.9340114

Ifedapo, A., Luiz, J., Judy, M., & Kenneth, A. (2020). Business ethics in africa: The role of institutional context, social relevance, and development challenges. *Journal of Business Ethics*, *161*(4), 717-729. http://dx.doi.org.ezproxy.regent.edu/10.1007/s10551-019-04338-x

Issler, K. D. (2009). Inner core belief formation, spiritual practices, and the willing-doing gap. *Journal of Spiritual Formation and Soul Care*, *2*(2), 179–198. doi:10.1177/193979090900200203

Ivancevich, J. M., Konopaske, R., & Matteson, M. T. (2005). *Organizational behavior and management* (7th ed.). McGraw-Hill Higher Education.

Jackson, D. L., Gillaspy, J. A., & Purc-Stephenson, R. (2009). Reporting practices in confirmatory factor analysis: An overview and some recommendations. *Psychological Methods*, *14*(1), 6–23. doi:10.1037/a0014694 PMID:19271845

Jacobs, T. O. (1970). *Leadership and exchange in formal organizations.* Human Resources Research Organization. doi:10.21236/AD0725584

Jain, P., Sachdev, A., Singhal, A., Svenkerud, P. J., & Agrawal, S. (2019). A positive deviance inquiry on effective communicative practices of rural Indian women entrepreneurs. *The Journal of Development Communication, 30*(1), 10–22. http://jdc.journals.unisel.edu.my/ojs/index.php/jdc/article/view/137

James, E. H., & Wooten, L. P. (2005). Leadership as (Un) usual: How to display competence in times of crisis. *Organizational Dynamics, 34*(2), 141–152. doi:10.1016/j.orgdyn.2005.03.005

James, E. H., & Wooten, L. P. (2010). *Leading under pressure: From surviving to thriving, before, during, and after a crisis.* Routledge.

James, P., & Steger, M. B. (2014). A genealogy of "globalization": The career of a concept. *Globalizations, 11*(4), 417–434. doi:10.1080/14747731.2014.951186

Janakova, M., Suchanek, P., Padysak, P., & Botlik, J. (2020). The KPI hierarchy for CRM and marketing. *GIS Business, 15*(1), 263–277. doi:10.26643/gis.v15i1.18378

Jin, S. A. A., & Phua, J. (2014). Following celebrities' tweets about brands: The impact of twitter-based electronic word-of-mouth on consumers' source credibility perception, buying intention, and social identification with celebrities. *Journal of Advertising, 43*(2), 181–195. doi:10.1080/00913367.2013.827606

Jividen, S. (2020). *5 Online COVID-19 Courses For Nurses.* https://nurse.org/articles/online-nurse-training-courses-covid-19-coronavirus/

John, O. P., & Srivastava, J. (1999). The big- five trait taxonomy, History, measurement, and theoretical perspectives. In Handbook of personality: Theory and research (2nd ed.). New York: Guilford Press.

Johnson, B. T., & Eagly, A. H. (1989). Effects of involvement on persuasion: A meta-analysis. *Psychological Bulletin, 106*(2), 290–314. doi:10.1037/0033-2909.106.2.290

Johnson, B. T., & Eagly, A. H. (1990). Involvement and persuasion: Types, traditions, and the evidence. *Psychological Bulletin, 107*(3), 375–384. doi:10.1037/0033-2909.107.3.375

Johnson, R., Silverman, S., Shyamsunder, A., Swee, H., Rodopman, O., & Bauer, E. (2010). Acting Superior But Actually Inferior?: Correlates and Consequences of Workplace Arrogance. *Human Performance, 23*(5), 403–427. doi:10.1080/08959285.2010.515279

Jones, K. E. (2005). *A quantitative study: Leadership attributes of effective ministers* (Doctoral dissertation). Available from ProQuest Dissertations and Theses database. (UMI No. 3194292)

Jones. (2007). *Nursing Leadership and Management: Theories, Processes, and Practice.* F.A. Davis Co. http://0-search.ebscohost.com.library.regent.edu/login.aspx?direct=true&db=nlebk&AN=188356&site=eds-live

Jöreskog, K. G. (1971). Simultaneous factor analysis in several populations. *Psychometrika, 36*(4), 409–426. doi:10.1007/BF02291366

Joshi, A., Kale, S., Chandel, S., & Pal, D. K. (2015). Likert scale: Explored and explained. *Current Journal of Applied Science and Technology,* 396-403. doi:10.9734/BJAST/2015/14975

Joyce, W. F., & Slocum, J. W. Jr. (1984). Collective climate; Agreement as bases for defining aggregated climates in organizations. *Academy of Management Journal, 27,* 721–742.

Joynt, S. (2017). Exodus of clergy: Responding to, reinterpreting or relinquishing the call. *Verbum et Ecclesia, 38*(1), 1–6. doi:10.4102/ve.v38i1.1664

Joynt, S. (2018). Exodus of clergy: "When the fight is just not worth it anymore" – The role of conflict in responding to the call. *Die Skriflig, 52*(1). Advance online publication. doi:10.4102/ids.v52i1.2331

Kahn, R. L., Wolfe, D. M., Quinn, R. P., Snoek, J. E., & Rosenthal, R. A. (1964). *Organizational stress: Studies in role conflict and ambiguity*. John Wiley.

Kaiser, R. B., & Kaplan, R. E. (2007). *Leadership versatility index: Facilitator's guide*. Kaplan DeVries.

Kalton, G. (2019). Developments in survey research over the past 60 Years: A personal perspective. *International Statistical Review, 87*(S1), S10–S30. doi:10.1111/insr.12287

Kane, C., & Cunningham, J. (2013). Leadership Changes and Approaches During Company Turnaround. *International Studies of Management & Organization, 42*(4), 52–85. doi:10.2753/IMO0020-8825420403

Kaplan, R. S., & Mikes, A. (2012). *Managing risks: A new framework*. Harvard Business Review. https://hbr.org/2012/06/managing-risks-a-new-framework

Kaplan, R. S., & Norton, D. P. (1992). The balanced scorecard: Measures that drive performance. *Harvard Business Review, 70*(1), 71–79. PMID:10119714

Kaplan, S. A., Luchman, J. N., & Mock, L. (2013). General and specific question sequence effects in satisfaction surveys: Integrating directional and correlational effects. *Journal of Happiness Studies, 14*(5), 1443–1458. doi:10.100710902-012-9388-5

Kaplowitz, M., Hadlock, T., & Levine, R. (2004). A comparison of web and mail survey response rates. *Public Opinion Quarterly, 68*(1), 94–101. doi:10.1093/poq/nfh006

Karakas, F. (2010). Spirituality and performance in organizations: A literature review. *Journal of Business Ethics, 94*(1), 89–106. doi:10.100710551-009-0251-5

Karasek, R. (1979). Job demands, job decision latitude, and mental strain: Implications for job re-design. *Administrative Science Quarterly, 24*(2), 285–306. doi:10.2307/2392498

Kasemaa, A. (2016). The adaptation of the motivation to lead instrument to the Estonian military context. *Journal of Management and Business Administration. Central Europe, 24*(1), 64–88.

Kay, W. K. (2000). Role conflict and British Pentecostal ministers. *Journal of Psychology and Theology, 28*(2), 119–124. doi:10.1177/009164710002800204

Kelman, H. (1958). Compliance, identification, and internalization: Three processes of attitude change. *The Journal of Conflict Resolution, 2*(1), 51–60. doi:10.1177/002200275800200106

Kelman, H. (1961). Process of opinion change. *Public Opinion Quarterly, 25*(1), 57–78. doi:10.1086/266996

Kerlinger, F. N., & Lee, H. B. (2000). *Foundations of Behavioral Research* (4th ed.). Cengage Learning.

Kerlinger, F. N., & Lee, H. B. (2000). *Foundations of behavioral research* (4th ed.). Nelson Thomson Learning.

Keusch, F., Bähr, S., Haas, G., Kreuter, F., & Trappmann, M. (2020). Coverage error in data collection combining mobile surveys with passive measurement using apps: Data from a German national survey. *Sociological Methods & Research*, 1–38. doi:10.1177/0049124120914924

Kezar, A. J., Chambers, A. C., & Burkhardt, J. C. (2005). *Higher education for the public good: Emerging voices from a national movement.* Jossey-Bass.

Kidd, P. T. (1984). *A 21st century paradigm in agile manufacturing: Forging new frontiers.* Addison-Wesley.

Kim, H.-Y. (2013). Statistical notes for clinical researchers: assessing normal distribution (2) using skewness and kurtosis. *PMC Website.* https://www.ncbi.nlm.nih.gov/pmc/articles/PMC3591587/

Kimberlin, C. L., & Winterstein, A. G. (2008). Validity and reliability of measurement instruments used in research. *American Journal of Health-System Pharmacy, 65*(23), 2276–2284. doi:10.2146/ajhp070364 PMID:19020196

Kim, H. Y. (2013). Statistical notes for clinical researchers: Assessing normal distribution (2) using skewness and kurtosis. *Restorative Dentistry & Endodontics, 52-54*(1), 52. Advance online publication. doi:10.5395/rde.2013.38.1.52 PMID:23495371

Kim, J., Egan, T., & Tolson, H. (2015). Examining the dimensions of the learning organization questionnaire: A review and critique of research utilizing the DLOQ. *Human Resource Development Review, 14*(1), 91–112. doi:10.1177/1534484314555402

Kim, J., & Song, H. (2016). Celebrity's self-disclosure on Twitter and parasocial relationships: A mediating role of social presence. *Computers in Human Behavior, 62,* 570–577. doi:10.1016/j.chb.2016.03.083

King, J. E. Jr. (2008). (Dis)missing the obvious: Will mainstream management research ever take religion seriously? *Journal of Management Inquiry, 17*(3), 214–224. doi:10.1177/1056492608314205

Kirkpatrick, D. L. (1994). *Evaluating training programs.* Berrett-Koehler Publishers.

Kirkpatrick, D. L. (1998). *Evaluating training programs: The four levels* (2nd ed.). Berrett-Koehler Publishers.

Kirkpatrick, D. L., & Kirkpatrick, J. D. (2007). *Implementing the four levels.* Berrett-Koehler Publishers.

Kirkpatrick, J. D., & Kirkpatrick, W. K. (2010). *Training on trial: How workplace learning must reinvent itself to remain relevant.* AMACOM.

Kisslinger, S. A. (2007). *Burnout in Presbyterian clergy of southwestern Pennsylvania* (Publication No. 3252060) [Doctoral dissertation, Indiana University of Pennsylvania]. Proquest Dissertation Abstracts and Theses.

Kjaergaard, M., & Ravasi, D. (2011). Mediating identity: A Study of Media Influence on Organizational Identity Construction in a Celebrity Firm. *Journal of Management Studies, 48*(3), 514–543. doi:10.1111/j.1467-6486.2010.00954.x

Klann, G. (2003). *Crisis leadership: Using military lessons, organizational experiences, and the power of influence to lessen the impact of chaos on the people you lead.* Center for Creative Leadership.

Kleinig, J., & Evans, N. G. (2013). Human flourishing, human dignity, and human rights. *Law and Philosophy, 32*(5), 539–564. doi:10.100710982-012-9153-2

Klever, G., & Dyble, J. (1972). *Report to ad hoc ministry study committee.* Unpublished manuscript, Office of Research, Board of Christian Education, United Presbyterian Church in the U.S.A., Philadelphia, PA.

Klimmt, C., Hartmann, T., & Schramm, H. (2006). Parasocial interactions and relationships. In J. Bryant & P. Vorderer (Eds.), *Psychology of entertainment* (pp. 291–314). Routledge.

Kline, P. (1993). *The handbook of psychological testing.* Routledge.

Kline, P. (1994). *An easy guide to factor analysis.* Routledge.

Kline, R. B. (2011). *Principles and practice of structural equation modelling.* Guilford.

Kline, T. (2005). *Psychological testing: A practical approach to design and evaluation.* Sage Publications.

Kling, F. R. (1958). A study of testing as related to the ministry. *Religious Education (Chicago, Ill.), 53*(3), 243–248. doi:10.1080/0034408580530301

Knapp, M. S., & Feldman, S. B. (2012). Managing the intersection of internal and external accountability. *Journal of Educational Administration, 50*(5), 666–694. doi:10.1108/09578231211249862

Knowledge@Wharton. (2019, June 17). *With high-deductible employer health plans, who wins?* https://knowledge.wharton.upenn.edu/article/high-deductible-health-plans-pros-and-cons/

Kohut, A., Keeter, S., Doherty, C., Dimock, M., & Christian, L. (2012). *Assessing the representativeness of public opinion surveys.* Pew Research Center. https://www.pewresearch.org/politics/2012/05/15/assessing-the-representativeness-of-public-opinion-surveys/

Kolarik, J. M. (1954). *A study of the critical requirements of the Lutheran ministry* (Doctoral dissertation). Available from ProQuest Dissertations and Theses database. (UMI No. 302015094)

Krabbe, P. F. M. (2017). *The Measurement of Health and Health Status.* Elsevier. doi:10.1016/B978-0-12-801504-9.00006-4

Krejcir, R. J. (2016). *Statistics on pastors: 2016 update.* Francis L. Schaeffer Institute of Church Leadership Development. https://files.stablerack.com/webfiles/71795/pastorsstatWP2016.pdf

Kristof, A. L. (1996). Person-organization fit: An integrative review of its conceptualizations, measurement, and implications. *Personnel Psychology, 49*(1), 1–49. doi:10.1111/j.1744-6570.1996.tb01790.x

Kristof-Brown, A. L., Zimmerman, R. D., & Johnson, E. C. (2005). Consequences of individuals' fit at work: A meta-analysis of person–job, person–organization, person–group, and person–supervisor fit. *Personnel Psychology, 58*(2), 281–342. doi:10.1111/j.1744-6570.2005.00672.x

Labrecque, L. I. (2014). Fostering consumer–brand relationships in social media environments: The role of parasocial interaction. *Journal of Interactive Marketing, 28*(2), 134–148. doi:10.1016/j.intmar.2013.12.003

Lai, C. K., Skinner, A. L., Cooley, E., Murrar, S., Brauer, M., Devos, T., Calanchini, J., Xiao, Y. J., Pedram, C., Marshburn, C. K., Simon, S., Blanchar, J. C., Joy-Gaba, J. A., Conway, J., Redford, L., Klein, R. A., Roussos, G., Schellhaas, F. M. H., Burns, M., ... Nosek, B. A. (2016). Reducing implicit racial preferences: II. Intervention effectiveness across time. *Journal of Experimental Psychology. General, 145*(8), 1001–1016. doi:10.1037/xge0000179 PMID:27454041

Laird, S. P., Snyder, C. R., Rapoff, M. A., & Green, S. (2004). Research: "Measuring private prayer: Development, validation, and clinical application of the multidimensional prayer inventory. *The International Journal for the Psychology of Religion, 14*(4), 251–272. doi:10.120715327582ijpr1404_2

Lance, C. E., Butts, M. M., & Michels, L. C. (2006). The sources of four commonly reported cutoff criteria: What did they really say? *Organizational Research Methods, 9*(2), 202–220. doi:10.1177/1094428105284919

Landis, J., & Koch, G. (1977). The measurement of observer agreement for categorical data. *Biometrics, 33*(1), 159–174. doi:10.2307/2529310 PMID:843571

Lashbrook, W. B., Snavely, W. B., & Sullivan, D. L. (1977) The effects of source credibility and message information quantity on attitude change of apathetics. *Communication Monographs, 44*, 252-261. doi:10.1080/03637757709390136

Lasswell, H. D. (1931). The measurement of public opinion. *The American Political Science Review, 25*(2), 311–326. doi:10.2307/1947659

Lasswell, H. D. (1965). *World politics and personal insecurity*. Free Press. (Original work published 1935)

Lavrakas, P. J. (2012). *Encyclopedia of survey research methods*. SAGE Publications.

Law, E. H. F. (2000). *Inclusion: Making Room for Grace*. Chalice Press.

Lazarova, S. (2017). Business intelligence approaches to the design of key performance indicators. In *Proceedings of the 2nd Conference on Innovative Teaching Methods* (ITM 2017, pp. 90-96). University of Economics – Varna.

Lee, A. A. (2017). *Ministry longevity, family contentment, and the male clergy family: A phenomenological study of the experience of ministry* (Publication No. 10599056) [Doctoral dissertation, Liberty University]. Proquest Dissertations.

Lee, C., Czaja, S. J., & Sharit, J. (2009). Training Older Workers for Technology-Based Employment. *Educational Gerontology*, *35*(1), 15–31. doi:10.1080/03601270802300091 PMID:20351795

Lee, J. J., & Miller, S. E. (2013). A Self-Care Framework for Social Workers: Building A Strong Foundation for Practice. *The Journal of Contemporary Social Services*, *94*(2), 96–103. doi:10.1606/1044-3894.4289

Lee, K., & Ashton, M. (2005). Psychopathy, Machiavellianism, and Narcissism in the Five-Factor Model and the HEXACO Model of Personality Structure. *Personality and Individual Differences*, *38*(7), 1571–1582. doi:10.1016/j.paid.2004.09.016

Lee, M., Walker, A., & Chui, Y. L. (2012). Contrasting effects of instructional leadership practices on student learning in a high accountability context. *Journal of Educational Administration*, *50*(5), 586–611. doi:10.1108/09578231211249835

Leiter, M., Price, S., & Spence Laschinger, H. (2010). Generational differences in distress, attitudes and incivility among nurses. *Journal of Nursing Management*, *18*(8), 970–980. doi:10.1111/j.1365-2834.2010.01168.x PMID:21073569

Lenz, E. (1996). Middle range theory: Role in research and practice. In: *Proceedings of the Sixth Rosemary Ellis Scholar's Retreat, Nursing Science Implications for the 21st century*. Cleveland, OH: Frances Payne Bolton School of Nursing, Case Western Reserve University.

Levy, M. (1979). Watching television news as parasocial interaction. *Journal of Broadcasting*, *23*(1), 69–80. doi:10.1080/08838157909363919

Lewis, A. E., & Steinhoff, J. C. (2019). The next frontier in government accountability: Impact reporting. *Journal of Government Financial Management*, *68*(1), 22–27.

Lewis, M. (2000). Self-conscious Emotions: Embarrassment, Pride, Shame, and Guilt. In *M. Lewis, & J. M. Haviland-Jones, Handbook of emotions* (pp. 623–636). Guilford.

Lichtman. (1989). *Ministerial effectiveness as a function of personal preferences and job expectancies* (Doctoral dissertation). Fuller Theological Seminary.

Liden, R. C., Wayne, S. J., Zhao, H., & Henderson, D. (2008). Servant leadership: Development of a multidimensional measure and multi-level assessment. *The Leadership Quarterly*, *19*(2), 161–177. doi:10.1016/j.leaqua.2008.01.006

Lie, H. C., Rueegg, C. S., Fosså, S. D., Loge, J. H., Ruud, E., & Kiserud, C. E. (2019). Limited evidence of non-response bias despite modest response rate in a nationwide survey of long-term cancer survivors—Results from the NOR-CAY-ACS study. *Journal of Cancer Survivorship: Research and Practice*, *13*(3), 353–363. doi:10.100711764-019-00757-x PMID:30993649

Likert, R. (1933). The Method of Constructing an Attitude Scale. In the Appendix to A Technique for the Measurement of Attitudes. *Archives of Psychology*, (140), 44-53. Downloaded February 5, 2021, from http://www.sfu.ca/~palys/Likert-1933-TheMethodOfConstructingAnAttitudeScale.pdf

Lilienfeld, S. (2016). *Forensic interviewing for child sexual abuse: Why psychometrics matters.* Springer International Publishing. doi:10.1007/978-3-319-21097-1_9

Lincoln, Y. S., & Guba, E. G. (1985). Naturalistic inquiry. *Sage (Atlanta, Ga.).*

Lindell, M. K., & Whitney, D. J. (2001). Accounting for common method variance in cross-sectional research designs. *The Journal of Applied Psychology, 86*(1), 114–121. doi:10.1037/0021-9010.86.1.114 PMID:11302223

Lindsay, A. C., Sussner, K. M., Greaney, M., Wang, M. L., Davis, R., & Peterson, K. E. (2012). Using qualitative methods to design a culturally appropriate child feeding questionnaire for low-income, Latina mothers. *Maternal and Child Health Journal, 16*(4), 860–866. doi:10.100710995-011-0804-y PMID:21512780

Little, T. (1997). Mean and covariance structures (MACS) analyses of cross cultural data: Practical and theoretical issues. *Multivariate Behavioral Research, 32*(1), 53–76. doi:10.120715327906mbr3201_3 PMID:26751106

Little, T. (2013). *Longitudinal structural equation modeling.* Guilford.

Liu, S.-F., Courtenay, B., & Valentine, T. (2011). Managing Older Worker Training: A Literature Review and Conceptual Framework. *Educational Gerontology, 37*(12), 1040–1062. doi:10.1080/03601277.2010.500576

Liu, Y., Wu, A. D., & Zumbo, B. D. (2010). The impact of outliers on Cronbach's coefficient alpha estimate of reliability: Ordinal/Rating scale item responses. *Educational and Psychological Measurement, 70*(1), 5–21. doi:10.1177/0013164409344548

Livingston, E. H., & Wislar, J. S. (2012). Minimum response rates for survey research. *Archives of Surgery, 147*(2), 110. doi:10.1001/archsurg.2011.2169 PMID:22351903

Liwski, N. T. (2010). *College Students' Television Friends: Parasocial Relationships as Attachment Bonds* (Doctoral dissertation). Purdue University.

Locht, M. V. D., Dam, K. V., & Chiaburu, D. S. (2013, July). Getting the most of management training: The role of identical elements for training transfer. *Personnel Review, 42*(4), 422–439. doi:10.1108/PR-05-2011-0072

Locke, E. A. (1991). *The essence of leadership.* Lexington Books.

Locke, E. A., & Latham, G. P. (1990). Work motivation and satisfaction: Light at the end of the tunnel. *Psychological Science, 1*(4), 240–246. doi:10.1111/j.1467-9280.1990.tb00207.x

Locke, E. A., & Latham, G. P. (2002). Building a practically useful theory of goal setting and task motivation: A 35-year odyssey. *The American Psychologist, 57*(9), 705–717. doi:10.1037/0003-066X.57.9.705 PMID:12237980

Loehlin, J. C. (1998). *Latent variable models: An introduction to factor, path and structural analysis.* Erlbaum.

Lombardo, M. M., & Eichinger, R. W. (2000). *The leadership machine.* Lominger Limited.

London, H. B., & Wiseman, N. B. (2011). *Pastors at greater risk.* Baker.

Lord, F. M. (1955). Estimating Test Reliability. *Educational and Psychological Measurement, 15*(4), 325–336. doi:10.1177/001316445501500401

Lubit, R. (2002). The Long-term Organizational Impact of Destructively Narcissistic Managers. *Academy of Management Review, 16*, 127–138.

Lukat, J., Margraf, J., & Lutz, R. (2016). Psychometric properties of the Positive Mental Health Scale (PMH-scale). *BMC Psychology, 4.* http://dx.doi.org.ezproxy.regent.edu/10.1186/s40359-016-0111-x

Lund, S., Madgavkar, A., Manyika, J., Smit, S., Ellingrud, K., Meaney, M., & Robinson, O. (2021). *The future of work after COVID-19*. https://www.mckinsey.com/featured-insights/future-of-work/the-future-of-work-after-covid-19

MacCallum, R., Widaman, K., Zhang, S., & Hong, S. (1999). Sample size in factor analysis. *Psychological Methods*, *4*(1), 84–99. doi:10.1037/1082-989X.4.1.84

Maccoby, M. (2000). Narcissistic Leaders-The Incredible Pros, The Inevitable Cons. *Harvard Business Review*, *78*, 69–77.

Ma, H., & Karri, R. (2005). Leaders Beware: Some Sure Ways to Lose Your Competitive Advantage. *Organizational Dynamics*, *34*(1), 63–76. doi:10.1016/j.orgdyn.2004.11.002

Majovski, L. F. (1982). *The role of psychological assessment in ministerial selection* (Doctoral dissertation). Available from ProQuest Dissertations and Theses database. (UMI No. 8223416)

Malony, H. N., & Hunt, R. A. (1991). *The psychology of clergy*. Morehouse.

Maltby, J., Day, L., McCutcheon, L. E., Gillett, R., Houran, J., & Ashe, D. D. (2004). Personality and coping: A context for examining celebrity worship and mental health. *British Journal of Psychology*, *95*(4), 411–428. doi:10.1348/0007126042369794 PMID:15527530

Maltby, J., Giles, D. C., Barber, L., & McCutcheon, L. E. (2005). Intense-personal celebrity worship and body image: Evidence of a link among female adolescents. *British Journal of Health Psychology*, *10*(1), 17–32. doi:10.1348/135910704X15257 PMID:15826331

Maltby, J., Houran, J., Lange, R., Ashe, D., & McCutcheon, L. E. (2002). Thou shalt worship no other gods - unless they are celebrities: The relationship between celebrity worship and religious orientation. *Personality and Individual Differences*, *32*(7), 1157–1172. doi:10.1016/S0191-8869(01)00059-9

Maltby, J., Houran, J., & McCutcheon, L. E. (2003). A clinical interpretation of attitudes and behaviors associated with celebrity worship. *The Journal of Nervous and Mental Disease*, *191*(1), 25–29. doi:10.1097/00005053-200301000-00005 PMID:12544596

Manfreda, K., Berzelak, J., Vehovar, V., Bosnjak, M., & Haas, I. (2018). Web surveys versus other survey modes: A meta-analysis comparing response rates. *International Journal of Market Research*, *50*(1), 79–104. doi:10.1177/147078530805000107

Mankey, R. C. (2007). *Understanding holistic leadership: A collaborative inquiry* (Order No. 3269093). Available from ProQuest Central; ProQuest Dissertations & Theses Global. (304859685). Retrieved from http://eres.regent.edu:2048/login?url=https://search-proquest-com.ezproxy.regent.edu/docview/304859685?accountid=13479

Manners, A. T. (2008). *Influence of transformational, autocratic, democratic, and laissez-faire leadership principles on the effectiveness of religious leaders* (Doctoral dissertation). Available from ProQuest Dissertations and Theses database. (UMI No. 3370948)

Mantzana, V., Themistocleous, M., Irani, Z., & Morabito, V. (2007). Identifying healthcare actors involved in the adoption of information systems. *European Journal of Information Systems*, *16*(1), 91–102. doi:10.1057/palgrave.ejis.3000660

Mantzaris, E. (2016). Development and trust in ethical leadership and the fight against corruption: The case of South Africa. *European Conference on Management, Leadership & Governance*. Kidmore End: Academic Conferences International Limited.

Marcus, L. J., McNulty, E. J., Henderson, J. M., & Dorn, B. C. (2019). *You're it: Crisis, change, and how to lead when it matters most*. PublicAffairs.

Markel, D., McCann, M., & Wasserman, H. M. (2015). Catalyzing fans. *Harvard Journal on Sports & Entertainment Law*, *6*(1), 1–40.

Markow, F., & Klenke, K. (2005). The effects of personal meaning and calling on organizational commitment: An empirical investigation of spiritual leadership. *The International Journal of Organizational Analysis*, *13*(1), 8–27. doi:10.1108/eb028995

Marr, B. (2020). *What is the difference between key performance indicators (KPIs) and critical success factors (CSFs)?* https://www.bernardmarr.com/default.asp?contentID=1406

Marshall, P. D., Moore, C., & Barbour, K. (2019). *Persona studies: An introduction.* Wiley-Blackwell.

Marsh, H. W., Hau, K.-T., Balla, J. R., & Grayson, D. (1998). Is more ever too much? The number of indicators per factor in confirmatory factor analysis. *Multivariate Behavioral Research*, *33*(2), 181–220. doi:10.120715327906mbr3302_1 PMID:26771883

Marsh, H. W., & Hocevar, D. (1985). Application of confirmatory factor analysis to the study of self-concept: First-and higher-order factor models and their invariance across groups. *Psychological Bulletin*, *97*(3), 562–582. doi:10.1037/0033-2909.97.3.562

Marwick, A. E., & boyd. (2011). I tweet honestly, I tweet passionately: Twitter users, context' collapse, and the imagined audience. *New Media & Society*, *13*(1), 114–133. doi:10.1177/1461444810365313

Maslow, A. (1987). A theory of human motivation. In *Motivation and personality* (pp. 15–34). Harper & Rob Publishers.

Mason, G. (1996). Recent advances in questionnaire design for program evaluation. *The Canadian Journal of Program Evaluation*, *11*(1), 73–84.

Mayerl, J., & Giehl, C. (2018). A closer look at attitude scales with positive and negative items and response latency perspectives on measurement quality. *Survey Research Methods*, *12*(3). Advance online publication. doi:10.18148rm/2018.v12i3.7207

McCrimmon, M. (2006). *Burn! 7 leadership myths to ashes.* Self Renewal Group.

McCutcheon, L. E., Ashe, D. D., Houran, J., & Maltby, J. (2003). A cognitive profile of individuals who intend to worship celebrities. *The Journal of Psychology*, *137*(4), 309–322. doi:10.1080/00223980309600616 PMID:12943182

McCutcheon, L. E., Lange, R., & Houran, J. (2002). Conceptualization and measurement of celebrity worship. *British Journal of Psychology*, *93*(1), 67–87. doi:10.1348/000712602162454 PMID:11839102

McDonald, R. (1999). *Test theory: A unified treatment.* Lawrence Erlbaum Associates.

McDuff, E. M., & Mueller, C. W. (2000). The ministry as an occupational labor market: Intentions to leave an employer (church) versus intentions to leave a profession (ministry). *Work and Occupations*, *27*(1), 89–116. doi:10.1177/0730888400027001005

McGregor, D. (1975). An uneasy look at performance appraisal. *Harvard Business Review*, *5*(7), 27–31.

McGregor, S. L. T., & Murnane, J. A. (2010). Paradigm, methodology and method: Intellectual integrity in consumer scholarship. *International Journal of Consumer Studies*, *34*(4), 419–427. doi:10.1111/j.1470-6431.2010.00883.x

McIntosh, G., & Rima, S. (2007). *Overcoming the Darkside of Leadership: How to Become an Effective Leader by Confronting Potential Failures.* Baker Books.

McLean, B., & Elkind, P. (2003). *Smartest guys in the room: The amazing rise and scandalous fall of Enron.* Portfolio/Penguin Group.

McNaught, W., & Barth, M. (1992). Are older workers good buys? A case study of Days Inn of America. *Sloan Management Review*, *33*(3), 1–17.

McNeal, R. (2000). *A work of heart: Understanding how god shapes spiritual leaders*. Jossey-Bass.

Medicine, J. H. U. o. (2021). *Coronavirus Resource Center*. https://coronavirus.jhu.edu/map.html

Mehrabi, N., Morstatter, F., Saxena, N., Lerman, K., & Galstyan, A. (2019, September). *A survey on bias and fairness in machine learning*. https://arxiv.org/pdf/1908.09635.pdf

Meindl, J. (1993). Reinventing leadership: A radical, social psychological approach. In J. K. Murnighan (Ed.), *Social Psychology in Organizations*. Prentice-Hall.

Men, L. R., & Tsai, W. S. (2015). Infusing social media with humanity: Corporate character, public engagement, and relational outcomes. *Public Relations Review*, *41*(3), 395–403. doi:10.1016/j.pubrev.2015.02.005

Meredith, W. (1993). Measurement invariance, factor analysis and factorial invariance. *Psychometrika*, *58*(4), 525–543. doi:10.1007/BF02294825

Merriam Webster. (2021, April). https://www.merriam-webster.com/

Merton, R. K. (1946). *Mass persuasion: The social psychology of a war bond drive*. Harper & Brothers Publishers.

Merton, R. K. (1968). On sociological theories of the middle range. In R. K. Merton (Ed.), *Social Theory and Social Structure* (pp. 39–72). Free Press.

Messick, S. (1995). Validity of psychological assessment: Validation of inferences from persons' responses and performances as scientific inquiry into score meaning. *The American Psychologist*, *50*(9), 741–749. doi:10.1037/0003-066X.50.9.741

Meyers, M. C., Adams, B. G., Sekaja, L., Buzea, C., Cazan, A.-M., Gotea, M., Stefenel, D., & van Woerkom, M. (2019). Perceived Organizational Support for the Use of Employees' Strengths and Employee Well-Being: A Cross-Country Comparison. *Journal of Happiness Studies*, *20*(6), 1825–1841. doi:10.100710902-018-0026-8

Milfont, T. L., & Fischer, R. (2010). Testing measurement invariance across groups: Applications in cross-cultural research. *International Journal of Psychological Research*, *3*(1), 111–130. doi:10.21500/20112084.857

Miller, D. M., & Krieshok, T. S. (1989). Sex differences in the second-order factor structure of the 16 PF: A confirmatory maximum likelihood analysis. *Measurement & Evaluation in Counseling & Development*, *2*(2), 73–80. doi:10.1080/07481756.1989.12022914

Mills, G. E., & Gay, L. R. (2019). *Educational Research: Competencies for analysis and applications* (12th ed.). Pearson Education, Inc.

Milyavsky, M., Krunglanski, A., Chemikova, M., & Schori-Eyal, N. (2017). Evidence of Arrogance: On the Relative Importance of Expertise, Outcome, and Manner. *PLoS One*, *12*(7), 1–31. doi:10.1371/journal.pone.0180420 PMID:28683114

Ministry retrains 'exited' pastors. (1997). *Christianity Today, 41*(7), 67. https://www.christianitytoday.com/ct/1997/june16/7t767b.html

Mircioiu, C., & Atkinson, J. (2017). A comparison of parametric and non-parametric methods applied to a Likert scale. *Pharmacy (Basel, Switzerland)*, *5*(2), 26–38. doi:10.3390/pharmacy5020026 PMID:28970438

Mitroff, I. I. (2004). *Crisis leadership: Planning for the unthinkable*. Wiley.

Mitroff, I. I. (2005). Crisis leadership: Seven strategies of strength. *Leadership Excellence*, *22*, 11.

Mohr, A. T., & Puck, J. F. (2007). Role conflict, general manager job satisfaction and stress and the performance of IJVs. *European Management Journal*, *25*(1), 25–35. doi:10.1016/j.emj.2006.11.003

Molinaro, V. (2017). *The leadership accountability gap: A global study exploring the real state of leadership in organizations today*. Lee Hecht Harrison.

Molinaro, V. (2018). *The leadership contract: The fine print to becoming an accountable leader* (3rd ed.). John Wiley & Sons.

Monod, S., Brennan, M., Rochat, E., Martin, E., Rochat, S., & Büla, C. J. (2011). Instruments measuring spirituality in clinical research: A systematic review. *Journal of General Internal Medicine*, *26*(11), 1345–1357. doi:10.100711606-011-1769-7 PMID:21725695

Monroe, K. R. (1994). A fat lady in a corset: Altruism and social theory. *American Journal of Political Science*, *38*(4), 861–893. doi:10.2307/2111725

Montiel-Overall, P. (2006). Implications of missing data in survey research. *Canadian Journal of Information and Library Science*, *30*(3/4), 241–269.

Moos, D., & Azevedo, R. (2009). Learning With Computer-Based Learning Environments: A Literature Review of Computer Self-Efficacy. *Review of Educational Research*, *79*(2), 576–600. doi:10.3102/0034654308326083

Mortensen, M., & Neeley, T. B. (2012). Reflected knowledge and trust in global collaboration. *Management Science*, *58*(12), 2207–2224. doi:10.1287/mnsc.1120.1546

Mo, S., & Shi, J. (2017). Linking ethical leadership to employee burnout, workplace deviance and performance: Testing the mediating roles of trust in Measuring Holistic Ethical Leadership 138 leader and surface acting. *Journal of Business Ethics*, *144*(2), 293–303. doi:10.100710551-015-2821-z

Moxcey, M. E. (1922). *Some qualities associated with success in the Christian ministry*. Teachers College, Columbia University.

Moy, A. C. (1985). *The relationship between leadership and ministerial effectiveness* (Doctoral dissertation). Fuller Theological Seminary.

Mueller, C. W., & McDuff, E. (2004). Clergy–congregation mismatches and clergy job satisfaction. *Journal for the Scientific Study of Religion*, *43*(2), 261–273. doi:10.1111/j.1468-5906.2004.00231.x

Mui, C. (2012, January 18). How Kodak Failed. *Forbes*. Retrieved from https://www.forbes.com/sites/chunkamui/2012/01/18/how-kodak-failed/?sh=2941395a6f27

Mull, M. (2018). *Testing an adapted and integrated model of Motivation to Lead and intention to apply* [Unpublished doctoral dissertation]. University of Texas, Tyler, TX.

Mundfrom, D., Shaw, D., & Ke, T. L. (2005). Minimum sample size recommendations for conducting factor analyses. *International Journal of Testing*, *5*(2), 159–168. doi:10.120715327574ijt0502_4

Murrell, K. L. (1997). Emergent theories of leadership for the next century: Towards relational concepts. *Organization Development Journal*, *15*(3), 35–42.

Muthén, B. O., & Christoffersson, A. (1981). Simultaneous factor analysis of dichotomous variables in several groups. *Psychometrika*, *46*(4), 407–419. doi:10.1007/BF02293798

Nauss, A. H. (1972). Problems in measuring ministerial effectiveness. *Journal for the Scientific Study of Religion*, *11*(2), 141–151. doi:10.2307/1384926

Nauss, A. H. (1974). The relation of pastoral mobility to effectiveness. *Review of Religious Research*, *15*(2), 80–86. doi:10.2307/3510237

Nauss, A. H. (1983). Seven profiles of effective ministers. *Review of Religious Research, 24*(4), 334–346. doi:10.2307/3511012

Nauss, A. H. (1989). Leadership styles of effective ministry. *Journal of Psychology and Theology, 17*(1), 59–67. doi:10.1177/009164718901700109

Nauss, A. H. (1994). Ministerial effectiveness in ten functions. *Religious Research Association, 36*(1), 58–69. doi:10.2307/3511652

Nauss, A. H. (1996). Assessing ministerial effectiveness: A review of measures and their use. In J. M. Greer, D. O. Moberg, & M. L. Lynn (Eds.), *Research in the social scientific study of religion* (Vol. 7, pp. 221–252). JAI Press.

Nauss, A. H., Schmiel, D., & Sohns, W. (1992). *Clergy evaluation instrument.* Board for Higher Education Services, The Lutheran Church-Missouri Synod.

Ndlovu, C. (2013). *Examining relationships between balanced scorecard effectiveness and nursing leaders' accountability* (Publication No. 3599543) [Doctoral Dissertation, Capella University]. ProQuest Dissertations and Theses Global.

Neal, J. (2000). Work as service to the divine. *The American Behavioral Scientist, 43*(8), 1316–1333. doi:10.1177/00027640021955883

Neely, J. (2021). *7 sales KPIs (key performance indicators) you should measure in 2021.* https://toggl.com/blog/sales-kpi

Nelson, S. J., & Reierson, J. L. (2013). New leader, new path: BP's redemption through a post-crisis shift in rhetorical strategies following the Deepwater Horizon oil rig explosion and spill. *Journal of the Communication. Speech & Theatre Association of North Dakota, 25,* 37–52.

Netemeyer, R. G., Bearden, W. O., & Sharma, S. (2003). Scaling procedures: Issues and applications. *Sage (Atlanta, Ga.).*

Nevicka, B., De Hoogh, A., Van Vianen, A., Beersma, B., & McIlwain, D. (2011). All I Need is a Stage to Shine: Narcissists' Leader Emergence and Performance. *The Leadership Quarterly, 22*(5), 910–925. doi:10.1016/j.leaqua.2011.07.011

Nicolae, M., Ion, I., & Nicolae, E. (2013). The research agenda of spiritual leadership. Where do we stand? *Journal of International Comparative Management, 14*(4), 551–566.

Noonan Hadley, C., Pittinsky, T. L., Sommer, S. A., & Zhu, W. (2011). Measuring the efficacy of leaders to assess information and make decisions in a crisis: The C-LEAD scale. *The Leadership Quarterly, 22*(4), 633–648. doi:10.1016/j.leaqua.2011.05.005

Northouse, P. G. (2004). *Leadership: Theory and practice* (4th ed.). Sage.

Northouse, P. G. (2016). *Leadership theory and practice* (7th ed.). Sage.

Nunnallly, J. C. (1978). *Psychometric theory* (2nd ed.). McGraw-Hill.

Nunnally, J. (1975). Psychometric theory. 25 years ago and now. *Educational Researcher, 4*(10), 7–21. doi:10.2307/1175619

Nunnally, J. (1978). An Overview of Psychological Measurement. In B. B. Wolman (Ed.), *Clinical Diagnosis of Mental Disorders.* Springer., doi:10.1007/978-1-4684-2490-4_4

Nunnally, J. (1978). *Psychometric Theory.* McGraw-Hill.

Nye, C. D., Chernyshenko, O. S., Stark, S., Drasgow, F., Phillips, H. L., Phillips, J. B., & Campbell, J. S. (2020). More than g: Evidence for the Incremental Validity of Performance-Based Assessments for Predicting Training Performance. *Applied Psychology: An International Review, 69*(2), 302–324. doi:10.1111/apps.12171

O'Keefe, D. J. (1990). *Persuasion.* Sage.

Olbrych, J. C. (2012). *The bonds of affection: Assessing clergy leadership effectiveness using adult attachment theory* (Doctoral dissertation). Available from ProQuest Dissertations and Theses database. (UMI No. 3529297)

Olckers, C. (2013). Psychological ownership: Development of an instrument. *SA Journal of Industrial Psychology, 39*(2), 1–13. doi:10.4102ajip.v39i2.1105

Oney, R. M. (2009). *Exploring the causal relationship of emotional intelligence to clergy leadership effectiveness* (Doctoral dissertation). Retrieved from Regent University database. (UMI No. 3392554)

Oroviogoicoechea, C., Roger, W., Beortegui, E., & Remirez, S. (2010). Nurses' perception of the use of computerised information systems in practice: Questionnaire development. *Journal of Clinical Nursing, 19*(1–2), 240–248. doi:10.1111/j.1365-2702.2009.03003.x PMID:20500261

Oyeniran, S. T., Jayesimi, O. S., Ogundele, R. A., & Oyeniran, O. A. Computer mediated communication for effective and efficient organization service delivery amid Covid-19 pandemic. *International Journal of Engineering and Artificial Intelligence, 1*(3), 44-49.

Ozgen Novelli, S., Laginess, A., & Viswesvaran, C. (2017). The Motivation to Lead Questionnaire: A meta-analytic examination of score reliability. *Academy of Management Proceedings, 2017*(1).

Page, D., & Wong, P. (2000). A conceptual framework for measuring servant-leadership. In S. Adjibolosoo (Ed.), *The human factor in shaping the course of history and development.* University Press of America.

Page, K. M., & Vella-Brodrick, D. A. (2009). The 'What,' 'Why,' and 'How' of employee well-being: A new model. *Social Indicators Research, 90*(3), 441–458. doi:10.100711205-008-9270-3

Pallant, J. (2006). *SPSS survival manual* (2nd ed.). Open University Press.

Pallant, J. (2010). *SPSS survival guide: A step-by-step guide to data analysis using the SPSS program* (4th ed.). McGraw-Hill.

Pallant, J. (2010). *SPSS survival manual: A step by step guide to data analysis using the SPS program* (4th ed.). McGraw-Hill.

Pallant, J. F. (2005). *SPSS survival manual: A step-by-step guide to data analysis using SPSS for Windows (Versions 12-14).* Allen & Unwin.

Palser, S. J. (2005). *The relationship between occupational burnout and emotional intelligence among clergy or professional ministry workers* (Publication No. 3162679) [Doctoral dissertation, Regent University]. Proquest Dissertation Abstracts and Theses.

Papaloizos, A., & Nicholls, J. (1970). An approach to measuring the effectiveness of participative methods in teaching managerial skills. *Training and Development Journal, 24*(6), 10.

Parent-Rocheleau, X., Bentein, K., & Simard, G. (2020). Positive together? The effects of leader-follower (dis) similarity in psychological capital. *Journal of Business Research, 110,* 435–444. doi:10.1016/j.jbusres.2020.02.016

Parker, S., & Hyratus, K. (2011). Priorities in nursing management. *Journal of Nursing Management, 19*(5), 567–571. doi:10.1111/j.1365-2834.2011.01285.x PMID:21749530

Parmenter, D. (2019). *What is a KPI (introduction to key performance indicators)?* https://kpi.davidparmenter.com/defining-kpis/

Parmenter, D. (2015). *Key performance indicators: Developing, implementing, and using winning KPIs* (3rd ed.). John Wiley and Sons.

Pater, R. (2013, November). Overcoming Leadership ADD: The Flaws of Arrogance, Distraction and Disconnection. *Professional Safety,* 30–34. www.asse.org

Patterson, K. (2003). *Servant Leadership: A theoretical model* [Unpublished doctoral dissertation]. Regent University, VA.

Patton, M. Q. (2002). *Qualitative research & evaluation methods* (3rd ed.). Sage.

Paycor. (2020, December 24). *The biggest cost of doing business: A closer look at labor costs*. https://www.paycor.com/resource-center/a-closer-look-at-labor-costs

Payne, J., McDonald, S., & Hamm, L. (2013). Production teams and producing racial diversity in workplace relationships. *Sociological Forum, 28*(2), 326–349. doi:10.1111ocf.12021

Payne, V. L., & Hysong, S. J. (2016). Model depicting aspects of audit and feedback that impact physicians' acceptance of clinical performance feedback. *BMC Health Services Research, 161*(12). doi:10.118612913-016-1486-3

Pearce, C., & Conger, J. (2003). *Shared leadership: Reframing the how's and why's of leadership*. Sage.

Pearson, C. M., & Mitroff, I. I. (1993). From crisis prone to crisis prepared: A framework for crisis management. *The Academy of Management Executive, 7*(1), 48–59. doi:10.5465/ame.1993.9409142058

Pedersen, R. D., Pallay, A. G., & Rudolph, R. L. (2002). Can improvement in well-being and functioning be distinguished from depression improvement in antidepressant clinical trials? *Quality of Life Research: An International Journal of Quality of Life Aspects of Treatment, Care and Rehabilitation, 11*(1), 9–17. doi:10.1023/A:1014441826855 PMID:12003058

Peeters, M., & van Emmerik, H. (2008). An introduction to the work and well-being of older workers. *Journal of Managerial Psychology, 23*(4), 353–363. doi:10.1108/02683940810869006

Pense, B. C. (1996). *Leadership styles and pastoral effectiveness* (Masters thesis). Available from ProQuest Dissertations and Theses database. (ProQuest No. 1380374)

Pergert, P., Bartholdson, C., Wenemark, M., Lützén, K., & Af Sandeberg, M. (2018). Translating and culturally adapting the shortened version of the hospital ethical climate survey (HECS-S) - retaining or modifying validated instruments. *BMC Medical Ethics, 19*(1), 35–35. doi:10.118612910-018-0274-5 PMID:29747639

Perloff, R. M. (1993). *The dynamics of persuasion*. Lawrence Erlbaum. doi:10.4324/9781410606884

Perrewé, P. L., Zellars, K. L., Ferris, G. R., Rossi, A. M., Kacmar, C. J., & Ralston, D. A. (2004). Neutralizing job stressors: Political skill as an antidote to the dysfunctional consequences of role conflict stressors. *Academy of Management Journal, 47*(1), 141–152. doi:10.2307/20159566

Pervin, L. A. (1968). Performance and satisfaction as a function of individual–environment fit. *Psychological Bulletin, 69*(1), 56–68. doi:10.1037/h0025271

Peter, J. P. (1981). Construct validity: A review of basic issues and marketing practices. *JMR, Journal of Marketing Research, 18*(2), 133–145. doi:10.1177/002224378101800201

Peterson, J. J. (2019). *StoryBrand narrative marketing: An examination of the influence of narrative marketing on organizations* (Unpublished doctoral dissertation). Virginia Beach, VA: Regent University.

Peterson, M. F., Smith, P. B., Akande, A., Ayestaran, S., Bochner, S., Callan, V., Jesuino, J. C., D'Amorim, M., Francois, P.-H., Hofmann, K., Koopman, P. L., Mortazavi, S., Munene, J., Radford, M., Ropo, A., Savage, G., & Setiadi, B. (1995). Role conflict, ambiguity, and overload: A 21-nation study. *Academy of Management Journal, 38*(2), 429–452. doi:10.2307/256687

Petronio, S. (1991). Communication boundary management: A theoretical model of managing disclosure of private information between martial couples. *Communication Theory, 1*(4), 311–335. doi:10.1111/j.1468-2885.1991.tb00023.x

Petronio, S. (1994). Privacy binds in family interactions the case of parental privacy invasion. In W. R. Cupach & B. H. Spitzberg (Eds.), *The Dark Side of interpersonal communication* (pp. 241–258). Lawrence Erlbaum. doi:10.4324/9781315807010-10

Petronio, S. (2002). *Boundaries of privacy: Dialectics of disclosure*. SUNY Press.

Petronio, S. (2013). Brief status report on communication privacy management theory. *Journal of Family Communication*, *13*(1), 6–14. doi:10.1080/15267431.2013.743426

Petronio, S. (2015). Communication privacy management theory. In C. R. Berger, M. E. Roloff, S. R. Wilson, J. P. Dillard, J. Caughlin, & D. Solomon (Eds.), *The International Encyclopedia of Interpersonal Communication*. doi:10.1002/9781118540190.wbeic132

Pett, M., Lackey, N., & Sullivan, J. (2003). Making sense of factor analysis: The use of factor analysis for instrument development in health care research. *Sage (Atlanta, Ga.)*.

Peytchev, A. (2013). Consequences of survey nonresponse. *The Annals of the American Academy of Political and Social Science*, *645*(1), 88–111. doi:10.1177/0002716212461748

Peytchev, A., Carley-Baxter, L. R., & Black, M. C. (2011). Multiple sources of nonobservation error in telephone surveys: Coverage and nonresponse. *Sociological Methods & Research*, *40*(1), 138–168. doi:10.1177/0049124110392547

Phillips, J. J. (1996). How much is the training worth? *Training & Development*, *50*(4), 20–24. https://www.questia.com/magazine/1G1-18434799/how-much-is-the-training-worth

Phillips, J. J., & Phillips, P. P. (2008). *Beyond learning objectives: Develop measurable objectives that link to the bottom line*. ASTD Press.

Phillips, J., & Stone, R. (2002). *How to measure training results: A practical guide to tracking the six key indicators*. McGraw-Hill.

Phillips, P. P. (2012). *Bottomline on ROI* (2nd ed.). HRDQ Press.

Phillips, P. P. (Ed.). (2010). *ASTD handbook of measuring and evaluating training*. ASTD Press. Available from https://www.td.org/Publications/Books/ASTD-Handbook-of-Measuring-and-Evaluating-Training

Piedmont, R. L. (1999). Does spirituality represent the sixth factor of personality? spiritual transcendence and the five-factor model. *Journal of Personality*, *67*(6), 985–1013. doi:10.1111/1467-6494.00080

Poggi, I., & D'Errico, F. (2011). Types of Pride and their Expression. In A. Esposito, A. Vinciarelli, K. Vicsi, C. Pelachaud, & A. Nijholt (Eds.), *Analysis of Verbal and Nonverbal Communication and Enactment* (pp. 434–448). Springer-Verlag.

Polit & Beck. (2010). Generalization in quantitative and qualitative research: Myths and strategies. *International Journal of Nursing Studies*, *47*(11), 1451-1458.

Pontius, K. D. (1992). *A descriptive study of motivational and personality characteristics in evangelical pastors* (Doctoral dissertation). Available from ProQuest Dissertations and Theses database. (UMI No. 9307480)

Ponton, M. K. (1999). *The measurement of an adult's intention to exhibit personal initiative in autonomous learning* [Unpublished doctoral dissertation]. The George Washington University, Washington, DC.

Porter, M. (1998). *Competitive advantage*. The Free Press. doi:10.1007/978-1-349-14865-3

Porter, S. R., Whitcomb, M. E., & Weitzer, W. H. (2004). Multiple surveys of students and survey fatigue. *New Directions for Institutional Research*, *2004*(121), 63–73. doi:10.1002/ir.101

Posner, B. Z. (2009). From inside out. *Journal of Leadership Education, 8*(1), 1–10. doi:10.12806/V8/I1/TF1

Poulsen, S., & Ipsen, C. (2017). In times of change: How distance managers can ensure employees' well-being and organizational performance. *Safety Science, 100*, 37–45. doi:10.1016/j.ssci.2017.05.002

Praslova, L. (2010). Adaptation of Kirkpatrick's four level model of training criteria to assessment of learning outcomes and program evaluation in higher education. *Educational Assessment, Evaluation and Accountability, 22*(3), 215-225. doi:10.100711092-010-9098-7

Prensky, M. (2001). Digital Natives, Digital Immigrants Part 1. *On the Horizon, 9*(5), 1–6. doi:10.1108/10748120110424816

Priesmeyer, R. H., Seigfried, R. J., & Murray, M. A. (2012). The supply chain as a wholistic system: A case study. *Management & Marketing, 7*(4), 551–564.

Privitera, G. J., & Ahlgrim-Delzell, L. (2019). *Research methods for education* (1st ed.). Sage.

Pulakos, E. D. (2004). *Performance management: A roadmap for developing, implementing and evaluating performance management systems*. Society for Human Resource Management Foundation.

Puls, T. R. (2011). *Authentic leadership and its relationship to ministerial effectiveness* (Doctoral dissertation). Available from ProQuest Dissertations and Theses database. (UMI No. 3498652)

Puls, T. R., Ludden, L. L., & Freemyer, J. (2014). Authentic leadership and its relationship to ministerial effectiveness. *The Journal of Applied Christian Leadership, 8*(1), 55–75.

Raelin, J. A. (2003). *Creating leaderful organizations*. Berrett-Koehler.

Ramani, S., & Krackov, S. K. (2012). Twelve tips for giving feedback effectively in the clinical environment. *Medical Teacher, 34*(10), 787-791. doi:10.3109/0142159X.2012.684916

Ranft, A. L., Zinko, R., Ferris, G. R., & Buckley, M. R. (2006). Marketing the image of management: The costs and benefits of CEO reputation. *Organizational Dynamics, 35*(3), 279–290. doi:10.1016/j.orgdyn.2006.05.003

Rattray, J., & Jones, M. C. (2007). Essential elements of questionnaire design and development. *Journal of Clinical Nursing, 16*(2), 234–243. doi:10.1111/j.1365-2702.2006.01573.x PMID:17239058

Rea, L., & Parker, A. (2014). *Designing and conducting survey research: A comprehensive guide* (4th ed.). John Wiley & Sons, Inc., Jossey-Bass.

Reave, L. (2005). Spiritual values and practices related to leadership effectiveness. *The Leadership Quarterly, 16*(5), 655–687. doi:10.1016/j.leaqua.2005.07.003

Rediger, G. L. (2003). Managing depression. *The Clergy Journal, 79*(9), 15-16. https://www-proquest-com.ezproxy2. apus.edu/trade-journals/managing-depression/docview/230520595/se-2?accountid=8289

Reed, A. (2016). Rooted in relationship: Longevity in congregational ministry. *Review & Expositor, 113*(3), 303–314. doi:10.1177/0034637316659304

Reilly, N. P., & Orsak, C. L. (1991). A career stage analysis of career and organizational commitment in nursing. *Journal of Vocational Behavior, 39*(3), 311–330. doi:10.1016/0001-8791(91)90041-J

Reinius, M., Wettergren, L., Wiklander, M., Svedhem, V., Ekstrom, A., & Eriksson, L. E. (2017). Development of a 12-item short version of the HIV stigma scale. *Health and Quality of Life Outcomes, 15*(1), 115. doi:10.118612955-017-0691-z PMID:28558805

Renberg, T., Kettis-Lindblad, A., & Tully, M. (2018). Testing the validity of a translated pharmaceutical therapy-related quality of life instrument, using qualitative 'think aloud' methodology. *Journal of Clinical Pharmacy and Therapeutics, 33*(3), 279–287. doi:10.1111/j.1365-2710.2008.00921.x PMID:18452415

Revelle, W., & Zinbarg, R. E. (2009). Coefficients alpha, beta, omega, and the glb: Comments on sijtsma. *Psychometrika, 74*(1), 145-154. http://dx.doi.org.ezproxy.regent.edu/10.1007/s11336-008-9102-z

Revelle, W., & Rocklin, T. (1979). Very simple structure: An alternative procedure for estimating the optimal number of interpretable factors. *Multivariate Behavioral Research, 14*(4), 403–414. doi:10.120715327906mbr1404_2 PMID:26804437

Reynolds, R. A. (2020). The centrality of evidence in the communication discipline. *Western Journal of Communication, 84*(5), 521-527. doi:10.1080/10570314.2020.1771411

Reynolds, J. L., & Lawrence, D. (2018). Is diversity & inclusion training really training? Rethinking New Models. In S. K. Camara, M. P. Orbe, K. S. Makai, & L. Gilinets (Eds.), *Communication & Training & Development: Exploring the Cutting Edge*. Kendall Hunt.

Reynolds, R. A. (2017). Begin with the end in mind: Conducting post training evaluations. In S. K. Camara (Ed.), *Communication training and development: Exploring the cutting edge*. Kendall/Hunt Publishing Co.

Reynolds, R. A., & Reynolds, J. L. (2002). Evidence. In J. P. Dillard & M. Pfau (Eds.), *The persuasion handbook: Developments in theory and practice* (pp. 427–444). Sage. doi:10.4135/9781412976046.n22

Richardson, H. A., Simmering, M. J., & Sturman, M. C. (2009). A tale of three perspectives: Examining post hoc statistical techniques for detection and correction of common method variance. *Organizational Research Methods, 12*(4), 762–800. doi:10.1177/1094428109332834

Rieder, K. L. (1991). *Vocational interests as predictors of effectiveness in the ministry* (Doctoral dissertation). Available from ProQuest Dissertations and Theses database. (UMI No. 9217952)

Rijsenbilt, A., & Commandeur, H. (2013). Narcissus Enters the Courtroom: CEO Narcissism and Fraud. *Journal of Business Ethics, 117*(2), 413–429. doi:10.100710551-012-1528-7

Robbins, S. P., & Judge, T. A. (2012). *Organizational Behavior* (15th ed.). Prentice Hall.

Rogers, G., Mentkowski, M., & Hart, J. R. (2006). Adult holistic development and multidimensional performance. In C. H. Hoare (Ed.), *Handbook of adult development and learning* (pp. 498–534). Oxford University.

Roof, R. A. (2016). *The relationship between spiritual engagement and authentic leadership: Exploring the core of leadership* (1791976131) [Doctoral dissertation, Regent University]. Proquest Dissertations & Theses Global.

Roof, R. (2014a). Authentic leadership questionnaire (alq) psychometrics. *Asian Journal of Business Ethics, 3*(1), 57–64. doi:10.100713520-013-0031-2

Roof, R. A. (2014b). The association of individual spirituality on employee engagement: The spirit at work. *Journal of Business Ethics, 130*(3), 585–599. doi:10.100710551-014-2246-0

Roof, R. A., Bocarnea, M. C., & Winston, B. E. (2017). The spiritual engagement instrument. *Asian Journal of Business Ethics, 6*(2), 215–232. doi:10.100713520-017-0073-y

Rosanas, J. M. (2020). The dehumanization and demoralization of management control systems: Can we possibly re-humanize and re-moralize them? *European Accounting and Management Review, 6*(2), 56–80.

Rosendahl, D. K. (2019). *Causes, consequences and cures of role stress among Swedish Free-Church pastors* [Unpublished doctoral dissertation]. Trinity College of the Bible and Trinity Theological Seminary.

Ross, D. L. (1987). *Similarity among ratings of ministerial effectiveness and its relationship to interpersonal responsiveness* (Doctoral dissertation). Available from ProQuest Dissertations and Theses database. (UMI No. 8801949)

Rosseel, Y. (2012). lavaan: An R Package for Structural Equation Modeling. *Journal of Statistical Software, 48*(2), 1–36. doi:10.18637/jss.v048.i02

Rost, J. C. (1991). *Leadership for the twenty-first century.* Praeger.

Roth, J. (2011). *The relationship between emotional intelligence and pastor leadership in turnaround churches* (Doctoral dissertation). Available from ProQuest Dissertations and Theses database. (UMI No. 3487845)

Rothwell, W., Sterns, H., Spokus, D., & Reaser, J. (2008). *Working longer: New strategies for managing, training, and retaining older employees.* American Management Association.

Rubin, A. M., Perse, E. M., & Powell, R. A. (1985). Loneliness, parasocial interaction, and local television viewing. *Human Communication Research, 12*(2), 155–180. doi:10.1111/j.1468-2958.1985.tb00071.x

Rubin, R. B., & McHugh, M. P. (1987). Development of parasocial interaction relationships. *Journal of Broadcasting & Electronic Media, 31*(3), 279–292. doi:10.1080/08838158709386664

Rubin, R. B., Palmgreen, P., & Sypher, H. E. (Eds.). (1994). *Communication Research Measures: A Sourcebook.* The Guilford Press.

Ruona, W., Lynham, S., & Chermack, T. (2003). Insights on emerging trends and the future of human resource development. *Advances in Developing Human Resources, 5*(3), 272–282. doi:10.1177/1523422303254667

Russell, D., Peplau, L. A., & Cutrona, C. E. (1980). The revised UCLA loneliness scale: Concurrent and discriminant validity evidence. *Journal of Personality and Social Psychology, 39*(3), 472–480. doi:10.1037/0022-3514.39.3.472 PMID:7431205

Ryan, R. M., & Deci, E. L. (2001). On happiness and human potentials: A review of research on hedonic and eudaimonic well-being. *Annual Review of Psychology, 52*(1), 141–166. doi:10.1146/annurev.psych.52.1.141 PMID:11148302

Sakalaki, M., Richardson, C., & Thepaut, Y. (2007). Machiavellianism and Economic Opportunism. *Journal of Applied Social Psychology, 37*(6), 1181–1190. doi:10.1111/j.1559-1816.2007.00208.x

Salant, P., & Dillman, D. A. (1994). *How to construct your own survey.* John Wiley & Sons, Inc.

Salles, A., Cohen, G. L., & Mueller, C. M. (2014). The relationship between grit and resident well-being. *American Journal of Surgery, 207*(2), 251–254. doi:10.1016/j.amjsurg.2013.09.006 PMID:24238604

Salmon, C. T. (1986). Perspectives on involvement in consumer and communication research. In B. Dervin & M. J. Voigt (Eds.), *Progress in communication sciences* (Vol. 7, pp. 234–268). Ablex.

Sanders, C. G. (2012). *Measurement of the intention to exhibit leadership behavior: Development of a scale* [Unpublished doctoral dissertation]. Regent University, Virginia Beach, VA, USA.

Sanders, J. O. (2007). *Spiritual leadership: Principles of excellence for every believer* (1st ed.). Moody.

Sandstrom, C. R. (1991). *The components of empowerment and personality of effective clergy leaders* (Doctoral dissertation). Available from ProQuest Dissertations and Theses database. (UMI No. 9129207)

Sass, J. S. (2000). Characterizing organizational spirituality: An organizational communication culture approach. *Communication Studies, 51*(3), 195–217. doi:10.1080/10510970009388520

Scarpello, V., & Vandenberg, R. J. (1992). Generalizing the importance of occupational and career views to job satisfaction attitudes. *Journal of Organizational Behavior*, *13*(2), 125–140. doi:10.1002/job.4030130203

Schaufeli, W. B., & Van Dierendonck, D. (1993). The construct validity of two burnout measures. *Journal of Organizational Behavior*, *14*(7), 631–647. doi:10.1002/job.4030140703

Schein, E. (.-B. (2010). Organizational culture and leadership (4th ed.). San Francisco, CA: Jossey-Bass.

Schiappa, E., Gregg, P. B., & Hewes, D. E. (2005). The parasocial contact hypothesis. *Communication Monographs*, *72*(1), 92–115. doi:10.1080/0363775052000342544

Schmidt, J. E. (1993). *Transformational leadership: The relationship between consciousness, values and skills* (Publication No. 9412221) [Doctoral dissertation, Western Michigan University]. Proquest Dissertation Abstracts and Theses. https://scholarworks.wmich.edu/cgi/viewcontent.cgi?article=2902&context=dissertations

Scholl, M. L. (2009). *The relationship between church effectiveness and pastoral management behavior* (Doctoral dissertation). Available from ProQuest Dissertations and Theses database. (UMI No. 3385075)

Schuller, D. S., Strommen, M. P., & Brekke, M. L. (Eds.). (1980). *Ministry in America: A report and analysis, based on an in-depth survey of 47 denominations in the United States and Canada, with interpretations by 18 experts.* Harper and Row.

Schunk, D. (1984). Self-efficacy perspective on achievement behavior. *Educational Psychologist*, *19*(1), 48–58. doi:10.1080/00461528409529281

Schwanda, T. (2010). "Hearts sweetly refreshed": Puritan spiritual practices then and now. *Journal of Spiritual Formation and Soul Care*, *3*(1), 21–41. doi:10.1177/193979091000300103

Schweitzer, L., & Lyons, S. (2008). The market within: A marketing approach to creating and developing high-value employment relationships. *Business Horizons*, *51*(6), 555–565. doi:10.1016/j.bushor.2008.03.004

ScienceDaily. (2013). *Big data, for better or worse: 90% of world's data generated over last two years.* https://www.sciencedaily.com/releases/2013/05/130522085217.htm

Scouller, J. (2014). The three levels of leadership. Oxford, UK: Management Books 2000.

Scuderi, N. F. (2010). *Servant leadership and transformational leadership in church organizations* (Doctoral dissertation). Available from ProQuest Dissertations and Theses database. (UMI No. 3413541)

Selznick, P. (1957). *Leadership in administration: A sociological interpretation.* Row, Peterson.

Senander, A. (2017). Beyond scandal: Creating a culture of accountability in the Catholic church. *Journal of Business Ethics*, *146*(4), 859–867. doi:10.100710551-016-3217-4

Sendjaya, S., & Sarros, J. C. (2002). Servant leadership: It's origin, development, and application in organizations. *Journal of Leadership & Organizational Studies*, *9*(2), 57–64. doi:10.1177/107179190200900205

Sergiu, G. (2015, March). Developing the Organizational Culture. *Review of International Comparative Management*, *16*(1), 137–143.

Shadish, W. R., Cook, T. D., & Campbell, D. T. (2002). *Experimental and quasi-experimental designs for generalized causal inference.* Houghton Mifflin.

Shalev-Shwartz, S., & Ben-David, S. (2014). *Understanding machine learning: From theory to algorithms.* Cambridge University Press.

Sharkness, J., & Deangelo, L. (2011). Measuring student involvement: A comparison of Classical Test Theory and Item Response Theory in the construction of scales from student surveys. *Research in Higher Education, 52*(5), 480–507. doi:10.100711162-010-9202-3

Sheep, M. L., & Foreman, P. O. (2012). An integrative framework for exploring organizational identity and spirituality. *Journal of Applied Business and Economics, 13*(4), 11–29.

Sheffield, B. (2008, July). *Avoid the top 5 reasons for pastoral termination, Part 5, Who runs the church?* LifeWay Christian Resources. http://www.lifeway.com/lwc/article_main_page/0%2C1703%2CA %25 253D167900%252526M %25253D200829%2C00.html

Shefner-Rogers, C. L., Rogers, E. M., & Singhal, A. (1998). Parasocial interaction with the television soap operas 'Simplemente Maria' and 'Oshin.'. *Keio Communication Review, 20*, 3–18. Retrieved January 30, 2021, from http://utminers.utep.edu/asinghal/ Articles%20and%20Chapters/ shefnerrogers_rogers_singhal.pdf

Shehan, C., Wiggins, M., & Cody-Rydzewski, S. (2007). Responding to and retreating from the call: Career salience, work satisfaction, and depression among clergywomen. *Pastoral Psychology, 55*(5), 637–643. doi:10.100711089-006-0064-8

Shen, F. (2017). Multitrait-Multimethod matrix. In The International Encyclopedia of Communication Research Methods. John Wiley & Sons. doi:10.1002/9781118901731.iecrm0161

Sherman, K., Eaves, E., Ritenbugh, C., Hsu, C., Cherkin, D., & Turner, J. (2014). Cognitive interviews guide design of a new CAM patient expectations questionnaire. *BMC Complementary and Alternative Medicine, 14*(1), 39–55. doi:10.1186/1472-6882-14-39 PMID:24460709

Shmailan, A. S. B. (2016). The relationship between job satisfaction, job performance and employee engagement: An explorative study. *Issues in Business Management and Economics, 4*(1), 1–8.

Shore, L., & Shore, T. (1995). Perceived organizational support and organizational justice. In R. S. Cropanzano & K. M. Kacmar (Eds.), *Organizational politics, justice, and support: Managing the social climate of the workplace* (pp. 149–164). Quorum.

Shultz, K., Wang, M., Crimmins, E., & Fisher, G. (2010). Age differences in the demand–control model of work stress: An examination of data from 15 European countries. In *Journal of applied Gerontology* (pp. 21–47). NIH Public Access. doi:10.1177/0733464809334286

Siddiq, K., Meyer, E., & Ashleigh, M. (2013, February). What is the impact of authentic leadership on leader accountability in a non-profit context? In *International Conference on Management, Leadership & Governance*. Academic Conferences International Limited.

Siewiorek, A., & Lehtinen, E. (2011). Exploring Leadership Profiles from Collaborative Computer Gaming. *International Journal of Leadership Studies, 6*(3), 357–374.

Silliman, D. (2021, January 5). *Inside RZIM, staff push leaders to take responsibility for scandal.* Retrieved February 16, 2021, from https://www.christianitytoday.com/news/2021/january/rzim-ravi-zacharias-turmoil-spa-allegations-investigation.html

Sills, S. J., & Song, C. (2002). Innovations in survey research. An application of web survey. *Social Science Computer Review, 20*(1), 22–30. doi:10.1177/089443930202000103

Singhal, A., & Svenkerud, P. J. (2018). Diffusion of evidence-based interventions or practice-based positive deviations. *The Journal of Development Communication, 29*(2), 54–64. http://jdc.journals.unisel.edu.my/ojs/index.php/jdc/article/view/134

Sink, C. A. (2018). School Counselors as Accountability Leaders: Another Call for Action. *Professional School Counseling, 13*(2), 68–74. Advance online publication. doi:10.5330/PSC.n.2010-13.68

Smith, S., & Lilienfeld, S. (2013, March-April). Psychopathy in the Workplace: The Knowns and Unknowns. *Aggression and Violent Behavior, 18*(2), 204–218. doi:10.1016/j.avb.2012.11.007

Snyder, C. R. (2000). Genesis: The birth and growth of hope. In C. R. Snyder (Ed.), *Handbook of hope, theories, measure and applications* (pp. 25–36). Academic Press.

Snyder, C. R., Harris, C., Anderson, J. R., Holleran, S. A., Irving, L. M., Sigmon, S. T., Yoshinobu, L., Gibb, J., Langelle, C., & Harney, P. (1991a). The will and the ways: Development and validation of an individual-differences measure of hope. *Journal of Personality and Social Psychology, 60*(4), 570–585. doi:10.1037/0022-3514.60.4.570 PMID:2037968

Snyder, C. R., Irving, L., & Anderson, J. (1991b). Hope and health. In C. R. Snyder & D. Forsyth (Eds.), *Handbook of social and clinical psychology: The health perspective* (pp. 285–305). Pergamon.

Snyder, C. R., & Lopez, S. J. (2007). *Positive psychology: The scientific and practical explorations of human strengths.* Sage Publications.

Snyder, H. (1979). *The problem of wineskins: The church in a technological age.* InterVarsity Press.

Sokolova, K., & Kefi, H. (2020). Instagram and YouTube bloggers promote it, why should I buy? How credibility and parasocial interaction influence purchase intentions. *Journal of Retailing and Consumer Services, 53*, 1-16. doi: .2019.01.011 doi:10.1016/j.jretconser

Soland, J. (2017). Is Teacher Value-Added a Matter of Scale? The Practical Consequences of Treating an Ordinal Scale as Interval for Estimation of Teacher Effects. *Applied Measurement in Education, 30*(1), 52–70. doi:10.1080/0895734 7.2016.1247844

Solas, J. (2016). The Banality of Bad Leadership and Followership. *Society and Business Review, 11*(1), 12–23. doi:10.1108/SBR-09-2015-0049

Somers, M. J., & Birnbaum, D. (1998). Work-related commitment and job performance: It's also the nature of the performance that counts. *Journal of Organizational Behavior, 19*(6), 621–634. doi:10.1002/(SICI)1099-1379(1998110)19:6<621::AID-JOB853>3.0.CO;2-B

Song, J., & Erdem, M. (2011). *M-learning in hospitality: An exploration of older workers needs and attitudes.* http://scholarworks.umass.edu/cgi/viewcontent.cgi?article=1273&context=gradconf_hospitality&seiredir=1&referer=http%3A%2F%2F0-scholar.google.com.library.regent.edu%2Fscholar%3Fhl%3Den%26q%3DSong%2Band%2BM-learning%2Bin%2Bhospitality%253A%2BAn%2Bexploration%2Bof%2Bolder%2Bworkers%2Bneeds%2Band%2Battitudes%26btnG%3DSearch%26as_sdt%3D0%252C47%26as_ylo%3D%26as_vis%3D0#search=%22Song%20M-learning%20hospitality%3A%20An%20exploration%20older%20workers%20needs%20attitudes%22

Sonnenfeld, J. (1991). *The hero's farewell: What happens when CEOs retire.* Oxford University Press. doi:10.1093/acprof:oso/9780195065831.001.0001

Sood, S., & Rogers, E. M. (2000). Dimensions of parasocial interaction by letter-writers to a popular entertainment-education soap opera in India. *Journal of Broadcasting & Electronic Media, 44*(3), 386–414. doi:10.120715506878jobem4403_4

Sorböm, D. (1974). A general method for studying differences in factor means and factor structure between groups. *British Journal of Mathematical & Statistical Psychology, 27*(2), 229–239. doi:10.1111/j.2044-8317.1974.tb00543.x

Spector, P. E. (1992). Summated Rating Scale Construction. In Quantitative Applications in the Social Sciences. Sage Publications. doi:10.4135/9781412986038

Spector, B., & Lane, H. (2007). Exploring the Distinctions between a High Performance Culture and a Cult. *Strategy and Leadership*, *35*(3), 18–24. doi:10.1108/10878570710745794

Spector, P. (2006). Method variance in organizational research: Truth or urban legend? *Organizational Research Methods*, *9*(2), 221–232. doi:10.1177/1094428105284955

Speight, D. E., & Speight, S. W. (2017). Exploring the lived experience of forced termination among Southern Baptist clergy couples: A retrospective study. *Journal of Psychology and Christianity*, *36*(2), 149–160.

Spencer, J. L. (2010). *Vision conflict within pastoral ministry* (Publication No. 3425735) [Doctoral dissertation, Regent University]. Proquest Dissertation Abstracts and Theses.

Spencer, J. L., Winston, B. E., & Bocarnea, M. C. (2012). Predicting the level of pastors' risk of termination/exit from the church. *Pastoral Psychology*, *1*(61), 85–98. doi:10.100711089-011-0410-3

Spencer, J. L., Winston, B. E., Bocarnea, M. C., & Wickman, C. A. (2009). *Validating a practitioner's instrument measuring the level of pastors' risk of termination/exit from the church: Discovering vision conflict and compassion fatigue as key factors* [Unpublished manuscript]. School of Global Leadership and Entrepreneurship, Regent University.

Standish, T., & Umbach, P. D. (2019). Should we be concerned about nonresponse bias in college student surveys? Evidence of bias from a validation study. *Research in Higher Education*, *60*(3), 338–357. doi:10.100711162-018-9530-2

Starr, S. (2012). Survey research: We can do better. *Journal of the Medical Library Association: JMLA*, *100*(1), 1–2. doi:10.3163/1536-5050.100.1.001 PMID:22272152

Stawarski, C. A. (2012). *What's the difference between return on expectations and return on investment?* https://www.td.org/Publications/Blogs/L-and-D-Blog/2012/10/Whats-the-Difference-Between-Return-on-Expectations-and-Return-on-Investment

Steenkamp, J. E. M., & Baumgartner, H. (1998). Assessing measurement invariance in cross-national consumer research. *The Journal of Consumer Research*, *25*(1), 78–90. doi:10.1086/209528

Steinbauer, R., Renn, R. W., Taylor, R. R., & Njoroge, P. K. (2014). Ethical leadership and followers moral judgment: The role of followers perceived accountability and self-leadership. *Journal of Business Ethics*, *120*(3), 381–292. doi:10.100710551-013-1662-x

Sterns, H., & Miklos, S. (1995). The aging worker in a changing environment: Organizational and individual issues. *Journal of Vocational Behavior*, *47*(3), 248–268. doi:10.1006/jvbe.1995.0003

Stever, G. S. (2009). Parasocial and social interaction with celebrities: Classification of media fans. *Journal of Media Psychology*, *14*(3), 1–39. https://gstever. sunyempirefaculty.net/ parasocial-and-social-interaction-with-celebrities/

Stever, G. S. (2017). Evolutionary theory and reactions to mass media: Understanding parasocial attachment. *Psychology of Popular Media Culture*, *6*(2), 95–102. doi:10.1037/ppm0000116

Stever, G. S., & Lawson, K. (2013). Twitter as a way for celebrities to communicate with fans: Implications for the study of parasocial interaction. *North American Journal of Psychology*, *15*, 339–354.

Stogdill, R. M. (1948). Personal factors associated with leadership: A survey of the literature. *The Journal of Psychology*, *25*(1), 35–71. doi:10.1080/00223980.1948.9917362 PMID:18901913

Stogdill, R. M. (1974). *Handbook of leadership: A survey of the literature.* Free Press.

Stoklasa, J., Stoklasa, J., Talášek, T., Talášek, T., Stoklasová, J., & Stoklasová, J. (2019). Semantic differential for the twenty-first century: Scale relevance and uncertainty entering the semantic space. *Quality & Quantity, 53*(1), 435–448. doi:10.100711135-018-0762-1

Stonecipher, P. (2012). The development of the leader and the spirit. *Journal of Leadership Education, 11*(2), 88–101. doi:10.12806/V11/I2/RF5

Strack, G., & Fottler, M. D. (2002). Spirituality and effective leadership in healthcare: Is there a connection? *Frontiers of Health Services Management, 18*(4), 3–18. doi:10.1097/01974520-200204000-00002 PMID:12087690

Strauss, M. E., & Smith, G. T. (2009, April 27). Construct validity: Advances in theory and methodology. *Annual Review of Clinical Psychology, 5*(1), 1–25. doi:10.1146/annurev.clinpsy.032408.153639 PMID:19086835

Streiner, D. L. (2006). Building a better model: An introduction to structural equation modelling. *Canadian Journal of Psychiatry, 51*(5), 317–324. doi:10.1177/070674370605100507 PMID:16986821

Streiner, D. L., & Norman, G. R. (2008). *Health measurement scales: A practical guide to their development and use.* Oxford University Press. doi:10.1093/acprof:oso/9780199231881.001.0001

Swanson, H. P. (1999). *Pastoral effectiveness: A study of differences among comparison groups of Seventh-day Adventist clergy* (Doctoral dissertation). Available from ProQuest Dissertations and Theses database. (UMI No. 9937628)

Swart, C. (2012). Building organisation–public relationships: Towards an understanding of the challenges facing public relations. *Communicatio, 38*(3), 329–348. doi:10.1080/02500167.2012.687751

Sykes, J. B. (Ed.). (1980). *The concise Oxford dictionary of current English.* Clarendon.

Tabachnick, B. G., & Fidell, L. S. (2019). *Using Multivariate Statistics* (7th ed.). Pearson Publishing.

Tabachnik, B. G., & Fidell, L. S. (2001). *Using multivariate statistics* (4th ed.). Allyn & Bacon.

Taber, K. S. (2018). The use of Cronbach's alpha when developing and reporting research instruments in science education. *Research in Science Education, 48*(6), 1273–1296. doi:10.100711165-016-9602-2

Tait, A. R., & Voepel-Lewis, T. (2015). Survey research: It's just a few questions, right? *Paediatric Anaesthesia, 25*(7), 656–662. doi:10.1111/pan.12680 PMID:25929546

Tamborini, R., Bowman, N. D., Eden, A., Grizzard, M., & Organ, A. (2010). Defining media enjoyment as the satisfaction of intrinsic needs. *Journal of Communication, 60*(4), 758–777. doi:10.1111/j.1460-2466.2010.01513.x

Tanner, M. N. (2016). Learning from clergy who have been forcibly terminated. *Journal of Management, Spirituality & Religion, 14*(3), 179–195. doi:10.1080/14766086.2016.1253496

Taylor, T. E., Poston, W. S. C., II, Haddock, C. K., Blackburn, G. I., Heber, D., Heymsfield, S. B., & Foreyt, J. P. (2003). Psychometric characteristics of the general well-being schedule (GWB) with African-American women. *Quality of Life Research, 12*(1), 31–39. doi:http://dx.doi.org.ezproxy.regent.edu:2048/10.1023/A:1022052804109

Taylor, R. (1990). Interpretation of the Correlation coefficient: A basic review. *Journal of Diagnostic Medical Sonography: JDMS, 1*(January/February), 1–39. doi:10.1177/875647939000600106

Taylor, S., Haywood, M., & Shulruf, B. (2019). Comparison of effect between simulated patient clinical skill training and student role play on objective structured clinical examination performance outcomes for medical students in Australia. *Journal of Education Evaluation Health Professionals, 16*(3), 30665274. doi:10.3352/jeehp.2019.16.3 PMID:30665274

Teh, K. P., Kareem, O. A., & Tai, M. K. (2017). *Identifying and interpreting the servant leadership dimensions for educational leadership and management.* UKM Journal of Management.

Tekin, A., & Polat, E. (2016). A scale for E-content preparation skills: Development, validity and reliability. *Eurasian Journal of Educational Research, 16*(62), 143. doi:10.14689/ejer.2016.62.9

Tetlock, P. E. (1992). The impact of accountability on judgment and choice: toward a social contingency model. In M. P. Zanna (Ed.), Advances in Experimental Social Psychology (vol. 25). Harcourt Brace Jovanovich. doi:10.1016/S0065-2601(08)60287-7

The Barna Group. (2008, October 7). *American spirituality gives way to simplicity and the desire to make a difference.* http://www.barna.org/barna-update/article/12-faithspirituality/19-american-spirituality-gives-way-to-simplicity-and-the-desire-to-make-a-difference

Thompson, L. M. (2013). *A quantitative comparative study of organizational culture and leadership accountability within public and private organizations* (Publication No. 3572907) [Doctoral Dissertation, University of Phoenix]. ProQuest Dissertations Publishing.

Thompson, B. (1997). The importance of structure coefficients in structural equation modeling confirmatory factor analysis. *Educational and Psychological Measurement, 57*(1), 5–19. doi:10.1177/0013164497057001001

Thompson, J. J., Kelly, K. L., Ritenbaugh, C., Hopkins, A. L., Sims, C. M., & Coons, S. J. (2011). Developing a patient-centered outcome measure for complementary and alternative medicine therapies II: Refining content validity through cognitive interviews. *BMC Complementary and Alternative Medicine, 11*(1), 136–153. doi:10.1186/1472-6882-11-136 PMID:22206409

Thurstone, L. (1947). *Multiple factor analysis.* University of Chicago Press.

Tiberius, V., & Walker, J. (1998). Arrogance. *American Philosophical Quarterly, 35*(4), 379–390.

Tinkelman, S. N. (1971). Planning the objective test. In R. L. Thorndike (Ed.), *Educational measurement* (2nd ed., pp. 46–80). American Council on Education.

Tjosvold, D., & Wong, A. S. H. (2000). The leader relationship: Building teamwork with and among employees. *Leadership and Organization Development Journal, 21*(7), 350–354. doi:10.1108/01437730010377890

Toosi, N. R., Sommers, S. R., & Ambady, N. (2012). Getting a word in group-wise: Effects of racial diversity on gender dynamics. *Journal of Experimental Social Psychology, 48*(5), 1150–1155. doi:10.1016/j.jesp.2012.04.015

Tourangeau, A., & McGilton, K. (2004). Measuring Leadership Practices of Nurses Using the Leadership Practices Inventory. *Nursing Research, 53*(3), 182–189. doi:10.1097/00006199-200405000-00005 PMID:15167506

Treviño, L. K., & Ball, G. A. (1992). The social implications of punishing unethical behavior: Observers' cognitive and affective reactions. *Journal of Management, 18*(4), 751–768. doi:10.1177/014920639201800409

Treviño, L. K., Hartman, L. P., & Brown, M. (2000). Moral person and moral manager: How executives develop a reputation for ethical leadership. *California Management Review, 42*(4), 128–142. doi:10.2307/41166057

Treviño, L. K., & Weaver, G. R. (2003). *Managing ethics in business organizations: Social scientific perspectives.* Stanford University Press.

Triandis, H. C., Bontempo, R., Villareal, M. J., Asai, M., & Lucca, N. (1988). Individualism and collectivism: Cross-cultural perspectives on self-ingroup relationships. *Journal of Personality and Social Psychology, 54*(2), 323–338. doi:10.1037/0022-3514.54.2.323

Trizano-Hermosilla, I., & Alvarado, J. M. (2016). Best alternatives to Cronbach's alpha reliability in realistic conditions: Congeneric and asymmetrical measurements. *Frontiers in Psychology, 7*, 769–769. doi:10.3389/fpsyg.2016.00769 PMID:27303333

Tsai, W. H. S., & Men, L. R. (2017). Social CEOs: The effects of CEOs' communication styles and parasocial interaction on social networking sites. *New Media & Society, 19*(11), 1848–1867. doi:10.1177/1461444816643922

Tsikriktsis, N. (2005). A review of techniques for treating missing data in OM survey research. *Journal of Operations Management, 24*(1), 53–62. doi:10.1016/j.jom.2005.03.001

Turgeon, P. (2019). *Identifying the leadership skills needed to develop the competencies to lead in a postcrisis organization: A Delphi study* (Corpus ID: 212980785) [Doctoral dissertation, Brandman University]. ProQuest Dissertations and Theses Global.

Turner, J. R. (1993). Interpersonal and psychological predictors of parasocial interaction with different television performers. *Communication Quarterly, 41*(4), 443–453. doi:10.1080/01463379309369904

U.S. Bureau of Labor Statistics. (2020, December 17). *Employer costs for employee compensation summary.* https://www.bls.gov/news.release/ecec.nr0.htm

Uhl-Bein, M. (2006). Relational leadership theory: Exploring the social processes of leadership and organizing. *The Leadership Quarterly, 17*(6), 654–676. doi:10.1016/j.leaqua.2006.10.007

Underwood, L. G. (2011). The daily spiritual experience scale: Overview and results. *Religions, 2*(1), 29–50. doi:10.3390/rel2010029

Underwood, L. G., & Teresi, J. A. (2002). The daily spiritual experience scale: Development, theoretical description, reliability, exploratory factor analysis, and preliminary construct validity using health-related data. *Annals of Behavioral Medicine, 24*(1), 22–33. doi:10.1207/S15324796ABM2401_04 PMID:12008791

Uraschi, G., Horodnic, I., & Zait, A. (2015). How reliable are measurement scales? External factors with indirect influence on reliability estimators. *Procedia Economics and Finance, 20*, 679-686. doi:S2212567115001239

van Dierendonck, D. (2011). Servant leadership: A review and synthesis. *Journal of Management, 37*(4), 1228–1261. doi:10.1177/0149206310380462

van Dierendonck, D., & Nuijten, I. (2011). The Servant Leadership Survey: Development and Validation of a Multidimensional Measure. *Journal of Business and Psychology, 26*(3), 249–267. doi:10.100710869-010-9194-1 PMID:21949466

van Eerde, W., & Thierry, H. (1996). Vroom's expectancy models and work-related criteria: A meta-analysis. *The Journal of Applied Psychology, 81*(5), 575–586. doi:10.1037/0021-9010.81.5.575

van Rooij, S., & Merkebu, J. (2015). Measuring the business impact of employee learning: A view from the professional services sector. *Human Resource Development Quarterly, 26*(3), 275-297. doi:10.1002/hrdq.21211

van Sonderen, E., Sanderman, R., & Coyne, J. C. (2013). Ineffectiveness of reverse wording of questionnaire items: Let's learn from cows in the rain. *PLoS One, 8*(7). Retrieved from https://search-proquest-com.ezproxy.regent.edu/docview/1440999743/fulltextPDF/A7D6467A73644490PQ/1?accountid=13479

Vandenberg, R. J., & Lance, C. E. (2000). A review and synthesis of the measurement invariance literature: Suggestions, practices, and recommendations for organizational research. *Organizational Research Methods, 3*(1), 4–70. doi:10.1177/109442810031002

Vardaman, D. L. (2013). *Leading change: Exploring the relationship between transformational, transactional, and change-oriented leadership and their impact on leadership effectiveness among pastors in a protestant denomination in the mid-western United States* (Doctoral dissertation). Available from ProQuest Dissertations and Theses database. (UMI No. 3613541)

Vasconcelos, A. F. (2010). The effects of prayer on organizational life: A phenomenological study. *Journal of Management & Organization, 16*(3), 369–381. doi:10.5172/jmo.16.3.369

Vasle, J. J., Beaman, J., & Sonarski, C. C. (2017). Rethinking Internal Consistency in Cronbach's Alpha. *Leisure Sciences, 39*(2), 163–173. doi:10.1080/01490400.2015.1127189

Verčič, A. T., & Verčič, D. (2007). Reputation as matching identities and images: Extending Davies and Chun's (2002) research on gaps between the internal and external perceptions of the corporate brand. *Journal of Marketing Communications, 13*(4), 277–290. doi:10.1080/13527260701300151

Vicente, P., & Reis, E. (2012). Coverage error in internet surveys: Can fixed phones fix it? *International Journal of Market Research, 54*(3), 323–345. doi:10.2501/ijmr-54-3-323-345

Vidgen, R., Sims, J. M., & Powell, P. (2013). Do CEO bloggers build community? *Journal of Communication Management (London), 17*(4), 364–385. doi:10.1108/JCOM-08-2012-0068

Vorderer, P., Hefner, D., Reinecke, L., & Klimmt, C. (Eds.). (2018). *Permanently Online, Permanently Connected. Living and Communicating in a POPC World.* Routledge.

Vroom, V. H. (1964). *Work and motivation.* Wiley.

Vygotsky, L. S. (1978). *Interaction between learning and development. Mind in society: the development of higher psychological processes.* Harvard University Press.

Wagner, J. (2019, May 29). 'A grandstander and a showboat': Kellyanne Conway attacks Comey for op-ed. *The Washington Post.* Retrieved from https://www.washingtonpost.com/politics/a-grandstander-and-a-show-boat-kellyanne-conway-attacks-comey-for-op-ed/2019/05/29/863b0594-8214-11e9-933d-7501070ee669_story.html

Walsh, S. L. (2019, October 29). Accountability would help in PG&E fiasco. *Wall Street Journal Online.* Retrieved February 16, 2021, from https://search-proquest-com.ezproxy.regent.edu/abicomplete/publication/publications_10598 3?accountid=13479

Walters, S., Winston, B., Dean, D., & Winner, W. (2021). *Gauging the Validation of An Instrument To Measure the Impact of Hope in Strategic Plan Implementation* [Unpublished doctoral dissertation]. Regent University, Virginia Beach, VA, United States.

Walther, J. B. (2011). Theories of computer-mediated communication and interpersonal relations. The handbook of interpersonal communication, 4, 443-479.

Walther, J. B. (1996). Computer-mediated communication: Impersonal, interpersonal, and hyperpersonal interaction. *Communication Research, 23*(1), 3–43. doi:10.1177/009365096023001001

Walther, J. B., Van Der Heide, B., Ramirez, A., Burgoon, J. K., & Peña, J. (2015). Interpersonal and hyperpersonal dimensions of computer-mediated communication. In S. Shyam Sundar (Ed.), *The handbook of the psychology of communication technology* (pp. 1–22). John Wiley & Sons Inc. doi:10.1002/9781118426456.ch1

Walumbwa, F. O., Avolio, B. J., Gardner, W. L., Wernsing, T. S., & Peterson, S. J. (2008). Authentic leadership: Development and validation of a theory-based measure. *Journal of Management, 34*(1), 89–126. doi:10.1177/0149206307308913

Wang, D. (2016). *The Buck Stops Where? Examining Leader and Collective Accountability in Teams* (Publication No. 10106401) [Doctoral Dissertation, Arizona State University]. ProQuest Dissertations Publishing.

Wang, B., Liu, Y., & Parker, S. K. (2020). How does the use of information communication technology affect individuals? A work design perspective. *The Academy of Management Annals, 14*(2), 695–725. doi:10.5465/annals.2018.0127

Wang, B., Liu, Y., Qian, J., & Parker, S. K. (2020). Achieving effective remote working during the COVID-19 pandemic: A work design perspective. *Applied Psychology, 70*(1), 16–59.

Wang, D., Whittaker, T. A., & Beretvas, S. N. (2012). The impact of violating factor scaling method assumptions on latent mean difference testing in structured means models. *Journal of Modern Applied Statistical Methods; JMASM, 20*(1), 108–130. doi:10.22237/jmasm/1335844920

Wang, J., & Hutchins, H. M. (2010). Crisis management in higher education: What have we learned from Virginia Tech? *Advances in Developing Human Resources, 12*(5), 552–572. doi:10.1177/1523422310394433

Wapner, S., & Demick, J. (2003). Adult development: The holistic, developmental, and systems-oriented perspective. In J. Demick & C. Andreoletti (Eds.), *Handbook of adult development* (pp. 63–83). Kluwer Academic/Plenum.

Wasberg, G. D. (2013). *Differentiation of self and leadership effectiveness in Christian clergy: A mixed methods study* (Doctoral dissertation). Available from ProQuest Dissertations and Theses database. (UMI No. 3602885)

WASC Senior College and University Commission. (2015). *2013 Handbook of Accreditation (revised).* https://www.wscuc.org/resources/handbook-accreditation-2013

Waters, R. D., & Tindall, N. T. J. (2010). Marketing churches on the Internet: An analysis of the dialogic potential of Christian web sites. *Journal of Philanthropy and Marketing, 15*(4), 369–381. doi:10.1002/nvsm.400

Watkins, M. W. (2018). Exploratory factor analysis: A guide to best practice. *The Journal of Black Psychology, 44*(3), 219–246. doi:10.1177/0095798418771807

Weick, K. E. (1995). *Sensemaking in organizations.* Sage Publications.

Weick, K. E., Sutcliffe, K. M., & Obstfeld, D. (2005). Organizing and the process of sensemaking and organizing. *Organization Science, 16*(4), 409–421. doi:10.1287/orsc.1050.0133

Weijters, B., & Baumgartner, H. (2012). Misresponse to reversed and negated items in surveys: A review. *JMR, Journal of Marketing Research, 49*(5), 737–747. doi:10.1509/jmr.11.0368

Wen-Chung Wang, W., Chen, H., & Jin, K. (2015). Item Response Theory Models for Wording Effects in Mixed-Format Scales. *Educational and Psychological Measurement, 75*(1), 157–178. doi:10.1177/0013164414528209 PMID:29795817

Werner, S., Praxedes, M., & Kim, H.-G. (2007). The reporting of nonresponse analyses in survey research. *Organizational Research Methods, 10*(2), 287–295. doi:10.1177/1094428106292892

Wesemann, K. R. (1995). *Predicting ministerial effectiveness* (Doctoral dissertation). Available from ProQuest Dissertations and Theses database. (UMI No. 9536609)

Wheeler, B. G. (2001). Fit for ministry? *Christian Century (Chicago, Ill.), 118*(12), 16–23. https://www.christiancentury.org/article/fit-ministry

Wheeler, J. V. (2013). A Holistic, Organic Process of Personal Growth and Leadership. *OD Practitioner, 45*(4), 38–42.

Whitney, D. S. (2014). *Spiritual disciplines for the Christian life.* NavPress.

Wickman, C. A. (2004). *Pastor in residence: At-risk pastor profile*. Regent University, School of Global Leadership & Entrepreneurship. https://www.regent.edu/acad/global/pir/pir_section1.cfm

Wickman, C. A. (2014). *Pastors at risk: Protecting your future, guarding your present*. Morgan James.

Wiggins, G., & McTighe, J. (2005). Understanding by design (2nd ed.). Alexandria, VA: Association for Supervision and Curriculum Development (ASCD).

Wigglesworth, A. (2018, April 15). From 'nut job' to 'slimeball': A timeline of Trump's insults aimed at Comey. *Los Angeles Times*. Retrieved from https://www.latimes.com/politics/la-na-pol-trump-comey-insults-20180415-htmlstory.html

Wildhagen, T., Mueller, C. W., & Wang, M. (2005). Factors leading to clergy job search in two Protestant denominations. *Review of Religious Research*, *46*(4), 380–403. doi:10.2307/3512168

Williams, A. (2003). How to write and analyse a questionnaire. *Journal of Orthodontics*, *30*(3), 245–252. doi:10.1093/ortho/30.3.245 PMID:14530423

Willis, G. (2005). *Cognitive interviewing: A tool for improving questionnaire design*. Sage Publications. doi:10.4135/9781412983655

Winston, B. (n.d.). The *Relationship of Servant Leadership, Perceived Organizational Support and Work-family Conflict with Employee Well-being* (Working paper).

Winston, B. E., Bekker, C., Cerff, K., Eames, D., Helland, M. R., & Garnes, D. (2005). *Hope as a possible factor in the implementation of strategic plans*. Unpublished manuscript.

Winston, B.E., Cerf, K., Eames, D., Helland, M., & Garnes, D. (2008). An instrument to measure the impact of hope in strategic plan implementation. *International Leadership Journal*, 39-56.

Winston, B. (2020). *Correlation of Essential Servant Leadership Behaviors*. Perceived Organizational Support, and Employee Well-Being., doi:10.20944/preprints202003.0222.v1

Winston, B. E. (2017). The stage is set for African Renaissance. In K. Patterson & B. E. Winston (Eds.), *Leading an African Renaissance: Opportunities and challenges* (p. 186). Palgrave Macmillan. doi:10.1007/978-3-319-40539-1_11

Winston, B. E., & Fields, D. (2015). Seeking and measuring the essential Behaviors of Servant Leadership. *Leadership and Organization Development Journal*, *36*(4), 413–434. doi:10.1108/LODJ-10-2013-0135

Wirth, W. (2006). Involvement. In J. Bryant & P. Vorderer (Eds.), *Psychology of entertainment* (pp. 199–214). Routledge.

Wood, J. A. Jr, & Winston, B. E. (2005). Toward a new understanding of leader accountability: Defining a critical construct. *Journal of Leadership & Organizational Studies*, *3*(11), 84–94. doi:10.1177/107179190501100307

Wood, J. A., & Winston, B. E. (2007). Development of three scales to measure leader accountability. *Leadership and Organization Development Journal*, *28*(2), 167–185. doi:10.1108/01437730710726859

Wood, R., & Locke, E. (1987). The relation of self-efficacy and grade goals to academic performance. *Educational and Psychological Measurement*, *47*(4), 1013–1024. doi:10.1177/0013164487474017

Wooten, L. P., & James, E. H. (2008). Linking crisis management and leadership competencies: The role of human resource development. *Advances in Developing Human Resources*, *10*(3), 352–379. doi:10.1177/1523422308316450

Wright, S. D. (2004). *The social phenomenon of transformational leadership among clergy* (Doctoral dissertation). Available from ProQuest Dissertations and Theses database. (UMI No. 3111407)

Wu, H., & Leung, S. (2017). Can Likert scales be treated as interval scales? A simulation study. *Journal of Social Service Research*, *43*(4), 527–532. doi:10.1080/01488376.2017.1329775

Xie, J. L. (1996). Karasek's model in the People's Republic of China: Effects of job demands, control, and individual differences. *Academy of Management Journal*, *39*(6), 1594–1619. doi:10.5465/257070

Xie, J. L., & Johns, G. (1995). Job scope and stress: Can job scope be too high? *Academy of Management Journal*, *38*(5), 1288–1310. doi:10.5465/256858

Yang, Y., & Green, S. B. (2011). Coefficient alpha: A reliability coefficient for the 21st century? *Journal of Psychoeducational Assessment*, *29*(4), 377–392. doi:10.1177/0734282911406668

Yelon, S., Ford, J. K., & Bhatia, S. (2014). How trainees transfer what they have learned: Toward a taxonomy of use. *Performance Improvement Quarterly, 27*, 27-52. doi:10.1002/pfi.21605

York, D. E. (2016). *Not Saul's armor: Introversion and effective pastoral leadership* (Doctoral dissertation). Available from ProQuest Dissertations and Theses database. (ProQuest No. 10156648)

Yue, C. A., Thelen, P., Robinson, K., & Men, L. R. (2019). How do CEOs communicate on Twitter? A comparative study between Fortune 200 companies and top startup companies. *Corporate Communications*, *24*(3), 532–552. doi:10.1108/CCIJ-03-2019-0031

Yukl. (2006). *Leadership in organizations* (6th ed.). Prentice Hall.

Yukl, G. (2006). *Leadership in organizations* (6th ed.). Pearson-Prentice Hall.

Yukl, G. (2010). *Leadership in Organizations*. Prentice Hall.

Yuksel, M., & Labrecque, L. I. (2016). "Digital buddies": Parasocial interactions in social media. *Journal of Research in Interactive Marketing*, *10*(4), 305–320. doi:10.1108/JRIM-03-2016-0023

Zellars, K., Hochwarter, W., Perrewe, P., Miles, A., & Kiewitz, C. (2001). Beyond self-efficacy: Interactive effects of role conflict and perceived collective efficacy. *Journal of Managerial Issues*, *13*, 483–499.

Zhao, Y., Hryniewicki, M. K., Cheng, F., Fu, B., & Zhu, X. (2018). Employee turnover prediction with machine learning: A reliable approach. In *Proceedings of SAI Intelligent Systems Conference* (pp. 737-758). Academic Press.

Zheng, X., Zhu, W., Zhao, H., & Zhang, C. (2015). Employee well-being in organizations: Theoretical model, scale development, and cross-cultural validation. *Journal of Organizational Behavior*, *36*(5), 645–647. doi:10.1002/job.2033

Zhu, D., & Chen, G. (2015). Narcissism, Director, Selection, and Risk-taking Spending. *Strategic Management Journal*, *36*(13), 2075–2098. doi:10.1002mj.2322

Zojceska, A. (2018, December 19). Top 10 Benefits of Diversity in the Workplace. *Talent Lyft*. https://www.talentlyft.com/en/blog/article/244/top-10-benefits-of-diversity-in-the-workplace#:~:text=What%20are%20the%20benefits%3F%20 1%20Variety%20of%20different,5%20Better%20decision%20making.%20...%20More%20items...%20

Zondag, H. J. (2004). Knowing you make a difference: Result awareness and satisfaction in the pastoral profession. *Review of Religious Research*, *45*(3), 254–269. doi:10.2307/3512263

Zorzi, M., Priftis, K., & Umilita, C. (2002). Brain damage: Neglect disrupts the mental number line. *Nature*, *417*(09), 138–139. doi:10.1038/417138a PMID:12000950

About the Contributors

Mihai C. Bocarnea, originally from Romania, came to Regent University in 1995 and currently serves as an associate professor in the School of Business & Leadership. He is an expert in the areas of communication, research methods, quantitative analysis and statistics. Dr. Bocarnea, co-editor of Online instruments, data collection, and electronic measurements: Organizational advancements, has co-authored such book chapters and articles as "Seven Scales to Measure the Seven Beatitudes in Leaders," " An Online Measure of Discernment," "Uncertainty Management's Impact on Job Satisfaction and Innovation," "Student-specific Characteristics as Predictors of Retention and Attrition in an Online Doctoral Leadership Program," "Constructivism in Online Distance Education," "Teaching and Instruction Online: Conceptual Foundations and Practical Applications," "Measurement in Organizational Behavior," "Leadership of Organizational Networks," and "Servant-leadership as a Predictor of Job Satisfaction and Organizational Commitment with the Moderating Effects of Organizational Support and Role Clarity among the Filipino Engineering, Manufacturing, and Technology Workers." He has also presented at numerous academic conferences both in the U.S. and overseas in Canada, Germany, India, Israel, Italy, Lithuania, the Netherlands, South Korea, the United Kingdom and Romania. Bocarnea's research interests include organizational communication, cross-cultural leadership, servant leadership, organizational change and pedagogy of online learning. Prior to his teaching career at Regent University, Bocarnea served as an Internet technology consultant, statistical analyst and consultant, principal researcher, and software engineer. He has also served as research analyst for various organizations in the U.S. and overseas.

Bruce Winston has been part of Regent University since 1991, both with the School of Business and the School of Business & Leadership. He led the School of Leadership as dean for one year and led the School of Business & Leadership as dean for seven years. He currently serves as Professor of Business and Leadership and is the director of the Ph.D. in Organizational Leadership program. His research interests include servant leadership, organizational development and transformation, leadership development, distance education, person-environment fit, employee well-being, and technology in higher education.

***

Jason D. Baker, Ph.D. serves Regent University as a Professor and Senior Technology Strategist. He holds a B.S. in Electrical Engineering from Bucknell University, an M.A. in Educational Technology Leadership from The George Washington University, a Ph.D. in Communication from Regent University, and recently earned a Master of Computer & Information Technology from the University of Pennsylvania. His primary area of research and practice has been online learning and educational technology within higher education. He has authored and edited numerous books, chapters and articles, and consulted with organizations regarding the development and management of online learning programs.

Tanesia R. Beverly, Ph.D., is a Measurement Scientist at the Law School Admission Council. Her research is related to instrument development and validation, and response time modeling. She holds a Ph.D. in Educational Psychology from the University of Connecticut.

William J. Brown is Professor and Research Fellow in the School of Communication and the Arts at Regent University.

Jamie Brownlee-Turgeon has been immersed in the higher education industry for over 20 years. Her experience includes student development, enrollment management, academics, student services, and student retention. In addition, she has also held multiple adjunct positions at a variety of institutions, including Assistant Professor of Business at Vanguard University. Jamie's experience provides her with the ability to see strategy through the eyes of multiple institutional stakeholders. From navigating complex systems in order to improve operational efficiencies, to developing learning organizations; she has a track record of consistent, increased enrollment and retention for both on-campus and online populations - in traditional and post-traditional university environments. Jamie is a passionate and innovative change agent, as well as a transformational leader, that places focused attention on maximizing human potential and system overhauls. Jamie is currently an Associate Vice President for Graduate and Professional Studies Enrollment, Student Services, and partnerships at Point Loma Nazarene University. Jamie also currently serves as an Adjunct Professor in the Fermanian School of Business at PLNU and Southern New Hampshire University. Previously, she taught at Brandman University. Prior to her current role, she served in leadership positions at Los Angeles Pacific University, Brandman University, and Vanguard University. Jamie Brownlee-Turgeon holds a Ph.D. in Organizational Leadership from Regent University with a research focus on Crisis Leadership. She earned an MA in Human and Organizational Development and a BA in Spanish from Azusa Pacific University. Additionally, she earned a Certificate in Evidenced Based Coaching from Fielding Graduate University. Jamie has presented on crisis leadership at a number of conferences and has consulted with the Southern California Child Welfare Department Services. Jamie, her husband, and two kids reside in Orange County, California.

Karen Cerff, PhD. Organizational Leadership (Regent University, USA); Post-doctoral qualification in Executive Coaching & Consulting (Regent University); MEd. Leadership (Cum Laude) (University of Stellenbosch, South Africa); Master Coach Trainer; Business, Leadership and Life Coach (LifeForming Leadership Coaching International). Dr Cerff is co-vocational as COO of Transformational Leadership Institute integrating coaching, consulting and training in interaction globally with organizational leaders and community development leaders, while serving in an academic capacity and as a Board member. Her research interests include transformational and servant leadership, organizational and leadership development, organizational communication, hope theory, and cross-cultural leadership dimensions.

Debra J. Dean is founder of His Kingdom Matters. She has a Ph.D. in Organizational Leadership from Regent University and decades of experience in corporate. She received the 2020 Women of Influence award by The Colorado Springs Business Journal and the 2020 Most Influential Business Consultancy CEO (USA) by Global CEO Excellence Award. Dr. Dean is a published author and sought-after speaker on topics of Diversity and Inclusion, Faith at Work, Respectful Pluralism (respecting all people), Leadership, and Followership.

Sam Dobrotka serves as campus pastor at Grace Covenant Statesville (NC). In addition to his role as pastor, he also teaches as an Adjunct Professor at Southeastern University, SUM Bible College & Theological Seminary, and Development Associates International. Dr. Dobrotka earned his Ph.D. in Organizational Leadership from Regent University and holds MA degrees (Theology and Cross-Cultural Studies) from Fuller Theological Seminary. His research interests lie in the areas of clergy effectiveness, strategic planning, organizational change, team building, and conflict management.

Dail Fields, PhD serves as an adjunct professor for doctoral programs at Regent and Franklin Universities. He is also a consultant in management and leadership for commercial and non-profit organizations. He has previously served as tenured full-time professor and program director for the Regent University PhD in Organizational Leadership and as Senior Research Scientist at the University of Georgia Institute for Behavioral Research. Dr. Fields was a Fulbright Scholar based in Lithuania in 2006-7 and completed a Fulbright Specialist assignment in Nepal in 2017. He is the author of "Taking the Measure of Work", a guide to measurement and assessment in organizations (Sage Publications). He has also published over 50 research studies in management and leadership research journals. Dr. Fields has been a guest speaker for management and educational organizations in Hong Kong, Lithuania, Russia, India, Singapore, Malaysia, China (P.R.C.), Nepal, and Guatemala. Prior to undertaking an academic career, Dr. Fields worked in business for over 20 years, holding senior management positions in such firms as Deloitte-Touche and MCI Communications Corporation. He also started and developed a small business. Dr. Fields holds a PhD from the Georgia Institute of Technology [1994], and BA with honors from Johns Hopkins University [1968].

Tariku Fufa Gemechu, PhD, is from Ethiopia and holds a PhD in Organizational Leadership from Regent University. He teaches master-level classes as adjunct faculty at Africa Leadership and Management Academy (ALMA) in Zimbabwe, International Leadership University Kenya (ILU–Kenya), and International Leadership University Ethiopia (ILU–Ethiopia). He also serves as adjunct faculty at the Global Academy for Transformational Leadership (GATL), based in Orlando, Florida. His research interests include ethical leadership, holistic leadership, human resource development and organizational effectiveness.

Mary A. Hansen, Ph.D., is a university professor in the Education Department at Robert Morris University. Her research interests lie in the areas of educational measurement, assessment, and program evaluation. She conducts research related to technical issues and validity of large-scale assessments, classroom assessment practices, and the impact of instruction as measured through outcomes assessment instruments; and has served as the program evaluator for several projects. She previously worked on a statewide alternate assessment, and has taught undergraduate, master's, and doctoral level courses in the areas of program evaluation, quantitative research methodology, and statistical analysis. She holds Masters Degrees in Statistics and Research Methodology and a Ph.D. in Research Methodology from the University of Pittsburgh, PA, U.S.A.

C. Victor Herbin III, Ph.D., is a leadership development program manager that draws from more than 20 years of proven leadership as a United States Army Officer. He commanded at every level and served in a myriad of senior strategic, operational, and tactical leadership positions, including the Department of the Army, the White House Communications Agency, and three combat tours supporting

Operation Iraqi Freedom. Dr. Herbin directed human resources operations while leading teams globally and utilizing innovative leadership strategies to maximize growth and development in complex, fast-paced environments. He led groundbreaking research that coined organizational arrogance and validated a theory-based instrument that measures this phenomenon. Dr. Herbin earned a Ph.D. in Organizational Leadership from Regent University, an M.A in Journalism with an emphasis in Strategic Communication from the University of Missouri, an M.A in Human Resources Management from Webster University, and a B.A in History and minor in Sociology from the University of Southern California.

Janet Reynolds has taught communication at Old Dominion University, Pepperdine University, and Fuller Theological Seminary. She retired as the Associate Director of the Brehm Center for Worship, Theology and Art in Pasadena, California. Her research areas are interpersonal and intercultural communication. She has taught Minorities in the Mass Media, Intercultural Communication and Communication Ethics. Her communication degrees are from Abilene Christian University, University of Hawaii and Regent University. She is currently assisting small nonprofit organizations in using communication strategies to fund raise and network in their communities.

Rodney A. Reynolds, PhD (Michigan State University), is a retired professor of Communication (with an emphasis on research methods, interpersonal relations, and persuasion/social influence). He served as a professor for forty-four years. The last eleven of those years he served as a university administrator over institutional research and effectiveness. He has consulting experience on legal communication, survey research, health administration/training, and educational administration.

Rick Roof is Dean of the School of Aeronautics and instructs doctoral students at the Liberty University School of Business in ethical leadership. He presents and publishes widely on spiritual engagement, identity-based leadership development, employee engagement, authentic leadership, and multicultural leadership. Dr. Roof earned a Ph.D. in Organizational Leadership from Regent University.

Charles Sanders is a Principal Modeling and Simulation Consultant for the Defense Modeling and Simulation Coordination Office and Army Modeling and Simulation Office. With over 30 years of experience in modeling and simulation, organization development, management and leadership, strategic policy and planning, and training and learning concepts; to include corporate staff support at all levels, he has provided advice to Office of Secretary of Defense, Joint Chiefs of Staff, U.S. Navy Staff, Joint Forces Command, and other executive level government and industry. Dr. Sanders led studies of emerging technologies for the M&S community, including cloud-based simulation, modeling frameworks and development of a persistent simulation test bed for 5Eyes partner nations. He previously provided strategies and plans support to Joint Staff J7 and ODUSD-P&R for over ten years, including initiation and development of the Department of Defense Training Transformation Program, and strategic support of the DoD Advanced Distributed Learning Initiative. Dr. Sanders served over twenty years the US Navy as a nuclear propulsion engineer and surface warfare officer. In addition to his many ship tours, experience included command of a mobile training team, member of the Nuclear Propulsion Examining Board and Fleet Training Policy and Plans analyst on the Navy Staff, where he served as the requirements and resource sponsor for Joint Simulation System (JSIMS) Maritime, and Operational Test Director for the Navy Operational Test and Evaluation Force (OPTEVFOR). Dr. Sanders earned a Doctor of Philosophy in Organizational Development, a Master of Science in Information Resources Management, and a Bachelor of Science in Chemistry.

J. Louis Spencer, Ph.D., serves as a program chair and professor at American Public University System, drawing from over two decades in higher education concurrent with over four decades of ministry leadership, including service as a senior pastor, church planter, and divisional leader and coach of other pastors and prospective leaders. He has served as a reviewer with the Academy of Management and on accrediting teams with Association of Biblical Higher Education. He has significant experience with course development and program evaluation. Dr. Spencer holds a Ph.D. in Organizational Leadership from Regent University, an M.A. in Religion from Azusa Pacific University, and a B.A. in Bible and Ministry from Life Pacific University.

Gaelebale Nnunu Tsheko (Ph.D.) is currently a Senior Lecturer at the University of Botswana teaching both undergraduate and graduate courses in measurement, research statistics and evaluation. She holds a Masters Degree and a Ph.D. from University of Pittsburgh, PA, U.S.A (1995 and 2001 respectively) with specialization in Research Methodology. Dr Tsheko's research interests include validation of (research) instruments, gender, and HIV/AIDS and she conducts research in all these areas. She is quite well rounded in the research process as it is her area of specialization. Dr Tsheko has participated in many research studies both as a team member and leader. She serves in various boards within the University of Botswana and at national level. She is a member of various professional bodies such as Botswana Educational Research Association (BERA) and African Evaluation Association.

Heidi R. Ventura serves as Associate Dean for the School of Graduate and Continuing Studies at Trevecca Nazarene University. She has taught and/or developed courses in research design, business, leadership, management, and interdisciplinary studies. Her research interests include higher education, accreditation, adult learner experience, faculty engagement, accountability, authentic leadership, and exegetical study of scriptural leadership theory and praxis.

Sarah Walters completed her BS in Athletic Training from the University of Central Arkansas. She then went on to receive a Masters degree in Organizational Leadership from Evangel University and recently finished her PhD in Organizational Leadership at Regent University. Walters oversees the Masters of Organizational Leadership Program at Evangel University and serves on many academic and administrative committees which support the functions of the University. Walters was also named one of Springfield Business Journal's 40 under 40 recipients in 2020 in the Springfield, MO community.

B. J. Weathersby-Holman, Ph.D., is the founder of Rutland & Associates, LLC a leadership development and personal coaching firm. Her firm is the exclusive provider of the Flourishing Pathways a Holistic Wellness program that focuses on Life Purpose, Career Development, and Health and Wellness. She is a Gallup® Certified Strengths-Based Coach and Certified Positive Psychology Practitioner (CAPP) She is a former adjunct with Peninsula and Milligan Colleges facilitating Undergraduates, MBA, and Doctoral students in classes such as Strategic Management, Leading Change, and Organizational Change and Leadership. She volunteers on the board of a large non-profit in Alexandria, VA. She is a practitioner currently leading the training & development and culture change effort for a large federal agency transitioning to a mobile workforce.

W. David Winner, Ph.D., currently teaches and is the coordinator of the Human Resource Development concentration in the Organizational Leadership Ph.D. program in the School of Business at Regent University. He also served 20 years in churches working with teenagers and young adults. Dave has a BA in Youth Ministry from Eastern University, a MDIV from Palmer Theological Seminary and my PhD in Organizational Leadership with a major in Human Resource Development from Regent University.

Andy Wood is the managing partner of the LifeVesting Group in Mobile, Alabama, offering professional coaching, consulting, counseling and communication services to individuals and organizations throughout the world. He also serves as an adjunct professor of leadership at Regent University and the Alabama School of the Arts at the University of Mobile. As a university professor, both full-time and adjunct, he has taught over 400 sections at every level in various universities and seminaries. He also has 32 years of church ministry experience as a senior pastor, church planter, men's pastor, worship leader, and youth pastor in Texas, Alabama, Mississippi, and Manitoba.

Index

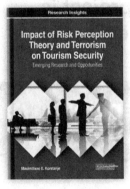

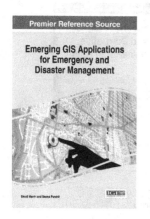

IGI Global
PUBLISHER of TIMELY KNOWLEDGE
www.igi-global.com

Publisher of Peer-Reviewed, Timely, and
Innovative Academic Research Since 1988

IGI Global's Transformative Open Access (OA) Model:
How to Turn Your University Library's Database Acquisitions Into a Source of OA Funding

Well in advance of Plan S, IGI Global unveiled their OA Fee Waiver (Read & Publish) Initiative. Under this initiative, librarians who invest in IGI Global's InfoSci-Books and/or InfoSci-Journals databases will be able to subsidize their patrons' OA article processing charges (APCs) when their work is submitted and accepted (after the peer review process) into an IGI Global journal.

How Does it Work?

Step 1: **Library Invests in the InfoSci-Databases:** A library perpetually purchases or subscribes to the InfoSci-Books, InfoSci-Journals, or discipline/subject databases.

Step 2: **IGI Global Matches the Library Investment with OA Subsidies Fund:** IGI Global provides a fund to go towards subsidizing the OA APCs for the library's patrons.

Step 3: **Patron of the Library is Accepted into IGI Global Journal (After Peer Review):** When a patron's paper is accepted into an IGI Global journal, they option to have their paper published under a traditional publishing model or as OA.

Step 4: **IGI Global Will Deduct APC Cost from OA Subsidies Fund:** If the author decides to publish under OA, the OA APC fee will be deducted from the OA subsidies fund.

Step 5: **Author's Work Becomes Freely Available:** The patron's work will be freely available under CC BY copyright license, enabling them to share it freely with the academic community.

Note: This fund will be offered on an annual basis and will renew as the subscription is renewed for each year thereafter. IGI Global will manage the fund and award the APC waivers unless the librarian has a preference as to how the funds should be managed.

Hear From the Experts on This Initiative:

"I'm very happy to have been able to make one of my recent research contributions *freely available* along with having access to the *valuable resources* found within IGI Global's InfoSci-Journals database."

– Prof. Stuart Palmer,
Deakin University, Australia

"Receiving the support from IGI Global's OA Fee Waiver Initiative *encourages me to continue my research work without any hesitation.*"

– Prof. Wenlong Liu, College of Economics and Management at Nanjing University of Aeronautics & Astronautics, China

For More Information, Scan the QR Code or Contact:
IGI Global's Digital Resources Team at eresources@igi-global.com.

IGI Global
PUBLISHER of TIMELY KNOWLEDGE

Printed in the United States
by Baker & Taylor Publisher Services